The Holy Roman Empire

The Holy Roman Empire

A DICTIONARY HANDBOOK

edited by Jonathan W. Zophy

GREENWOOD PRESS Westport, Connecticut ● London, England

Library of Congress Cataloging in Publication Data

Zophy, Jonathan W. 1945-
  The Holy Roman Empire.

  Includes index.
  1. Holy Roman Empire—History—Dictionaries.
I. Title.
DD84.Z66   943'.0003   79-8282
ISBN 0-313-21457-3

Library of Congress Catalog Card Number: 79-8282
ISBN: 0-313-21457-3

First published in 1980

Greenwood Press
A division of Congressional Information Service, Inc.
88 Post Road West, Westport, Connecticut 06881

Printed in the United States of America

10 9 8 7 6 5 4 3 2 1

Contents

List of maps

Acknowledgments

This volume owes its genesis to Arthur H. Stickney, editor for Research and Professional Books of Greenwood Press. A former reference librarian, Art Stickney recognized the need for such a work and first approached me about compiling and editing it. His assistance and that of the staff at Greenwood at every phase of the production of *The Holy Roman Empire* has been invaluable.

I would like to offer deepest thanks to Tim Peterson for his fine maps and to Karen Gray, Roger Meslar, Randy Nehls, Barry Rabe, and Dana Runestad for their help in proofreading. Lorilee Herrmann, Roberta Odegaard, and Kathy Zuehlsdorf graciously assisted in typing the manuscript. Colleagues and friends John Bailey, Larry Buck, Harold Grimm, Bill Gunderson, Kim G. House, David A. Krueger, Don Michie, Randy Miller, John Neuenschwander, Tom Noer, Dave Rhoads, Sandy Roberts, and Bonnie Smith gave me a great deal of aid and encouragement. The Zophy and Howard families provided a full measure of kindness and support. Modest financial assistance was supplied by the Johnson Fund of the American Philosophical Society and Carthage College.

Finally I would like to thank and commend all of the authors whose essays can be found in this volume (see "notes on contributors"). I have been continually gratified by their scholarship and their willingness to assist in this project. My part of this book is dedicated to Angela Howard Zophy, a continuing source of affection, assistance, and inspiration.

Abbreviations

AHR	*American Historical Review*
ADB	*Allgemeine deutsche Biographie*
ARG	*Archiv für Reformationsgeschichte*
Bl	Blatt, Blätter
BW	*Biographisches Wörterbuch zur Deutschen Geschichte*
CEH	*Central European History*
CHR	*Catholic Historical Review*
ChH	*Church History*
DGD	*Die Grossen Deutschen: Deutsche Biographie*
dtsch	deutsche, deutschen, deutsches
DRTA	*Deutsche Reichstagsakten*
ed	editor, edited, edition
EWA	*Encyclopedia of World Art*
Forsch	Forschung, Forschungen
germ	germanisches
gesch	Geschichte, geschichtliche
hist	historisch, history
HZ	*Historische Zeitschrift*
inst	Institut, institute
int	international
introd	introduced, introduction
j	journal
Jb	Jahrbuch
JMH	*Journal of Modern History*
med	medieval, medievales
MGH	*Monumenta Germaniae Historica*
MIÖG	*Mitteilungen des österreichischen Instituts für Geschichtsforschung*
Mitt	Mitteilungen
MQR	*Mennonite Quarterly Review*
MVGN	*Mitteilungen des Vereins für Geschichte der Stadt Nürnberg*
NDB	*Neue deutsche Biographie*
no	number
nos	numbers
quel	quellen
rpr	reprint
SCJ	*The Sixteenth Century Journal*
Schaff-Herzog	*The New Schaff-Herzog Encyclopedia of Religious Knowledge*

Spec	*Speculum*
SS	*Scriptores*
SRG	*Scriptores rerum Germanicorum*
tr	translator, translated, translation
ver	Verein, vereinigung, Vereins
Z	Zeitschrift, Zeitschriften

Introduction

This reference book is concerned with the Holy Roman Empire from the time of Charlemagne to the Napoleonic dissolution in 1806. The Holy Roman Empire, or the Old Reich, is a historical oddity and a controversial one at that. Almost every aspect of imperial history has been the subject of great debate. As Robert E. Herzstein has noted in his *The Holy Roman Empire in the Middle Ages: Universal State or German Catastrophe?* even the term *Holy Roman Empire* was "not prevalent until the twelfth century." Voltaire's oft-quoted quip that the Empire was "neither Holy, nor Roman, nor an Empire" is certainly true in some sense for many phases of imperial history, especially after 1648.

Surprisingly, recent scholarship has rather neglected the study of the Old Reich. Much of the passion has gone out of the debate over the nature and utility of the Empire even for those dwindling numbers of scholars who still care about the subject. Modern scholarship has become more preoccupied with the empires of Bismarck and Adolf Hitler; even the medievalists in England and North America have largely abandoned the topic except as it relates to the problems of the Church or the Renaissance and Reformation movements. The result has been a great paucity of materials written about the Empire for the English-speaking world. This book makes an effort to fill that gap in the reference field. I hope it will stimulate renewed interest in the Empire.

Interest in the English-speaking world in the Empire has never totally died out, however. The recent republication of a number of classic German works in English translations, including books by Karl Hampe and Josef Fleckenstein (see the bibliography at the close of this volume, which gives special attention to works in English), attests to that continued interest. The existence of an English-language version of Friedrich Heer's beautifully illustrated, *The Holy Roman Empire* (1968) and a number of more limited studies of various aspects of imperial history produced in the last few decades indicates that at least some scholars are aware of the importance of the Old Reich for understanding the modern world. In addition, many students and scholars interested in German history are becoming aware that the Holy Roman Empire and its culture are more characteristic of German genius than are the aberrations of the Third Reich.

Time is working in favor of the Old Reich and will eventually lessen the shadows cast by the recent horrors perpetrated by the Nazis. Not so surprisingly given the horrors perpetrated by modern nation-states in the name of religion or nationalism, the ideals represented by the Universal Christian Empire, as the Old Reich's leaders at times liked to think about it, are beginning to take on a fresh appeal. For too long some historians contrasted the Empire unfavorably with the strong national monarchies that emerged in late medieval England and France, among others. It was further argued that the Empire retarded the development of both Germany and Italy as nation-states and that because they were late in developing in the national mode, they later became overly nationalistic, which paved the way for the rise of fascism. The Old Reich is also held responsible for World Wars I and II, the Great Depression, and the Holocaust.

This tortured historical logic is coming to appear increasingly farfetched and unfair to the larger, infinitely complex reality of the Holy Roman Empire. Perhaps Frederick Barbarossa has little to do with Hitler and Goebbels. Such linkages, even those that also include Alexander the Great, Augustus Caesar, Charlemagne, Otto I, and Napoleon I, are patently absurd and do a great injustice to the historical process as it seeks to understand how the world functions. Total history, soon to be cosmic history, has helped give us a better perspective on the political history of the last two thousand years. Freed from the fears and partisan passions of World War II, we no longer need allow the catastrophes of the eighteen years of the Third Reich dwarf the realities of the one thousand years of the Old Reich.

Despite the attractiveness of the concept of a universal monarchy headed by an elected emperor with rather circumscribed powers, we will not argue that the Empire "was the greatest achievement of the German people" or that it was the most intelligent political system yet devised. Benevolent as some of the emperors were, the imperial system (and the term *system* is really too modern a concept) did not work to provide maximum economic benefits for the masses. However, the emperors did do a great deal to help the economic life of the Empire by defending it against outside aggressors and by trying to keep internal peace, though with limited success. In addition, politically astute as the emperors were, one of their objectives was not to increase political expression opportunities for their subjects. The objectives of modern political states differ sharply in many respects from the concerns of the Holy Roman emperors. Many moderns have little sympathy with defenders of the faith or those who wish to recapture the glory of ancient Rome. Even though our world view is different in some respects, we can still learn much from those who lived in central Europe between 800 and 1806.

The Holy Roman Empire, 800 to 1806 represents an effort to increase our understanding of this complex phenomenon. It contains short essays with brief bibliographies on many of the persons, places, terms, and events of importance for the history of the Empire. The book is designed for the general public, students, and scholars. Some will use it to supplement and update standard German reference works such as Bruno Gebhardt's four-volume *Handbuch der deutschen Geschichte,* or the fifty-six volumes of the *Allgemeine deutsche Biographie.* Obviously a single-volume reference work on such a broad topic cannot claim to be comprehensive, although a strong effort has been made to be at least somewhat representative.

Individual essays on the emperors and their predecessor kings from Charlemagne to Francis II are included. These imperial sketches provide some of the skeleton that helps to hold the book together just as the emperors served as the most important personification of the Empire itself. Certainly the emperors were not always the most important figures in the Empire; nevertheless their lives are worthy of our attention, and they do tell us something about the larger life of the Empire. It must always be kept in mind what a symbolic entity the Empire was and how much was symbolized in the office of the emperor. All of the lesser emperors shared some of the reflected glory of Charlemagne and Otto I and the larger imperial tradition with its many legends and myths. All states rest on certain shared illusions, as well as certain inescapable realities. Sometimes the illusion is more powerful than even the most basic of realities, including military force and taxation.

The story of the Empire, nevertheless, is more than the saga of the emperors. It is also illustrated by the lives of thousands of less-exalted individuals. This is especially true for a structure like the Old Reich, where power was so diffused. Therefore we have included biographical studies of seventeen ecclesiastical princes; twenty-four secular princes; twenty-eight nonruling political leaders; and fifteen military men. These categories provide for some overlapping since many of the emperors, for example, were also military leaders and much else. Furthermore, to provide a suitable working vocabulary for those new to the subject of the Empire, a number of important terms and institutions, such as *Roman law* and *Imperial Cameral Court,* are defined and explained. The political history of the Empire is further illuminated by fifteen entries on wars, ten on major battles, and fourteen on significant treaties.

Despite the extensive coverage of political and military history, other important developments are included. Thus the volume provides brief essays about thirty-seven prominent theologians and philosophers, sixteen humanists, twenty-four authors, fifteen artists and musicians, and several scientists. Many more in each category could have been included except for limitations of space. Happily other English-language reference works, such as the *Dictionary of Scientific Biography,* make up for many of the omissions of nonpolitical figures, as well as providing greater coverage for some of those included.

An effort has been made to present essays of interest to students of social, economic, urban, and women's history. These are among the areas that have not received as much attention from historians as imperial political and cultural history but are now drawing increasing attention. A great deal remains to be done and redone in all phases and aspects of research on the Holy Roman Empire. This volume includes ten histories of cities; ten essays on individual women, many of whose lives illustrate larger issues; an essay on Jews in the Empire; an essay on witchcraft; and an important essay on the Peasants' War of 1524–1526, which sheds light on the wider social and economic implications of that event. Prominent capitalists like Jacob Fugger are covered, as well as

Maps
of the Holy Roman Empire
circa 843 to circa 1810

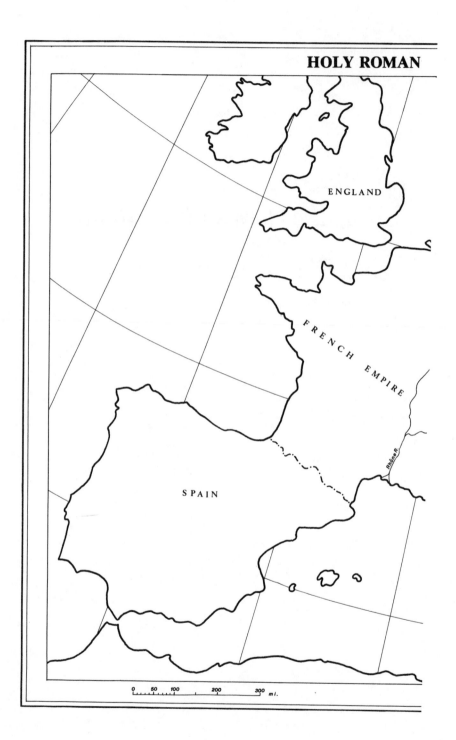

HOLY ROMAN

ENGLAND

FRENCH EMPIRE

Rhône R.

SPAIN

0 50 100   200   300 mi.

EMPIRE CIRCA 843 *1810*

RUSSIA

Rhine R.

CONFEDERATION

of the

RHINE

PRUSSIA

Oder

D. of WARSAW

AUSTRIAN EMPIRE

HELVETIC REP.

ILLYRIAN PROV.

K. of ITALY

OTTOMAN

Danube R.

EMPIRE

K. of NAPLES

TCP'71

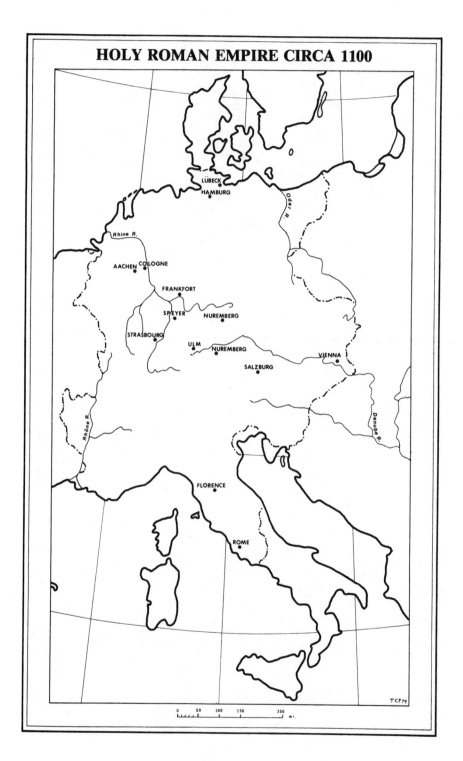

HOLY ROMAN EMPIRE CIRCA 1100

LÜBECK
HAMBURG

Rhine R.

AACHEN COLOGNE

FRANKFORT

SPEYER   NUREMBERG

STRASBOURG

ULM
NUREMBERG

VIENNA

SALZBURG

Oder R.

Rhône R.

Danube R.

FLORENCE

ROME

0   50   100   150   250
                          mi.

TCP79

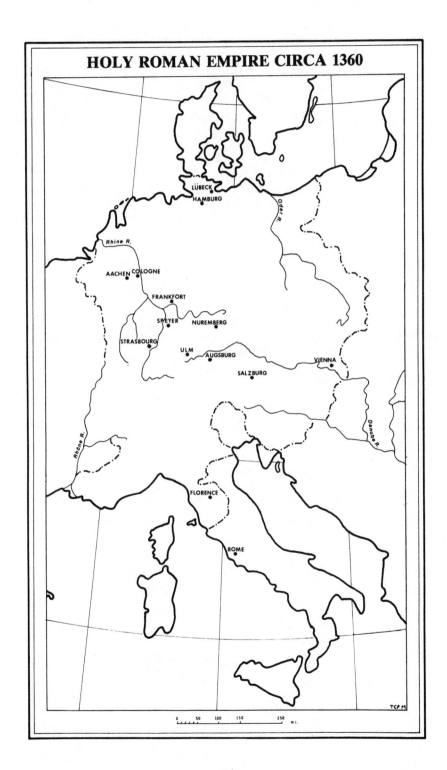

HOLY ROMAN EMPIRE CIRCA 1360

LÜBECK

HAMBURG

Rhine R.

Oder R.

AACHEN COLOGNE

FRANKFORT

SPEYER NUREMBERG

STRASBOURG

ULM AUGSBURG

VIENNA

SALZBURG

Rhône R.

Danube R.

FLORENCE

ROME

TCP 79

0   50   100   150   250
                            mi.

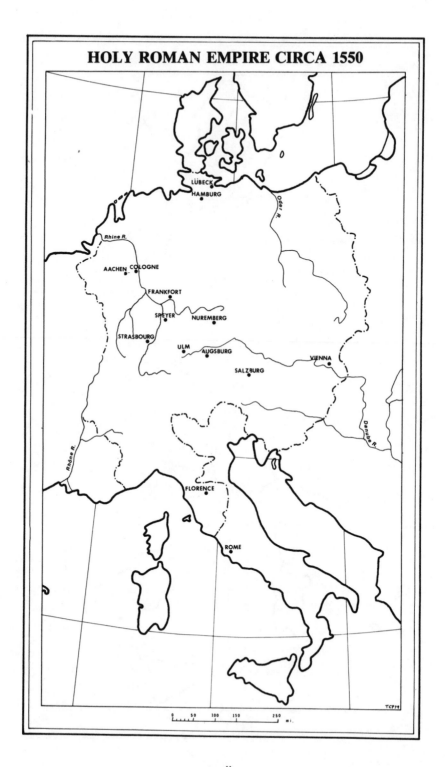

HOLY ROMAN EMPIRE CIRCA 1550

LÜBECK
HAMBURG

Oder R.

Rhine R.

AACHEN COLOGNE

FRANKFORT

SPEYER   NUREMBERG

STRASBOURG

ULM
AUGSBURG   VIENNA

SALZBURG

Rhône R.

Danube R.

FLORENCE

ROME

0   50   100   150   250
                              mi.

TCP79

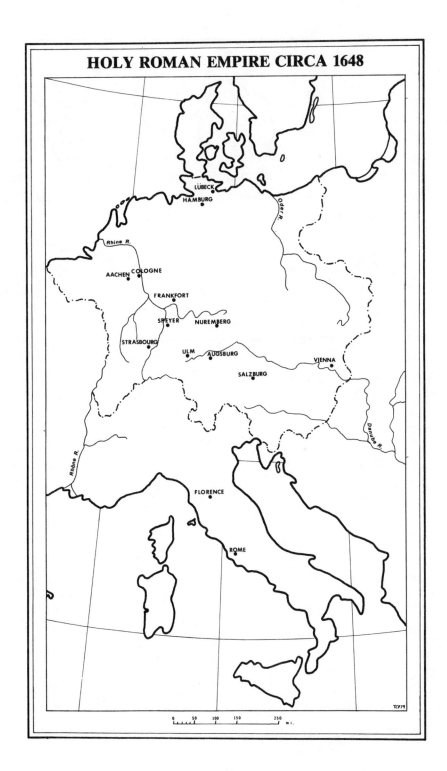

HOLY ROMAN EMPIRE CIRCA 1648

LÜBECK
HAMBURG

Oder R.

Rhine R.

AACHEN COLOGNE
FRANKFORT
SPEYER NUREMBERG
STRASBOURG
ULM AUGSBURG
SALZBURG
VIENNA

Rhône R.

Danube R.

FLORENCE

ROME

0   50   100   150   250   mi.

TCP79

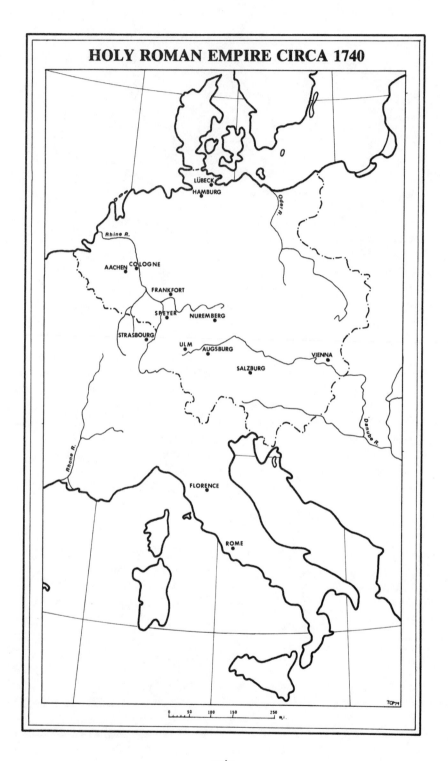

HOLY ROMAN EMPIRE CIRCA 1740

LÜBECK
HAMBURG

Rhine R.
Oder R.

AACHEN COLOGNE

FRANKFORT

SPEYER NUREMBERG

STRASBOURG

ULM AUGSBURG
VIENNA

SALZBURG

Rhone R.

Danube R.

FLORENCE

ROME

0   50   100   150   250
m.i.

TCP71

HOLY ROMAN EMPIRE CIRCA 1801

LÜBECK

HAMBURG

Rhine R.

Oder R.

AACHEN COLOGNE

FRANKFORT

SPEYER NUREMBERG

STRASBOURG

ULM AUGSBURG

VIENNA

SALZBURG

Rhône R.

Danube R.

FLORENCE

ROME

0 50 100 150 250 mi.

TCP71

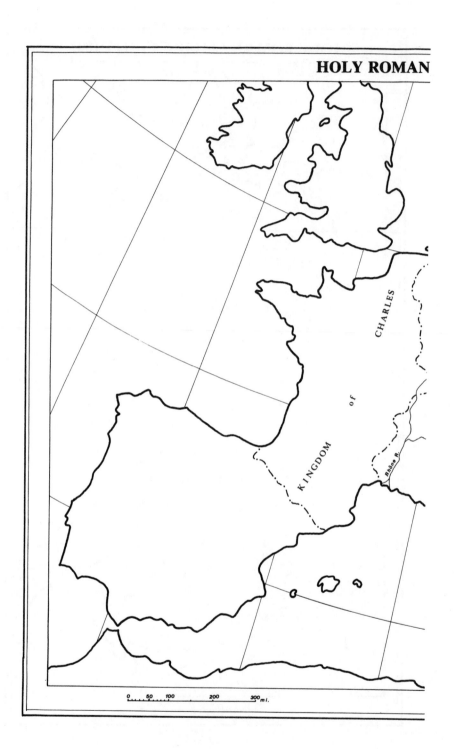

CHARLES

o f

KINGDOM

Rhône R.

0   50   100   200   300 mi.

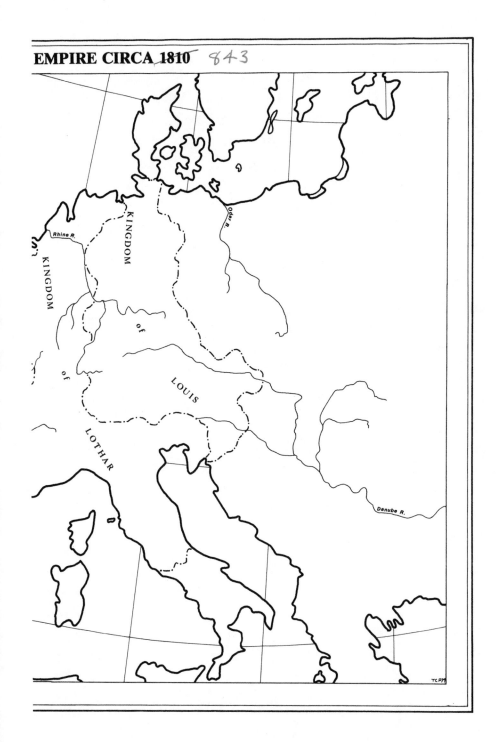

EMPIRE CIRCA 1810 843

KINGDOM

Rhine R.

Odor R.

KINGDOM

of

of

LOUIS

LOTHAR

Danube R.

TCP9

The Holy
Roman
Empire

a

AACHEN (Aix-la-Chapelle) was the capital of Charlemagne's Empire. According to his biographer Einhard, Charlemagne decided to build his palace at Aachen because of his love of swimming in the warm mineral springs. After his imperial coronation in the year 800, Charlemagne considered Aachen to be the "new Rome." Rarely leaving the city after 807, Charlemagne embarked on an ambitious building program, including the construction of the imperial chapel, Capella Palatina, patterned after San Vitale in Ravenna. However, the most enduring moment created at Aachen was cultural and intellectual, not material. It was from the Palace School at Charlemagne's court at Aachen that the movement known as the Carolingian Renaissance was begun.

Although some form of school had existed at court from the days of Charles Martel, prior to 782 the school was primarily a place where young nobles learned knightly virtues and the arts of warfare. Charlemagne widened the curriculum to include intellectual training by organizing and centralizing the cultural activities taking place at scattered local schools. Scholars were gathered from the provinces, Spain, and, especially, England, where numerous monastic centers of learning were still very active.

Charlemagne's determination to spread Christianity through an educated clergy provided the initial inspiration for the revival of learning, but the training of administrators was the primary function of the Palace School. In an age of almost universal illiteracy, Charlemagne needed literate men to write and enforce the laws if his vast Empire of different peoples and dialects was to be held together by more than the sheer force of his army.

Alcuin, an English scholar, served as a sort of chief minister for ecclesiastical and educational affairs. He knew the liberal arts and organized a curriculum that included grammar, arithmetic, geometry, and astronomy. Other well-known scholars at the school included Peter of Pisa, a grammarian and poet; Paul the Deacon, a Lombard historian; Theodolf from Spain, a classicist; and the Franks Angilbert and Einhard.

Much of the new learning was devoted to a mastery of Latin, which had fallen into decay in the centuries since the end of the Roman Empire. A usable form of handwriting known as Carolingian miniscule was developed. These basic tools enabled the palace scholars to study and copy many works of the Church fathers and selected classical authors. By encouraging the dissemination of this new learning throughout the Empire, the preservation of the thoughts of some ancient authors and early Church fathers was ensured.

The most original thought that developed at the Palace School was in the area of political theory. The imperial coronation of Charlemagne raised the issue of universal Christian authority. Court scholars attempted to define the proper roles of emperor and pope. Although these works had little if any immediate effect (Charlemagne completely dominated the Church), they did provide a starting point from which the great battles concerning imperial-papal power would grow in the eleventh and twelfth centuries. Undoubtedly the ideas of the churchmen associated with the Palace School had a tremendous influence on Charlemagne's son Louis the Pious, whose reign was dominated by a conflict between his imperial responsibilities and his perceived duty as a Christian emperor to submit to the higher spiritual authority of the Church.

With few exceptions, the work of the court scholars was unoriginal. Literature and poetry generally followed the content and style of the ancients and the Church fathers very closely. Architecture tended to be a fusion of Roman, Byzantine, and Oriental styles. Even in the field of political theory, which produced the most original ideas, thought at any given time was determined chiefly by existing conditions.

Despite its severe limitations, the Carolingian Renaissance made western Europe more aware of its cultural heritage and spread learning beyond the confines of a few isolated monasteries. The idea that education was necessary for good government, Church administration, and the community in general was firmly planted.

Aachen never became the new Rome that Charlemagne had envisioned, but the town did continue as an important ceremonial center until the end of the Empire. It became customary for the emperors to be elected at Frankfurt, but they continued to be crowned at Aachen. Especially brilliant coronations were held for Otto I in 962 and Charles V in 1520. Napoleon received the reliquary of Charlemagne at Aachen. The presence of the emperors on ceremonial occasions and at other times, the cathedral, and the many imperial traditions associated with Aachen helped to keep the community alive despite its lack of development in trade and industry and the attention the emperors paid to other cities such as Nuremberg and Vienna. The Carolingian capital endured as an important symbol of imperial continuity and tradition.

Works About: E. S. Duckett, *Alcuin, Friend of Charlemagne* (New York, 1951); M. Laistner, *Thought and Letters in Western Europe, A.D. 500–900* (Ithaca, N.Y., 1931); P. Mennicken, "Der Aachener Dom," in *Aachen zum Jahre 1951* (Aachen, 1951); K. F. Morrison, *The Two Kingdoms* (Princeton, 1964); H. Schnitzler, *Der Dom zu Aachen* (Düsseldorf, 1950); P. E. Schramm, *Die Anerkennung Karls des Grossen als Kaiser* (Munich, 1952); R. E. Sullivan, *Aix-la-Chapelle in the Age of Charlemagne* (Norman, Oklahoma, 1963).   D. B. Mapes

See CHARLEMAGNE; CHARLES V; FRANKFURT AM MAIN; LOUIS I; NUREMBERG; OTTO I; VIENNA.

ADELHEIDE OF BURGUNDY (c. 931–999), wife of Emperor Otto I, the Great (912–973), was the daughter of Rudolf II of Burgundy and Bertha of

Swabia. Soon after the death of her father in 937, Bertha married King Hugo of Italy. At an early age Adelheide was betrothed to Hugo's son, Lothar. Hugo fell from power in 945, but with the support of Margrave Berengar of Ivrea, Lothar became king of Italy. Adelheide married Lothar in 947 and bore him a daughter, Emma, later queen of France. Lothar died on November 22, 950. When Adelheide refused to marry Berengar II's son, Adalbert, Berenger held her prisoner for four months in Como (April–August 951). She escaped, traveled to Canossa, and visited Atto, a relative of Matilda, the mother of Otto I. At Canossa Adelheide received a marriage proposal from Otto I, whose first wife, the Anglo-Saxon princess, Edgitha, had died in 946. Adelheide and Otto I were married in Italy late in 951, and Otto I asserted his claim to the throne of Italy.

Four children were born to Adelheide and Otto I: Emperor Otto II (955–983); Matilda (955–999), first abbess of Quedlinburg; Adelheide (?–974), abbess of Essen; and Liutgard (?–?).

In 962 Otto I and Adelheide returned to Italy for their imperial coronation by Pope John XII. A third trip to Italy lasting six years (966–972) was necessary for Otto I to establish his authority in Italy and to defeat the Greeks lodged in southern Italy. To ease tensions with the east, a marriage between Otto II, coemperor since 967, and Theophano, daughter of the eastern emperor Romanus II, was arranged (972).

Adelheide was one of Otto I's close advisers, and she remained at the imperial court during the first half of the reign of her son, Otto II (973–983). For unknown reasons Adelheide chose after 978 to live in Italy or at the court of her brother, Conrad of Burgundy. Adelheide and Otto II were reconciled at a meeting in Pavia (980). Shortly before Otto II's death in 983, Adelheide was made viceroy in Italy. When Otto II died, his successor, Otto III (980–1002), was three years old. Henry II, the Quarrelsome, duke of Bavaria, tried to establish himself as regent for the young emperor. Adelheide quickly returned from Italy to oppose Henry II and together with Theophano and Archbishop Willegis of Mainz assumed responsibility for the administration of the Empire. She became estranged from Theophano and left the imperial court, returning after Theophano's death in 991. Adelheide was regent until Otto III took over the government in 995.

Adelheide devoted her energy to the Church in her final years. Abbots Majolus and Odilo of Cluny were her close friends and spiritual advisers. She founded a number of churches and cloisters, among them the convent of St. Peter and St. Paul in Salz, Alsace, where she was buried in 999.

Works About: Gertrud Bäumer, *Otto I. und Adelheid* (Tübingen, 1951); J. Bentzinger, *Das Leben der Kaiserin Adelheid* (Turin, 1842); W. von Giesebrecht, *Gesch. der dtsch. Kaiserzeit* (Leipzig, 1881), vol. 1; Hermann Hüffer in "Das Leben der Kaiserin Adalheid von Odilo von Cluny," *Geschichtschreiber der dtsch. Vorzeit*, 2d ed. (Leipzig, 1891) vol. 8; R. Köpke and E. Dümmler, *Jb. des dtsch. Reichs unter Otto I.* (Leipzig, 1876); Giovanni-Battista Semeria, *Vita politico-religiosa de santa Adelaide* (Turin, 1842); E. Steindorff, "Adelheid," *ADB* 1:75–77; K. Uhlirz, *Jb. des dtsch. Reichs unter Kaiser Otto II.* (Berlin, 1837–1840); R. Wilmans, *Jb. des dtsch. Reichs* *unter Kaiser Otto III.* (Berlin, 1837–1840); F. P. Wimmer, *Kaiserin Adelheid, Gemahlin Ottos I. des Grossen* (Regensburg, 1889).   *J. W. Gates*

See MATILDA OF QUEDLINBURG; OTTO II; OTTO III.

ADOLF OF NASSAU (1255–1298) was the son of Count Walfram II. He was elected king of the Germans in 1291 and ruled until his deposition by the German princes in 1298. Like his predecessor, Rudolf of Habsburg, Adolf did not come from a house that had attained princely rank. The two dominant features of his reign were poverty and reliance upon the Church for support.

Adolf did not come to the throne until the two most prominent candidates, Albert, son of Rudolf I, and Wenceslaus IV, king of Bohemia, son of Ottocar (r. 1278–1305), had been rejected. Although Albert's reputation for cruelty may have played some part in his rejection, it is more likely that the electors took into consideration the fact that the election of either Albert or Wenceslaus IV was almost sure to bring about a war between Austria and Bohemia. After nine months of intrigue, the electors met at Frankfurt and elected Adolf of Nassau. The presence of Gerhard of Eppstein, archbishop of Mainz and a close relative of Adolf, as one of the electors probably contributed to his election. The election took place May 1, 1291, and was unanimous. Adolf I was crowned on June 24 at Aachen.

Adolf's financial problems began even before his coronation when he was forced to pledge his castle at Cobern in return for the two thousand marks needed to pay for his election expenses. Soon after, he had to pledge a portion of the imperial domain to Wenceslaus IV as a security for the marriage settlement of his daughter Guta, who was to marry Rupert, Wenceslaus' son. It was hoped that this marriage would cement a family alliance against the Habsburgs.

Adolf's chronic need of money and lack of prudence led him to make a treaty in 1294 with Edward I, king of England. In return for thirty thousand marks, Adolf agreed to attack the French forces of Philip the Fair with whom Edward I was engaged in war. Adolf kept his word and attacked the French. Immediately his rival, Albert of Habsburg, declared for the French. There was little bloodshed, but the German princes began to complain that their king was nothing more than a mercenary for the English. Plans for Adolf's deposition began to be formed.

Another source of discontent involved Adolf's subservience to the Church, the papacy as well as the German ecclesiastical princes. Adolf's obligations to the Church were shown when he renounced the power of intermeddling with ecclesiastical suits and confirmed to the archbishop and clergy all their immunities, secular and spiritual. He also bound himself as surety for Archbishop Gerhard to the pope in a sum that he failed to pay and that rendered Adolf liable at every moment to papal dictation.

By 1298 the German princes began to make definite plans for Adolf's deposition. They offered the crown to Albert of Habsburg and asked Pope Boniface

VIII to assent to the deposition. Given Adolf's obligations to the papacy, it is not surprising that Boniface refused to agree to his removal. Nevertheless the princes made arrangements for a diet at Frankfurt on May 1 to which both Adolf and Albert were summoned.

On June 23 a court at Mainz formally deposed Adolf and bestowed the crown on Albert. Adolf was charged with general incapacity and uselessness, destruction of churches, corruption of virgins, serving the king of England for pay, and cruelties exercised in Thuringia and Meissen. The accusations were made and sentence pronounced by the electors of Mainz, Saxony, and Brandenburg. Although these electors claimed to have the protection and authority of the pope and the consent of the other electors, Adolf did retain the support of the Count Palatine and the archbishop of Trier.

Adolf hurried to fight for his throne and ten days after the deposition met his enemy in force at Göllsheim near Worms, where he was killed in battle. Adolf was buried at Speyer.

Works About: G. Barraclough, *The Origins of Modern Germany* (New York, 1946); Adolf Gauert, "Adolf von Nassau," *NDB*, 1:74–75; F. Heer, *The Holy Roman Empire*, tr. Janet Sondheimer (New York, 1968); *MGH Legum Sectio IV, Constitutiones et Acta Publica*, ed. Jakob Schwalm (Hanover, 1904–1906), vols. 2–4; W. Stubbs, *Germany in the Later Middle Ages* (London, 1908); Wegele, "Adolf von Nassau," *ADB*, 1:89–92.   *D. B. Mapes*

See AACHEN; ALBERT I; RUDOLF I.

ADRIAN VI (1459–1523), pope, born Adrian Florenz Dedal in Utrecht and educated at Zwelle and Deventer by the Brethren of the Common Life, studied and taught theology at the University of Louvain, becoming dean of St. Peter's Church and chancellor of the university in 1947. Margaret of Burgundy chose him as a member of her household, and the Emperor Maximilian I appointed him tutor to his grandson, Charles of Spain, later Charles V. He probably began his duties as Charles' teacher in 1510, and Charles was always grateful to Adrian for his religious instruction. Sent on a diplomatic mission to Spain, on the death of Ferdinand V, Adrian was appointed administrator of the kingdom, made bishop of Tortosa (1516), viceroy of Spain and Castile (1517), and inquisitor of Aragon and Navarre (1517) and Castile and Leon (1518). At the request of Emperor Charles, he was created cardinal by Leo X in 1517, and after Leo's death (1522) the cardinals elected Adrian the first non-Italian pope of the century. He died twenty months after his accession to the papacy.

Adrian attempted to deal with the reform of the Church, the impact of the Lutheran revolt, and the Turkish threat. Humanists such as Juan Luis Vives, Pirckheimer, Aegidius of Viterbo, and even Erasmus looked to Adrian as the needed agent of Church reform. Although he had endorsed the condemnation of Luther's writings by the faculty of theology in Louvain, he sought reform of such abuses as pluralities and opposed simony and nepotism; yet his call for a general council was rejected. He tried to get Erasmus—who considered him an enemy of "good letters"—to write against Luther and was unsuccessful in winning over Zwingli. At the diet of Nuremberg (1522), his *Instructio* admitted to abuses in the curia, but the diet refused his request to execute the Edict of Worms against German heretics. Unable to reconcile the Christian princes— Francis I and Charles V were at war against one another—Adrian was also unable to prevent the fall of Belgrade and Rhodes to the Turks.

Works By: L. P. Gachard, ed., *Correspondence de Charles-Quint et d'Arien VI* (Brussels, 1859); A. Mercati, ed., *Dall'Archivo vaticano: . . . Diarii di concistori del pontificato di Adriano VI* (Rome, 1951). **Works About:** C. Burman, *Hadrianus VI, sive analecta historica* (Utrecht, 1727); J. Coppens, *Paus Adriaan VI* (Louvain, 1959); P. Declerkc, "Adriaan van Utrecht (1459–1523)," *Collationes Burgenses et Gandavenses* 6 (1960); 3–35; *Ephem. Theol. Lovanienses* 35 (1959); 513– 629; C. A. C. von Höfler, *Papst Adrian VI* (Vienna, 1880); A. Lapitre, *Adrien VI* (Paris, 1880); G. Moringus, *Vita Hadriani VI* (Louvain, 1536); R. R. Post, "Studien over paus Adriaan VI," *Arch. Gesch. Kath. Kerk Nederland* 3 (1960): 12–61, 341–51; E. H. J. Reusens, *Syntagma Doctrinae Theologicae Adriani sexti* (Louvain, 1862); D. Van der Perre, "Paus Adrianus VI en Erasmus," *Hist. Documentatie* 12 (1970): 16–35.   *A. M. McLean*

See CHARLES V; ERASMUS MAXIMILIAN I; NUREMBERG, DIETS OF 1522–1524.

AGNES OF POITOU (c. 1025–1077), second wife of Emperor Henry III (1017–1056), was the daughter of Duke William V of Aquitaine (?–1031) and his second wife, Agnes of Burgundy. After the death of her father, who was one of the most powerful lords in France, Agnes of Burgundy defeated her two stepsons, William the Fat of Aquitaine and Odo, and ruled first for and later with her own two sons. During her early years, Agnes of Poitou is mentioned twice in contemporary records: once at the court of William the Fat (1031) and a second time at the side of his wife, Eustacia, in a cloister (1036–1037) after William's fall from power. She was in Besançon at the court of her uncle Reginald in 1042 when Bruno, bishop of Würzburg, came to seek her hand for Henry III, whose first wife, Gunhilda of Denmark, had died in Italy in 1038. Henry III met Agnes at the Burgundian border in October 1043. They traveled to Mainz where she was crowned queen. With great pomp the two were married in Ingelheim late in November 1043. Agnes accompanied Henry III to Italy in 1046, and the two were crowned emperor and empress by Pope Clemens II on Christmas Day. Five children were born to Henry III and Agnes: Matilda (1045– 1060), wife of Rudolf of Swabia; Judith–Sophia (1047–1097), wife of Salomon of Hungary (d. 1068) and later of Vladislav of Poland; Adelheide (1048–?), from 1062 abbess of Quedlinburg and Gandersheim; Emperor Henry IV (1050– 1106); and Conrad (1052–1055).

Agnes was usually at Henry III's side. She is mentioned in many imperial documents, but no contemporary chroniclers characterize her influence at court. Most historians agree that Henry III held the reigns of political, military, and ecclesiastical power in his own hands. Nevertheless Agnes administered the Empire as regent for Henry IV between 1056 and 1062. She tried to preserve the Empire and the policies of Henry III. Like Henry III Agnes chose her advisers from the ecclesiastical hierarchy and traveled extensively within the Empire.

Agnes' regency was plagued with misfortune. She placed the administration of some imperial territories in the hands of powerful nobles who later rebelled against her son, Henry IV. For example, Rudolf of Rheinfelden received Swabia. Agnes tried to strengthen Rudolf's ties to the imperial court by arranging his marriage to her eldest daughter, Matilda, in 1059. Matilda died the following year, however, and Rudolf of Swabia became one of Henry IV's most rebellious vassals.

In 1060 Agnes sent an army led by King Andreas to help her son-in-law Salomon of Hungary. Andreas was killed, the army was defeated, and Judith and Salomon were forced to flee to Melk. When Pope Victor II died in 1057, his successor, Stephen IX (Frederick of Lower Lorraine, abbot of Monte Cassino), was chosen without her participation. Stephen IX visited the imperial court and was on good terms with Agnes, but the reform papal party precipitated crises in church politics for her son.

In the spring of 1062, Agnes' regency ended abruptly. Bishop Anno of Cologne kidnapped the twelve-year-old Henry IV. Henry tried unsuccessfully to break away from his captors. Agnes made no attempt to resist the transfer of power and withdrew to her own lands. The following winter Agnes traveled to Italy, arriving in Rome in 1063 dressed as a penitent. Peter Damiani became her close friend and spiritual adviser. Agnes quickly won the trust of Pope Alexander II, who sent her several times to the imperial court to gain support for his papacy. She was closely associated with Hildebrand who became Pope Gregory VII in 1073. Agnes defended the papal position and tried to conciliate between Gregory VII and Henry IV until her death in 1077.

Works About: Marie Luise Bulst–Thiele, *Kaiserin Agnes, Beiträge zur kulturgeschichte des mittelalters und der renaissance* (Leipzig, 1933) vol. 52; G. Meyer von Knonau, *Jb. des dtsch. Reiches unter Heinrich IV.* (Leipzig, 1890); T. Lindner, "Agnes von Poitou," *ADB* 1:138–40; Karl Seipoldy, *Die Regentschaft der Kaiserin Agnes von Poitiers* (Berlin, 1887); E. Steindorff, *Jb. des dtsch. Reiches unter Heinrich III.* (Leipzig, 1874–1881):   *J. W. Gates*

See GREGORY VII; HENRY III; HENRY IV; INVESTITURE CONTROVERSY; STEPHEN IX.

AGRICOLA, RUDOLF (1444–1485), humanist, was born near Groningen in Frisia. A precocious intellect, Rudolf began his university career at Erfurt at age twelve. He also studied at Cologne and Louvain, where he developed a strong interest in classical Greek. This interest was fully realized between 1496 and 1979, a decade Agricola spent in Italy, where he mastered Greek and wrote a biography of Petrarch.

When he returned to the north in 1479, Agricola found himself sought after as a leading link with the intellectual life of the south. He represented his home town at the court of Emperor Maximilian for half a year in 1482. Finally, elector Philip of the Palatinate and Bishop John von Dalberg won his services and brought him to Heidelberg. His last years were spent studying, lecturing, and informally presiding over a circle of younger humanists. His most important work was an introductory manual, *On Dialectical Invention*. Agricola was one of the founding fathers of German humanism.

Works By: P. S. Allen, "The Letters of Rudolf Agricola," *English Historical Review* 21 (1906): 302–17. **Works About:** Friedrich von Bezold, *Rudolf Agricola* (Munich, 1884); L. W. Spitz, *The Religious Renaissance of the German Humanists* (Cambridge, Mass., 1963); H. E. J. M. van der Velden, *Rodophus Agricola* (Leiden, 1911).   *J. W. Zophy*

See HUMANISM; MAXIMILIAN I.

ALBERT I (1225–1308) who ruled the Empire from 1298 to 1308, was the eldest son of the founder of the Habsburg imperial dynasty, Rudolf I, and Gertrude von Hohenberg. In 1298, he became imperial regent of the duchies of Steiermark and Austria; in 1282, he ruled them together with his brother Rudolf and, by the Rheinfelder agreement of 1283, became their sole ruler. He proved to be both a capable military leader and competent administrator and was widely regarded as the chief contender for the imperial crown, although his father was unable to secure his succession.

Rudolf's death in 1292 brought Albert additional Habsburg holdings in the Upper Rhineland and Swabia. But the Rhenish ecclesiastical electors, led by Archbishop Gerhard of Mainz, found him too powerful and independent to be trusted. Instead they elected Adolf of Nassau, a vassal of Cologne and the count Palatine, in May 1292. Adolf proved to be less of a "cleric's king" than anticipated, and his alliance with Edward I of England against Philip IV of France in 1295 was opposed by Pope Boniface VIII. Boniface gradually moved into Albert's camp. With the support of his brother-in-law Wenceslaus II of Bohemia, Gerhard of Mainz, and most of the ecclesiastical and lay princes, Albert deposed Adolf in 1298, ostensibly because he had despoiled Church property. The issue was settled with Adolf's defeat and death at the Battle of Göllsheim, and Albert was elected king of the Germans on July 27, 1298, at Frankfurt and crowned a month later at Aachen.

Albert quickly intervened in imperial politics, confirming the privileges of the imperial princes wrested from the cities and mollifying the cities, in turn, by reducing tolls on commerce at the diet at Nuremberg in 1298–1299. He defended the Jews from persecution. In August 1300, he beat a hasty retreat from Nimwegen before Count John of Hainault could compel royal recognition of his usurpation of the vacant imperial fiefs of Holland and Zeeland. And he agreed to submit conflicting French and imperial claims in the Burgundian territories to arbitration and sealed the peace with a marriage alliance at Quatrevaux near Tours in December 1299.

Boniface VIII did not look favorably upon a relaxation of tension between France and Germany. Nor would he recognize Albert, although he had helped to depose Adolf, until he renounced imperial rights in northern Italy. In October 1300, Boniface organized yet another league against a German king, this time composed of the remaining adherents of Nassau and led by Adolf's brother, Archbishop Diether of Trier. In turn, Albert drew upon the support of the Rhenish towns, to whom he promised further reductions in princely tolls, and was able to secure the peace in a long series of campaigns along the Rhine. Despite threats of excommunication and an outstanding charge of the murder of Adolf, Boniface clearly needed Albert's support against France. With a few perfunctory diplomatic gestures, papal recognition was secured on April 30, 1303, and the whole issue became moot when Boniface was captured at Anagni and then died in Rome on October 11.

Settlement with the pope freed Albert to strengthen his dynastic position within the Empire, and this required that he turn his attention to the east. Albert's brother-in-law, Wenceslaus II of Bohemia, king of Poland since 1300, now looked to the Hungarian succession for his son Wenceslaus III. Albert was acutely aware of the danger that Premyslid ambition held for his dynastic position in Austria and the possibility of a French-Bohemian alliance held at least as much danger for the Empire. He marched into Hungary late in 1304, but Wenceslaus' death in 1305 forced his son to renounce his claim. Wenceslaus III was murdered in 1306, thus ending the dynasty in Bohemia. Albert was able to secure both Bohemia and Moravia as imperial fiefs for his son Rudolf.

Like Adolf of Nassau before him, Albert attempted to claim Thuringia as a fief of the Empire and sent forces to invade the lands of the Wettin Margrave Frederick. Their defeat at Lucka in May 1307, combined with the death of Rudolf in July, which left Bohemia to Duke Henry of Carinthia, seemed to signal a general unrest in the Empire. Swabia and the Swiss cantons, the Rhineland, were all in revolt, and Albert was compelled to turn his attention to the restoration of his authority in the west. He was assassinated by three young nobles while making preparations for his campaigns near Brugge in Baden on May 1, 1308. Among the conspirators was his disaffected nephew Duke John of Swabia, the son of his younger brother Rudolf, called John the Parricide.

Works About: Hermann Henneberg, *Die politischen Beziehungen zwischen Deutschland und Frankreich unter König Albrecht I* (Strasbourg, 1891); Alfred Hessel, *Jb. des dtsch. Reichs unter Konig Albrecht I von Habsburg* (Munich, 1931): M. Lintzel, "Das Bundnis Albrechts I mit Bonifaz VIII," *HZ* 151 (1935): 457–85; H. L. Lucas, "Diplomatic Relations of Edward I and Albrecht of Austria," *Spec.* 9 (1934): 125–34; *MGH Legum Sectio IV, Constitutiones et Acta Publica* ed. Jakob Schwalm (Hanover, 1904–1906): vols. 3, 4 and supplementum 4, pt. 2; Alfred Niemeier, *Untersuchungen über die Beziehungen Albrechts I zu Bonifax VIII* (Berlin, 1900). S. A. Garretson

See ADOLF OF NASSAU; RUDOLF I.

ALBERT II (1397–1439), who ruled the Empire from 1438 to 1439, was the first in an unbroken succession of Habsburg monarchs that lasted until 1740, ending with Charles VI. The son of Albert IV of Austria and Johanna of Bavaria-

Straubing, Albert ruled Austria in regency from 1404 to 1411 and proved himself to be a competent military leader during the Hussite wars. A capable administrator, he imposed a relatively successful territorial peace in Austria and developed a strong territorial church after Pope Martin V granted him the right to reform Austrian cloisters in 1418. His death in 1439 and the death of his unlucky son, Ladislaus Posthumous, in 1457 ended the Albertine line of the Habsburgs.

Albert's career was tied to the fortunes of the last Luxembourg king of Germany, Sigismund. Not only did Albert assist him in his wars against the Hussites in 1420 and 1421, but he broke from the Electoral Union of 1424, a body of imperial princes who sought to act as a regency council to rule the western Empire in Sigismund's stead. He married Sigismund's daughter Elizabeth on April 19, 1422, and was designated heir in Bohemia and Hungary by both the marriage and by an interdynastic pact dating from the reign of Charles IV and confirmed by Sigismund in 1402. He enjoyed Sigismund's sponsorship when he attempted in October 1423 to assert his authority over the imperial fiefdom of Moravia, which nevertheless ended in his defeat by the Hussites at Tauss in 1431.

Sigismund's death on December 9, 1437, left Albert the chief claimant for the imperial crown. His election in Hungary followed immediately on December 18, 1438, and he was crowned at Stuhlweissenburg on January 1 with little difficulty, except for the electoral concession that he would reside in Hungary. The crown of Germany came almost as easily, and Albert was elected at Frankfurt on March 18, 1438, accepted the invitation late in April, and was approved without delay by Pope Eugenius IV, who needed an ally in his fight with the Council of Basel. The imperial princes of Germany were interested in gaining concessions, however, and they would have required Albert to reduce the power and independence of the imperial cities, consult them on major decisions concerning the Empire, reform the courts, remove Sigismund's Bohemian chancellor Caspar Schlick and replace him with a German prelate less favorably inclined toward the cities, and maintain neutrality between pope and council for at least six months.

The crown of Bohemia posed greater problems. Under the aegis of Sigismund's succession agreement, Albert was elected by a majority of the Bohemian estates on December 27, 1437, at Prague. But a significant minority of the Czech-Nationalist party, among whom George Podiebrady first made his appearance, favored an alliance with Poland and invited King Vladislav to claim Bohemia for his thirteen-year-old brother Casimir. Albert attempted to avoid Polish intervention by marrying his daughter Elizabeth to Casimir, but the Hussites elected him nonetheless at Prague on May 29, 1438. In the war that followed, Albert had the support of Saxony, Bavaria, and Brandenburg. He drove the Poles back to Silesia and Moravia before Pope Eugenius IV established an armistice in January 1439.

Eugenius' hopes that Albert would intervene against the Council of Basel proved to be groundless, and when Albert put the electoral requirements made of him in March before the diet at Nuremberg in July 1438, only the point of neutrality was confirmed. Worse, the diet at Mainz in 1439 promulgated anti-papal reform decrees from Basel, while preserving its neutrality on the conciliar issue. Indeed the imperial diets were still inflamed by the reforming impulse evident in the 1420s during the reign of Sigismund. At the diet at Nuremberg in 1438, the electors again proposed division of the Empire into four circles, using the princely estate to enforce imperial peace, ban the vendetta, and reform the royal courts. Again, as in Sigismund's reign, the cities guardedly opposed such a diffusion of imperial authority and its investment in their princely opponents.

In April 1438, Turkish forces under Sultan Muras II advanced from Siebenbürgen, forcing Albert to search among the Hungarian estates for support. His demands for assistance were met by counter demands for concessions of royal prerogatives and lands, accompanied by anti-German riots. The weak imperial army was unable to defend Serbia. While waiting for reinforcements on the plains of Bacska, Albert II contracted dysentery and died en route to Vienna on October 27, 1439, at Langendorf.

Works About: Wilhelm Altmann, *Die Wahl Albrechts II zum römischen Könige*, Hist. Untersuchungen, vol. 2 (Berlin, 1886); *DRTA, Altere Reihe*, ed. Gustave Beckmann and Helmut Weigel (Stuttgart, 1908–1916), vols. 13, 14; Wilhelm Pückert, *Die Kurfürstliche Neutralität während des Basler Konzils* (Leipzig, 1858); Wilhelm Wostry, *Kaiser Albrecht II* (Vienna, 1906), vols. 1, 2.

S. A. Garretson

See CHARLES IV; FREDERICK III; HUS; SIGISMUND.

ALBERT V (1528–1579), duke of Bavaria from 1550 to 1579, was not only one of the most influential German princes in the Counter Reformation but also one of the founders of the Bavarian absolutist state in the late sixteenth and later seventeenth centuries.

Although little concrete is known about his early childhood, his education and later life were heavily influenced by his training in the Jesuit college at Ingolstadt. The Jesuits imbued the young Bavarian heir with a strong sense of Catholicism and legalism along with a deep appreciation of Renaissance humanism. Often accused of sluggishness, which in part stemmed from Albert's good-natured life-style, he nevertheless displayed energy and ability in dealing with the political and religious problems in his territory. He was a ruler who thoroughly enjoyed the pleasures of life, especially the hunt and banquets. His devotion to Renaissance art, sculpture, music, and architecture was excessive. In fact his extravagant spending seriously strained the resources of his state and left his heir, William V, on the verge of bankruptcy.

Albert's father, William IV, held high political hopes for his son. Albert's marriage to Anna, the eldest daughter of Emperor Ferdinand I, for instance, might have brought an electoral title to Bavaria. Yet as William's only legitimate son, Albert's reign marked the first time the Bavarian decree on primogeniture was put into effect. This decree, promulgated by Duke Albert IV on July 8,

1506, declared that the Bavarian lands were indivisible. Albert V therefore ruled a unified Bavaria over which he steadily tightened political control.

Politics and religion went hand in hand during Albert and his successors' rules. Under Albert V the interconnection of the political and family interests of the Wittelsbachs with that of the Catholic church became a characteristic of the Bavarian dukes.

Centralization of ducal authority partially hinged on the question of Protestantism. Albert's excessive tastes had given the Protestant factions in the Bavarian diet the opportunity to win religious concessions from Albert. The duke had attempted to compromise with the Protestants. In fact he was instrumental in convincing the pope to allow communion in both forms in his lands. When the Protestants remained adamant and resistance within the diet began to grow against Albert's centralizing efforts, Albert moved to crush the Protestants and reduce the power of the Bavarian assembly. In 1563 he accused several leading Lutheran nobles of a conspiracy against him and had them excluded from the diet. In addition, Catholic nobles who thought themselves free of Bavarian authority within the Empire lost their independence. Using a body known as the Spiritual Council, which was largely controlled by Albert's secular advisers, the duke suppressed the Protestant movement within his lands. Every Bavarian church was inspected annually. Strict censorship was imposed, and the Jesuits were given control of the Bavarian schools and universities.

Albert's dogmatic Catholicism not only enabled him to lay the foundations of an absolutist state, but also extended the influence of Bavaria beyond its borders into the Empire. Typical of this Wittelsbach policy was Albert's efforts to acquire bishoprics for Wittelsbach candidates. The attempt to acquire the important territory of Salzburg in 1565 for his youngest son, Ernest, failed, but he did have success in acquiring Freising. Under Albert's successor, William V, Ernest became bishop not only of Hildesheim, Münster, Halberstadt, and Lüttich but also archbishop of Cologne.

Works About: Berndt Baader, *Der Bayerische Renaissancehof Herzog Wilhelms V. (1568–1579)* (Leipzig, 1943); Julius Cohen, *Der Kampf der Bayernherzoge gegen die reformatorische Bewegung in sechzehnten Jahrhundert* (Nuremberg, 1930); Richard Dunn, *The Age of Religious Wars, 1559–1689* (New York, 1970); W. Goetz, *Beiträge zur Gesch. Herzog Albrechts V. und des Landsberger Bundes 1556–1598* (Munich, 1898); K. Hartmann, *Der Prozeb gegen die protestanten Landstande in Bayern unter Herzog Albrechts V., 1564* (Munich, 1904); Hajo Holborn, *A History of Germany: The Reformation* (New York, 1964); Heinrich Lutz, "Die Herzoge Wilhelm IV and Albrecht V," in *Handbuch der Bayerischen Gesch.*, ed. Max Spindler (Munich, 1969), vol. 2.   *C. T. Eby*

See WILLIAM V.

ALBERT ("Alcibiades") (1522–1557), margrave of Brandenburg-Kulmbach, a major figure in the domestic wars of the mid-sixteenth century, was outlawed as a threat to public order, hence the nickname after a dissolute pupil of Socrates. Albert was born into the Frankish Hohenzollerns, but he was orphaned at the age of five and received a haphazard education under the guardianship of his uncle Margrave George. Albert came to power suddenly in 1541 by forcing a partition of his father's principality between himself and his uncle.

In order to play a role in national politics and to master the heavy debts that he had inherited from his father, Albert entered military service under Emperor Charles V. He distinguished himself in Charles' Marne campaign of 1544 and was commissioned to raise a large force against the Protestant League of Schmalkalden in 1546. Although his dashing campaign against his fellow Lutherans ended with his own defeat and capture, Albert received rewards after Charles V's victory. Albert's effort to impose the Interim on his Lutheran subjects almost led to revolt.

In 1549, since Charles V had not kept up his subsidy, Albert accepted an English commission against the French. When the campaign was cancelled, Albert switched to the growing princely opposition to the emperor, and he negotiated a subsidy for the league from Henry II of France. Along with this change in political loyalty, Albert suddenly became an ardent evangelical. In the war against the emperor, Albert plundered and extorted large payments from Franconian neighbors who sided with Charles V. After the defeated emperor had made peace, Albert refused to recognize the treaty, and he marched into the Rhineland. Charles V then took Albert's large army into his service to help in the abortive siege of Metz in the winter of 1552–1553.

The emperor's refusal to enforce the treaties that Albert had extorted from the Franconian estates led Albert into rebellion in spring 1553. An alliance of Protestant and Catholic estates gathered against Albert, who was seen as a threat to public order. He was defeated at Sievershausen on June 9, 1553, though his opponent, elector Maurice of Saxony, was fatally wounded in the battle. Outlawed, Albert fled to France. His efforts to negotiate or force a return to his principality ended when his health suddenly collapsed, and he died at Pforzheim on January 8, 1557.

Works About: Karl Brandi, *The Emperor Charles V*, tr. C. V. Wedgwood (London, 1939); Erich, Freiherr von Guttenberg, *NDB*, 1:163; Otto Kneitz, *Albrecht Alcibiades Markgraf von Kulmbach 1522–1557*, Die Plassenburg, no. 2 (Kulmbach, 1951); W. Maurenbrecher, "Albrecht Alcibiades" *ADB*, 1:252–57; Johann Voight, *Markgraf Albrecht Alcibiades von Brandenburg-Kulmbach*, 2 vols. (Berlin, 1852).   *S. W. Rowan*

See CHARLES V; MAURICE; NUREMBERG; SCHMALKALDIC LEAGUE.

ALBERT THE GREAT (c. 1200–1280) philosopher and scientist, was born at Lauingen on the Danube near Ulm of a noble family. After studying the liberal arts at Padua, Albert was recruited into the Dominicans by their master general, Jordan of Saxony, over the strong opposition of his family. He taught theology at various schools in Germany and at Paris from 1245 to 1248, where he held the chair for foreigners in theology. In the summer of 1248, he went to Cologne to establish a *studium generale,* a kind of medieval think-tank for brilliant young Dominicans. His greatest student was the brilliant Thomas Aquinas (1225–1274).

Albert then began an administrative career as provincial of the German Dominicans from 1253 to 1256 and bishop of Regensburg from 1260 to 1262. The later part of his life was spent preaching and teaching, mainly at Cologne. He took part in the Council of Lyons of 1274 and in 1277 journeyed to Paris in an unsuccessful effort to block the condemnation of some of the teachings about Aristotle.

A scholar of wide-ranging interests, Albert made important contributions to natural science, especially biology. He not only introduced Greek and Arab science into medieval schools, but he stressed and practiced empirical observation. A master of Aristotelian thought, Albert attempted to purge Aristotle of the heretical taint of Averroism and to reconcile reason and faith.

Works By: *Omnia Opera*, ed. Bernhard Geyer, 40 vols. (Cologne, 1951–). **Works About:** S. M. Albert, *Albert the Great* (Oxford, 1948); T. M. Schwertner, *St. Albert the Great* (Milwaukee, 1932); W. A. Wallace, "Albertus Magnus," *DSB*, 1:99–103; J. A. Weispheipl, "Albert the Great," *New Catholic Encyclopedia* (New York, 1967) 1:254–58.   *J. W. Zophy*

See COLOGNE; DANTE

ALDRINGER (after 1620, Aldringen) JOHN VON (1588–1634), count and imperial military commander, was born in Luxembourg and died in Landshut, Bavaria. A self-made soldier who had served briefly as secretary in the Luxembourg chancellory, Aldringer began his military career in the imperial army in upper Italy. He fought in the Thirty Years War, during the Bohemian campaign as an officer in Spanish pay, and after 1621, as a lieutenant colonel in the Catholic League army of Duke Maximilian of Bavaria. In 1623 he rejoined Ferdinand's army. His tactical abilities and organizational talents were important for the imperial war effort during the next decade.

Aldringer was named war councillor and colonel commissioner for the army. In 1625 he was given command over a regiment. He played a leading part in Wallenstein's victory over Ernest von Mansfeld at the Dessau Bridge (1626). In 1628 Wallenstein entrusted him with the takeover of Mecklenburg. When Ferdinand II issued the Edict of Restitution (1629), he chose Aldringer as one of the three commissioners to supervise the execution of the edict in the Lower Saxon Circle. In the same year Aldringer also participated in the peace negotiations with King Christian IV of Denmark at Lübeck. He distinguished himself in the Mantuan war (1630). As commanding officer of Ferdinand's forces in the upper imperial circles, he forced the capitulation of Württemberg (1631). The emperor showed his gratitude by promoting Aldringer to field marshal. During the 1633 campaign against Sweden, Aldringer grew increasingly suspicious of Wallenstein's behavior and tactics. He belonged to the circle of officers who remained loyal to the emperor during the Wallenstein conspiracy and contributed decisively to the general's fall in 1634. Only a few months later, Aldringer himself was fatally injured in a battle with the Swedes at Landshut in Bavaria.

Work By: Friedrich Parnemann, ed., *Der Briefwechsel der Generale Gallas, Aldringen und Piccolomini im Januar und Februar 1634* (Berlin, 1911). **Works About:** "Aldringer," *BW*, 1:66ff; Ernst Brohm, *Johann von Aldringen* (Halle, 1882); Arno Duch, "Aldringen," *NDB*, 1:188–90; Hermann Hallwich, *Johann Aldringen* (Leipzig, 1805); Janko and Schoetter, "Aldringen," *ADB*, 1:327–29; J. Krebs, "Zur Beurteilung Holks und Aldringens," *Hist. Vierteljahrschrift*, 3 (1900): 321–78.   *Bodo Nischan*

See EDICT OF RESTITUTION; FERDINAND II; THIRTY YEARS WAR; WALLENSTEIN, ALBERT.

ALEXANDER OF ROES (second half of thirteenth century), imperial theorist, was probably from a Cologne patrician family. He became a canon and joined the retinue of Cardinal Jacob Colonna in the papal curia in the early 1280s. He witnessed the death of Pope Nicholas III in 1280, the election and coronation of Pope Martin IV in 1281, and the Sicilian vespers in 1282.

Three works are now attributed to Alexander of Roes: the scholarly *De translatione imperii* and *Noticii seculi* and a dramatic parable in hexameters, *Pavo*. Alexander's writings demonstrate German patriotism and Christian conviction and reveal originality, humor, and an excellent power of observation, which is especially evident in his knowledge of the character of the German, Italian, and French peoples. He defended the right of the Germans to imperial power and denounced papal claims to temporal supremacy. One fundamental idea in his presentations involved his plan for the establishment and maintenance of world order. He sought to bring all nations into a balance of power in which the greatest states had special responsibilities. The Italians were responsible for spiritual rule, the Germans for secular rule, and the French for intellectual rule. Together and in concert, they maintained the world order.

The works of Alexander of Roes were spread in Germany in the fifteenth century through the imperial reform movement. Some historians believe that Alexander, as a theorist of the Holy Roman Empire, indirectly influenced Emperor Maximilian I's idea of universal rule.

Works About: H. Heimpel, "Alexander von Roes," *NDB*, 1: 194–95; W. Schraub, *Jordan von Osnabrück und Alexander von Roes* (Heidelberg, 1910).   *J. J. Spielvogel*

See MAXIMILIAN I.

ALTDORFER, ALBRECHT (1480–1538), artist, was born probably in Regensburg, the son of a painter. Most of his life seems to have been spent in Regensburg, where he became a city councillor in 1519 and city architect in 1526. As a painter, draftsman, printmaker, and architect, he developed an excellent reputation and generally prospered. A supporter of the Reformation, he along with Lucas Cranach the elder was part of the Danubian school. Altdorfer also contributed a great deal to the development of landscape painting.

Works About: Adolf Jannasch, "Albrecht Altdorfer," *DGD*, 1:377–86; Gisela Noehles and Karl Noehles, "Altdorfer," *EWA*, 1:222–26.   *J. W. Zophy*

See CRANACH.

AMSDORF, NICHOLAS VON (1483–1565), conservative Lutheran reformer, was born at Torgau to a noble family. He commenced his university career at Leipzig but eventually transferred to Wittenberg, where his uncle, John von Staupitz, was a professor and dean. Amsdorf did well at Wittenberg, becoming canon of the university church, earning a licentiate in theology, and teaching on the faculty.

One of the earliest supporters of his colleague Martin Luther, Amsdorf accompanied him to the Leipzig debate in 1519 and to Worms in 1521. He also assisted Luther in his attempts to reform the university's theological curriculum. Called to Magdeburg in 1524 by the city council on Luther's recommendation, Amsdorf oversaw ecclesiastical reform as superintendent. He also assisted in establishing the reform in Goslar and Einbeck.

Amsdorf became noted as a conservative defender of Luther's doctrines in disputes not only with radical reformers like Melchior Hofmann but also with his fellow Lutherans, who were more open to compromise. He opposed the Wittenberg Concord, which attempted to reconcile the positions of the Lutherans and the Reformed on the eucharist.

His friend, Elector John Frederick of Saxony, installed him as bishop of Naumburg/Zeitz in 1541 despite the opposition of Julius von Pflug. This unhappy period was ended by the Schmalkaldic War, when he was driven into exile. During the following years he served as adviser to the elector and his sons. Amsdorf also assisted in the founding of the University of Jena in opposition to Wittenberg, where the teachings of the irenic Melanchthon now held sway. He later was forced to move on the Eisenach, where he died after having promoted the Reformation there.

Works By: *Nikolaus von Amsdorff: Ausgewählte Schriften,* ed. Otto Lerche (Gütersloh, 1938). **Works About:** Peter Brunner, *Nikolaus von Amsdorf als Bischof von Naumburg* (Gütersloh, 1961); Robert Kolb, *Nikolaus von Amsdorf (1483–1565), Popular Polemics in Preserving Luther's Legacy* (Nieuwkoop, 1977); Otto Nebe, *Reine Lehre: Zur Theologie des Niklas von Amsdorff* (Göttingen, 1935); Theodor Pressel, *Nicolaus von Amsdorf* (Elberfeld, 1862); David Steinmetz, *Reformers in the Wings* (Philadelphia, 1971); Hans Stille, *Nikolaus von Amsdorf* (Zeulenroda, 1937).

J. W. Zophy

See JOHN FREDERICK; LUTHER; MELANCHTHON; STAUPITZ.

ANABAPTISM, from the Greek word for *rebaptism*, was a term applied to several sectarian movements in the era of the Reformation whose adherents professed adult baptism as opposed to the infant baptism practiced by the Church of Rome and the major Protestant churches. Adult baptism was a consequence of the belief that individuals had to accept Christianity freely and consciously. Baptism was a sign of that acceptance, a view contrary to orthodox Christian teaching, which viewed baptism as a sacrament commanded by God to remove original sin.

Although controversy remains as to the origin of the movement in the sixteenth century, the first appearance seems to have been in Switzerland under the leadership of Conrad Grebel, but it may have developed simultaneously in south Germany and other areas. The first recorded baptism was administered by Grebel in Zurich in January 1525, and many of his views on Christianity became common to the majority of the Anabaptist sects.

As with baptism, most Anabaptists believed that the ritual of the Last Supper was not a true sacrament. Instead it was a symbolic act of fellowship and a remembrance of Christ's promise and suffering and, for many, an acknowledgment that all Christians must endure pain and suffering, as Christ did. From this view came the concept of the Church as a suffering church with all true Christians having to undergo three baptisms: by spirit, by water, and by blood. The Anabaptists viewed the church as a visible church of true believers. Most congregations made extensive use of the ban, banishing members who were perceived as unbelievers. The Anabaptists also placed a heavy emphasis upon personal piety and ethics, urging that true Christians should live according to the principles set forth by Christ in the Sermon on the Mount. Following this, many of the congregations professed a Christian communism that all material goods should be shared equally among the body of believers.

Because of their religious views, the Anabaptists faced the immediate hostility of both the orthodox churches and the secular state. The Swiss brethren were persecuted severely from their inception. But the worst persecution seems to have been generated by certain extremist views of the secular state. Most Anabaptists viewed the secular state as evil by its very nature and urged, at most, passive obedience to secular authorities. Some of the early leaders of the movement, however, notably Hans Hut in south Germany, incorporated a chiliastic view in their teachings, which predicted the imminent Day of Judgment when the children of God would rise up to slay all nonbelievers, preparing the way for the return of Christ. Following this, some apparently preached violent resistance to all secular authority and a complete political and economic restructuring of society. To such views the secular authorities reacted with alarm, and hundreds, ultimately thousands, of leaders and adherents were arrested, imprisoned, and executed. Such policy was confirmed by the imperial diets of Speyer (1529) and Augsburg (1530) when representatives of the estates reiterated the Justinian Code's condemnation of rebaptism as punishable by death.

Such persecution had a severe effect upon the already small movement, forcing thousands into exile from Switzerland and Germany. Of the surviving sects, the largest was the Hutterite brethren, founded by Jacob Hutter in Moravia. The Hutterites lived in strict communistic societies, prospered as farmers, and still survive in North America and the Ukraine. Other groups, such as the followers of Melchior Hofmann in the Rhineland, became more and more extreme in their views. The extremist movement reached its climax in the city of Münster in Westphalia, where, in 1534, Jan Matthys of Haarlem and Joh Beukelsz of Leiden led their followers to a successful takeover of the government and the establishment, by Beukelsz, of an Anabaptist dictatorship noted for its brutality, extremism, and immorality through the introduction of polygamy. After fourteen months, the Anabaptists were driven out by the Lutheran prince, Philip of Hesse, and their leaders were executed.

Following the debacle of Münster, Anabaptism was finally purged of its radical elements by the Dutch reformer Menno Simons (1496–1561). Simons successfully synthesized Anabaptist theology to establish a peaceful and pious movement. His followers, called Mennonites, grew to become the largest and most enduring of the Anabaptist sects, exercising considerable influence on latter-day Quakers, independents, and Baptists. Renewed persecution of the Anabaptists in the seventeenth and eighteenth centuries resulted in the migration of thousands to North America, where the Mennonites continue to exist in large numbers.

The great suffering of the generally peaceful Anabaptists at the hands of Catholic and Protestant authorities alike gradually made an impact upon many religious and secular leaders and thereby contributed to the concept of religious toleration in Western thought and practice. Many have argued that the concept of the congregationally controlled church also contributed much to the development of democratic ideas in the West.

Works About: Rollin S. Armour, *Anabaptist Baptism* (Scottdale, Pa., 1966); Claus-Peter Clasen, *Anabaptism: A Social History, 1525–1618* (Ithaca, N.Y., 1972); Peter James Klassen, *The Economics of Anabaptism* (The Hague, 1964); Franklin H. Littell, *The Anabaptist View of the Church* (Chicago, 1952), and *The Origins of Sectarian Protestantism* (New York, 1964); *Quel. und Forsch. zur Reformationgesch.: Quel. zur Gesch. der Wiedertäufer,* 11 vols. (Leipzig and Gütersloh, 1930–1964); W. Packhull, *Mysticism and the Early South German-Austrian Anabaptist Movement* (Scottdale, Pa., 1977).   *D. M. Hockenbery*

See DENCK; HUBMAIER; HUT; MÜNSTER AFFAIR; MUNTZER; PHILIP OF HESSE; SYMONDS; WESTERBURG.

ANDREAE, JACOB (1528–1590), was the son of an itinerant Bavarian blacksmith who finally settled his family in Waiblingen near the city of Stuttgart in Württemberg. Andreae's significance for German and imperial history lay in the fact that as adviser to princes and as an irenic theologian, he helped to prevent a collapse of Luther's Reformation church during the troubled years of civil war and theological strife following Luther's death in 1546. Andreae took his B.A. degree at the University of Tübingen in 1543 and earned an M.A. in 1545. He became a doctor of sacred theology in 1553. His first pastorate was at Stuttgart, and he remained there until his city was captured by Spanish troops in the Schmalkaldic War. Later he became a superintendent at Goeppingen, a short distance to the east of Stuttgart.

Much of Andreae's career as a preacher and theologian coincides with the severe disruptions generated by the religious civil wars in Germany between 1546 and 1552. The internecine wars added to the natural tendency of theologians to quarrel over doctrine. As a counselor to Duke Christopher of Württemberg, Andreae attended a number of imperial diets, theological colloquies, and disputations. Some of the problems to which he tried to find common ground in order to cool the controversies were the following issues: the role of faith and works in salvation, the importance of Adiaphora in liturgy, the nature of the Eucharist, types of church organization and administration, the issue of predestination, and the nature of Christ. Andreae wrote over two hundred pamphlets in the vernacular to present his views to the widest possible audience in the Empire. Andreae's official importance coupled with the sheer volume and quality of his published works make him one of the important Lutheran pamphleteers in sixteenth-century German history.

As recognition of Andreae's skill and scholarship, Duke Christopher in 1561 named him chancellor of the University of Tübingen. Probably Andreae's most significant and famous contribution to the religious stability of the Empire was his part in the creation of the Formula of Concord of 1577, which was included in the famous *Book of Concord* in 1580. The *Book of Concord* was accepted by a number of princes, by imperial cities, and by many theologians. The Formula of Concord helped to unify many of the factious Lutherans and prevented them from becoming hopelessly fragmented. Thus the essential thrust of Martin Luther's powerful religious statements was maintained and transmitted to the future. Andreae's notable achievements as an irenic theologian are well illustrated in his summary statement of the Formula of Concord, as well as by his printed sermons and tracts.

Works By: Robert Kolb, ed. and tr., *Andreae and the Formula of Concord: Six Sermons on the Way to Lutheran Unity* (St. Louis, 1977). **Works About:** Ernst Henke, "Jakob Andreae," *ADB*, 1:436–41; Peter Meinhold, "Andreae," *NDB*, 1:277; Arthur E. Peipkorn, "Jakob Andreae," *Encyclopedia of the Lutheran Church*, 1:74.   R. G. Cole

See CHRISTOPHER; LUTHER; SCHMALKALDIC WAR.

ANDREAE, JOHN VALENTIN (1586–1654) was a leading intellectual and theologian in the Holy Roman Empire during the late Reformation. He was born into a Lutheran pastor's family at Herrenberg, a short distance northwest of Tübingen in Württemberg. Andreae's formal training was at the University of Tübingen where his grandfather had been chancellor. He took his B.A. in 1603 and his M.A. in 1605. Leaving the university, Andreae led a restless and wandering life, visiting Strasbourg, Geneva, France, and Italy. In 1614 he became a preacher in Vaihingen, fifteen miles northwest of Stuttgart. Six years later he moved to the nearby city of Calw and was promoted to the high pastoral office of superintendent. The plundering forces of the imperial army fell upon Andreae while he was pastor at Calw. His home was plundered, and his library was burned by the army of John von Werth. In 1639 John Valentin Andreae moved to Stuttgart and became court preacher. He finished his career as an abbot and pastor at the old monastaries of Bebenhausen and Adelburg. His last years were busy ones; Andreae devoted much of his remaining energies to helping rebuild ruined and disorganized Lutheran churches disrupted by the long years of civil and religious warfare.

Andreae is especially important for his role in maintaining the vigor of Reformation ideas in an age when Lutheran doctrines were assaulted by both mystics and cold rationalists. Martin Luther's idea of justification by faith and faith active in love are clearly demonstrated by Andreae's utopian work *Christianopolis* (1619). In the seventeenth century, Andreae's utopian thoughts had little effect outside the Empire, but they seemed to persist within. In the late eighteenth century near the town of Vaihingen, where Andreae had preached as a young pastor, the famous utopian leader George Rapp began to reiterate a number of Andreae's utopian ideas and proceeded to recruit many disciples who ultimately moved to the United States in the nineteenth century to found the towns of Old Economy, Pennsylvania, and New Harmony, Indiana. The ideal held by many "high orthodox" theologians such as Andreae of finding practical applications for Christian ideas was carried out by the Rappites to a degree beyond the point that conditions in Andreae's time would have permitted. Yet Andreae, while pastor at Calw, organized a society whereby Christian workers became part of an organization to help the needy, ill, and lame. The worker groups consisted primarily of textile dyers and came to be known as the *Färberstift*.

Another area of Andreae's interest was the body of ideas found in the *Corpus Hermeticum*. Renaissance humanists and scholars such as Andreae believed that Hermetic ideas were the ancient source of Plato's wisdom, an exciting though erroneous assumption. Andreae's book *The Chemical Wedding* (1616) is a just reflection of the mysteries of the Hermetic tradition and is an interesting attempt to relate early seventeenth-century science to the Christian religion. One spinoff from Andreae's knowledge of Hermetic ideas was his interest in the use of pictorial devices in the education of children. As did the ancient Hermes, Andreae believed that children might profit more at an early age from the study of pictorial emblems than from the study of rhetorical abstractions. In some ways Andreae anticipated and may have influenced the most famous teacher of the late Reformation, John Commenius (d. 1670).

Without question John Valentin Andreae was one of the most influential reformers, theologians, and intellectuals during a troubled part of the history of the Holy Roman Empire in the seventeenth century. Moreover, he is a fine example of the diversity of interests to be found in one orthodox Lutheran pastor.

Works By: Felix Held, ed. and tr., *Christianopolis: An Ideal State of the Seventeenth Century* (New York, 1916); John Warwick Montgomery, *Cross and Crucible: Johann Valentin Andreae (1586–1654) Phoenix of the Theologians*, 2 vols. (The Hague, 1973). Vol. 2 is a critical edition of Andreae's *The Chemical Wedding*. **Works About:** John C. Christianson, "The Pilgrim's Quest," *Cresset*, 40:6–9 (1977); Ernst Henke, "Andreae," *ADB*, 1:441–47; Otto Schottenloher, "Johann Valentin Andreae," *NDB* 1:277–78.   R. G. Cole

See LUTHER.

ARNIM, HANS GEORGE VON (1583–1641), Protestant military commander and statesman during the Thirty Years War, who at different times served Sweden, Poland, Saxony, and the emperor, was born at Brandenburg and died in Dresden. He began his military career in the army of Gustavus Adolphus of Sweden (1613–1617), fought for Sigismund III of Poland against the Turks, and joined the imperial forces as a colonel in 1626. He distinguished himself in the reconquest of Silesia. As Wallenstein's right-hand man, he played an important role in the occupation of Mecklenburg and Pomerania. In 1628, he was made field marshal. When Ferdinand II issued the Edict of Restitution (1629), Arnim left the imperial service to become commander-in-chief of the Saxon forces. A devout Lutheran and ardent German constitutionalist, Arnim devoted himself from this time on to the formation of a Protestant third party between the imperial and foreign armies.

Tilly's threat to Saxony forced the elector to enter into an alliance with Gustavus Adolphus (which Arnim negotiated). The Saxon army fought on the Swedish side in the Battle at Breitenfeld (September 17, 1631), and it occupied Bohemia and Silesia during the following months. Arnim, however, was distrustful of the Swedes and therefore receptive to Wallenstein's peace overtures (1632). But the talks with the imperial commander-in-chief remained fruitless, largely because Wallenstein was simultaneously intriguing with the Swedes, Bohemians, and French. What little chances for success these negotiations may have had came to naught when Wallenstein was assassinated in February 1634; Arnim barely escaped getting caught in the catastrophe. His third party program had been discredited shortly afterward, the elector signed a separate peace with the emperor (Prague, 1635). Arnim, who opposed the treaty, quit Saxony to return to his family estate at Boitzenburg. There, the Swedish chancellor, Axel Oxenstierna, charging that Arnim had conspired against his government, had him arrested in March 1637. Arnim was taken to Sweden but escaped a year later. After a brief stopover in Hamburg, he reentered the imperial Saxon service to help fight the foreign armies in Germany. He died in 1641 at Dresden while preparing a military campaign against France and Sweden.

Works About: Heinz Gollwitzer, "Hans Georg A. v. Boitzenburg," *NDB*, 1:372 ff; Hermann Hallwich, ed., *Briefe und Akten zur Gesch. Wallensteins*, 4 vols. (Vienna, 1912); H. G. Helbig, "v. Arnim," *ADB* 1:568–70; Georg Irmer, ed., *Die Verhandlungen Schwedens und seiner Verbündeten mit Wallenstein und dem Kaiser von 1631 bis 1634*, 3 vols. (Leipzig, 1888–1891); Georg Irmer, *Hans Georg von Arnim* (Leipzig, 1894).   *Bodo Nischan*

See EDICT OF RESTITUTION; FERDINAND II; THIRTY YEARS WAR; TILLY; WALLENSTEIN, ALBERT.

ARNULF (850–899), who ruled from 887 to 899, was the illegitimate son of Carloman (the son of Louis the German) and a woman of noble birth named Liutswind. After 876 he was granted Carinthia and Pannonia by his father.

Nevertheless, when Carloman died in 880, Arnulf did not succeed him. Bavaria instead went to Louis III, Carloman's brother, who confirmed Arnulf in Carinthia. When Louis died in 882, Arnulf became subject to Charles the Fat, for whom he served as a commander with Count Henry in the campaign against the Vikings the same year. Despite that campaign, Arnulf remained a promising general. Zwentibold (Svátopluk), prince of Moravia, ravaged Pannonia in 883 and 884 because Arnulf refused (successfully) to hand over two vassals. Previously relations between the two had been good (Arnulf named an illegitimate son Zwentibold), and peace was restored in 885. The eastern front was often tense.

The political downfall of Liutward, previously the closest advisor to Emperor Charles the Fat, in July 887 turned out to be a blessing. Liutward retired to Arnulf's court and advised him how he might take power. That November Arnulf succeeded in getting the support of the east Frankish nobility at Frankfurt. Shortly afterward Charles the Fat was deposed at Tribur near Darmstadt. The details are obscure. One later source says Hildigard, the daughter of Louis III, played an essential role. The weakness of Charles and the Empire in the face of strong opponents—Vikings, Slavs, and Bulgars—undoubtedly had its effect. The Empire now was faced with a number of smaller kingdoms. Odo, who had defended Paris against the Vikings, was chosen king of the West Franks. Berengar of Friuli and Guy (Guido) of Spoleto were fighting for the crown in Italy. Louis, son of Boso, held Provence up to Lyons, while Rudolf, the son of Conrad, count of Auxerre, claimed Upper Burgundy (around the Alps and beyond the Jura). At Worms (August 888) Odo met with Arnulf, who received him well. Arnulf also sent Odo a crown that was used for his coronation on November 13. Odo may have recognized Arnulf as his nominal superior to make his own position more secure. Then Arnulf marched against Rudolf of Burgundy, who was claiming greater Lorraine and had even been crowned king of Lorraine by the bishop of Toul. His forces were no match for Arnulf's, and he retreated. Later in October Rudolf went to Regensburg and came to terms with Arnulf. The latter became his lord, and Rudolf was confirmed in Burgundy. In November Arnulf was in Italy. There was a truce in force until January 6, 889, between Berengar and Guy; Arnulf supported the former, who acknowledged him as lord. Guy won and was subsequently crowned emperor (February 11, 891) by Pope Stephen V.

A revolt by Bernard, the illegitimate son of Charles the Fat, was put down in 890, and Bernard was killed by Rudolf, count of Rhaetia. In May an embassy came from the Moravians to renew the peace. The major event of the year, however, was a Viking invasion in the neighborhood of Liège and Aachen. On June 26 they inflicted a bloody defeat on Archbishop Sunderold of Mainz and a count, named Arnulf, at La Gueule. Arnulf (the king) avenged this in October in a battle on the banks of the Dyle River; two Viking kings were killed. The spring of 892 saw the last Viking raid. In July was another expedition against the Moravians; in September Vladimir, king of the Bulgars, renewed a peace with Arnulf. August 893 was again the occasion for a campaign against the Moravians. In October Arnulf received an appeal from Pope Formosus (elected September 891) to save him from the tyranny of Guy. Arnulf sent his son, Zwentibold, ahead with an army; he and Berengar caught Guy in Pavia, but nothing was accomplished (some cite a bribe as one reason). In 894 Arnulf and Berengar captured Bergamo and received an oath of fealty from the lords at Pavia and Milan. He then returned, defeating Rudolf of Burgundy on his way back. In August of that year his nemesis Zwentibold, whom one chronicler called the "womb of all treachery," died, as did Guy of Spoleto.

Arnulf's popularity with the Church continued as he held a synod at Tribur. About the same time at Worms, his son, Zwentibold, was elevated to the kingship of Lorraine. The same summer the Abodrites made peace, and the Bohemian Slavs were subdued. In September Formosus again urged Arnulf to come to Rome. He did, took the city around January, was appropriately showered with honors, and was crowned emperor the next month. In March, as he prepared to advance against Spoleto, he was stricken with paralysis and returned home. On April 4 Formosus died, and Arnulf's success in Italy evaporated. He did succeed in securing the throne (897) for his four-year-old son, Louis the Child, and died on December 8, 899, at Regensburg.

Works About: *Annales Fuldenses*, ed. F. Kurze, *SRG* (Hanover, 1891); G. Barraclough, *The Crucible of Europe* (Berkeley, 1976); J. Böhmer and E. Mühlbacher, *Regesta Imperii I.*, rev. ed. by C. Brühl and H. Kaminsky (Hildesheim, 1966); E. Dümmler, *Gesch. des Ostfranken Reiches*, *Jb. der Dtsch. Gesch.* (Leipzig, 1887, rpr. 1960), vol. 1; *MGH Diplomata regum Germaniae ex stirpe Karolinorum III, Die Urkunden Arnolfs*, ed. P. Kehr (Berlin, 1940).   *C. J. Dull*

See CARLOMAN; CHARLES II; LOUIS II; LOUIS III.

AUGSBURG, one of the great cities of southern Germany, was founded by the Romans about 30 A.D. at the confluence of the rivers Lech and Wertach. *Augusta Vindelicum* served as a provincial capital for over three centuries. After the Romans abandoned Germany early in the fifth century, the settlement virtually disappeared, but by the late eighth century it had reemerged as the seat of a bishopric and a center of Carolingian administration. During the long episcopate of Saint Ulrich (923–973), the bishop's authority as secular lord of Augsburg was noticeably strengthened. It was also during Ulrich's reign, in 955, that a Magyar invasion of Germany was turned back at the Lechfeld just outside Augsburg.

The eleventh century saw the emergence of a community of traders and artisans adjacent to the episcopal settlement. The traders' struggle to assert their political autonomy was first rewarded in 1156 when Emperor Frederick Barbarossa granted a charter that limited episcopal control over the secular community. The following century saw a steady growth in the citizens' privileges, culminating in the *Stadtrechtsbuch* of 1276 by which Rudolf of Habsburg confirmed their rights of self-government. A charter granted by Emperor Louis the Bavarian in 1316 affirmed Augsburg's status as a free imperial city.

The struggle against the bishop was superseded in the fourteenth century by emerging conflicts among the citizens themselves. Attacks against exclusive rule by the old patrician families came to a climax in 1368 when armed protests led to the adoption of a new constitution under which guild masters were guaranteed a majority of seats on the city council. Augsburg joined the league of Swabian cities in 1379 and participated in the league's subsequent war against the rulers of Bavaria and other south German territories; in 1462–1463 Augsburg was again at war with Bavaria. The city emerged from these conflicts with its autonomy intact, but it never succeeded in acquiring any significant territory beyond its own walls.

In the late fifteenth century, Augsburg emerged as the leading commercial and financial center of southern Germany. Two Augsburg families—the Fuggers and the Welsers—rose to prominence as international merchants and bankers. Their rise was closely tied to the fortunes of the Habsburg emperors, from whom they received generous mining and colonial concessions but to whom they were required to make extensive loans. Jacob Fugger the Rich (1459–1525) is also noted for his endowment of the *Fuggerei*, an unique city-within-the-city for penurious older citizens of Augsburg.

Augsburg's involvement in the history of the Reformation began in 1518, when Luther's interview with Cardinal Cajetan took place in the city. Lutheran doctrine found its classic expression in the Augsburg Confession, submitted by Protestants to Charles V at the imperial diet of 1530 in Augsburg. The city itself underwent the Reformation beginning in 1534, but some influential Augsburgers—notably the Fuggers—remained loyal to the Catholic cause. In 1548, to punish Augsburg for participating in the Schmalkaldic War, Charles V abolished the guilds and abrogated the constitution of 1368; henceforth three-quarters of the council seats were to be held by patricians. At the same time Catholicism was reintroduced, though not exclusively. Under the Peace of Augsburg of 1555, Augsburg itself became one of the few German cities in which Protestant and Catholic forms of worship were to coexist side by side.

The later sixteenth century was a period of internal strife and economic retreat. Disputes over the introduction of the Gregorian calendar and over the appointment of Protestant ministers led to bitter political conflicts from 1583 on. The Fuggers, by now ennobled, gradually withdrew from financial activity into the life of landed aristocrats. The Welsers, less astute, went bankrupt in 1614. Nevertheless the city was still prosperous enough to erect numerous civic buildings, notably the imposing city hall built between 1615 and 1620.

The Thirty Years War brought an abrupt end to Augsburg's prosperity. Repeated military occupations, as well as outbreaks of the plague, reduced Augsburg's population from about thirty-five thousand before the war to some twenty thousand in 1648. The war also brought about violent reversals in religion as the city alternated between imperial and Swedish occupations. The Peace of Westphalia, however, confirmed the rights of both religions and introduced a system of strict parity under which Catholics and Protestants had equal representation in every branch of the city government.

Augsburg gradually recovered from the war. A short-lived attempt by the elector of Bavaria to annex the city in 1704 did not impede the general revival of prosperity. By the early eighteenth century, the city had achieved wide renown as a center for the gold and silver crafts. Large-scale cotton manufacturing was introduced in the late eighteenth century; consequent changes in the structure of the textile industry led to an unsuccessful weavers' uprising in 1794. Growing dissatisfaction with the civic administration, especially its financial mismanagement, robbed the patrician government of popular support as it struggled to sustain the city's autonomy during the Napoleonic era. Under the *Reichsdeputationshauptschluss* (major resolution of an imperial deputation from the Diet) of 1803, the city retained its independence, but in 1806, under French supervision, Augsburg was annexed to the kingdom of Bavaria.

Works About: Ingrid Bátori, *Die Reichsstadt Augsburg im 18. Jahrhundert: Verfassung, Finanzen und Reformversuche* (Göttingen, 1969); Richard Ehrenberg, *Capital and Finance in the Age of the Renaissance: A Study of the Fuggers and Their Connections*, tr. H. M. Lucas (London, 1928); Rolf Kiessling, *Bürgerliche Gesellschaft und Kirche in Augsburg im Spätmittelalter: Ein Beitrag zur Strukturanalyse der oberdeutschen Reichsstadt* (Augsburg, 1971); Leonhard Lenk, *Augsburger Bürgertum im Späthumanismus und Frühbarock, 1580–1700* (Augsburg, 1968); Christian Meyer, ed., *Urkundenbuch der Stadt Augsburg* [1104–1399], 2 vols. (Augsburg, 1874–1878); Hermann Rinn, ed., *Augusta 955–1955* (Munich, 1955); Friedrich Roth, *Augsburgs Reformationsgeschichte*, 4 vols. (Munich, 1901–1911); Wolfgang Zorn, *Augsburg: Geschichte einer deutschen Stadt* 2d ed. (Augsburg, 1972).   *C. R. Friedrichs*

See AUGSBURG, DIET OF 1530; AUGSBURG, PEACE OF; CHARLES V; FREDERICK I; FUGGER; IMPERIAL CITIES; LUTHER; RUDOLF I; THIRTY YEARS WAR; WESTPHALIA.

AUGSBURG, DIET OF 1530, was the first meeting of Emperor Charles V with the imperial estates since the diet of Worms in 1521. Charles returned to the Empire in favorable circumstances as a victorious sovereign who had just received papal coronation as emperor. He was determined to settle the religious situation in the Empire and to acquire aid from the estates to counter Turkish military endeavors. Although the diet legislated against Jewish activities, price cartels, and speculative trading and took other measures in support of the emperor's wishes, its significance is largely found in the religious sphere.

Charles announced in advance his intention to conclude religious diversity in the Empire. Accordingly evangelical estates drew up their articles of faith, which they submitted to the emperor and the diet. Most important of these was the Lutheran Confession, subsequently known as the Augsburg Confession, almost entirely the work of Philip Melanchthon albeit approved by Luther. This Confession, although rejected at the diet, was signed by the princes who had protested at the diet of Speyer in 1529 and by the cities of Nuremberg and Reutlingen.

It was and remained a doctrinal statement of Lutheran belief. A second confession, known as the Tetrapolitana and composed by Wolfgang Capito and Martin Bucer, was also submitted. Since both statements were rejected by Charles and the Catholics, there appeared no hope for reconciliation.

Catholic scholars had also come prepared to participate in the proceedings at Augsburg. Most notable among these were probably the papal legate, Cardinal Campeggio, Eck, Cochlaeus, and Faber, each an ardent opponent of Luther and evangelical teachings. Campeggio seemed convinced that force alone would solve the religious schism, although he was willing to try other means. Eck submitted a polemical treatise listing more than four hundred Protestant errors. All of these men, on Charles' suggestion, worked to produce the *Confutatio*, or refutation of the Augsburg Confession.

When attempts at mediating the religious crises failed, most Protestants left Augsburg. The recess (*Abschied*), dated September 22, was passed therefore by Catholic estates, and it forbade all deviations from Catholicism. By reaffirming the provisions of the Edict of Worms in 1521 and by negating the religious statements contained in recesses issued between that of Worms and the present one, the recess aimed at suppressing Lutheranism as well as Zwinglianism and Anabaptism. By also legislating against evangelical practices and the means used to spread the Protestant Reformation, the recess seemed to promise a quick demise to the evangelical movement. Finally the document declared that Protestants had to submit to these decisions by April 15, 1531. If they refused, they would be attacked legally through the Imperial Cameral Court (*Reichskammergericht*). As a result of these provisions and threats made against them, most Protestant estates felt that they had to ally. Their discussions led to the creation of the Schmalkaldic League early in 1531.

Works About: Carl Brettschneider, ed., *Corpus Reformatorum*, vol. 2: *Philippi Melanthonis Opera Quae Supersunt Omnia* (Halle, 1835); Carl Eduard Forstemann, ed. *Urkundenbuch zur Gesch. des Reichstags zu Augsburg 1530*, 2 vols. (Hildesheim, 1966); Herbert Grundman, *Landgraf Philipp von Hessen auf dem Augsburger Reichstag 1530* (Gütersloh, 1959); Hubert Jedin, *A History of the Council of Trent*, tr. Ernest Graf, 2 vols. (St. Louis, 1957–1961); E. W. Mayer, "Forsch. zur Politik Karls V. während des Augsburger Reichstags von 1530," *ARG* 13 (1916): 40–73; J. M. Reu, ed. *The Augsburg Confession: A Collection of Sources with a Historical Introduction* (Chicago, 1930); Hans von Schubert, *Der Reichstag von Augsburg im Zusammenhang der Reformationsgeschichte* (Leipzig, 1930); J. H. Stuckenberg, *The History of the Augsburg Confession* (Philadelphia, 1897); Valentin von Tetleben *Protokoll des Augsburger Reichstages*, ed. H. Grundman (Gütersloh, 1958); J. von Walter, "Der Reichstag zu Augsburg," *Luther–Jahrbuch* (1930): 1–90. *P. N. Bebb*

See BUCER; CAPITO; CHARLES V; ECK; IMPERIAL CAMERAL COURT; MELANCHTHON; SCHMALKALDIC LEAGUE; SPEYER, DIET OF 1529.

AUGSBURG, RELIGIOUS PEACE OF, 1555, recognized adherents of Catholicism and of Lutheranism. With regard to the latter, the peace extended legal recognition to those who accepted the Augsburg Confession of 1530 and guaranteed them the right to exercise their religion. Such provisions were part of the recess of the diet of Augsburg that met from February to September 1555. By acknowledging Lutheranism, the peace concluded a stage in the development of Protestantism in the Empire that had begun with Luther's protest in 1517. Emperor Charles V (1519–1556) was neither present at Augsburg nor did he have much to do with this solution to the religious problems; he had left the Empire permanently in January 1553. His brother, King Ferdinand, supervised the diet and issued its recess.

The peace was essentially a political solution to the religious divisions in the Empire, and it largely resulted from the initiative of the princes—electors and many other imperial estates refused to attend the diet—working in conjunction with Ferdinand. This solution provided that in the secular territories of princes and imperial knights, the ruler had the right to determine the religion of his subjects. This was a recognition of the principle *cuius regio, eius religio* subsequently elaborated. Since only Lutheranism and Catholicism received official acknowledgment and were promised secure existence, practitioners of other forms of Protestantism and sectarians were implicitly banned. At the princes' insistence, imperial cities that had adopted Lutheranism had to allow and protect the rights of minority Catholics to worship in the Catholic institutions reopened after the 1548 Interim.

With regard to ecclesiastical estates, the peace stated that those secularized before the Peace of Passau of August 1552 were to remain Lutheran and that spiritual princes who became Protestant in the future forfeited their lands, titles, and privileges and that the legal bodies responsible for these princes had the right to appoint Catholic successors. This was the famous ecclesiastical reservation clause. The effects of this *reservatio ecclesiastica* were partially offset by Ferdinand's secret declaration (*declaratio Ferdinandae*) to Protestant estates existing in ecclesiastical principalities that they would not be attacked, although this understanding was not part of the formal recess.

By imposing a solution to the religious divisions in the Empire, the religious peace began a period of relative calm. The peace, however, was not particularly satisfying to either Catholics or Lutherans because each side felt it had made too many concessions, and various imperial estates believed that the recess impugned their own freedoms and privileges. Nevertheless although the peace advanced the cause of particularism in the Empire, it also brought about some stability in imperial affairs and it endured for more than fifty years.

Works: B. J. Kidd, ed., *Documents Illustrative of the Continental Reformation* (Oxford, 1911), pp. 362–64; **Works About:** Gerhard Pfeiffer, "Der Augsburger Religionsfriede und die Reichsstädte," *Z. des Hist. Ver. für Schwaben und Neuburg* 61 (1955): 211–321; Matthias Simon, *Der Augsburger Religionsfriede* (Augsburg, 1955); Lewis W. Spitz, "Particularism and Peace, Augsburg—1555," *ChH* 25 (1956): 110–26; Gustav Wolf, *Der Augsburger Religionsfriede* (Stuttgart, 1890).   *P. N. Bebb*

See AUGSBURG, DIET OF; CHARLES V; FERDINAND I; LUTHER; SCHMALKALDIC WAR.

AUSTERLITZ (Czech Slavkov), a town in Moravia, was the site of French Emperor Napoleon Bonaparte's victory over the combined Austro-Russian forces on December 2, 1805, in the so-called Battle of the Three Emperors during the Napoleonic wars. Having captured an Austrian army at Ulm (October 20) and entered Vienna (November 13), Napoleon advanced into Moravia, where the remnants of Emperor Francis II's (I of the Austrian Empire) forces were joined by the Russians. Not strong enough himself to attack the Austro-Russian force, Napoleon determined to entice his enemies into attacking him by feigning weakness and retreating.

Encouraged, Czar Alexander and Emperor Francis had their armies advance to the village of Austerlitz, west of which Napoleon had taken up position behind the south-flowing Goldbach Creek. Napoleon had deliberately left the commanding Pratzen heights in the center unoccupied, as if his retreat were to continue. On the evening of December 1, the allies held a war council at which the Austrian chief of staff, General Weyrother, outlined a plan to cross the Goldbach and intercept Napoleon's retreat, an optimistic plan encouraged by a confused commotion in the French camp that night. Russian General Michael Kutusov (1745–1813), the allied field commander, suspected a trick but was overruled and registered his disapproval by falling asleep during the conference.

The commotion in the French camp was actually a torchlight procession celebrating the anniversary of Napoleon's coronation, for the French leader was now concentrating his forces for battle, calling in Bernadotte's I Corps via Brünn (Brno) and Davout's III Corps from Vienna to increase his army to 67,400 against the allied 85,400. Before dawn on December 2, the allied movement began, Buxhöwden's left wing advanced in three massive columns, with Kienmayer's cavalry in the lead. They were followed by Kollowrath and Miloradovitch, while Bagration engaged Lannes' V Corps on the right astride the Brünn-Olmütz road at the Santon hill. Alexander and Francis were on the Pratzen heights, watching the allied advance, when the rising sun of Austerlitz burned off the mist in the creek valley to reveal the French infantry ascending the plateau that was the center of the allied position.

Napoleon had left Legrande's division to delay back across the marshy Goldbach, counting on Davout's III Corps to arrive in time, watched the allies cross his front, and then struck for the center with the rest of Soult's IV Corps and Bernadotte's I. Kutusov swung Miloradovitch around and called up Liechtenstein's cavalry and the Russian Imperial Guard under Grand Duke Constantine, but by 10 A.M. Soult had the plateau. Napoleon now committed Murat's cavalry, Bessieres' Imperial Guard, and Oudinot's grenadiers to split the allied army. Buxhöwden's wing was driven south over the frozen lakes and marshes of the Litava, and Napoleon positioned twenty-five cannon on the heights, smashing the ice under them and completing their destruction. By nightfall the battle was over, with 27,000 allied casualties, including 12,000 prisoners, to 8,818 French casualties.

Napoleon's campaign had culminated in his battle of decision, and within twenty-four hours a broken Emperor Francis sued for peace. The Treaty of Pressburg (Bratislava) was signed December 26, 1805. The news of Austerlitz killed English Prime Minister William Pitt, shattered the Third Coalition, forced the Russians out of central Europe, and isolated the Prussians to be dealt with at Napoleon's leisure the next year.

Works About: D. Chandler, *Campaigns of Napoleon* (New York, 1966); H. Lachouque, *Napoléon à Austerlitz* (Paris, 1960); C. Manceron, *Austerlitz* (Paris, 1962); Emperor Napoleon I, *La Correspondence de Napoléon Ier*, 32 vols. (Paris, 1858–70); General P., Comte de Ségur, *Histoire et Mémoires* (Paris, 1837).   *A. H. Ganz*

See FRANCIS II; NAPOLEONIC WARS.

AUSTRIAN SUCCESSION, WAR OF THE (1740–1748), was a worldwide European conflict begun with the occupation of Silesia by Frederick II of Prussia in 1740 and ended by the Treaty of Aix-la-Chapelle (Aachen) in 1748. It was a confusing war characterized by dynastic ambitions and by alliances and agreements cynically made and broken, but it was also a limited war of small professional armies that seldom affected the civilian populations. France and Prussia, allied with Spain and Bavaria, were generally opposed to Austria, supported by England and the United Netherlands, France's traditional enemies, and Sardinia and Saxony. The Pragmatic Sanction (April 19, 1713) of Holy Roman Emperor Charles VI (1685–1740), extorted and bribed from the estates of the Empire and nations of Europe, guaranteed the succession of his daughter, Maria Theresa (1717–1780), to the Habsburg lands; but no sooner did he die on October 20, 1740, than the succession was contested by the elector of Bavaria, Charles Albert Wittelsbach (1697–1745), by Philip V Bourbon of Spain (1683–1746), by Augustus III Wettin (Albertine line) of Poland and Saxony (1696–1763); even the other powers of Europe sought to take advantage of the new twenty-three-year-old monarch.

Frederick II Hohenzollern of Prussia (1712–1786), himself only twenty-eight, had just become king (May 1740) and was determined to increase Prussia's power and prestige. Taking advantage of Russia's internal confusion, occasioned by the death of Czarina Anna (1693–1740) on October 28 and the succession of the two-month-old Ivan VI (1740–1764), marched his army into the Austrian province of Silesia on December 16, 1740, an act of aggression exceptional even in that Machiavellian age. Frederick raised a spurious claim to the former duchies of Liegnitz, Brieg, Jägerndorf, and Wohlau based on a testamentary union between the duke of Liegnitz and the elector of Brandenburg in 1537. Leaving his minister Count Henry von Podewils to draft the legal details and negotiate the fait accompli with Vienna, Frederick fully expected Maria Theresa, given her political difficulties, to accept a financial indemnification, a promise to support her other claims, and Brandenburg's vote to elect her husband, Francis of Lorraine (1708–1765), Holy Roman emperor as compensation. Indeed the

Silesians, especially the Lutheran Protestants, welcomed Prussian liberation from Catholic Austria. But Maria Theresa, proving to be strong and capable, and especially bitter regarding Frederick's aggression, had a field army formed under Count William von Neipperg (1684–1774) to retake Silesia. At Mollwitz on April 10, 1741, the Austrians routed the Prussian cavalry and sent Frederick fleeing, but the disciplined Prussian infantry finally drove the Austrians from the field.

This victory by a small state encouraged Austria's enemies to take advantage of its weakness. Louis XV of France (1710–1774) and his chief minister, the eighty-seven year old Cardinal André Fleury (1653–1743), were unwilling to intervene, especially because another conflict for empire with England seemed imminent; but the war party, led by the count (later marshal and duke) de Belle-Isle (1684–1761), engineered an anti-Habsburg coalition. The French reinforced Bavaria and supported the elector's candidature as Holy Roman emperor (Treaty of Nymphenburg, May 1741), initiated a treaty with Prussia, the Treaty of Breslau, June 5, 1741, recognizing Frederick's acquisition of Silesia, escorted the Neapolitans and Spaniards against the Milanese, intimidated Hanover and Saxony, and spurred on the Swedes to occupy the Russians. A Franco-Bavarian army under old Marshal François duke de Broglie (1671–1745) advanced on Vienna but then crossed into Bohemia, as a Saxon force moved up the Elbe, stormed Prague on November 26, 1741, and there saw the elector of Bavaria elected Holy Roman Emperor Charles VII (January 24, 1742; crowned February 12).

Although forced to flee Vienna, Maria Theresa rallied the Habsburg cause. England, at war with Spain since 1739 over Jenkins' ear and finding the French escalating the conflict, voted Austria 300,000, though unable to help otherwise. Neipperg's forces in Silesia were released to fight the allies by the curious truce of Kleinschellendorf (October 9, 1741), by which the fortress of Neisse was surrendered to the Prussians after a mock siege. The Hungarians proclaimed their loyalty after an emotional appeal by the young Maria before the Hungarian parliament at Pressburg (Bratislava, in Slovakia) on September 11 and furnished an invaluable force of light troops. Field Marshal Ludwig Khevenhüller (1683–1744) thus was able to lead an army up the Danube into Bavaria that took Munich on Charles VII's coronation day, strategically flanking the Franco-Bavarian army in Bohemia. Encouraged, Maria Theresa revealed and denounced the terms of the truce with Frederick. Upset by the revitalized Austrian war effort, Frederick reentered the war in December 1741, driving through Moravia to within sight of Vienna. But Broglie was inactive, the Saxons went home, the Bavarians went south to defend their country, and, when he learned that an Austrian army under Prince Charles of Lorraine (1712–1880), the empress' brother-in-law, was marching to cut him off, Frederick retreated. On May 17, 1742, the Austrians attacked him at Chotusitz (Czaslau) but were defeated; and when Broglie won a minor engagement on May 24 at Sahay, near Budweis, Maria Theresa ceded Silesia to Prussia in the preliminary Treaty of Breslau

(June 11, 1742), confirmed by the Treaty of Berlin, July 28, ending the First Silesian War.

Prince Charles' Austrian forces were now free to converge upon Prague, and the French evacuated that city on December 16, 1742. Habsburg success continued with the campaigns of 1743. In addition an Anglo-German "Pragmatic Army" under King George II (1683–1760) formed at Ostend, advanced south up the Rhine, and defeated French Marshal Noailles at Dettingen on the Main (June 27). France itself was threatened with invasion when winter finally ended the campaigning. In Italy the Habsburgs were equally successful. The Royal Navy neutralized the Neapolitans and Marshal Otto von Traun (1677–1748) held the Spaniards, which encouraged Charles Emmanuel III of Sardinia to put 40,000 troops into the field in return for £200,000 a year from England and some Lombardy territories from Austria (Treaty of Worms, September 1743).

France came to the assistance of Spain in the Italian conflict by the Treaty of Fontainebleau (October 1743) and finally officially declared war on England, Austria, and Sardinia in spring 1744. A corps was assembled at Dunkirk to support the Jacobite cause of the Young Pretender, Charles Edward ("Bonnie Prince Charlie") Stuart (1720–1788), and an army was deployed to invade the Austrian Netherlands. The Austrians under Prince Charles and Traun, however, dislocated the French strategy by crossing the Rhine on July 1. But the French concentrated against the new threat, while Frederick of Prussia, disquieted by the Habsburg successes, concluded a new secret alliance with Louis XV. In August 1744, he marched through Saxony and invaded Bohemia, taking Prague on September 16. But then, harassed on all sides by Austrian hussars and Croatians, the Prussians retreated, their army almost destroyed by desertion, sickness, starvation, and exhaustion. Frederick's campaign did at least provide relief for France. In Italy the French assisted the Spanish and Neapolitans in defeating the Austrians and Sardinians in a series of engagements, but by autumn had failed to win the Po Valley.

On January 20, 1745, Charles VII died, and the new Bavarian elector had no desire to become Holy Roman emperor. On January 8, 1745, Maria Theresa's position had been further strengthened by the signing in Warsaw of the Quadruple Alliance with England, Holland, and Saxony. Austrian armies overran Bavaria again, and in the Peace of Füssen (April 22), the elector agreed to support the candidature of Francis as emperor in return for regaining his lands. But France and Prussia displayed renewed vigor. The French besieged Tournai in the Austrian Netherlands, the brilliant Marshal Maurice, count de Saxe (1696–1750), decisively defeating the English duke of Cumberland at Fontenoy on May 11, 1745. Maria Theresa still hoped to recover Silesia, but on June 4 Frederick's revitalized cavalry broke Prince Charles' Austro-Saxon army at Hohenfriedberg near Breslau, earning him recognition as "the Great."

Prussia and England were ready to recognize Maria's husband as emperor (elected Francis I on September 13), but Maria persisted in reclaiming Silesia. Frederick had to defeat Prince Charles a third time at Soor, Bohemia, on September 30 and march on Dresden, while the Old Dessauer (Prince Leopold of Anhalt-Dessau, 1676–1747) routed Marshal Rutowski's Saxons at Kesselsdorf (December 15). Maria Theresa had to acknowledge defeat, ending the Second Silesian War with the Peace of Dresden (December 25, 1745).

In the Po Valley the Franco-Spanish forces defeated the Sardinians but were in turn defeated at Piacenza (June 16, 1746). The Austrians took, but could not hold, Genoa, and a stalemate obtained until the conclusion of peace. Elsewhere the English defeated the Jacobites at Culloden Moor (April 16, 1746) and began to prevail against France and Spain on the high seas. In the Low Countries, French Marshal Saxe defeated his English, Dutch, and Austrian opponents, but France was impoverished. A Russian army marched to the Rhine to aid the allies but did not affect the general peace of Aix-la-Chapelle (Aachen), signed October 18, 1748, ending the drawn-out conflict. The peace was inconclusive, confirming only the succession of Maria Theresa and the rise of Frederician Prussia. Austria, of course, lost Silesia.

Works About: *Die Kriege unter der Regierung der Kaiserin Marie Theresia: Gesch. des österrei-chischen Erbfolgekrieges* 9 vols. (Vienna, 1896–1914); Prussian official *Die Kriege Friedrichs des Grossen*, 20 vols. (Berlin, 1890–1914), esp. *Der Erste Schlesische Krieg*, vol. 1 and *Der Zweite Schlesische Krieg*, vol. 13.   *A. H. Ganz*

See CHARLES VI; FRANCIS I; MARIA THERESA; PRAGMATIC SANCTION.

b

BACH, JOHANN SEBASTIAN (1685–1750), composer and musician, was born in Eisenach, Thuringia, a member of a highly talented musical family. His early life was made painful by the early death of both his parents. His oldest brother gave him keyboard lessons until he joined the poor boys' choir in Lüneburg; he was a fine student. In 1703 Bach became the organist at the New Church in Arnstadt on the northern edge of the Thuringian forest.

The year 1707 was eventful for the young Lutheran organist for he obtained a post at Mühlhausen and married his cousin, Maria Barbara Bach. A year later he became court organist at Weimar and a member of the orchestra. He received encouragement from Duke William Ernest, whose nephews Bach gave music lessons. After being passed over as musical director at Weimar, Bach moved on to Käthen as musical director to Prince Leopold. He continued composing during this period, concentrating mostly on chamber and orchestral music. It was a happy four years, though marred by the death of his wife.

In 1721 Bach became the director of church music for Leipzig, where he remained for fifteen years until becoming court composer for the elector of Saxony. In May 1747 he played before Frederick the Great at Potsdam. His health was undermined by two eye operations performed by John Taylor, oculist to King George III of England, who also numbered Handel among his victims. Bach achieved his greatest fame as a composer long after his demise.

Works By: H. David and A. Mendel, ed. *The Bach Reader* (New York, 1966) H. Müller and E. von Asow, ed., *J. S. Bach, Briefe* (Regensburg, 1950). **Works About:** Karl Geiringer and Irene Geiringer, *Johann Sebastian Bach* (New York, 1966); Albert Schweitzer, *J. S. Bach* (London, 1952); P. Spitta, *J. S. Bach* (New York, 1957); C. S. Terry, *Bach* (London, 1928); Percy M. Young, *The Bachs,* 2 vols. (London, 1970). *J. W. Zophy*

See FREDERICK II, THE GREAT; HANDEL.

BALDUNG-GRIEN, HANS (1484/85–1545), an outstanding painter and designer of woodcuts and stained glass, was born in Schwabisch Gmünd, the son of a university-educated jurist. During his formative years, Hans seems to have trained in the workshop of Albrecht Dürer.

Arriving in Strasbourg on April 1, 1509, he married and joined the guild of goldsmiths, painters, printers, and glaziers. For a while Baldung worked as an illustrator for several local printers and executed commissions for regional notables. From late 1512 to 1517, he lived in Freiburg im Breisgau, where he executed his most famous work, the great retable for the high altar of the cathedral. He spent the rest of his career in Strasbourg, where he rose to prominence in his guild, invested his earnings wisely, and generally prospered. His paintings and drawings reveal an extraordinarily gifted and imaginative artist.

Works About: Thomas A. Brady, Jr., "The Social Place of a German Artist: Hans Baldung-Grien (1484–85–1545) at Strasbourg," *CEH,*8 (1975): 295–315; O. Fischer, *Hans Baldung-Grien* (Munich, 1939); Carl Koch, "Hans Baldung-Grien," *DGD,* 1:401–17; Margaretta M. Salinger, "Baldung-Grien, Hans," *EWA,* 2:206.   *J. W. Zophy*

See STRASBOURG.

BAUMGARTNER, HIERONYMUS (1498–1565), an early supporter of Lutheranism within the Nuremberg government, was born in Nuremberg, the son of a prominent patrician. After spending five years at Ingolstadt, Baumgartner continued his studies of philosophy, mathematics, and jurisprudence at Leipzig and from 1518 on at Wittenberg. There he studied with Philip Melanchthon and became an early enthusiast for the teachings of Martin Luther. While in Wittenberg, Baumgartner became engaged to a former nun, Katherine von Bora. Because of the objections of his family, the engagement was broken off, and he later married Sybilla Dichtlin. Katherine became the bride of Luther.

Baumgartner returned to Nuremberg and joined the city council in 1525, where he became an influential supporter of Lutheranism. As early as 1524 he had urged his former mentor, Philip Melanchthon, to found a school in Nuremberg, which was eventually accomplished; the school opened on Easter 1526. He was also one of the founders of the Nuremberg public library, to which he donated his personal book collection in 1538.

As a statesman, he represented his native city at the diets of Speyer in 1529 and 1544 and at Augsburg in 1530, as well as at numerous other diplomatic gatherings, where he continued to defend the Lutheran movement staunchly. On some of these missions, he was accompanied by his able elder brother, Bernard, who was also a distinguished member of the city council. Within the Nuremberg government, Hieronymus rose to the highest rank, becoming city treasurer in 1558. His description of his fourteen-month imprisonment at the hands of the knight, Albert von Rosenberg, remains his most important literary accomplishment.

Works By: H. W. Caselmann, ed., "Ein eigenhandiger Bericht Hieronymus Paumgartners über seine Gefangennahme durch Albrecht von Rosenberg," *Jahresbericht des Hist. Ver. von Mittelfranken,*[33] *(1865); N. Müller, ed., "Beiträge zu Briefwechsel der älteren Hieronymus Baumgartner uber seiner Familie," MVGN, 10 (1893).*
Works About: Wilhelm Krag, *Die Paumgartner von Nürnberg und Augsburg: Ein Beitr. zur Handelsgesch, des XV. und XVI. Jahrhunderts* (Munich, 1919); Victor Kraus, "Baumgartner," *ADB,* 2:168–69; Otto Puchner, "Hieronymus Baumgartner," *NDB,* 1:664–65; G. E. Waldau, ed., *Joachimi Camerarii de vita Hieronymus Paumgartner* (Nürnberg, 1785), and "Lebensgeschichte des ersten Kirchenpflegers zu Nürnberg, Herrn Hieron. Paumgartner," *Vermischte Beyträge zur Gesch. der Stadt Nürnberg* (1789), vol. 4.   *J. W. Zophy*

See AUGSBURG, DIET OF; LUTHER; NUREMBERG.

BAVARIAN SUCCESSION, WAR OF THE (1778–1779), an almost blood-less conflict nicknamed the Potato War, was initiated with the death of the childless Maximilian III Joseph, Bavarian elector since 1745, on December 30, 1777, and the extinction of the Bavarian Wittelsbach line. The succession passed to elderly Charles Theodore (1724–1799), elector of Palatine (1733). This in-crease in power of a belligerent neighbor upset the Holy Roman emperor, Joseph II (1741–1790) of Austria, and his mother, Maria Theresa (1717–1780), who sent Austrian troops into Bavaria, claiming a number of lordships as lapsed fiefs of their crowns. The annexations had been planned with Charles Theodore who desired to elevate his natural children as princes of the Empire, having no legitimate heirs himself. This accretion in Austrian power in turn upset elderly King Frederick II of Prussia (1712–1786), who mobilized his armies in support of the next heir, Charles, duke of Pfalz-Zweibrücken (Deux-Ponts), supported by the Saxon troops of Elector Frederick Augustus III (1750–1827).

Two Prussian armies under Frederick and his brother, Prince Henry (1726–1802), invaded Bohemia in July 1778, but the Austrians, under Field Marshal Gideon Ernst von Loudon (1717–1790), withdrew behind the Elbe, and the Prussians spent their time foraging. Neither side was eager for a decision, though Prussian detachments were surprised and defeated at Dittersbach (November 8, 1778), Habelschwerdt (January 18, 1779), and Cämmerswalde (February 7, 1779). In November 1778 Czarina Catherine II (1729–1796) of Russia offered to mediate the quarrel, and a peace was signed at Teschen on May 13, 1779. Frederick had lost forty thousand troops, mostly from sickness and desertion; but the Austrians had to give up their designs on Bavaria, being compensated with the little district of Burghausen on the Inn, and acknowledge the Prussian claim to the margraviates of Ansbach and Bayreuth; and Charles of Zweibrücken was designated successor to childless Charles Theodore (though he died in 1795 and his brother actually succeeded in 1799 as Maximilian IV Joseph, 1756–1825, king of Bavaria, and Maximilian I after 1806). Emperor Joseph II con-tinued intriguing to exchange the remote Austrian Netherlands for Bavaria, by which Charles Theodore would become king of Burgundy. Frederick of Prussia thwarted this project as well by forming the League of Princes in 1785 to defend the threatened imperial constitution.

Works About: A. Buchner, *Gesch. von Baiern* (Munich, 1820–1853); S. Riezler, *Gesch. Bayerns* (Gotha, 1878–1899); G. F. Schmettau, *Ueber den Feldzug der preussischen Armee in Böhmen im Jahre 1778* (Berlin, 1789). *A. H. Ganz*

See FREDERICK II, THE GREAT; JOSEPH II; MARIA THERESA.

BEATRICE OF TUSCANY (c. 1015–1076), daughter of Frederick II of Upper Lorraine, married a powerful north Italian lord, Boniface II of Tuscany (c. 1037). Boniface II's holdings included Tuscany, Mantua, Parma, Ancona, Reg-gio, Piacenza, Ferrara, Modena, Spoleto, and Verona. Three children were born to Beatrice and Boniface II: Frederick (?–1055), Beatrice (?–1053), and Matilda of Tuscany (1046–1115). Boniface II, who had incurred the mistrust of Emperor Henry III, was murdered in 1052.

Two years later Beatrice married Gottfried II, the Bearded, of Lower Lorraine (?–1069). Gottfried II had twice rebelled against Emperor Henry III because of disagreements over the distribution of the inheritance of Gottfried II's father. Henry III refused to recognize Gottfried II's marriage to Beatrice because, according to canon law, they were too closely related to marry. Henry III took Gottfried II prisoner in 1055 and had Beatrice and her daughter Matilda brought to Germany. By June 1056, Gottfried II and Henry III settled their differences, Beatrice and Matilda were released, and Henry III recognized the marriage.

In 1057 it was agreed that Beatrice's daughter Matilda should marry Gottfried II's son, Gottfried III, the Hunchback. Beatrice and Matilda accompanied Gottfried II in 1067 when he fought the Normans in Italy on behalf of the young emperor Henry IV. Matilda and Gottfried III were married late in 1069(?), perhaps shortly before the death of Gottfried II in December of that year. Matilda and Gottfried III were estranged after a short period. Beatrice, accompanied by Matilda, returned to Tuscany in 1072.

Beatrice, Gottfried II, and Matilda played important roles in support of the papal reform party. Gottfried II's brother, Frederick, became Pope Stephen IX (August 1057–March 1958). Gregory VII was a close friend of Beatrice and Matilda. Henry IV's humiliating audience with Gregory VII on January 28, 1077, took place at Matilda's castle in Canossa. Beatrice, who died in 1076, left her lands to her daughter Matilda, who ruled them for thirty-nine years.

Works About: Alfred Overmann, *Gräfin Mathilde von Tuscien* (Innsbruck, 1895); Karl Reindel, "Gottfried II. der Bärtige," *NDB*, 6:662; E. Steindorff, *Jb. des dtsch. Reichs unter Heinrich III* (Leipzig, 1874–1881).   *J. W. Gates*

See GREGORY VII; HENRY III; HENRY IV; STEPHEN IX.

BEAUFORT, HENRY (c. 1375–1447), an English cardinal, was papal legate in Germany during a phase of the Hussite wars. Henry was the second of four children born to John of Gaunt, duke of Lancaster, by his mistress Katharine Roelt. These children were legitimized by the pope under the name of Beaufort in February 1397, a year after their parents married. Henry Beaufort studied at Oxford, Cambridge, and Aachen before becoming bishop of Lincoln in 1398. His half-brother became king of England as Henry IV in 1399, and the Beauforts held important positions in his government as well as under the subsequent Lancastrian administrations of Henry V and Henry VI. Beaufort was moved from Lincoln to the wealthier see of Winchester in 1405, and he gained an almost legendary reputation for financial management.

As ranking prelate in the Order of the Garter, Beaufort inducted King Sigismund of Germany into the order at Windsor during Sigismund's tour of the western countries to gain support for the Council of Constance. In 1417, Beaufort arrived in Constance while ostensibly on a pilgrimage to the Holy Land, and he negotiated with Sigismund to arrange the election of a new pope. Although himself a candidate for the papacy in early balloting, Beaufort was looked upon by the new pope, Martin V, as a man who had helped him to gain election. In gratitude for his support, Martin named Beaufort a cardinal and papal legate in the British Isles, honors that Beaufort later had to decline on the order of King Henry V.

Tensions within the regency council for young Henry VI led to Beaufort's departure from England in 1427, again ostensibly on a pilgrimage. He finally received the red hat of a cardinal and the commission as papal legate for Germany, Bohemia, and Hungary to lead the crusade against the Hussites. Cardinal Beaufort arrived at the Bohemian frontier in July 1427 to find the crusade army in retreat, and his efforts to rally the troops caused only a brief pause in their rout. The cardinal convoked an imperial diet at Frankfurt am Main in November and December 1427 to consider ways and means of combatting the heretics. The princely estates approved the cardinal's plan for a direct poll tax on the residents of the Empire, and they forced the urban estates to accept the proposal lest they be thought soft on heresy. This was the first general direct tax in imperial history and it was to serve as the model for taxation projects over the next century referred to as the Common Penny. Cardinal Henry attempted to collect the tax rapidly, using ecclesiastical penalties to whip the estates into line. When many estates protested against such harshness, Beaufort was convinced to reverse his mass excommunications and to lower his expectations of German readiness to obey national authorities. Over thirty thousand guilders were collected, mostly from ecclesiastical estates, but further efforts to collect the tax stagnated when Beaufort left Germany without appointing a deputy in his stead.

Cardinal Henry was convinced that he needed English troops to stiffen German resistance to the Hussites, and he returned to England in September 1428 to raise these soldiers. He recruited a force and made a fruitless journey to Scotland seeking donations for the crusade. Beaufort's troop was then diverted to Paris in July 1429 to bolster the garrison of the duke of Bedford against the resurgent French army led by Joan of Arc. The sacrifice of a crusading unit to English political interests shocked Martin V and brought Cardinal Henry Beaufort's activities as a papal legate in Germany to an end. The rest of his long career was passed as a figure in English political life, and he was never again to play a major role in larger European affairs.

Works About: Frederick G. Heymann, "The Crusades against the Hussites," in Kenneth Setton, ed., *A Hist. of the Crusades* (Madison, 1975), 3:586–646; William Hunt, *Dictionary of National Biography,* (Oxford 1921–22), 2:41–8; E. F. Jacob, *The Fifteenth Century* (Oxford 1961); K. B. McFarland, "Henry V, Bishop Beaufort and the Red Hat, 1417–1421," *English Hist. Review* 60 (1945); 316–48; František Palacký, *Urkundl. Beitr. zur Gesch. des Hussitenkrieges* (Prague, 1873); DRTA, 1st series, vol. 9; Lewis Bostock Radford, *Henry Beaufort* (London, 1908).

S. W. Rowan

See COMMON PENNY; SIGISMUND.

BEETHOVEN, LUDWIG VAN (1770–1827), composer, was born in Bonn, the eldest surviving child of John and Mara van Beethoven. Although the Beethovens were of Flemish descent, they had established themselves in Bonn as musicians for two generations. Because of his father's alcoholism, which impoverished the family, Ludwig was forced to leave school at age eleven. Through the auspices of his teacher, Christian Gottlob Neefe, Beethoven got his first composition published and began work as Neefe's assistant organist at the court of the elector of Cologne, Maximilian Francis, the brother of the Emperor Joseph II.

Maximilian Francis admired Beethoven's talent and sent him to Vienna in 1787 to study with Mozart. His stay in Vienna was cut to two months by the death of his mother. He remained in Bonn for five more years playing viola in the theater orchestra. Beethoven was hired by the widow of Chancellor Joseph von Breuning as music teacher to two of her children, and through her influence he acquired a number of other wealthy pupils.

In the autumn of 1792 Beethoven left Bonn to study with Haydn in Vienna. With the help of his friend, Count Ferdinand von Waldstein, he was well received in aristocratic circles. His tours as a concert pianist and composer were successful until progressive deafness caused his playing to degenerate. His famous *Third Symphony* of 1804 was dedicated to Napoleon, but Beethoven struck out the dedication when he learned that the Corsican had taken the title *emperor*, which outraged his republican sensibilities. He found a generous patron in Prince Karl Lichnowsky, who helped support him and get his works published. Beethoven achieved great fame even before his death in Vienna of cirrhosis of the liver.

Works By: Emily Anderson, ed., *The Letters of Beethoven*, 3 vols. (New York, 1961). **Works About:** H. C. Fischer, *Ludwig van Beethoven* (London, 1973); Theodor von Frimmel, *Ludwig van Beethoven* (Berlin, 1922); H. C. Robbins Landon, *Beethoven* (New York, 1970); G. R. Marek, *Beethoven* (New York, 1969); A. W. Thayer, *The Life of Beethoven*, 2 vols. (Princeton, 1967).   *J. W. Zophy*

See HAYDN; JOSEPH II; MOZART; VIENNA.

BERLICHINGEN, GÖTZ VON (c. 1480–1562), knightly soldier of fortune, was born at Castle Hornberg to a noble family. For a number of years, he served at the court of the margrave of Brandenburg-Ansbach. In 1504 Götz lost his right hand in battle during the War of the Bavarian Succession. He replaced it with an iron hook and became known as the man with the iron hand, who struck terror in his enemies. His foes multiplied as he entered into lengthy feuds with cities such as Nuremberg and archbishoprics such as Mainz. In 1519 he fought with Duke Ulrich of Württemberg and was enmeshed in his fall.

During the Peasants' Revolt of 1525, he threw his lot in with the peasants in the campaigns against Bamberg and Mainz and succeeded in getting the latter to accept the demands of the peasants' Twelve Articles. He deserted the peasants in May, fleeing to his castle at Hornberg and thereby avoided participating in their disastrous defeat. Nevertheless he was imprisoned a number of times and had to engage in a great deal of litigation to regain his lands and freedom. Although placed under imperial ban on four occasions, Berlichingen served Emperor Charles V in the campaign of 1542 against the Turks and in 1544 against the French.

Goethe's romantic drama, *Götz von Berlichingen*, of 1773 was based on the knight's misleading autobiography and presents Götz as a heroic foe of priest and prince, defender of the poor and downtrodden. In reality, he was an opportunist of mixed motives, one of which was monetary gain.

Works By: *The Autobiography of Götz von Berlichingen,* ed. H. S. M. Stuart (London, 1962). **Works About:** F. W. G. von Berlichingen-Rossach, *Gesch. des Ritters Götz von Berlichingen mit der eisernen Hand und seiner Familie* (Leipzig, 1861); Johann Kamann, *Die Fehde des Götz von Berlichingen mit der Reichsstadt Nürnberg und dem Hochstifte Bamberg 1512–1514* (Nuremberg, 1893); Wilhelm Nestle, "Götz von Berlichingen," *Württemb. Vierteljahrshefte für Landesgesch.* 18 (1909): 373–97; Helgard Ulmschneider, *Götz von Berlichingen: Ein adeliges Leben der dtsch. Renaissance* (Sigmaringen, 1974); H. Zoepfl, *Die Hauptmannschaft des Götz von Berlichingen im Grossen Bauernkrieg vom Jahre 1525* (Heidelberg, 1850).   *J. W. Zophy*

See GOETHE; PEASANTS' WAR; ULRICH OF WÜRTTEMBERG.

BERNHARD, DUKE OF SAXE-WEIMAR (1604–1639), Protestant military leader in the Thirty Years War, was born in Weimar and died in Neuenburg on the Rhine. A man of deep religious piety, Bernhard belonged to a small but militant group of German Lutheran princes who advocated the use of military force to defend their constitutional and religious liberties. He fought in the Palatinate and Danish phases of the war, but his talents as a military leader did not become evident until after Gustavus Adolphus had intervened in the conflict (1630). Bernhard was one of the first German princes to join the Swedish king and fight under his command, first as a colonel and, after April 1632, as a general.

Bernhard's willfulness and jealousy of his brother William, who ranked militarily above him, made him cantankerous and difficult to deal with. When Gustavus Adolphus was killed in the Battle of Lützen (November 16, 1632), Bernhard assumed command of the Swedish army and won a victory over Wallenstein's forces. As an award for his services he received the duchy of Franconia (newly created from the bishoprics of Würzburg and Bamberg) as a fief of the Swedish crown in 1633. Sweden's war effort, now directed by Chancellor Axel Oxenstierna, suffered from the rivalry and disagreements between Bernhard and the Swedish generals. Bernhard favored a continuation of Gustavus' offensive strategy, while the other generals (especially Gustav Horn) preferred defensive holding operations against the leaguist and imperialist forces. In spite of these differences, the Swedes conquered Regensburg in November 1633. But a few months later they suffered a disastrous defeat at Nördlingen (September 6, 1634) in which they lost control of southern Germany. Bernhard was deprived of Franconia.

Bernhard was one of the few German princes who did not support the Peace of Prague that Emperor Ferdinand II negotiated with Elector John George of Saxony in 1635. Instead he signed a contract with Richelieu (Treaty of St. Germain, October 27, 1635), in which he agreed to lead a French-subsidized army of eighteen thousand men. In return, he was promised the landgravate of Alsace and the county of Hagenau as independent territories. During the next few years, Bernhard conducted successful military operations in Lorraine and Burgundy and along the Upper Rhine. In 1638 he won crushing victories at Rheinfelden and Breisach, both key positions along the Rhine providing France with a gateway into Germany. Bernhard was at the height of his career. By refusing to compromise over the Alsace region, he earned for himself a reputation as a German patriot. Bernhard's sudden death of a fever (July 18, 1639) permitted the French to seize control of the principality; his army, the "Bernhardines" or "Weymariens," also came under French command.

Works About: Gustav Droysen, *Bernhard von Weimar*, 2 vols. (Leipzig, 1885); Georg Irmer, ed., *Die Verhandlungen Schwedens und seiner Verbündeten mit Wallenstein und dem Kaiser von 1631 bis 1634*. 3 vols. (Leipzig, 1888–1891); K. Menzel, "Bernhard, Herzog zu Sachsen–Weimar," *ADB*, 2:439–50; A.M.R.A. Vicomte de Noailles, *Bernhard de Saxe–Weimar (1604–1639) et la réunion de L'Alsace à la France (Paris, 1908); "Saxe–Weimar,"* in J. F. Michaud, *Biographie Universelle* (Paris, 1854–1865), 38:165–72; F. Schubert, "Bernhard, Herzog von Sachsen," *NDB*, 2:113–15.

Bodo Nischan

See THIRTY YEARS WAR; WALLENSTEIN, ALBERT.

BERTHOLD OF HENNEBERG (1442–1504), elector and archbishop of Mainz, was the son of George, count of Henneberg. He studied law at the University of Erfurt and in Italy. He pursued an ecclesiastical career, beginning as cathedral canon in Mainz in 1464 and becoming cathedral dean in 1474. He was made archbishop of Mainz in 1484 gaining a reputation as a careful and dedicated administrator of his ecclesiastical state. He established law and order, practiced thrift in government, and worked for moral improvement in the clerical establishment. Being dedicated to reform of the Church, he turned against the abuses connected with indulgences, church offices, and papal finances. As archbishop of Mainz and hence an elector and archchancellor of the Holy Roman Empire, he began to play a leading role in the Empire. In 1486, he was actively involved in gaining the election of Maximilian as king of the Romans. During the reign of Emperor Frederick III, he had demonstrated his interest in the issue that would make him one of the leading political figures in the early reign of Emperor Maximilian I: the administrative reform of the Holy Roman Empire.

As leader of the reform movement, Berthold of Mainz was basically a politically conservative figure who represented the aristocratic constitutionalism of the later Middle Ages. His aim was to establish effective organs of central government with a leading role for the princes as councillors of the emperor. Berthold's vision was one of a federal Empire in which the estates, and especially the great princes, and emperor ruled together. In order to make possible the growth of the new institutions, a period of peace would be necessary. Thus the armed forces of the Empire would be used only to maintain domestic order while foreign war was avoided. Berthold's idea of reform was fundamentally medieval and ran counter to the emerging early modern trend of strong monarchy.

The first concrete manifestations of the reform movement were achieved at the diet of Worms in 1495. The *ewiger Landfrieden,* or perpetual internal peace, was proclaimed, outlawing all personal feuds and requiring the estates to seek a peaceful settlement of disputes. To do this, a new institution, the *Reichskammergericht,* or Imperial Cameral Court, was created by the diet. This court of the Empire, dominated by the princes, was to apply the rule of law and stamp out feuds among the German estates. A general tax, the so-called Common Penny, was also established by this diet to provide funds for the support of an imperial army and the *Reichskammergericht.* However, efforts at collecting this tax proved to be largely unsuccessful because of the unwillingness of the estates to bolster the authority of the emperor with an imperial army. Since the estates wanted to play an active role in foreign and internal policy, Berthold's reform party at Worms tried to establish a *Reichsregiment,* or Imperial Council of Regency, which would cooperate directly with the emperor in governing the Empire. Maximilian's opposition to this check on his monarchical authority thwarted the efforts of the reformers.

The difficult political situation of the emperor forced him to acquiesce at the diet of Augsburg in 1500 in the formation of a *Reichsregiment.* This achievement was the high point of the reform movement's efforts under Berthold of Mainz's leadership to establish a federal Empire. This council, as Berthold and his colleagues developed it, was composed of twenty-one members. It was presided over by the emperor or his deputy but could proceed with business without the presence of either one. The council was responsible for the administration of the Empire, financial policy, justice, foreign policy, and the armed forces. To provide for defense, a new program was followed. Cavalry would be provided by the nobility and the subjects of the princes would be taxed to form a militia. Contributions from the towns and clergy would finance the expenses of the new institutions of federal government. Basically the *Reichsregiment* claimed full authority to run the Empire and virtually reduced the emperor to a figurehead monarch. He had become the formal president of a committee dominated by Berthold of Mainz and his electoral colleagues. Even the command of the military was taken away from the emperor. However, the *Reichsregiment* failed to become permanently established. Neither the emperor nor the estates cooperated with the new institution, and it lacked money and staff to impose its will upon the Empire. Its foreign policy was meaningless and undermined by Maximilian's independent role in handling foreign affairs. By 1502, Maximilian felt strong enough to demand the surrender of the imperial seal from Berthold of Mainz as archchancellor of the Empire. Berthold's attempts to persuade the electors to form a union to uphold the reforms of 1495 and 1500 against their violation by the emperor were of no effect. In fact, Maximilian even accused Berthold of being a traitor in the pay of the king of France. The *Reichsregiment* ceased to function, and Maximilian established his own *Hofrat,* or privy council, to take over the imperial administrative functions. Berthold of Mainz's vision for reorganizing imperial administration had been a failure. His health, which had already begun to suffer in 1502, continued to deteriorate, and he died near the end of 1504. Without his leadership and dedication the reform movement totally collapsed.

Works About: Heinz Angermeier, "Die Reichsregimenter und ihre Staatsidee," *HZ 211* (1970): 265–315; Karl Bader, *Ein Staatsmann vom Mittelrhein. Gestalt und Werk des Mainzer Kurfürsten und Erzbischofs Berthold von Henneberg* (Mainz, 1955); Hans Baron, "Imperial Reform and the Habsburgs, 1486–1504," AHR 44 (1938–1939):293–303; Fritz Hartung, "Berthold von Henneberg, Kurfürst von Mainz," *HZ 103* (1909): 527–551 and "Die Reichsreform von 1485 bis 1495: Ihr Verlauf und ihr Wesen." Hist. *Vierteljahrschrift* 16 (1913): 24–53; Viktor von Kraus, *Das Nürnberger Reichsregiment 1500–1502* (Innsbruck, 1883); Erich Molitor, *Die Reichsreformbestrebungen des 15. Jahrhunderts bis zum Tode Kaiser Friedrichs III* (Breslau, 1921); Alfred Schröcker, *Unio atque concordia. Reichspolitik Bertholds von Henneberg 1484–1504* (Würzburg, 1970); J. Weiss, *Berthold von Henneberg, Erzbischof von Mainz* (1889); Eduard Ziehen, *Mittelrhein und Reich im Zeitalter der Reichsreform 1356–1504,* 2 vols. (Frankfurt, 1934–1937).   *J. J. Spielvogel*

See COMMON PENNY; FREDERICK III; IMPERIAL CAMERAL COURT; IMPERIAL COUNCIL OF REGENCY; MAXIMILIAN I.

BLENHEIM (Battle of or Second Battle of Hochstädt, August 1704) took place during the War of the Spanish Succession (1701–1714) when John Churchill, duke of Marlborough, commander-in-chief of the English forces, and Prince Eugene of Savoy, imperial commander, defeated a Franco-Bavarian force near Hochstädt, Bavaria, and forced the elector Max Emmanuel out of the war.

The Franco-Bavarian forces intended to join the Hungarian rebels under Francis II Rákóczi in order to invade the Holy Roman Empire and seize the capital at Vienna. The elector of Bavaria's seizure of Passau in January 1704 highlighted the ineffectiveness of the imperial military effort and spotlighted the weakness of the Empire. With a mere nineteen hundred men, the commander at Passau had been unable to withstand the elector's ten thousand troops. Because of Passau's strategic location as key to the hereditary countries, its easy capitulation highlighted the danger that the Empire was facing and impelled Emperor Leopold I to request military aid from his allies, particularly the maritime powers, England and the United Provinces.

In order to mislead the French, the plan was carried out in the greatest secrecy. In a brilliant strategic maneuver, Marlborough transferred a whole body of troops from the Low Countries up the Danube to Bavaria. On June 22, 1704,

Marlborough met the imperial commanders, Prince Eugene of Savoy and Prince Louis of Baden, near Ulm. Prince Louis and Marlborough went on to defeat the Bavarians in a bloody battle at Donauwörth, while Eugene of Savoy guarded Stollhofen. Louis of Baden with fifteen thousand troops besieged Ingolstadt, then held by the Bavarians. Meanwhile Eugene and Marlborough marched with approximately fifty-five thousand troops to Hochstädt, where they encountered a Franco-Bavarian army of approximately sixty thousand under the command of marshals Tallard and Marsin and the elector Max Emmanuel of Bavaria. Marlborough and Eugene rotated the command every other day. On August 13, 1704, it was Marlborough's turn to command. He led the attack on Tallard's forces and routed the cavalry while Eugene launched a holding attack on the right flank. The destruction of Tallard's troops forced Marsin and the elector to retreat with their contingents largely intact. Blenheim was one of the bloodiest battles in the war; about twelve thousand on each side were killed or wounded. The resultant victory was but the first of a series of military reverses for Louis XIV: it punctured the image of French military invincibility, prevented the Habsburgs from leaving the war, pushed the French behind the Rhine, raised the morale of the German princes, forced Bavaria out of the war, and removed the danger threatening the Holy Roman Empire.

Works About: C. T. Atkinson, *Marlborough and the Rise of the British Army* (New York, 1921), pp. 193ff; Max Braubach, *Prinz Eugen von Savoyen,* 5 vols. (Vienna, 1963–65); David Chandler, *Marlborough as Military Commander* (London, 1973); Winston S. Churchill, *Marlborough: His Life and Times* (London, 1947), 1:72ff; Philip Roder von Diersberg, ed., *Kriegs-und Staatschriften über der spansichen Erbfolgekrieg, 1700–1707* (Karlsrühe, 1850); Eugene Francis, *Feldzüge* (Vienna, 1876–1892), 5:460ff; Onno Klopp, *Der Fall des Hauses Stuart* (Vienna, 1879); George Murray, ed., *The Letters and Dispatches of John Churchill, First Duke of Marlborough from 1702–1712* (London, 1845); Frank Taylor, *The Wars of Marlborough* (Oxford, 1921); B. Van T'Hoff, ed., *The Correspondence of John Churchill, First Duke of Marlborough, and Anthonie Heinsius, Grand Pensionary of Holland* (The Hague, 1951).   *L. S. Frey and M. L. Frey*

See EUGENE OF SAVOY; LEOPOLD I; SPANISH SUCCESSION, WAR OF.

BOCCACCIO, GIOVANNI (1313–1375), foremost Italian prose writer and Latin encyclopedist, was born in Tuscany, most probably Florence, the illegitimate son of a merchant banker from Certaldo who was associated with the Bardi banking house. Boccaccio spent his youth (1327–1341) in Naples, first as a merchant's apprentice and then as a student of canon law at the university. He absorbed the cultural and artistic life of the city, met the greatest jurists, artists, and men of letters, and read the classics and their medieval commentators, as well as collections of French and Provençal lyrics available in the royal library. Here began his literary career, which blossomed upon his return to Florence.

After his father's bankruptcy (1345) and death (1349), Boccaccio lived in straitened circumstances. His fame as a poet enabled him to fulfill many offices in the Florentine government. In 1350 he was ambassador to the lords of Romagna and was later sent by the Company of Or San Michele with a gift of ten florins for Suora Beatrice, Dante Alighieri's daughter, a nun in Ravenna. Boccaccio took part in the Office of the Chamberlains (the treasury) in 1351 and treated with Jacopo di Donato Acciaiuoli for Florence in the city's purchase of Prato from Naples. During the same year, he failed in his embassy to form an alliance with Ludwig of Bavaria against the Visconti of Milan. In 1354 the Comune sent him first to Innocent VI in Avignon to sound out the pope's position on the descent into Italy of Charles IV and then to bribe the marauder and renegade, Friar Moriale, whose plundering bands threatened Florentine possessions. From May to August 1355, the writer registered the absences of soldiers in the Office of the Militia. He probably went as ambassador "ad partes Lombardie" in 1359. The year 1356 found him again in Avignon with Urban V, and 1367 in Rome congratulating the pontiff for (temporarily) reestablishing the Holy See in the city.

In 1350 Boccaccio first met Petrarch in Florence; their friendship and reciprocal influence lasted until 1374. In 1351, Boccaccio tried unsuccessfully to persuade his friend to accept a chair in the Florentine Studium (University). After some of his acquaintances were implicated in a conspiracy concerning the issue of admonishment, by which Florentine citizens could be unfairly disenfranchised and proscribed, the writer removed his residence to Certaldo, where he received visits from Coluccio Salutati and the Villani. For Leonzio Pilato, who was then translating Homer in Boccaccio's house in Florence, the writer obtained the first Western chair of Greek in the Studium. In 1362 the posthumous message of a Carthusian monk, Pietro Petroni, caused Boccaccio extreme alarm: both he and Petrarch would be damned for pursuing profane literary studies. But, upon Petrarch's persuasion, Boccaccio resumed his literary career with a more moral and spiritual commitment.

In the same year, invited by Niccolò Acciaiuoli, his boyhood friend, now grand seneschal of Naples, Boccaccio returned to that city with the hope of financial aid but was treated shamefully by his host. From there he fled to Venice to visit Petrarch (1363) and retired again to Certaldo, where he resided until 1366. Five years after Niccolò's death, he was to visit Naples more pleasantly in 1370, before his final retirement to Certaldo in 1371. Here, refusing invitations from Petrarch and offers of protection from Ugo di San Severino (on behalf of Queen Giovanni of Naples), Giacomo d'Aragona (the queen's husband), and Niccolò Orsini, count Palatine and count of Nola, Boccaccio devoted himself to the revision of his encyclopedic works and to copying his youthful masterpiece, the *Decameron* (completed c. 1351–1352). In October 1373, he began to lecture on Dante's *Comedia* in the church of Santo Stefano di Badia of Florence, but illness forced his return to Valdelsa in January 1374. Plagued with various diseases, scabies, and obesity, Boccaccio died in Certaldo in 1375.

Works By: Giovanni Boccaccio, *Decameron,* ed. Charles S. Singleton, 2 vols. (Bari, 1955); *Decameron: Edizione diplomatico-interpretiva dell' autografo Hamilton 90,* ed. Charles S. Singleton

(Baltimore, 1974); *Tutte le opere di Giovanni Boccaccio, a cura di Vittore Branca,* 12 vols. (Milan, 1964–). **Works About:** Alvatore Baltaglia, "Elementi autobiografici nell'arte del Boccaccio." *La Cultura* 9 (1930); Giuseppe Billanovich, *Restauri boccacceschi* (Rome, 1945, repr. 1947); Vittore Branca, *Boccaccio medievale* (Florence, 1965, rev. 1970), and "Giovanni Boccaccio: Profilo biografico,"in *Tutte le opere di GB,* 1:3–203, in *Boccaccio: The Man and His Works,* ed. Richard Monges and Dennis J. McAuliffe (New York, 1976); Vittore Branca and Pier Giorgio Ricci, "Notizie e documenti per la biografia del Boccaccio," *Studie sul Boccaccio* 3 (1965): 5–24, 5 (1969): 1–18, and 6 (1971): 1–10; E. G. Léonard, *Boccace et Naples* (Paris, 1944) Carlo Musecetta, "Giovanni Boccaccio e i novellieri," in *Il Trecento, storia della letteratura italiana,* ed. Emilio Cecchi and Natalino Sapegno (Milan, 1965), 2: 317–558; Natalino Sapegno, *Il Trecento* (Milan, 1934); A. della Torre, *La giovinezza di Giovanni Boccaccio* (Città di Castello, 1905). *A. K. Cassell*

See CHARLES IV; DANTE; PETRARCH.

BOEHME, JACOB (1575–1616), mystic and theosophist, was a native of Alt-Seidenberg near Görlitz in Silesia. His parents were pious Lutherans of peasant backgrounds. Despite limited formal schooling, young Jacob developed scholarly interests through contacts with learned friends and through voracious reading. He especially enjoyed Luther's German Bible, the ideas of Paracelsus, and a number of works by German mystics. Because of his modest physical stature, Boehme had to abandon heavy agricultural work for the shoemaking trade to which he was apprenticed in his fourteenth year. After a serious visionary experience, the young shoemaker resolved to lead a godly and virtuous life. He eventually settled in Görlitz, where he opened up a shoemaking shop and married.

His domestic tranquility was disturbed by periods of religious melancholy. Boehme's restless soul found little satisfaction in the sterile dogmatism of his local Lutheran church. After a series of divine illuminations, the shoemaker found himself compelled to write a book, *The Aurora,* which told of the ceaseless struggle between good and evil. Circulated privately among friends, a copy of the unfinished manuscript fell into the hands of Gregor Richter, a local minister who feared heresy. Richter maneuvered the town council into exacting a pledge from Boehme that he refrain from writing on theological matters or leave Görlitz.

Boehme's efforts in the yarn and woolen gloves trade proved unsuccessful, and he chafed under the writing prohibition. Finally in 1619 Boehme accepted the urgings of his friends that he resume writing and not waste his gift for prose. A series of influential and compelling volumes emerged, including the *Mysterium-Magnum* (1623) and *The Way to Christ Discovered* (1624). Boehme wrote of God as a will that seeks to realize itself in nature. In God, forces such as darkness and anger are governed by light and love. Man must surrender his will to God as Christ has done.

The greatest linguistic innovator in German since Luther, Boehme had a profound impact upon later mystics, philosophers such as Hegel, romanticists, pietists, and even Quakers in England. In May 1624 he traveled to Dresden, where the philosopher-mystic was widely acclaimed and offered help from influential persons in promoting a new Reformation. The congenial Boehme died a short time later at home in Görlitz proclaiming, "Now I am going to Paradise."

Works By: *Sämtliche Schriften,* ed. Will-Erich Peukert, 11 vols. (Stuttgart, 1955–1961); *Concerning the Three Principles of the Divine Essence* (London, 1910); *The Confessions of Jacob Boehme* (New York, 1954); *The Forty Questions of the Soul and the Clavis* (London, 1911); *The Way to Christ* (London, 1947). **Works About:** G. M. Alleman, *A Critique of Some Philosophical Aspects of the Mysticis of Jacob Boehme* (Philadelphia, 1932); Heinrich Bornkamm, *Luther und Böhme* (Bonn, 1925); A. M. Guinsberg, "Jacob Boehme from Orthodoxy to Enlightenment" (Ph.D. diss., Stanford University, 1971); Alexander Koyré, *La Philosophie de J. Boehme* (Paris, 1929); H. L. Martensen, *Jacob Boehme* (New York, 1949).   *J. W. Zophy*

See LUTHER; ECKHART; PARACELSUS; SILESIUS.

BRANT, SEBASTIAN (c. 1458–1521), poet and lawyer, was born an innkeeper's son in Strasbourg. After private tutoring, Sebastian entered the University of Basel, where he received a doctorate in canon and civil law in 1489. Until 1500 he stayed in Basel as a professor of law and then served as dean as well as an editor for a local publisher. In 1494 Brant published his *Ship of Fools,* which became the most popular work of German literature before Goethe. This and his other satirical writings earned him lasting fame.

When Basel decided to leave the Empire and join the Swiss Confederation, Brant, an ardent admirer of Emperor Maximilian, left for Strasbourg. Back in his home town, he became a legal adviser and then city secretary for the city council. Brant continued to write poetry and legal treatises and was named a member of the imperial council by Maximilian. In his writings, Brant showed a great concern for restoring political and social stability to the Holy Roman Empire, which he felt was in a state of decline.

Works By: Sebastian Brant, *The Ship of Fools,* tr. E. H. Zeydel (New York, 1944). **Works About:** Gerhard Dünnhaupt, "Sebastian Brant," in *The Renaissance and Reformation in Germany,* ed. G. Hoffmeister (New York, 1977); Ulrich Gaier, *Studien zu Sebastian Brants Narrenschiff* (Tübingen, 1966); William Gilbert, "Sebastian Brant: Conservative Humanist," *ARG* 46 (1955): 145–67; Barbara Könneker, *Sebastian Brant* (Munich, 1966); Edwin Zeydel, *Sebastian Brant* (New York, 1967).   *J. W. Zophy*

See MAXIMILIAN I; STRASBOURG.

BRENZ, JOHN (1499–1580), a major Protestant reformer, began life as a member of a baker's family in Weilderstadt near Stuttgart. A student at Heidelberg, which remained a Roman Catholic stronghold, he witnessed and was impressed by Martin Luther's disputation there in 1518. His growing Lutheranism almost cost him a heresy trial, which he avoided by accepting a call to the parish of Schwabish Hall in 1522. Remaining there for more than a quarter of a century, Brenz quietly but effectively ushered in and institutionalized the Reformation. Although siding with Luther in the controversy over the Eucharist, he differed with the Wittenberger in advocating a state church. The author of influential catechisms, Brenz became the foremost spokesman for Lutheranism in south Germany. He helped to write important church orders for Brandenburg and Nuremberg.

Duke Ulrich of Württemberg invited Brenz in 1536 to establish the Reformation throughout his territory and to help reorganize the University of Tübingen. He also participated in most of the major religious colloquies of his day, from Marburg in 1529 to Regensburg in 1541. After the defeat of the League of Schmalkalden and the imposition of the Augsburg Interim, Brenz was forced to go into hiding for a time.

In 1550 he was commissioned to draw up the *Confessio Virtembergica* by Duke Christopher of Württemberg. This confession was intended to explain the Lutheran position to the Roman Catholic leaders assembled at Trent, but Brenz was not allowed to present his document in person. Following the abolition of the Interim, Brenz became provost of the cathedral in Stuttgart in 1553 and visitor-general of the cloisters in 1557. From this position, he completed the institutionalization of the Reformation in Württemberg, culminating in his church order of 1559.

Works By: *Predigten des Johannes Brenz,* ed. E. Bizer (Stuttgart, 1955); Johannes Brenz, *Werke,* ed. Martin Brecht and Gerhard Schafer (Tübingen, 1970–). **Works About:** Martin Brecht, *Die Frühe Theologie des Johannes Brenz* (Tübingen, 1966); James M. Estes, "Church Order and the Christian Magistrate according to Johannes Brenz," *ARG* 59 (1968): 5–24 and "Johannes Brenz and the Institutionalization of the Reformation in Württemberg," *CEH* 3 (1973): 44–59; H. Hermelink, *Johannes Brenz als lutherischer und schwäbisher Theologe* (Stuttgart, 1949); F. W. Kantzenbach, "Der Anteil des Johannes Brenz an der Konfessionspolitik und Dogmengeschichte des Protestantismus," in *Reformatio und Confessio: Festschrift für D. Wilhelm Maurer* (Berlin, 1965), pp. 113–29; D. C. Steinmetz, *Reformers in the Wings* (Philadelphia, 1971).   *J. W. Zophy*

See CHRISTOPHER OF WÜRTTEMBERG; LUTHER; ULRICH OF WÜRTTEMBERG.

BRÜCK, GREGOR (1485/86–1557), Saxon jurist and statesman of the Reformation period, was born in the small town of Brück (north of Wittenberg) where his father, Gregor Heinze, was burgomaster. The son, who eventually adopted the name of his birthplace, studied at the universities of Wittenberg and Frankfurt on the Oder, becoming a doctor of both civil and canon law. He was called from a promising legal career into the service of his prince, Frederick the Wise, elector of Saxony. He quickly rose to the position of chancellor (1520/21), an office that he held until 1529. Although he bore only the title of councillor after this date, his influence and authority remained undiminished throughout most of his lifetime. Following his resignation from the chancellorship, Brück resided for many years in Wittenberg where he proved to be a very effective intermediary between the religious reformers and the electoral government. He was highly regarded by Luther, who referred to him as "the only pious jurist" and "the Atlas of our principality." By his distinguished service to three successive electors of Saxony, he established a solid reputation as one of the most important figures in Reformation politics and diplomacy.

Brück played a significant role at the diet of Worms (1521), where he carried on negotiations concerning Luther with Father Glapion, confessor to Emperor Charles V. For the next two decades Brück actively participated in most of the major political assemblies in Germany where Saxon and Reformation interests were at stake. He was the chief author of the famous protest issued by the evangelical party at the diet of Speyer (1529). His importance as spokesman for the Protestant estates of the Empire was even greater at the diet of Augsburg (1530). As well as helping to draw up the momentous Augsburg Confession, Brück successfully defended the right of the Protestant party to have the document publicly read at the diet. He also compiled a report of the proceedings at Augsburg, an important source for the history of those events.

The emperor's threatening response to the Augsburg Confession caused the German evangelicals to take up the matter of self-defense. Brück made a decisive contribution to the subsequent founding of the Schmalkaldic League by persuading Luther that on legal grounds the Protestant princes were justified in forming an alliance to offer resistance to a tyrannical emperor. On behalf of the Schmalkaldic League, Brück conducted numerous negotiations with Catholic princes and the imperial government. He generally sought peaceful solutions to the crises of his day and thereby helped to postpone the outbreak of religious warfare until the 1540s.

Brück strongly influenced internal Saxon affairs as well as the course of Reformation diplomacy. As a legal adviser and judge, he promoted the administration of justice in the civil courts. His contributions toward the establishment of parish visitations and consistory courts helped shape the organizational structure of the Lutheran territorial church. He also served as an overseer of the University of Wittenberg and drew up the 1536 charter that reorganized it.

Works By: *Gesch. der Handlungen in der Sache des heiligen Glaubens auf dem Reichstage zu Augsburg im J. 1530 von Dr. Gregorius Heinse, genannt Brück, Churfürstl. Sächs. Cantzler,* ed. Carl Eduard Förstemann (Halle, 1831); Philipp Melanchthon, "Oratio de Gregorio Pontano, Doct. Iuris, Cancellario Ducum Saxoniae Electorum," in *Philippi Melanthonis Opera* (Halle, 1844), vol. 12. **Works About:** Ekkehart Fabian, "Gregor Brück," *NDB,* 2: 653–54, *Die Entstehung des Schmalkaldischen Bundes und seiner Verfassung* (Tübingen, 1962), and *Dr. Gregor Brück 1557–1957: Lebensbild und Schriftwechselverzeichnis* (Tübingen, 1957); Theodor Kolde, "Der Kanzler Brück und seine Bedeutung für die Entwicklung der Reformation," *Z. für hist. Theologie* 44 (1874): 343–408; Georg Mentz,"Beiträge zur Charakteristik des kursächsischen Kanzlers Dr. Gregor Brück," *Arch. für Urkundenforschung* 6 (1918): 299–322; Theodor Muther, "Gregor Brück," *ADB* 3:388–92.   *C. C. Christensen*

See CHARLES V; FREDERICK III, THE WISE; JOHN FREDERICK; JOHN OF SAXONY; LUTHER; SCHMALKALDIC LEAGUE.

BUCER, MARTIN (1491–1551), a major Protestant leader, was born in Schlettstadt near Strasbourg, the son of a cobbler. After finishing Latin school, he entered the Dominican cloister in Strasbourg at age fifteen. In 1516 Bucer

was transferred to the cloister of the Blackfriars in Heidelberg, where he continued his education in Greek, theology, and the writings of the humanists,
especially Erasmus. At Heidelberg he encountered Luther in 1518 and was
profoundly impressed. His interest in Luther eventually resulted in his departure
from the monastery for service as a parish priest at Landstuhl, the parish of
Franz von Sickingen. There he married Elizabeth Silbereisen, a young nun.

Endangered by the failure of Sickingen's campaign against Trier, Bucer was
forced to leave Landstuhl for Weissenburg, where he assisted in the cause of
reform. As the Knights' War moved into that area, he left for Strasbourg. There
Bucer became one of the great leaders of the reform movement in that important
city through his preaching, writing, organizing, and educational activities. His
influence on reform extended into Hanau-Lichtenberg, Baden, Württemberg,
and Hesse.

In 1529 Bucer, with the aid of Philip of Hesse, attempted to mediate between
Martin Luther and Ulrich Zwingli, with whom he had been in contact with since
1523. Although union was not achieved at the resulting Marburg colloquy of
1529, Bucer did succeed in 1536 in having a Wittenberg Concord accepted,
which united his ideas on the Lord's Supper with those of the Lutherans. The
Swiss went their own way confessionally. His efforts toward reconciliation also
extended to the Roman Catholics as a leading participant in the discussions at
Regensburg in 1541.

After the defeat of the Schmalkaldic League in 1547, Strasbourg was compelled by Emperor Charles V to accept the Augsburg Interim, which Bucer
believed was much too favorable to the teachings and practice of the Roman
Catholic Church. When Thomas Cranmer, archbishop of Canterbury, invited
him to England in 1549, he readily accepted. There he assisted Cranmer in his
revision of the *Book of Common Prayer,* lectured at Cambridge University, and
composed his most famous treatise, *De Regno Christi.* Shortly after receiving
a doctor of divinity degree from Cambridge, he became seriously ill and died.

Works By: Wilhelm Pauck, ed., *Melanchthon and Bucer* (Philadelphia, 1969); J. V. Pollett, *Martin Bucer: Etudes sur la correspondence* (Paris, 1958–1963); Robert Stupperich et al., eds., *Martin Bucers Deutsche Schriften,* 4 vols. (Gütersloh, 1960–); Francois Wendel, ed., *Martini Buceri Opera Latina* (Paris, 1954–1955). **Works About:** H. Bornkamm, *Martin Bucers Bedeutung für die europäischen Reformationsgeschichte* (New York, 1941); Hastings Eells, *Martin Bucer* (New Haven, 1931); Constantin Hopf, *Martin Bucer and the English Reformation* (New York, 1941); J. M. Kittelson, "Martin Bucer and the Sacramentarian Controversy," *ARG* 64 (1973): 166–83; Ernst-Wilhelm Kohls, *Die Schule bei Martin Bucer* (Heidelberg, 1963); Friedhelm Krüger, *Bucer und Erasmus* (Wiesbaden, 1970); C. Mitchell, "Martin Bucer and the Sectarian Dissent" (Ph.D. diss., Yale University, 1960); G. J. van der Poll, *Martin Bucer's Liturgical Ideas* (Assen, 1954); W. P. Stephens, *The Holy Spirit in the Theology of Martin Bucer* (Cambridge, Mass., 1970).   *J. W. Zophy*

See LUTHER; MARBURG COLLOQUY; SICKINGEN; STRASBOURG; ZWINGLI.

BUGENHAGEN, JOHN (1485–1558), a leading Lutheran reformer and an
able organizer of the Lutheran churches in northern Germany and parts of Scan-

dinavia, was born on the Baltic island of Wollin to a prominent patrician family. His education culminated at the University of Greifswald where he came under the influence of humanism. He was attracted by humanist emphases, especially the love of the classical languages, the advocacy of an excellent literary style, the study of the Christian classics, and the concern for renewal in the Church. These ideals remained priorities throughout his life.

Bugenhagen's appointment as rector of the city school at Treptow on the Rega in 1504 marks the beginning of an educational career that lasted half a century. Under his tutelage, the school prospered and attained an admirable reputation. Except for his educational activity, little information is available concerning his life until 1520. There is evidence that he was ordained a priest in 1509 and that he became the leader of an intellectual and reforming circle in Treptow. His biblical studies, his humanist interests, and his own inclinations awakened a reform spirit in Bugenhagen long before he came into contact with Martin Luther. He was an ethical reformer, however, and did not challenge the theology of the Church. In typically humanist fashion, he promoted education as the essential means of achieving reform in Church and society.

Bugenhagen's lengthy and fruitful association with Luther and the Lutheran Reformation began in 1520. It was then that he was introduced to Luther's revolutionary attack on the sacramental system of the Church, *The Babylonian Captivity of the Church*. After studying the work carefully, he decided to join the Lutheran movement and traveled to Wittenberg in the spring of 1521.

His intention was to study with Luther, but he quickly emerged as a leading evangelical reformer. He was welcomed into the inner circle of the Wittenberg theologians and immediately began his diligent labors on behalf of the Reformation. Shortly after his arrival, he resumed his teaching activity as a lecturer at the University of Wittenberg. His faculty status was officially recognized in 1533, when he was also awarded the degree of doctor of theology. In 1523 he was chosen pastor of the city church and functioned in that office until 1557. As city pastor he was Luther's pastor and most intimate spiritual councillor, roles that Luther deeply appreciated. He also served as a theological adviser and writer, as a translator of the Scriptures into High and Low German, and as the general superintendent for electoral Saxony. He declined invitations to become bishop of Schleswig (1541) and bishop of Cammin (1544) in his native Pomerania because of his desire to remain in Wittenberg.

Bugenhagen's most visible accomplishments were in the areas of organization and administration. Between the years 1528 and 1543 he traveled to Braunschweig, Hamburg, Lübeck, Pomerania, Denmark, Schleswig-Holstein, Hildesheim, and Braunschweig-Wolfenbüttel and organized the evangelical movement in these areas. His organizational work was codified in the church orders, which were intended to and often did serve as the legal bases for the Lutheran churches in these territories. Bugenhagen's Lübeck church order, for example, was operative into the nineteenth century. In the church orders Bugenhagen provided models for the evangelical worship services, addressed the problem of poor relief by providing guidelines for the establishment of common chests and poor chests, and formulated an extensive educational system whose central institution was the Latin school. Bugenhagen cooperated closely with the evangelical secular authorities, both city councils and princes, in his organizational work. That work had important implications for the future relationship of Lutheranism to the Emperor Charles V and the Holy Roman Empire. It facilitated the gradual maturation of the Lutheran reform movement into the Lutheran church. This development was one factor that enabled the Lutherans to survive the emperor's belated military offensive against them and to recover from a major military defeat at Mühlberg in April 1547.

Although he did not attend the various imperial diets held during the 1520s and 1530s, Bugenhagen did participate in the planning of them. He also accompanied Luther and Melanchthon to Schmalkalden in 1537 where the Lutheran estates prepared for the expected imperial and papal offensive. Although he struggled with the question, Bugenhagen very early defended the right of resistance against the emperor. Already in 1523 he asserted that a prince must protect his subjects against illegal activity, including unjust religious persecution by the emperor. In 1529 he further explicated his poisition and again defended the lower magistrate's right to resist an unjust higher magistrate. He noted that citizens must obey their rulers, even if those rulers are not Christians. However, if the rulers, to whom God has given authority, disobey the Word of God, suppress it, or drive people from it, then they need not be recognized as legitimate magistrates. Individuals, including princes, must bear as much injustice as possible without resistance. When the welfare of their subjects is at issue, however, princes must defend those subjects if a higher authority misuses its power. This is the princes' God-given right and responsibility. For the Lutheran estates, such arguments served as the theological and theoretical justification for organizing the Schmalkaldic League and ultimately for military conflict with Emperor Charles V.

The years between Luther's death in 1546 and his own death during the night of April 19–20, 1558, were difficult ones for Bugenhagen. The Schmalkaldic War (1546–1547) brought physical hardships. But more taxing were the aftereffects of the war. Bugenhagen was unfairly accused of betraying the elector John Frederick because he cooperated with Maurice of Saxony in hopes of quickly reopening the University of Wittenberg after the war. With the unitive force of Luther gone, bitter theological conflicts erupted in the Lutheran camp. Although Bugenhagen and Melanchthon felt that only adiaphora had been compromised in the Leipzig Interim (1548), Flacius Illyricus (1520–1575) and Nicholas von Amsdorf accused them of forsaking true Lutheranism and bitterly chastised them for accepting the Interim. Bugenhagen defended his Lutheran orthodoxy but refused to become involved in a literary battle. Instead he devoted his energies to what he considered to be constructive activity on behalf of the

Lutheran churches. He continued to preach, lecture, write, ordain pastors, and administer ecclesiastical affairs. His devotion to the Reformation was complete after the pivotal year 1520, and his contributions to the movement were both diverse and substantial.

Works By: Emil Sehling, ed., *Die evangelischen Kirchenordnungen des XVI. Jahrhunderts,* 7 vols. (Leipzig and Tübingen, 1902–1961); Otto Vogt, ed., *Dr. Johannes Bugenhagens Briefwechsel* (Stettin, 1888). **Works About:** Klaus Harms, *D. Johann Bugenhagen* (Bielefeld, 1958); Kurt Hendel, "Johannes Bugenhagen's Educational Contributions" (Ph.D. diss., Ohio State University, 1974); Hermann Hering, *Doktor Pomeranus, Johannes Bugenhagen* (Halle, 1888); Frank Lane, "Poverty and Poor Relief in the German Church Orders of Johann Bugenhagen" (Ph.D. diss. Ohio State University, 1973); Karl A. T. Vogt, *Johannes Bugenhagen Pomeranus* (Elberfeld, 1867).   *K. K. Hendel*

See CHARLES V; JOHN FREDERICK; LUTHER; SCHMALKALDIC WAR.

BULLINGER, HENRY (1504–1575), church reformer, was born in Bremgarten (Canton Aargau) where his father was dean. After attending the Latin schools at Bremgarten and at Emmerich (Cleves), Henry studied at the University of Cologne, where he received the bachelor of arts and master's degrees in 1520 and 1522, respectively. By the time he returned to Bremgarten in April 1522, Bullinger had already accepted the new evangelical teaching. In January 1523, he became head teacher at the abbey school of the Cistercian monastery at Kappel, where he first reformed the curriculum of the Latin school and then effected an evangelical reform of the monastery. The Mass was abolished on September 4, 1525. Bullinger accepted ordination and a part-time pastorate at Hausen am Albis, near Kappel, in 1528. In 1529 he became pastor of his home parish; within a month Bremgarten was committed to the Reformed teaching. During the same year Bullinger married Anna Adlischwyler. The defeat of Zurich by the Catholic states at Kappel in October 1531 greatly affected Bullinger; according to the Second Treaty of Kappel, he and his family were exiled from Bremgarten. They went to Zurich, where Bullinger was no stranger. He had gone there to meet Zwingli in 1523, he had been present at all three disputations with the Anabaptists in 1525, and he had spent five months there in 1527. When he arrived there after Kappel in November 1531, he was offered Zwingli's position, which he accepted on December 13.

During his forty-five year tenure at first minister of the Zurich church, Bullinger's influence in Reformed circles was surpassed perhaps only by Calvin. This impact was largely due to Bullinger's voluminous correspondence and writings: over twelve thousand extant letters to and from nearly every prominent ecclesiastical and civil leader of the period and 119 published works. Bullinger also authored the Second Helvetic Confession, which became the most accepted of all Reformed confessions, not only in the confederation but in France and the Empire as well. During this time Zurich became a haven for refugees from all over Europe, including the Empire.

Bullinger inherited Zwingli's controversy with the Lutherans over the Eucharist. Luther, a few months after Zwingli's death, attacked the Zwinglians in an open letter to Margrave Albert of Brandenburg, referring to them as fanatics and blaming their defeat at Kappel on false teaching. Bullinger's reply, to Albert, was swift but conciliatory. He would not attack Luther, but he did defend Zwingli. Then in 1536, the First Helvetic Confession, largely written by Bullinger, was the Swiss response to the Wittenberg Concord. This conflict with the Lutherans, although muted at times, continued throughout Bullinger's lifetime. But despite Bullinger's efforts, the Zwinglian teaching slowly lost its hold on the south German cities and territories, which either were forced back into Catholicism or moved closer to Lutheranism.

Bullinger's relationships with the rulers of cities and territories in the Empire were many and varied: Philip I and William IV of Hesse; Herman von Wied, archbishop of Cologne; Frederick III, elector of the Pfalz; Ludwig von Sayn-Wittgenstein; and the dukes of Württemberg. His contacts with Württemberg illustrate his continuing efforts to defend the Zwinglian point of view in the Empire. Duke Ulrich, who had been deposed in 1520, regained his throne in 1534 with the aid of Philip of Hesse. Bullinger urged Ulrich to effect a thorough Zwinglian reformation. Although for several years Württemberg hung in the balance between the Lutheran and Reformed points of view, the Lutherans won out. In 1547, in the face of the imperial army, Duke Christopher and Count George, the son and brother of Ulrich, fled for refuge, first to Zurich and then to Basel. In 1552 Bullinger wrote a short treatise, dedicated to George, in which he argued that the Zwinglians were not heretical but orthodox in their teaching. However, George's death in 1558 marked the end of any Reformed influence in Württemberg. Christopher, a strong Lutheran, issued an edict banning both the Anabaptists and protestants of the Reformed persuasion. In 1561 Bullinger sent Christopher a copy of his *Tractatio verborum Domini,* which elicited a response from John Brenz, setting off a war of words concerning the Eucharist and Ubiquity that lasted into the 1570s. By that time, the encroachments of Lutheranism and the subsumption of Zwinglianism within Calvinism had nearly destroyed the earlier Zwinglian influence in the Protestant cities and territories of the Empire.

Works By: Ulrich Gabler and Endre Zsindely, eds., *Heinrich Bullinger Briefwechsel,* vol. 1, *Heinrich Bullinger Werke* (Zurich, 1973); Joachim Staedtke and Erland Herkenrath, eds. *Heinrich Bullinger Bibliographie, Heinrich Bullinger Werke. Erste Abteilung,* 2 vols. (Zurich, 1972, 1977). **Works About:** Fritz Blanke, *Der junge Bullinger, 1504–1531* (Zurich, 1942); Heinhold Fast, *Heinrich Bullinger und die Täufer. Ein Beitrag zur Historiographie und Theologie im 16: Jahrhundert* (Weierhof, 1959); Ulrich Gäbler and Erland Herkenrath, eds., *Heinrich Bullinger, 1504–1575. Gesammelte Aufsätze aum 400. Todestag. Erster Band: Leben und Werk. Zweitzer Band: Beziehungen und Wirkungen* (Zurich, 1975); Carl Pestalozzi, *Heinrich Bullinger. Leben und ausgewählte Schriften. Nach handschriftlichen und gleichzeitigen Quellen* (Elberfeld, 1858); Johann Martin Usteri, "Vertiefung der Zwinglischen Sakraments und Tauflehre bei Bullinger," *Theologische Studien und Kritiken* 56 (1883): 730–58.   *J. W. Baker*

See CHRISTOPHER OF WÜRTTEMBERG; LUTHER; ZWINGLI.

BURGKMAIR, HANS (1473–c. 1531), one of the most distinguished artists of the Augsburg school, was born in Augsburg and studied under his father, Thomas Burgkmair, and under Martin Schongauer. He was a member of the painters' guild in Strasbourg in 1490 and in Augsburg in 1498. He is best known for his woodcuts, of which he produced over seven hundred. They include some of the first chiaroscuro woodcuts. He did woodcuts for several of Emperor Maximilian's books, including the *Weisskunig* and *Theuerdank*. His main work is a series of prints portraying the triumphs of the emperor. In 1507 Burgkmair translated the scheme of Conrad Celtis for a program uniting the arts and sciences under the patronage of the emperor into a visual form by designing a double-headed imperial eagle crest accompanied by the emblems of the Celtis Society.

Burgkmair's visit to Venice and northern Italy in 1505 helped other German masters become aware of the Italian achievement. In fact, he is one of the earliest German painters to show the influence of the Italian Renaissance. In general, his paintings demonstrate a lively sense of color and a careful modeling and execution of detail, although many of his works present a hard and mechanical character. The subjects of his portraits include Elector Frederick the Wise of Saxony and Duke William of Bavaria. Burgkmair had a strong influence upon the painting of Hans Holbein the Younger and Christoph Amberger.

Works About: M. Salinger,"Burgkmair," *EWA*, 2:732; P. Strieder, "Burgkmair," *NDB*, 3:47–9.
                                                                                    J. J. Spielvogel

See CELTIS; FREDERICK III, THE WISE; HOLBEIN; MAXIMILIAN I.

C

CAJETAN, THOMAS DE VIO (1469–1534), was a cardinal, a skilled opponent of Luther, and a noted Thomist theologian and scholar. Born as Jacopo de' Vio at Gaeta, from which he acquired his surname, he entered the Dominican order in 1484, taking the name of Thomas. He studied theology, philosophy, natural science, and medicine at Naples, Bologna, and Padua. At a general meeting of the chapter in Ferrara, he engaged in debate with Pico della Mirandola, a result of which was his promotion to master of sacred theology at the request of Duke Ercole. Summoned to the University of Pavia in 1497, he taught there and, later, at the Sapienza in Rome. He became procurator general of the Dominicans in 1500, vicar-general in 1508, cardinal in 1517, and bishop of Gaeta in 1519. An erudite man who espoused papal supremacy and infallibility, he wrote more than one hundred and fifty works, perhaps the most significant of which was *De divina institutione pontificatus Romani pontificis*, his interpretation of St. Thomas' *Summa theologica*.

Faithful to the traditions of the Dominicans, Cajetan served pope, Church, and order in a variety of ways. He preached for Alexander VI, Julius II, and Leo X; he served as legate to Germany in 1518–1519 and to Hungary, Bohemia, and Poland in 1523–1524; he composed Clement VII's response to King Henry VIII's appeal for a divorce from Catharine of Aragon in 1530; he helped settle certain difficulties with followers of Savonarola and sent the first Dominican missionaries to the Western Hemisphere; he played a major role at the Fifth Lateran Council (1512–1517), where he defended the mendicant orders and championed the cause of papal infallibility; and he was instrumental in the elevation of Adrian VI to the chair of St. Peter. He was a major Catholic reformer whose numerous exegetical writings indicated Erasmian influences.

With regard to the Empire, Cajetan was best known for his confrontations with Luther and his participation in the 1520 consistory, which condemned Luther. Sent as legate to Germany in 1518, Cajetan's mission was to win support for a new crusade against the Turks. To further this goal, he was empowered to enlist the aid of prominent princes by granting awards, to reconcile the recalcitrant Bohemian heretics, to honor Emperor Maximilan I, to raise Archbishop Albert of Mainz to the cardinalate, and to seek a new tax levy for the war effort from the diet meeting at Augsburg. He was also to bring Luther back into the church. With the exception of the honors bestowed on Maximilian and Albert, Cajetan's mission was unsuccessful, although the reasons for his failure were beyond his control. The assembled estates at Augsburg refused the crusade and tax largely because of anti-Roman sentiments. In Luther's case, Cajetan's instructions were not to debate with the reformer; Luther was either to recant or to be sent to Rome. Due to Luther's and Cajetan's positions on the authority of the pope, the two did not agree. Cajetan had more success at Frankfurt in 1519, however, when he worked behind the scenes for the election of Charles V as king of the Romans.

Convinced of Luther's errors, Cajetan participated in the consistory in 1520, which led to the formulation of the *Exsurge domine,* the first bull against Luther. At the same time he studied the Protestant arguments carefully. He realized the insufficiency of the Vulgate Bible for a serious study of the Scriptures, and in subsequent investigation he used Erasmus' Greek text and the humanists' exegetical tools. After the Sack of Rome in 1527, during which he was imprisoned, Cajetan retired to Gaeta. Recalled to Rome by Clement VII in 1530, Cajetan spent his remaining years there as a papal adviser. He was regarded by many as a likely successor to Clement for the papal throne.

Works By: Thomas de Vio Caietanus, *De divine institutione pontificatus Romani pontifices (1521),* ed. Friedrich Lauchert, Corpus Catholicorum, Werke Katholischer Schriftsteller im Zeitalter der Glaubensspaltung, vol. 10 (Münster/Westphalen, 1925); Jared Wicks, ed., *Cajetan Responds* (Washington, D.C., 1978). **Works About:** Aluigi Cossio, *Il cardinale Gaetano e la riforma* (Cividale, 1902); Facoltà de Filosofia dell' Universita Cattolica del Sacro Cuore, ed., *Il cardinale Tomaso de Vio Gaetano nel quarto centenario della sua morte* (Milano, 1935); Theodor Kolde, "Cajetan," in *Schaff-Herzog,* ed. S. M. Jackson et al. (New York, 1908), 2:338–39; J. A. Weisheipl, "Cajetan," in *New Catholic Encyclopedia* (New York, 1967) 2:1053–55.   *P. N. Bebb*

See ADRIAN VI; LUTHER.

CAMPEGGIO, LORENZO (1472–1539), cardinal, distinguished canonist, and papal diplomat to the Empire and England, was the son of a famous lawyer, Giovanni Campeggio. Lorenzo studied and taught law at Padua and Bologna. After the death of his wife in 1509, he entered the ecclesiastical state and rapidly advanced. He became auditor of the Rota, bishop of Feltre in 1512, nuncio to the imperial court from 1513 through 1517, cardinal in 1517, legate to England in 1518 and 1519, member of the Segnatura, archbishop of Bologna in 1523, and legate to the Empire in 1524 and 1525. In his remaining years he served on the papal commission investigating the affairs of the Teutonic Knights, as legate to England to resolve the Henry VIII–Catharine of Aragon marriage dispute, as legate to the Empire in 1530–1532, and as Paul III's representative to convene the council at Vicenza in 1538. Because of his influence on Henry VIII during his first legatine mission to England, Campeggio received appointment as bishop of Salisbury in 1524, a post he held until Parliament revoked it after the introduction of the English Reformation.

The cornerstone of Campeggio's imperial diplomacy was his reliance on the power of the emperor. Although he recognized the necessity of Church reform— he submitted one of the most noted plans for Catholic reform to Adrian VI in which he claimed, among other things, that the chief source of evil in the Church was the Roman curia—and earned a prominent place on the roster of Catholic reformers, Campeggio argued insistently for the enforcement of the Edict of Worms and the forceful suppression of Protestants. Both at the diets of Nuremberg in 1524 and Augsburg in 1530, he advanced the edict; in the former case he made no notable headway because of the arguments contained in the estates' grievances, while in the latter he believed that Charles V's bearing at Augsburg augured well for the future of Catholicism in the Empire. At the same time he realized that to counter successfully the Protestants, ecclesiastical reform in the Empire must occur.

Campeggio's most notable influence on the political fate of Germany came shortly after the conclusion of the diet of Nuremberg in 1524. In June he summoned to a meeting at Regensburg Archduke Ferdinand, the dukes of Bavaria, and twelve prince-bishops (Salzburg, Trent, Regensburg, Bamberg, Speyer, Strasbourg, Augsburg, Constance, Basel, Freising, Brisen, and Passau). The result was the Regensburg Union, the first alliance of a confessional nature in the Empire. The union's goals were to enforce the Edict of Worms, to halt the spread of Lutheranism, and to introduce reform in the exercise of religious life in Germany. This league served as a precedent for the subsequent creation of the Catholic League of Dessau in the north and the Protestant League of Torgau, the predecessor of the Schmalkaldic League.

Works By: Campeggio, *Concilium Tridentinum: Diariorum, actorum, epistularum, tractatuum. Nova collectio,* ed. Societas Goerresiana (Freiburg, 1901–1938); Gerhard Müller, ed., *Nuntiaturberichte aus Deutschland,* Abt. 1, suppl. 1: *Legation Lorenzo Campeggios, 1530–1531 und Nuntiatur Girolamo Aleandros, 1531* (Tübingen, 1963). **Works About:** E. V. Cardinal, "Campeggio," *New Catholic Encyclopedia* (New York, 1967) 2:1113 and *Cardinal Lorenzo Campeggio, Legate to the Courts of Henry VIII and Charles V* (Boston, 1935); T. B. Scannell, "Campeggio," *Catholic Encyclopedia* (New York, 1913) 3:223–24.   P. N. Bebb

See CHARLES V; FERDINAND I; NUREMBERG, DIETS OF 1522–1524.

CAMPO FORMIO, TREATY OF (October 17, 1797), ended Austria's participation in the First Coalition (1792–1797) against revolutionary France. The Austro-Prussian alliance had been the nucleus of that coalition. The combined armies under the command of the duke of Brunswick had invaded France in 1792. Prussia had left the alliance by the Peace of Basel (1795) agreeing to abandon the left bank of the Rhine. Austria continued fighting until defeated by French armies in Germany and in Italy, the latter commanded by Napoleon. In 1796, Bonaparte conquered northern and central Italy and broke into Carniola and Styria. He took the diplomatic initiative as he had the military, with little interference from the directors in Paris; at Leoben he dictated the preliminaries to the court of Vienna. After lengthy negotiations throughout the summer and fall of 1797, the treaty was signed. It redrew the map of Italy: Austria annexed the Venetian Republic, including its possessions across the Adriatic Sea, Dalmatia, and littoral Istria; the districts between the Adige and Ticino rivers went to the newly constituted Cisalpine Republic; and the Republic of Genoa was replaced by the Ligurian Republic. The Italian republics served as satellites for France, which also received the Venetian fleet and the Ionian Isles. Emperor Francis renounced his claims to the Netherlands, ceded Breisgau to the duke of Modena, and recognized the independence of the Cisalpine Republic. In the secret provisions, Austria promised support for French acquisition of the left bank of the Rhine, with the exception of the Prussian territories, and France undertook to secure Austrian compensation, which would include the archbishopric of Salzburg and part of Bavaria. Austria and France agreed to compensate the dispossessed German princes with territory on the right bank of the Rhine. The emperor would summon a congress at Rastadt to settle German affairs and to conclude the final peace. The congress that convened included representatives of France, Austria, Prussia, and other German states. Austrian attempts to gain new concessions from France failed. The quarreling among the German princes disrupted the congress. The Treaty of Campo Formio proved to be merely a truce in the continuing war against France. In 1799, Austria joined Great Britain and Russia in the Second Coalition. A definitive peace was not achieved until the Congress of Vienna.

Works About: Felgel, "Franz II," *ADB,* 7:285–90; David Chandler, *The Campaigns of Napoleon* (New York, 1966); Somerset de Clair, *Napoleon's Memoirs* (New York, 1949); Hugo Hantsch, *Die Gesch. Österreichs,* 2 vols. (Vienna, 1955); John Eldred Howard, ed., *Napoleon I, Emperor of France: Letters and Documents* (New York, 1961); Hugo Hantsch, "Franz II," *NDB,* 5:358–61; Carlile A. Macartney, *The Habsburg Empire, 1790–1918* (New York, 1969); F. M. H. Markham, *Napoleon and the Awakening of Europe* (New York, 1965); Robert B. Mowat, *The Diplomacy of Napoleon* (London,1924); J. M. Thompson, ed., *Letters of Napoleon* (London, 1934).

L. S. Frey and M. L. Frey

See FRANCIS II; FRENCH REVOLUTIONARY WARS.

CAPITO, WOLFGANG (1478–1541), humanist and reformer, began life in Hagenau near Strasbourg as the son of a moderately prosperous blacksmith. Educated in the Latin school at Pforzheim, Wolfgang went on to study at Ingolstadt and later Freiburg, where he received an M.A. in 1506. Following this he went to Strasbourg, working as a proofreader and moving in humanist circles.

Always interested in religion, Capito returned to Freiburg, took minor orders, and was ordained a priest. In 1512 he was called to Bruchsal to serve as canon and preacher to the Benedictine foundation. Three years later he moved on to Basel as cathedral preacher. In that busy intellectual center, Capito prospered as a churchman and as a scholar, teaching at the university from which he received a doctorate in theology in 1515. His reputation as a biblical and Hebrew scholar brought him into contact with the great Erasmus.

Capito also made the acquaintance of Martin Luther, corresponding with him as early as 1518. This did not prevent him from being appointed chaplain and adviser to Albert, elector and archbishop of Mainz, where he attempted to mediate between the archbishop and Luther. Tiring of the role of courtier, Capito left in February 1523 to become provost at St. Thomas in Strasbourg. There he eventually became one of the key leaders in the reform movement along with Martin Bucer and the politician Jacob Sturm. His activity as a reformer was highlighted by his authorship with Bucer of the *Confessio Tetrapolitana,* presented at the 1530 diet of Augsburg.

Works About: J. W. Baum, *Capito und Bucer* (Elberfeld, 1860); Paul Kalkoff, *W. Capito im Dienste Erzbischof Albrecht von Mainz* (Berlin, 1907); James M. Kittelson, *Wolfgang Capito: From Humanist to Reformer* (Leiden, 1975); Beate Stierle, *Capito als Humanist* (Gütersloh, 1974); O. E. Strasser, *La Pensée théologique de Wolfgang Capiton* (Neuchâtel, 1938). *J. W. Zophy*

See BUCER; ERASMUS; LUTHER; STRASBOURG; STURM.

CARLOMAN (c. 830–880), who ruled the Empire from 876 until 880, was the oldest son of Emperor Louis II and Emma. Much of his early life was given over to military and administrative training and activity. It was a period of instability as the various descendants of Charlemagne plotted against one another in order to secure and enlarge their holdings. In addition, Louis II and his sons had to defend the Empire against attacks by the neighboring Slavs.

Carloman's life was further complicated by the fact that his mother openly favored him over his younger brothers, Louis and Charles, and intrigued to have her husband bestow lands and honors upon him. The envy and ambition of his brothers eventually resulted in mutinies in 866, 871, and 873. Louis and Charles were placated only by grants of land and promises for the future. Throughout these revolts Carloman stayed loyal to his father and helped him in his various enterprises, such as the efforts to incorporate some of the territory of Lothar II in greater Lorraine into the Empire. Carloman journeyed with his father to Italy in 875 in an effort to consolidate imperial claims there and to insure his succession to the crown.

When Louis II died on August 28, 876, at Frankfurt, Carloman was recognized as his successor and was officially titled king of Bavaria. Louis was named king of Saxony until his death in 882 and Charles was named king of Swabia. Louis and Charles also partitioned Lotharingia between them. Carloman's illegitimate son, Arnulf, received Carinthia and Pannonia.

Despite these settlements, the fraternal plotting continued, and Carloman's last years were times of troubles. Various Italian states and an aggressive Pope John VIII attempted to reduce the Carolingian presence south of the Alps. Carloman met with John VIII late in the summer of 877 in an effort to come to some sort of understanding. These efforts were unsuccessful, and in 879 Carloman was forced to cede Italy to his brother Charles, who had been plotting with the pope. While in Italy Carloman contracted illness that continued to afflict him until his death on March 22, 880. His son, Arnulf, was temporarily bypassed, and the bulk of Carloman's possessions fell into the hands of his ambitious brother Charles, who ruled the Empire from 880 to 887.

Works About: E. Dümmler, *Gesch. des Ostfranken Reiches,* 3 vols. (Leipzig, 1887, rpr. 1960); Josef Fleckenstein, *Die Hofkappel der dtsch. Könige I* (Freiburg, 1959) and *Early Medieval Germany,* tr. B. Smith (New York, 1978); Theodor Schieffer, "Karlmann," *NDB,* 11:275–76.

                                                                                          J. W. Zophy

See ARNULF; CHARLES III; LOUIS II.

CATHOLIC LEAGUE was founded on July 10, 1609, under the leadership of Duke Maximilian of Bavaria to counter the Protestant Union (1608) and to protect the interests of Germany's Catholic rulers. The league included Bavaria, the prince-bishops of Bavaria, Franconia, and Swabia, and the three Rhenish archbishop-electors (Cologne, Trier, Mainz). Maximilian, director of the alliance, contributed most of the troops to the twenty-thousand-man league army commanded by Count John Tserclaes von Tilly. The league prudently refrained from intervening militarily in the Jülich-Cleves succession dispute in 1609 and 1610; however, Maximilian supported Wolfgang William of Neuburg, the Catholic claimant in the dispute, a convert from Lutheranism who had married his sister. Austria's attempt to exert greater control over the alliance and use it as an instrument of Habsburg family politics led to Maximilian's resignation in 1616 and the temporary dissolution of the league. But a year later he reorganized the league as an alliance of south German Catholic estates.

The Bohemian revolt, which sparked the Thirty Years War, forced Emperor Ferdinand II to seek the support of the league. In the Treaty of Munich (October 1619), which he negotiated with Maximilian, the Catholic princes pledged their support to the emperor. Ferdinand, in return, recognized Maximilian as head of the alliance and vouched to reimburse him for the league's expenses and reward him for his services. With the aid of French diplomats, Maximilian also negotiated the Treaty of Ulm (1620) in which the Protestant Union promised to remain neutral while the Catholics intervened in Bohemia.

In November 1620 the league forces defeated the army of Frederick V, elector of the Palatinate and king of Bohemia, at the White Mountain (near Prague), thereby contributing decisively to Ferdinand's victory over the rebels. The league army conquered the Upper and Rhenish Palatinates, occupied Hesse-Cassel (1622–1623), and fought in the Lower Saxon and Danish wars (1623–1630). Tilly won important victories in northern Germany against Protestant armies commanded by Count Ernest von Mansfeld, "Bishop" Christian of Halberstadt, and King Christian IV of Denmark. His forces also helped carry out Catholic restitutions in Protestant territories. The league's influence, however, began to decline after 1626 as it was increasingly overshadowed by the imperial army of Duke Albert von Wallenstein. Hoping to regain some of their earlier influence, Maximilian and the other princes forced Ferdinand to dismiss Wallenstein and name Tilly as his commander-in-chief (1630). But Sweden's intervention and victories over the league (especially at Breitenfeld, 1631), Tilly's death (1632), and, finally, Wallenstein's recall as imperial general signified the continued decline of the league. It was officially dissolved with the Peace of Prague (1635), which forbade all special confederations in the Empire.

Works About: *Briefe und Akten zur Gesch. des dreissigjährigen Krieges* 11 vols. (Munich, 1870–1909, n.s. 1907–); Walter Goetz, "Die Kriegskosten Bayerns und der Ligastände im Dreissigjährigen Krieg," *Forsch. zur Gesch. Bayerns* 12 (1904):109–25; Franziska Neuer-Landfried, *Die katholische Liga. Gründung, Neugründung und Organisation eines Sonderbundes 1608–1620* (Kallmünz, 1968); Johann Setterl, *Die Ligapolitik des Bamberger Fürstbischofs Johann Gottfried von Aschhausen 1609–1617* (Diss., Würzburg, 1916).   *Bodo Nischan*

See FERDINAND II; MANSFELD, ERNEST; MAXIMILIAN I, DUKE; THIRTY YEARS WAR; TILLY.

CELTIS, CONRAD (1459–1508), humanist poet, began life as the son of a peasant in a village near Würzburg. After running away from home, Conrad managed to get educated at the universities of Cologne, Heidelberg, Rostock, and Leipzig. His reputation as a poet resulted in Emperor Frederick III's crowning him as the first German poet laureate of the Empire. He then began a ten-year period of wandering, which took him to Italy where he came to resent Italian pretensions of cultural superiority. Celtis returned to the north to study mathematics and poetry at Cracow. Later he took a post as a professor of rhetoric at the University of Ingolstadt. In 1497 Celtis accepted the invitation of Emperor Maximilian to join the faculty of the University of Vienna. There he established the College of Poets and Mathematicians, wrote poems and plays, and taught until his death as a result of syphilis.

Conrad Celtis became known as the finest lyric poet among the German humanists. Like Ulrich von Hutten, Celtis was a kind of a cultural nationalist and wanted the Germans to outstrip the Italians culturally. Toward that end, he had many of his humanist friends contribute to his *Germany Illustrated,* a topographical-historical work. His epic poem, *Ligurinus,* praised Emperor Frederick Barbarossa, as his *Norimberga* praised Nuremberg.

Works By: Leonard Forster, *Selections from Conrad Celtis* (Cambridge, 1948); Hans Rupprich, ed., *Der Briefwechsel des Konrad Celtis* (Munich, 1934); Albert Werminghoff, *Conrad Celtis und sein Buch über Nürnberg* (Freiburg, 1921). **Works About:** Friedrich von Bezold, "Konrad Celtis, der dtsch. Erzhumanist," *HZ* 49 (1883); 1–46, 193–229; Michael Seidlmayer, "Konrad Celtis," *Jb. für Frankische Landesforsch.* 19 (1959): 395–416; L. W. Spitz, *Conrad Celtis, the German Arch-Humanist* (Cambridge, Mass., 1957); Ludwig Sponagel, *Konrad Celtis und das dtsch. Nationalbewuszsein* (Bühl-Baden, 1939).   *J. W. Zophy*

See FREDERICK I; FREDERICK III; HUMANISM; MAXIMILIAN I.

CHARLEMAGNE (c. 742–814), French for Carolus Magnus, Charles the Great, and Karl der Grosse, is the name posterity bestowed upon Charles, king of the Franks and first emperor of the Holy Roman Empire.

Both the place and the year of Charles' birth are disputed. He was born either in Aachen or Liège, and a case can be made for a birthdate of 745, although most recent scholarship agrees with the earlier 742 date.

Charles was the eldest son of Pepin the Short, mayor of the palace to King Childeric III, the Merovingian king of the Franks. Pepin, as the actual power behind the throne, began a series of political intrigues with Pope Zachary and the Frankish nobility, which culminated in 754 with the deposition of the Merovingian dynasty and the anointing by Pope Zachary of Pepin the Short along with his two sons, Charles and Carloman, as the rightful rulers of the Franks. Pepin ruled as king of the Franks until his death in 768. Shortly before he died, Pepin, like all other Frankrish rulers (who held to no theory of primogeniture), divided his kindgom equally between his sons, Charles and Carloman.

The two brothers never got along as rulers, and Carloman tried on at least one occasion to undermine his brother's rule. Carloman died providentially on December 4, 771. The Franks did not have a system of filial succession; rather the Frankish nobility elected the king of the Franks from among the eligible male members of the royal house. Hence although Carloman left two sons by his wife, the lords bypassed Carloman's children in the succession and elected his brother, Charles, as king, thereby reuniting Pepin's original kingdom.

Along with being king of the Franks, Charles had also inherited from his father the title and office of *Patricus Romanus,* which carried with it the responsibility of serving as the temporal defender and protector of the lands and rights of the Roman papacy. In the eighth century, this was no idle office, as the patrimony of St. Peter bordered on the kingdom of Lombardy, whose King Desiderius coveted the land belonging to the papacy and waged war to conquer it.

With the obligation of defending the pope on his southern border, Charles also faced the threat of the hostile and still pagan Saxons on his northern and eastern borders. In July 772, Charles mounted an invasion of the Saxon lands with much success, destroying a major city and a principal pagan cult site in the process.

The situation in Italy called him away from his campaign against the Saxons. In January 772, a new pope, Adrian I, had been elected. Adrian was an enemy of King Desiderius of Lombardy, and the Lombard king wasted little time in invading the newly acquired papal lands of his foe. In a matter of months Desiderius had captured the northern plains of the patrimony and was threatening Ravenna. At this critical juncture, Pope Adrian called upon Charles for aid.

Charles sent envoys to Italy to investigate the situation and, upon being convinced that the pope was indeed in the right and had been maliciously attacked by the Lombards, prepared to fight. Charles organized a powerful Frankish army and marched on Lombardy in the spring of 773. King Desiderius was defeated in open combat and forced to retreat with half of his army to his walled capital of Pavia, while his son, Adelghis, with the remainder of the army, fell back to

Verona. Charles laid siege to both cities, capturing Verona shortly after Christmas 773 and Pavia in June 774. When Pavia fell, Charles assumed the crown of Lombardy and added the kingdom of Lombardy to his domains. During this time, Charles also paid his first visit to Rome, where he met Pope Adrian I. The two became friends, and on Easter Sunday, 774, Pope Adrian consecrated Charles as the champion of the Catholic church. Charles took his commission extremely seriously and came to see himself as the divinely ordained soldier of the Church whose duty it was to defend the Church and bring Christianity to the pagan. From 774 to 785, Charles waged a long series of some fifty-three campaigns against internal and external enemies, all but twelve of which were undertaken in the name of advancing or defending the Church. The most important of these were the eighteen campaigns against the Saxons, all aimed at subjecting the Saxon peoples to the Catholic church under the political auspices of Charles.

The campaigns against the Saxons in 774 and 775 were militarily successful but had to be broken off when Lombardy rose in revolt in 776, led by the son and son-in-law of the former King Desiderius, Adelghis and Areghis of Beneventum. Charles marched on Lombardy and quickly quelled the uprising.

In 777, Charles' attention was turned toward Moslem Spain, which he invaded with only minor success and no lasting impact. This invasion has been immortalized in the famous *Chanson de Roland*.

Meanwhile in Charles' absence, the Saxons regrouped their forces and attacked the Frankish kingdom under the command of their charismatic leader, Wittekind. Wittekind was something of a folk hero in his own time, who welded together the various Saxon tribes by his own dynamic personality, rallying them to fight against the Franks in defense of the Saxon's age-old liberty and religion. From 779 to 785 Charles and Wittekind fought for control of Saxony. Wittekind proved to be an adept commander and defeated Charles in several engagements. But Charles managed to win several major battles against Wittekind and was further aided by a revolt in the Saxon forces. The decisive battle of the war with Wittekind was that fought at Osnabrück, where Charles roundly defeated the Saxon forces under their heroic leader. With the defeat at Osnabrück, Wittekind conceded that the God whom Charles worshipped was stronger than Odin, and in 785 Wittekind was baptized into the Christian faith, with Charles, king of the Franks, as his godfather. The Christianized Saxons became part of Charles' realm.

The years between 785 and 800 were comparatively peaceful, filled with minor military campaigns to strengthen and solidify Charles' newly won lands. The only major military effort mounted during this time was the campaign in 791 against the Avars, a powerful people on the eastern extremity of Charles' domains and the last serious threat to his dominions. With the conquest of the Avars and their incorporation into Charles' ever-growing lands, the period of military expansion ended.

A series of intrigues in Rome during this period triggered the succession of events that would lead to the crowning of Charles as emperor. In 795, Pope Adrian I died, and Pope Leo III was elected. Leo was a native Roman, and his election caused jealousy and made enemies for the new pope. Intrigues were launched against the pope, and on April 25, 799, Pope Leo was waylaid on the streets of Rome, beaten, and left for dead. Leo fled Rome to the safety of the man charged with defending the Church, Charles.

Charles immediately dispatched a corp of his personal representatives (*missi dominici*) to accompany Leo back to Rome, investigate the conspiracy against the pope, and bring its perpetrators to justice. Charles himself went to Rome as soon as he could free himself from administering his kingdom and was met at the Italian border by Pope Leo, who accompanied the Frankish king on the rest of the journey to Rome. In Rome, Charles' *missi* had done their job well, and most of the conspirators had been taken. Pope Leo publicly proclaimed a solemn oath denying the charges of grave moral misconduct brought against him by the conspirators, and this oath was considered evidence enough of the pope's innocence. The exonerated Pope Leo then magnanimously spared his accusers the death penalty and sentenced them only to banishment.

The more immediate concern of the pope was that such a conspiracy should never happen again. In order to ensure this, some neutral party was needed to have sovereign rule over the city of Rome. But in the minds of most people, the only person who could have legitimate control of Rome was a Roman emperor, and the person who stylized himself as emperor of Rome was the emperor ruling in Constantinople. By the eighth century, however, the separation between East and West was virtually complete; the Eastern Roman Empire was in reality impotent in the West, and no one in Western Europe seriously considered the emperor of the Byzantine Empire to be their liege. This was further compounded by a general disgust for the political intrigues, palace revolts, collapsing fiscal policy, and general tumultuous history that plagued the Byzantine emperors. As late as 797, Emperor Constantine VI had been deposed by his own mother, Irene, who set herself up as empress after blinding and imprisoning her son. Western Europeans found this Eastern court intrigue distasteful and considered the Byzantine emperors unfit to rule. The Church had its own particular argument with the East, as the Roman Catholic church considered the Eastern Orthodox church heterodox on some points and heretical on others. Thus the rulers of the political entity that styled itself as the Roman Empire were really never seriously considered for the protectorship of Rome. There was, then, only one other possibility, and that was Charles, king of the Franks, whose military conquests had created a new empire in the West. And so on Christmas Day in 800, Pope Leo III crowned Charles as Holy Roman emperor, thereby reconstituting the Western Empire under the auspices of the papacy. At the same time, Charles' son, who was also named Charles (the Younger), was crowned king of the Franks and groomed to be successor to the imperial crown.

Neither Pope Leo nor Charles ever claimed that the imperial office in Constantinople had been made invalid by the crowning of Charles as emperor, and both pope and emperor kept up diplomatic relations with Byzantium. The Holy Roman Empire was a new entity built on an old foundation, applying the titles and powers of the Roman emperor to a new political entity centered upon the Christian church and the Roman papacy. Nonetheless the Byzantine emperors never acknowledged the imperial title or claims of Charles or his successors.

The imperial title made Charles in theory what he already was in fact: the principal ruler of Western Europe. But the office of emperor also made Charles the supreme temporal protector of Western Christendom and, especially, the Roman Catholic church. Charles took this responsibility, as he did all religious responsibility, with zealous seriousness and spent the remainder of his life trying to achieve governmental cooperation with the Church.

The final thirteen years of Charles' life were spent ordering his Empire and preparing for the succession. Charles, like his father, Pepin the Short, and true to his Frankish heritage, did not follow any pattern of primogeniture but simply divided his Empire equally between his three sons: Louis the Pious received the collection of small principalities that make up much of what is today modern France; Charles the Younger received Frankland (as king of the Franks), Frisia, Saxony, Hesse, and Franconia; and Pepin received Lombardy, Bavaria, and southern Alemannia. All of this was duly documented in Charles' will of 806. This plan never reached fruition, however. Charles the Younger and Pepin both died before their father, and upon the death of Charles, the lords of the Franks voted his only surviving son, Louis the Pious, to be king of the Franks, who later also succeeded to the imperial throne.

One of Charles' favorite imperial projects was the systematization and codification of the traditional laws of the peoples within his Empire. As king he had codified the laws of his own people, the Franks; as emperor, he codified the laws of the Frisians, Thuringians, and Saxons by 802.

Charles proved to be a genius at administration. To administer his vast Empire, Charles divided it into counties and hundreds and appointed counts and hundredmen to be governors of their respective districts. Along with this Charles instituted the annual parliament or diet, held each spring, as a gathering of temporal and spiritual lords (Charles included bishops and priests in much of his political activity) meeting to discuss the administration of the empire. Charles also reorganized and expanded the old Frankish office of *missi dominici* from mere royal messengers to that of itinerant governors and royal pleni-potentiaries. There were two *missi* assigned to each province, one a layperson and one a cleric, both of whom were under orders to visit their territory at least four times per year. Apart from these overseers, justice was usually administered by the local count or hundredman, with an appeals process ending with the emperor.

Much of Charles' time was spent in supporting and patronizing the Church. He sought to improve, refine, and unify the Church through imperial legislation, thus providing a series of laws in support of the Church and clergy; enforced tithing to support the clergy; clerical immunity from prosecution; regular visits of bishops throughout their diocese; standard religious instruction in the vernacular for the laity; schools attached to each cathedral and abbey for the training of clergy, teaching the seven liberal arts plus scriptural exegesis. Charles also charged his brilliant Anglo-Saxon court scholar, Alcuin, to supervise the editing of the Scriptures then in use in order to bring them into conformity with the best available texts. Charles was also an avid patron of Church music, and on his trips to Rome was so impressed by Gregorian chant and the Roman Mass that he standardized these forms of worship throughout his Empire and established schools of Church music taught by Church musicians from Rome in order to implement the new chants and Mass setting.

Charles had a high appreciation for learning, which he channeled into the cultural revival known as the Carolingian Renaissance. Charles himself could read and speak Latin (although he never learned to write) and also understood Greek. He gathered at his court the greatest scholars from England, Italy, Ireland, and Spain, all under the leadership of Alcuin. These scholars collected and copied manuscripts from classical Rome as well as the Patristic era, taught others, and produced original tracts, Scripture commentaries, poetry, and histories, little of which had been done since the collapse of the Western Empire. Charles also patronized art and architecture and instituted a large-scale program of church building and decorating, introducing Byzantine and Oriental motifs, which would later evolve into Romanesque architecture.

Charles died peacefully at Aachen at age seventy-two, having reigned as king and emperor for forty-seven years. He was buried in the octagonal church he had built at Aachen.

Works About: S. Abel and B. Simson, *Jb. des frankischen Reiches unter Karl dem Grossen*, 2d ed., 2 vols. (Leipzig, 1883–1888); J. F. Böhmer and E. Mühlbacher, *Regesten des Kaiserreichs unter den Karolingern*, 2d ed. (Innsbruck, 1908); D. Bullough, *The Age of Charlemagne* (New York, 1966); A. Cabaniss, *Charlemagne* (New York, 1972); Einhard and Notker the Stammerer, *Two Lives of Charlemagne*, tr. Lewis Thorpe (Baltimore, 1969); H. Fichtenau, *The Carolingian Empire* (Oxford, 1957); L. Halphen, *Charlemagne et l'Empire Carolingien* (Paris, 1949); F. Heer, *Charlemagne and His World* (New York, 1975); P. Jaffé, ed., *Bibliotheca Rerum Germanicarum. Monumenta Carolina* (Berlin, 1867); A. Kleincausz, *Charlemagne* (Paris, 1934); E. Mühlbacher, ed., *Die Urkunden der Karolinger. MGH. Diplomata Karolinorum* (Berlin, 1906); Richard Winston, *Charlemagne* (New York, 1954).   M. E. Chapman

See AACHEN; GISLA OF CHELLES; IMPERIAL REGALIA; LOUIS I; TITLES; VERDUN.

CHARLES III, THE FAT (839–888), who ruled the Empire from 880 to 887, was the youngest son of Louis the German and Emma. The epithet *fat* did not occur until the middle of the twelfth century. From 875 on, Italians had called him "little Charles" (Karoleto, Karlito, Carolus Minor) to distinguish him from Charles the Bald. In 862 he married Richardis, the daughter of Count Erc(h)anger of Alsace. Three years later he was given Swabia and Churwalch and then appeared afterward as count of Breisgau. The revolt of himself and his brother Louis against their father took place in 871, and the plotting continued in 873. Much of the friction was caused by the parental treatment of Carloman, the oldest son and their mother's favorite. After the reconciliation, Charles served as his father's envoy to Charles the Bald (874) and led a futile expedition into Italy against the same Charles the following year. When his father died (876), he became king of Swabia; he also received part of Lothringia (878) in a partition with his brother, Louis III. The same year he began communicating with Pope John VIII to replace as emperor his brother, Carloman, whose position in Italy was becoming hopeless. In 879 Carloman ceded Italy to Charles, who entered Italy without opposition that November and was crowned king of Italy early in 880 at Ravenna. (Carloman died March 22, 880.) The rest of the year was spent in negotiations with the West Frankish kings and a military venture with them against Boso, a Burgundian pretender. Besieging Vienne (in Provence) forced Boso to flee without his family and part of his troops, although he remained in power. In Rome on February 12, 881, Charles was crowned emperor by Pope John VIII.

A Viking invasion at the beginning of 882 forced him to leave Italy and head north. The Vikings had taken a number of cities (including Cologne, Aachen, and Trier) and plundered widely. At an assembly at Worms in May, Charles gathered an army of Franks, Swabians, Thuringians, Saxons, and Lombards to combat the invasion. While besieging their camp at Elsloo, he decided to negotiate. He gave one chief, Godefried, Frisia as a fief (once he had been baptized) and other honors; Godefried also married Gisla, an illegitimate daughter of Lothar II. The other, Sigefrid, settled for more than two thousand pounds of gold and silver and left. In another respect it was a profitable year; his brother, Louis the Younger, died on January 20, 882, and Charles became the sole ruler of the East Franks. Louis III of France also died on August 5, 882.

Charles spent the summer of 883 in Italy, where he dealt with a rebellion by Guy (Guido), duke of Spoleto. Guy was arrested but escaped, and a plague spoiled Charles' plan to plunder his territory. Charles returned north to witness a civil war between two Thuringian dukes. The Vikings also reappeared, and Count Henry defeated a group attacking Saxony (February 884). The next year began with a reconciliation with Guy of Spoleto, but the most important event of the year took place in April when an embassy of West Franks came to offer Charles their throne. Their young king, Carloman, had died on December 12, 884, and the only successor was the five-year-old son of Louis the Stammerer, Charles the Simple. Furthermore their kingdom had been impoverished by paying the Vikings twelve thousand pounds of silver. Charles had now reunited the Empire of Charlemagne except for that which Boso ruled. Also in 885 Charles invited Pope Adrian III to visit France; above all Charles wanted to arrange for his illegitimate son, Bernard, to succeed him. The invitation was futile, because the pontiff died shortly after. Since his successor, Stephen V, was chosen without Charles' consultation, the emperor sent Liutward, bishop of Vercelli, and some Roman bishops to depose the new pope, but they were unsuccessful.

Again in 886 Charles marched against the Vikings, led by Sigefrid, now besieging Paris. Charles returned from Italy, held an assembly at Metz, and then sent his best general, Count Henry, against them. Henry died on August 28, and Charles himself was forced to move against them. Rather than attempt to crush the Vikings, who were caught between the besieged and Charles' army, he opened negotiations in November. That same month it was agreed that the Vikings would raise the siege for seven hundred pounds of silver (due the next March) and permission to winter in Burgundy, which they plundered. From Paris Charles went to Alsace, where he was ill (perhaps he was epileptic) for a considerable period. It had not been a good year. Much of Mainz and Lower Frisia had been devastated by floods from May to July. The Slavs attacked in September. An unusually severe winter followed.

Boso's death on January 11, 887, removed a chronic problem. Provence submitted, and Charles adopted Boso's young son, Louis. Even though the Vikings had received their money, they did not depart as planned and devastated and plundered such cities as Troyes, Reims, Toul, and Verdun. Signs of dissatisfaction with the sick and ineffective emperor began to appear. A major blow was the removal of Liutward, his most important adviser; he was charged with heresy and adultery (with the empress) and removed in July. The emperor's illness continued to render him incapable of performing his duties, and in November at Frankfurt his vassals offered the crown to Arnulf, margrave of Carinthia, an illegitimate son of Carloman, Charles' brother, and one of Charles' best generals. Shortly afterward Charles was officially deposed at Tribur near Darmstadt. Charles died on January 13, 888, at Neidingen (on the Danube near Constance). The last few months of his life were spent on the lands assigned him by Arnulf. He was the last to have the Empire of Charlemagne, a tribute more to his longevity than ability. The choice of Odo by the West Franks rather than Arnulf ensured the permanent split of the Empire.

Works About: *Annales Fuldenses,* ed. F. Kurze, *SRG* (Hanover, 1891); J. F. Böhmer and E. Mühlbacher, *Regesta Imperii I,* ed. C. Bruhl and H. H. Kaminsky (Hildesheim, 1966); E. Dümmler, *Gesch. des Ostfranken Reiches* (Darmstadt, 1960); *MGH, Diplomata regum Germaniae ex stirpe Karolinorum II, Die Urkunden Karls III.,* ed. P. Kehr (Berlin, 1937).   *C. J. Dull*

See ARNULF; CARLOMAN; CHARLEMAGNE; LOUIS II.

CHARLES IV (1316–1378), the first of Germany's modern kings who ruled from 1347 to 1378, was the eldest son of the Luxembourg king John of Bohemia and Elizabeth, sister of the Premyslid king Wenceslaus III. He was the father of two succeeding kings of Germany, Wenceslaus I, born in 1361, and Sigismund, born in 1368. Charles spent much of his youth, from 1323 to 1331, at the court of Charles IV of France, where he changed his name from Wenceslaus to Charles and took Blanche, the sister of Philip VI, as his wife in 1324. He was well acquainted with French culture and politics.

In 1331, at the age of fourteen, he was called to lead his father's supporters in northern Italy. In 1333, Charles returned to Bohemia, where he was made margrave of Moravia and assumed a growing role in the governance of Bohemia and in imperial politics. He strengthened his dynasty's fortunes by arranging the marriage of his fourteen-year-old brother John Henry to Margaret Maultasch of Tyrol in 1336. Acting as regent, his thorough management of ducal finances and his assertion of authority against the nobility led to a revolt against him, the expulsion of his brother from the country, and the flight of Margaret to the Wittelsbach emperor, Louis, who was already interested in asserting prior Wittelsbach claims. With Louis' marriage of Margaret to his eldest son, Louis of Brandenburg, the conflict between the Bohemian Luxembourgs and the Wittelsbach emperor, which was to take place on a much broader scale had begun.

In April 1346, Charles accompanied King John to Avignon, where he met with his former teacher Clement VI and agreed to terms that would gain him papal assistance and make him emperor. With the support of his great-uncle Baldwin of Trier and his father, along with the Rhenish ecclesiastical electors and Saxony-Wittenberg, Charles was elected at Rhense on July 11, 1346. But before confronting Louis, the blind king John of Bohemia and his son fought in the Battle of Crècy in August 1346. John was killed; Charles was wounded twice. Now Charles of Bohemia and thirty years old, he was crowned king of Germany at Bonn on November 26 and, after agreeing to confirm the pope in his Italian lands, renounce all participation in Italian affairs, and annul all the acts of Louis against the papacy, Clement confirmed his election (but did not invite him to Rome for coronation as emperor).

The threat of imminent confrontation between Louis and Charles ended with Louis' death on October 11, 1347. The Wittelsbach party continued to oppose Charles and, after offering their support to Edward III of England and Frederick of Meissen-Thuringia, elected Gunther, count of Schwarzburg, on January 30, 1349. Charles' cautious diplomacy and clear military superiority made his reign short. Charles' second marriage to Anna, the daughter of the count Palatine Rudolf II, brought this major prince to his faction. Most of the others followed. And Charles enjoyed the aid of the Rhenish urban leagues, who were least desirous of seeing the Wittelsbachs become their imperial lords as well as their most avaricious territorial neighbors. Gunther agreed to settle his claim at Eltvil on May 26, 1349, and a more general agreement secured the peace at Bautzen on February 14, 1350. This agreement accorded the Wittelsbachs gracious terms, dropping all charges and confirming them in their territorial holdings. It was clearly in Charles' interest to gain their support, and he, in turn, ended his sponsorship of the pretender to the Askanian crown of Brandenburg, the "false Woldemar," which he had proclaimed in 1348. Finally he confirmed Louis of Brandenburg in his claim to Tyrol and Carinthia.

Charles is to be credited with a modern disregard of the imperial ideal, which allowed him to restore a working relationship with the papacy in exchange for hegemony in Italy. Relations with Clement were difficult nevertheless, in part because of Charles' renewed peace with the Wittelsbachs and his support of the deposed Wittelsbach archbishop, Henry of Mainz, who had seized the temporalities of the see. It was left to Clement's successor, Innocent VI, to confirm Charles' imperial claim and invite him to Rome for coronation. But Charles was to come without troops and stay in Rome only for a day.

In preparation for his departure from the Empire, Charles took advantage of disunity among the Wittelsbachs to remove the electoral vote from Bavaria, which had jointly exercised it with the Palatinate, and confine its use to the count Palatine. He toured Germany, bestowing royal favor in all directions and proclaiming temporary public peace to compose the estates while he was in Italy. He confirmed the rights of the Swabian Urban League to defend its members. And he had the good sense to ignore Florentine invitations and Petrarch's exhortations to intervene in Italian politics. He politely listened to Cola di Rienzi, the Roman tribune at Prague in 1350. Then he imprisoned him and eventually sent him to Avignon instead of returning with him to Rome as a liberator.

Charles crossed the Alps without an imperial army, was crowned king of the Lombards in Milan on January 6, 1355, and then moved on to Rome for his imperial coronation. Staying only one day, as prescribed, Charles was crowned at St. Peter's by Cardinal Peter of Ostia on April 5. Then he returned to Germany. He remained above the Guelf and Ghibelline factions, took oaths and taxes, but made no attempt to reestablish imperial government in Italy.

The emperor's strategy was ultimately successful. Independent of Italian politics, Germany stood once more as the protector of the Church against France. Charles' visit to Pope Urban V in Avignon to escort him to Rome in 1365 succeeded only in gaining him the kingdom of Burgundy (Arles, June 4, 1365). But he returned again to Italy to accompany Urban on his brief return to Rome in 1368, a visit that foreshadowed Gregory IX's final break with Avignon in 1377.

Prior to his coronation, Charles had tried to regulate the Wittelsbach electoral vote. The events of Louis the Bavarian's reign, not to mention his own election, had made the need for a set electoral procedure clear. At the imperial diets at Nuremberg and Metz between November 1355 and December 1356, such an ordinance was drafted, debated, and finally published. Known as the Golden Bull, it went far beyond electoral procedure, although this was rigorously defined. It granted special regalian rights to the electoral territories, including rights to mint currency, rights to mining, and judicial autonomy (*ius de non evocando et de non appellando*). It declared electoral lands indivisible and descending under primogeniture. It denied the right of defensive or offensive association to the estates, although the right of self-help or feud was only slightly curtailed. And it proposed, with little success, an annual meeting of the electors to discuss the affairs of the Empire, which was to occur after each Easter and last for four weeks. The Golden Bull thus established a model for princely territorial states and their prerogatives, which was energetically pursued by all princes, regardless of their status in the Empire.

Princes such as the Habsburg duke Rudolf IV envied the electoral princes and redoubled their efforts to compete as major territorial states. The son of Duke Albert of Austria, the nineteen-year-old Rudolf, was married to one of Charles' daughters and, anxious to stand on an equal footing with the electors, presented five forged documents purporting to be ancient imperial confirmations of similar rights extended to the Habsburgs by Nero and Julius Caesar. Although Charles' friend Petrarch soon proved the documents fraudulent, Rudolf continued to assert his claims. The death of Louis of Brandenburg in 1361 and, shortly thereafter, the death of his son Meinhard, duke of Upper Bavaria and count of Tyrol, left Rudolf's sister, Margaret Maultasch of the Tyrol, in a position to cede these lands to her brother, despite Luxembourg claims through her first husband, John Henry. Again Charles was diplomatic and realistic. He secured the favor of a major dynastic opponent in the agreement at Brünn in 1364, which ceded Tyrol to the Habsburgs and settled upon a formula of union if either line should fail.

The agreement at Brün was no deterrent to Charles' pursuit of his own dynastic interest, since he already had an heir, Wenceslaus, and would soon have another, Sigismund. He focused his efforts upon the construction of a strong Bohemian monarchy. His impressive fiscal and administrative talents, along with those of his chancellor, John von Neumarkt, made Bohemia one of the most advanced of the early modern territorial states. He imposed a codification of the Bohemian law, the *Maiestas Carolina,* upon the Bohemian estates. The code went far beyond the Golden Bull in abolishing the feud, and it strengthened royal finances and extended the prerogatives of the royal courts. And he founded the University of Prague in 1348, creating an eastern competitor to the academic hegemony of Paris.

Charles was an acquisitive monarch. In 1355, he purchased part of the Upper Palatinate and annexed Lower Lusatia in 1367. He secured succession in Brandenburg for his son Wenceslaus in 1373; his third marriage to Anna of Schweidniz-Jauer in 1362 brought the eventual annexation of Silesia to the Bohemian crown. He arranged a strategic marriage for Sigismund, who married a daughter of the Angevin king Louis of Hungary. Charles' fourth marriage to Elizabeth of Pomerania helped to secure his position in the north, where commercial relations with the Hanseatic League were a major consideration.

On the other hand, Charles weakened his dynasty in 1377 when he divided his lands among his sons and nephews. One year before his death, he granted Wenceslaus the kingship of Bohemia, Luxemburg, and Silesia. He gave Sigismund the margraviate of Brandenburg and Görlitz to John Henry. He divided Moravia between his nephews, Jobst and Procopius. In his last years Charles paid little attention to the affairs of the Empire, save to concern himself with the succession of his eldest son, Wenceslaus, as king of the Romans, which he accomplished in 1376. Charles IV died in Prague on November 29, 1378.

Works About: Johann Friedrich Böhmer, *Die Regesten des Kaiserreichs unter kaiser Karl IV, 1346–1378* (Innsbruck, 1887); Otto Fischer, *Karl IV Dtsch. Kaiser, König von Böhmen* (Bremen, 1941); Bede Jarrett, *The Emperor Charles IV* (London, 1935); *MGH: Legum Sectio IV, Const et Acta*, ed. Karl Zeumer and Richard Soloman, vol. 8 (Hanover, 1910–1926); E. L. Petersen, "Studien zur Goldene Bulle Von 1356," *Deutsches Archiv für Erforschung des Mittelalters* 22 (1966):227–53; F. Seibt, *Karl IV* (Munich, 1978); S. H. Thomson, "Learning at the Court of Charles IV," *Spec.* 29 (1950):1–20; Emil Werunsky, *Gesch. Kaiser Karls und seiner Zeit*, (Innsbruck, 1880–1892), vols. 1–4; Eduard Winter, *Frühhumanismus, seine Entwicklung deren Bedeutung für Kitchenreformbestrebungen der 14. Jahrhunderts* (Berlin, 1964); Karl Zeumer, *Die Goldene Bulle Kaiser Karls IV* (Weimar, 1908), vols. 1–2.   *S. A. Garretson*

See GOLDEN BULL; HANSEATIC LEAGUE; LOUIS IV; NUREMBERG; PETRARCH; SIGISMUND; WENCESLAUS I.

CHARLES V (1500–1558), Holy Roman emperor from 1519 to 1556, was born on February 24, 1500, in Ghent, Flanders. His father was Philip the Handsome, son of Emperor Maximilian I and Mary of Burgundy. His mother was Joan the Mad, daughter of Ferdinand and Isabella of Spain. After his father's death in 1506, Charles was raised by his aunt, Margaret of Austria, regent of the Netherlands. As a youth he was especially influenced by two men. His spiritual mentor was Adrian of Utrecht, a representative of the reform-minded modern devotion movement; who inculcated in him a simple, steadfast religious faith that he maintained throughout his life. The noble Guillaume de Croy, sieur de Chièvres, served as a surrogate father. Guillaume told the young Charles tales of chivalry and explained the missionary ideals of Burgundy. These remained with Charles during his long public career. In 1515, at the age of fifteen, he began that career when he came of age as duke of Burgundy, but he did not remain there long.

In 1517 Charles went to Spain to claim his Spanish inheritance. He had been proclaimed king of Spain after the death of his maternal grandfather, Ferdinand, in 1516. He spoke no Spanish and soon met with opposition from Spaniards, who resented the young foreigner who was surrounded by Burgundians and who ignored the rights of the provinces and their estates in establishing central organs of government. Some, such as the Comuneros, a group of Castilian cities that had the support of nobles, began a revolt, which lasted from 1520 to 1522. After a lengthy visit to Germany to begin his reign as Holy Roman emperor, Charles returned to Spain and bloodily suppressed the revolt. Eventually Charles gained the support and trust of his Spanish subjects. During his stay in Spain from 1522 to 1529, he learned Spanish and became a Spaniard. Later it was said of him by the Spanish that Charles spoke French with his ambassadors, Italian with his wives, German with his grooms, but Spanish with God. Castilian grandees now replaced Burgundians in the administration of the government.

During his long rule, Charles developed a deep understanding with his Spanish subjects, and it was Spanish money and Spanish troops that executed his policies and maintained his wars.

Upon the death of his grandfather, Holy Roman Emperor Maximilian I, in 1519, Charles became the leading candidate for the imperial throne. With the help of the German banking firms of the Fuggers and Welsers of Augsburg for bribes, Charles was the unanimous choice of the seven electors. He was crowned at Aachen on October 23, 1520. Charles ruled an enormous empire. He held over sixty royal and princely titles, including emperor, archduke of Austria, duke of Burgundy, king of Castile and Aragon, which included the rule of southern Italy and possessions in the New World, and king of Hungary. As ruler of such an empire, he also fell heir to a host of problems.

As Holy Roman emperor, Charles' first and the major task throughout his reign was to solve the problem of Luther and the Protestant Reformation. After his confrontation with Luther at the diet of Worms in 1521, Charles made it clear that he intended to crush the Lutheran Reformation. In many ways Charles' stand at Worms was just as dramatic as Luther's: "I am descended from a long line of Christian emperors of this noble German nation, and of the Catholic kings of Spain, the archdukes of Austria, and the dukes of Burgundy. They were all faithful to the death to the Church of Rome, and they defended the Catholic faith and the honor of God. I have resolved to follow in their steps. A single friar who goes counter to all Christianity for a thousand years must be wrong. Therefore I am resolved to stake my lands, my friends, my body, my blood, my life, and my soul." By the Edict of Worms, Luther was put under the ban of the Empire, and the printing of Lutheran literature was forbidden. However, little was accomplished, and Charles delegated further solution of the Lutheran problem to his brother Ferdinand, whom he designated as his representative in the Empire, granting him the Habsburg lands in the Empire as a hereditary possession. That Charles was unable to settle this Lutheran issue as quickly as he thought was due in part to external problems, including papal opposition, the dynastic struggle with the French monarchy, and the pressure of the Turks, and in part to internal problems, namely the opposition of German Protestant princes and even Catholic princes who feared an overly strong emperor.

Charles' relations with the papacy were largely determined by the emperor's conciliar policy. Beginning in 1529, Charles pressed the papacy for the summoning of a general Church council. Initially he hoped that a council could settle the religious controversy and thus solve the Lutheran problem in the Empire. But as Lutheranism continued to spread, his goals shifted, and he wanted a council to undertake the reform of the Church in head and members so that he could better carry out his struggle with Lutheranism. Pope Clement VII feared a council and as an Italian prince feared even more the union of Naples and Milan in the hands of the emperor. Clement's antiimperial policy, however, failed disastrously; Rome was sacked, and the pope was captured by the troops of Charles V in 1527. As a result of their forced reconciliation, Charles V was crowned emperor by the pope at Bologna in 1530, the last time a Holy Roman emperor was crowned by a pope. This same year saw Charles at the height of his power in Italy and signals the beginning of Habsburg rule in Italy, which lasted until the eighteenth century. Despite his successes with Clement, Charles was still not able to gain the pope's cooperation in convening a council. He finally achieved his goal with Clement's successor, Paul III, after years of wrangling. The Council of Trent met on December 13, 1545, but failed to provide the kind of reform that Charles wanted. Charles' relationship with the papacy demonstrates great irony. Both sides were dedicated to maintaining the Catholic cause against Luther, but papal politics could easily work against that goal as Charles repeatedly experienced frustration. Papal fear of Spanish domination of Italy resulted in continual efforts to thwart Charles' plans and hence hobbled the one ruler who was genuinely committed to crushing the Lutherans.

The struggle of Charles V with the French king, Francis I, was long and costly. Charles' aims were the restoration of old imperial territories, including the duchy of Burgundy and Milan. Francis I felt that France was surrounded on all sides by Habsburg possessions and wished to break out of this encirclement by allying himself with the pope, other Italian rulers, German Protestant princes, and even the Turks. Charles V and Francis I became brothers-in-law through the marriage of Charles' sister Eleanor to Francis, but this connection failed to achieve any peace. Charles and Francis fought a series of intermittent wars for the hegemony of western Europe. Hostilities broke out in 1521 and ended at Pavia in 1525 when Charles defeated Francis I and took the French king as prisoner. This victory assured Spanish supremacy in Italy. By the Treaty of Madrid of 1526, Francis gave his sons as hostages and married the emperor's oldest sister, Eleanor. But once free, Francis sabotaged the treaty and resumed the war, now allying himself with Pope Clement VII, who feared the ambitions of Charles V, in the League of Cognac. The result was the sack of Rome in 1527 and the imprisonment of Clement VII until 1528. The war continued until both sides agreed to the so-called ladies' peace, the Peace of Cambrai of 1529, negotiated by the mother of Francis and the emperor's aunt Margaret. By this peace treaty Charles renounced his claim to Burgundy, Francis his claims to Milan and Naples. The compromise solution was not satisfactory and certainly not permanent, for in 1536, now allied with the Turks, Francis I invaded Savoy in order to reconquer Milan; another Habsburg-Valois war erupted. After a challenge of personal combat, which Francis I refused, Charles invaded Provence, hoping thereby to force the French to withdraw in Italy, but the military operation was inconclusive. Peace was concluded in May 1538, reaffirming the provisions of the Treaty of Cambrai and thus leaving the major issues unresolved. In 1542, war broke out again over Milan. When the emperor invaded

France and appeared within sight of Paris, Francis agreed to make peace. The Peace of Crépy of 1544 basically confirmed the status quo.

In addition to his struggle with the French, the pressure of the Turks forced Charles to neglect the Lutheran problem periodically. The siege of Vienna by the Turks in 1529 demonstrated that Charles could not allow the German situation to deteriorate into war. In 1532, faced with a Turkish threat to the hereditary Habsburg lands, Charles granted a religious truce to the Protestants. In return for additional religious concessions, he received armed support to fight the Turks. Charles faced Sultan Suleiman's forces before Vienna but did not have the strength to give decisive battle. After returning to Spain in 1533, he prepared a counteroffensive against the Turks in the Mediterranean. He captured Tunis in North Africa in 1535, but this did little to diminish overall Turkish strength, and his continuing problems in Germany kept him from executing additional campaigns against the Turks.

At the diet of Worms, Charles had indicated his determination to crush Luther and his supporters. Because of his other problems, Charles was not able to return to Germany until 1530. At the diet of Augsburg, Charles tried to find an accommodation with the Protestants. The Catholic responded to the Augsburg Confession, the basic confessional statement of the Lutheran church, with the Confutation, which Charles approved. The final decree of the diet confirmed the resolutions of the Edict of Worms of 1521, and Charles demanded that the Lutherans return to the Catholic church by April 15, 1531. The Protestant princes reacted by forming the defensive Schmalkaldic League in 1531. Because of a renewed Turkish threat in Austria, the emperor was forced to grant some concessions in return for armed support against the Turks. By the Peace of Nuremberg in 1532, it was agreed that no attacks were to be made against the Lutherans before the meeting of a general church council. Once again, Charles was driven to compromise on the religious issue to meet an external problem. Charles came to realize that the Lutherans could not simply be exterminated as the Catholic extremists wished. Consequently in the 1530s and 1540s he attempted to follow a path of moderation. His goal was to reach a compromise with the Lutherans through a series of religious conferences, with a general church council attended by both Protestants and Catholics providing the final settlement. Religious conferences were held at Hagenau, Worms, and Regensburg, where moderate Catholics and moderate Protestants took steps to reconcile their differences. Ultimately there was no grand compromise due to Luther's intransigence, opposition from Catholic Rome, and political opposition to Charles that was developing in Germany. Charles, finally despairing of compromise, decided to use force to settle the Lutheran problem.

It was not until 1546 that Charles was finally free of his other problems and able at last to bring an army with him to Germany. Charles was enormously successful at first. At the Battle of Mühlberg (April 1547), Elector John Frederick of Saxony, the leader of the Protestant princes, became the emperor's prisoner. Philip of Hesse, another Protestant leader, also surrendered. The victory of Charles V in Germany seemed complete. At the diet of Augsburg in 1547–1548, he imposed the Augsburg Interim, under which, in return for adhering again to Catholicism, Lutherans were granted communion in both kinds and clerical marriage, pending the decision of a general council. But this victory of Charles soon proved to be his undoing. He frightened not only Lutheran princes but also the Catholic princes of the Empire who feared that Germany would become Spanish, under a Spanish emperor, and a Spanish army of occupation. Consequently Maurice of Saxony, a Protestant general but a supporter of Charles, deserted the emperor. With this defection a league of German princes, in alliance with King Henry II of France, was able to defeat and drive Charles from Germany in 1552. Late in 1552, after he had been forced to grant further concessions to the Protestant princes in the Treaty of Passau, he left Austria to carry on the struggle in western Germany. This campaign also failed, and in 1553 he recognized the inevitable, handing over all responsibility for German affairs to his brother Ferdinand and ultimately accepting the religious Peace of Augsburg in 1555. The settlement recognized Lutheranism as equal to Catholicism and determined that the governing authorities in each state within the Holy Roman Empire would determine the religion of the state.

Charles had spent a lifetime attempting to reform the Holy Roman Empire. He wished to maintain its federal structure and wanted to establish an imperial league as the new form of organization regulating relations between the king and princes and among the princes themselves. Already in existence was the *Reichsregiment,* the Imperial Governing Council. The leading princes felt that the *Reichsregiment* should exercise the emperor's powers in his presence as in his absence and advise and decide on all matters affecting the Empire. Charles found this unacceptable and, at the diet of Worms in 1521, the compromise was reached in which the *Reichsregiment* would act only in the absence of the emperor and would represent the supreme governmental authority in the Empire. In the decades after 1521, the *Reichsregiment* disintegrated. Charles attempted repeatedly, as in 1547–1548 and 1552–1553, to form an imperial league that would cover the whole of Germany but always without success. His hopes for reform were destroyed not only by the princes but also by the conflicting aims of Habsburg policy in the Empire. While it is true that Charles wanted to rebuild Germany on a stronger base, one cannot overlook that Charles wanted support for specifically Habsburg policy, which the princes regarded as outside their concern.

Charles V's view of the Empire was essentially medieval. He asserted that world peace could only be guaranteed through the *imperium* of the Holy Roman Empire with the emperor as a supreme sovereign. Mercurino Gattinara, his close political adviser, had especially emphasized this conception of empire. The Burgundians at Charles' court were the chief spokesmen for this imperial conception. Charles does not seem, however, to have interpreted this in the context of universal monarchy, involving the conquest of additional territories. His wars against the French were fought, in his view, to protect the rightful inheritance and possessions of Burgundy and Milan as part of the Holy Roman Empire. In addition, when Cortés, the conqueror of Mexico, offered Charles an imperial title equal to his German title, the emperor refused, a reminder that he was never overly interested in his overseas possessions. He did not think of them in the same imperial terms he applied to European lands. The colonies merely enhanced the power image of the Habsburgs without being integrated into any imperial scheme. Although the colonies were thought of in terms of exploitation, it was not until the 1550s that any significant sum of gold and silver reached Charles' Spain from America.

By the time of the Peace of Augsburg in 1555, Charles was exhaused by his decades of struggle and made the final decision to abdicate his ruling power. On October 25, 1555, he handed over his power in the Netherlands to his son Philip, and on January 16, 1556, he abdicated in favor of Philip in Spain, the Italian lands, and the colonies. He offered his resignation of the imperial crown on September 12, 1556, but this abdication was not ratified until February 1558. He retired to seclusion in Spain at his country house at San Geronimo de Yuste, where he died on September 21, 1558.

Works By: Lothar Gross, ed., *Die Reichsbücher Karls V, 1519–1556* (Vienna and Leipzig, 1930); A. Kluckhohn and A. Wrede, eds. *DRTA unter Karl V, Jüngere Reihe* (Munich, 1893–1905, 1929), vols. 1–4, 7; Karl Lanz, ed., *Correspondenz des Kaisers Karl V*, 3 vols. (Leipzig, 1844–1846). **Works About:** M. F. Alvarez, *Charles V* (London, 1975); Jean Babelon, *Charles-Quint* (Paris, 1947); Karl Brandi, *The Emperor Charles V*, tr. C. V. Wedgwood (New York, 1939); Helmut G. Koenigsberger, *The Habsburgs and Europe, 1516–1660* (Ithaca, N.Y., 1971); John Lynch, *Spain under the Habsburgs*, vol. 1: *Empire and Absolutism, 1516–1598* (New York, 1964); Ramon Ménéndez Pidal, *Idea imperial de Carlos V* (Madrid, 1941); Volker Press, *Kaiser Karl V, König Ferdinand und die Entstehung der Reichsritterschaft* (Wiesbaden, 1976); Peter Rassow, *Die politische Welt Karls V* (Munich, 1945), and *Karl V. Der Kaiser und seine Zeit* (Cologne, 1960); Martti Salomies, *Die Pläne Kaiser Karls V für eine Reichsreform* (Helsinki, 1953); Royall Tyler, *The Emperor Charles the Fifth* (London, 1956).   *J. J. Spielvogel*

See ADRIAN VI; GATTINARA; FUGGER; LUTHER; MAXIMILIAN I; SCHMALKALDIC WAR; WORMS.

CHARLES VI (1685–1740), Holy Roman emperor from 1711 through 1740, was the second and favorite son of Leopold I and his third wife, Eleanore of Pfalz-Neuburg. Like his father and his brother Joseph, Charles was a talented musician and patron of the opera. He too had a strong sense of duty toward both his family and the Holy Roman Empire. An ugly, short man, Charles had the typical Habsburg lip and brown hair. Taciturn, reticent, and on occasion stubborn like his father, he was not particularly fond of governing. He spent most of his time with his family playing billiards or cards. He was also an avid collector of books and coins. Charles was very attached to his family, particularly his wife, the beautiful Elizabeth Christina of Brunswick-Wolfenbuttel

(1691–1750), whom he used to address as his "White Lizzy" because of her clear complexion. Concerned about the succession, he was deeply grieved when he lost his only son, Leopold, in 1716. He was determined to safeguard the inheritance of his eldest daughter, Maria Theresa, just as his father had tried, but failed, to secure Charles' succession to the Spanish empire.

On the death of Carlos II of Spain, Leopold I, at the urging of both his sons, pressed Archduke Charles' claims to the Spanish empire and immediately went to war with Louis XIV of France. As Habsburg claimant to the Spanish lands, Charles and his wife went to Spain in order to garner support for his reign as Carlos III. Unfortunately he was not able to win much backing in Spain outside of Barcelona and Catalonia. He directed the Habsburg campaign in Spain while his brother, on the death of their father, fought on the Rhine, in the Netherlands, and in Italy. Upon the death of Joseph in 1711, the allies refused to support Charles VI's claims to the Spanish empire; they opposed a personal union of Spain and the Habsburg lands. After the allies deserted Charles and concluded a separate peace with France at Utrecht in 1713, Charles was forced to negotiate with France and sign the treaties of Rastatt and Baden in 1714, which ended the war and partitioned the Spanish lands. Philip V retained Spain and the overseas empire, while Charles acquired Milan, Naples, and the Netherlands.

Although Charles had not been successful in pressing Habsburg claims to Spain, he did not reconcile himself to that loss for more than a decade, just as Philip V had not accepted the loss of Milan, Naples, and the Netherlands. While Charles VI was preoccupied with war in the east against the Turks, Spain seized Sardinia and Sicily (1717 and 1718). In order to avoid upsetting the balance of power, England, France, the United Provinces, and Austria went to war. In the short conflict that ensued, Austria retook Sicily. Philip, recognizing the futility of the war, made peace at the Treaty of the Hague in 1720. By this compromise, Philip acknowledged the cession of the Netherlands to Austria, and Charles recognized Bourbon rule in Spain and the right of Don Carlos (the elder son of Philip V and Elizabeth Farnese) to Parma, Piacenza, and Tuscany. Charles exchanged Sardinia, which Savoy had received at Utrecht, for Sicily. Still hoping to bring Spain back into the Habsburg orbit, Charles concluded a short-lived, unsuccessful alliance with Spain (Treaty of Vienna of 1725). Charles never intended to fulfill his part of the agreement: his promise to marry his eldest daughter to the son of Philip V and Elizabeth Farnese.

After Charles had accepted the impossibility of regaining Spain, he was determined to ensure that the Habsburg territories would pass intact to his heirs. In 1713 Charles issued the Pragmatic Sanction, which declared that all of the Habsburg possessions were indivisible and hereditary in both the male and female line. The problem of securing recognition for his eldest daughter, Maria Theresa, preoccupied Charles throughout his reign. In order to obtain the consent of the various estates in his realm and the major European powers to the Pragmatic Sanction, Charles was forced to make concessions. In exchange for England's consent, he abandoned the Ostend Company. He supported Frederick Augustus' candidacy to the Polish throne in order to obtain Saxony's assent. The War of the Polish Succession (1773–1735) was as much a disaster for Charles as the second Turkish war was later to be. France supported the candidacy of Stanislaus Leszcynski, the father-in-law of Louis XV, while Russia and Austria supported Augustus II of Saxony. In the subsequent fighting, France, Spain, and Sardinia declared war on the Holy Roman Empire and Russia. In spite of the leadership of Prince Eugene, Austria and its allies fared miserably; Philippsburg, Naples, and Sicily were taken. In the subsequent peace (1738), Austria ceded Naples and Sicily to Spain and in return received Parma and Piacenza; Francis Stephen of Lorraine, Maria Theresa's husband, lost Lorraine to France but received Tuscany as compensation.

Charles had concentrated on obtaining paper guarantees to the Pragmatic Sanction rather than on reforming his administration and building up his army and treasury. Debacles like the War of the Polish Succession were the unfortunate result. In contrast, earlier in his reign Charles had fared relatively well in his first Turkish war. The Turks, who were attempting to undo the settlement at Karlowitz (1699), tried to take Morea and went to war with Venice in 1714. Charles, realizing that Turkish inroads in the Adriatic would endanger the Habsburg position in Hungary, allied with Venice. Under Prince Eugene of Savoy, the imperialists won a series of victories over the Turks. For example at Peterwardein (1716) the imperialists with 70,000 troops annihilated the Ottoman army of 120,000. In the peace of Passarowitz (1718) the Turks kept the Morea and Charles VI acquired the banat of Temesvár, the northern part of Serbia, including Belgrade, and part of Wallachia and Bosnia, plus trading rights in the Turkish empire. Unfortunately Charles lost all of these territories, except for the banat of Temesvár, in the second of his Turkish wars (1737–1739).

The second Turkish war, like the War of the Polish Succession, was a series of disasters that revealed the military and financial weaknesses of Charles' regime. In spite of the creditable effort of Gundaker Thomas von Stahrremberg, director of Austrian finance, and what proved to be calamitous and drastic military cutbacks, Austria was near bankruptcy in the 1730s. Economically Charles had tried to strengthen Austria's financial position by the abolition of some trade barriers and by the building of roads such as the one over the Semmering Pass, linking Trieste with the Vienna basin. When Charles VI died unexpectedly in 1740, he left his heir with a depleted treasury and a demoralized and greatly weakened army. The contingency that Charles had tried so hard to avoid occurred a few months after his death. The War of the Austrian Succession broke out as various European powers tried to dismember Maria Theresa's inheritance.

Works About: ADB, 15:206-09; L. Bittner, ed., *Chronologisches Verzeichnis der österr. Gesch. Staatsverträge* (Vienna, 1903); Max Braubach, *Prinz Eugen von Savoyen*, 5 vols. (Vienna, 1963–1965); Hajo Holborn, *A History of Modern Germany, 1648–1840* (New York, 1969); W. H.

McNeill, *Europe's Steppe Frontier, 1500–1800* (Chicago, 1964); *NDB*, 11:211 -18; Oswald Redlich, *Das Werden einer Grossmachet, Österreich von 1700 bis 1740* (Vienna, 1942); Karl P. Roider, Jr. *The Reluctant Ally: Austria's Policy in the Austro–Turkish War, 1737–1739* (Baton Rouge, 1972 J. W. Stoye, *Emperor Charles VI* (New York, 1962); Gustav Truba, ed., *Die Pragmatische Sanktion, Authentische Texte samt Erläuterungen und Übersetzungen* (Vienna, 1913). L. S. Frey and M. L. Frey

See EUGENE: KARLOWITZ: LEOPOLD I: MARIA THERESA: PRAGMATIC SANCTION: STAHREMBERG: UTRECHT.

CHARLES VII (1697–1745), Holy Roman emperor from 1742 through 1745, and Charles Albert, elector of Bavaria (1726–1745), was the son of the dashing, heroic Maximilian Emmanuel, elector of Bavaria, and his second wife, Theresa Cunigunda, daughter of John Sobieski, king of Poland. During Charles' infancy Bavaria was despoiled by imperial troops because the elector had sided with Louis XIV against Emperor Leopold I in the War of the Spanish Succession (1701–1714). When the imperialists occupied Munich, Charles and his brother were taken as prisoners to Vienna. After peace was concluded and Maximilian Emmanuel was restored to his electorate, Charles was released. In 1717 Charles even aided the Habsburgs in their struggle against the Turks; he led a Bavarian contingent and served courageously under Prince Eugene of Savoy. At the seizure of Belgrade, he was particularly noted for his bravery. In 1722 this amiable, friendly, rather phlegmatic prince, married the younger daughter of the deceased Holy Roman emperor Joseph I, Maria Amalia. At that time upon the insistence of her uncle, Emperor Charles VI, she renounced her rights to the Habsburg inheritance. Neither Maximilian Emannuel of Bavaria nor Frederick Augustus of Saxony, whose son Frederick Augustus II had married the eldest daughter of Joseph I, Maria Josepha, in 1719, intended to respect these disclaimers.

In 1726 Charles succeeded his father as elector. He tried to rival the French court in grandeur and at the same time introduce moderate reforms. Like his father, Charles vacillated between supporting the Bourbons and the Habsburgs. In 1732 both Charles Albert and Frederick Augustus I of Saxony recognized the Pragmatic Sanction. Bavaria did so with secret reservations and protests. At the same time the elector was trying to secure French support for his claims on the Habsburg inheritance, which dated from the sixteenth century. His father had signed a treaty with France as early as 1714 in which Louis XIV had pledged to support Wittelsbach claims, particularly for the Bohemian crown lands.

As soon as Charles VI died, the elector put forward his claims and refused to recognize the succession of Maria Theresa, Charles VI's eldest daughter. Bavaria, along with Prussia, Saxony, Spain, and France, hoping to dismember its inheritance, went to war (War of the Austrian Succession, 1740–1748). With French support, Charles was elected Holy Roman emperor in 1742. This was the first time since 1438 that a Habsburg had not held the imperial throne. George, elector of Hanover (George II of England), had promised his vote in order to protect the neutrality of his electorate; Frederick of Brandenburg had pledged his in exchange for recognition of his right to Lower Silesia. Although Charles did succeed in being crowned Holy Roman emperor, the war went disastrously for him; his electorate was overrun and occupied by Habsburg troops. His success in Bohemia, where he declared himself king (1741), was short-lived; he was forced to flee in 1742. With Frederick II's assistance, he finally returned to Munich where he died in January of the following year, a broken, impoverished man. His son Maximilian Joseph, supported by his mother, sued for peace and subsequently signed the Treaty of Füssen with Maria Theresa in 1745.

Works About: *ADB*, 15:219–26; A. von Arneth, *Gesch, Maria Theresias* (Vienna, 1863–1879); Eugen Guglia, *Maria Theresia: Ihr Leben und ihre Regierung*, 2 vols. (Munich, 1917); P. T. Heigel, *Der österr Erbfolgestreit und die Kaiserwahl Karls VII* (Munich, 1877); Hajo Holborn, *A Hist. of Modern Germany, 1648–1840* (New York, 1969); *NDB*, 11:218–19; Max Spindler, ed., *Handbuch der bayer Gesch.*, 2 vols. (Munich, 1966).   *L. S. Frey and M. L. Frey*

See AUSTRIAN SUCCESSION; CHARLES VI: EUGENE; MARIA THERESA; PRAGMATIC SANCTION.

CHRISTOPHER (1515–1568), duke of Württemberg and universally acclaimed as the father of his country *(Landesvater, pater patriae)*, was responsible for firmly implanting the Lutheran Reformation in his territories and for consolidating it for three centuries thereafter by means of fundamental laws and institutions. Born in Urach, the son of Duke Ulrich of Württemberg and Duchess Sabina of Bavaria, Christopher spent much of his early life in exile from his native soil following the conquest of Württemberg in 1519 by the Swabian League and its subsequent occupation by Austrian forces. His early education under the tutelage of Michael Tiffernus, an outstanding Latinist, was regulated by a treaty between his uncle, the duke of Bavaria, and Holy Roman Emperor Charles V. The young man accompanied Charles to the diet of Augsburg in 1530 and on other journeys until he escaped to his Bavarian relatives in 1532.

Because of the continuing hostility that the father displayed toward his young son, Christopher remained in exile for another decade, despite his conversion to Ulrich's Lutheran faith. From 1534 until 1542 he won high praise at the court of King Francis I. A treaty of reconciliation with the father at Reichenweiler (Riquewihr) in Alsace in 1542 secured for Christopher the right of succession to Ulrich's lands in exchange for a promise to maintain the evangelical faith in Württemberg after Ulrich's death. In 1544 Christopher married Anna Maria, daughter of Margrave George of Brandenburg-Ansbach, while serving as governor *(Statthalter)* of Mömpelgard (Montbéliard), a small Swabian principality west of the Rhine. From this happy marriage issued four sons and eight daughters, including his immediate successor, Ludwig.

Upon the death of Ulrich in 1550, Christopher moved to Stuttgart and began his ambitious eighteen-year reign. A steady stream of ordinances and regulations for church and state alike began flowing from his chancellery, all intended to consolidate the Lutheran Reformation and his control within and to win friends and useful allies abroad. Central to Christopher's foreign policy was his unswerving friendship with the Habsburg house and the Holy Roman emperors, first Charles V and later Maximilian II (who visited Christopher in Stuttgart on at least one occasion).

In later life the duke became increasingly concerned about the spread of Calvinism in the neighboring Palatinate and the persistence of sectarian religious sympathies within his own lands. From 1599 on, with the active assistance of such court theologians as John Brenz and Jacob Andreae, he promoted Lutheran unity while turning his country into a Lutheran bulwark for generations to come. Christopher's notable refusal to intervene in the French wars of religion strengthened his hand as a mediator between the opposing camps and religious parties. His crowning legislative achievement was the great ecclesiastical ordinance *(Grosse Kirchenordnung)* and the school ordinance *(Schulordnung)* of 1559, whereby the Augsburg Confession was declared the sole religious confession to which servants of church and state were expected to swear allegiance. Only in the educational program for his firstborn son, Eberhard, which he personally planned and supervised, did Christopher experience frustration and disappointment; the young prince preceded his father in death in 1568 at the age of twenty-three. In the words of a later Swabian historian, "Christopher became the prince on the evangelical side most worthy of confidence and trust; he really had no enemies, and wherever a mediator's services were needed, there he was."

Works By: Viktor Ernst, ed., *Briefwechsel des Herzogs Christoph von Wirtemberg,* 4 vols. (Stuttgart, 1899–1907). **Works About:** Balthasar Bidembach, *Herzog Christophs Leben* (Schwäbisch Hall, 1817); Bernhard Kugler, *Christoph, Herzog zu Wirtemberg,* 2 vols. (Stuttgart, 1868–1872); Hans-Martin Maurer, "Herzog Christoph als Landesherr," *Bl. für wurttemb. Kirchengesch.* 58–59 (1968–1969): 112–38; J. C. Pfister, *Herzog Christoph zu Wirtemberg,* 2 vols. (Tübingen, 1819–1820); Louis Reith, "Prince Eberhard and His Preceptors: The Education of Princes in Sixteenth-Century Württemberg" (Ph. D. diss., Stanford University, 1976); P. F. Stälin, "Christoph," *ADB,* 4:243–50; R. Uhland, "Christoph," *NDB,* 3:248;–49; Karl Weller and Arnold Weller, *Württembergische Geschichte im südwestdtsch. Raum,* 6th ed. (Stuttgart, 1971).   *L. J. Reith*

See ANDREAE; BRENZ; CHARLES V; LUDWIG III; MAXIMILIAN II; PHILIP OF HESSE; ULRICH.

COLOGNE played an influential role in the history of the Holy Roman Empire both as a free imperial city and as an electoral archbishopric. The city traces its heritage to the first century B.C. when the Romans constructed it as a military camp. After the fall of the Empire, Cologne slowly grew during the early Frankish kingdoms and was especially favored during the rule of Charlemagne. From the tenth to the thirteenth centuries, the city, located on the northern Rhine, developed as an important center for trade and commerce. Cologne was a crossroads between commerce with the southern German territories and the Netherlands, as well as the Baltic regions. It later became a member of the Hanseatic

League. By the thirteenth century the city of Cologne had grown to be the largest and most prosperous of the medieval German cities. It continued to hold this dominance until the sixteenth century when wars, economic depressions, and several other factors contributed to its decline as a commercial center.

An important feature of Cologne's political life from the eleventh to the thirteenth centuries was the almost constant struggle between its townspeople and their overlord, the archbishop of Cologne. Although generally the revolts were not bloody, with the exception of the uprising in 1138, the interests of Cologne's citizens and its archbishop could not be reconciled. Recent scholarship has determined that the archbishop was largely responsible for the development of political independence in the city. Forced to neglect the governing of the city because of his involvement in high imperial politics in the eleventh and twelfth centuries, the archbishop permitted the middle class to assume the reins of daily administration and government. The twelfth and thirteenth centuries witnessed the final struggles of the archbishop to regain control over the city; by 1288, he was forced to grant Cologne's independence, demonstrated in his change of residence from Cologne to Bonn.

The next conflict centered on the attempt of the lower classes to break the patrician monopoly of city office. A serious challenge to the patricians took place in 1371 when the wool weavers seized the city government for several months. Although the patricians were able to regain their position after a brutal supression of the weavers, the nonpatrician elements continued their demands. In 1396 the old families could no longer resist the political pressures of the other social groups, and their monopoly of office was finally broken in their acceptance of a city constitution.

The late fifteenth and sixteenth centuries again saw numerous social and political conflicts within the city. The lower guilds demanded a greater share in political life, which an oligarchy of established guild masters and families denied to them. In 1482, 1513, and 1525 riots swept through the city. The insurrection of the lower guilds in 1525 was indicative that the German Peasants' Revolt of 1524–1525 also had urban manifestations.

Despite this internal dissension, Cologne grew in political importance within the Empire. On September 19, 1475, the Emperor Frederick III granted Cologne privileges which gave the city a greater degree of autonomy.

During the Reformation, the city of Cologne remained staunchly Catholic. It was the major center of opposition to two attempts in 1546 and 1583 on the part of its archbishop-electors to convert to Protestantism. While the city largely resisted Protestantism because of a strong Catholic revival, a secondary motive might have been the fear that the city could lose the freedoms of its imperial charter and once more come under the secular control of the archbishop.

In the seventeenth and eighteenth centuries, Cologne suffered a gradual decline in political and economic importance. The destruction caused by the Dutch War of Independence and later by the Thirty Years War partially helped to account for the decline of trade in this region. In addition, new trade routes that bypassed Cologne were established in northern Europe. The city became a backwater.

In 1794 French troops occupied the area, and three years later the city swore an oath of allegiance to the French Republic. With the dissolution of the Empire in 1806, its charter ended, and in the settlement of 1814 the city passed into Prussian hands.

The history of the archbishopric of Cologne was equally colored. Already a leading German ecclesiastical center in the second century, Cologne rose to prominence under the Carolingian empire. By the eighth century, the archbishopric's influence throughout north central Germany and into the Netherlands had expanded. The bishoprics of Liège, Utrecht, Munster, Osnabruck, Minden, and Bremen were under its sway. This sizable territory was impossible for the archbishop to administer effectively, so beginning in the twelfth century he delegated his authority to several archdeacons, the most important being those of Cologne, Bonn, Xanten, and Soest.

As early as the tenth century, the archbishopric of Cologne became involved in imperial politics. One of its first great archbishops, Bruno I (reigning, from 953 to 965), was the brother of the Emperor Otto I. The Cologne archbishops served the Holy Roman emperors in various high capacities, especially as chancellors of the Italian area of the German empire. This involvement in imperial affairs gave the Cologne archbishops an advantage in their territorial acquisitions; moreover they were not without an eye to personal gain. Cologne began its major territorial expansion in the twelfth century when two successive archbishops, Rainald, of Dassel (1156–1167) and Philipp of Heinsberg (1168–1191), served Frederick Barbarossa as imperial chancellors. Rainald of Dassel was able to acquire significant territories on both sides of the Rhine, while Philipp of Heinsberg annexed the Duchy of Westphalia.

In 1356 the Golden Bull of Emperor Charles IV made Cologne one of the privileged seven electors of the Holy Roman emperor.

In the fifteenth century the vast territories that Cologne had acquired gradually won their freedom. The duchies of Jülich, Berg, Cleves, and Mark evolved, the city of Cologne was completely free in 1475, and numerous smaller territories—collectively known as the *Unterherrschaften* (about seventy-five)–had won either complete or partial independence from the archbishop.

In the sixteenth century Cologne nevertheless remained the leading German episcopate. During the Reformation, the archbishopric of Cologne was one of the first German areas to show signs of a healthy Catholic revival, but Catholicism had to face two serious threats of near Protestantization before it finally triumphed. Cologne's location in Germany and bordering on the Netherlands, as well as being an electoral seat, made it an attractive territory for Protestant and Catholic powers. The main reason for Catholicism's success in Cologne was the support of the Bavarian Wittelsbachs, who through Ernest of Bavaria, placed their candidate on the episcopal throne after Gebhard Truchsess's failure to protestantize Cologne in 1583. Thereafter the fate of the archbishopric was tied with the politics of the Wittelsbachs. Ernest was replaced by his nephew, the able and reform-minded Ferdinand (1612–1650), but after Ferdinand's leadership, its archbishops–among them Maximilian Henry (1650–1688), Joseph Clemens (1688–1723), and Clemens August (1723–1761)–were notably dull and ineffective. The promising career of the last archbishop-elector of Cologne, Maximilian Francis of Austria (1781–1801), the youngest son of Maria Theresa, was cut short by the French invasion in 1794.

In 1801 the left bank of Cologne became part of the French empire, and finally in 1803 the final history of the archbishopric of Cologne as an imperial electorate began when secularization was introduced.

Works About: Leonard Ennen, *Gesch. der Stadt Köln*, 5 vols. (Cologne, 1869–1880); August Franzen, *Bischof und Reformation (Münster, 1971)*; Axel Kuhn, *Jakobiner im Rhineland* (Stuttgart, 1976); E. Podlich, *Gesch. der Erzdiözese Köln* (Mainz, 1879); O. R. Redlich, *Staat und Kirche am Niederrhein zur Reformationszeit* (Leipzig, 1939); Wilhelm Schönfelder, *Die Wirtschaftliche Entwicklung Kölns von 1370–1513* (Cologne, 1970); Hugo Stehkämpfer, *Köln Das Reich und Europa* (Cologne, 1973), and, with others, *Revolution in Köln, 1074–1918* (Cologne, 1973); Paul Strait, *Cologne in the Twelfth Century* (Gainesville, 1974); Paul Weiler, *Die kirchliche Reform in Erzbistrum Köln* (Münster, 1931).   C. T. Eby

See CHARLEMAGNE: COLOGNE CRISES: HANSEATIC LEAGUE: HERMAN V: IMPERIAL CITIES: RAINALD.

COLOGNE CRISES OF 1547 AND 1583 presented similar issues and political-religious implications for the history of the archbishopric of Cologne and the Holy Roman Empire. In both instances the archbishop-elector of Cologne tried to convert the Catholic territory of Cologne to the Protestant side. If these attempts had been successful, the political and religious complexion of the Holy Roman Empire would have been dramatically changed in the sixteenth century. In addition to being the most influential Catholic archbishopric in northwestern Germany, Cologne offered the prestigious seat of imperial elector. Cologne's conversion would have given the Protestants the upper hand in the imperial electoral college during this crucial period of the Reformation. In addition, the Protestantization of Cologne might have influenced those territories neighboring it, such as the united duchies of Jülich-Berg-Cleves and Mark, the bishoprics of Münster, Osnabrück, and Minden, and several other smaller German holdings in the northwest.

The first Cologne crisis began in the late 1530s. After the failure of his attempt to reform the archbishopric in 1538, Herman V of Wied decided to expose Cologne to Protestant thought. Wied's motivation is not clear. Religiously he had only a superficial understanding of the differences between Catholicism and Protestantism. Perhaps he was hoping to steer a middle road in the growing hostility between Emperor Charles V and the Protestant Schmalkaldic League.

Early in 1542 the noted Protestant Martin Bucer was invited by Herman of Wied to Cologne to discuss religious issues with him and his advisor, John Gropper. In December 1542 Bucer returned and began a series of sermons at Bonn. Immediately his preaching was resisted by the cathedral chapter, the university, and the city council of Cologne. Despite this resistance Wied threw his support to Bucer's efforts in cooperation with Philip Melanchthon to prepare a new religious ordinance. The core of opposition to Wied centered on the city council of Cologne, which was motivated by its traditionally strong Catholic sentiments and the fear that if Cologne became Protestant, it would lose its imperial charter as a free city of the Empire. The estates of the electorate, on the other hand, sided with Wied.

Pope Paul II encouraged Catholic opposition, and, more importantly, Emperor Charles V actively intervened in the matter. He invoked the law of the Empire against further reform moves in Cologne and in May 1545 visited the city. Petitions from Wied and the estates were ignored until the calling of an imperial diet. Charles V warned Herman that his electoral power was dependent upon his holding of his religious office. Herman of Wied still refused. He believed that his estates would continue to support him and that he could rely upon the Schmalkaldic League's promises to intervene should force be used against him.

Charles V acted quickly. He declared that the demands of the estates in the electorate were invalid and the league backed down at the diet of Regensburg in the face of the emperor's political strength. Wied's fate was sealed shortly after. In April 1546 he was suspended from office and on July 3, 1546, formally deposed and excommunicated. On February 25, 1547, Herman of Wied resigned his office and retired to his family estates. Cologne was securely back in Catholic hands.

Like his predecessor, Herman of Wied, Gebhard Truchsess of Waldburg, archbishop of Cologne from 1577 to 1583, nearly brought the archbishopric to the brink of disaster. His conversion to the Protestant faith in 1583 resulted in a bitter conflict, the Cologne crisis of 1583, better known as the Cologne war. When elected as archbishop in 1577, Gebhard appeared to be a solid Catholic candidate for that position. The papacy would have preferred the nomination of Ernest of Bavaria but was nevertheless initially satisfied with Gebhard's behavior. Soon it became apparent that Truchsess was not interested in furthering Catholic fortunes in Cologne. His life was filled with wordly pleasures, especially his love affair with Countess Agnes of Mansfeld. The situation worsened in December 1582 when Gebhard publicly announced that he would permit freedom of conscience in Cologne and embraced the Protestant faith. On February 2, 1583, he married Agnes of Mansfeld.

Although there is no doubt about the legality of Truchsess' conversion, the fact that he refused to step down from his episcopal office was a violation of the ecclesiastical reservation of the Peace of Augsburg. Urged by his Protestant friends, such as Count Adolph of Neuenahr, Adolph of Solms, and John of Nassau, Gebhard believed that he could find support among other Protestant princes to uphold his rash move. His chances were meager. Within the archbishopric, the city council of Cologne, the university, the cathedral chapter, and the estates were united in opposition to him. The papacy under Pope Gregory XIII acted with speed; on March 22, 1583, after a secret session Gebhard was formally deposed from office. The papacy was also instrumental in the nomination of Truchsess' successor, Ernest of Bavaria, in June 1583.

The struggle did not end with Ernest's election. Although the support from major Protestant princes, such as Duke Augustus of Saxony, was not forthcoming, Gebhard did have help from Elector Louis VI of the Palatinate, Count John Casimir of the Palatine, the counts of Wetterau, and a few cities. After a few months of war, Truchsess' cause collapsed, and he was forced to flee to the Netherlands in 1584.

The final result of the second Cologne crisis was the involvement of Bavarian political power in this area of the Empire. Papal policy had envisioned that by committing Bavarian power to the defense of the German lower Rhine in cooperation with the Spanish fight in the Netherlands, Catholicism might be restored in these important territories of northwestern Germany. The house of Wittelsbach also gained significant political prestige through the control of these lands.

Works About: A. Franzen, *Bischof und Reformation* (Münster, 1971); Joseph Hansen, ed., *Der Kämpf um Köln, 1576–1584* (Berlin, 1892); Hermann Kelm, "Zum Begriff 'Kölner Reformation,'" *Monatschefte für Evangelische Kirchengesch, des Rheinlandes* 20–21 (1971–1972); Franz Lau and Ernst Bitzer, *Hist. of the Reformation in Germany,* tr. B. A. Hardy (London, 1969); Max Lossen, *Der Kölnische Krieg, 1565–1586,* 2 vols. (Munich and Gotha, 1882, 1897); C. Varrentrapp, *Hermann von Wied und sein Reformationsversuch in Köln* (Cologne, 1878).   *C. T. Eby*

See AUGSBURG, RELIGIOUS PEACE OF; BUCER; COLOGNE: HERMAN V.

COMMON PENNY *(gemeiner Pfennig),* a graduated tax levied on all adult subjects of the Empire, male and female fifteen years of age and older, was based on their individual worth. *Common Penny* generally referred to any head tax during the fifteenth and early sixteenth centuries, but it specifically denoted that tax passed at the diet of Worms in 1495 and lasting until 1499. The extent of its success has been variously interpreted, and it constitutes an important source of investigation today.

The Common Penny was part of Maximilian's attempted constitutional reform of the Empire. Proceeds from this tax—the only direct, national tax paid to the Empire by subjects—were to finance the contemporaneously created Imperial Chamber Court and to offset expenditures for military campaigns. A central treasury was created at Frankfurt am Main. Like most other taxes within the Empire, collection of this one was difficult, and it was soon discontinued.

Works About: Steven W. Rowan, "The Common Penny (1495–99) as a Source of German Social and Demographic Hist.," *CEH* 10(1977): 148–64. Karl Zeumer, ed., *Quel zur Gesch. der dtsch. Reichsverfassung im Mittelalter,* 2d ed. (Tübingen, 1913), 2:294–96.   *P. N. Bebb*

See IMPERIAL CAMERAL COURT; MAXIMILIAN I.

CONCILIARISM profoundly affected the Western church, particularly during the fourteenth and fifteenth centuries. Its principles also touched the political arena and constituted an essential background for later constitutional developments. Conciliar thought held that the council, rather than the pope, is the supreme authority within the Church. This assertion was based on the conviction that authority is ultimately inherent in the whole community of believers. The community exercises that authority through a properly constituted representative assembly, the general council. Every member of the Church, including the pope, is subject to the authority of the whole and therefore to the authority of its representative, the council. While these basic themes were generally affirmed, there is a great deal of diversity among the various conciliar thinkers as they explicated and interpreted them. A variety of opinions persisted concerning the precise nature and extent of conciliar and papal power. Conciliarism therefore consists of a number of related but certainly not uniform theories.

As Brian Tierney has so ably demonstrated, the foundations of conciliar ideas must be sought in the canonist literature of the twelfth and thirteenth centuries. Although papal monarchy was the dominant tradition within canon law, Hostiensis and Zabarella, for example, proposed a corporation theory of ecclesiastical government. This theory, as well as opinions expressed by Huguccio and others concerning the feasibility of deposing a heretical pope, serve as fertile background for later conciliar thought.

The ruminations of the canonists were essentially theoretical. It was not until the volatile fourteenth and fifteenth centuries that conciliar ideas took on practical significance and were explicated fully. The persistent conflicts between Church and state, continuing papal centralization of power within the Church and, finally, the Great Schism (1378–1417) gave impetus and prominence to conciliarism. The centers of conciliar thought were the court of Emperor Louis of Bavaria (1282–1347) and the University of Paris.

In the early years of the fourteenth century, John of Paris argued that the pope is not lord *(dominus)* of the Church but rather its servant and steward *(dispensator)*. He receives his jurisdictional powers from the community when he is elected to his office. The general council, representing the whole Church, is above the pope and has power to depose him if he fails to fulfill the responsibilities of his office. The most radical explicator of the conciliar position was a revolutionary political theorist, Marsiglio of Padua, who enjoyed the protection and support of Emperor Louis IV. In his *Defensor pacis* (1324) he asserted that the legislator must be sovereign. The legislator is the people. The ruler can be appointed, corrected, and even deposed by the legislator. Thus he is clearly subordinate to the will of the people. Applying these basic principles to the Church, Marsiglio maintained that the Church consists of all the faithful and that the general council, which best represents them, is the supreme authority in matters of faith. The papacy is clearly subservient to the council, which can elect and depose a pope.

After 1378 the urgency with which conciliar ideas were articulated became more pronounced, though those ideas were no more revolutionary. During the Great Schism, two and finally three popes simultaneously claimed to be the earthly head of Christendom. The Church faced a crisis, and a solution had to be found. The conciliarists proposed such a solution. They maintained that a general council could resolve the schism. However, they were faced with a legal dilemma. According to canon law, only the pope could convene a legitimate council. In his *Epistola concordiae* (1380) Conrad of Gelnhausen cited the Aristotelian principle of equity *(epieikeia)* as a justification for circumventing canon law. Noting that necessity and justice may require going beyond the letter of the law, Conrad maintained that the cardinals or the emperor could call a council. William of Occam, Henry of Langenstein, John Gerson, Peter d'Ailly, Dietrich of Nieheim, and Nicholas of Cusa were other leading proponents of conciliarism.

Through the efforts of these individuals and the ultimate cooperation of the cardinals and the secular leaders of Europe, the schism was resolved at the Council of Constance. The three rival popes either abdicated or were deposed, and Martin V was elected pope in November 1417. The council also adopted a moderate statement of the conciliar position in the decree *Haec sancta* (1415) and stipulated regular meetings of a general council in the decree *Frequens* (1417).

It appeared that conciliarism had won the day. However, Martin V and his successors refused to accept conciliar claims of superiority. A prolonged struggle resulted from which the papacy emerged victorious. In 1460 Pope Pius II, a former conciliarist, issued the bull *Execrabilis,* which condemned the conciliar position.

The papal victory was achieved with the support of the secular princes who were the ultimate beneficiaries of the struggle between papacy and council. A number of secular leaders, including Emperor Louis of Bavaria and Philip IV of France, had tolerated conciliar thinkers and had employed conciliar ideas in their conflicts with the papacy. Later the majority, including the Emperor Sigismund, had promoted conciliar efforts to end the schism. The papacy argued, however, that the basic principles of authority and government articulated by the conciliar thinkers could readily be applied to the secular sphere. Theories of popular sovereignty could be addressed against secular monarchy, as well as papal monarchy. While formulating such arguments, the papacy also agreed to surrender more and more control over the Church in its territories to the princes in return for their support of papal monarchy. As a result, the secular leaders abandoned the conciliar movement during the first half of the fifteenth century, although the full impact of the issues raised by conciliarism was not felt within the political sphere until the constitutional developments of the seventeenth and eighteenth centuries. When the call for a council was resurrected by a prince or an emperor after 1450, it was generally employed as a political tool to extract further concessions from the papacy. Vestiges of conciliar thought have continued to surface and to exercise some influence, but the basic goals of conciliarism have not been achieved within the Church. Its principles of sovereignty and government were more fully implemented in the political context, though conciliarism cannot be given primary credit for this development.

Works About: Remigius Bäumer, ed., *Die Entwicklung des Konziliarismus* (Darmstadt, 1976); Antony Black, *Monarchy and Community* (Cambridge, 1970); E. F. Jacob, *Essays in the Conciliar Epoch,* rev. ed. (Notre Dame, Ind., 1963); Francis Oakley, *Council over Pope?* (New York, 1969); P. E. Sigmund, *Nicholas of Cusa and Medieval Political Thought* (Cambridge, Mass., 1963); and Brian Tierney, *Foundations of Conciliar Theory* (Cambridge, 1955).   *K. K. Hendel*

See LOUIS IV; MARSIGLIO OF PADUA; NICHOLAS OF CUSA; PIUS II; SIGISMUND.

CONCORDAT OF WORMS is the name given to the agreement reached in 1122 between Pope Calixtus II and Emperor Henry V which put an end to the investiture controversy that had begun in 1075. The investiture controversy was essentially a dispute between the papacy and the emperors as to the respective rights of each in the selection and installation of bishops and abbots in the Empire. The difficulty was created as a result of the dual role that had come to be expected of such churchmen. By definition, they clearly had spiritual functions to perform, and since at least the days of Otto I, 962–973, they also had had numerous administrative and bureaucratic functions to perform for the imperial government since the German kings' only hope of controlling the turbulent German nobility and the powerful particularist dukes was by allying closely with the German Church. Clearly both emperor and pope had an important stake in determining who would hold the position of bishops and abbots within the Empire.

The Concordat of Worms was basically a compromise agreement, as neither side had proven capable over the previous fifty years of implementing completely its wishes. By the terms of the concordat, the emperor guaranteed free election of bishops and abbots by their respective clergy or monks and surrendered his claim to be able to invest them with the ring and staff—the symbols of their spiritual office—at their installation. Previously the emperor had given the ring and staff to a prelate in a feudal ceremony when he accepted him as a vassal, thus granting him control over the lands and endowments associated with the position. The terms of the agreement still left the emperor with considerable powers over Church matters in Germany. He was permitted to be present at all elections of bishops and abbots and retained the right to invest the elected candidate as a vassal and confer upon him his lay rights and obligations that came with the land and endowments associated with the ecclesiastical post. Moreover the emperor could intervene directly in disputed elections, not a negligible factor since there was no general consensus that a majority constituted election and there was a longstanding custom of preference being given to the sounder of the candidates. Thus only in a virtually unanimous election did the emperor not have a voice. What was more, German bishops and abbots could not be consecrated until the emperor had received their homage and fealty as vassals, a fact that effectively gave him a veto power over an elected candidate since he could refuse to accept a man as a vassal. In Burgundy and Italy, the emperor received the man's homage after he was consecrated; this situation gave him less control over the election of a candidate but was of little consequence since the emperor's power was already relatively limited in those areas because of other factors.

The Concordat of Worms was essentially a compromise victory for the papacy, which, over the long term, was able to undermine the emperor's control of the German Church. Nonetheless in the hands of a powerful sovereign such as Frederick Barbarossa, the powers remaining to the emperor could be formidable if exercised to their legal limit. Weaker kings, however, lost considerable ground. The eventual collapse of the alliance between the German monarchy and the Church had serious repercussions, for the royal power was slowly eroded, and the king became more isolated and increasingly at the mercy of the dukes and powerful nobles.

The Concordat of Worms took the form of an imperial diploma granted to God and the pope by the emperor, and a papal bull granted to the emperor by the pope.

Works: W. Fritz, ed., *Quel. zum Wormser Konkordat* (Berlin, 1955). **Works About:** A. Hofmeister, "Das Wormser Konkordat: Zum Streit um seine Bedeutung," *Forsch. und Versuche zur Gesch. des Mittelalters und der Neuzeit: Festschrift Dietrich Schäfer* (Jena, 1915); pp. 64–148; *MGH Const.*, 1.1:159–61; Ian S. Robinson, *Authority and Resistance in the Investiture Contest* (New York, 1968).   *D. S. Devlin*

See FREDERICK I; HENRY V; INVESTITURE CONTROVERSY.

CONRAD OF FRANCONIA(?–918) was king of East Frankland from 911 to 918. When Louis the Child, last Carolingian king of the East Franks, died in 911 the German dukes were presented with the problem of electing a non-Carolingian king. The dukes had gained great independence during the previous half-century and were torn between their desire for a weak king who would not interfere in their duchies and the need for unified leadership against the Magyar invaders. The Church wanted a strong king, feeling that it would be much easier to deal with one monarch than with several dukes. Finally the desire for independence overcame the influence of the Church and the need for a strong leader to repel the Magyars. The weakest duke, Conrad of Franconia, was elected by the nobles of Franconia and Saxony assembled at Forcheim on November 10, 911. Bavaria and Swabia accepted the choice. The Lotharingian nobles refused to accept a non-Carolingian king and yielded their duchy to France and their homage to another Carolingian, Charles the Simple. The Church, despite its desire for a strong king, gave its support to Conrad.

Most of Conrad's short reign was spent dealing with rebellions in Saxony, Bavaria, and Swabia and in attempts to recapture the duchy of Lotharingia. His only real support came from the nobles of Franconia and the Church.

Conrad's difficulties in Saxony began in 912 when Henry, son of Otto, became duke upon his father's death. Henry refused to bow before Church or crown and was soon involved in a quarrel with Hatto, archbishop of Mainz and former chief counselor of Louis the Child. Conrad intervened and in 915 Henry rebelled against Conrad. According to the contemporary accounts of Widukind, the royal army led by Conrad's brother Eberhard marched into Saxony and was defeated by the Saxons.

Duke Arnulf of Bavaria was equally independent of his bishops and the king. Conrad marched into Bavaria in 914, and in 916 the royal army laid seige to Arnulf's capital at Regensburg. When they captured and looted the city, Arnulf was forced to seek refuge among his Hungarian enemies.

The situation in Swabia though basically similar was complicated by a power struggle between the layman Burchard I and Salamo III, bishop of Constance. When Burchard I died in 911, his successor, Erchanger, continued the struggle. In 914 he captured and imprisoned the bishop. This act offended the crown, which leaned heavily on episcopal support and involved Conrad in the local power struggle. Erchanger eventually regained the dignity of duke and remained opposed to the king.

By 916 the forces of disintegration had become so strong that the bishops of Germany attempted to bring the independent heads of the duchies to loyalty and submission, calling an assembly at Hohenatcheim in Swabia. The bishops ordered many of the priests and abbots of their diocese to attend, and a papal legate was sent by Pope John X. Henry of Saxony avoided being brought to trial by making a nominal peace with Conrad. Arnulf of Bavaria and Erchanger of Swabia treated the council's acts with contempt. In retaliation Conrad issued a sentence of death against Erchanger, who was arrested and executed in January 917. Arnulf was temporarily driven from his capital of Regensburg. He retaliated by plundering monasteries and dividing the treasure with his liege men, thus gaining the name Arnulf the Bad. Despite Conrad's campaign against him in 918, Arnulf returned to his capital and continued to hold his position as duke.

When Conrad died in December 918, Germany was in a state of anarchy. The Hungarian assaults continued year after year, Lotharingia was lost, and Saxony, Bavaria, and Swabia were in a state of almost constant rebellion against the crown. Before his death, Conrad ordered his brother Eberhard to convey the crown to Henry, duke of Saxony, indicating his realization that only a strong king could save the German kingdom.

Works About: G. Barraclough, *The Crucible of Europe* (Berkeley, 1976); J. F. Böhmer and E. Mühlbacher, *Regesta Imperii I*, ed. C. Bruhl and H. H. Kaminsky (Hildesheim, 1966); E. Duckett, *Death and Life in the Tenth Century* (Ann Arbor, 1967); E Dümmler, *Gesch. des Ostfranken Reiches*

(Darmstadt, 1960); F. L. Ganshof, *Feudalism* (New York, 1964); Widukind, *Res Gestae Saxoni-carum*, ed. G. Waitz, *MGH SS*, 3 (Berlin, 1882).   *D. B. Mapes*

See HENRY I; LOUIS III.

CONRAD II (c. 990–1039), duke of Franconia, from 1024 to 1039 German king, and from 1027 to 1039 Holy Roman emperor, was the founder of the Salian dynasty of emperors. He succeeded Henry II as king and emperor. The Saxon dynasty ended with Henry, and thus it was necessary to choose a successor from among the matrilinial descendants of Henry I. Conrad's primary support for election came from certain segments of the nobility and from the great prelates of Germany, despite strong opposition from the powerful monastic reform party, which claimed that Conrad was unsympathetic to the Cluniac-inspired monastic reform movement then current in Germany.

Conrad's earliest years as monarch were spent in consolidating his position and suppressing rebellions led by his stepson, Ernest of Swabia, the magnates of Lorraine, and the Italians. He succeeded at these tasks by 1027, and having forced northern Italy into submission was crowned emperor both at Milan and Rome. Through war and negotiation, he expanded the borders of the Empire by annexing Lusatia (1031) and Burgundy (1033). He took seriously his title of Holy Roman emperor and king of the Romans, believing that Italy and Rome should be integral parts of the Empire, though the Italian magnates, churchmen, and commercial towns resented any domination by the Germans. The last years of his reign were spent subduing opposition in northern Italy where he took the side of the lesser nobility in a war against the magnates and prelates. He deposed several powerful bishops, restricted the power of the magnates, and made the fiefs of the lower nobility hereditary as a reward for their support. At his death, he left a relatively pacified Italy and Germany.

Conrad was instrumental in the reorientation of the administration of the Empire under the Salian emperors. In Germany, and later in Italy, he intended to favor the lesser nobility against the higher nobility, thus reversing the policy of the Saxon emperors. This policy was, however, later abandoned by his successor when it proved unworkable as a result of the incomplete feudalization of Germany and the consequent social order that made an alliance between monarchy and free nobility feasible elsewhere. Conrad did understand that the greater nobility and prelates were untrustworthy allies, and though the attempted alliance with the free nobility ultimately failed, his policy of replacing ecclesiastics in administrative positions was more successful. He initiated the policy of promoting his serfs to high palace offices and relied increasingly on royal agents in important military and administrative positions. These policies, which brought such officials under more direct royal control than had been the case with their ecclesiastic predecessors, were followed by the later Salian emperors and tended to make the monarchy more independent of the Church. In another break with the policies of his predecessors, Conrad appropriated Church lands and revenues for the crown's use, though in many cases such land and revenue had once belonged to the royal demesne and had been alienated over the previous century. Conrad was one of the more energetic, farsighted, and competent rulers of the medieval Empire, though he could be quite ruthless with prelates and nobility who opposed or blocked his policies. On his death, Conrad left the imperial treasury wealthier than ever before and the power of the emperor at its height.

Works About: *Annales Hildesheimenses,* ed., G. Waitz, *MGH SS* (Berlin, 1878); *Die Urkunden Konrads II.,* ed., H. Bresslau, *MGH Dip.* 4:1–417 (Berlin, 1889); B. Gebhardt, ed., *Handbuch der dtsch. Gesch.* 9th ed. (Stuttgart, 1970), 1:299–307; K. Hampe, *Germany under the Salian and Hohenstaufen Emperors,* tr. R. Bennett (Totowa, N.J., 1973); B. H. Hill, *Medieval Monarchy in Action* (New York, 1972); T. Schieffer, "Heinrich II. und Konrad II.," *Dtsch. Archiv* 8 (1951): 384–437; H. Vogt, *Konrad II. i, Vergleich zu Heinrich II, und Heinrich III.* (Frankfurt am Main, 1957); Wipo, *The Deeds of Conrad II,* tr. T. Mommsen and K. Morrison, in *Imperial Lives and Letters of the Eleventh Century* (New York, 1962).   *D. S. Devlin*

See GISELA; HENRY II; HENRY III.

CONRAD III (c. 1093–1152), duke of Swabia, and from 1138 to 1152 German king, was the founder of the Hohenstaufen dynasty of German rulers. Conrad succeeded to the crown in much the same way as had his immediate predecessor, Lothar, whom Conrad had opposed as antiking from 1127 to 1135. Thus the elective principle again triumphed over heredity and with much the same decentralizing consequences. Lothar's reign had resulted in a vast augmentation of the power of his very capable son-in-law, Henry the Proud, duke of both Saxony and Bavaria. The German nobility and prelates fully realized that they were electing the weaker of the two candidates but very much feared granting the crown to Duke Henry lest he establish a new family dynasty based on the power of the Welfs.

Conrad immediately made the grave mistake—not his only one—of depriving Henry of his two duchies and granting them to others. The result was a bitter civil war, continued after Henry's death by his brother, Welf, and later by his son, Henry the Lion. Conrad thus precipitated the Welf-Hohenstaufen feud, which continued into the next century and eventually spread into Italy where it formed the basis for political antagonism between the various city-states into the Renaissance as the Guelph (Welf)-Ghibelline party alliances.

Conrad, elected by the same faction of powerful ecclesiastics and particularist nobles who had supported Lothar, inherited the same policies as had his predecessor. Not only did dukes like the Welfs oppose the monarchy, but many local nobility as well pursued their own interests in full realization that neither the king nor the higher nobility had the strength or resources to spare to control them. The great prelates exercised increasingly more power as Conrad was even less successful than Lothar in implementing the monarchy's rights over the

Church as guaranteed by the Concordat of Worms, with the general result that the German Church became even more independent of the king. Despite his basically good relationship with the papacy and Church leaders like the head of the Cistercian order, Bernard of Clairvaux, Conrad had so little control in Germany that he dared not venture to Italy for imperial coronation lest his position at home deteriorate completely. He wisely spurned all attempts to enlist him in the Second Crusade sponsored by Bernard and Pope Eugenius III until the former personally convinced him to go to the Holy Land by extracting promises of peaceful behavior from the German nobility while the king was absent from his realm. Conrad's part in the disastrous and largely unsuccessful crusade was insignificant, though he did succeed in forging an alliance with the Byzantine emperor, Manuel I Comnenus, to attempt to dislodge the powerful Norman king, Roger II of Sicily, from southern Italy. His attempts to aid Pope Eugenius and obtain imperial coronation were frustrated by Welf and Henry the Lion, both in the pay of Roger, by the general disorganization in Germany and by the increasing unrest and desire for political independence among the populace of Rome and the northern Italian merchant communes.

Conrad died in 1152, his health broken by the time spent on crusade, predeceased by his eldest son and joint king, Henry. Although energetic and active, Conrad's reign was marked by numerous unsuccessful struggles and thwarted schemes that resulted in a further decline in the power and prestige of the German monarchy, leaving the Empire in a state of disarray. He was a popular monarch, remembered for his kindness and knightly qualities by contemporaries. One of his most important contributions was the appointment as his successor of his nephew, Frederick Barbarossa, who became one of the most competent men ever to rule the Empire.

Works About: W. Bernhardi, *Konrad III.* (Leipzig, 1883); K. Hampe, *Germany under the Salian and Hohenstaufen Emperors,* tr. R. Bennett (Totowa, N.J., 1973); I. Jastrow and G. Winter, *Dtsch. Gesch. im Zeitalter der Hohenstaufen, 1125–1273* (Stuttgart, 1897–1901); Otto of Freising, *The Two Cities,* tr. C. C. Mierow (New York, 1928), and *The Deeds of Frederick Barbarossa,* tr. C. C. Mierow (New York, 1953).   *D. S. Devlin*

See FREDERICK I; HENRY III; HENRY THE LION; LOTHAR II; WELF-WAIBLINGEN CONTROVERSY.

CONRAD IV (1228–1254), Holy Roman emperor from 1250 to 1254, was the son of Frederick II and his second wife, Yolanda (or Isabella) of Brienne. At the age of seven days, Frederick bestowed the kingdom of Jerusalem on the young prince Conrad. Conrad was elected king of the Romans during his father's lifetime and was bequeathed the kingdom of Sicily in his father's will. Despite his impressive inheritance, Conrad's short reign was plagued by three problems: the implacable hatred of the papacy toward the Hohenstaufen, his talented and ambitious illegitimate half-brother Manfred, and the independence of the German princes.

Conrad never exercised any real power over the kingdom of Jerusalem. In 1250 the actual government of Jerusalem was exercised by Louis IX (St. Louis) of France who was still in the East after his Egyptian crusade.

In Germany Conrad's power was limited by the considerable authority Frederick had surrendered to the German princes in order to pursue his Italian goals. One example of the erosion of imperial power in Germany concerned the persistent battles between the nobles and the rising towns and communes. Between 1213 and 1235, Frederick supported the activities of the princes indirectly through tax exemptions to knights and monasteries. When Conrad relaxed the antimunicipal policy of his father, his efforts proved to be too late, inconsistent, and halfhearted. The loyalty of many towns was lost, and they would later bargain with various antikings, such as Henry Raspe and William of Holland.

After restoring order in Germany, Conrad crossed the Alps in January 1251. Conrad's half-brother Manfred, an illegitimate favorite of Frederick II, was already active in southern Italy. In Frederick's will Manfred, age eighteen at the time, was given a great appanage in southern Italy and appointed *balio*, or governor, of all Italy until Conrad came and set up his own administration. He was also put in succession for the kingdom of Sicily if the legitimate line should die out. In the autumn of 1251, Manfred suppressed a revolt of the nobility and cities of the Terra di Lavoro. Conrad's growing suspicion of Manfred's ambition was confirmed when he attempted to control Sicily by sending an uncle, Galvano Lancia, to replace Conrad's loyal governor, Peter Ruffo, in southern Italy. This was unsuccessful when Peter Ruffo was confirmed in 1252 as vicar of Sicily and Calabria. Most of 1252 and 1253 were spent dealing with rebellions in Terra di Lavoro and Capua and Naples.

The biggest obstacle Conrad found in trying to establish his power in Italy was the constant opposition of the papacy. The animosity between the papacy and the Empire was an old problem involving questions of a theoretical nature, in addition to the very real problem of political control of central Italy. The papacy claimed that political authority descended from God; since the pope was the vicar of Christ on earth, this power resided in the papal office, to be granted at the discretion of the pope. Imperial claims rested on a dualistic theory of authority in which the spiritual and temporal spheres were separate, with the power of the papacy restricted to spiritual matters. These conflicting ideas produced a flood of literature on the nature of political power and authority in the eleventh and twelfth centuries.

On a temporal level, the papacy feared encirclement. If Conrad or any other German emperor could effectively control both Germany and Italy, the papacy would be forced to submit to imperial control. The positions of both Conrad and the papacy were further complicated by local Italian conditions. The cities of northern Italy were preoccupied with quarrels among themselves and lent little aid to either the papal or the imperial cause. The city of Rome had formed itself into a commune and elected Brancaleone degli Andalo, a Bolognese lawyer with Ghibelline sympathies, as a temporary head of state.

Conrad, who needed papal neutrality in order to keep control of Germany, began negotiations with the pope. These negotiations were doomed to fail because of papal demands that Conrad give up Sicily. Conrad would not and could not. Innocent IV then considered offering the throne to Conrad's half-brother Henry but nothing came of it except the rumor, encouraged by the pope in 1253, that Conrad poisoned Henry at age eighteen. By January 1254 Conrad publicly accused the pope of usurpation and heresy, and in February Innocent responded by excommunicating Conrad. The pope then began to preach a new crusade against the Hohenstaufen. Like previous attempts to launch crusades against Christian monarchs, this one was rejected by the kings of Europe. The French queen regent, Blanche, went so far as to threaten to confiscate the lands of anyone who responded to the call, and in Germany papal agents were openly derided.

Conrad prepared for war. His army was in good condition, and his treasury was full because of heavy taxation in his Italian lands. His plans to march north were cut short when he died on May 21, 1254, at Lavello on the borders of Apulia at the age of twenty-six. Leaving only a two-year-old-son, Conradin, in Germany, Conrad IV's death meant the end of the Hohenstaufen dynasty.

Works About: G. Barraclough, *The Origins of Modern Germany* (New York, 1946); O. H. Becker, *Kaisertum, dtsch. Königswahl und Legitimitatsprinzip* (Frankfurt, 1975); Karl Hampe, *Germany under the Salian and Hohenstaufen Emperors,* tr. Ralph Bennett (Totawa, N.J. 1973); Ernst Kantorowicz, *Frederick the Second,* tr. E. O. Lorimer (New York, 1957); *MGH, Constitutiones et acta publica imperatorum et regnum, Tom. II (1198–1272),* ed. L. Weiland (Hanover, 1896). S. Runciman, *The Sicilian Vespers* (Baltimore, 1960); D. M. Smith, *Medieval Sicily, 800–1713* (New York, 1968).   *D. B. Mapes*

See FREDERICK II, INTERREGNUM.

CRANACH, LUCAS, THE ELDER (1472–1553), painter and engraver, was born at Kronach in northern Franconia. Lucas learned the art of engraving from his father. Active in Vienna from 1500 to 1503, he was appointed court painter by Frederick the Wise of Saxony in 1505. There he became a city councillor and a friend of Martin Luther and Philip Melanchthon. Cranach lent his artistic talents to the Reformation by illustrating and publishing a number of evangelical writings. His son, Lucas the Younger (1515–1586), was also a fine painter.

Works About: Carl C. Christensen, *Art and the Reformation in Germany* (Athens, Ohio, 1979); Max J. Friedländer and Jakob Rosenberg, *The Paintings of Lucas Cranach* (Ithaca, 1978). Gisela Noehles and Karl Noehles, "Cranach," *EWA,* 4:64–70; Christian Schuchardt, *Lucas Cranach des Älteren Leben und Werke,* 3 vols. (Leipzig, 1851–1871); Hildegard Zimmermann, *Lucas Cranach d. A.* (Halle, 1929).   *J. W. Zophy*

See FREDERICK III, THE WISE; LUTHER; MELANCHTHON.

CUSPINIAN, JOHN (1473–1529), German humanist and diplomat, was born in Schweinfurt to an upper-middle-class family. He studied at Leipzig, Würzburg, and Vienna, where, in 1493, he was crowned poet laureate by Emperor

Maximilian I. He was chosen rector of the University of Vienna in 1500, and after the death of his friend Conrad Celtis in 1508, he took over the latter's professorial chair of poetry and rhetoric. Cuspinian's activity demonstrates well two of the major preoccupations of German humanists; diplomacy and scholarship. He served Maximilian I as a diplomat and was especially successful in the succession treaty concluded at Vienna in 1515 between the Habsburgs and Jagiellos. In 1526, after the Battle of Mohács, he made a stirring appeal to the German princes to rescue the Empire and Christendom from the Turks.

Possessing great wealth, Cuspinian used his position as head of the Viennese humanist circle to spread humanistic ideas through a voluminous correspondence and to discover ancient manuscripts. He edited the two great historical works of Otto of Freising. In addition to his poems and orations, he also wrote histories of the Roman consuls and the Roman, Greek, and Turkish, emperors, which were published after his death. His historical geography of lower Austria was not finished in his lifetime.

Cuspinian is significant for the diffusion of humanism in southeastern Europe. The knowledge of eastern Europe and the Byzantine area that he provided for the Germans aided them in their struggles with the Turks.

Works By: H. Ankwitz von Kleehoven, ed., *Johannes Cuspinianus Briefwechsel* (Munich, 1933).
Works About: H. A. von Kleehoven, *Der Wiener Humanist Joh. Cuspinian* (Graz, 1959).   *J. J. Spielvogel*

See CELTIS; HUMANISM; MAXIMILIAN I; OTTO OF FREISING.

d

DANTE ALIGHIERI (1265–1321), foremost Italian poet and political theorist, was born in Florence of a bourgeois family of ancient and noble heritage. Little is known of his childhood. From his works we know that his education was much influenced by earlier contemporaries, particularly Brunetto Latini, the poetic encyclopedist and statesman, Guido Guinizelli, the Bolognese jurist and poet, and Dante's "first friend," Guido Cavalcanti, with whom he exchanged ideas and examples of philosophical love poetry. He had firm friendships with the poets Forese Donati (with whom he exchanged scurrilous verse), Lapo Gianni, and Gianni Alfani, as well as acquaintance with masters of other arts, such as Giotto, Odorisi di Gubbio, Casella, Ciacco, and Capocchio. Provençal poetry, particularly the verses of Arnaut Daniel, also influenced him. Among the classics, Dante studied Aristotle, Virgil, Horace, Ovid, Cicero, Satius, and Boethius along with their medieval commentators and amplifiers. He frequented the religious schools of the Franciscans and Dominicans and read such Church writers as St. Augustine, St. Bernard of Clairvaux, the Victorines, Albert the Great, St. Bonaventura, and St. Thomas Aquinas.

The poet did not divorce himself from the political life of his city; he records taking part in his youth in the Battle of Campaldino against the Aretines on June 11, 1298, where the Tuscan Ghibellines were defeated, and in the same year in the Battle of Caprona where the Pisans surrendered.

In the *Vita nuova (The New Life)* the poet informs us that in his ninth year, he met his guide in love, righteousness, and inspiration, Beatrice, who died in 1290. Early commentators identify her as Bice di Folco Portinari, later the wife of Simone de' Bardi. At the end of this short work, Dante pledges to write of Beatrice "that which had never been written of any woman," a promise usually taken as fulfilled in his *Commedia (Divine Comedy)*.

From the poet's marriage to Gemma di Manetto Donati, there issued at least three children, two sons, Jacopo and Pietro, both of whom later wrote commentaries on their father's *Commedia,* and a daughter, Antonia, who later became a nun and assumed the religious name of Suora Beatrice. A document in Lucca from 1308 refers possibly to a third son, Giovanni. In 1293 the Florentine Priors (the governmental system that had ruled since 1282), under the influence of Giano della Bella, had promulgated the Ordinances of Justice, which disenfranchised the males of all magnate families of old wealth and permitted active citizenship only to members of the guilds. In consequence, a violent feud split the Guelph party: one side, later designated the Whites, headed by the rich merchant Vieri de' Cerchi, and the other, later the Blacks, led by the hotheaded

Corso Donati. Taking advantage of a 1295 mitigation of the ordinances that permitted the lower nobility to gain eligibility to hold office through membership in a guild, Dante enrolled, if only nominally, in the greater guild of physicians and apothecaries. From November 1295 until April 1296, the poet belonged to the special Council of the Captain of the people. In December 1295 he was among those consulted concerning the election of priors, and from May to September 1296 he sat on the Council of One Hundred. Although the minutes of city meetings from July 1298 until February 1301 are not extant, we know that Dante took an active part in the government during the White ascendancy until 1301.

On May 7, 1300, the commune sent the poet as ambassador to San Gimignano with a triple mission: to consolidate the Tuscan Guelphs in support of the pope's war in Romagna against the Aldobrandeschi of Santa Fiora, to warn against the pope's domination of the Guelph league, and to invite the San Gimignesi to send representatives to elect a new Guelph captain. Dante achieved his highest office in 1300 when he was nominated prior for the term between June 15 and August 15. His success ended with the renewal of civil strife. On June 23, the eve of St. John's Day, certain Black magnates attacked the White consuls of the guilds as they marched in procession to make traditional offerings to the patron saint of Florence. Pope Boniface VIII, requested to act as mediator between the two rival groups, first sent Cardinal Matteo d'Aquasparta under the guise of peacemaker but with the secret mission of aiding the Black-Donati faction. The cardinal arrived in Florence on June 27 just as Dante took office as prior. The prelate failed in his mission, but the priors banished the leaders of the warring factions in opposite directions from the city: the Blacks to Città della Pieve, and the Whites, including Dante's"first friend," Guido Cavalcanti, to Sarzana in Lunigiana. Dante was unavoidably responsible for his friend's death for Guido contracted malaria there and died soon upon his return to Florence in 1300. Boniface then requested Charles of Valois, brother of Philip IV of France, to invade Tuscany. Dante, seeing the future danger, urged the Council of One Hundred to recall Florentine troops engaged in the Aldobrandeschi campaign in Maremma. The poet's opposition to the pope gained no support.

On All Saints' Day (November 1), 1301, Charles of Valois arrived at the gates of Florence ostensibly as pacifier; the listless, indecisive Whites permitted him entrance. At nightfall four days later, the banished Black leader, Corso Donati, with several cohorts forced his way into the city. With tacit support from Charles and guarantees from the pope, Corso vindictively plundered his wealthy enemies and freed prisoners from the jails. The triumphant Blacks appointed a new *podestà*, Cante de' Gabrielli of Gubbio, under whose authority were banished six hundred Whites. According to Dino Compagni and Leonardo Bruni, Dante had left the city earlier in September on an embassy to soothe the wrath of the pope. On January 27, 1302 (new style), the poet and four of his party were charged in absentia before Cante with trumped-up charges of barratry and peculation in office and were fined five thousand *lire picciole*. Were the fines to remain unpaid for three days, the property of those found guilty was to be confiscated and razed; were they paid, the condemned were to be exiled for two years from Tuscany and forever vanished from holding public office. Dante's fine went unpaid, and on March 10, the poet and fourteen others were condemned to be burned alive; the death sentence was reiterated in September 1311 and in Ocotber 1315.

The exiled Dante joined the disaffected Whites and Florentine Ghibellines in Siena. He was probably at Forlì in Romagna in 1303. Sometime during this period, disgusted with his fellow exiles' desultory attempts to gain entrance into Florence by force, Dante broke with them "to make a party for himself." In the same year, either as White ambassador or merely to take refuge, the poet journeyed to the head of the Ghibelline league in northern Italy, Bartolomeo della Scala, lord of Verona. Dante henceforth traveled alone. He certainly spent some time with Count Guido Salvatico in the Casentino and with Uguccione in the castle of Faggiuola in the Urbino hills. Between 1304 and 1306 he was in Bologna, where he may have set plans for the philosophical work, the *Convivio (The Banquet)* and his treatise on language, the *De vulgari eloquenta* (On the Vernacular). After the White Guelph expulsion from Bologna in 1306, he is recorded as being in Padua on August 27. On October 6, 1306, the poet mediated peace between his current benefactor, Marchese Franceschino Malaspina, and the bishop of Luni at Sarzana in Lunigiana. From here Dante may have journeyed to Lucca and whence returned to Casentino. Dante's hopes for a return to Florence rose when Corso Donati allied himself with Uguccione della Faggiuola; but the poet was disappointed again when Corso's tempestuous nature turned even the Blacks against their former hero, forcing him to flee and causing his death by their Catalan mercenaries in 1308.

In the same year Henry of Luxembourg became the Holy Roman emperor, Henry VII. Dante's enthusiastic vision of him as the messiah king is preserved in his *Epistola (Letters)* V of 1310 to all the princes and peoples of Italy proclaiming Henry as "the comfort of nations." In another missive, *Epistola* VI, dated March 31, 1311, from Casentino, Dante rebuked the "most iniquitous Florentines" for their obstinacy in resisting the emperor. His countrymen retaliated by excluding him from the amnesty of September 3, 1311. A further letter of April 17, 1311, *Epistola* VII, scolded the emperor himself for remaining in Lombardy at the seige of Cremona instead of descending to the Arno. Henry passed through Genoa and South through Pisa to be crowned in the Church of St. John the Lateran on June 20, 1312, since the Vatican was being held by the emperor's enemy, King Robert of Naples. The emperor reached Florence on September 19 but instead of attacking the city returned to Pisa in November, preparing to conquer the kingdom of Naples in the coming year. Henry died suddenly, however, on August 12, 1313, at the monastery of Buonconvento, and Dante's faith in the renewal of the Empire was crushed.

Here again the progress of Dante's wanderings is unclear. He may have stayed at Gubbio with Bosone de' Rafaelli and later at Lucca with Uguccione della

Faggiuola who had recently conquered that city, only to lose it again in 1315. In this year the Florentines offered the poet the opportunity of reentering their city, but their price was exorbitant: Dante would have had to pay a steep fine and walk in sackcloth to the baptistry of San Giovanni to do penance. We learn from his *Epistola* IX that Dante scornfully rejected the ignominy and retired to the protection of Can Grande della Scala, the Ghibelline leader and ruler of Verona. Here on January 20, 1320, Dante delivered his philosophical discourse, *De situ et forma aque et terre (Questions on the Height and Form of Water and Earth)*. In 1320, perhaps after the defeat of Can Grande in Padua, Dante finally retired to the protection of Guido da Polenta of Ravenna. Here joined by his children, the poet wrote two Latin eclogues to Dante del Virgilio, who invited him to be crowned as poet in Bologna. In Ravenna Dante finished his masterpiece, the *Commedia*, afterward styled as "divine," and performed embassies for his protector. The poet's last mission was a delicate and unsuccessful embassy to Venice in consequence of which the Venetians refused him return sea passage and thus condemned him to journey through malaria-infested lagoons of the northern Adriatic. Probably as a result of contracting that disease, Dante died in Ravenna on September 14, 1321.

Dante's chief political text, apart from the fragmentary *Convivio* (especially IV, iv–ix) and the political philosophy pervading the *Commedia*, is his completed Latin treatise in three books, the *De Monarchia (On Monarchy)*, most probably written around 1310–1313, though some date it at 1317. Championing the German imperial cause, the poet affirms that the government of universal empire is essential for mankind's well-being; the supreme authority of the sole Holy Roman emperor derives from the divinely ordained supremacy of the Roman people as world rulers; the emperor's power is drawn directly from God himself and not indirectly from the Church. Dante follows the conviction set forth in the *Convivio* that a sole temporal ruler owning everything would covet nothing and thus would initiate a state of peace and pure justice. Since man's nature is dual, mortal and immortal, he must have two rulers to fulfill his potential: as the emperor guides the world to earthly happiness, the pope guides man to the blessedness of the world to come. These two discrete goals of temporal and eternal happiness find hierarchical tempering only in the last lines of Dante's treatise: the emperor must honor the pope as a firstborn son honors his father. Dante follows these views with some modifications in the *Commedia*.

Works By: Paolo Milano, ed., *The Portable Dante* (New York, 1968); *Codice diplomatico dantesco*, ed. Renato Piattoli (Florence, 1950); *La Commedia secondo l'antica vulgata*, ed. Giorgio Petrocchi, 4 vols. (Milan, 1966–1967); *The Divine Comedy*, tr. Charles S. Singleton, 6 vols. (Princeton, N.J., 1970–1975); *Le Opere di Dante: Testo critico della Società Dantesca Italiana*, 2d ed. (Florence, 1960). **Works About:** Charles T. Davis, *Dante and the Idea of Rome* (Oxford, 1957); Alessandro Passerin d'Entreves, *Dante as a Political Thinker* (Oxford, 1952); Francesco Ercole, *Il pensiero politico di Dante*, 2 vols. (Milan, 1927–1928); Etienne Gilson, *Dante and Philosophy*, tr. David Moore (New York, 1963); Hans Kelson, *Die Staatslehre des Dante Alighieri* (Vienna and Leipzig, 1905); Fritz Kern, *Humana civilitas (Staat, Kirche und Kultur): eine Dante-untersuchung* (Leipzig, 1913); Arrigo Solmi, *Il pensiero politicio di Dante: studi storici* (Florence,

1922); Paget Toynbee, *Dante Alighieri: His Life and Works,* ed. Charles S. Singleton (New York, 1965).   *A. K. Cassell*

See HENRY VII; PETRARCH; WELF-WAIBLINGEN CONTROVERSY.

DEFENESTRATION OF PRAGUE (May 23, 1618) marked the beginning of the Bohemian revolt against the Habsburgs that triggered the Thirty Years War. Relations between Bohemia's Protestant nobility and the country's Habsburg rulers had deteriorated steadily before this incident. In an effort to strengthen the Catholic church and its own position in Bohemia, the Austrian government increasingly had curtailed the rights and liberties of Protestants that had been guaranteed by Emperor Rudolf II's *Letter of Majesty* (1609). Tensions between the crown and the nobility reached an almost feverish pitch after Archduke Ferdinand of Styria, nephew of Emperor Matthias, had been accepted as king designate by the Bohemian estates. Ferdinand, a zealous Catholic who had stamped out heresy in his domain, clashed almost immediately with the nobility. Early in 1618, he sought to stop the Protestants from building churches at the towns of Klostergrab and Braunau. On May 23, 1618, about a hundred Protestant noblemen, spurred on by Count Henry Matthias Thurn, appeared at the Hradschin castle, the seat of the Habsburg government in Prague, to protest to the royal governors, William Slavata and Jaroslav Martinitz, both fanatical Catholics. The meeting was stormy. In the ensuing physical scuffle, the two governors and a secretary were thrown out of a window of the royal castle (apparently in deliberate imitation of the defenestration that had started the Hussite revolt two centuries earlier). Miraculously all three survived the fall; only Slavata suffered some bodily injury. The incident was significant, though, for it constituted a coup d'etat against the Habsburgs. The Protestant nobility immediately proceeded to organize a provisional government headed by Wenzel von Ruppa. To protect the new regime, they voted the raising of an army of sixteen thousand men under the command of Thurn. The revolt soon ended with a complete Habsburg victory (Battle of the White Mountain, November 8, 1620). The international conflict triggered by this incident, however, was to continue for three more decades and greatly alter the power balance and map of Europe.

Works About: *Briefe und Akten zur Gesch. des Dreissigjährigen Krieges,* N.F. II: Jan. 1618-Dec. 1620 (Munich, 1966); *Documenta Bohemica Bellum Tricennale Illustrantia* (Prague, 1972), vol. 2; Frank N. Magill, ed., *Great Events from History* (Englewood Cliffs, N.J., 1973), 1:250–53; J. V. Polišenský, *The Thirty Years War* (Berkeley and Los Angeles, 1971), pp. 98–132; Hans Sturmberger, *Aufstand in Böhmen: Der Beginn des Dreissigjährigen Krieges* (Munich, 1959). *Bodo Nischan*

See FERDINAND II; HUS; RUDOLF II; THIRTY YEARS WAR.

DENCK (DENK), HANS c. 1495–1527), was called variously by his contemporaries the Apollo, the abbot, the bishop, and the pope of the Anabaptists. Influenced by humanism, German mysticism, especially the *German Theology,* (author unknown) and the Protestant Reformation, he exercised considerable influence on south German Anabaptism through personal contact with a relatively few Anabaptist leaders and through eleven written confessions, translations, and theological treatises. He is equally well known for having abandoned his Anabaptist position shortly before his death in 1527. Denck was a strong advocate of freedom of the will, and his theology can best be described as spiritualistic. Some call him a forerunner of Unitarianism.

Born in Habach in upper Bavaria, Denck's early career was common for a young humanist. He matriculated at the University of Ingolstadt (1517–1519) spent a year among the humanist circle in Augsburg, and taught for a year in Regensburg. In 1522–1523, he was in Basel, making the acquaintance of the famous humanist Oecolampadius, and earning a living as proofreader and editor for the printers Cratander and Curio. With the recommendation of Oecolampadius, Denck secured a position in Nuremberg in 1523 as headmaster at the school of St. Sebald.

A skilled linguist who was proficient in Latin, Greek, and Hebrew, Denck's sensitive religious character led him into involvement in the theological issues of his day. Seeing potential dangers of legalism and institutionalization in Lutheranism, Denck leaned toward a subjective norm. In Nuremberg, probably influenced by Andreas Bodenstein von Karlstadt and, possibly, Thomas Müntzer, Denck began to develop a concept of continuing revelation through the inner word and a decidedly spiritual interpretation of the sacraments of baptism and Holy Communion. Denck's religious views were discovered by the city council during investigation of a number of religious disturbances in the city. Believing him to be the spiritual leader of a circle of "godless painters" in the city, the council summarily expelled him from Nuremberg in January 1525 without even time to take with him his wife, child, and material possessions.

From Nuremberg, Denck traveled first to Mühlhausen, at the invitation of Müntzer, but had to flee before the Peasants' War. He next went to St. Gall and finally to Augsburg. In Augsburg, he apparently accepted rebaptism at the hands of the Swiss leader Balthasar Hubmaier. At the same time, he seems to have been instrumental in converting Hubmaier from his Zwinglian predestinarian position. Denck also performed his only recorded adult baptism in Augsburg, on the fiery Hans Hut, who went on to become the most dynamic and successful of the Anabaptist evangelists in south Germany. The evidence suggests that Denck helped to mollify Hut's sociorevolutionary tendencies.

When Hubmaier left Augsburg for Nikolsburg, Moravia, Denck became the spokesman for the Augsburg Anabaptist community. He engaged in a disputation with the Lutheran clergy there but left Augsburg before a second scheduled disputation. In November 1526, he disputed with the reformer Martin Bucer in Strasbourg, to be expelled from that city in the following month. During the next year, Denck attempted to resolve growing differences among Anabaptist leaders, presiding over the Martyrs' Synod in Augsburg in August 1527. With the failure of that meeting to unify the Anabaptists, Denck left the city disillusioned with the movement. He then wrote to Oecolampadius, asking permission to stay in Basel. Oecolampadius then asked for, and received, a statement of faith from Denck, which was published as *Hans Denks Widerruf.* In this famous document, Denck abandoned his Anabaptist position, his mysticism and rational spiritualism proving stronger than his Anabaptism. In November 1527, Denck died of the plague, but his influence continued through his written works, the most important being *Von der waren Liebe,* of 1527.

Works By: Walter Fellman, ed., *Hans Denck: Schriften* (Gütersloh, 1956), vols. 6, 24; *Geburtstag Gewidmet* (Leipzig. 1888). **Works About:** George Baring, "Hans Denck und Thomas Müntzer in Nürnberg, 1524," *ARG,* 50:145–81; Austin Patterson Evans, *An Episode in the Struggle for Religious Freedom: The Sectaries of Nürnberg, 1524–1528* (New York, 1924); Jan Kiwiet, "The Life and Theology of Hans Denck, ca. 1500–1527," *MQR* 31(1957):227–59, 32(1958): 3–27; Theodor Kolde, "Hans Denk und die gottlosen Maler von Nürnberg," *Beitrage zurbayerischen Kirchengesch.,* 8 (1902):1–31, 49–72; and "Zum Prozess des Johann Denk und der 'drei gottlosen Maler' von Nürnberg, in *Kirchengesch. Stud.: Hermann Reuter zum 70; Geburtstag Gewidmet* (Leipzig, 1888). *D. M. Hockenbury*

See ANABAPTISM; HUBMAIER; HUT; MUNTZER; NUREMBERG; PEASANTS' WAR.

DIETRICH OF NIEHEIM (1340–1418), late medieval reformer, was the son of a patrician family from Nieheim. After receiving minor orders in the diocese of Paderborn and legal studies in Rome, he spent almost his entire life in the service of the papal curia in Avignon and Rome. After serving as bishop of Verden from 1395 to 1401, he returned to curial activity in Rome and helped to prepare reform proposals for the Council of Constance. He accompanied Pope John XXIII to the Council of Constance, for which he was active as a legal adviser from 1415 to 1417.

Dietrich authored a number of reform and historical works. *De schismate* (1409) is a history of the Great Church Schism after 1378 and contains portraits of the leading figures, many of whom, including popes, Dietrich knew personally. In his *Dialogus* (1410), he proved to be a passionate champion of Church reform. He embraced conciliarism and placed the right to call and lead a council in the hands of the emperor. He also denied the spiritual institution of papal primacy. His writings on German history emphasized the work of Charlemagne and other emperors for the unity and purity of the Church and their crusading activity. In general, his works show a concern for Church reform along conciliar lines and a defense of the medieval imperial tradition. Some historians believe that Maximilian I's idea of universal rule was indirectly dependent on the work of Dietrich of Nieheim.

Works About: Hermann Heimpel, *Dietrich von Nieheim* (Münster 1932) and "Dietrich," *NDB,* 3:691–92. *J. J. Spielvogel*

See CONCILIARISM: MAXIMILIAN I.

DIETS *(Reichstage),* meetings of representatives of the German estates, akin to Parliament in England, evolved from the medieval *curia regis,* or council of the king. By the thirteenth century they contained two houses, electors and greater princes. Their function was to advise and aid the emperor in the administration of the Empire. Occasionally the emperor summoned representatives of the free imperial cities to a diet, although it was not until 1489 that the cities were formally acknowledged as a regular part of the organ; even then, however, it was not until the late sixteenth century and, subsequently, the Peace of Westphalia, that the two upper houses recognized the cities' vote as coequal. After 1489 diets contained three colleges or curiae, known as imperial estates *(Reichsstände):* (1) the six electors (the king of Bohemia generally attended only the election of a new emperor); (2) the princes, which also included prelates, counts, and lords; and (3) representatives of the free imperial cities. Theoretically these three houses acted as a representative of the German nation. In practice, they were interest groups opposed to each other and often divided internally.

The Golden Bull of 1356 empowered the archbishop of Mainz as archchancellor of the Empire to summon the imperial estates to the diet. Originally only the emperor could call a diet, but by the time of Charles V (1519–1556) the emperor needed the electors' consent. After the diet opened the imperial proposition was read, which contained the subjects to be debated by the estates. In most cases each curia consulted and voted separately on these points, although there were rare cases of intercurial cooperation. If the estates reached agreement, the archchancellor transmitted the advice to the emperor or his representative, who had the right to accept or reject such counsel; by the eighteenth century, however, this proviso had become a formality. When the diet finished its business—which, depending upon the inclination of the archchancellor, might deviate from the proposition or supplement it—its conclusions and the emperor's assent appeared in the form of a recess *(Abschied* or *Reichsabschied).* The recess, preparation of which belonged to the archchancellor's authority, applied to the Empire as a whole and constituted the normal means of making known imperial legislation. After the conclusion of the diet of 1654, the last recess appeared *(Jüngster Reichsabschied).* Even though a perpetual diet *(Immerwährende Reichstag)* came into existence at Regensburg in 1663 and lasted until the end of the Empire, imperial legislation and decisions now were issued from the emperor's chancellory.

A number of problems exist with respect to the diet, among which are the degree to which it was a formal institution; the extent to which its decisions were binding on absent estates, present estates that held minority views, and recalcitrant inclinations of the emperor and his advisers; and the role it played as a consultative versus a legislative body. Given the scope of these problems, only a few generalizations appear to apply to the diet. First, its competence was never completely established, and this was made manifest by myriad meetings and special committees devised within estates, territories, and the Empire at large. Second, the electoral curia constituted the real power within the diet, at least for most of its history. The Golden Bull provided that each new sovereign had to reaffirm the electors' privileges, and this affirmation maintained their position. It was also the electors' power that resulted in extracting the capitulation of election—promises from the emperor previous to his election, which he was obliged to fulfill—from the time of Charles V on. Finally the Reformation itself highlighted and exacerbated these problems. With the division of the Empire into Catholic and Protestant estates, the Reformation added a new form of particularism into the imperial scene. While the religious Peace of Augsburg (1555) and the Peace of Westphalia (1648) tended to alleviate religious contentions as a whole, confessional preferences remained significant in the diet.

Works About: Hermann Conrad, *Dtsch. Rechtsgeschichte*, 2 vols. (Karlsruhe, 1962–1966); Walter Fürnohr, *Der immerwährende Reichstag zu Regensburg* (Regensburg, 1963); Hist. Kommission bei der Bayerischen Akademie der Wissenschaften, ed., *DRTA, ältere Reihe*, (Munich, 1868–rpr. 1956), vols. 1–17,19,22, *DRTA, mittlere Reihe: DRTA unter Maximilian I* (Göttingen, 1972–1973), vol. 3, *DRTA, jüngere Reihe: DRTA unter Karl V* (Munich, 1893–, rpr. Göttingen, 1962–), vols. 1–4, 7, 8; Hajo Holborn, *A Hist. of Modern Germany* (New York, 1959–1969), vols. 1–2; Helmut Neuhaus, *Reichstag und Supplikations–ausschuss: Ein Beitrag zur Reichsverfassungsgeschichte der ersten Hälfte des 16. Jahrhunderts,* Schriften zur Verfassungs–geschichte, vol. 24 (Berlin, 1977); Friedrich H. Schubert, *Die dtsch. Reichstage in der Staatslehre der frühen Neuzeit, Schriftenreihe der Hist. Kommission bei der Bayerischen Akademie der Wissenschaften* (Göttingen, 1966).   *P. N. Bebb*

See AUGSBURG, DIET OF; CHARLES V; GOLDEN BULL; NUREMBERG, DIETS OF 1522–1524; SPEYER, DIET OF 1526; SPEYER, DIET OF 1529; WESTPHALIA; WORMS.

DISPUTED ELECTION OF 1198 involved the struggle for the German throne between Philip of Swabia and Otto of Brunswick. When Henry VI died on September 28, 1197, he left one son, three-year-old Frederick, already elected king of the Romans but uncrowned, then living at Foligno, Italy. His mother, Constance, took him to Palermo where he was crowned king of Sicily by hereditary right, at Pentecost 1198. Constance, and after her death the child's guardian, Pope Innocent III, had no desire to maintain Frederick's rights in Germany where his uncle, Duke Philip, was already campaigning on his behalf. Many of the princes closely associated with the Hohenstaufen dynasty were on crusade. Those present did not relish the idea of a child ruler and urged Philip to accept the crown himself. On March 8, 1198, at Mühlhausen they elected him king, and on September 8 at Mainz the archbishop of Tarantaise crowned him.

The lower Rhine princes and the Welf faction, stirred to action by Archbishop Adolf of Altena of Cologne, sought a candidate to oppose Philip. After several others declined, Otto of Brunswick, Henry the Lion's son, accepted this position. A handful of nobles elected Otto on June 9, 1198; Adolf crowned him at Aachen on July 12. Richard I and then John of England aided their nephew

Otto; Philip II of France allied with Philip of Swabia. Educated, cultured, and chivalric, Philip surpassed in personal gifts the inexperienced and boorish Otto, but Otto won the support of Pope Innocent III in 1201 largely because of traditional Hohenstaufen clashes with the papacy. Otto paid a high price for papal approbation: by the Concessions of Neuss (June 8, 1201) he surrendered to Innocent most of the imperial claims to territory in central Italy. In Germany Innocent's intervention and excommunication of the Hohenstaufen faction had little effect. Archbishop Adolf, Henry of Brabant, and Henry of Brunswick actually changed sides and joined Philip. On January 6, 1205, Adolf crowned Philip again, this time in Aachen. In 1206 Philip forced Landgrave Herman of Thuringia and Ottocar I of Bohemia to desert Otto, and on July 27 at Wassenberg, he defeated Otto himself, causing him to retreat to Brunswick.

Innocent III prepared to accommodate himself to the military situation by opening negotiations with Philip. In 1207 papal legates lifted the ban, arranged an armistice, and moved toward recognition of Philip, but force, not diplomacy, ended the struggle. For personal reasons the Bavarian Count Palatine Otto of Wittelsbach assassinated Philip at Bamberg on June 21, 1208. His partisans gave up the struggle. Otto agreed to a new, unanimous election at Frankfurt on November 11, 1208, and thus became the universally acknowledged king. The decline in the royal power through dissipation of resources from 1198 through 1208, along with the disruption of the Hohenstaufen administrative system, proved disastrous to the German monarchy.

Works About: J. Jastrow and G. Winter, *Dtsch. Gesch. im Zeitalter der Hohenstaufen, 1125–1273,* 2 vols. (Berlin, 1893–1901); Friedrich Kempf, ed., *Regestrum Innocentii III papae super negotio Romani imperii* (Rome, 1947) Helene Tillmann, *Papst Innocenz III.* (Bonn, 1954); E. Winkelmann, *Philipp von Schwaben und Otto IV. von Braunschweig,* 2 vols. (Leipzig, 1873–1878, repr. 1963); Caspar Wolfschläger, *Erzbischof Adolf I. von Köln als Fürst und Politiker, 1193–1205* (Münster, 1905).   *R.H. Schmandt*

See HENRY VI; INNOCENT III; OTTO IV.

DÜRER, ALBRECHT (1471–1528), one of the greatest artists of the northern Renaissance, was born in Nuremberg, the son of a goldsmith, Dürer was first apprenticed to his father. Having shown early signs of a talent for drawing, he was sent to the workshop of the Nuremberg master painter and woodcut designer, Michael Wolgemut, in November 1486. He remained with Wolgemut for four years until he started on his travels. Like his contemporary Leonardo da Vinci, Dürer remained a lifelong learner, who hungered for additional knowledge of art and life. The exact route of his travels remains a mystery until he surfaced in Commar early in 1492. By summer he was in Basel working in woodcut workshops prior to his departure for Strasbourg in the fall of 1493.

In the spring of 1494 Dürer returned to Nuremberg and married Agnes Frey, a modest and attractive young woman, who failed to understand her husband's expanding intellectual horizons and who developed an intense dislike for Albrecht's closest friend, the patrician humanist, Willibald Pirckheimer. He left for Italy in the fall, visiting Pirckheimer in Pavia and studying the glories of Venice.

Upon his return to Nuremberg in the spring of 1495, he opened his own workshop, where he completed the famous *Apocalypse* cycle, among other works, by 1498. In 1505 he made his second journey to Italy and stayed primarily in Venice. Back home two years later, he eventually was employed by Emperor Maximilian I, a result in part of the auspices of Christoph Kress, an influential Nuremberg politician. Dürer cooperated in the creation of the giant woodcut, *The Triumphal Arch of Maximilian I* (1515–1517), and of its counterpart, *The Triumphal Procession of Maximilian I,* which was not finished because of the emperor's death in 1519. He did complete a beautifully decorated prayer book with forty-five drawings done according to Maximilian's ideas.

In July 1520 Dürer journeyed to the Netherlands hoping to obtain from the new sovereign, Charles V, a continuation of the yearly salary of one hundred florins granted to him by Maximilian I. He stayed almost a year and learned a great deal studying the works of the Dutch masters. But there he contracted malaria fever while studying a beached whale in the mosquito-infested swamps of Zeeland; this undermined his health for the rest of his life.

Back in Nuremberg, Dürer found himself involved in the Reformation movement as one of Luther's early humanist supporters. He celebrated the city's official adoption of Lutheranism and the defeat of the rebellious peasants in 1525 by dedicating his painting of the *Four Apostles* to the city fathers. One of the apostles bears a close resemblance to Luther's colleague, Philip Melanchthon, and the others look like Nuremberg supporters of the Reformation. The artist very much admired Luther's clear exposition of the Bible.

Despite bouts of melancholia and ill health, Dürer labored unceasingly until his death. He left behind more than six dozen paintings, more than a hundred engravings, about two hundred and fifty woodcuts, more than a thousand drawings, and three printed books on geometry, fortification, and the theory of human proportions, the last of which appeared six months after his death. His friend Pirckheimer wrote his epitaph:"Whatever was mortal of Albrecht Dürer is covered by this tomb." Much that is immortal of Dürer still lives today in his art and writings.

Works By: *Albrecht Dürer: Diary of His Journey to the Netherlands* (Greenwich, Conn., 1971); *Dürers schriftlicher Nachlass,* ed. Hans Rupprich (Berlin, 1956); *The Writings of Albrecht Dürer,* ed. and tr. W. M. Conway (New York, 1958). **Works About:** *Albrecht Dürers Umwelt: Festschrift zum 500. Geburtstag Dürers* (Nuremberg, 1971); Jan Bialostocki, "Dürer," *EWA,* 4:512–32; E. Flechsig, *Albrecht Dürer,* 2 vols. (Berlin, 1928–1931); Erwin Panofsky, *The Life and Art of Albrecht Dürer* (Princeton, 1955); Moritz Thausing, *Albert Dürer,* 2 vols. (London, 1882); W. Waetzold, *Dürer und sein Zeit* (London, 1938); F. Winkler, *Albrecht Dürer* (Berlin, 1958); H. Wölfflin, *Die Kunst Albrecht Dürers* (Munich, 1943).   *J. W. Zophy*

See CHARLES V; LUTHER; MAXIMILIAN I; MELANCHTHON; PIRCKHEIMER, WILLIBALD.

e

EBERHARD (1445–1496), also known as Eberhard the Bearded *(im Barte, barbarus),* first duke of Württemberg and founder of Eberhard Karls University in Tübingen, was born in Urach, the son of Count Ludwig of Württemberg and Countess Palatine Mechthild. Upon the sudden death of his father in 1450, the youth was entrusted to the guardianship of relatives in Stuttgart. Although his formal education was neglected, Eberhard displayed a zeal for Christian doctrine and a lifelong dedication to the advancement of learning. After a pilgrimage to the Holy Land in 1468 in the company of several noble youths, he visited Italy in 1482, where he was received in Florence by Lorenzo de' Medici and in Rome by Pope Sixtus IV (who presented him with a golden rose).

At a time when other territories were threatened with disintegration, Eberhard managed to secure, by means of family treaties, the indivisibility of his lands and the establishment of a firm regulation of inheritance rights for his successors. The key element in this consolidating activity was Eberhard's decision to join the Swabian League, a step that won him the general approval of the Holy Roman emperor, Frederick III. Eberhard demonstrated his concern for religion by his reform of the monasteries and by his promotion of the Bretheren of the Common Life, for whom he founded many new houses. Because he never mastered Latin, Eberhard had many scholarly works translated into German and surrounded himself with scholars and poets. Perhaps his most notable achievement was the founding of a university in Tübingen in 1477. This new institution of higher learning, modeled after the University of Paris, soon became the home of such leading intellects as Gabriel Biel and John Vergenhans. Eberhard visited his school regularly and loved to hold open house for the professors in the home of Vergenhans, his former tutor and the university's first rector.

At the diet of Worms in 1495, Holy Roman Emperor Maximilian I, a close friend of Eberhard, conferred upon him the dignity of a duke *(Herzog)* and designated his land an imperial dukedom *(Reichsherzogtum).* In November 1495 the new duke promulgated a territorial ordinance *(Landesordnung)* as the first uniform legal code for his newly consolidated lands.

Married happily to Barbara, daughter of Ludovico of Mantua, of the Gonzaga family, in 1474, Eberhard left no descendants other than the esteemed university that bears his name. It has been said the "many bitter experiences made him intelligent; travels and a talented wife completed his transformation." Eberhard's motto, appropriate to his achievements, was: *Attempto!* ("I dare to do it!").

Works About: Ernst Fritz, *Eberhard im Bart: Die Politik eines dtsch. Landesherrn am Ende des Mittelalters* (Stuttgart, 1933); Eberhard Gönner, "Eberhard im Bart," *NDB*, 4:234–36; Karl Pfaff, *Gesch. Wirtenbergs* (Stuttgart, 1819), vol. 1; J. C. Pfister, *Eberhard im Bart, erster Herzog zu Würtemberg* (Tübingen, 1822); J. F. Rösslin, *Leben des ersten merkwürdigen Herzogs von Würtemberg Eberhard im Bart* (Tübingen, 1793); C. F. Sattler, *Gesch. des Herzogthums Würtenberg unter der Regierung der Graven,* 4th ed. (Tübingen, 1777), vols. 2–3; Eugen Schneider, *Eberhard im Bart* (Freiburg, 1875); C. F. von Stälin, *Wirtembergische Gesch.* (Stuttgart, 1856); P. F. Stälin, "Eberhard im Bart," *ADB*, 5:557–59; Karl Weller and Arnold Weller, *Württembergische Gesch. im südwestdeutschen Raum,* 6th ed. (Stuttgart and Aalen, 1971).   *L. J. Reith*

See FREDERICK III; MAXIMILIAN I.

EBERLIN, JOHN (c. 1465–c. 1533), reformer and pamphleteer, was born in the margraviate of Burgau in the small village of Kleinkötz about three miles south of the city of Günzburg. Eberlin's family background is obscure; his parents were impoverished lower nobility, and he was orphaned at an early age. By the time Eberlin was thirty years old, he had become a priest in the diocese of Augsburg and the holder of the M.A. degree from the University of Basel. Coming under the influence of Dr. John Scherdine, city preacher at Heilbronn, Eberlin took monastic vows and became a member of the Franciscan Observants, a strict and well-disciplined begging order of monks.

Prior to the Lutheran Reformation, Eberlin was allowed by his cloister at Ulm to travel to Tübingen where he served as a preacher and a schoolmaster in the Tübingen school for advanced studies. Ultimately Eberlin was attracted to the Reformation movement by reading the pamphlets of Martin Luther. Breaking his ties with the Franciscans, Eberlin embarked upon a remarkable career as a reformer, pamphleteer, and political theorist. His first pamphlet was addressed to the young and newly elected emperor of the Holy Roman Empire, Charles V. Eberlin, as did a number of the Swabian members of the ranks of the lower nobility, had a loyalty to the concept of the Empire and saw great promise and hope for German lands under the rule of Charles V. Eberlin hoped that the university-educated sons of the lower nobility would make loyal and useful employees of the emperor in governing of German lands. Very quickly the hopes of Eberlin for a happy imperial government were thwarted by the throes of the Reformation.

Eberlin continued to publish a variety of pamphlets. According to surviving data on the nature of sixteenth-century publications, his work was written and published in a quantity second only to that of Martin Luther in the greatest decade of pamphlet printing, the 1520s. In 1521, Eberlin published a series of vernacular pamphlets, which he called the "Fifteen Friends," and was published in three editions by three different printers in scattered locations. The eleventh pamphlet was a blueprint for a utopian society named Wolfaria, a place where life goes well. Wolfaria reflects the influence of Platonic ideas, the ideas of Thomas More, and his own Christian perspective. Eberlin's utopia is the first utopian work to be printed in a vernacular language. There is some evidence to indicate that Eberlin's utopian thought helped to shape the utopian scheme of the seventeenth-century Württemburg theologian, John Valentin Andreae.

By 1525, Eberlin entered the court of George II of Wertheim. Wertheim was one of the few places in German lands where there was no suppression of the peasants after the painful years of revolt (1524–1526). After George II died, Eberlin moved for the final time to Leuterhausen near Ansbach where he died, somewhat disillusioned with the slow nature of change.

An overview of Eberlin's writings testifies to the wide range of his interests in the social, political, and intellectual life of the Holy Roman Empire. Not only did he champion Lutheran ideas, but he worked hard at solving some of the economic problems besetting lands within the Empire. In 1524 he wrote a popular and well-received satire on economic life, *I Wonder Where All the Money Went*. Internal evidence indicates that Eberlin is the likely author of another satire suggesting a solution to the serious threat of Turkish invasion from the southeast. Eberlin writes that the monks or cloister people in Wolfaria all turn out with their bodies and resources and battle the Turks, an action that was sufficient to solve the Turkish problem.

Eberlin's total impact on German-speaking lands is difficult to calculate, but all authorities agree that he was a friend of the people, a popular preacher, and a fighter for Reformation. He was alive and sensitive to the whole range of problems affecting the everyday life of those living within the confines of the Holy Roman Empire in the first three decades of the sixteenth century.

Works By: Johann Eberlin von Günzburg, *Ausgewählte (sämtliche) Schriften,* ed. Ludwig Enders, 3 vols. (Hakle, 1896–1900). **Works About:** Richard G. Cole, "Johann Eberlin von Günzburg and the German Reformation" (Ph.D. diss., Ohio State University, 1963), and "The Reformation in Print," *ARG* 66:93–102; William P. Hitchcock, *The Background of the Knights' Revolt, 1522–1523* (Berkeley, 1958); Bernhard Riggenbach, *Johann Eberlin von Günzburg und sein Reform program* (Tübingen, 1874); Lewis Spitz, "Johannes Eberlin," *New Catholic Encyclopedia* (New York, 1967) 5:28–29; Ernst Wolf, "Eberlin," *NDB,* 4:247–48.   *R. G. Cole*

See ANDREAE; CHARLES V; LUTHER.

ECCLESIASTICAL RESERVATION (reservatum ecclesiasticum), part of the religious Peace of Augsburg, was accepted by King Ferdinand I and the German estates on September 25, 1555. The purpose of the ecclesiastical reservation was to prevent the further secularization of Catholic church properties in the Empire. It stated that an ecclesiastical prince who turned Lutheran would lose his rights and privileges. Instead of forcing his subjects to convert with him (like a secular prince could), he had to vacate his post and permit the local Catholic chapter to elect a new bishop (archbishop or abbot).

The Lutherans opposed this reservation but eventually permitted its inclusion in the Augsburg treaty. There it appeared not as part of the compact between the emperor and the estates but as an announcement based on imperial authority. The ecclesiastical reservation was important because it saved many Church properties and thus helped the survival of German Catholicism. However, it was never fully accepted by the Protestants, who continued to secularize Catholic bishoprics and abbeys, especially in northern Germany in such places as Bremen, Lübeck, Minden, Magdeburg, and Halberstadt. After the Protestant defeats in the Thirty Years War, Emperor Ferdinand II sought to return to a stricter enforcement of the ecclesiastical reservation by issuing the Edict of Restitution in 1629. The reservation was confirmed in the Peace of Westphalia (1648), though only for Church lands that had been Catholic in 1624.

Works About: Karl Brandi, *Der Augsburger Religionsfriede* (Göttingen, 1927); Fritz Dickmann, "Das Problem der Gleichberechtigung der Konfessionen im Reich im 16. und 17. Jahrhundert," *HZ* 201 (1965): 265–305; J. Heckel, "Augsburger Religionsfriede," *RGG,* 1:736ff; Theo Hoyer, "The Religious Peace of Augsburg," *Concordia Theological Monthly* 26 (1955):820–30; Matthias Simon, *Der Augsburger Religionsfriede* (Augsburg, 1955); Hermann Tüchle, "Der Augsburger Religionsfriede: Neue Ordnung oder Kampfpause," *Z. des Hist. Ver. für Schwaben* 61 (1955): 323–39.   *Bodo Nischan*

See AUGSBURG, RELIGIOUS PEACE OF; EDICT OF RESTITUTION; FERDINAND I; FERDINAND II; THIRTY YEARS WAR; WESTPHALIA.

ECK, JOHN (1484–1543), one of the most important figures in Europe during the Reformation, was born at Egg in Swabia, the son of a peasant named Mayer. He began his formal studies at Heidelberg in 1498 and attended universities at Tübingen, Cologne, and Freiburg im Breisgau, concentrating on law and theology. At Freiburg in 1505 he entered the teaching profession in which he remained throughout his life. Ordained to the priesthood at Strasbourg in 1508 where he made the acquaintance of that city's humanist circle, he moved to Ingolstadt in 1510; he received the doctorate in theology and became professor of theology at the university in this same year. Ingolstadt remained Eck's formal residence until his death, although he traveled extensively and attended most of the major political and religious meetings of his day. He became a city preacher in 1519 and served his city in this and similar posts until 1540.

A contentious man with a tenacious memory, Eck engaged in numerous debates. He first received attention by attacking the medieval prohibition on usury in a series of writings and disputations. Arguing that a charge of 5 percent interest on loans was acceptable, Eck defended his views at Bologna, Vienna, and elsewhere. Probably his most notable debate was the Leipzig disputation (June 27–July 16, 1519) with Luther and Karlstadt. Here Eck forced Luther to clarify further his evangelical theology. In the process Eck became convinced that Luther was wrong; he remained Luther's bitter opponent until the end, incurring the wrath and hostility, sometimes unjustly, of proponents of Protestantism. At Leipzig, Eck's ability won over Duke George of Saxony (d. 1539), a man who became a strong political opponent of the new theology.

Because of the close connection between political and religious life at this time, religious views and affiliations had political ramifications, and vice versa.

It is thus difficult to separate Eck's political activity from his opposition to the Protestants. One might argue that Eck's agitation for Luther's excommunication, his successful campaign to this end in Rome in 1520, which resulted in the first papal bull *(Exsurge domine)* against Luther, and his role as nuncio in charge of the bull's publication brought about the Edict of Worms in 1521. It is certain that Eck's activities on behalf of Catholicism served to harden the political lines in the Empire during the Reformation. This is evident by his participation at Nuremberg and Regensburg in 1524; his opposition to Melanchthon's writings and irenicism, expecially at Augsburg in 1530 and during the religious discussions at Hagenau, Worms, and Regensburg in 1540 and 1541; and his attempt, with Campeggio, to enlist the support of King Henry VIII of England against the Protestants.

A scholar, Eck wrote extensively. Much of his writing was polemical in nature. Perhaps the best known were his personal attacks on Luther, his coauthorship of the *Confutatio* or *Refutation* of the Augsburg Confession in 1530, his list of more than four hundred Lutheran errors, and his *Manual of Common Doctrines Against Luther and Other Enemies of the Church*. The last, reprinted many times in the sixteenth century, served as a polemical handbook of Catholicism. He also translated the Bible into German and wrote against the Jews.

Works By: Wilhelm Gussmann, ed., *D. Johann Ecks vierhundertundvier Artikel zum Reichstag von Augsburg 1530,* Quel. und Forsch zur Gesch. der Augsburgischen Glaubensbekenntnisses, vol. 2 (Cassel, 1930). Johannes Metzler, ed., *Tres Orationes Funebres in Exequiis Ioannis Eckii Habitae,* Corpus Catholicorum, vol. 16 (Münster, 1930). **Works About:** Brecher, "Eck," *ADB,* 5:596–602; E. Iserloh, "Eck," *NDB,* 4:273–75; Theodor Wiedemann, *Dr. Johann Eck, Professor der Theololgie an der Universität Ingolstadt* (Regensburg, 1865).   *P. N. Bebb*

See AUGSBURG, DIET OF; CAMPEGGIO; LUTHER; MELANCHTHON.

ECKHART, MEISTER (c. 1260–1327), mystic and theologian, was born in the Thuringian town of Hochheim. At an early age he entered the Dominican order in Erfurt. He went on to study at Cologne, then very much influenced by the scholasticism of Albert the Great and Thomas Aquinas, and at Paris. In 1294 Eckhart became prior of the Dominican cloister in Erfurt and vicar of the order in Thuringia. He was given the title *magister* or *meister,* during a teaching mission to Paris in 1300. In 1303 he became the provincial for the Dominicans in Saxony and founded a number of convents. From 1314 to 1323 he belonged to the Dominican house in Strasbourg, where he became an extremely popular and influential preacher using the German vernacular. Because many of his views were controversial, the archbishop of Cologne summoned Eckhart to his court in 1326. The scholar defended himself by arguing that his sermons and writings had been misunderstood by the ignorant. Nevertheless a bull issued by Pope John XXII in 1329 condemned twenty-eight of Eckhart's propositions, though it also stated that Eckhart had subjected himself to papal authority prior to his death.

Meister Eckhart is regarded as the most learned and systematic of the great German mystics. His central theme was the relationship between God as the only true reality, and the human soul as the only place in the universe where God can reveal Himself in the truth of His being. Eckhart argued that God may enter a human life through the soul and take over its direction. He implied that the Church was not necessary as a mediator between God and man. Because much of his writing was in German, Meister Eckhart helped to establish that language as a literary vehicle suitable for conveying abstract thought.

Works By: Meister Eckhart, *Die dtsch. Werke,* ed. Josef Quint et al., 9 vols. (Stuttgart, 1938–); *Selected Writings,* ed. J. M. Clark (London, 1958). **Works About:** J. M. Clark, *Meister Eckhart* (London, 1957); C. F. Kelly, *Meister Eckhart on Divine Knowledge* (New Haven, 1977); Josef Quint, *Meister Eckhart* (Munich, 1955). *J. W. Zophy*

See ALBERT THE GREAT.

EDICT OF RESTITUTION (March 6, 1629), a decree issued by Emperor Ferdinand II during the Thirty Years War, ordered the immediate restitution of all illegally secularized church properties to the Catholic church. The edict, promulgated after Wallenstein's and Tilly's victories in the Lower Saxon War, expressed Ferdinand's conviction that he had a divine mandate to impose both his will and his religion on the German Protestants.

The edict ordered the strict enforcement of the ecclesiastical reservation of the Peace of Augsburg (1555), stipulating that all church goods that had become Protestant after 1552 be re-Catholicized. Another provision of that same treaty, Ferdinand's declaration, which guaranteed Lutherans living in ecclesiastical principalities freedom from Catholic persecution, was, however, declared null and void. The 1555 agreement was interpreted to apply only to Lutherans and Catholics; Calvinists were specifically excluded. The Imperial Cameral Court was instructed to apply the emperor's ruling to all litigations involving church property rights. Special execution commissioners were appointed to supervise the decree's enforcement.

Had it been rigorously enforced, this edict would have counter reformed two archbishoprics, twelve bishoprics, and more than fifty major convents. It would have entailed the alteration of boundaries all over north and central Germany and the survival of Protestantism would have been seriously jeopardized. Württemberg, Brunswick, and the imperial free city of Augsburg became the edict's first victims. But no immediate attempts were made to execute the decree in Pomerania, Brandenburg, and Saxony. Wallenstein's overwhelming military power in northern Germany, however, left no doubt that these principalities too were greatly threatened.

While momentarily strengthening Ferdinand's position, the edict actually helped to undermine his power. The emperor's military might and territorial acquisitions alarmed his league allies, particularly Maximilian of Bavaria. Fear of the edict radicalized Germany's more moderate princes, especially the electors of Brandenburg and Saxony, who in the past had generally cooperated with the emperor. The vagaries of war soon forced Ferdinand to modify (Peace of Prague, 1635) and eventually to abandon his decree altogether (Peace of Westphalia, 1648). The Edict of Restitution, however, remains an important watermark of imperial power and ambition in the Thirty Years War.

Works About: Michael C. Lundorp, ed., *Der Römischen Kayserlichen Majestät und Dess Heiligen Römischen Reichs . . . Acta Publica* (Frankfurt am Main, 1618–1721), 3:1048–1055); Moriz Ritter, "Der Ursprung des Restitionsedikts," *HZ* 76 (1895):62–102; Theodor Tupetz, "Der Streit um die geistlichen Güter und das Restitutionsedikt," *Sitzungberichte der Philosophisch-Hist. Klasse der Kaiserlichen Akademie der Wissenschaften* 102 (Vienna, 1883): 315–566; Helmut Urban, *"Das Restitutionsedikt: Versuch einer Interpretation* (Ph.D. diss., Berlin, 1968); A. M. Ward, "The Edict of Restitution and the Dismissal of Wallenstein (1628–1630)," in *The Cambridge Modern History* (New York, 1934), 4:109–17.   *Bodo Nischan*

See ECCLESIASTICAL RESERVATION; FERDINAND II; THIRTY YEARS WAR; WALLENSTEIN; WESTPHALIA.

ELIZABETH OF THURINGIA (Elizabeth of Hungary) (1207–1231), daughter of King Andreas II of Hungary (d. 1235) and Gertrude of Meran (d. 1213), was sent at the age of four to the court of Landgrave Herman I of Thuringia (1190–1217). Elizabeth was betrothed to Herman I's son, Ludwig IV of Thuringia (1200–1227), and the two children were raised together at Wartburg castle near Marburg. Elizabeth's piety and compassion for the poor, diseased, and outcast in society was evident in her childhood years. In 1221 Elizabeth and Ludwig IV were married in Eisenach. A son, Herman II of Thuringia (1222–1241) and two daughters, Sophie (c. 1224–1279), wife of Duke Henry II of Brabant, and Gertrude (1227–1297) abbess of Altenberg near Wetzlar, were born to them.

When Ludwig IV was away on military campaigns, Elizabeth devoted herself to good works. Her generosity and service to the sick and poor aroused the criticism of her brother-in-law, Henry Raspe (c. 1204–1247), who administered Ludwig IV's territory in his absence. Ludwig IV, however, respected and shared Elizabeth's religious and humanitarian sympathies and always supported her charitable work. At her request he built a home for lepers not far from the Wartburg. In 1226 famine struck while he was attending an imperial diet in Cremona. Elizabeth opened granaries, ordered bread to be baked, established soup kitchens, and distributed money among the subjects. Henry Raspe reported to Ludwig IV that Elizabeth was impoverishing his estates. Nevertheless Ludwig IV endorsed Elizabeth's actions. Ludwig IV left the following year on a crusade to the Holy Land. He died of a fever on a ship off the Italian coast near Otranto in 1227. Shortly after word of Ludwig IV's death reached the Wartburg, Elizabeth and her children were expelled from Ludwig's court by Henry Raspe. She found refuge for a short time with her uncle Egbert, bishop of Bamberg, but returned to Thuringia when her dowry was restored to her.

Elizabeth's spiritual adviser was the controversial Master Conrad of Marburg (d. 1233), papal visitor to German monasteries. He crusaded so fervently against heretics among the laity, as well as among the clergy, that contemporary chroniclers greeted his violent death with relief.

In 1228 Elizabeth renounced her children and kin to become a member of the third order of St. Francis. She lived the remaining years of her short life in simple lodgings and spent her days caring for lepers, the aged and the poor. Four years after her death, Elizabeth was declared a saint by Pope Gregory IX.

Works About: A. Borst, "Elisabeth," *NDB*, 4:452; W. Canton, *The Story of Saint Elizabeth* (Boston, 1913); Edith Deen, *Great Women of the Christian Faith* (New York, 1959); Walter Nigg, *Elisabeth von Thüringen* (Munich, 1958); E. Ranke, "Elisabeth" *ADB*, 6:40–5; Elizabeth von Schmidt-Pauli, *Saint Elizabeth* (New York, 1932); Reinhold Schneider, "Elisabeth von Thüringen" *DGD*, 1:130–53; Leo Weismantel, *Elisabeth* (Leipzig, 1957).   *J. W. Gates*

See FREDERICK II.

ENGELBRECHT, PETER (?–1491), tutor of Emperor Maximilian I, was made Maximilian's second teacher by Emperor Frederick III after the death of Jacob von Fladnitz in 1466. Engelbrecht, who came from Passail, had been a canon in Wiener Neustadt. He was remembered as a worldly cleric who knew how to dress fashionably. As Maximilian's teacher, Engelbrecht was straightforward and pedantic. He attempted to drum a scholastic training into a pupil who was very active and disliked school routine, especially the methods of his teacher. Engelbrecht was encouraged by Maximilian's father, Frederick III, to use strong measures to enforce his pupil's submission. His subsequent cruelty caused Maximilian to suffer psychological disturbances and to have difficulties in speaking. Maximilian always retained a strong dislike for Engelbrecht. In later life he said, "If Peter my teacher still lived, I would make him live near me, in order to teach him how children should be brought up." However, Frederick III seems to have been satisfied with Engelbrecht and rewarded him by having him made the first bishop of Wiener Neustadt in 1477. Peter remained in this position until his death in 1491.

Works About: Heinrich Fichtenau, *Der junge Maximilian* (Munich, 1959), and *Die Lehrbücher Maximilians I und die Anfänge der Frakturschrift* (Hamburg, 1961).   *J. J. Spielvogel*

See FREDERICK III; MAXIMILIAN I.

ERASMUS, DESDERIUS (c. 1466–1536), humanist, probably illegitimately born at Gouda (near Rotterdam), educated at Deventer and later at s'Hertogenbosch by the Brethren of the Common Life, entered the Augustinian monastery of canons regular at Steyn (c. 1486) and was ordained in 1492. Through the patronage of the bishop of Cambrai, he began his studies at the University of Paris in 1495, residing at Montaigu College, where he developed an aversion to scholasticism. In 1499 he made his first of several trips to England

and met Thomas More, Archbishop Warham, and John Colet, the last encouraging him to study Greek. Erasmus' concern to apply to the great Christian texts those exegetical methods the Italian humanists had applied to classical texts dates from this first trip. He returned to the Continent, spending time in France and the Low Countries, returned to England (1505–1506), and then spent three years in Italy (1506–1509). He returned to England (1511–1514) to Queen's College, Cambridge, went to Basel (in 1514), spent time in Louvain and Holland, and settled in Basel from 1521 through 1529, where he was associated with the publisher Froben. After Basel accepted the Reformation, he went to Freiburg im Breisgau where he remained until 1535. He then returned to Basel where he died.

Erasmus' view of politics was developed from his belief as a Christian humanist that sound learning *(bona literae)* should be applied to the administration of public affairs in a Christian state and from his knowledge of politics in the Low Countries. The story of Erasmus' strictly political opinions ends in 1521 following his direct contact with court life and men of state in the Netherlands. For a short time he was aligned with the national party in the Netherlands and believed that each *patria* should be governed by a national prince of its own, yet he held in contempt the tradition of the aristocracy and the Burgundian culture of chivalry, and he believed that moral decisions, formed in one's youth, flow from one's character.

Perhaps Erasmus' moral concern clouded his understanding of the dynamics of power and his ability to understand the relations between states. In the *Paraclesis,* the preface to his edition of the Greek New Testament (1516), he makes it clear that Christian people could be spared many wars if the Gospel were truly preached. His concern with an enlightened, reformed, theologically purified Church is expressed in the *Enchiridion Militis Christiani* (1503), where the highest expression of religious devotion, he states, is found in the practice of virtue motivated by inward piety. The oration given before Archduke Philip the Fair in 1504, the *Panegyricus,* states that peace requires greater bravery than war and that it is a prince's duty to maintain peace. The *Institutio Principis Christiani* [Institution of a Christian Prince], written for Charles V in 1516, emphasizes the necessity for a ruler to receive an education that inculcates in him a duty to care for his people. It states that the prince is a servant of the people and that Christian princes should never engage in war against one another; instead they should submit to arbitration. Erasmus' case against war is more fully developed in *Querela Pacis* [The Complaint of Peace], published in 1517 at the request of John Le Sauvage, where he argues that an unjust peace is more honorable for the pious prince than the most just war. Other references to the matters of state are scattered in his *Epistolae* and *Adagia*.

Dulce bellum inexpertis ("sweet is war to those who know it not"), a lengthy adage in the 1515 edition, provides an account of the historical degeneration of man to explain pagan wars and present practices and argues that war violates

Christian man's true nature. Reason, and the model found in Christ's life, dictates that war is too costly; everyone suffers ruin. Additions to this adage in 1523 identify contemporary princes as tyrannous war gods, while Erasmus sharpens his attack in the 1526 edition on Church authorities who justify war, and he demonstrates how pagan warriors practiced a more humane art of war than did contemporary Christian monarchs. Other adages are antimonarchical (among them "Scarabaeus" and "Aut regem aut fatuum nasci oporlet," both separately printed), while *Sileni Alcibades* observes how governors are inwardly contemptuous of their subjects.

Erasmus' *Colloquia,* which he continually revised and expanded, contain social and political criticism; "The Funeral" comments on the unstable peace after Pavia, "On Fish Eating" observes the strife among Christians, "Charon" foresees world ruin as the result of mass war, and "Of a Soldier's Life" satirizes the military. As a counterpoint to his pacifism and desire to restore unity to a humanistically reformed Christendom, Erasmus calls for a revitalized Scripture-oriented faith, the root of which lies in the Gospels where the *philosophia Christi* is to be found in all its purity and simplicity. This theme finds expression in such works as the "Inquiry Concerning Faith" (1535), "Explanation of the Apostle's Creed" (1533), and "The Preacher" (1535). For Erasmus the Church consisted of the whole range of Christian people; he believed that man is restored by grace (as embodied in Christ), which becomes effective through faith.

While Erasmus, as an independent scholar, tried to avoid taking sides in Reformation polemics, he has justly been charged with laying the egg that Luther hatched. His *New Testament* (1516) was the first published version of the Greek text and was the basis for many vernacular translations, while the *Encomium Moriae* [Praise of Folly] (1509), the *Colloquies,* and other writings were imbued with criticism of clerical abuses and social injustices of the kind the reformers also wanted to change. In addition Erasmus' editions of the Church fathers (Jerome, Basil, Cyrill, Chrysostum, Irenaeus, Ambrose, Augustine, and Origen) provided reliable texts used by the disputants in their Reformation debates. Erasmus' sermon, *De Immensa Dei Misericordia* [On the Immense Mercy of God] (1524), had dealt with the relation of justification and good works, while the *Inquisitio de Fide* [An Inquiry Concerning Faith] (1524) clearly showed sympathy with Luther's doctrines. However, Erasmus professed ignorance of Luther's writings, and his fear of change in the doctrine of the Church finally led him to break publicly with Luther in 1524 with the *De libero arbitrio* [Diatribe on Free Will], which analyzes the limitations of Luther's position on human freedom. Luther repudiated Erasmus' theological arguments in *De servo arbitrio* [Bondage of the Will] (1525), which Erasmus answered in the first and second *Hyperaspistes*.

Despite bitter controversy during the last years of his life and the mistrust of both Catholics and Protestants, Erasmus continued his scholarly work. The *Ecclesiastes* [The Preacher] (1533), which emphasizes how preaching is the most important function of the Christian priest, underscores Erasmus' lifelong concern to restore man's perfect nature through the grace of Christ. When man is so restored, a gradually reformed Christendom can live in peace and harmony. Erasmus' determination to remain above religious partisanship is reflected in the *De Sacrienda Ecclesiae Concordia* [On Restoring the Peace of the Church](1533), which advocates tolerance, that men live well, and not lightly disregard tradition and treats the major subjects of dissension. Erasmus' cultural idea of *eruditio* and *pietas* permeated his religious and political writings; he could not separate the need for men of state—especially the princes—to act on the basis of Christian principles found in the Gospels and revealed to men in the life of Christ.

Works By: P. S. Allen, *Opus epistolarum Des. Erasmi Roterodami*, 11 vols. (Oxford, 1906–1963); *Collected Works of Erasmus: The Correspondence* (Toronto, 1974–); H. Holborn, ed., *Erasmus Ausgewählte Werke* (Munich, 1933). **Works About:** R. H. Bainton, *Erasmus of Christendom* (New York, 1969); E. von Koerber, *Die Staatstheorie des Erasmus von Rotterdam* (Berlin, 1967); Margaret Mann Philips, *Erasmus and the Northern Renaissance* (New York, 1950); James D. Tracy, *The Politics of Erasmus: A Pacifist Intellectual and His Political Milieu* (Toronto, 1978).   *A. M. McLean*

See CHARLES V; HUMANISM; LUTHER.

ESSLINGEN on the Neckar was a free imperial city from the thirteenth century until 1802. Esslingen is first mentioned in 777 as the site of a monastic cell affiliated with the great Carolingian abbey of St. Denis. In the tenth century Esslingen was held by the dukes of Swabia, who minted coins there. By 1100 it had passed to the Hohenstaufen, who promoted the community's development, authorized the construction of a wall, and raised Esslingen to the status of a city by 1219. The *Municipal Law Code* of Esslingen, first mentioned in 1229, not only provided the young city with the framework for its own legal development but also served as a model for the *Municipal Law Code* subsequently granted to Ulm and other Swabian cities.

With the decline of the Hohenstaufen after 1250, Esslingen successfully asserted its status as a free imperial city. The fourteenth century was an era of economic growth and political evolution in Esslingen. Extensive vineyards made the city a major center for trade in wine. Constitutional changes instituted in the course of the fourteenth century guaranteed representatives of the guilds a prominent role in the city's government.

Eager to expand its territory, Esslingen was plunged into repeated conflicts with the surrounding county (later duchy) of Württemberg. As an ally of Emperor Henry VII, Esslingen occupied Stuttgart and other Württemberg cities in 1312 but was forced to return these acquisitions in 1316. After joining the league of Swabian cities in 1377, Esslingen was again pitted against Württemberg until the cities' defeat at the battle of Döffingen in 1388. Esslingen's participation in the great War of the Cities of 1448–1454 was equally unfruitful. By 1473 the city had given up all hopes of expanding its territory and signed a treaty that placed it under Würtemberg's protection but did not compromise its status as a free city. The treaty was periodically renewed until 1802, although this did not preclude further incidents of friction. As a member of the Swabian League, founded in 1488, Esslingen was involved in the effort to expel Duke Ulrich of Württemberg from his duchy in 1519 and was subjected to a brief siege by Ulrich before his departure.

Protestant sentiments were widely voiced in Esslingen during the 1520s, but the magistrates initially took a hesitant position toward the Reformation. Their caution was partly dictated by the fact that Esslingen was the seat of two organs of the imperial administration, the *Reichsregiment* and the *Reichskammergericht,* from 1524 to 1527. In 1531, however, after a poll of the citizenry showed overwhelming support for the Protestant cause, the magistrates authorized the introduction of the Reformation. In 1552 Charles V abrogated the old guild-based constitution of Esslingen and replaced it with one giving the patricians control of the city council; the Reformation, however, remained in force.

From the mid-sixteenth century onward, Esslingen suffered a steady decline in political and economic importance. An economic blockade of the city by Württemberg from 1541 to 1557 vividly demonstrated Esslingen's dependence on peaceful relations with its powerful neighbor. Already heavily indebted by 1618, the city government fell even further into debt during the Thirty Years War. The wars of Louis XIV, which brought French incursions in 1688, 1693, and 1707, contributed further to the city's economic distress, as did a fire that destroyed two hundred houses in 1701. The eighteenth century was characterized by mounting dissatisfaction among the citizenry with the inefficiency and financial mismanagement of the patrician government. Constitutional changes to allow greater citizen participation were introduced in 1793, only to be rendered meaningless in 1802 when, with French approval, the city of Esslingen lost its imperial status and was annexed to Württemberg.

Works About: Otto Borst, *Gesch. der Stadt Esslingen am Neckar* (Esslingen, 1977); Adolf Diehl, ed., *Urkundenbuch der Stadt Esslingen,* 2 vols. (Stuttgart, 1899–1905); *Esslinger Studien,* vols. 1– 9 (1956–1964); Bernhard Kirchgässner, *Wirtschaft und Bevölkerung der Reichsstadt Esslingen im Spätmittelalter, Nach den Steuerbüchern 1360–1460* (Esslingen, 1964); Eberhard Naujoks, *Obrigkeit, Zunftverfassung und Reformation: Studien zur Verfassungsgeschichte von Ulm, Esslingen und Schwäbisch Gmünd* (Stuttgart, 1958).   *C. R. Friedrichs*

See CHARLES V; HENRY VII; IMPERIAL CAMERAL COURT; IMPERIAL CITIES; IMPERIAL COUNCIL OF REGENCY; SWABIAN LEAGUE; ULRICH OF WÜRTTEMBERG.

EUGENE OF SAVOY, PRINCE FRANCIS (1663–1736), a prominent imperial field marshal and statesman, served Leopold I, Joseph I, and Charles VI. Born in Paris in October 1663, Eugene was the son of Olympia Mancini, a niece of Cardinal Mazarin, and Prince Eugene Maurice of Savoy-Carignan, count of Soissons. In Paris Louis XIV dubbed him *le petit abbé* because Eugene, a man of small stature, was destined for a career in the Church. Eugene, however, wanted a military commission. After Louis repeatedly refused to grant him a military assignment and his mother was disgraced at court, Eugene left

Paris and went to Vienna to serve Louis XIV's cousin and archrival, Leopold I, the Holy Roman emperor. Embittered, Eugene never forgot or forgave Louis XIV. At Vienna, Count John Wenzel Wratislaw, the Bohemian chancellor, and his cousin, Ludwig William, margrave of Baden (the Turkenlouis), befriended Eugene and helped him advance in the military.

Eugene served with distinction in the Turkish war (1683–1699) and the War of the League of Augsburg (1688–1697). He aided in the relief of Vienna under Duke Charles V of Lorraine (1683), the capture of Budapest (1686), and the siege of Belgrade (1688). In acknowledgment of his achievements, Leopold made him a field marshal in the imperial army. When the War of the League of Augsburg broke out in 1688, Eugene succeeded in winning the temporary alliance of his cousin, Victor Amadeus II of Savoy, to Leopold's cause. Eugene served bravely on both the Rhine and in Italy, raising the siege of Coni, seizing Carmagnola, and defeating the French commander Catinat until Victor Amadeus abandoned the emperor and concluded a separate treaty with France. In 1697 he succeeded Augustus the Strong as commander-in-chief of the imperial army in Hungary where, at the Battle of Zenta, he annihilated a Turkish army three times larger than his own. This notable victory effectually ended the Turkish war.

During the War of the Spanish Succession, he served Leopold I as commander-in-chief of the imperial forces in Italy and as president of the council of war. Prince Eugene was part of the younger coterie, including Count Gundaker Thomas von Stahremberg, president of the Chamber and Count John Wenzel Wratislaw, who advocated reform of the governmental and military administration. Eugene and Wratislaw were close friends and furthered each other's careers. Eugene's support occasioned the witticism that "formerly St. Christopher [Wratislaw was a very large man] carried little Jesus [Eugene] but now the picture is reversed." During Leopold's reign, Prince Eugene had pressed for war against Louis XIV; he opposed the growing ascendancy of France and advocated consolidating and increasing the power of the Habsburg lands as a basis of imperial strength.

When war broke out, Leopold immediately appointed Eugene imperial commander in Italy. As such he brilliantly defeated Marshal Catinat, forcing him to retreat to the Oglio, and Catinat's successor, the duke of Villeroi, whom he outmaneuvered at Chiari and later seized at Cremona. Because of the shortage of troops, Eugene was unable to corner Vendôme, a much more astute foe, who had ample reinforcements. Eugene was later sent to Hungary to assess the danger from the rebellion, led by Francis II Rákóczi. Still later, Eugene joined John Churchill, duke of Marlborough, commander of the allied forces to defeat a Franco-Bavarian force at Blenheim; that victory ended the danger of a Franco-Bavarian-Hungarian invasion of the Holy Roman Empire and forced Bavaria out of the war. Prince Eugene and Marlborough thereafter became close friends and military collaborators. In 1705 and 1706 Eugene again returned to Italy where he easily defeated Vendôme's successor and drove the French out of

Italy. In recognition of his success in Italy, Joseph named him lieutenant general in 1707. He failed to take Toulon in 1707 but did succeed, with Marlborough, in defeating the French at Oudenarde and seizing Lille (1708). In 1709 Eugene again cooperated with Marlborough and achieved a somewhat equivocal victory over Marshal Villars at the bloody battle of Malplaquet (1709). After the allies had abandoned Emperor Charles VI and concluded a separate peace at Utrecht (1713), Eugene counseled him to end the war with France. The emperor reluctantly assented and sent Eugene to negotiate with Villars at the castle of the deceased margrave of Baden at Rastatt (Peace of Rastatt and Baden, 1714).

Less than two years later when war again broke out with the Turks, Charles appointed Eugene to command the army in Hungary. He defeated the Turks at Peterwardein (1716), Temesvár (1716), and Belgrade (1717). The Treaty of Passarowitz in 1718 ended the war. In the 1730s, even though Eugene had opposed involvement in the War of the Polish Succession (1733–1735), he loyally agreed to take command of the army on the Rhine. Old, ill, and hampered by numerically inferior forces, he was unable to achieve any victories on the field. He was forced to carry out a purely defensive strategy, but was able to prevent enemy penetration of Bavaria.

A year after the war ended, the "first soldier of the empire" died unmarried at Vienna (1736) and was buried in St. Stephen's Cathedral. Cold, austere, taciturn, extremely loyal to the Habsburgs, Eugene was a trustworthy soldier and administrator. Besides serving as imperial general and president of the Council of War, he had also been governor of the Austrian Netherlands and vicar-general of Italy. An ineffectual administrator, Eugene excelled as a soldier; his passion was war. His black animated eyes reflected his fiery vitality. His mastery of the art of movement and his keen insight into the intentions and limitations of his men and his enemies marked him as one of the greatest of the Habsburg generals.

Works By: F. Heller, ed., *Militärische Korrespondenz des Prinzen Eugen von Savoyen,* 2 Vols. (Vienna, 1848); Eugène François, prince of Savoy, *Feldzüge des Prinzen Eugen von Savoyen,* 20 vols. (Vienna, 1876–1892); Philip Roder von Diersburg, ed., *Kriegs-und Staatschriften über der spanischen Erbfolgekrieg, 1700–1707* (Karlsruhe, 1850). **Works About:** Antoine Béthouart, *Le Prince Eugène de Savoie, Soldat, Diplomate, et Mécène* (Paris, 1975); Max Braubach, *Prinz Eugen von Savoyen* 5 vols. (Vienna, 1963–65); A. Gaedeke, *Die Politik Österreichs in der spanischen Erbfolgefrage,* 2 vols. (Leipzig, 1906), Nicholas Henderson, *Prince Eugene of Savoy* (London, 1964); Derek McKay, *Prince Eugene of Savoy* (London, 1977).   L. S. Frey and M. L. Frey

See CHARLES VI; JOSEPH I; LEOPOLD I; SPANISH SUCCESSION; VIENNA, SIEGE OF; ZENTA.

EUGENIUS III (1145–1153), formerly Abbot Bernard Paganelli of the Cistercian monastery of St. Anastasius in Rome, was elected pope on February 15, 1145. His most pressing problem was the revolutionary Roman republic proclaimed in 1143 in defiance of papal authority. Less immediate but no less significant was the ambition of Roger II of Sicily who was steadily expanding his realm and consolidating his power. Since both the Roman and the Sicilian issues also impinged on imperial rights in Italy, Eugenius hoped to induce King Conrad III to commit German forces in the peninsula. Unexpectedly, however, Conrad enlisted in the Second Crusade, and so Eugenius spent much time between 1146 and 1148 in exile in France.

As soon as Conrad returned from the East in 1149, Eugenius reopened contact with him and his intimate adviser, Abbot Wibald of Stavelot-Corbey. Frequent correspondence and several embassies passed back and forth. Eugenius hoped to lure Conrad to Rome by offering him the imperial coronation, which Conrad had never received. The Roman republic, dominated by Arnold of Brescia whom the Church had condemned as a heretic, competed for Conrad III's favor, but the republicans' pompous assertions of their political fantasies elicited Conrad's contempt. Simultaneously Eugenius, who resided in the Campania between June 1150 and December 1152, gingerly avoided complications arising from the alliances that grew out of the Second Crusade: Louis VII of France with Roger of Sicily against Manuel of Constantinople, and Conrad III with Manuel against the Norman king. In late 1151 Eugenius and Conrad came to terms about the king's forthcoming journey to Rome, but Conrad died on February 15, 1152.

Eugenius enthusiastically greeted the accession of Frederick I whose concern for his imperial rights and dignity made him anxious to receive the crown of the Empire without delay. Eugenius cleverly played on Frederick's sensitivities by revealing Arnold of Brescia's plot to promote someone else as emperor, a puppet crowned by the republic. An exchange of embassies between pope and king soon produced agreements incorporated into the Treaty of Constance (February 23, 1153). The pope proposed to bestow the imperial crown whenever Frederick could come to Rome and to employ the Church's resources against whomever should threaten the honor of the Empire. For his part, Frederick contracted to overthrow the Roman republic, and thus restore the pope's temporal power, and to defend the honor of the papacy and its regalian rights. Each party committed itself to make no territorial concessions in Italy to the Byzantine emperor. To ensure Frederick's goodwill, Eugenius' legates, evidently carrying out his instructions, acceded to the king's request for an annulment of his marriage to his first wife, Adela of Vohburg, suspended his enemy Archbishop Henry of Mainz, and confirmed several of his episcopal nominees, but not Wichmann of Magdeburg. Although Eugenius thus cleared the way for Barbarossa's first Italian journey, he himself died on July 8, 1153, a year before that event took place.

Works: P. Jaffé, *Regesta Pontificum Romanorum ab condita Ecclesia ad annum post Christum natum MCXCVIII,* 2d ed., ed. W. Wattenbach et al. (Leipzig, 1885–1888, repr. 1956). **Works About:** H. Gleber, *Papst Eugen III. (1145–1153) unter besonderer Berücksichtung seiner politischen Tätigkeit* (Jena, 1936); J. Haller, *Das Papsttum: Idee und Wirklichkeit* (Basel, 1952), vol. 3; M. Maccarone, *Papato e Impero della elezione di Federico I alla Morte di Adriano IV (1152–1159)* (Rome, 1959); H. K. Mann, *Lives of the Popes in the Early Middle Ages* (London, 1913), vol. 9.   *R. H. Schmandt*

See CONRAD III; FREDERICK I.

f

FERDINAND I (1503–1564), Holy Roman emperor from 1558 to 1564, was born on March 10, 1503, at Alcalá de Henares in Spain. He was the second son of Philip the Handsome, son of Emperor Maximilian I and Mary of Burgundy, and of Joan the Mad, daughter of Ferdinand and Isabella of Spain. He was raised in Spain under the direction of his grandfather Ferdinand. His education by Pedro de Guzman and the Dominican Alvaro Osorio de Moscoso in the tradition of Spanish scholasticism may have contributed to his later political pragmatism. The plans of his grandfather to have him succeed to the throne of Spain failed when the throne went to Charles in 1516. After a meeting with his brother upon the latter's arrival in Spain, Ferdinand went to the Netherlands in 1518 where his education was completed under the care of his aunt Margaret. He also came into contact with the ideas of Erasmus, which would influence his later political and religious positions.

By a treaty concluded in Worms on April 28, 1521, Charles V recognized his brother Ferdinand as ruler of the hereditary Austrian possessions of Upper and Lower Austria, Styria, Carinthia, and Carniola. In an agreement made in Brussels in January and February 1522, he was made regent of all the German Habsburg possessions in southeastern Germany and of the duchy of Württemberg. In effect, the agreements established a new German branch of the Habsburg family beside the Burgundian-Spanish one. Charles, of course, expected close cooperation of the Habsburgs in ruling a large part of Europe, and Ferdinand generally recognized his brother's position and greater political vision. Although Ferdinand was originally a stranger to things German, he learned German once he arrived in Austria in 1521 and came to identify himself with German interests.

In 1521 Ferdinand married Anna, daughter of King Vladislav II of Bohemia and Hungary. After the death of her childless brother, Louis II, at the Battle of Mohács in 1526, Ferdinand claimed the succession to the crowns of Bohemia and Hungary for himself. He was elected unanimously to the throne of Bohemia in 1526. The visit of Ferdinand to Prague in that same year marked the reopening of the Bohemian lands to the Habsburgs. He built a summer palace for his wife, Anna, and began the process of gaining Bohemian loyalty to his dynasty. Ferdinand's bid for Hungary was not as successful. Only a minority offered the crown to Ferdinand, which he received in November 1527. A majority elected the rival claimant, John Zápolya. This split helped to bring the greater part of Hungary under Turkish rule. Consequently Ferdinand was faced with a Turkish threat throughout his reign. The Turks laid siege to Vienna in 1529 and threatened the Austrian lands in 1532 and 1541. In 1538, by treaty arrangement, Ferdinand secured the right to succeed Zápolya, but when the latter died in 1540, the Hungarians and the Turks took up the cause of John Sigismund, Zápolya's infant son. By a peace treaty in 1547, Ferdinand paid tribute to the Turks for his part of Hungary.

With Charles gone from Germany during much of the 1520s, Ferdinand was left to oversee Habsburg interests. In the absence of the emperor, he was made president of the *Reichsregiment*, the Imperial Governing Council, and acted as his brother's representative in imperial business. At the same time he was occupied with the government of the Austrian lands. After the imperial coronation of Charles in Bologna, Ferdinand was elected king of the Romans in January 1531 at Cologne and thus became heir to the imperial throne. The election was opposed by the Protestant princes and also brought discord to the Catholic side since it seemed to establish the Habsburgs on a hereditary throne. Ferdinand had earned the honor of this election by his efforts on behalf of his brother. Although he had at first attempted to suppress the Protestant reformers and their teachings in Austria and the neighboring duchies, Ferdinand, probably because of the Turkish danger, now became inclined to follow a middle course between the Catholics and Protestants. In 1532, he agreed to the religious peace at Nuremberg, which stated that no attacks were to be made against the Lutherans before the meeting of a general Church council. In return, he received some help from the Protestants for the war against the Turks. He suffered a blow to his prestige in 1534 over the duchy of Württemberg, which had first been placed under Habsburg administration in 1519 after the military defeat and exile of Duke Ulrich. Ferdinand had become its regent in 1522. In 1534, the political leader of Lutheranism, Landgrave Philip of Hesse, with the aid of French money, succeeded in conquering Württemberg and in returning Ulrich to power. In order to avoid an attack of Philip's troops on Austria, Ferdinand had to accept the loss. Ferdinand was forced to accept the Treaty of Cadan, by which Ulrich received the duchy, though as a fief from Austria. But the loss of Württemberg did not keep Ferdinand from further involvement in German politics.

Although Ferdinand helped Charles against the Protestant Schmalkaldic League in 1546 and 1547, he began nevertheless to adopt a more independent position. Ferdinand was offended when his brother, after crushing the Schmalkaldic League, refused to restore Württemberg to him. Ferdinand also felt that his brother provided him inadequate assistance against the Turks. Ferdinand was especially upset when Charles indicated his desire to have his son Philip succeed to the imperial throne. Ferdinand had been a loyal lieutenant for Charles for almost thirty years, generally subordinating his own judgment to Charles' desires. During this time Ferdinand had become a German prince, both personally and politically. It was obvious that the defense of the frontier against the Turks depended on support from the Empire. Naturally he thought of himself and his family as the successors to Charles in Germany. In 1551, Ferdinand reluctantly agreed to the plan that upon Charles' abdication, Philip should be chosen king of the Romans and then succeed Ferdinand as emperor. Charles paid the price for these schemes when Ferdinand was a spectator and mediator rather than a participant in Charles' war with Maurice of Saxony in 1552. In the same year Ferdinand negotiated the Treaty of Passau with Maurice, which declared a truce in the religious wars. In the following year Charles agreed to drop his plans for Philip and recognized that Ferdinand would be succeeded by his son Maximilian. Harmony was then restored between the brothers, and Charles virtually turned the conduct of imperial business over to Ferdinand.

Ferdinand received full authority to "act and settle." Thus it was he who was primarily responsible for the religious Peace of Augsburg, which brought an end to the German religious wars in 1555. It established the equality of Lutheranism with Catholicism, the right of the German princes to determine the religion of their states, and the ecclesiastical reservation, which stipulated that every ecclesiastical prince, archbishop, bishop, or abbot who became Protestant would lose his title, lands, and privileges. To gain the support of the Protestants for the ecclesiastical reservation, Ferdinand made a secret concession, known as the Declaration of Ferdinand, in which he gave the assurance that Lutheran subjects would not be molested in the Catholic ecclesiastical territories. After Charles finally carried out his intention to abdicate as emperor in 1558, Ferdinand was crowned emperor at Frankfurt on March 24. Pope Paul IV refused to recognize the new emperor, but Pius IV, his successor, did so in 1559. The few remaining years of Ferdinand's reign as Holy Roman emperor were spent in trying to settle the religious differences of Germany and in attempts to press the Turkish war more strongly. For a while his hopes for peaceful religious settlement revolved around the Council of Trent, which resumed its sessions in 1562. He sent representatives to the council to demand communion in both kinds for the laity, removal of clerical celibacy, and a genuine reform of the Church and the Church's properties and possessions. His demands demonstrated his hopes for the return of the Lutherans to a reformed Catholic church. But by this time the idea of using the council for a reconciliation with the Protestants had faded, and the requests of Ferdinand were easily pushed aside. Ferdinand was also unsuccessful in inducing the Protestants to be represented at the council.

It is apparent in his political dealings in Germany that Ferdinand tended to be somewhat more pragmatic than his brother Charles. By the beginning of the 1550s Ferdinand had come to realize that Lutheranism could not be crushed by military force. Even earlier, he demonstrated a willingness to find a peaceful solution to the Protestant problem. He was inclined to Erasmian ideas, and his princely ideal was essentially defined by Erasmus' *Handbook of the Christian Prince*. In fact, the second edition of this work was dedicated to Ferdinand. There were Erasmians, such as his chancellor Bernhard of Cles and two bishops of Vienna, John Faber and Frederick Nausea, in his immediate circle. And in his opposition to a great war to exterminate the Protestant heretics in Germany as some wanted, Ferdinand basically manifested the Erasmian virtues of compromise and reconciliation. He was also guided by the practical realization that such a war would ruin the Empire and produce a collapse of the Bohemian-Austrian-Hungarian defense system, which kept the Turks from the heart of central Europe.

In his attempts to compromise, Ferdinand was willing to make some concessions to the Protestants. He permitted Protestant administrators in former Catholic bishoprics. He secured from Pope Pius IV the privilege of communion in both kinds for the laity in Bohemia and in some parts of Germany. The treaties with the Protestants of the Empire, culminating in the Peace of Augsburg in 1555, owed much to his energetic efforts. At the same time, Ferdinand remained a loyal son of the Roman Catholic church and sought compromises as a way to restore the unity of the Church. He refused to conciliate Lutherans by giving in to their request to abrogate the clause concerning the ecclesiastical reservation in the Peace of Augsburg. The Jesuits, who were uncompromising in their stand against Protestantism, were heartily supported by the emperor when he opened the University of Vienna to them in 1551. Before allowing his son Maximilian to be elected as king of the Romans in 1562, he forced him to renounce his Protestant inclinations.

In the administration of the hereditary Austrian lands, Ferdinand continued the centralization and standardization of his grandfather Maximilian I. Although these attempts were not overly successful, Ferdinand revealed administrative gifts in the creation of a central *Hofrat*, or aulic council, in 1522 and the *Kriegsrat*, or war council, in 1556. Through the division of the Austrian lands among his three sons, he undermined his own efforts at centralization.

Ferdinand died in Vienna on July 25, 1564. Hard working and intelligent, Ferdinand showed greater political realism than his brother Charles V and was rewarded with greater popularity among the people and princes of Germany. Historians have especially regarded his reign as significant for establishing the hereditary Habsburg monarchy in Bohemia and Hungary and thus securing the basic boundaries of the Habsburg empire to 1918, as well as the rebuilding of the Holy Roman Empire as a community to which both Catholics and Protestants could legally belong.

Works By: Wilhelm Bauer and Robert Lacroix, eds., *Die Korrespondenz Ferdinands* I, pt. 1: *Familienkorrespondenz*, 2 vols. (Vienna, 1912–1930). **Works About:** Wilhelm Bauer, *Die Anfänge Ferdinands I* (Vienna, 1907); F. B. von Bucholtz, *Gesch. der Regierung Ferdinands des Ersten*, 9 vols. (Vienna, 1831–1838); Wolfgang Hilger, *Ikonographie Kaiser Ferdinands I* (Vienna, 1969); Alphons Lhotsky, *Das Zeitalter des Hauses Österreich. Die ersten Jahre d. Regierung Ferdinand I in Österreich* (Vienna, 1971); Karl Oberleitner, *Österreichs Finanzen und Kriegswesen unter Ferdinand I* (Vienna, 1859); Volker Press, *Kaiser Karl V, König Ferdinand und die Entstehung der Reichsritterschaft* (Wiesbaden, 1976); Anton Rezek, *Gesch. der Regierung Ferdinands I in Böhmen* (Prague, 1878); Eduard Rosenthal, *Die Behördenorganisation Kaiser Ferdinands I* (Vienna, 1887);

Alexander Thiry, "The Regency of Archduke Ferdinand, 1521–31" (Ph.D. diss., Ohio State University, 1970)

J. J. Spielvogel

See CHARLES V; ERASMUS; MAXIMILIAN II; PHILIP; ULRICH OF WÜRTTEMBERG.

FERDINAND II (1578–1637), Holy Roman emperor from 1619 and grandson of Ferdinand I, was born in Graz, Austria, on July 9, 1578, the eldest son of fifteen children of Archduke Charles (1540–1590), ruler of inner Austria, and Maria, daughter of Albert IV, duke of Bavaria. He was educated in the Jesuit University of Ingolstadt (1590–1595) and, under the guidance of his Jesuit confessor, Father William Lamormaini, became the pattern prince of the Counter Reformation, imbued with the absolutist and Catholic doctrine of one church, one king.

On December 2, 1596, he received the homage of the estates of inner Austria (his father having died in 1590), undertaking the government of Styria, Carinthia, Carniola, and Gorizia. After a visit to Italy, he mounted an organized attack on Protestantism in the archduchies, which had spread under the religious pacification granted by his father in 1578. He compelled his Protestant subjects to choose between exile and conversion, entirely suppressing Protestant worship (the astronomer John Kepler fled to the patronage of Rudolf II at Prague); and as the estates were largely Protestant, Ferdinand thus also broke the forces resisting the political absolutism of the Habsburgs.

In April 1606 Ferdinand joined with the other archdukes in recognizing his cousin Matthias (1557–1619) heir presumptive because Emperor Rudolf II was childless and mentally incompetent; but he was unwilling to help depose the emperor. Neither Matthias, however, nor the other brothers, the archdukes Maximilian and Albert, had direct heirs. But Ferdinand did have two sons from his marriage in 1600 to his cousin Maria Anna, daughter of William V, duke of Bavaria, and sister of Maximilian I of Bavaria (1573–1651), founder of the Catholic League (1609). The elder archdukes renounced their rights of succession in favor of Ferdinand and engineered his coronation as king of Bohemia (June 29, 1617) and Hungary (July 1, 1618). But he failed to be elected king of the Romans, or imperial successor designate because of the opposition of the Protestant electors and of Matthias' adviser, Cardinal Melchior Klesl (Khlesl), who favored a conciliatory policy toward the Protestants. Maximilian and Ferdinand then had Klesl seized on July 20, 1618, and imprisoned in Ambras Fortress in Tyrol (though he was allowed to return to Vienna in 1627); and when Matthias died on March 20, 1619, Ferdinand was unanimously elected emperor at Frankfurt on August 28, 1619.

The Empire was already disintegrating. The Protestant Bohemians, believing their religious and civil liberties menaced by Ferdinand and his Jesuit officials, had been in revolt since the defenestration of Prague (May 23, 1618) and their deposition of Ferdinand as king. Count Henry Matthias Thurn's forces skirmished with two imperial armies, which then retreated before the advance of Ernest von Mansfeld, who took Pilsen on November 21; and on August 26, 1619, the Protestant diet elected Frederick V, elector of the Palatinate (1596–1632), as king of Bohemia (mocked by the Jesuits as the Winter King), initiating the Thirty Years War. At the same time the Protestant prince of Transylvania, Gabriel Bethlen (Bethlen Gabor) (1580–1629), invaded Hungary, taking Bratislava (Pressburg) on September 15 and securing his own election as king of that territory.

Ferdinand's fortunes were restored when Spanish troops of his brother-in-law Philip III (1578–1621) (by marriage to his sister Margarette) overran the Palatinate; and the Catholic League of his former brother-in-law Maximilian I of Bavaria (Maria Anna had died in 1616 and Ferdinand married his second wife, Eleonora Gonzaga of Mantua, in 1622), under the command of Count John von Tilly (1559–1632), routed the Protestants at the White Mountain near Prague (November 8, 1620), in reward for which Maximilian was named an elector. Another brother-in-law (married to sister Anna), Sigismund III of Poland (1566–1632), forced Bethlen to renounce the Hungarian throne and retreat to Transylvania. By 1627 all worship in Bohemia except Roman Catholicism had been banned and all Protestants ordered banished. A new constitution made the kingdom hereditary in the house of Habsburg and effectively eliminated the political and national liberties of the Bohemians.

The intervention of Christian IV of Denmark (1577–1648), as much to rival Swedish control of the Baltic littoral as to champion Protestantism, subsidized by Charles I of England (1600–1649) and the Dutch, initiated the Danish War (1625–1629). The defeat of the anti-Habsburg coalition by the Catholic League under Tilly and the imperial army under the enigmatic Albert von Wallenstein (Waldstein) (1583–1634), resulting in the Peace of Lübeck (May 22, 1629), encouraged Ferdinand to issue the Edict of Restitution on March 6, 1629. This document decreed that all ecclesiastical lands that had been secularized since 1552 (by the Peace of Passau) be restored to Church control.

The edict was perceived as threatening not only to Protestant princes but also to Catholic rulers, for it seemed to imply the reassertion of the imperial prerogative within the political structure of the Empire. At the electoral diet of Regensburg in 1630, the elector Maximilian of Bavaria and the Saxon Lutherans forced Ferdinand to dismiss his brilliant and powerful general, Wallenstein, on August 13, ostensibly because of the latter's failure to take Stralsund in 1628.

Thus the imperial forces were handicapped when Gustavus II Adolphus of Sweden (1594–1632), who had taken Karelia and Ingria from Russia, Livonia from Poland, and the ports of Memel and Pillau from Prussia, landed in Pomerania on July 6, 1630. The escalating conflict was as much a national and dynastic struggle as it was a religious one, and Gustavus, though a devout Lutheran, was subsidized by Catholic France's Cardinal Richelieu (1585–1642). Due to the mobility of his ordnance and of his army and the genius of his tactics,

Gustavus overran northern Germany and shattered Tilly's army at Breitenfeld in Saxony (September 17, 1631).

When Tilly was mortally wounded in an engagement along the Lech River, Bavaria, in April 1632, Ferdinand in desperation recalled Wallenstein. The politically ambitious Wallenstein, who had even secretly negotiated with Gustavus, demanded absolute control over the army and military policy. He maneuvered the Swedes out of Bavaria, but at Lützen in Saxony on November 16, 1632, gout-ridden Wallenstein's army was destroyed, though the Swedish king was killed. Mutual exhaustion stalemated the fighting, and Wallenstein's continuing political machinations caused Ferdinand to dismiss him and probably have him assassinated (February 25, 1634).

Although the Swedes were defeated at Nördlingen (September 5–6, 1634), which dissolved the League of Heilbronn, the Peace of Prague, signed May 30, 1635, with John George I, elector of Saxony, was an admission by Ferdinand of his failure to crush Protestantism in the Empire. This agreement, soon assented to by other princes, modified the Edict of Restitution by making 1627, not 1552, the criterion of Church ownership of land.

Ferdinand was now fifty-seven years old but prematurely aged, and his son, the future Ferdinand III (1608–1657), had primarily arranged the Peace of Prague. This most Catholic emperor was also at odds with Urban VIII (pope from 1623 to 1644), who opposed Habsburg hegemony in Italy. In the conflict over the succession to the duchies of Mantua and Monferrato, the papacy supported the French claimant, Charles Gonzaga, duke of Nevers, who prevailed by the Treaty of Cherasco (June 19, 1631). Having secured his son's election as king of Rome and hence successor at Regensburg (December 22, 1636), Ferdinand II died in Vienna on February 15, 1637. He was a Catholic of intense devotion but a statesman of only meager talent, who tried to rule the Empire in a time of great crisis; and he died just as a rising France actively joined his enemies.

Works By: B. Dudik, ed., *Korrespondenz Kaiser Ferdinands II. mit P. Becanus und P. W. Lamormaini* (Vienna, 1848 ff.). Works About: F. van Hurter, *Gesch. Kaiser Ferdinands II.* (Schaffhausen, 1850–1855); F. C. Kevenhiller, *Annales Ferdinandei* (Regensburg, 1640–1646); M. Ritter, *Dtsch. Gesch. im Zeitalter der Gegenreformation und des Dreissigjährigen Krieges*, 3 vols. (1889–1908).   *A. H. Ganz*

See DEFENESTRATION OF PRAGUE; ECCLESIASTICAL RESERVATION; FERDINAND I; KEPLER; THIRTY YEARS WAR; TILLY; WALLENSTEIN, ALBERT.

FERDINAND III (1608–1657), Holy Roman emperor from 1637, was born in Graz, Austria, on July 13, 1608, the second son (John Charles died in 1619) of six children of the future Emperor Ferdinand II (1578–1637), and Maria Anna, sister of Maximilian I of Bavaria (1573–1651), later elector. He was educated by the Jesuits while the Thirty Years War was breaking out and crowned king of Hungary on December 8, 1625, and of Bohemia on November 21, 1627. His father recognized his ability and allowed him an increasing role in imperial affairs.

The imperial army generalissimo, Albert von Wallenstein (1583–1634), however, refused to allow Ferdinand to hold military command; hence Ferdinand played an important role in the dismissal of the famous general, succeeding him in 1634. As commander-in-chief of the imperial forces, he followed the advice of Field Marshal Matthias von Gallas (1584–1647) but was at least nominally responsible for the capture of Regensburg and Donauwörth and for defeating the Swedes at Nördlingen (September 5–6, 1634).

Ferdinand, less fanatic than his father, was instrumental in drawing up the compromise Peace of Prague (May 30, 1635), which modified the 1629 Edict of Restitution. His father secured his election as king of the Romans, or successor designate to the emperor, at Regensburg on December 22, 1636, despite the opposition of Bavaria and Urban VIII (pope 1623–1644), and was elected emperor upon his father's death in February 1637. He was eager to end the Thirty Years War on the basis of the Peace of Prague but was reluctant to grant religious freedom to the Protestants or act apart from the Spain of Philip IV (1605–1665) (whose sister, the Infanta Maria Anna, he had married on February 26, 1631).

But powerful France was emerging as the arbiter of Europe, and fresh French forces under the brilliant leadership of the Prince de Condé (1621–1686) defeated the long-invincible Spanish *tercios* at Rocroi in 1643, crossing the Rhine to defeat the imperial forces at Freiburg in 1644 and at Nördlingen in 1645. Cardinal Richelieu had died in 1642 (as did Louis XIII in 1643), but his anti-Habsburg policy was continued by his protégé, Cardinal Jules Mazarin (1602–1661), during the regency for Louis XIV.

Danish concern at Swedish expansion did provide a respite for Ferdinand's armies. Christian IV (1577–1648) came to an understanding with the emperor, and the Swedes redirected General Lennart Torstensson's (1630–1651) army from marching on Vienna to overrun Jutland in 1644. But when Gallas marched to assist the Danes, he was routed by Torstensson at Jüterbog (November 23, 1644), who then invaded Bohemia and destroyed a second imperial army at Jankov (Jankau) on March 6, 1645, threatening Prague and Vienna.

At the same time, however, negotiations were in progress that would result in the Peace of Westphalia, ending the Thirty Years War in 1648. Some 150 representatives were involved, imperial interests were represented by Maximilian Trauttmansdorff, Catholic envoys met in Münster, and the Protestants met in Osnabrück. The treaty that was signed on October 24, 1648, reflected the failure of the Habsburgs to restore either imperial or Catholic control over the territories of the Holy Roman Empire. Politically the members of the Empire received full sovereignty, and the emperor was to be bound by the decisions of the imperial diet (in permanent session at Regensburg after 1663) regarding matters of war and peace. Religiously equality of rights was allowed among

Catholics, Lutherans, and Calvinists in the Empire (though not in the Habsburg possessions), with Protestants sitting on the supreme court and the Aulic Council.

Ferdinand continued to seek the pacification of the Empire, advanced by the Nuremberg agreement of July 1650, by conceding much toleration to the Hungarian Protestants. He had three sons by Maria Anna: Ferdinand, for whom he secured election as king of Hungary (1647) and as king of the Romans (1653), but who died of smallpox in 1654 at the age of twenty-one, breaking his father's spirit; Leopold (1640–1705) who was elected king of Hungary (1655) and of Bohemia (1656) and who succeeded his father as emperor; and Charles Joseph (died 1664), bishop of Passau and Breslau and grandmaster of the Teutonic Knights. After Maria Anna died in 1646, Ferdinand married his cousin, Maria Leopoldina of Tyrol, daughter of the Archduke Leopold, in 1648, but who died the following year; and then Eleanora of Mantua, of the Nevers branch of the Gonzaga dynasty, in 1651 (who died in 1687).

The Habsburgs were still a potent force in international affairs, and in 1656 Ferdinand dispatched an army to Italy to assist Spain in its conflict with France (a conflict ended with the Peace of the Pyrenees in 1659). He had also just negotiated an alliance with Poland to check Swedish aggression under Charles X (1622–1660) when he died on April 2, 1657.

Although a more realistic and less fervently Catholic ruler than his father, Ferdinand III had to preside over the decline in Habsburg power. A well-cultured individual, the musical works that he composed, together with those of the emperors Leopold I and Joseph I, have been published by G. Adler (Vienna, 1892–1893).

Works About: K. Eder, "Ferdinand III," *NDB*, 5:85–86; M. Koch, *Gesch. des dtsch. Reiches unter der Regierung Ferdinands III.*, 2 vols. (Vienna, 1865–1866).   *A. H. Ganz*

See FERDINAND II; LEOPOLD I; MÜNSTER TREATY; OSNABRÜCK TREATY; THIRTY YEARS WAR; WESTPHALIA.

FISCHER VON ERLACH, JOHN BERNHARD (1656–1723), imperial architect and sculptor, was born in Graz, Austria, and trained as a sculptor by his father. John received further training in Rome, where he met Bernini, among others. Returning to Austria in 1686, Fischer worked as a medalist, sculptor, and designer of stucco decorations, gardens, and vases. In 1689 he was appointed to give daily lessons in architecture to Joseph I, king of Hungary, then eleven years old. In that same year, Fischer achieved public recognition for the two triumphal arches he erected to honor his pupil's entrance into Vienna as the newly crowned king of Germany.

As the king's architect, Fischer received many important commissions. In 1692 he began a town palace in Vienna and a chateau for Chancellor Strattmann. From 1693 on he worked for the archbishop of Salzburg and for many other ecclesiastical and secular dignities, such as Prince Eugene of Savoy. Following the coronation of Emperor Joseph I, Fischer von Erlach was appointed super-intendent of imperial buildings. He was reappointed to that post by Emperor Charles VI in 1712 after presenting the manuscript of a monumental series of engravings. His design for the Karlskirche in Vienna won him great praise. After his demise, his son, Josef Emmanuel (born 1693), succeeded him and completed his father's unfinished buildings including the imperial library and the Karlskirche.

Works About: H. Aurenhammer, *Johann Bernhard Fischer von Erlach* (Vienna, 1957); G. Kun-roth, *Die hist. Architektur Fischers von Erlach* (Munich, 1956); H. V. Lancaster, *Fischer von Erlach* (London, 1924); Hans Sedlmayr, "Fischer von Erlach," *EWA*, 5:396–400, and *Johann Bernard Fischer von Erlach* (Munich, 1956).   *J. W. Zophy*

See CHARLES VI; EUGENE OF SAVOY; JOSEPH I; VIENNA.

FRANCIS I (1708–1765), Francis Stephen of Lorraine, grand duke of Tuscany, and Holy Roman emperor (1745–1765), married Maria Theresa (1736), the eldest daughter of Charles VI, Holy Roman emperor (1711–1740). Francis was the second son of Leopold Joseph, duke of Lorraine, and Elizabeth Charlotte, daughter of Philip, duke of Orleans. He was betrothed to his cousin, Maria Theresa, and living in Vienna when the War of the Polish Succession (1733–1735) broke out. Cardinal Fleury of France, who intended to acquire Lorraine before Francis could succeed the aging duke, ordered Marshal Villars to occupy that land quickly. When peace was finally concluded in 1738, Frederick Augustus of Saxony was recognized as King Augustus III of Poland and Stanislaus Leszcynski was given the duchy of Lorraine. After Stanislaus' death Lorraine, still legally part of the Holy Roman Empire, would become part of France. In exchange for Lorraine, Francis Stephen was to receive the grand duchy of Tuscany after the expected expiration of the Medici dynasty (1737).

On the death of his father-in-law in 1740, war again broke out, the War of the Austrian Succession (1740–1748). During this conflict, a Wittelsbach, Charles Albert, was elected Holy Roman emperor (Charles VII) in 1742; this was the first time since 1438 that a Habsburg had not held the imperial throne. Charles' reign, however, was as short-lived as it was disastrous. When he died in January 1745, Maria Theresa, who could not hold the imperial title since she was a woman, was able to get her husband elected Holy Roman emperor despite the protests of the Palatinate and Brandenburg. Francis' election increased the prestige of the house of Habsburg, though theoretically he was from the house of Lorraine. On her husband's election, Maria Theresa became empress consort. In the peace of Aachen (Aix-la-Chapelle) Francis Stephen's election as Holy Roman emperor and Maria Theresa's succession as archduchess of Austria and queen of Hungary and Bohemia were recognized.

Although Maria Theresa was deeply in love with her husband, she did recognize his limitations; Francis Stephen was gay, friendly, easy-going, but undistinguished and unsuited to governing. Maria Theresa served as coregent but never really shared her power as ruler of the Habsburg hereditary lands with her husband. Maria Theresa and her husband had sixteen children. The eldest male, Joseph, became king of the Romans in 1763. On the death of his father he became Holy Roman emperor and coregent with his mother, who continued to hold the real power in the state.

Works About: A. von Arneth, *Gesch. Maria Theresias* (Vienna, 1863–1879); H. Benedikt, "Franz I," *NDB*, 5:358; Flegele, "Franz I," *ADB*, 7:278–85; G. P. Gooch, *Maria Theresa and Other Studies* (London, 1951); Eugen Guglia, *Maria Theresa* (Munich, 1917); Joseph Kallbrünner, ed., *Kaiserin Maria Theresia politisches Testament* (Vienna, 1952); C. A. Macartney, *Maria Theresa and the House of Austria* (Mystic, Conn., 1969); Robert Pick, *Empress Maria Theresa: The Earlier Years, 1717–1757* (New York, 1966); Friedrich Walter, ed., *Maria Theresia: Briefe und Aktenstücke in Auswahl* (Darmstadt, 1968).   *L. S. Frey and M. L. Frey*

See AUSTRIAN SUCCESSION; CHARLES VII; JOSEPH I; MARIA THERESA; PRAGMATIC SANCTION; POLISH SUCCESSION.

FRANCIS II (1768–1835), last Holy Roman emperor (1792–1806) and as Francis I, emperor of Austria from 1804, was born in Florence on February 12, 1768, the oldest of sixteen children born to Leopold II (1747–1792), then grand duke of Tuscany and later emperor, and Maria Luisa, daughter of Carlos III of Spain (1716–1788). He was brought to Vienna to be educated as heir to the throne in 1784 by his uncle, the childless Emperor Joseph II (1741–1790), who was, however, repelled by his reserved and timid nephew. Francis did see some military service in the Turkish campaigns. On February 18, 1790, his wife of two years, Elizabeth of Württemberg, died in childbirth; and his uncle, the emperor, died two days later. Francis acted as regent under the guidance of the elderly Prince von Kaunitz (1711–1794) until his father came up from Italy to become Leopold II.

On September 19 Francis was married to his first cousin, Maria Theresa, daughter of Ferdinand, king of Naples, and Queen Caroline, his father's sister. This marriage of double first cousins required a papal dispensation. Only seven of the twelve children born to the couple lived to adulthood including the feebleminded epileptic Ferdinand (1793–1875), who succeeded to the throne, and Maria Anna, an imbecile who was kept at Schönbrunn.

On March 1, 1792, Leopold died, leaving the Empire and the Habsburg lands to Francis. Immature at twenty-four, the emperor was faced with the upheavals of the French Revolution and the Napoleonic expansion. Scarcely a month after his accession, France declared war on Austria in retaliation for the Declaration of Pillnitz (August 27, 1791). The Prussian defeat at Valmy (September 20, 1792) was followed by the loss of the Austrian Netherlands. In 1793 when the revolutionaries executed Louis XVI and later Queen Marie Antoinette, Francis' aunt, Austria joined in the First Coalition against them. Nonetheless Austrian forces were consistently defeated, and General Napoleon Bonaparte's Italian campaign resulted in the Treaty of Campo Formio (October 17–18, 1797). Austrian participation in the Second Coalition witnessed the defeat of Russia at Zurich in September 1799 and the epic retreat of Field Marshal Alexander Suvorov across the Alps, Melas' defeat by Napoleon at Marengo (June 14, 1800), and Kray's defeat by Moreau at Hohenlinden (December 3, 1800), all leading to the Peace of Luneville (February 2, 1801).

Despite the military disasters, Francis' popularity mounted at home, especially in Vienna. Austrian nationalism was rising, reflected in Joseph Haydn's anthem "God Keep Kaiser Franz." Though the melancholic emperor was hardly a heroic figure, he manifested the enduring patience to survive his enemies. Politically he had never sympathized with the liberalism of his father and his uncle, and the confusion resulting from Joseph's reforms and the chaos of the French Revolution convinced him more firmly of the correctness of absolutism.

Out of preference as much as necessity, Francis, foreseeing the demise of the Holy Roman Empire, unified the Habsburg lands as the Austrian Empire (August 10, 1804). Thus when the war of the Third Coalition led to disaster at Ulm (October 20, 1805), Austerlitz (December 2), and the Treaty of Pressburg (December 26), and the Napoleonic Confederation of the Rhine supplanted the Holy Roman Empire the following year, the Habsburgs still had an imperial throne. On August 6, 1806, the end of the millennial Empire was announced in Vienna in the square Am Hof, and the medieval regalia and vestments were stored away in the treasury of the Hofburg. The Viennese, preoccupied with the two-step waltz and the lively Maria Theresa, seemed hardly to notice.

In 1809 Austria declared war on France again and, though Francis' able brother the Archduke Charles won a victory at Aspern-Essling (May 21–22), was as quickly defeated by Napoleon at Wagram (July 5–6). Francis' new foreign minister, Clemens von Metternich (1773–1859), softened the terms of the Peace of Schönbrunn (October 14) by arranging the marriage of the emperor's daughter, Marie Louise, to the "Corsican ogre" by proxy, in March 1810. (She dutifully provided Napoleon with an heir but quickly left him in 1814.) It was Metternich who maneuvered Austrian policy to help defeat Napoleon in the war of liberation (1813–1814), and it was he who was the shrewd architect of the Congress of Vienna (September 1814–June 1815). While the visiting sovereigns and their entourages enjoyed the hunts and dances of the Hofburg, the Council of Four (Talleyrand made it five) redrew the map of Europe in the baroque Ballhaus, the adjoining chancellery building. Austria gave up some of its western territories but emerged as a more compact entity, retaining its prestige in German affairs with the presidency of the new German Confederation.

Francis politely adhered to the Holy Alliance of Czar Alexander I but strongly supported the reactionary policies it implied, as practiced by Metternich. While Vienna enjoyed the comfortable Biedermeier age of Schubert and Strauss, political liberals were suppressed by a secret police system made notorious by the fortress prison of the Spielberg. Francis had only reluctantly agreed to the mass mobilization of 1809, fearing the dangers of an armed citizenry, and was hesitant to support the Tyrolean revolt of Andreas Hofer (1767–1810) against Napoleon's satellite, Bavaria. (Rewarded with the Austrian governorship of the Tyrol, Hofer was later betrayed to the French and shot at Mantua.).

Opposed to change in general, Francis ironically retained many of Joseph II's reforms, as modified by Leopold II, including state control of the Church, though he ultimately sympathized with (but did nothing about) the restoration of ecclesiastical powers. In this he was pressed by his fourth wife, Charlotte of Bavaria, the empress Caroline Augusta. Maria Theresa had died in 1807, and Francis had married a third time, barely eight months later, a beautiful young cousin, Maria Ludovica of Modena-Este. But she was ill with tuberculosis and, exhausted by entertaining royalty at the Congress of Vienna, died on a trip in Verona in 1816. Six months later he married Charlotte of Bavaria, twenty-four years his junior (died 1873).

Francis was unwilling to change the succession to pass over his retarded son, Ferdinand, in favor of his unimaginative but healthy second son, Francis Charles, who fathered the future Francis Joseph I (1830–1916). Metternich intrigued to prevent any regency by the emperor's brothers, the archdukes Carl and John, who opposed him, even marrying Ferdinand to Marianna of Savoy. But when Francis II died on March 2, 1835, succeeded by Ferdinand, Metternich was one of the regents named to govern the Austrian Empire.

Works About: V. Bibl, *Francois II, le beau-père de Napoléon* (Paris, 1936); J. A. Helfert, *Kaiser Franz und die österreichischen Befreiungs-Kriege* (Vienna, 1867); W. C. Langsam, *Francis the Good: The Education of an Emperor, 1768–1792* (New York, 1949); F. Maass, *Der Josephinismus, 1760–1850* (Vienna, 1957–1961), vols. 4–5; H. Rössler, *Oesterreichs Kampf um Deutschlands Befreiung, 1805–1815*, 2 vols., 2d ed. (Hamburg, 1945); F. Walter, *Gesch. der österreichischen Zentralverwaltung unter Franz I und Ferdinand I*, 2 vols. (Vienna, 1956).   *A. H. Ganz*

See HAYDN; JOSEPH II; LEOPOLD II; NAPOLEONIC WARS; VIENNA.

FRANKFURT AM MAIN, was one of the most important free imperial cities in the Empire whose significance rested on constitutional and economic bases. A military settlement during the Roman Empire, the city became a favorite of emperors in the high Middle Ages, and, as a consequence, it received a large number of privileges. Among these were the right to host semiannual fairs, one in the autumn (granted 1240) and the other during Lent (granted 1330); constitutional recognition in the Golden Bull of 1356 as the traditional site of the emperor's election; and maintenance of its free imperial status until the demise of the Empire. Even after 1806 it—along with Lübeck, Hamburg, and Bremen— remained free. In the later sixteenth century, Frankfurt became the seat of the emperor's coronation, as well as of his election. So important was the city that its native son Goethe (1749–1832) referred to Frankfurt as the secret capital of Germany.

The city's favorable geographical location accounted for its greatness. Situated on the lower Main east of the river's confluence with the Rhine, the city was accessible by the two most important water routes bisecting the Empire. It was also the focal point of landed trade routes from north to south and east to west. This location tied Frankfurt's economic fate to supraregional and international commerce, and these in turn motivated the policies of its patrician government. Such policies manifested themselves in the city's adherence to authorities who granted Frankfurt's privileges, for the government felt that only by maintaining these freedoms would the city retain its status.

Because of its semiannual fairs, Frankfurt became a center of the exchange of ideas, as well as of goods and money. This was most apparent in the prominence of its book fairs, part of the larger fairs and attended by publishers and dealers from around Europe. Although the city's introduction of the Reformation did not ultimately damage the right to host these fairs, it led to harassment of the book trade by the Imperial Book Commission that operated under the influence of the Counter Reformation. Largely because of this, Leipzig began to supersede Frankfurt in the late seventeenth and eighteenth centuries as the book center of the Empire.

During the Reformation, the city's government experienced severe difficulties in appeasing those powers upon which its strength rested. It was pushed from below by its citizenry who were pro-evangelical and wished the government to declare that faith openly, and it was pulled from above by threats from the emperor and the archbishop of Mainz, the city's ordinary and archchancellor of the Empire, if it gave in to the populace. In this situation the government tried to find a middle ground. Belatedly, in 1533, Frankfurt declared itself Lutheran and joined the Schmalkaldic League. At the same time it lodged complaints and appeals with the Imperial Cameral Court (*Reichskammergericht*) in order to stave off final judgments on complaints made against the city. Although the government was seriously tested, in the long run such practices were successful, verified by the subsequent importance of Frankfurt as an international industrial and banking capital. Until the end of the Empire, it remained Lutheran while it tolerated relatively large numbers of Calvinists, Catholics, and Jews.

Works About: Friedrich Bothe, *Gesch. der Stadt Frankfurt am Main* (Frankfurt, 1913); Alexander Dietz, *Frankfurter Handelsgeschichte*, 4 vols. (Glashütten im Taunus, 1910–1925, rpr. 1970); Sigrid Jahns, *Frankfurt, Reformation und Schmalkaldischer Bund* (Frankfurt, 1976); Georg L. Kriegk, *Frankfurter Burgerzwiste und Zustände im Mittelater* (Frankfurt, 1862; repr., 1970); Günter Rauch, *Pröpste, Propstei und Stift von Sankt Bartholomäus in Frankfurt 9. Jahrhundert bis 1802* (Frankfurt, 1975); Gerald L. Soliday, *A Community in Conflict: Frankfurt Society in the Seventeenth and Early Eighteenth Centuries* (New Hampshire, 1974); J. W. Thompson, ed. and tr., *The Frankfort Book Fair* (Chicago, 1911; repr. New York, 1968). *P. N. Bebb*

See GOETHE; GOLDEN BULL; IMPERIAL CAMERAL COURT; IMPERIAL CITIES; SCHMALKALDIC LEAGUE.

FREDERICK I, BARBAROSSA (1125–1190), German king (1152–1190), and Holy Roman emperor (1155–1190), was the son of Frederick of Hohenstaufen and nephew and successor of Conrad III. He was virtually a unanimous choice of the German nobility because of his background. His chivalric reputation and sympathy for the lower nobility made him acceptable to that group, while his relationship to both the Welf and Hohenstaufen families through his mother and father, respectively, made him acceptable to the greater nobility as a unifying factor and mediator between these two powerful families whose feuding had brought the Empire to civil war in the previous century. Frederick was charismatic, intelligent, energetic, and ambitious. His accession to the throne encouraged the German nobility and people to believe that in him they had found the leader who could restore order to the Empire and recapture the past glories of the Ottos.

Frederick's policies were in most respects dictated and colored by the past and a romantic view of the present. He was determined to restore imperial authority and thus bring peace and order to Germany. He desired to reimpose an eroded royal authority over the German Church and to make good again the imperial claims over Italy and Rome. In essence, he believed in the myth of the universal empire with its Roman center and viewed himself not only as the heir of Charlemagne but of Augustus as well. Frederick's goals as king and emperor thus show him more to be a captive of the past—in reality, a romanticized past that never was—than a forward-looking statesman of the future.

Before being able to embark on more ambitious and universal plans, however, Frederick found it necessary to deal with the difficult situation in Germany first. He had two fundamental objectives for Germany in his first years as ruler: he wanted to restore general peace and order among the nobility, which meant ending private warfare and healing the rift between Welf and Hohenstaufen, and he wanted to exercise in full the rights granted to the crown in Church relations by the Concordat of Worms. A first step toward the pacification of Germany was taken with Frederick's declaring a general land peace in 1152, an act that virtually outlawed private warfare. While this measure was unevenly enforced over the following forty years, largely depending upon whether the king was absent from the realm, it nonetheless limited and restricted private warfare since transgressions of the peace were usually ruthlessly punished once Frederick returned to Germany. In 1158 Frederick extended the land peace throughout the entire Empire and in 1186 at the diet of Nuremberg promulgated supplementary laws restricting private warfare even further.

The key to the enforcement of the land peace lay in the cooperation between the monarchy and the dukes, for as long as the king and the most powerful members of the nobility were united in enforcement, the prosecution of private warfare was very difficult. Indeed the dukes were often the chief sponsors of private warfare as a result of particularist interests. Such had been the case during Conrad III's reign with the Welf-Hohenstaufen dispute, which at times threatened to plunge Germany into complete civil war. The cessation of private warfare and the return of peace and order thus was contingent on a successful mediation of the Welf-Hohenstaufen feud, a task that was of paramount importance at the time of Frederick's accession. The dispute had originated when Conrad III had deprived the Welf, Henry the Proud, of his duchies of Saxony and Bavaria, granting the former to the Billung, Albert the Bear, and the latter to the Babenberg, Leopold of Austria. Frederick, being related to both the Welf and Hohenstaufen families, was the ideal mediator, and early in his reign he began the lengthy negotiation necessary to solve the problem. The Welf, Henry the Lion, the king's cousin, was confirmed as duke of Saxony with extensive powers in the Slavic lands to the east. Henry was also granted the duchy of Bavaria in 1154, which satisfied his demands but left the Babenberg descendant, Henry Jasomirgott, in a difficult situation. After two years of negotiation Frederick succeeded in separating Austria from Bavaria and granting the former to Henry Jasomirgott with considerable privileges allowing him virtual autonomy. Albert the Bear received the mark of Brandenburg, with permission to extend his authority into Slavic lands, and the king's uncle, Welf VI, was satisfied with the grant of extensive imperial fiefs in northern Italy. Thus by 1157 Frederick had satisfied the desires of the leaders of both the Welf and Hohenstaufen families, obtained peace in Germany, and restored order and imperial authority throughout the kingdom.

In regard to the crown's relationship to the German Church, Frederick took advantage of a temporary lack of strong international ecclesiastical leadership to extend his influence over the leading German prelates and abbots. The death of Bernard of Clairvaux in 1153, disorganization in the papacy, and Arnold of Brescia's recent establishment of the Roman commune provided him the opportunity. Frederick admitted the concessions made to the Church by previous emperors and agreed to the terms of the Concordat of Worms but stubbornly insisted on exercising the considerable rights and prerogatives still available to him by custom and law. Through disputed and double elections, his presence at several elections, approval of nomination procedures, and the application of indirect pressure, he was able to control the appointment of most bishops and abbots. Moreover, many German churchmen were not necessarily opposed to the reestablishment of the old Ottonian crown-Church alliance, especially under the leadership of an able and energetic young king, a situation far superior to the continued growth of an international institutional Church ruled out of Rome. The result was the speedy re-creation of the German Church on the model originally established by Otto I two hundred years before, where the German bishops functioned in a dual secular-spiritual role. Indeed under Frederick, German prelates came again to function increasingly as imperial officials and give first precedence to their political duties. For forty years, the essential requirement in the selection of bishops was their political and administrative abilities more than their piety and devotion to spiritual ideals. Through their stricter inclusion in the feudal structure, the German prelates became increasingly dependent on the king, and Church resources became more available for royal utilization.

While considerably successful in his attempts to restore the imperial ideal to Germany and the eastern frontiers, Frederick met with much less success in his activities and undertakings in Italy. There were essentially two areas of Italy of crucial interest to the young German king. One was the city of Rome, the seat of the papacy, headquarters of the international Church, and the symbolic capital of the Empire. The other was Lombardy and its leading city of Milan, a wealthy territory comprising much of northern Italy, the control of which could potentially have provided the emperor the means to operate far more independently in Germany than would otherwise have been the case. In effect, Frederick's control of Lombardy was half of his policy for the revival and extension of the royal power in Germany where, other than the somewhat unreliable alliance with the dukes and leading prelates, the king's only power base was his practice of consolidating royal and family demesne through the acquisition of additional lands, especially in Swabia.

Frederick's first Italian expedition in 1154–1155, though not particularly outstanding, did meet some of his limited objectives. With an army of only eighteen hundred knights, the king was unable to confront directly the defiant and rebellious Milanese but did range up and down Lombardy attacking and destroying several small towns, including Tortona, a key ally of Milan. He thus made quite clear his future intentions of exercising his rights as king of Lombardy and of bringing the cities of northern Italy under his sway. Frederick's immediate objective in this expedition was Rome and the imperial crown, which he was to receive from Pope Eugenius III in return for an alliance formed in 1153 at Constance against the Normans of the south and the heretical Arnold of Brescia's Roman commune. By the time Frederick reached Rome, Eugenius had been replaced by the energetic reformer Adrian IV, who solved the Roman commune problem by laying an interdict on the city during Holy Week, which led to the expulsion of Arnold. Frederick showed his good faith by capturing the heretic and turning him over to Roman authorities, who executed him. Following a disturbing and foreboding meeting with the new pope at Sutri, Frederick was crowned emperor in June 1155 amid hostile demonstrations by the Roman populace, which were harshly repulsed by the emperor's troops. Rather than meet the invasion from the south by the Norman king, William I, however, the new emperor withdrew his small, malaria-infested army to Germany, thereby leaving Adrian IV in difficult straits. Left with no alternative, the pope was forced to conclude an alliance with the Normans at Benevento in 1156.

Strained relations between emperor and pope reached the breaking point in 1157 at the diet of Bescançon when the papal chancellor, Roland Bandinelli, presented a letter to the German court in which Adrian IV seemingly claimed the Empire to be a fief granted by the pope to the emperor as his vassal. Actually Adrian's letter was open to two different interpretations, depending upon the translation of the key word *beneficia*. By one interpretation, the pope said he was pleased to crown Frederick emperor and hoped to grant him even further benefits (*beneficia*). By the other, the pope said he was pleased to have crowned Frederick emperor and would like to give him even more fiefs (*beneficia*). The emperor's chancellor, the able and ambitious Rainald of Dassel, translated *beneficia* as *fiefs*, thus implying a papal claim of lordship over the Empire. The German nobility was enraged, the emperor insulted, and Cardinal Roland barely escaped with his life. Although Adrian promptly claimed that his letter had been misunderstood, it was widely known that both he and Roland were great admirers of the policies of Gregory VII and disturbed about events in the German Church. Indeed it is not impossible that the pope deliberately chose a word that could be counted harmless if need arose or that could be used later as the foundation for broader claims of papal authority. In any event, the German bishops were alienated from the papacy, and Frederick issued a declaration echoing Henry IV's claim to hold the throne "by election of the princes and the hand of God alone." He then prepared to invade Italy in force where Milan, seizing on the split between pope and emperor, had begun its reconquest of Lombardy.

Frederick's primary objective in his Italian expedition of 1158–1162 was the assertion of his imperial rights over Lombardy, which meant controlling the wealthy and powerful city of Milan whose expansionist interests had led to economic, political, and military oppression of its smaller neighbors. Facing an army of ten thousand knights, Milan quickly capitulated to a compromise allowing Milanese self-government, and at the diet of Roncoglia in 1158 the emperor began the necessary job of reorganizing Lombardy. Frederick severely restricted the self-government of most towns, insisting on appointing their administrators, and claimed full feudal jurisdiction over the territory, which included lucrative financial advantages for the imperial government. The rapacity, incompetence, and insensitivity of many of Frederick's appointed German officials, plus his insistence that Milan surrender half its territory, resulted in a revolt of several cities, led by Milan and encouraged by Pope Adrian. The death of the pope late in 1159 did not alleviate the situation since a divided College of Cardinals elected Roland Bandinelli as Alexander III while an imperialist minority settled on Victor IV as an antipope, later confirmed by the emperor at the Council of Pavia in 1160. Despite his excommunication by Pope Alexander, Frederick pressed on with the war against the rebellious Lombard cities, finally subduing and razing Milan in 1162 and destroying the walls of its major allies. With the installation of imperial *podestas* throughout Lombardy, it appeared that the emperor had finally succeeded in acquiring that rich territory, which had always remained just outside the grasp of earlier emperors.

The major obstacle remaining to thwart Frederick's plans was Pope Alexander, who out of desperation had forged an alliance with the Normans of Sicily, the Byzantines, and Venice, which felt its power and independence threatened by the emperor's successes in Lombardy. Through skillful negotiation and power politics, Frederick and his advisers had succeeded by 1166 in stripping Alexander of his support in the German Church and from the English and French crowns. Even the death of Victor in 1163 and his replacement by a new antipope, Pascal, did not deter his progress. A new Italian expedition in 1166 succeeded in capturing Rome by spring 1167, forcing Alexander to seek refuge with the Normans. In the flush of success, however, events suddenly took a disastrous turn for the emperor. A serious epidemic devastated his army in Rome, while the cities of Lombardy reasserted themselves in the face of heavy-handed imperial rule by forming the Lombard League. Only with great difficulty was Frederick able to withdraw the remnants of his supporters and army to the safety of Germany, where he spent the next seven years continuing his consolidation of power there and awaiting another opportunity to intervene in Italy.

Frederick's final attempt to restore effective imperial authority in Italy began with his expedition of 1174. This time he lacked the support of his powerful cousin Henry the Lion, whose policies had led to a minor rift between the two and who refused to aid his feudal lord when begged to do so in 1176. Moreover he was faced by a powerful alliance of the Lombard League and Venice, encouraged and assisted by the pope and his Norman allies. Failing to capture the key fortress of Alessandria, Frederick took the offensive in the field only to meet a disastrous and humiliating defeat at Legnano in May 1176. After Legnano, all hope of direct imperial domination of Italy was lost, and the emperor wisely realized the value of diplomatic measures to obtain at least some part of his goals. At the Treaty of Agnani late in 1176, Frederick agreed to recognize Alexander as the true pope and the following summer at Venice reached a temporary agreement with the Lombards, which was later expanded and ratified at the Peace of Constance in 1183 whereby the Italian cities recognized his sovereignty but retained their self-government. In fact, from this point onward, the alliance between Milan and the Empire strengthened, with the papacy as the opposition, and in his last years Frederick concentrated his Italian policy on affirming his control of the center of the peninsula. In addition, Frederick concluded a marriage alliance with the Normans of Sicily in 1186.

Following the war with the Lombard League, Frederick returned to Germany to continue his policy of consolidating the royal power. Effectively reaffirmed in his control of the German Church by his recent accommodation with Pope Alexander, the emperor now set about destroying the power of the powerful dukes. Henry the Lion's aloofness and independence in previous years showed the necessity for this action, and in 1179 Frederick moved against his Welf cousin. The result was the banishment of Henry, the dismembering of his duchies, and the destruction of his power in Germany. The chief beneficiaries were the territorial princes who now were free to operate relatively independently in their lands with but little direct control from above. Indirectly the royal power was augmented through a more solid establishment of a feudal system and the elimination of powerful vassal dukes. In his last years, Frederick reigned over a relatively peaceful and prosperous Germany.

With his position in the Empire safely protected, Frederick decided in 1188 to lead the Third Crusade to attempt the recapture of Jerusalem, which had been taken by the Saracens in 1187 under the able leadership of Saladin. Frederick's view of himself as the head of a universal Christian empire and the secular leader of Western Christendom almost dictated the necessity of his playing a leading role in a new crusade. Leaving a peaceful and well-ordered Empire in the hands of his son, Henry, the emperor departed for the Holy Land in 1189. Despite numerous difficulties, the aging though still capable and charismatic emperor managed to lead his army to Celicia, where in June 1190 he drowned while bathing.

Frederick Barbarossa was one of the most capable men ever to rule the Holy Roman Empire. Although he had to overcome many obstacles, he nonetheless succeeded in repairing and restoring much of the power and prestige of the German monarchy and Empire. Under his rule Germany was generally peaceful and prosperous. Trade expanded, new towns were founded, and the Slavic lands to the east were colonized and Christianized. His political reforms tended to facilitate the administration of the government. Although generally unsuccessful and perhaps unwise in the pursuit of his objectives in Italy, he was adhering to the same imperial policies followed by his predecessors for centuries.

German legend refused to allow the death of the popular Frederick and has him miraculously alive in the Kyffhäuser, to reappear at the unification of Germany. Among German rulers, Frederick has made one of the deepest and most lasting impressions on the German mind. He was succeeded as king and emperor by his son, Henry VI.

Works About: *Constitutiones et Acta publica*, vol. 1: *MGH Legum Sectio IV*, ed. Ludwig Weiland (Hanover, 1893, rpr. 1963); W. von Giesebrecht, *Gesch. der dtsch. Kaiserzeit*, ed. W. Schild (Leipzig, 1888, 1895), vols. 5–6; Helmold, *The Chronicle of the Slavs*, tr. F. J. Tschan (New York, 1966); Karl Jordan, *Freidrich Barbarossa* (Göttingen, 1959); Peter Munz, *Frederick Barbarossa, A Study in Medieval Politics* (Ithaca, N.Y. 1969); E. Otto, *Friedrich Barbarossa* (Potsdam, 1943); Otto of Freising, *The Deeds of Frederick Barbarossa*, tr. C. C. Mierow with R. Emery (New York, 1966) and *Two Cities: A Chronicle of Universal History to the Year 1146 A.D.*, ed. and tr. C. C. Mierow (New York, 1966); Marcel Pacaut, *Frederick Barbarossa*, tr. A. J. Pomerans (New York, 1970); Peter Rassow, *Honor imperii, die neue Politik Friedrich Barbarossas*, 1152–1159 (Munich, 1961); Henry Simonsfeld, *Jb. des Dtch. Reiches unter Friedrich I* (Leipzig, 1908), vol. 1.   D. S. Devlin

See CONRAD III; HENRY VI; HENRY THE LION; HENRY THE PROUD; RAINALD; WELF-WAIBLINGEN CONTROVERSY.

FREDERICK II (1194–1250), emperor, a Hohenstaufen, elected king in Germany in 1211, was crowned at Mainz in 1212 and at Aachen in 1215 after the defeat of Otto IV, and coronated at Rome in 1220. An understanding of Frederick's genealogy and youth helps to explain in large measure his complex rule.

Son of Emperor Henry VI (d. 1197) and the Sicilian heiress Constance (d. 1198), Frederick immediately had contact with two most influential European families. On the paternal side he was the grandson of Emperor Frederick (I) Barbarossa of Hohenstaufen (d. 1190), and on the maternal side his grandfather was Roger II (d. 1154) of Sicily, a Norman. Left as a ward of Innocent III, Frederick was reared in Sicily to become its king. Here he came under the diverse cultures that characterized the kingdom and that in turn marked his reign: Arabic, Byzantine, Norman, Jewish, Saracen, and Italian. With considerable justification, many regarded him as an Oriental ruler; his practice of traveling about with his harem and menagerie added to that image.

Although the Hohenstaufen faction in the Empire pushed his election before it was finally successful in 1211, Frederick spent little time in German territories. Altogether he was present less than ten years—from 1212 to 1220 and for some months during the middle of the 1230s. Yet his very elevation to the imperial dignity more than any other single cause spelled the demise of the Hohenstaufen family and, after his death, brought about the interregnum that lasted until 1273. As king of Sicily and emperor, Frederick became sovereign of territories that caught the papal states and Lombard communes in a vise. In order for them to maintain their independence, these states, often under papal leadership, intrigued with Frederick's opponents, and this led to turmoil in his territories. By excommunicating Frederick, the pope fomented rebellion in the Empire, and a Church council officially deposed him in 1245, thereby setting off a new round of civil wars.

During Frederick's reign it became clear that German affairs played only a minor role in his policy. His control of Sicily and Italy, the success of which necessitated favorable relations with both the papacy and Lombardy, was the cornerstone. An outline of his endeavors after his return from Germany in 1220 confirms this observation. Until 1224, he reorganized the government of Sicily, and then he spent the next two years attempting to pacify northern Italy. In the process he endangered his relationship with Rome because the pope feared imperial encirclement. To conciliate the pope who had excommunicated him in 1227, Frederick undertook a successful crusade to the Holy Land. Upon his return to Sicily, he placated the inhabitants and the pope, and the papal ban was lifted by the Treaty of San Germano and the Peace of Ceperano (1230). Until 1235, Frederick remained in Italy and his southern kingdom where he began an extensive building program and instituted governmental reform, represented by the famous *The Constitutions of Melfi* (1231). After quelling a rebellion in Germany led by his son, King Henry VII, who had the support of the Lombard League, Frederick returned to Italy. Once again he began to pursue his Italian policy, and this led to his second excommunication in 1239. He did not venture north of the Alps for the remainder of his life. Thus only indirectly did Frederick involve himself in German affairs, yet it would be too facile to maintain that he was not concerned about them.

Although Italy was the center of Frederick's imperial vision, any disturbances in Germany detracted him from the pursuit of his goal, a realization that his opponents were quick to note. In order to pacify his German principalities and gain their support, Frederick granted extensive concessions to the princes, spiritual and secular, and also to his antagonists. By the privileges of 1213, 1220, and 1232, he advanced the growing tendency of the princes—already launched on their paths by the civil wars of 1197–1212—to independent action. Similar was his conciliation of Otto of Welf, heir of Henry the Lion, to whom he granted the newly created duchy of Brunswick-Lüneburg in 1235. These grants help explain the princes' support for Frederick in 1235–1236 when he put down his son's rebellion. At the same time, however, he had alienated the independent sources of imperial power and made it virtually impossible for the sovereign to pursue an autonomous German policy.

During his reign in the Empire, Frederick concluded an epoch in German history and began another. By subordinating German interests to his own Italian concerns, Frederick allowed the creation of a power vacuum into which ecclesiastical and secular princes poured their self-interest. While tensions had always existed between the imperial sovereigns on the one hand and the greater princes on the other, the goal of imperial policy from the time of Otto I had been to find an equilibrium between the two, one that preserved public authority and respect for the king. Frederick, however, allowed such a tenuous equilibrium to fall. Because he was apparently indifferent to German demands, the princes appropriated power, and their acquisition prepared the foundations of the subsequent imperial structure elaborated in the Golden Bull of 1356 and experienced in the Empire until its demise. While he may have envisioned a reorganization of the imperial government along the lines of his Sicilian success—indeed his proposals in 1235 to the diet at Mainz seemed to indicate this—his difficulties in Italy prevented him from its implementation.

Judgments vary on Frederick's abilities as a ruler and his effect on the Empire. There is little disagreement, however, on the fact that he was educated. He evinced an avid interest in mathematics, natural sciences, architecture, and horticulture, among other things, and he spoke several languages. Although pudgy and rather myopic, he loved the hunt and his aviary. In some respects his Sicilian court became a precursor of the Renaissance state, and Frederick a Renaissance prince. In addition to *The Constitutions of Melfi*, two of his most notable acts were the founding of the University of Naples in 1248 and his *The Art of Hunting with Birds*. Married at least three times and fathering a number of children, the house of Hohenstaufen died out within two decades of Frederick's death.

Works By: *The Art of Falconry*, tr. and ed. C. A. Wood and F. M. Fyfe (Stanford, 1943, rpr. 1955). **Works About:** Patience Andrewes, *Frederick II of Hohenstaufen* (New York, 1970); E. Horst, *Friedrich der Staufer* (Dusseldorf, 1977); A. Huillard–Breholles, ed., *Historia diplomatica Friderici secundi*, 7 vols. (Paris, 1852–1861); Ernst Kantorowicz, *Frederick the Second*, tr. E. O. Lorimer (New York, 1957); Konstanzer Arbeitskries für mittelalter Gesch. ed., *Studien und Quel.*

zur Welt Kaiser Friedrichs II, 4 vols. (Sigmaringen, 1972–1974); Georgina Masson, *Frederick II of Hohenstaufen* (London, 1957); J. M. Powell, "Frederick II and the Church: A Revisionist View," *CHR* 48 (1962–1963): 487–97; T. C. Van Cleve, *The Emperor Frederick II of Hohenstaufen* (Oxford, 1972); L. Weiland, ed., *MGH, Constitutiones et acta publica imperatorum et regnum, Tom. II (1198–1272)* (Hanover, 1896); E. Winkemann, *Kaiser Friedrich II*, 2 vols. (Leipzig, 1889–1897).   *P. N. Bebb*

See FREDERICK I; HENRY VI; HENRY VII; HENRY THE LION; INNOCENT III; VIGNA.

FREDERICK III (1415–1493), Duke Frederick V of Steiermark and emperor from the death of his cousin Albert II in 1440 until his son Maximilian succeeded as king of the Romans in 1486, presided over a chaotic period in German history. The disasters of his reign occurred in part because of the posthumous birth of an heir to Albert's three crowns of Hungary, Austria, and Bohemia. Ladislaus Posthumous' very existence lost Frederick the use of a substantial Habsburg-Luxembourg patrimony, which might have enabled firmer direction of the Empire and which instead embroiled him in succession disputes in the eastern Empire. But in part they were caused by weakness, vacillation, and a preference to retire from imperial politics. Frederick spent nearly the whole of his reign, from 1444 to 1471, east of his hereditary lands in Austria and Steiermark. His preoccupation with the fortuitous coincidence of the Latin and German phrases *Austriae est imperare orbis universo* and *Alles Erdreich ist Österreich untertan* with the sequence of vowels, now considered legendary in any case, was hardly emblematic of his substantive goals or policy.

Frederick was elected king on February 2, 1442, with the unanimous support of the Rhenish ecclesiastical electors, assisted by his brother-in-law Frederick II of Saxony and the count Palatine Louis IV. The electors of Brandenburg and the king of Bohemia, who were inclined to support the landgrave Louis of Hesse, found him nearly as acceptable, and Frederick's succession was undisputed. The same could not be said of his succession to the Habsburg patrimony. Albert's will established a regency council including his widow, Elizabeth, the eldest Habsburg claimant, and a body of councillors from each of his three crowns to guard the throne for his son. Ladislaus was crowned king of Hungary on May 15, 1440, but a group of nobles, mindful of the Turkish threat, preferred the king of Poland, Vladislav II, who accepted the crown on July 17. Frederick lost the civil war that followed but regained Ladislaus' crown when Vladislav was killed at Varna in 1444. Refusing, however, to surrender his ward to the Hungarian royal council, Frederick lost his rights as regent when the Hungarians turned to John Hunyadi, the national hero of the Turkish campaigns, and made him regent. In November 1446, Hunyadi led an invasion of Austria to reclaim Albert's heir but was instead convinced by the papal legate Cardinal Carvajal to lead another crusade against the Turks.

Ladislaus also complicated the succession in Bohemia, where the estates attempted first to offer the crown to Albert of Bavaria or to Frederick himself.

They finally acknowledged Ladislaus in 1443, but again Frederick refused demands that he reside at Prague. In 1452, the Bohemian diet recognized the moderate Hussite leader George Podiebrady.

Austria presented a problem for other reasons. From 1379 the Habsburg inheritance had been split into two lines: the Albertine in Austria and the Leopoldine in the rest. In 1411, the Leopoldine line had again split into Styrian and Tyrolese branches, and Frederick IV of Tyrol had left an eleven-year-old heir, Sigismund, under Frederick's guardianship in 1439. The diet of Tyrol acquiesced to Frederick's regency only if Sigismund stayed in Tyrol, a condition that Frederick promptly ignored. When Albert II, of the Austrian line, died, Frederick secured confirmation as his successor, hoping to reunite all three branches of the Habsburgs. Now regent of Tyrol and Austria, he gained full control of Styria by granting his brother Albert VI a generous pension. But his fiscal exactions in the Habsburg lands, inflated by the demands of imperial office, brought Tyrol to revolt in 1446, and Frederick was forced to return the territory to Sigismund. His brother Albert, a participant in the uprising, gained Habsburg lands on the Rhine. And the Austrian estates demanded that Ladislaus reside at Vienna. On December 12, 1451, the Austrians demanded that Ladislaus assume his crown and govern with an Austrian royal council. Frederick ignored them long enough to travel to Rome for his imperial coronation and marriage to Eleanora of Portugal, but when he returned to his residence at Wiener Neustadt in June 1452, he was greeted with a full-scale rebellion led by Ulrich von Cilli, Ladislaus' cousin. He acquiesced to the Austrians, surrendered Ladislaus to Cilli, and returned to Vienna. There Cilli quickly lost his popularity when his close relationship to Ladislaus gained him the reputation of a despot. He was nearly deposed by the council when Ladislaus, claiming his majority at age fifteen, reinstated him.

In 1453 Constantinople fell; in 1456 John Hunyadi led the heroic defense of Belgrade. While the emperor was busy with futile negotiations with the imperial diets for assistance against the Turks, Ladislaus led an army against them. During the relatively insignificant campaign, Ulrich von Cilli was killed by Hunyadi's son Ladislaus, and King Ladislaus violated his promise not to prosecute him for murder, executing him in March 1457. With Hunyadi's younger son, Mathias Corvinus, imprisoned, Ladislaus returned to Prague and died there suddenly on November 23. His death ended the Albertine line and, with it, direct Habsburg claim to the threefold monarchy. Frederick acceded to the election of George Podiebrady on March 2, 1458, as king of Bohemia and confirmed his electoral vote the following year. He lost the Hungarian crown to Mathias Corvinus in 1463 but retained the title and a pension. The settlement included rights of succession if Hunyadi's line should end. In Austria Frederick faced his brother Albert VI, who had granted Sigismund his lands on the Rhine in exchange for his claims to Tyrol. Frederick successfully defended his crown with the assistance of Matthias Corvinus, but Lower and Upper Austria were partitioned once again. In June 1461, unrest in Austria caused by poor harvests and

Frederick's debasement of the currency put Albert at the head of another revolt. He beseiged Frederick at his Vienna residence in November 1462 and forced the emperor to mortgage his Austrian title for eight years. Albert's death in December 1463 restored a united Austria once more.

Frederick had more than one reason to rejoice. On March 31, 1462, Pius II opened heresy charges against George Podiebrady, who had tolerated the moderate Hussites in Bohemia for political as well as religious reasons. Excommunicated in 1466, he faced revolts in Silesia and Moravia and invasion from Hungary by Matthias Corvinus. In a bid for allies, he offered succession to the crown to Casimir of Poland's son, Vladislav, but died on March 22, 1471. Vladislav pursued his claim, and warfare spilled over into Austria. Matthias Corvinus established his residence at Vienna in 1485, and Frederick was once again ejected from his lands. Vladislav became king of Bohemia on July 15, 1490, following Corvinus' death on April 6, 1488; Maximilian I, pushed to assume imperial office against his father's wishes, on February 16, 1486, retrieved Austria. By the Peace of Pressburg, arranged in 1491, Maximilian dropped his claim to the Hungarian and Bohemian crowns in exchange for succession in both if Vladislav should die without an heir.

While Frederick was absorbed in the east with his patrimony, he could spend little time on the affairs of the Empire. This had been the intent of the electors when they elected a monarch with so few resources that he would be unable to interfere with their own projects. But on one issue Frederick was assertive, although it must be said that it cost him nothing. When Frederick was elected, the schismatic Council of Basel had important friends in the Empire, and the electors favored its support. Frederick, on the other hand, supported the Roman Pope Eugenius IV. First he intervened at the imperial diet at Nuremberg in August 1444 to postpone an electoral statement in favor of Basel. This unpopular position was sweetened by extensive rights of appointment and visitation in the Habsburg lands, which Eugenius granted to the emperor. The other princes in Germany rushed to make similar arrangements before Eugenius died in February 1447. His successor, Nicholas V, reached an agreement with the emperor in the Concordat of Vienna in February 1448, which excluded Habsburg lands from external episcopal jurisdiction, granted the right of presentation for benefices, and shared ecclesiastical taxes. The document was a model for the revolution of the princes and for the development of territorial churches later expressed in the Reformation.

Along with Church reform, imperial reform was again a major issue. With the Turkish threat looming, Frederick could either defend the Empire with his own resources, which he could not secure, or he could turn to the imperial estates for aid. Unfortunately he was indifferent to calls for imperial reform, and the period from 1454 to 1471, when he finally appeared at an imperial diet, was filled with proposals to fill his functions with an electoral council. The count Palatine, Frederick I, who was especially inclined to depose Frederick, was guilty of arrogating his title (that is, substituting himself as elector instead of acting as regent for his nephew Philip). The emperor's refusal to recognize the arrogation created an impasse, which incapacitated the electoral college. Both the electors of Saxony and Brandenburg were unwilling to take any drastic measures to force Frederick to attend the diets. Nor did the free imperial cities want to see imperial reform led by the electors and territorial princes.

The diet of Regensburg in 1454 attempted to establish an imperial government based upon an electoral proposal to create a standing imperial council, establish a permanent imperial court with salaried judges, and establish an imperial tax. Sending the proposal to Wiener Neustadt with Archbishop Jacob of Trier in February 1455, the electors heard nothing more of it. The Rhenish princes went so far as to summon Frederick to attend the next diet at Nuremberg, threatening deposition in favor of George Podiebrady or the count Palatine. They were ignored; Frederick proclaimed imperial peace and asked for subsidies, but refused to barter with his royal prerogatives.

The fiscal support necessary for Frederick's opposition to reform came from the cities, which submitted to forced levies and loans rather than see their neighboring territorial princes infused with imperial authority. Their position was precarious in the face of expanding princely states. Nuremberg was involved in a running battle with the margrave Albert-Achilles, brother of Frederick II of Hohenzollern, elector of Brandenburg, from 1448 to 1453. Appealing to the emperor for protection, Nuremberg found him unwilling to arbitrate the dispute and, despite promises made to both parties, Frederick failed to commission a royal court to decide the case and instead sent Duke Louis IX of Bavaria-Landshut to mediate a truce. In 1441, the Swabian League had reassembled; by 1446 there were over thirty-one members. The league still allowed Louis of Bavaria-Landshut to seize Donauwörth in 1458 and Adolf II, archbishop of Mainz, to repress Mainz into a territorial city in 1462.

The princes too needed the emperor to settle disputes among them. In northwestern Germany a dispute between Archbishop Dietrich of Cologne and Adolf of Cleves over Westphalian lands went on for five years until the pope settled it in 1449. Even then it continued by proxy, with the duke of Hoya, a vassal of Cleves, quarreling with Dietrich over prerogatives in Münster from 1450 to 1457. Further, the imperious Albert-Achilles involved himself in a tripartite quarrel with the dukes of Bavaria and the count Palatine. Albert-Achilles' intrigues with the emperor, in alliance with Württemburg, Baden, and Mainz, against the Bavarian party was balanced by George Podiebrady. Both Bavaria and the count Palatine prevailed in decisive battles in June and August 1462, and Podiebrady negotiated a peace in August 1463 at Prague. Frederick thus raised his prestige in the Empire and became an even more likely candidate now that the electoral reformers had just beaten the emperor's party on the field.

By the late 1470s the Turks again appeared in Carniola, and Frederick was caught up in the conflict over the Bohemian succession following George Podiebrady's death in 1471. Austria and even Frederick's own Styria were restive and near insurrection. All of these crises forced his appearance at the diet of

Regensburg in June 1471 for the first time since 1444. Now Frederick was willing to address the need for imperial reform in exchange for help against the Turks, assistance that he received only in part. He again refused to trade imperial prerogatives for aid, thus limiting the possibility of reform, and the estates had to content themselves with a four-year imperial peace, some strictures against recourse to the feud, and a standing imperial court under Archbishop Adolf of Mainz.

Frederick still hoped to reverse his fortunes. He began negotiations with the powerful Charles the Bold, duke of Burgundy, for a marriage alliance between his daughter Mary and Maximilian. This would have brought Charles closer to the Habsburg party on the Rhineland, in opposition to Frederick I, the count Palatine. It would head off conflict with Charles over his claims to lands affiliated with the Swiss confederacy and, it was suggested, make him into a military agent for Habsburg interests in the area. The negotiations at Trier in September 1473 collapsed when Charles made it clear that he would settle for no less than joint possession of the royal title. The marriage, which eventually brought Maximilian the Burgundian lowlands, was concluded on August 14, 1477, after Charles' death. Upon his accession to the imperial crown, Maximilian recovered Austria for his father, who played only a nominal role in imperial politics thereafter and died at Linz on August 19, 1493.

Works About: Adolf Bachmann, *Dtsch. Reichsgesch. im Zeitalter Friedrich III und Maximilian I* (Leipzig, 1884–1894); *DRTA, Altere Reihe*, ed. Hermanne Herre and Ludwig Quidde (Stuttgart, 1915, 1928), vols. 15–16; Brigitte Haller, *Kaiser Friedrich III im Urteil der Zeitgenossen* (Vienna, 1965); Hugo Hantsch, *Gestalter der Gesch. Österreiches* (Innsbruck, 1962); Alphons Lhotsky, *Aufsätze und Vorträge*, ed. Hans Wagner and Heinrich Koller (Munich, 1971), vol. 2; *MGH, SRG, Nova Series XIII, Thomas Ebendorfer, Chronica Austria*, ed. Alphons Lhotsky (Zurich, 1967); Otakar Odlozilik, *The Hussite King: Bohemia in European Affairs, 1440–1471* (New Brunswick, 1965); Eduard Ziehen, *Mittelrhein und Reich im Zeitalter der Reichs reform, 1356–1504* (Frankfurt, 1934).   *S. A. Garretson*

See ALBERT II; MAXIMILIAN I; NUREMBERG; SWABIAN LEAGUE.

FREDERICK II, THE GREAT (1712–1786), was the eldest son of Frederick William I, king in Prussia, and Sophie Dorothea of Hanover. Frederick William, who ruled his family as a despot, could not countenance an heir whose tastes and ambitions conflicted with his. The contrast between the father and the son became more and more marked. Frederick William, a gruff, inarticulate man, found himself confronting an extremely bright son who was critical and caustic in speech. To guarantee the very existence of the state, the heir had to share, so Frederick William thought, his iron resolution, his devotion, his principles, his beliefs. Frederick did not share the king's love of soldiering. He was, in his father's mind, a "coward," a "milksop," a man who would "ruin all I have done." Frederick did not hide the fact that he acted under compulsion, that he hated his father's harsh regime. The desperation of the young prince was reflected in his attempted flight from Prussia to England in 1730. He was caught and court-martialed. His friend Katte was arrested and executed before his eyes. Fearing that that was to be his own fate, he became a master of dissimulation. To prove his loyalty to his father, he served a two-year apprenticeship in the state bureaucracy and married "that horrible creature" Elizabeth Christiana, whom he castigated as "a dullard as stupid as a bundle of straw and without the least education." The unwanted marriage proved an unhappy one, and there were no children. Frederick and Frederick William did become reconciled. By the time the king was forty, he was ill with dropsy and gout. He died in 1740, content, as he said, "since I have so worthy a son and successor." The Austrian ambassador wrote concerning the heir that "he told me that he is a poet and can write a hundred lines in two hours. He could also be a musician, a philosopher, a physicist, or a mechanician. What he never will be is a general or a warrior." This diplomat, normally so astute, was indeed proven wrong.

The cynical, ambitious Frederick came to the throne at the age of twenty-eight, "a motley composition of barbarity and humanity." Those who expected a change of government were doomed to disappointment. He essentially followed his father's lead but pursued an aggressive foreign policy and maintained a far larger military establishment. Upon the death of Charles VI on October 20, 1740, Frederick planned to seize the Austrian province of Silesia, a wealthy and populated land that was strategically located. Maria Theresa, however, would not agree to its loss. To her, Frederick was not merely an adversary; he was an enemy, a perfidious prince who had betrayed the Empire. In December 1749, Frederick led his troops into Silesia. "I have crossed the Rubicon," he wrote. When the Austrian and Prussian armies met at Mollwitz, the Prussian cavalry was routed, and Frederick fled. The infantry commanded by Schwerin held firm and saved the day. Frederick would never again leave a battle. France and Bavaria allied with Prussia in mid-1741, but Frederick double-crossed them by suspending hostilities in the secret convention of Kleinschnellendorf. In the Treaty of Berlin (1742) Maria Theresa ceded all of Silesia except three counties to Frederick. She could now concentrate on waging war against Charles VII, whose election as Holy Roman emperor she disputed.

The war reopened in August 1744. While the Austrian forces were invading French Alsace, Frederick launched an attack on Bohemia. Maria Theresa, "that man in Vienna" as Frederick called her, now concentrated her troops against Prussia. Frederick's allies would give him little assistance: Charles VII had died and his heir had made peace; the French were engaged in fighting Great Britain. Frederick nevertheless held his own by victories at Hohenfriedberg in Silesia (June), Soor in Bohemia (September), Hennersdorf (November), and Kesseldorf (December). He had outmaneuvered the troops of Austria but remained on the defensive. The war-weary Maria Theresa made peace with Frederick in December 1745. Reluctantly she ceded Silesia. In exchange, Frederick recognized her husband as Emperor Francis I.

The peace proved to be merely a truce in the long struggle. In August 1756, Frederick began the Seven Years War by invading Saxony. He feared the alliance building up against him of Austria, France, and Russia. Great Britain, Hanover, Hesse-Cassel, Brunswick, and Gotha allied with Prussia. Frederick had the advantage of inner lines of defense and of an enemy coalition wracked by dissension. The hard-pressed Frederick was forced to resort to emergency measures like exacting contributions from the occupied regions and debasing the coinage. During the summer of 1757, the Swedes invaded Pomerania, the Russians occupied East Prussia, and the Austrians reached Berlin. Frederick saved the situation by defeating a combined French imperial army at Rossbach and by outmaneuvering an Austrian army at Leuthen; he had prevented the reconquest of Silesia. The death of Elizabeth of Russia in 1762, his most implacable foe, saved him. He concluded a truce with Russia's new czar, Peter III. Without Russian aid, Maria Theresa could not continue the war. Austria, Prussia, and Saxony signed the Peace of Hubertusburg in 1763, which restored the *status quo ante bellum*. Maria Theresa conceded the loss of Silesia; Frederick returned Saxony to its elector and promised to vote for the election of Archduke Joseph as king of the Romans, successor to his still-reigning father. Maria Theresa had failed in her bid for German supremacy, but she had held her kingdom together. Prussia at great cost had won status as a European power. Frederick had won his reputation as a military genius by his use of rapid fire power, vigorous assaults, and various strategic maneuvers.

Frederick could now turn to rebuilding his state, to repairing the damage wrought by war, and to furthering Prussia's economic development. Over three hundred thousand colonists were settled in Prussia. In order to expand agriculture, the marshlands were drained and diked, and the cultivation of turnips, potatoes, and sugar beets encouraged. To spur industry, Frederick set up schools to train spinners and weavers, established cotton mills, and fostered iron production in Westphalia and mining in Upper Silesia. He increased state revenues by devising a system of indirect taxation (the *Régie*), by raising the excise on beer, salt, tobacco, and coffee, and by establishing state monopolies in salt, sugar, porcelain, tobacco, and coffee.

Although complete law reform was not achieved until 1781, Samuel von Cocceji (d. 1755), with Frederick's support, was able to simplify judicial procedure and to replace the jurisdiction of the nobility with a body of officials. A deist himself, Frederick was famed for his religious toleration; he permitted Catholics to build a church in Berlin and even invited the expelled Jesuits to settle in his lands. He did not, however, extend that same toleration to Jews. In spite of the facade of enlightenment, Prussia remained a barracks state, the army its national industry. Militarism became rooted in the minds of the people and the functioning of the government.

In the later years of his reign, Frederick, though wary of Russia's power, allied with Catherine II. In the first partition of Poland (1772), Frederick received the bishropric of Ermeland and West Prussia, except Danzig and Thorn. Prussia was now connected with Pomerania and Brandenburg. Frederick became king of, not in, Prussia. In imperial politics he strove to inhibit Austrian expansion by participating in the Potato War of 1778–1779 and organizing the League of Princes in 1785. The man who made possible Prussia's eventual domination of central Europe died in 1786.

Frederick's priorities had always been those of a politician. He had described himself as "philosophe par inclination, politique par devoir." He was known as an enlightened despot because of his intellectual predilections; he read widely, wrote history and even poetry, and surrounded himself with men of letters. He acted, however, according to raison d'état, not pure raison. Believing himself "the first servant of the state," he rose at four in the summer and five in the winter, devoting ten hours a day to state affairs. He took personal control of the administration, attempting to mold the state and the society to his wishes. He set an example of devotion to duty, frugality, and simplicity.

He bequeathed to his successor, his nephew Frederick William II, a territory of 75,000 square miles, a population of 5 million, an army of 200,000, an annual revenue of 20 million talers, and a treasury of 70,000 talers. Frederick once related a dream he had. He was at Charlottenburg and there met his father. "Have I conducted myself well?" he asked him. Frederick William replied, "Very well." The dream was symbolic. Frederick William could have not wished for a better successor.

Works By: R. Köser et al., *Politische Korrespondenz*, 46 vols. (Berlin, 1879ff); J. D. E. Preuss, ed., *Oeuvres de Frédéric le Grand*, 33 vols. (Berlin, 1846–1847). **Works About:** W. L. Dorn, "The Prussian Bureaucracy in the Eighteenth Century," *Political Science Quarterly*, 46 (1931): 403–23, 47(1932):75–94; Carl Hinrichs, *Preussen als hist. Problem* (Berlin, 1964); Hubert Johnson, *Frederick the Great and His Officials* (New Haven, 1975); R. Köser, *König Friedrich der Grosse*, 4 vols. (Stuttgart, 1912); L. von Ranke, *Die dtsch. Mächte und der Fürstenband* (Leipzig, 1875); G. Ritter, *Frederick the Great*, tr. Peter Paret (Berkeley, 1974); Hans Rosenberg, *Bureaucracy, Aristocracy and Autocracy: The Prussian Experience, 1660–1815* (Cambridge, Mass., 1958); Otto Graf zu Stolberg-Wernigerode, "Friedrich II," *NDB*, 5:545–58.   *L. S. Frey and M. L. Frey*

See AUSTRIAN SUCCESSION; CHARLES VI; CHARLES VII; FRANCIS I; FREDERICK WILLIAM I; MARIA THERESA; PRAGMATIC SANCTION; SEVEN YEARS WAR.

FREDERICK III (1657–1713), elector of Brandenburg, literally crowned himself Frederick I, king in Prussia, on January 18, 1701, with the imperial sanction. As the second son of the Great Elector, Frederick William, and his wife, Louise Henrietta of Orange, Frederick became heir to the state on the death of his older brother, Charles Emil, in 1674 and elector of Brandenburg in 1688. Although Frederick inherited the features of Frederick William, his were smaller and more delicate. Unfortunately Frederick lacked not only the physical vigor of his father but also his strength of mind. His indecisiveness was heightened rather than mitigated by his religious and ethical ideals. Frederick thought that it was his duty to put religion before anything else. A pious man, he interpreted events as the will of God. Man could no nothing against fate, he must accept what God had sent him. This inclination to fatalism often allowed Frederick to avoid making difficult decisions. Frederick's vacillation and suspicions exacerbated the personal rivalries of his court, whose members sought to exploit him for their own ends. After the dismissal of Eberhard von Danckelmann in 1697, a coterie of corrupt favorites headed by Wartenberg dominated him until the reforms of 1711.

Frederick sought to hide his personal weakness through outward show of pomp and magnificence, so much so that he was dubbed the "ape of Louis XIV." He attempted to endow his newly established kingship with the magnificence found in Paris and used French as the language of his court. In imitation of the famous statue of Henry IV on the Pont Neuf, Frederick erected an equestrian statue of his father, Frederick William, on a bridge in Berlin. He even ordered his representative in Paris to procure the form and dimensions of Louis XIV's perruque so he could have an exact copy made. Berlin was to be a city of splendor and culture. He beautified his capital by enlarging his palace and building a massive arsenal (*Zeughaus*) and seven churches. He patronized engineers, architects, painters, and musicians, especially the famous baroque architect and sculptor Andreas Schlüter. During his reign, the Academy of Sciences at Berlin and the University of Halle were founded. He also adopted the new Gregorian calendar.

Frederick's achievements in foreign affairs were less notable. He was never able to make the army an effective arm of his foreign policy, although his troops rendered great assistance to the allies during the War of the League of Augsburg and the War of the Spanish Succession. This latter commitment brought him certain territorial gains, including Spanish Guelderland, Neuchâtel, and Lingen, the acknowledgment of his kingship, and allied subsidies, which helped maintain his army. Unequal to the dextrous manipulation so necessary in the Great Northern War, he did not commit his troops but maintained an uneasy neutrality and kept his lands free from the devastation of that war. His involvement in that conflict would have plunged the Holy Roman Empire, then at war with France, into that conflagration.

Frederick married three times: in 1679 to Elizabeth Henrietta of Hesse-Cassel (d. 1683), who bore him a daughter (d. 1705); in 1684 to Sophie Charlotte of Hanover (d. 1705), who bore him his only surviving child, Frederick William; and in 1708 to Sophie Louise of Mecklenburg, who outlived him.

It was Frederick's misfortune to be placed in history between a father and a son who would eclipse him by their superior talents. He lacked their personal energy, vigor, and aggression, their strength of body, and their force of mind. His weakness was accentuated by their strength. His physique appears even smaller in comparison with the stout robustness of his father and of his son. He lacked their strength and purpose, physically, mentally, personally, and administratively. They ruled, whereas he was ruled by his own weakness and indecision. Fettered by his own indecision and debilities, he was infatuated with the outward trappings of power. The mystique attached to his kingship reflected, nevertheless, the real power of the Prussian state.

Works By: Ernst Berner, ed., "Aus dem Briefwechsel König Friedrich I von Preussen und seiner Familie," *Quel. und Untersuchungen zur Gesch. des Hauses Hohenzollern* 1 (1901). **Works About:** *ADB*, "Friedrich III," 7:627–35; E. Berner, *Gesch. des preussichen Staates* (Bonn, 1896); J. Droysen, *Gesch. der preussischen Politik* (Leipzig, 1972); B. Erdmannsdorffer, *Dtsch. Gesch. von westfälischen Frieden bis zum Regierungsantritt Friedrichs des Grossen, 1648–1740* (Berlin, 1892–1893), vol. 3; Linda Frey and Marsha Frey, "The Foreign Policy of Frederick I: A Fatal Vacillation?" *East European Quarterly* 9 (1975); 259–69; Carl von Noorden, "Die preussischen Politik in spanischen Erbfolgekriege," *HZ* 18:197–358; Albert Waddington, *L'Acquisition de la couronne royale de Prusse par les Hohenzollerns* (Paris, 1888).   *L. S. Frey and M. L. Frey*

See FREDERICK WILLIAM; FREDERICK WILLIAM I; SOPHIE CHARLOTTE; SPANISH SUCCESSION; WAR OF THE LEAGUE OF AUGSBURG; WARTENBERG.

FREDERICK III, THE WISE (1463–1525), elector of Saxony, was the eldest son of Elector Ernest of Saxony and succeeded to the electoral title, as well as leadership of the Ernestine branch of the Wettin dynasty upon his father's death in 1486. He received an unusually good education for a prince of his day and evinced considerable interest in scholarly and artistic matters throughout his life. He possessed a strong sense of tradition, which expressed itself in a keen interest in German history and in the essentially medieval form of his deep religious piety.

His father's testament had stipulated that Frederick should rule all of his lands, except the portion known as the electoral circle (surrounding Wittenberg), jointly with his younger brother John. This arrangement worked surprisingly well, and the two cooperated with a rare degree of harmony. Frederick was clearly the dominant partner, however, and exercised a patriarchal type of rule. He took steps to modernize the administrative machinery of his state and was well served by a series of able advisers.

Frederick's efforts to expand his territorial power base in central Germany met with little success. Nonetheless by virtue of both his electoral title and his personal reputation for political sagacity, Frederick was destined to play an important role in national politics. His name is commonly linked with the promotion of reforms in the imperial constitution (1495), although, unfortunately, the sources are not clear concerning the degree to which Frederick actually supported the various proposals involved. In line with the traditional prerogatives of the Saxon electors, he held the title of imperial vicar and managed to extend somewhat the authority of this office. In 1500 he was appointed by Emperor Maximilian I to the position of president of the newly created Imperial Council of Regency (*Reichsregiment*). Although he declined to be a candidate himself, Frederick was a key figure in the imperial election of 1519. He finally cast his vote for the successful nominee, Charles V, after securing from him a pledge for the repayment of old debts owed to Saxony by the Habsburgs. Frederick also assumed a leading part in the negotiations by which the seven electors sought to limit certain of Charles' powers in advance by compelling him to sign an unprecedented election capitulation.

By this time, Frederick's relations with the Empire had acquired a new dimension through the emergence of the Saxon religious reformer Martin Luther. Luther, who was a professor of theology at the University of Wittenberg established by Frederick in 1502, found in the elector a patron without whose political protection the Reformation movement probably could not have survived. Frederick appears to have decided at an early date that the reformer must not be condemned without first being granted a fair trial on German soil. To this end he skillfully pursued a complicated series of negotiations with both the imperial government and the papacy. The high point of this diplomatic campaign was reached when he succeeded in gaining for Luther a safe public hearing at the diet of Worms (1521). Although Frederick was unable to prevent the subsequent issuing of the anti-Lutheran Edict of Worms, he did secure from the emperor an exemption of electoral Saxony from its enforcement.

A number of motives, political and personal, have been suggested for Frederick's continued protection of Luther: a reluctance to recognize any legal jurisdiction in the Reformation dispute higher than that of the increasingly sovereign Saxon state, a concern for the welfare of his new university, and hence its most illustrious faculty member, a sense of justice that forbade surrendering Luther to his enemies before he had been given an impartial hearing and refuted, and a genuine commitment to the person and perhaps also the teachings of the reformer. The matter remains the subject of scholarly controversy, due to the elector's somewhat enigmatic personality and highly cautious manner of proceeding. It is of interest that Frederick apparently did not receive Holy Communion in the evangelical form (in both kinds) until on his deathbed. Furthermore he carefully avoided all personal contact with Luther. It was left to Frederick's successors to promote actively adoption of the new patterns of theology and worship throughout the Saxon territories.

Frederick the Wise was one of the most influential princes in sixteenth-century Germany, and it would be inaccurate to suggest that he derives his historical significance solely from his association with the Protestant Reformation. It is this aspect of his long career, however, that attracted the greatest amount of attention.

Works About: Karlheinz Blaschke, "Kurfürst Friedrich der Weise von Sachsen und die Luthersache," in *Der Reichstag zu Worms von 1521*, ed. Fritz Reuter (Worms, 1971) pp. 316–35; *DRTA unter Kaiser Karl V* (Gotha, 1893ff); Carl Eduard Förstemann, *Neues Urkundenbuch zur Gesch. der ev. Kirchenreformation* (Hamburg, 1842), vol. 1; M. Grossmann, *Humanism in Wittenberg, 1485–1517* (Nieuwkoop, 1975); Christian Gotth. Neudecker and Ludwig Preller, eds., *Georg Spalatins hist. Nachlass und Briefe*, vol. 1: *Friedrichs des Weisen Leben und Zeitgesch.* (Jena, 1851); Paul Kirn, *Friedrich der Weise und die Kirche* (Leipzig, 1926); Anni Koch, "Die Kontroverse über die Stellung Friedrichs des Weisen zur Reformation," *ARG* 23 (1926): 213–60; Theodor Kolde, *Friedrich der Weise und die Anfänge der Reformation* (Erlangen, 1881); Hans Patze and Walter Schlesinger, *Geschichte Thüringens* (Cologne, 1967), vol. 3; Friedrich H. Schubert, *NDB* 5:568–72; M. M. Tutzschmann, "*Friedrich der Weise, Kurfürst von Sachsen* (Grimma, 1848).

C. C. Christensen

See BRÜCK; CHARLES V; JOHN OF SAXONY; LUTHER; SPALATIN.

FREDERICK V (1596–1632), elector of the Palatinate and king of Bohemia, the son of Frederick IV and Luise Juliane of Orange, was born and died in the Palatinate. He received his education at the Huguenot academy in Sedan. He stayed at the court of Duke Henry of Bouillon, the acknowledged leader of the Calvinist party in France, from 1605 to 1612. He learned French and became well versed in Reformed theology. In 1613 he married Elizabeth Stuart, daughter of King James I of England. The marriage, concluded to cement the political alliance of the Palatinate, the Netherlands, and England, turned out to be an unusually happy union. The young couple shared an interest in the arts and fine aesthetic judgment and brought a more refined and elegant French style to Heidelberg. Heidelberg castle was expanded and beautified with a magnificent terrace and garden. The city, already the intellectual center of German Calvinism, now also became known for its cultural and artistic tastes.

Since Frederick was only fourteen when his father died in 1610, the government was placed into the hands of a regent, Duke John of Zweibrücken. In 1614 the young prince reached his majority and assumed full control of his country. A trustworthy individual without much political acumen, he became easy prey for his not always very prudent political advisers. The most important of these was Prince Christian I of Anhalt, a man of superficial diplomatic excellence, who had also dominated his father's administration by effectively exploiting the Protestant cause for the aggrandizement of the Palatinate. Inside Germany, Anhalt's diplomatic masterpiece was the formation of the Protestant Union under Palatinate leadership (1608); outside Germany it was the English marriage. He and Frederick's other Calvinist advisers looked upon the Bohemian revolt against the Habsburgs (which sparked the Thirty Years War) as a further means to enhance the Palatinate's stature in international politics. They therefore encouraged the elector, who already sympathized with the rebels, to accept the royal crown that the Bohemian estates offered him in 1619 after they had deposed Ferdinand of Austria.

Frederick's acceptance of the crown was foolhardy and turned the local rebellion into an empire-wide conflict. The new king and his court arrived in Prague in October 1619, but neither his father-in-law, King James I of England, nor the Dutch, nor even the German Union princes were prepared to back his Bohemian venture. The only foreign aid he received came from Duke Charles Emanuel of Savoy who sent a small mercenary army under the command of Count Ernest von Mansfeld. His cause suffered a further blow when the German electors picked Ferdinand, the man whom the Bohemians had just jilted, as their new emperor. Ferdinand's elevation strengthened his hand in dealing with the rebels and their new king. Maximilian of Bavaria, head of the Catholic League and strongest among the German princes, and John George of Saxony, the foremost Lutheran prince in the Empire, immediately pledged their support to the new emperor. Frederick's Bohemian venture came to an ignominious end on November 8, 1620, in the Battle of the White Mountain (near Prague). Here a combined imperial-leaguist army won an overwhelming victory over the Bohemian rebels and their supporters. Frederick and his wife fled Prague via Breslau and Berlin to the Hague where the Oranges, their Dutch relatives, granted them refuge. Meanwhile Frederick's homeland, the Palatinate, was overrun by Spanish and Bavarian troops. The Protestant Union officially dissolved in May 1621. Frederick, whom Ferdinand had placed under the imperial ban, lost both his land and title. The emperor awarded Maximilian of Bavaria for his services by transferring to him the disgraced ruler's electoral dignity (1623) and the Upper Palatinate (1628).

Frederick, humiliated and ridiculed as the Winter King, could only hope and wait at the Hague for more fortuitous times. Anhalt, who was largely responsible for his predicament, no longer was with him, yet some of his other councillors remained faithful. His most trusted advisers now were Ludwig Camerarius and John Joachim von Rusdorff; both used their diplomatic influence to work for the restitution of Frederick's land and title. Their efforts appeared successful early in 1632 when Gustavus Adolphus of Sweden, after beating the league army at Breitenfeld, freed the Palatinate of Spanish and Bavarian forces. Frederick left his exile in the Netherlands to return to Germany but soon made the bitter discovery that Gustavus was prepared to grant him only limited sovereignty over his former country. His hopes dimmed even further when the king was killed in combat at Lützen (1632). Thirteen days later (November 29) Frederick died, heartbroken, of a violent fever while traveling through the Palatinate. Like his father he was only thirty-six years old at the time of his death; his burial site remains unknown to this day.

With Frederick V the political ambitions and aggressiveness of the Palatinate Calvinists reached both their high point and cataclysmic end. More than any other event, the elector's acceptance of the Bohemian crown transformed a local rebellion into a major international war that not only cost Frederick his land and title but also brought inestimable suffering and devastation to central Europe. When the war ended in 1648, the peacemakers at Westphalia returned the Rhenish Palatinate to Charles Louis, Frederick's oldest son, and created a new eight electorate especially for him. The Palatinate, however, never again exercised the intellectual and political influence that it had enjoyed in the late sixteenth and early seventeenth centuries.

Works About: L. M. Baker, ed., *The Letters of Elizabeth Queen of Bohemia* (London,1953); George Bromley, ed., *A Collection of Original Royal Letters, Written by King Charles the First and Second, King James the Second, and the King and Queen of Bohemia . . . from the Year 1619 to 1665* (London, 1787); Claus P. Clasen, *The Palatinate in European Hist. 1555–1618* (Oxford, 1966); *Documenta Bohemica Bellum Tricennale Illustrantia* (Prague, 1972), vol. 2; Samuel R. Gardiner, ed., *Letters and other Documents Illustrating the Relations between England and Germany*, 2 vols. (London, 1865–1868); M. Ritter, "Friedrich V," *ADB*, 7:621–27; Friedrich H. Schubert, "Friedrich V," *NDB*, 5:535f, *Ludwig Camerarius*, 1573–1651 (Kallmünz, 1955); Hans Sturmberger, *Aufstand in Böhmen: Der Beginn des Dreissigjährigen Krieges* (Munich, 1959); Frances A. Yates, *The Rosicrucian Enlightenment* (London, 1972).   *Bodo Nischan*

See FERDINAND II; JOHN GEORGE I; MANSFELD, ERNEST; MAXIMILIAN I, DUKE; THIRTY YEARS WAR; WESTPHALIA.

FREDERICK AUGUSTUS (1670–1733), the second son of John George III, became elector of Saxony as Frederick Augustus I after the death of his brother John George IV in 1694 and later Augustus II, king of Poland. His physical strength and courage earned him the title the Strong. He had fought against France and in 1695 and 1696 rather ineffectually against the Turks. Upon the death of John Sobieski in 1696, he became a candidate for the Polish throne. An ambitious, ruthless man, he adopted the Roman Catholic faith in order to gain the title. His wife, Christine Eberhardine, left him after his conversion. Elected and crowned in 1697, he ruled as Augustus II from 1697 to 1704 and from 1709 to 1733.

In 1699, he allied with Peter I, czar of Russia, and Frederick IV of Denmark-Norway in a scheme to partition the Swedish empire, then ruled by Charles XII. He had, however, underestimated his opponent. Augustus invaded Livonia but was defeated by the Swedes and driven across the Dvina. Charles resolved to punish the double-dealing Augustus and invaded Poland in 1701. A diet convened under Swedish auspices deposed the incalculable Augustus and elected in his stead Stanislaus Leszczynski, the palatine of Posen. Augustus' attempts to disrupt the coronation proved futile, and he fled to Saxony. When Charles struck at the elector's home base, Saxony, Augustus was forced to sign the Treaty of Altranstädt (1706) by which he recognized Stanislaus as king of Poland and abandoned the Russian alliance. After the Swedish defeat at Poltava in 1709, Augustus renewed the offensive league with Peter and Frederick and recovered his Polish throne. After Charles' death (1718), Augustus concluded peace with Sweden in 1719; by this pact he was recognized as king of Poland.

Augustus tried to change the constitution and administration and to convert the elective kingship of Poland into a hereditary one. He schemed to mediate a partition of Poland among Saxony, Austria, and Prussia by which the bulk of the republic would be ruled by the Saxon house. This too failed. A crafty, dissolute man, he became famous for his mistresses and his extravagances. He sired many illegitimate children, including the famous general, Maurice of Saxony. His legitimate son, Frederick Augustus, succeeded him as elector of Saxony and king of Poland.

Works About: Flothe, "Friedrick August I," *ADB*, 7:781–84; C. Gurlitt, *August der Starke*, 2 vols. (Dresden, 1924); Paul Haake, *August der Starke in Urteil seiner Zeit und der* Nachwelt (Dresden, 1922), *Konig August der Starke eine Charakterstudie* (Munich, 1902) and "Der erste Hohenzollernkönig und August der Starke vor und nach 1700," *Forsch zur brandenburg und preussischen Gesch*. 46 (1934): 381–90, H. Kretzschmar, "Friedrick August I," *NDB*, 5:572–73; W. F. Reddaway et al., *The Cambridge Hist. of Poland from Augustus II to Pilsudski, 1697–1935* (Cambridge, 1941).   *L. S. Frey and M. L. Frey*

See NORTHERN WAR.

FREDERICK WILLIAM (1620–1688), the Great Elector, margrave and elector of Brandenburg, was born and died in Berlin, the eldest son of Elector George William and Elizabeth Charlotte of the Palatinate, a granddaughter of

William of Orange. The chaos and destruction of the Thirty Years War, which he experienced as a child in Brandenburg, left a lasting impression on him. So did his stay in Holland (1634–1638) where he studied briefly at the University of Leiden, then the center of Calvinist and late humanist learning, and spent considerable time at the court of his uncle, Frederick Henry of Orange, the Dutch stadtholder. In the Low Countries, young Frederick William gained an appreciation for maritime and commercial power and a lifelong preference for Dutch art, architecture, and technology.

When Frederick William, completely inexperienced in politics, succeeded his father as elector of Brandenburg in December 1640, he took charge of a country ravaged and occupied by foreign armies. The Hohenzollern domains (Brandenburg; Prussia; and Mark and Cleves in the Rhineland), widely scattered and without suitable defensive forces, had easily fallen prey to foreign troops; the towns were devastated and the population drastically reduced. The country was in such complete shambles that Frederick William preferred to spend the first three years of his reign not in Berlin but in the remote, safer city of Königsberg (capital of Prussia). In order to ease the sufferings of his people, he began his rule by returning to a policy of unarmed neutrality. Troops hired to fight for the emperor were discharged, and a truce was signed with Sweden (July 1641). Neutrality, however, did not work any better than it had earlier in the war. The young elector, recognizing that he required an army in order to control his country and achieve greater freedom of action, soon began to build up his military forces again (1643). His new standing army, organized and financed after Dutch and Swedish models, often with taxes collected over the objections of the Junker estates, was to become the first and most important institution of an increasingly absolutist state. In addition, he sought the military support of the Dutch by marrying Louise Henrietta of Orange (1646). The marriage did not bring the anticipated aid, yet Louise Henrietta, an extraordinary woman, was to exert considerable influence on his reign. Lacking strong foreign support at the Westphalian peace congress (1648), Frederick William was unable to make good his claim to all of Pomerania (whose last duke had died without heirs in 1637). He had to be content with eastern Pomerania, while western Pomerania, with the important port city of Stettin and the Oder estuary, went to Sweden. As compensation, Frederick William gained the securalized bishoprics of Kammin, Halberstadt, and Minden and the promise of the archbishopric of Magdeburg, all of which were important links to his possessions in the Rhineland. Next to the Habsburgs, the Hohenzollerns now ruled the largest territory in the Empire.

Following the Thirty Years War, Frederick William continued to rebuild his country, reorganizing the privy council (1651) and the country's civil service and forcing the estates into greater submission. His leadership and military abilities were put to a severe test in the war between Poland and Sweden (First Northern War, 1655–1660) in which he supported both parties in turn. The Brandenburg army passed the test of fire in the three-day Battle of Warsaw (July

1656) and drove the Swedes from western Pomerania (1659). French intervention forced Frederick William to give up his Pomeranian conquest again. The Treaty of Oliva (1660), however, gave him full sovereignty over the duchy of Prussia, previously held as a fief of the Polish king.

The accession of Louis XIV in France (1661) ushered in an era of vast international struggles in Europe in which the elector sought to maintain the balance of power by preventing any one side from achieving predominance. To advance Brandenburg's interests, Frederick William generally joined the weaker state against the stronger, thus continuously shifting alliances among France, the Low Countries, and the Habsburgs (a policy referred to in the seventeenth century as Brandenburg's intermittent fever). With King Louis XIV alone, he concluded eight different treaties over a twenty-year period. He supported the Dutch republic in 1672 when this country was threatened by France, but a year later he made peace with Louis XIV at Vossem. In July 1674 he joined the anti-French alliance consisting of the emperor, Spain, and the Netherlands. At Fehrbellin (1675) he scored a major victory over the Swedish army, which, at the instigation of France, had entered eastern Pomerania and the Mark. By 1677, Frederick William's forces had captured Stettin and swept the Swedes from Pomerania, but under French pressure he again had to surrender western Pomerania in the Peace of Saint-Germain-en-Laye (1679). Frederick William, called the Great Elector in honor of his recent military triumphs, now decided to gain in alliance with France what he could not obtain by opposing it. He signed a secret treaty with Louis XIV (1679) committing himself, in return for subsidies, to support the French candidates in the next Polish and imperial elections and permitting French troops free passage through his domain. The pact allowed Louis' *chambres de réunion* a freer hand along the western frontier of the Empire but still did not give the Hohenzollerns all of Pomerania. The Great Elector therefore soon changed political partners again and signed a treaty with the Netherlands. This alliance with William of Orange was cemented by the Edict of Potsdam (1685) whereby Frederick William granted asylum to all Huguenots expelled from France by Louis XIV after the revocation of the Edict of Nantes. In January 1686, the elector also renewed his alliance with the emperor, pledging his military aid to the Habsburgs in Hungary in return for the district of Schwiebus.

Frederick William's greatness lay not only in his accomplishments as a military leader and diplomat but in other areas as well. Following Dutch economic models and French mercantilistic ideas, he paid great attention to agriculture, encouraged trade through canal construction, furthered the systematic colonization of his sparsely populated country, and even attempted to build a navy and start a colony on the Guinea coast of West Africa. A discriminating patron of the arts and education, he established the Royal Library and Art Gallery in Berlin, founded the University of Duisburg, and reorganized those at Königsberg and Frankfurt on the Oder. These policies were rooted in the elector's deep

Calvinist faith, which made him view power as something God given that had to be used with responsibility. Like Louis XIV of France, Frederick William regarded himself as an embodiment of the state and of his people. His most coveted prize, western Pomerania, kept eluding him throughout his reign, but that in no way diminished his very real accomplishments. He had attained power when the fortunes of the Hohenzollerns and the Mark Brandenburg were at their lowest ebb; in raising them, he laid the foundations for Prussian absolutism and power.

Works About: Francis L. Carsten, *The Origins of Prussia* (Oxford, 1954); C. A. Macartney, ed., *The Habsburg and Hohenzollern Dynasties in the Seventeenth and Eighteenth Centuries* (New York, 1970), pp. 228–74; Otto Meinardus, ed., *Protokolle und Relationen des Brandenburgischen Geheimen Rathes aus der Zeit des Kurfürsten Friedrich Wilhelm*, 7 vols. (Leipzig, 1889–1919); Gerhard Oestreich, "Calvinismus, Neustoizismus und Preussentum," *Jb. für die Gesch. Mittel — und Ostdeutschlands* 5 (1956): 157–81, "Friedrich Wilhelm," *NDB*, 5:495–501, and *Friedrich Wilhelm, der Grosse Kurfürst* (Göttingen, 1971); Ernst Opgenoorth, *Friedrich Wilhelm, der grosse Kurfürst von Brandenburg* (Göttingen, 1971–), vol. 1; Herman von Petersdorff, *Der Grosse Kurfürst*, 2d ed. (Leipzig, 1939); Martin Philippson, *Der Grosse Kurfürst Friedrich Wilhelm von Brandenburg*, 3 vols. (Berlin, 1897–1903); Ferdinand Schevill, *The Great Elector* (Chicago, 1947); *Urkunden und Actenstücke zur Gesch. des Kurfürsten Friedrich Wilhelm von Brandenburg*, 23 vols. (Berlin, 1864–1930).   *Bodo Nischan*

See FREDERICK III, ELECTOR; THIRTY YEARS WAR; WESTPHALIA.

FREDERICK WILLIAM I (1713–1740), king in Prussia, the son of Frederick I and his second wife, Sophie Charlotte, was born in 1688. His tutors, Count von Dohna and Count Finkenstein, imbued him with habits of punctiliousness, cleaniness, and thrift and a passion for the military that lasted throughout his life. Headstrong and aggressive, he was a child who would threaten to jump from a three-story window when denied his breakfast. He grew into a robust man with a ruddy face, blue eyes, and a high forehead. He possessed a great deal of physical energy and a violent temper, which he frequently vented on those around him. Completely different in temperament and taste from Frederick I, he was nevertheless a loyal son who always obeyed his father without question. Frederick William would later find his own son's disobedience and intractability incomprehensible. His passion for the military was strengthened by his acquaintance with John Churchill, duke of Marlborough, Prince Eugene of Savoy, and Prince Leopold of Anhalt-Dessau.

When he came to the throne in 1713, he dismissed every unnecessary official and governed the state with a strict discipline and unbending frugality. Contemptuous of art, poetry, philosophy, and letters, he was determined to prevent "the old histories of my father from awakening again." The king worked strenuously and expected others to follow his example. "Travailler pour le Roi de Prusse" became a proverbial saying for hard work and little pay. Undeterred by bad weather and terrible roads, he would tour his provinces, thus earning the sobriquet King of the Highroads. He spent his evenings in the so-called tobacco parliament, an informal gathering of close associates, punctuated with guard-room humor and practical jokes. For relaxation he also hunted with a vigor that daunted others.

By curtailing the expenses of the court and by extending rigid economies throughout the realm, he transformed Prussia into the Sparta of the north; he made Prussia independent of foreign subsidies, built up a large army, and created a substantial war chest. He instilled a new spirit, discipline, and efficiency into the troops and virtually created a professional army. He also mobilized the nobility into service in the army. He ended the diversity of weapons, uniforms, and regulations; he stipulated the color and cut of the uniforms, the number of buttons, even the yardage allowed. He had a childish obsession with tall soldiers who were enrolled, often forcibly, into the Potsdam giant regiment. His affection for the soldiers, whom he called his children, deterred him from using the army he had so painstakingly built up. As Peter the Great remarked, he liked to go fishing but did not like to get his feet wet.

Frederick William was one of Prussia's greatest administrators not only of the army but also of internal state affairs. He reorganized the government and fused the provincial organizations into one unified administration. In 1722 he wrote the instructions for the *Generaldirektorium* of war, finance, and domains. He merged the separate administrations of the domains, the mint, the postal service, and the customs into a general board of finance (*Generalfinanzdirektorium*). He subordinated local officials to the control of the central government and de-stroyed local autonomy. He consolidated the separate civil and military revenue administrations under a single supreme board and the provincial domains and commissariat administrations into collegial boards. The king decided matters from his private apartment or cabinet, not in council. Frederick William's reforms made possible the later reforms of his son. His reign represents the climax of the process of administrative evolution, which provided modern public offices staffed with a professional civil service. His establishment of a centralized hierarchy of administrative offices represented the capstone in the structure of absolutism.

In other spheres he converted the private estates of the king into crown domains, freed the serfs on royal lands, and converted hereditary leases of royal lands into short-term leases. This mercantilistic spirit was also manifested in the colonization of East Prussia, the improvement of municipal administration, and the encouragement of native industries, especially wool. Tolerant in an age of intolerance, he even welcomed Catholics into his lands.

His foreign policy was not as successful. He did gain Guelderland at the Peace of Utrecht and Stettin and the adjacent district in western Pomerania at the Peace of Stockholm, but his attempt to press Prussian claims to the duchies of Jülich and Berg failed. Too straightforward and religious a man for the diplomatic game, he became the dupe of both Austria and France. He generally remained loyal to the emperor and attempted to perpetuate the tradition of Hohenzollern friendship with the Habsburgs, though he did toy with a French alliance.

He had married Sophie Dorothea of Hanover in 1706. Their initial affection gave way to almost continual altercations. The woman, who bore him fourteen children, was discontented with the stern and parsimonious Frederick William, who ruled his family as a despot. She helped to turn the eldest son against his father. The king could not countenance an heir who did not share his likes and dislikes, his thoughts, and his beliefs. "Fritz is a piper and a poetaster, he cares nothing about soldiers and will ruin all I have done," Frederick William would bitterly remark. The contrast between the two was marked. Frederick was secretive, reserved, and when pressed, sarcastic, an effeminate fellow with long hair who could not ride a horse or shoot. The rift between father and son grew until Frederick attempted flight in 1730. The execution of his best friend before his eyes and his own imprisonment shocked him into unwilling obedience. After working as a clerk and demonstrating his loyalty, Frederick was gradually reconciled with his father. In his later years Frederick William was plagued with dropsy and gout, which only increased his bad temper. Frederick William, the man who created the Prussian army, died in 1740. His iron resolution, honest of purpose, love of justice, and unflagging dedication helped weld Prussia into a strong state, a state with an army that ranked third among the European powers and a civilian government and economy geared to support that army.

Works By: Otto Krauske, ed., *Die Briefe König Friedrich Wilhelms I an den Fürsten Leopold zu Anhalt-Dessau* (Berlin, 1905); W. M. Pantenius, *Erlasse und Briefe des Königs Friedrich Wilhelm I von Preussen* (Leipzig, 1913). **Works About:** *ADB*, 7:635–56; Wilhelm Altman, *Ausgewählte Urkunden zur brandenburgisch-preussischen Verfassungs-und Verwaltungsgesch* (Berlin, 1897), vol. 1; Gordon Craig, *The Politics of the Prussian Army, 1640–1945* (Oxford, 1955); Reinhold August Dorwart, *The Administrative Reforms of Frederick William I of Prussia* (Cambridge, 1953); J. G. Droysen, *Gesch. der preussischen Politik* (Leipzig, 1869), vol. 4; Robert Ergang, *The Potsdam Führer* (New York, 1941); David Fassmann, *Leben und Thaten Friedrich Wilhelms I.* (Hamburg, 1735); Friedrich Förster, *Friedrich Wilhelm I. König von Preussen* (Potsdam, 1835); F. Hartung, *König Friedrich Wilhelm I. von Preussen* (Berlin, 1942); Carl Hinrichs, *Preussen als hist. Problem* (Berlin, 1964); O. Krauske, "Vom Hofe Friedrich Wilhelms I," *Hohenzollern Jb.* 5 (1901): 173–201; Gerhard Oestreich, *Friedrich Wilhelm I, preussischer Absolutismus, Merkantilismus und Militarismus* (Göttingen, 1977) and *NDB*, 5:540–45; Albert Waddington, ed., *Recueil des instructions données aux ambassadeurs et ministres de France depuis les traités de Westphalie jusqu' à la révolution française.* vol. 16 (Paris, 1901).   L. S. Frey and M. L. Frey

See FREDERICK II, THE GREAT; FREDERICK III, ELECTOR; SOPHIE CHARLOTTE; UTRECHT.

FREIBURG IM BREISGAU, a town located on the chief east-west land route across the southern Black Forest, was founded in 1120 by the dukes of Zähringen. After the death of the last duke of Zähringen in 1218, Freiburg passed to the counts of Urach, who took the title of counts of Freiburg. Under these weak lords, Freiburg became virtually autonomous, and the town grew rapidly as a result of its control of a booming local silver industry. The community was under the control of a wealthy urban nobility in the high Middle Ages, though in 1293 an annual mayor (*Bürgermeister*) supplanted the permanent magistrate (*Schultheiss*) as the chief municipal officer. At the same time, guilds became public corporations with representation in the town council.

The prosperity of Freiburg declined in the second half of the fourteenth century, a result of the collapse of silver mining and the dispersal of the old urban nobility into the countryside. From 1366 to 1368, a feud with Count Egon IV ended with Freiburg's defeat in battle. Freiburg was allowed to buy out the count's interests but at such a high price that it had to give itself to the Habsburgs. In 1386 much of the Freiburg nobility was massacred by the Swiss at Sempach, and in 1388 a group of guildsmen established a new guild-dominated regime. Many, but not all, of the guildsmen's gains were reversed by the Habsburgs in 1392. Freiburg became the seat of the Avignonese antibishop of Constance during the Great Schism. When the Habsburg duke Frederick IV was outlawed for helping John XXIII flee Constance, Freiburg had a brief career (1416–1429) as an imperial city. From 1450 to 1458 and 1461 to 1463, Freiburg was the residence of Archduke Albert VI, who temporarily abolished the guilds in favor of a more oligarchical regime and founded Freiburg University. Like the rest of the Breisgau, Freiburg passed under Burgundian rule in 1469 but participated in the overthrow of the Burgundian governor, Peter von Hagenbach, and in the campaigns with the Swiss against Charles the Bold from 1474 to 1477.

The political and cultural apogee of Freiburg was from 1490 to 1519, when the town had a special relationship with King (later Emperor) Maximilian I. Freiburg was the meeting place of an imperial diet in 1497–1498. The town leaders suppressed a peasant conspiracy in nearby Lehen in 1513, and in the early Reformation period the town leaders were notorious gendarmes of regional religious and social reaction. Toward the end of the Peasants' War, in May 1525, Freiburg briefly capitulated to a peasant revolutionary army.

The constitution of the town was altered by Austrian authorities in 1557 to make it more oligarchical. In the mid-sixteenth century Freiburg recovered its late-medieval population losses, though it never fully regained its former prosperity.

From the Thirty Years War onward, Freiburg became part of the frontier between France and the Habsburg lands, and the town was economically exhausted and frequently besieged. Freiburg was occupied by the French from 1677 to 1698, during which time Marshal Sébastien de Vauban completely demolished the medieval suburbs in order to construct elaborate fortifications. The last French siege came in 1744, and the victorious French force leveled the town's defenses before withdrawing. The Breisgau again became a theater of war in 1792, but after French occupation the region passed to the duke of Modena in 1803. In 1806 Freiburg was finally incorporated into the Grand Duchy of Baden.

Works About: Friedrich Hefele, *Freiburger Urkundenbuch*, 3 vols. Freiburg, 1938–1957); Franz Laubenberger, "Die Freiburger Stadtverwaltung im 17. und 18. Jahrhundert und ihre gesellschaftliche Struktur," in Erich Maschke and Jürgen Sydow, eds., *Verwaltung und Gesellschaft in der südwestdeutschen Stadt des 17. und 18. Jahrhundert* (Stuttgart, 1969); Theodor Mayer, "The State of the Dukes of Zähringen," in Geoffrey Barraclough, ed., *Medieval Germany* (Oxford, 1938), 2:175–202; Steven Rowan, "The Common Penny (1495–99) as a Source of German Social and Demographic Hist.," *CEH* 10 (1970): 148–64; Walter Schlesinger, "Das älteste Freiburger Stadtrecht," *Z. für Rechtsgesch., Germ. Abt.* 83 (1966): 63–116; Heinrich Schreiber, *Gesch. der Stadt und Universität Freiburg im Breisgau*, 2 vols. (Freiburg, 1857–1860), and *Urkunden Buch der Stadt Freiburg im Breisgau*, 2 vols. (Freiburg, 1828–1829); Berent Schwineköper, "Bemerkungen zum Problem der städtischen Unterschichten aus Freiburger Sicht," in Erich Maschke and Jurgen Sydow, eds., *Gesellschaftliche Unterschichten in den südwestdeutschen Stadten* (Stuttgart, 1967). Statistisches Landesamt, Bad-Württ., *Freiburg im Breisgau Amtl. kreisbeschreibung* (Freiburg, 1965), vol. 7.   *S. W. Rowan*

See MAXIMILIAN I; PEASANTS' WAR.

FRENCH REVOLUTIONARY WARS (1792–1802), first half of a twenty-three year European conflict triggered by the French Revolution, ended with the Treaty of Amiens; the Napoleonic Wars proper ended at Waterloo in 1815. The radicalization of the French Revolution after 1789 caused the other nations of Europe, which had not been displeased initially at seeing their powerful neighbor weakened internally, to become increasingly concerned at the possible spread of the revolutionary ferment. After King Louis XVI's arrested flight to Varennes in June 1791, Queen Marie Antoinette's brother, the Emperor Leopold II, joined with King Frederick William II of Prussia (1744–1797) in issuing the Declaration of Pillnitz (August 27) appealing for the other states to use force against the revolutionaries. The Girondin faction got the assembly to declare war on Austria (but not on the Holy Roman Empire) on April 20, 1792, as much to draw attention from domestic problems as to protect and spread the revolutionary ideals.

As the Jacobins rose to power, Charles William Ferdinand, the duke of Brunswick (1735–1806), commanding the allied army, issued a manifesto on July 27 threatening Paris with reprisals should the king and queen be harmed. His force crossed the French frontier on August 19, but the advance was hesitant; Austria and Prussia were distracted by the Russian invasion of truncated Poland on May 19, and Brunswick retreated after exchanging cannonades with François Christophe Kellermann's (1735–1820) and Charles François Dumouriez' (1739–1823) French forces at Valmy in the Argonne on September 20, 1792. Dumouriez, encouraged by this victory, then drove back the Austrian army of the Netherlands at Jemappes on November 6, and while some French forces defeated the Sardinians in Savoy, others advanced across the Rhine and seized Frankfurt.

By the spring of 1793, the Jacobins had executed Louis XVI (January 21) and declared war on England and Spain. England responded by engineering the First Coalition with the Netherlands, Russia, Sardinia, Spain, Naples, Prussia (July 14), Austria (August 30), and Portugal between March and September.

The Jacobin Committee of Public Safety created the nation-in-arms with the *levée en masse* (universal conscription) of August 23 of Lazare Carnot (1753–1823). But Dumouriez' advance on the Netherlands was defeated at Neerwinden, west of Liège, by an Austrian army under Prince Josias of Saxe-Coburg-Saalfeld (on March 18) and defeated again at Louvain, whereupon Dumouriez concluded an armistice and shortly thereafter defected to the Austrians. Allied disunity and lack of strategic purpose, however, enabled the French to hold all fronts, from the Low Countries to Spain, though the revolt of the Vendée, which broke out in March and proved difficult to quell.

In 1794 Prussia and Russia were preoccupied with their second partition of Poland and then the revolt of Thaddeus Kosciuszko (1746–1817) in Warsaw; Coburg was forced to retreat before the French army of Sambre-et-Meuse, which cleared Belgium. But with the overthrow of Maximilien Robespierre (1758–1794), the new Directory signed treaties with Tuscany (February 9, 1795), with Prussia (at Basel, April 5–6), with the Dutch Batavian Republic (at the Hague, May 16), and with Spain (Second Peace of Basel, July 22). Austria, under Holy Roman Emperor Francis II (1768–1835), remained hostile, and after negotiating a third partition of Poland in January, concluded a treaty with England (May 20) to receive a subsidy of £600,000 to maintain two hundred thousand troops in the field, and drove the French from the Palatinate.

For 1796 Carnot conceived a coordinated offensive, with Jean Baptiste Jourdan's (1762–1833) army of Sambre-et-Meuse advancing southeast from the Low Countries and Jean Moreau's (1763–1813) army of Rhin-et-Moselle advancing east into southern Germany, while Kellermann's army of the Alps and Napoleon Bonaparte's (1769–1821) army of Italy cleared the Po valley. In the north the French advanced into Bavaria, but Jourdan was driven back by the Archduke Charles (1771–1847), and Moreau retreated. In Italy, however, Napoleon brilliantly drove between the Sardinians and Austrians, and Sardinia was forced to withdraw from the coalition and surrender Nice and Savoy by the armistice of Cherasco (April 28, 1796). Napoleon then maneuvered General Beaulieu out of Lombardy, winning at Lodi (May 10), and out of most of Venetia; he then besieged Mantua. Dagobert Sigismond Würmser (1724–1797) brought an army down from Germany but was defeated by Napoleon at Castiglione (August 5), and Baron Alvintzy (Joseph von Barbarek) took command but was defeated at Arcola on the Adige (November 15–17). In January 1797 Alvintzy advanced anew, but was routed by Napoleon at Rivoli, near Lake Garda, later in the month. The Archduke Charles came down from the Rhine to take command but was no more fortunate than his predecessors against Napoleon. On April 18, 1797, an armistice was negotiated at Leoben.

Napoleon's reorganization of northern Italy as the Cisalpine Republic under French protection was confirmed by the Treaty of Campo Formio (October 17–18). Austria ceded the Austrian Netherlands to France and promised it the left bank of the Rhine (confirmed at Rastatt, March 9, 1798), though receiving

Venetia east of the Adige. Naples had made peace with France on October 10, 1796; Czar Paul I (1754–1801) succeeded Catherine of Russia in November and ended Russian involvement; and when Portugal made peace on August 10, 1797, England's coalition had disintegrated.

In 1798 Napoleon mounted an expedition against Egypt, apparently to hurt England economically, but was stranded by Admiral Horatio Nelson's victory at Aboukir Bay on the Nile (August 1). Napoleon's subsequent failures in Syria, along with the French occupation of Rome (February 15, 1798) and Switzerland, stimulated the formation of the Second Coalition (England, Russia, Austria, Turkey, Portugal, and Naples) by 1799.

In March 1799 the French advanced to defeat the Austrians before the Russians arrived. But in Germany Jourdan was defeated by Archduke Charles at Stockach (March 25) and retreated back across the Rhine. In Italy Barthelemy Schérer was defeated by Major General Paul Kray von Krajova (1735–1804) at Magnano on April 5. In the center André Masséna (1756–1817) held Switzerland by repulsing the Archduke Charles at Zurich on June 4. The Austrians were soon reinforced by two Russian armies. Nonetheless the Archduke Charles was dispatched to the middle Rhine, and Alexander Korsakov was routed at second Zurich on September 25 by Masséna and driven north across the Rhine. Alexander Suvorov (1729–1800), who had forced the St. Gotthard Pass and advanced to Lake Lucerne, had to retreat eastward across the Alps, and Czar Paul ordered the campaign ended on October 23.

Napoleon Bonaparte had meanwhile returned from Egypt and overthrew the Directory in the coup d'état of Brumaire (November 9–10, 1799), establishing himself as first consul. He initiated peace overtures, but England and Austria remained steadfast opponents. The Austrians still held southern Germany with the one hundred thousand troops of Kray, and northern Italy with the ninety thousand troops of Michael Melas (1730–1806); but the decrepit Aulic Council (Austrian council of state) was incapable of conceiving the strategic situation on a Napoleonic scale.

Under cover of the peace negotiations, Napoleon created the Army of the Reserve at Dijon, which the Austrians were led to believe comprised old reservists and raw conscripts; actually it had a nucleus of veterans and was to play the principal role in Napoleon's strategy. Utilizing the pivotal position of Switzerland, this force was to coordinate with Moreau's 120,000–man Army of the Rhine to defeat Kray in southern Germany and march on Vienna; but with the opposition of the cautious Moreau, Napoleon decided to swing south instead, into the secondary theater of northern Italy and combine with Masséna's 36,000–man Army of Italy (Liguria) to defeat Melas in the Po River valley.

But on April 5, 1800, the Austrians moved first. The Aulic Council, ignoring the capabilities of the Reserve at Dijon, had Melas advance on Genoa, ultimately to lay siege to Toulon. Initially successful, Melas drove Masséna back into Genoa and besieged him there with the assistance of the Royal Navy; but he was now vulnerable to attack from the north. Urging Masséna to hold out until June 4, Napoleon began moving his 40,000 troops over the Alps by the Great St. Bernard pass, a passage of a week. There was still deep snow in the mountains and the cannon were transported only by dragging the guns on hollowed tree trunks. In addition Moreau, who only advanced across the Rhine on April 25, sent scarcely half the troops south originally planned for.

Napoleon might have marched directly on Turin, or to relieve Masséna, besieged in Genoa, but instead boldly marched southeast on Milan, entering it on June 2, to cut Melas' communications and trap him. Masséna capitulated on June 4 to lenient terms, thus releasing Melas to concentrate at Alessandria. But Napoleon was already across the Po and decisively defeated him at Marengo (June 14, 1800). Yet Marengo did not bring peace because Italy was not the decisive theater of operations. In Germany Moreau drove Kray from Ulm and Munich, achieving the armistice of Parsdorf (July 15). But English Prime Minister William Pitt (1759–1806) induced Emperor Francis II to stay in the coalition, and it was not until Moreau defeated Kray and the Archduke John at Hohenlinden (December 3) that the Austrians, by the armistice of Steyr (December 25), agreed to negotiate a separate peace with France. The fighting in Italy, where the French had occupied Tuscany and the Papal States and advanced across the Adige, ended with the armistice of Treviso (January 15, 1801). The peace negotiations at Leoben finally resulted in the peace of Luneville, signed February 9, 1801, basically reaffirming the settlement of Campo Formio.

England alone continued the struggle, clearing the remaining French from Egypt by the end of September 1801 and destroying the neutral Danish fleet at Copenhagen on April 2, 1801, lest it join Napoleon. But England was ready for peace, and with the resignation of the energetic William Pitt, the government agreed to the Treaty of Amiens (March 27, 1802) by which France recovered almost all the overseas territories that had been lost. Nonetheless the peace would prove impermanent because the underlying issues had not been resolved.

Works About: Austrian War Office, *Krieg gegen die französische Revolution* (Vienna, 1905–); Archduke Charles, *Grundsätze der Strategie* (1796 campaign) (Vienna, 1813), and *Gesch. des Feldzuges 1799 in Deutschland und der Schweiz.* (Vienna, 1819); A. Chuquet, *Les Guerres de la Révolution,* 11 vols. (Paris, 1886–1896).   *A. H. Ganz*

See CAMPO FORMIO; FRANCIS II; LEOPOLD II.

FRITZ, JOSS (c. 1476–1525), peasant leader in the *Bundschuh* (peasant's clog) and Peasants' Revolt, was born at Untergrombach near Bruchsal. Other than his place of birth, little is known of him until about 1501–1502 when he began to organize a general uprising of peasants and townspeople under the symbol of the Bundschuh. Along with the slogan, "God's Equal Justice Alone," the peasants pledged to pay no rents, tithes, taxes, or tolls; they demanded free streams, commons, and forests (as God made them) and the division of Church and monastic properties.

Fritz planned to commence the uprising on April 22, 1502. From the capture of Obergrombach castle, it was to become a general movement in southwest Germany without distinction between peasant and townsman. All was ready when Fritz was betrayed. A hundred were arrested; ten were executed, but Joss Fritz escaped.

He was next known ten years later as a field ranger near Freiburg in Lehen. Fritz retained his *Bundschuh* convictions and by 1513 was conspiring to lead another uprising. His program was directed primarily against the nobility: payments and labor reduced to absolute minimums; fishing and hunting to be free and the commons open; appropriate justices to replace Church and manorial courts; theft fines not to exceed the value of the article; and interest not to exceed 5 percent.

This new order was justified in the divine law but was Joss Fritz's work entirely. He was the center of the movement. Each co-conspirator—there were about forty in all—was personally selected by him to be representative of groups and elements within the peasant and urban lower classes. Paradoxically the group's demands were purely agrarian, and the movement was peasant in character throughout. Joss Fritz's second *Bundschuh* movement was also betrayed. Thirteen of the conspirators were executed, again not including Fritz, who escaped dressed as a pilgrim.

Between 1515 and 1517 Joss Fritz prepared yet another uprising, this time for the Rhineland. Reversing his mode of operation, he recruited a large number of itinerant missionaries from the beggars and gamblers circulating the land. His program was equally bold. The nobility would be overthrown, destroyed, and dispossessed; all rents, dues, and obligations would end except for minimal remittances to the emperor and the Church. But nothing happened, even though the impending *Bundschuh* was known in bits and pieces everywhere. Perhaps just fragmented knowledge of the movement brought sufficient counter measures from the authorities.

Over the next few years, peasant revolts broke out in many Rhineland locales. In the early moments of the great Peasants' Revolt of 1524–1525, the peasants of the Black Forest recorded the presence of an old and gray-bearded Joss Fritz saying he could not and would not die until the *Bundschuh* had attained its final setting forth. His work melded the concept of the divine justice into the grievances of the peasants.

Works About: W. Andreas, "Der Bundschuh," *Archiv Sozial Wissenschaftlich* 60 (1928); Gunther Franz, *Der dtsch. Bauernkrieg*, 7th ed. (Darmstadt, 1965), and "Fritz, Joss," *NDB*, 5:631; A. Rosenkranz, *Der Bundschuh* (Leipzig, 1927), vol. 1.   *K. C. Sessions*

See PEASANTS' WAR.

FUGGER, JACOB THE RICH (1459–1525), early capitalist, was a native of Augsburg, where his family had established itself in banking. Originally intended for an ecclesiastical career, Jacob was brought into the family business after the death of his elder brother, Peter, in 1473. He was sent to Venice to study bookkeeping and in 1485 was given charge of the Fugger agency in Innsbruck, where he involved the family in the Tyrolian mining industry. The Fugger influence was extended by making generous loans to Archduke Sigismund of the Tyrol and Emperor Maximilian I. By 1502 after extending the family's mining interests into Hungary and Silesia, Jacob became virtual head of the Fugger family business. He continued to load money to Maximilian, secured by the income from the royal salt mines, who rewarded him with the countships of Kirchberg and Weissenhorn. Jacob became a member of the imperial nobility and a count of the Empire in 1514. Of the 850,000 gulden needed to secure Maximilian's grandson Charles's election as Holy Roman emperor in 1519, Jacob the Rich personally raised 544,000 gulden.

True to his motto, "I shall gain while I am able," Fugger involved his family in all manner of commerce, including the East India spice trade. The Fuggers were also active in Church finance. It was Jacob who loaned Albert of Brandenburg the 34,000 gulden necessary to secure the archbishopric of Mainz. This led to the sale of indulgences in order to repay the loan, which triggered Martin Luther's protest. During the ensuing Reformation, Jacob stayed loyal to the Roman Catholic church.

In Augsburg Jacob Fugger founded the Fuggeri, the world's first social settlement house for poor workers. Despite imperial protests against monopolistic practices in 1522–1523, the childless Fugger willed a large fortune to his nephew Anton (1493–1560), who helped finance the Habsburg wars against the Turks, the French, and the Protestants.

Works About: Richard Ehrenberg, *Capital and Finance in the Age of the Renaissance: A Study of the Fuggers and their Connections* (New York, 1963); Ernst Hering, *Die Fugger* (Leipzig, 1939); Götz von Pölnitz, *Die Fugger* (Tübingen, 1970); Jakob Strieder, *Jacob Fugger the Rich*, tr. M. L. Hartsough (New York, 1931).   *J. W. Zophy*

See AUGSBURG; CHARLES V; LUTHER; MAXIMILIAN I; SIGISMUND.

9

GAISMAIR, MICHAEL (1491–1532), also Gaissmayr, was born in Sterzing (Tyrol). He was a leader in the Tyrolean Peasants' Revolt (1525), a visionary of political, social, economic democracy in a Tyrolean republic, and a diplomatist-advocate of Zurich-Tyrol anti-Habsburg axis in the Swiss and south German Reformation.

Gaismair was scribe for the military commander in Tyrol, secretary to the bishop of Brixen, and customs officer at Klausen. Rebellion arose in Brixen on May 10, 1525, and Gaismair was elected leader as the movement spread rapidly across Tyrol. But revolt faded quickly after the arrival of Archduke Ferdinand of Austria at the invitation of the province's parliament. Gaismair obeyed summons to Innsbruck, but discovering the revolt still alive in Trent and surrounding areas, he resumed leadership. Following military defeat, Gaismair fled into Switzerland in September 1525.

In early 1526 the rebel leader unveiled his proposal for a new order in Tyrol. The twenty-eight articles of his territorial ordinance (*Landesordnung*) foresaw a thoroughly leveled republic in his homeland, achieved through universal equality at law, an end to rule by nobility and clergy, election of the clergy by the people, dismantling of the merchant guilds, nationalizing of the mines, and extensive poor relief. Walls of cities and castles would come down, as would internal tolls; business and manufacture would be officially supervised; and swamplands would be drained for agricultural development. All effective power would be placed by representative democracy in the hands of the peasants, craftsmen, and miners.

Gaismair's reform plan was drawn from his government service, his studies, and Reformation and reform literature. The strongest outside influence was from Ulrich Zwingli, where religious provisions would dispense with pilgrimages, wayside shrines, the Mass, the decorations, the ceremony and the music, and replace it all with the stark biblical simplicity of the Zurich worship. This Reformation would be secured for the future by establishment of a Zwinglian college in Tyrol.

Zwingli's influence in Gaismair's reform plans is the result of refuge the rebel gained in Zurich over the winter 1525–1526. As the Tyrol uprising failed, Gaismair recognized that the ultimate enemy was Austria, and he sought support in the Swiss Confederation against the Habsburgs. This search brought him to Zurich and Zwingli. From their meeting arose tandem objectives. Zwingli would expand the Zurich Reformation and Gaismair would master Tyrol. Zurich, the forest cantons, Grisons, St. Gall, and eventually Tyrol in alliance would be the first stage. The union would expand to embrace the great south German cities such as Constance, Lindau, and Strasbourg. Gaismair's revolution in Tyrol would be carried out, and Zwingli's Reformation would penetrate the alliance. Eventual treaty with France and Venice would complete an anti-Habsburg, counter-Austria system in alpine Europe and south Germany.

Gaismair's elaborate plans became exposed in the spring of 1526, and the revolutionary fled once more. He emerged leading the second Salzburg revolt and again was trounced. Heading back to Tyrol, he realized that arrest awaited him and diverted his route into territory of the Venetian republic. Gaismair apparently prospered in Venetian soil, but his concern for his homeland continued, and his relationship with Zwingli and Zurich endured. Zwingli's activist politics led him to seek Venetian cooperation. In 1529 his representative approached the government of the Doge with alliance offers. The agent also had contact with Gaismair.

The fugitive counseled Zurich to remain fast upon the ultimate enemy and direct all energies against the Habsburgs; a Protestant-Venetian alliance could surely do that. Here Tyrol was crucial, for it sat astride the Habsburgs' alpine communications with Italy and was the treasure chest of imperial politics in south Germany. Thus any action by Zurich turned on separating Tyrol from the Habsburgs, and Gaismair stood ready to do just that, using Venetian troops and the help of exiled Duke Ulrich of Württemberg.

This projection of December 1529 did not come about, but it did not die away. Rather it matured as Gaismair and Zwingli met again in July 1530. The old plan of 1526 was revived. Tyrol, the linchpin, would be secured by Gaismair and an army of eighteen thousand launched from Grisons. Zwingli's expansionism, however, came abruptly to an end with his death at the Battle of Kappel on October 11, 1531.

Gaismair's life also came to an abrupt end as he fell to a Habsburg-bribed assassin in Padua in April 1532. His rebel patriotism, remarkable activity, and wide-ranging leadership in the alpine peasants' revolts are well known. He also earns recognition for his visionary statesmanship and his capacious diplomacy.

Works By: Günther Franz, ed., *Quel. zur Gesch. des Bauernkriegs* (Munich, 1963). **Works About:** G. Franz, *Der dtsch. Bauernkrieg*, 10th ed. (Darmstadt, 1975); Walter Klaassen, *Michael Gaismair* (Leiden, 1978); Josef Macek, "Zu den Anfängen des Tiroler Bauernkrieges," *Historica* 1 (1959): 135–95; Oskar Vasella, "Bauernkrieg und Reformation in Graubünden 1525–26," *Z. für Schweizische Gesch.* 20 (1940): 53–65, and *NDB*, 7:40; Ziessberg, "Gaismair," *ADB*, 8:313–14.   *K. C. Sessions*

See FERDINAND I; PEASANTS' WAR: ULRICH OF WÜRTTEMBERG; ZWINGLI.

GATTINARA, MERCURINO ARBORIO DI (1465–1530), a dominant figure in the early government of Emperor Charles V, was born and raised in the area of Vercelli in the Savoyard Piedmont. He studied law at Turin and made a name for himself as an advocate. In 1501 he was made chief adviser to Margaret of Habsburg, the wife of Duke Philbert the Handsome of Savoy. When Philbert died in 1504, Gattinara worked to obtain a good property settlement for Margaret from the Savoyard government, and he went north with Margaret when she became ruler of Austrian Burgundy and the Low Countries in 1506. Gattinara became president of the assembly of the Burgundian estates at Dôle, but his efforts to discipline the Burgundian nobility led to strong opposition and to attacks on Gattinara's feudal holdings in the Franche—Comté. He performed diplomatic missions both for Margaret and for the emperor Maximilian I, and in 1513 he was created count of Gattinara.

On October 15, 1518, Gattinara became grand chancellor to King Charles of Spain, and from the outset he pushed for Charles to pursue the imperial crown, despite the fact that Flemish and Spanish advisers were unenthusiastic about the idea. When Charles V was elected emperor in June 1519, Gattinara became imperial grand chancellor. After the death of Chièvres in 1521, Gattinara took his place as chief adviser to Charles V. Throughout the following decade, Gattinara wrote memoranda to Charles stressing the divine mission of the emperor to bring peace to Christendom and to wage war on the infidel abroad. His elevated concept of empire, derived largely from Roman law and the medieval Italian Ghibelline tradition, provided a working ideology for Charles' ramshackle state. Gattinara consistently saw Italy as the key to the imperial rule of Christendom, and he perceived the chief obstacles to pacifying Italy to be France and an independent papacy.

The policy of reducing French power in Italy culminated in the capture of King Francis I of France at the Battle of Pavia on February 24, 1525. Gattinara pushed for a settlement of all outstanding differences before the king was released, but the majority of the imperial council advocated releasing him as soon as he had signed a preliminary agreement. Gattinara refused to seal the Peace of Madrid on January 14, 1526, and he was not surprised when Francis immediately formed the hostile League of Cognac. Gattinara was on leave tending to private business when a runaway imperial army sacked Rome and imprisoned Pope Clement VII in the summer of 1527. Gattinara returned to Spain to take charge of the drifting imperial government there. In 1528 Gattinara helped negotiate the shift of the Genoese admiral Andrea d'Oria from the French to the imperial cause, and in 1529 Charles V and Gattinara traveled to a pacified Italy. Gattinara was made a cardinal in late 1529, and Charles V was crowned emperor in February 1530, at Bologna. Gattinara died the following June in Innsbruck on his way to the diet of Augsburg.

Gattinara advocated the calling of an universal council to reform the Church and pave the way for the destruction of Lutheranism in Germany. His concept of the imperial mission tended to assign a subordinate role to the pope in the leadership of Christendom. He was a correspondent of Erasmus and supported him against attacks by enemies at the Spanish court.

Works About: Marcel Bataillon, *Erasmo y España*, tr. Antonio Alatorre 2d ed. (Mexico City, 1966); Carlo Bornate, ed., "Historia vite et gestarum per dominum magnum cancellarium," *Miscellanea di storia italiana* 48 (1915): 231–582; Carlo Bornate, "L'apogeo della Casa di Absburgo e l'opera politica di un Gran Cancelliere di Carlo V," *Nuova rivista storica* 3 (1919):396–439, "La politica italiana del Gran Cancelliere di Carlo V," *Bolletino storico di Novara* 24 (1930):389–414 and *Enciclopedia italiana*, 16:451; Karl Brandi, *The Emperor Charles V*, tr. C. V. Wedgwood (London, 1939), and *Kaiser Karl V* (Munich, 1941); repr., Darmstadt, 1967), vol. 2; Hubert Jedin, *History of the Council of Trent*, tr. Ernest Graf (St. Louis, 1957), vol. 1; Edward D. McShane, *New Catholic Encyclopedia*, 6:301–2; Fritz Walser, *Die spanische Zentralbehörden und der Staatsrat Karls V.*, ed. Rainer Wohlfeil, Abhandl. der Akad. der Wiss. in Göttingen, Phil.-hist. Kl., 3d series, no. 43 (Göttingen, 1959).   *S. W. Rowan*

See CHARLES V; ERASMUS; MAXIMILIAN I.

GEORGE WILLIAM (1595–1640), margrave and elector of Brandenburg, was born in Kölln/Spree and died at Königsberg. He was the son of Elector John Sigismund who had opened a new chapter in Brandenburg's history when he converted to Calvinism in 1613. George William was married to Elizabeth Charlotte, sister of Frederick V of the Palatinate, Bohemia's ill-fated Winter King; his sister, Marie Eleonore, was the wife of King Gustavus Adolphus of Sweden. Before acceding to the government in Brandenburg in 1619, George William had served as regent of the Hohenzollern family's Rhenish territories (1614-1617). During his stay there he fell under the influence of the Catholic Count Adam zu Schwarzenberg who later became one of his leading advisers. George William was weak, unimaginative, vacillating, and easily influenced. Throughout his reign, which coincided with the Thirty Years War, he was torn between conflicting factions. Schwarzenberg and the elector's staunchly Lutheran mother, Anne, generally favored a pro-imperial policy, while his Calvinist advisers advocated neutrality or an anti-Habsburg stand. With Brandenburg already in a state of economic decline when the war began and the country's powerful Lutheran estates unwilling to appropriate additional funds for the military, the elector could not conduct an effective foreign policy. His problems were compounded by the fact that the Hohenzollern territories were scattered from Poland to the Rhine and therefore virtually indefensible.

Caught in the storm of the Thirty Years War, the helpless elector attempted a variety of policies, all without much avail. He began his reign proclaiming his neutrality but could not enforce it without a respectable army. During the Lower Saxon War large parts of Brandenburg were overrun and devasted by foreign armies (1625–1626), while in the east King Gustavus Adolphus of Sweden, fighting his own war with Poland, occupied the ports of Prussia (1626). On Schwarzenberg's advice George William therefore joined the emperor (1627). But the heavy contributions extorted by Duke Albert von Wallenstein's imperial forces and the emperor's Edict of Restitution (1629), which threatened Brandenburg's former bishoprics with re-Catholization, soon made the Habsburg alliance very unpopular. The elector again began listening more to his Calvinist

advisers and in 1630 returned to neutrality. Since his Calvinist councillors recognized that their country was too weak alone to maintain its neutrality, they
persuaded Germany's other Protestant princes at the Leipzig Convention (1631)
to create a defensive alliance that was supposed to stand as a neutral third force
amid the imperial, league, and foreign armies. Unfortunately the alliance, and
with it also Brandenburg's second attempt at neutrality, failed because of the
military superiority of the Swedes and the emperor. After seizing Pomerania
and capturing Frankfurt on the Oder, Gustavus' armies swept into Brandenburg
and forced the elector to join Sweden. Gustavus' death (1632) and the defeat of
the Swedish army at Nördlingen (1634) enabled Schwarzenberg to exert himself
once again. On his advice, George William signed the Peace of Prague (1635)
with the emperor and thereby became an enemy of the Swedes. Schwarzenberg
hoped to recruit an army to expel the Swedes and make good the elector's claim
to Pomerania, whose last duke had died without heirs in 1637. But the elector
received no aid from the emperor, and the army that Schwarzenberg raised was
undisciplined and no match for the foreign armies that continued to occupy and
devastate Brandenburg. In the fall of 1638, George William, thoroughly disillusioned, left Berlin for the greater safety of Königsberg (East Prussia) where
he died two years later of dropsy. Schwarzenberg, who had remained behind as
a virtual dictator, died only a few weeks later.

Works About: Francis L. Carsten, *The Origins of Prussia* (Oxford, 1954); *Documenta Bohemica
Bellum Tricennale Illustrantia,* (Prague, 1974–1977), vols. 4–5; J. Gustav Droysen, "Brandenbur-
gische Audienzen bei Gustav Adolf," *Zeit. für Preussische Gesch. und Landeskunde* 15 (1878): 1–
54; T. Hirsch, "Georg Wilhelm," *ADB,* 8:619–29; Thomas Klein, "Georg Wilhelm," *NDB,*
6:203ff; Georg Irmer, ed., *Die Verhandlungen Schwedens und seiner Verbündeten mit Wallenstein
und dem Kaiser von 1631 bis 1634,* 3 vols. (Leipzig, 1888–1891); Reinhold Koser, *Gesch. der
brandenburgischen Politik bis zum Westfälischen Frieden von 1648* (Stuttgart and Berlin, 1939);
Christian O. Mylius, ed. *Corpus Constitutionum Marchicarum,* 6 vols. (Berlin and Halle, 1737-
51); Bodo Nischan, "Brandenburg's Reformed Räte and the Leipzig Manifesto of 1631," *Journal
of Religious History* (in press); Johannes Schultze, *Die Mark Brandenburg* (Berlin, 1964), vol.
4.   *Bodo Nischan*

See EDICT OF RESTITUTION; LEIPZIG, CONVENTION OF; THIRTY YEARS WAR: WAL-
LENSTEIN, ALBERT.

GERMAN FACTORY IN VENICE (Fondacho dei Tedeschi) was a combination warehouse and hostel built in the thirteenth century next to the foot of
the Rialto Bridge, which spanned the Grand Canal. It was maintained by the
Venetians. During the high Middle Ages, large numbers of south German whole-
sale merchants, seeking a market for their goods, traveled by way of the Brenner
Pass to Verona, then made their way down the Adige to Venice, city of the
lagoons and trading capital of much of the Mediterranean. In order to supervise
these visitors more closely, the Venetian government constructed this factory
and had it managed by a superintendent who was accountable to the Venetian
senate. These merchants—who also included Hungarians, Poles, and Bohemi-

ans—were obliged to stay at the *fondacho,* which was centrally located at the major Venetian marketplace. Allowed to import only goods from their native regions, these merchants stored their wares here and purchased luxuries and spices brought to Venice by the city's traders.

Due to the success of the *fondacho,* it became an important place not only for the exchange of merchandise but also ideas. In 1500 statistics indicated that there were 62 arrivals from Augsburg, 5 from Strasbourg, and more than 230 from Nuremburg. Germans passing through Italy resided at the *fondacho* when they reached Venice. One significant example in this regard was the famous Albrecht Dürer who acquired knowledge of Italian Renaissance artistic techniques here. The fondacho thus served as a bridge between the Italian and northern Renaissance and between both of these the Reformation.

Although the original structure was destroyed by fire in 1505, the government had the *fondacho* rebuilt by 1508 because it was so significant to the economic life of the city. The new Renaissance palace, frescoed by Giorgione, remained the center of German merchant activity in Venice until its closure in 1805.

Works About: Henry Simonsfeld, *Der Fondacho dei Tedeschi in Venedig und die Dtsch-Vene- tianischen Handelsbeziehungen,* 2 vols. (Stuttgart, 1887); Leo Schuster, *Die Rolle der Nürnberger Kaufherren am Fondacho dei Tedeschi in Venedig* (Erlangen, 1962).   *P. N. Bebb*

See AUGSBURG; DÜRER; NUREMBERG; STRASBOURG.

GEYER, FLORIAN also Geier (c. 1490–1525), was a shadowy leader in the Tauber district of the Peasants' Revolt (1524–1526). Geyer was a well-situated and well-to-do nobleman of ancient and distinguished lineage. He subscribed to the reform plan of the peasants but took no major leadership role.

Early in life Geyer inherited a castle at Giebelstadt and part of Castle Ingolstadt, both near Würzburg, as well as sizable estates in the region. A controversy over rights to monastic properties in Würzburg resulted in his excommunication in 1517. He entered upon a life of noble service in the army of the Swabian League; for the ruler of Brandenburg, Margrave Casimir; and for Grand Master Albert of Prussia. Probably he was in the retinue accompanying Albert at his conference with Luther at Wittenberg in 1523, which may account for Geyer's fervent conversion to the evangelical faith.

Florian Geyer entered the revolt in mid-April 1525 during the Mergentheim Peasant Congress. The rebels employed him honorably; as their emissary to numerous cities, they were seeking to draw him into the uprising. His mission was successful with nine dependent towns of Mainz and with Kitzingen and Rothenburg. Why he aligned himself with the peasants has no ready explanation. He vowed the destruction of every castle, but he was not propertyless and had not led himself to the rebellion for expectation of gain. His actions, seen in the consequences of his negotiations, bespeak a respect for order and authority. He demanded full confiscation and dispossession of the Church. But his rage was against specific targets, the evildoers in high office and the exploiters of the faithful. For him, redistribution through Reformation meant evangelical equity, not leveling equality. In sum, Geyer seems to have possessed a mind and faith that endowed him with vision beyond his class into the need for overall change and with the conviction to act on the vision.

He did not seek converts or to lead. Convinced personal action seems for him to have been enough. Even so, his words and acts identified him with the rebels and earned him the animosity of his peers. As the Tauber revolt was collapsing after the decisive battles of Königshofen and Ingolstadt (June 2 and 4, 1525), Geyer unsuccessfully sought negotiations with Margrave Casimir. Deported from Rothenburg, he was heading toward the district of Halle when he and his party of loyal companions were assassinated by agents of his own brother-in-law.

Works About: Heinrich Barge, "Geyer," *Vergangenheit und Gegenwart* 19 (1929): 524–32; Wilhelm Benkert, "Florian Geyer," *ARG* 41 (1948):154–63; Günther Franz, "Florian Geyer," *Hist. Vierteljahrschrift* 24 (1928): 484–90; Gunther Franz, ed., *Quel. zur Gesch. des Bauernkrieges* (Munich, 1963), nos. 108, 109; Walter Peter Fuchs, "Florian Geyer," *Frankische Lebensbilder*, ed. Gerhard Pfeiffer (Würzburg, 1967), 3:109–40.   *K. C. Sessions*

See LUTHER; PEASANTS' WAR; SWABIAN LEAGUE.

GISELA (c. 990–1043), daughter of Duke Herman II of Swabia and Gerberga of Burgundy, was thrice married. Two marriages, first to Count Bruno of Braunschweig (m. 1013?) and then to Duke Ernest I of Swabia (?–1015), were shortlived. Gisela bore her first husband a son, Count Liudolf, and her second husband two sons, Duke Ernest II of Swabia (–1030) and Duke Herman IV of Swabia (–1039). In 1015 Emperor Henry II granted Gisela control of Ernest I's estate on behalf of her young son, Ernest II. After Gisela married Henry II's enemy, Salian count Conrad of Speyer, Henry II rescinded his approval of Gisela's guardianship and entrusted the boy to his father's brother, Archbishop Poppo of Trier. Henry II and ecclesiastical leaders disapproved of the marriage because both Gisela and Conrad were descendants of Henry I, the Fowler. In 1024 Conrad became the first of the Salian Franks to be elected king of the Germans. He was consecrated as Conrad II by Archbishop Aribo of Mainz on September 8, 1024. Aribo refused to crown Gisela, presumably because he, too, objected to the marriage. Archbishop Pilgrim of Cologne, who sought reconciliation with Conrad II after opposing his candidacy, crowned Gisela queen on September 21, 1024. In later years the archbishops of Cologne based their right to crown German kings on Pilgrim's precedent. At Easter 1027 Pope John XIX crowned Conrad II and Gisela emperor and empress.

Gisela and Conrad had three children: Emperor Henry III (1017–1056); Beatrice, a nun at Quedlinburg after 1025; and Matilda (–1034). Gisela was an able consort and played an important role in diplomacy and Church politics. She carried out negotiations between Conrad II and her uncle, Rudolf III of Burgundy, which led to a meeting near Basel in August 1027 at which Rudolf III named Conrad II his successor to Burgundy. Gisela brought about a compromise between Conrad II and Duke Mesko of Poland. She was less successful mediating between her husband and her rebellious son, Ernest II of Swabia. The latter was finally killed in a battle with Conrad II's troops in 1030.

Gisela carried responsibility for ecclesiastical patronage and politics. Her influence in the appointment of bishops and abbots is clearly documented. Gisela was better educated than was Conrad II, and she oversaw Henry III's formal education. Conrad II, on the other hand, made sure that Henry III was given military and administrative training at an early age.

There is evidence of an estrangement between Gisela and Henry III after he became emperor in 1039. The breach was healed by 1041, but Gisela's influence at court was not apparent between the reconciliation in 1041 and her death in February 1043. She was buried in the cathedral at Speyer.

Works About: Heinrich Appelt, "Gisela," *NDB* 6:413–14; Bresslau, "Gisela," *ADB* 9;193–95; N. Bischoff, "Über die Chronol. der Kaiserin Gisela ünd uber die Verweigerung ihrer Krönung durch Aribo von Mainz," *Mitt. des Instituts fur österr. Geschichtsforschung* 58 (1950); O. Blümcke, *Burgund unter Rudolf III. und der Heimfall der burgundischen Krone an Kaiser Konrad* II (Greifswald, 1869); E. Brandenburg, "Probleme um die Kaiserin Gisela," *Sächsische Akademie der Wissenchaften zu Leipzig, Philologiseh-hist. Klasse, Berichte* 80, no. 4 (Leipzig, 1928); H. Bresslau, *Jb. des dtsch. Reichs unter Konrad II.* (Leipzig, 1879–1884); O. V. Falke, *Der Mainzer Goldschmuck der Kaiserin Gisela* (Berlin, 1913); M. Pfenninger, *Die kirchliche Politik Kaiser Konrads II.* (Halle, 1880); H. J. Riekenberg, "Das Geburtsdatum der Kaiserin Gisela," *Dtsch. Archiv* 9 (1952); E. Steindorff, *Jb. des dtsch. Reichs unter Heinrich III.* (Leipzig, 1874–1881).   *J. W. Gates*

See CONRAD II; HENRY I; HENRY II.

GISLA OF CHELLES (Gisíla, Gislana) (757–810), daughter of Pepin and the only sister of Charlemagne, was dedicated to a religious life at an early age. The robes she wore at her baptism were sent to Pope Paul I as a symbol of her spiritual adoption. Reigning popes opposed proposals of marriage by Constantine Copronymus, eastern emperor, for his son, Leo, and by Adaelgius, king of the Lombards, for his son, Desiderius. Gisla became the ninth abbess of Chelles and built the Church of St. Mary and St. Savior.

Works About: Alcuin to Gisla in Migne, *Patr. Lat.* c. 362, 363; *Monumeta Carolina,* ed. P. *Jaffé (Aachen, 1867); Pope Paul I to Pippen in Migne, Patr. Lat.* lxxxix. 1183; Pope Stephan III (770) to Charlemagne in Migne, *Patr. Lat.* xcviii. 255. William Smith and Henry Wace, eds., *A Dictionary of Christian Biography, Literature, Sects and Doctrines* (New York, 1974); vol. 2.   *J. W. Gates*

See CHARLEMAGNE.

GOETHE, JOHN WOLFGANG (1749–1832), literary giant, was born into a middle-class family in Frankfurt. He received some of his early education from his father. In 1765 Goethe began his university training at Leipzig but was forced to leave three years later because of illness. He completed his formal education at Strasbourg, where he received a licentiate in law in 1771. While in Strasbourg Goethe came to know John Gottfried Herder, who introduced the broad-minded student to the most recent literary and artistic trends.

Goethe returned to Frankfurt as a practicing attorney, but the publication of his play *Götz von Berlichingen* in 1773 won him fame as a literary man. After a short stint as a legal councillor at Wetzlar, Goethe was invited to the small duchy of Sachsen-Weimar by its ruler, Karl August, who had been impressed by Goethe's enormously successful novel of 1774, *The Sorrows of Young Werther*.

Goethe's stay at Weimar proved to be permanent, punctuated only by travels such as his famous journeys to Italy and Switzerland. His relationship with Karl August was for the most part warm and long-lasting. He served the duke as a kind of minister of culture from 1776 to 1786, even presiding over the War Commission in 1779. During the invasion of France by the German states in 1792, Goethe accompanied Karl August and the Weimar contingent. He was also present at the siege of Mainz in 1793 and its recapture by the Germans.

Despite all this political activity, Goethe was largely indifferent to the fate of the Empire. He found the Empire a concept that was almost impossible to grasp and had little enthusiasm even for the reforms of Joseph I. Instead of the political Empire, Goethe preferred an empire of culture and a republic of the mind.

His own intellectual interests and activities were incredible in both range and scope. Goethe was interested in, among other things, anatomy, art, botany, literature, geology, history, mineralogy, optics, travel, and zoology. He wrote autobiography, drama, novels, and scientific treatises. As director of the court theater in Weimar, he staged some of his own plays as well as those of friends like Frederick Schiller, with whom he also collaborated on a literary magazine. In part because of Goethe's influences, Weimar became a kind of Renaissance court, attracting a cluster of poets and thinkers. Goethe himself became one of the giants of German literature and was revered during his lifetime throughout Europe.

Works By: Goethe, *Werke*, 133 vols. (Weimar, 1887–1919); *Goethe the Lyrist: 100 Poems*, ed. E. H. Zeydel, (Chapel Hill, 1958), and *Poems of Goethe* (Chapel Hill, 1957); *The Autobiography*, tr. John Oxenford (New York, 1969); *The Permanent Goethe*, Thomas Mann, ed. (New York, 1948). **Works About:** Liselotte Dieckmann, *Johann Wolfgang Goethe* (New York, 1974); Richard Friedenthal, *Goethe* (London, 1965); Hans Pyritz, *Goethe-Bibliographie*, 2 vols. (Heidelberg, 1955-68); Heinrich von Srbik, *Goethe und das reich* (Leipzig, 1940); Emil Staiger, *Goethe*, 3 vols. (Zurich, 1949).   *J. W. Zophy*

See BERLICHINGEN; FRANKFURT AM MAIN; HERDER; JOSEPH I; SCHILLER.

GOLDEN BULL (1356), a document proclaimed by Emperor Charles IV, became the major constitutional statement of the principles governing the Holy Roman Empire until its demise during the Napoleonic wars. Issued in two parts, the first and most substantive appeared at Nuremberg in January 1356, the second at Metz in December 1356. Together the bull established the procedures for electing the king of the Romans. It supplied a definition of the right to vote and provided for majority decisions. In addition, the bull regulated coinage, dealt with tolls, and established mechanisms for the maintenance of public peace.

With regard to the king, the Golden Bull remained silent on the contentious point of papal confirmation. Traditionally the king had two coronations, one at Aachen and the other at Rome. In the papal coronation, the pope acknowledged the election and conferred the title of Holy Roman emperor. In its refusal to mention papal confirmation, however, the bull must be viewed against the backdrop of preceding imperial-papal controversies. At Rense in 1338, the electors maintained that it was by their vote alone that the emperor acquired his sovereignty. This position, which ran counter to papal claims, was reaffirmed by the estates at two diets in Frankfurt in 1338 and 1339. Once elected, the estates' said, the emperor needed no papal coronation. This view persisted although kings until the time of Ferdinand I (1556–1564) attempted to obtain papal coronation.

The most significant part of the bull was the creation of the electoral college. For the first time in the history of the Empire, this college received legal, constitutional status. Previously there had always been a group of important princes within the Empire who elected the king, but the composition of this group had been ill defined. Furthermore the rights, privileges, and obligations of these electors remained hazy. In the early fourteenth century the number of electors was usually seven, but there were often diverse claimants for the seven positions. With the Golden Bull, the seven electors received clear definition, and provisions were made for rights of succession. No new electoral titles were added until the seventeenth and eighteenth centuries.

The seven officials selected by the bull were the most powerful princes in the Empire. There were three ecclesiastical and four secular ones: the archbishops of Mainz, Cologne, and Trier, the king of Bohemia, the duke of Saxony, the margrave of Brandenburg, and the count Palatine of the Rhine. Duties, rights, privileges, and order of precedence were clearly stated to allay confusion. Forms of letters convoking the college and empowering an elector's representative to act in his stead were included. The bull also contained the oath to be administered to the electors by the archbishop of Mainz when he opened the voting procedure.

The archbishop of Mainz, as archchancellor of the Empire, was responsible for convoking each election at Frankfurt am Main. In order to facilitate travel to and attendance at the election, the bull established that principalities had to furnish safe conduct and escort services to the electors or their representatives. Failure to provide these services resulted in crimes of perjury and penalties of outlawry. When the electors or their representatives assembled, they took the oath obliging them to cast their votes "for a person fitted to rule the Christian people." If no decision occurred within thirty days, the electors were to be placed on bread and water until they had made a decision. The archbishop of Mainz supervised these proceedings.

During the election a majority vote became decisive and was regarded as unanimous. Although it was not stated in the bull, this device hindered the possibility that the papacy might influence the ecclesiastical electors' votes; in this event, the votes of the secular princes outnumbered the archbishops and in this fashion made the office of the king independent of Rome.

Befitting an era concerned with decorum and ritual, the offices and duties of each elector were listed in the bull: Mainz was the archchancellor of the Empire for Germany; Cologne was the archchancellor of the Empire for Italy; Trier was the archchancellor the Empire for Gaul and the kingdom of Arles; Bohemia, which had priority among the secular princes because of the royal title, was the chief cup bearer; Saxony was the archmarshall of the Empire; Brandenburg was the archchamberlain of the Empire; and the count Palatine was the archseneschal. Each had specific duties to perform during royal ceremonies.

To inhibit contentions for the electoral dignity, the bull provided for the reaffirmation of each elector's privileges by a new king (confirmed again when the king became emperor), prescribed the inalienability of the electorate, and provided for electoral succession. The electoral dignity passed to the oldest male lay child; if he had died, it passed to his oldest male lay child. In default of this issue, the dignity went to the next oldest male lay child, and so on according to the laws of primogeniture. If the successor was less than eighteen years of age, provision was made for a guardian until he reached his majority. When there was no heir, the dignity reverted to the king-emperor who supplied a successor, except in the case of Bohemia, whose inhabitants chose their king.

In addition to these provisions, the bull granted other rights. Most dealt with the electors, although some also applied to nonelectoral members of the Empire. Within their territories, electors possessed all mines, metals, and saltworks; they received rights to tax the Jews; and their superior jurisdictional rights were specifically acknowledged. In the absence of royal authority from the Empire, the count Palatine and the duke of Saxony exercised the royal prerogative in their respective portions of the Empire. Finally the bull stated that Frankfurt was to serve as the place of election, Aachen as the site of coronation, and Nuremberg as the city where each new king must hold his first diet.

The effects of the Golden Bull have been variously interpreted by scholars. By making virtual sovereigns of the electors, the bull authorized princely particularlism and prohibited imperial centralization in the Empire, a realization made more manifest by the Peace of Westphalia (1648). In this sense, the bull kept the Empire disunified. On the other hand, it established a regular, orderly procedure for royal succession, which, with a few adjustments, remained in effect until 1806. Issued in the period following imperial-papal difficulties, it effectively halted further disintegration with the Empire and recognized the existence of political realities.

Works About: Geoffrey Barraclough, *The Origins of Modern Germany* (Oxford, 1946, rpr. 1963); James Bryce, *The Holy Roman Empire* (New York, 1904, rpr. 1961); Wolfgang Fritz, *Die Goldene Bulle Kaiser Karls IV vom Jahre 1356* (Weimar, 1972); E. F. Henderson, ed. and tr., *Select Hist. Documents of the Middle Ages* (London, 1925), pp. 220–61; Konrad Müller, *Die Goldene Bulle Kaiser Karls IV, 1356* (Bern, 1970); J. R. Tanner, C. W. Previté-Orton and Z. N. Brooke, *Cambridge Medieval Hist.* vol. 7: *The Decline of Empire and Papacy* (Cambridge, 1932), chaps. 3–5; O. J. Thatcher and E. H. McNeal, eds. *A Source Book for Mediaeval Hist.* (New York, 1905), pp. 283–305; E. Werunsky, *Gesch. Kaiser Karls IV und seiner Zeit,* 3 vols. (Innsbruck, 1880–1892); Karl Zeumer, *Die Goldene Bulle Kaiser Karls IV,* vol. 2: *Quel. und Studien zur Verfassungsgeschichte des Dtsch. Reiches in Mittelalter und Neuzeit* (Weimar, 1908).   *P. N. Bebb*

See CHARLES IV; COLOGNE; FERDINAND I; FRANKFURT AM MAIN; NUREMBERG; WESTPHALIA.

GOTTFRIED VON STRASBOURG (c. 1170–2220), epic poet, was born in

Strasbourg to an upper-middle-class family. Little is known of his life, but he seems to have had academic training because he expresses familiarity with scholastic thought, Latin, and French. His fame as the second greatest German epic poet following Wolfram von Eschenbach rests on a single surviving work, *Tristan and Isolde*. Gottfried's *Tristan* is a fierce, passionate love story, whose composition was much influenced by the work of Hartman von Aue.

Works By: Gottfried von Strasbourg, *Tristan and Isolde,* trs. A. T. Hatto (London, 1960). **Works About:** W. T. H. Jackson, *The Anatomy of Love: The Tristan of Gottfried von Strasburg* (New York, 1971); Gertrude Schoepperle, *Tristam and Isolt: A Study in the Sources of the Romances,* 2 vols. (New York, 1960); Hans-Hugo Steinhoff, *Bibliographie zu Gottfried von Strassburg* (Berlin, 1971); Gottfried Weber, *Gottfried von Strassburg* (Stuttgart, 1962).   *J. W. Zophy*

See HARTMANN VON AUE; WOLFRAM VON ESCHENBACH.

GREGORY V OR BRUNO (972–999), pope, was the second son of Duke

Otto of Carinthia and the great-grandson of Emperor Otto I. Bruno received a fine education, became a cleric, and served in the imperial chapel. When Pope John XV died in 996, Emperor Otto III appointed his twenty-four year old chaplain as pope and presented him as such to the Roman delegation that had come to Ravenna. Bruno styled himself Gregory V and was accepted in Rome without serious opposition. He thereby became the first German and non-Italian pope in a century.

One of his first acts was to crown Otto as emperor on Ascension Day, May 3, 996. In the fall of that year, Gregory was forced to flee Rome because of an aristocratic reaction led by Crescentius. An effort to promote an antipope, John XVI, with Byzantine aid failed as Otto in 998 assisted Gregory in his return to Rome. The emperor showed little mercy to the insurgents; Crescentius was beheaded, and John XVI was blinded and confined to a monastery. This campaign symbolized the possibilities for cooperation between pope and emperor and gave a temporary reality to the ideals of the Empire.

Gregory was more than an imperial lackey; he was quite capable of independent action when he felt the best interests of the Church mandated it. For example, he opposed the imperial candidate, Gerbert, later Pope Sylvester II, for the archbishopric of Reims. Gregory did approve Gerbert's subsequent appointment as archbishop of Ravenna. He also opposed Otto in restoring the see of Merseburg after it had been absorbed by Magdeburg. Regrettably the reign of this capable young pope ended in his early death.

Works About: F. Dressler, ''Gregory V,'' *New Catholic Encyclopedia*, 6:771; L. Duchesne, *Liber pontificalis*, 3 vols. (Paris, 1886-1892, rpr. 1956) 2:261–62; P. Jaffé, *Regesta pontificum romanorum*, ed. S. Löwenfeld et al., 2 vols. (Graz, 1956); H. K. Mann, *The Lives of the Popes in the Early Middle Ages*, 17 vols. (London, 1925), 4:389–446   *J. W. Zophy*

See OTTO I; OTTO III; SYLVESTER II.

GREGORY VII (c.1020–1085), pope 1073–1085, was the name taken by the Italian monk, Hildebrand, on his election as pope in 1073. He succeeded Alexander II and was the pope during the initial stages of the investiture contest between the papacy and the Holy Roman emperors. Most historians rank him among the greatest popes and consider his reign as pope to be one of the most significant periods in papal history. He set in motion the forces that eventually resulted in extensively broadening the power of the papacy and eroding the power of the Holy Roman emperor.

As a young monk, Hildebrand became chaplain and adviser to Pope Gregory VI. When Gregory was desposed by Emperor Henry III in 1046 in his reform of the papacy, Hildebrand accompanied his mentor to exile in Germany but was soon back in Rome serving as administrator of the papal states for the reformer pope, Leo IX. By 1050, Hildebrand had begun his program of clerical reform, directing his energies toward improving the situation in the territories near the papal states. His reforms were generally opposed by clergy and nobility alike, but he persevered, finding additional support among other cardinals of the curia like Humbert of Silva, Candida, and Peter Damiani, as well as from the reformer popes, Victor II, Stephen IX, and Nicholas II.

As long as Emperor Henry III lived, the papal reform program worked harmoniously with the emperor's attempted reform of the German Church. At Henry's death in 1056, however, the Empire fell under a regency until his son, Henry IV, reached his majority. Under the regency clerical abuses multiplied in Germany. Equally significant, the papacy took steps to gain its independence from the Empire. Pope Nicholas II placed the election of future popes in the hands of the College of Cardinals, thus limiting, theoretically, the emperor's rights in future papal selections to approving the cardinals' candidate. In addition, in 1059, Nicholas effected a treaty, engineered by Hildebrand, with the Normans of southern Italy to provide military assistance against the German monarchy in the event of an imperial invasion of Italy. In return, the Norman duke Robert Guiscard recognized the pope as his feudal lord and received the fief of southern Italy and Sicily. In addition, Hildebrand and Humbert brought the papacy to support the popular clerical reformers of the key imperial city of Milan, the Patarini, in their struggle with their imperially appointed archbishop, Wido, whose reinvestment by the pope raised the question of the legitimacy of his earlier appointment by the emperor.

During the papacy of Alexander II, Hildebrand's power steadily increased, and he gained an ever decisive control over papal policy. His determination to push forward his policy of clerical reform led to papal support of the Spanish Reconquista led by the Cid and the Norman invasion of England in 1066, both of which symbolized the further extension of the clerical reform movement sponsored by the papacy. Hildebrand's diplomatic successes of the 1060s thus slowly prepared the way for the creation of a power base from which the reform-minded papacy could launch an attack on the Salian monarchy to free the German Church from lay control and successfully reform it. The heart of the papacy's Church reform movement in which Hildebrand was a leading figure for over thirty years was the elimination of direct lay control over the clergy, especially over the appointment of bishops and abbots. While the fundamental objective of the reformers was the improvement of the morality and pastoral qualities of the lower clergy, it was felt that this goal could be achieved only with the ardent support of the direct supervisors of the clergy, the bishops and abbots. Thus the direct thrust of papal reform was an attempt by the pope and curia to ensure the cooperation of local prelates in the larger reform effort. Such cooperation could be assured, however, only if the prelates' loyalty and dedication to the reform cause was guaranteed by their being appointed by and dependent on the papacy. In the papal view, large-scale, effective Church and clerical reforms could succeed only if directed from Rome and implemented at the local level by competent, reform-minded bishops and abbots. Consequently it was crucial that the pope, and not lay magnates, appoint all prelates. Moreover lay appointment of bishops frequently resulted in the appointment of competent political and bureaucratic administrators who represented the interests of their secular lords more than they represented their spiritual interests. Nowhere was this situation more apparent than in the Empire where, since the days of Otto I, the bishops and abbots usually had been the appointees of the emperors and their staunchest allies against the decentralizing, particularist interests of the German nobility, often emphasizing their political duties over their spiritual duties.

It was to correct this situation and bring the German bishops under the control of the papacy so that clerical and Church reform could proceed in the Empire that Hildebrand entered into the investiture controversy with the emperor soon after his election as pope in 1073. His choice of Gregory VII as his papal name symbolically indicated his concern for returning to the days of Pope Gregory I (590–604) when, it was believed by the papal reformers, the Church had been directed and led by the pope as the true head of Christendom. Gregory VII served notice of his intentions by calling synods where he forbade clerical marriage, alienation of Church land, simony, and various other abuses. His appointed legates, largely chosen from the reform-minded Cluniac monks, were delegated the task of enforcing the new laws on clerical discipline, despite their great unpopularity in many quarters.

Gregory's direct conflict with Emperor Henry IV began in 1075 with the pope's publication of the *Dictatus Papae* where he proclaimed in twenty-seven items that, according to tradition, the pope was the supreme head of the Church and of all Christendom, having the power to depose and reinstate not only bishops but emperors as well. Later in the same year Gregory got to the heart of the matter with the promulgation of his investiture decree, which declared "that no one of the clergy shall receive the investiture with a bishopric or abbey or church by the hand of any emperor, king, or lay person." Thirty years earlier Cardinal Humbert had equated such investiture with simony. Gregory declared the penalty for lay investiture to be excommunication. The remaining years of his life were dedicated to attempted enforcement of the ban on lay investiture, a ban bitterly opposed by most European royalty and nobility.

The dispute with the Empire occurred when Henry IV appointed in late 1075 a new archbishop of Milan, a direct violation of the investiture decree. Gregory threatened to depose the emperor. Henry responded by calling a synod at Worms in January and deposing the pope, as Henry III had done forty years earlier with Gregory VI. But the emperor had miscalculated his strength and the pope's weakness, for Gregory responded in February with a deposition and excommunication of Henry and all the prelates who supported him. The German bishops deserted the imperal cause, while the Saxons and southern dukes organized opposition to the emperor. Henry was able to present himself to Gregory at Canossa, Italy, in January 1077 where, after standing in the snow for three days as a penitent asking forgiveness, he was absolved by the pope and restored to the Church. By March 1077, however, the rebellious dukes had elected an antiking, Duke Rudolf of Swabia, who promised to support the reform movement in Germany and to renounce imperial control of episcopal elections. In the civil war that followed, Henry slowly gained the upper hand while Gregory delayed in choosing a side until early 1080. By that time it was too late. Henry now gained quick control of Germany, painted the pope as a power-grasping autocrat, and with the Lombard and German prelates in support declared at a council in June the deposition of Gregory and elevation of the archbishop of Ravenna as antipope under the name Clement III. Gregory promptly turned to his Norman allies in the south for military aid, a need made more apparent with the death of Rudolf of Swabia and the collapse of the rebellious party in Germany in October 1080. Henry then invaded Italy, besieging Rome in 1081 and capturing it in 1083 when the Romans betrayed the previously popular pope who now fortified himself in the Castel Sant' Angelo. The Normans finally came to Gregory's aid in 1084, whereupon the emperor sacked Rome and withdrew northward rather than risk battle with the Normans who themselves also plundered the city before returning to Salerno with the pope. Gregory died in Salerno in May 1085, his last words reportedly being; "I have loved righteousness and hated iniquity; therefore I die in exile." He was succeeded as pope by Victor III.

Although at his death his cause seemed lost, Gregory VII had accomplished a great deal. His forty years of attempted Church reform, crowned by his papacy, had established a turning point in the history of both the Church and the Empire. Although not successful by his death, he had nonetheless clearly drawn the issues establishing papal supremacy over the Church, demarcating the lines of ecclesiastical reform for two centuries, and asserting the importance of the separation of Church and state, clerical and lay. Some historians have interpreted his struggle with Henry as an inordinate grasp for power and an attempt to establish the ecclesiastic sphere as superior to the secular. More frequently, his career is seen as a bold, stubborn defense of the Church and its rights against political domination by secular authorities. His reforming activities improved the moral quality of the Church and established an ideal that was followed by his successors in further reforms. While the immediate victory was the emperor's, Gregory had set in motion the forces that eventually undermined imperial power and eroded the emperor's ability to control the turbulent German nobility. In this regard, Gregory's pontificate marked the beginning of papal ascendancy in Europe as well as the beginning of the disintegration of the Empire, whose very foundations had been shaken. Gregory was later canonized a saint by the Church.

Works By: *The Correspondence of Pope Gregory VII*, ed. and tr. E. Emerton (New York, 1932, rpr. 1967); B. Tierney, ed., *The Crisis of Church and State, 1050–1300* (Englewood Cliffs, N. J., 1964); *Das Register Gregors*, ed. E. Caspar, (Berlin, 1955). *De Controversie Hildebrandi et Henirici, MGH,Lib. de lite*, vol. 1. **Works About:** Z. N. Brooke, *Lay Investiture and Its Relation to the Conflict of Empire and Papacy*, Proceedings of the British Academy 25 (London, 1939); E. Caspar, "Gregor VII in seinen Briefen," *HZ* 130 (1924): 1–30; Agnes B. Cavanaugh, *Pope Gregory VII and the Theocratic State* (Washington, D.C., 1934); K. Hampe, *Germany under the Salian and Hohenstaufen Emperors*, tr. R. Bennett (Totowa, N.J., 1973); A. MacDonald, *Hildebrand* (London, 1932); C. Mirft, *Die Wahl Gregors VII* (Marburg, 1892); K. F. Morrison, "Canossa: A Revision," *Traditio* 18 (1962):121–48; G. Tellenbach, *Church, State, and Christian Society at the Time of the Investiture Contest*, tr. R. Bennett, (Oxford, 1940); J. P. Whitney *Hildebrandine Essays* (Cambridge, 1932); Wido of Osnabrück, *Liber de Controversie Hildebrandi et Henirici, MGH, Lib. de lite*, vol. 1.   *D. S. Devlin*

See HENRY III; HENRY IV; INVESTITURE CONTROVERSY; LEO IX; MATILDA OF TUSCANY; STEPHEN IX.

GRIMMELSHAUSEN, HANS JACOB CHRISTOFFEL VON (c. 1621–

1676), novelist, was born at Gelnhausen the son of an innkeeper. Educated at an evangelical school, his early life was disrupted by the Thirty Years War. At age fifteen Hans joined the cavalry regiment of Baron John von Götz, possibly as a stable boy. In 1643 he joined the regiment of Baron Hans Reinhard von

Schauenberg, where he rose to the rank of regimental secretary and converted to Catholicism. His administrative competence was such that he stayed in the employ of Schauenberg as his steward following his military discharge in 1649.

During his service for Schauenberg, Grimmelshausen had the opportunity to travel throughout Germany, where he had a close look at the damage caused by the war. He also married Catharine Henninger and fathered many children by her. Grimmelshausen later worked as an innkeeper before securing a position as mayor of the village of Renchen near Strasbourg. There he continued his writing and was active in the opposition to the expansionist activities of Louis XIV of France. His most important literary accomplishment was the satirical novel *Simplicissimus,* which enjoyed great popularity and is the most important contemporary fiction to emerge from the Thirty Years War.

Works By: *The Adventurous Simplicissimus,* tr. A. T. S. Goodrick (Lincoln, Neb., 1962); *Gesammelte Werke in Einzelausgaben,* ed. Rolf Tarot, 9 vols. (Tübingen, 1967–); **Works About:** Kenneth Negus, *Grimmelshausen* (New York, 1974); Julius Peterson, "Grimmelshausen," *DGD,* 1:547–65; Gunther Weydt, *Hans Jacob Christoffel von Grimmelshausen* (Stuttgart, 1971).   *J. W. Zophy*

See THIRTY YEARS WAR.

GRÜNEWALD, MATTHIAS (c. 1480–1528), painter, was a native of Würzburg, whose early years are obscure. From 1485 to 1490, he lived in Aschaffenburg; from 1508 to 1527, he was attached to the court of Ulrich of Gemmingen, archbishop of Mainz, and his successor, Albert. Grünewald later found employment in Frankfurt, Halle, and Magdeburg as a waterworks specialist and mill builder. Considered one of the greatest artists of his generation, Grünewald was overshadowed in Germany only by Albrecht Dürer.

Works About: A. Burkhard, *Matthias Grünwald* (Cambridge, Mass., 1936); Karl Sitzmann, "Grünwald," *EWA,* 7:182–86; Thomas Stoll, "Matthias Grünewald," *DGD,* 1:343–63; W. K. Zülch, *Der hist. Grünwald* (Munich, 1938).   *J. W. Zophy*

See DÜRER.

GUTENBERG, JOHN (c. 1398–1468), inventor, was born in Mainz, although little else is known of his early life. His name appears in a document of March 3, 1430, which refers to his exile for his part in a dispute between patricians and guildsmen. Gutenberg eventually settled in Strasbourg, where he opened a goldsmith shop. Experimenting with metals, he seems to have discovered an alloy that could be poured into molds to form letters that would not shrink or twist upon cooling. The letter stamps could be assembled to form a page of lettering and then be broken down and reassembled to form another page. This movable type could be used to print many copies of the same book or many copies of different books.

Harassed by legal and financial problems, Gutenberg returned to Mainz in October 1448. By 1454 he began to print a Bible in double columns of type that resembled Gothic script, with forty-two lines in Latin to a page. Gutenberg's first printed edition of three hundred Bibles represents a glorious triumph of the printer's art. Yet the triumph was marred for the inventor by losing a legal suit for debt repayment. He was forced to hand over his tools and presses. The winners of the lawsuit, including an ex-partner, were the actual publishers of the first printed books. A bachelor, Gutenberg died in debt.

Printing proved a phenomenal success. Books could be produced for a fraction of the cost of manuscripts. By 1500 up to nine million printed copies of thirty thousand printed works were in circulation. A typographic revolution had been set in motion, and the world would never be the same. Without printing the Reformation of the sixteenth century and the rise of modern science are almost inconceivable.

Works About: R. G. Cole, "The Dynamics of Printing in the Sixteenth Century," in *The Social Hist. of the Reformation,* ed. L. Buck and J. Zophy (Columbus, 1972); Elizabeth L. Eisenstein, *The Printing Press as an Agent of Change,* 2 vols. (New York, 1978); R. Hirsch, *Printing, Selling and Reading, 1450–1550* (Wiesbaden, 1967); Marshall McLuhan, *The Gutenberg Galaxy* (Toronto, 1962); D. C. McMurtrie, *The Book* (Oxford, 1943); Aloys Ruppel, *Johannes Gutenberg* (Nieuwkoop, 1967).   *J. W. Zophy*

See EBERLIN; LUTHER.

♭

HANDEL, GEORGE FREDERICK (1685–1759), musician and composer, was born in Halle in Saxony, the son of a successful surgeon. His musical talents were noticed in 1696 by Elector Frederick III of Brandenburg and his wife, Sophie Charlotte. Although Handel enrolled as a law student at Halle in 1702, music remained his real love. He eventually left the university to join the Hamburg orchestra. His first opera was performed in 1705.

During a successful tour of Italy as a performer and composer, Handel met Prince Ernest Augustus of Hanover, who offered the young harpsichordist the post of court musical director. He remained in that capacity until 1716, when he went to England and became a favorite of Queen Anne and her successor, George I. Handel flourished in England as a musical director, impresario, composer, and virtuoso performer on harpsichord and organ. He also gave lessons and, although troubled by bad health and failing eyesight, continued to compose up to the time of his death.

Works About: O. E. Deutsch, *Handel: A Documentary Biography* (New York, 1974); J. S. Hall, *G. F. Handel* (London, 1963); P. H. Lang, *George Frederic Handel* (New York, 1966); Herbert Weinstock, *Handel* (New York, 1946). *J. W. Zophy*

See FREDERICK III; SOPHIE CHARLOTTE.

HANSEATIC LEAGUE was a loose federation of north German merchants and cities that combined to maintain commercial hegemony in the North and Baltic seas. Although *hanse* generally referred to merchant guilds and/or associations between cities, the Hanseatic League specifically referred to the German federation. Membership in it became restricted to German populated towns even though privileges often extended to merchants elsewhere. The league lasted roughly from the middle of the twelfth to the middle of the seventeenth centuries, and its origins predate the founding of many towns that subsequently became part of it. The league's heyday, which probably peaked about 1350, was past by the beginning of the sixteenth century.

At its height the Hanseatic League included about two hundred towns although, since it lacked the legal appurtenances associated with a formal organization, an exact tabulation remains impossible. Unquestionably Lübeck operated as its capital, and it was that city's officials who convoked the sporadic meetings of members and presided at the diets. In addition to Lübeck, the major Hanse towns were Cologne, Bremen, Hamburg, Dortmund, Munster, Osnabrück, Soest, Brunswick, Goslar, Hildesheim, Lüneburg, Magdeburg, Wismar,

Rostock, Stralsund, Stettin, Danzig, Königsberg, Thorn, Breslau, Cracow, Dorpat, Reval, Riga, Stockholm, Visby, Deventer, and Kampen. Many of these towns were colonized by north German merchants who migrated eastward during the high Middle Ages.

Lübeck's leading role in the federation was due largely to its geographical position on the Holstein isthmus that connected the North and Baltic seas. Since Denmark controlled the sound between the peninsula and the Scandinavian countries, European trade and exchange of goods in the Baltic would be managed by Danish interests save for Lübeck. Because of its strategic location and the maintenance of its independence, Lübeck became the center of an axis that ran from London to Novgorod and that bypassed the sound. When the Danish king attempted to conquer Holstein, many Hanse cities formed the Cologne Confederation in 1367, and, under the leadership of Lübeck, the confederation forced Denmark to sue for peace. This resulted in the Peace of Stralsund in 1370.

In many respects the Hanseatic League was the economic counterpart of the Italian maritime cities in the Mediterranean, although some Hanse cities were inland. The league concentrated on trade in consumer goods of western and northern Europe for the furs, timbers, ores, and grains of northeastern Europe and Russia.

A concatenation of forces in the late fifteenth century spelled the onset of the league's demise. Among the most obvious developments were the heightened political centralization appearing in England and Scandinavia and the emerging Muscovite state. Problems between the Teutonic Knights and Poland-Lithuania further disrupted Hanse trade in the Baltic. All of these were exacerbated by economic competition from the southern and northwestern parts of Europe. Finally the Reformation and the wars stemming from it, as well as the growth of the territorial state, produced economic policies at variance with the commercial activities of the league. Despite a few spurts of renewed economic vigor during the sixteenth century, the league was unable to combat such forces.

Interpretation of the Hanseatic Leauge has varied with the fate of Germany, and as a result it is difficult to generalize about the league's character and composition. Recent historiography tends to emphasize the Hanse involvement in interregional and international economic affairs and, conversely, to mitigate against its peculiar Germanic features. This is partially the result of post–World War II political phenomena in that many Hanse cities are now subject to Marxist ideologies.

Works About: Ver. für hansische Gesch., ed., *Hansische Geschichtsblätter*, (1871–), vol. 1; Ahasver von Brandt, "Recent Trends in Research in Hanseatic Hist.," *Hist.* 41 (1956):25–37; Philippe Dollinger, *The German Hansa*, tr. and ed. D. S. Ault and S. H. Steinberg (California, 1970); K. Pagel, *Die Hanse* (Braunschweig, 1952); Fritz Rörig, "Hanseatic League," *Encyclopaedia of the Social Sciences*, 7:261–67, and *The Medieval Town* (California, 1967); A. Weiner, "The Hansa," ed. J. R. Tanner, C. W. Previté Orton, and Z. N. Brooke, *Cambridge Medieval History*, (Cambridge, England, 1964) 7: chap. 8.   *P. N. Bebb*

See COLOGNE; STRALSUND; TEUTONIC KNIGHTS.

HARRACH, COUNT FERDINAND BONAVENTURA (1637–1706), a close personal friend of Leopold I, served the emperor as ambassador to Spain (1673–1676, 1697–1698), grand chamberlain (1699–1705), master of the horse, grandmaster of the Empire, and first minister. Harrach, whom Leopold I often referred to as his only friend, grew up and later hunted with the emperor. Neither an acute politician nor a good businessman, Harrach was nevertheless a charming, cultured, honorable minister. Conscientious and incorruptible, Harrach had powerful friends in Count Francis Joseph Lamberg, governor of upper Austria, and Count Ferdinand Wallenstein. He consistently opposed the policies of Count Andreas Kaunitz, vice-chancellor of the Empire. Harrach, along with Count Wallenstein, Count Julius Becelini, the chancellor of Austria, Count Wolfgang Öttingen, president of the Aulic Council, and Count Mansfeld, formed the center of the old ministerial party, whose members had served Leopold since his early days as emperor. They blocked attempts at reform and opposed war with France over the Spanish inheritance; they believed that Leopold did not have the financial or the military resources to engage in protracted conflict with France. They also maintained that the war effort should be centered on Italy, not Spain, the "tagg-end of God's creation," because of Italy's proximity to the hereditary countries.

Works About: Max Braubach, *Prinz Eugen von Savoyen,* 5 vols. (Vienna, 1963-65); Felgel, "Harrach," *ADB,* 10:629–32; Hugo Hantsch, *Die Gesch. Österreichs-Ungarns zur Grossmacht* (Freiburg im Breisbau, 1933); H. Kellenberg, "Harrach," *NDB,* 7:698–99; Oswald Redlich, *Das Werden einer Grossmacht, Österreich von 1700 bis 1740* (Vienna, 1942); John P. Spielman, *Leopold I of Austria* (New Brunswick, 1977); Heinrich Ritter von Srbik, *Wien und Versailles, 1692–1697* (Munich, 1944).   *L. S. Frey and M. L. Frey*

See LEOPOLD I.

HARTMANN VON AUE (c. 1170–1250), poet, came from a noble Swabian family. His early life remains obscure, but he may have spent his youth in a monastery, for he shows a thorough grounding in Latin, French, and the Bible, as well as strong religious convictions. After an unhappy love affair, Hartmann went crusading in 1197. He began his poetic career as a minnesinger, although lyric poetry was not his strong suit. His fame rests on two lengthy epics, *Erec,* written (c. 1192) before his participation in the crusade, and *Iwein,* his last work (c. 1202). Both works reflect the influence of Chrétien de Troyes and the Arthurian cycle. His religious sympathies are given full expression in his *Gregorius* (c. 1187–89) and his *Poor Henry* (c. 1190). Hartmann von Aue became the most imitated German poet of the Middle Ages.

Works By: Hartmann von Aue, *Erec,* ed. H. Leitzmann (Tübingen, 1957); *Gregorius: A Medieval Oedipus Legend,* ed. E. H. Zeydel and B. Q. Morgan (Chapel Hill, 1955); *Iwein,* ed G. F. Benecke and Karl Lachmann (Berlin, 1966). **Work About:** Peter Wapnewski, *Hartmann von Aue* (Stuttgart, 1962).   *J. W. Zophy*

See GOTTFRIED VON STRASBOURG; WOLFRAM VON ESCHENBACH.

HAYDN, FRANZ JOSEPH (1732–1809), composer and musician, began life in the village of Rohrau in eastern Austria. His father was a wheelwright, and his mother had been a cook. A schoolmaster cousin took him from home in order to obtain for him the musical education that his parents could ill afford. Young Franz sang in the church choir, learned basic music, and began to master a number of instruments. At age eight he was invited to become a chorister at St. Stephen's Cathedral in Vienna. He stayed there for nine years until his voice broke and he was dismissed from the choir school. Haydn then began to do a series of odd musical jobs to support himself and to continue his studies. His luck changed in 1758 when Count Ferdinand Maximilian von Morzin of Bohemia hired him as musical director and chamber composer.

A short while later Haydn entered the service of Prince Pal Antal Esterházy as assistant conductor for his orchestra at his castle at Eisenstadt, thirty miles from Vienna. In 1766 he advanced to musical director. Even Empress Maria Theresa attended the operas he staged and wrote for his great patron Prince Miklós Esterházy, for whom he worked for thirty years. A friend of Mozart, Haydn became internationally famous during his own lifetime.

After a successful stint in England, Haydn returned to the Empire in the summer of 1792 for the coronation of Emperor Francis II at Frankfurt. He continued to instruct (Beethoven among others) and compose until his death in Vienna.

Works By: H. C. Robbins Landon, ed., *The Collected Correspondence and London Notebooks of Joseph Haydn* (London, 1959) and *Haydn: Chronicles and Works*, 5 vols. (Bloomington, Indiana, 1976–). **Works About:** Karl Geiringer and Irene Geiringer, *Haydn* (New York, 1963); H. E. Jacob, *Joseph Haydn* (New York, 1950); C. F. Pohl, *Joseph Haydn*, 3 vols. (Berlin, 1875, 1882, Leipzig, 1927). *J. W. Zophy*

See BEETHOVEN; FRANCIS II; MARIA THERESA; MOZART; VIENNA.

HENRY I, THE FOWLER (c. 876–936), duke of Saxony-Thuringia, and from 919 to 936 king of the Germans, is generally considered to be the founder of the German monarchy. Designated king by his predecessor, Conrad I, and acclaimed by the Saxon and Franconian nobility, Henry was the first non-Frank to rule in the Holy Roman Empire. To continue traditions, however, he adopted Frankish customs, dress, and manners.

Henry was at first enthusiastically supported by the higher German nobility as a result of the independence and autonomy he showed as duke of Saxony against King Conrad and the German Church. He even refused to be crowned by the bishops, maintaining that the support of the nobility was sufficient to him. During his reign, however, his attitude toward the Church changed, and his relationship with the higher clergy became increasingly closer as he developed an awareness of the political importance of the Church and its traditional support of a strong monarchy. The most serious problem Henry faced as king was the relative freedom from royal control enjoyed by the greater nobility, an independence that had been much accelerated in the previous fifty years with the disintegration of the monarchical power. From 919 to 925 Henry concentrated on reestablishing royal control over the duchies of Swabia, Lotharingia, and Bavaria, succeeding through negotiation, compromise, and battle in being accepted by his fellow dukes as the head of a ducal federation with himself as king. During the remainder of his reign, he further consolidated royal control over the five duchies of Germany, especially through the appointment of the higher clergy to their posts, though he generally allowed the dukes a free hand in the administration of their own territories.

Henry also faced difficulties with the uncivilized tribes on the Empire's eastern borders, the Slavic Wends and the Hungarian Magyars. After 925, he undertook a series of wars of conquest against these peoples, thus initiating the *Drang nach Osten* ("Drive to the East") which would remain a part of the German political ethos for a millennium. He took the area of Brandenburg from the Wends and inflicted a severe defeat on the Magyars in 933. These frontier wars saw the completion of a series of military reforms that Henry had undertaken early in his reign. In the conquered lands to the east, he constructed fortified towns primarily for military purposes, and in Saxony he improved the defensive fortification of the towns. His Saxon army was transformed by the inclusion of unfree *ministeriales,* legally serfs, who were trained as heavy cavalry, thereby giving him a more mobile, efficient, and loyal striking force than the other dukes or the eastern tribes had.

Upon his death, Henry obtained from the other dukes and the nobility the recognition of his son, Otto, as his successor. Henry's successful reign restored much of the lost power and prestige to the monarchy, preparing the way for his son to restore the Empire to the fortunes it had enjoyed under the early Carolingians. Even his contemporaries recognized him as the founder of the new kingdom of Germany.

Works About: Charters and statutes in *MGH Dip* (Berlin, 1879), vol. 1; H. Heimpel, *Bemerkungen zur Gesch. König Heinriche I* (Leipzig, 1937); R. Holtzmann, *Gesch. der sachsischen Kaiserzeit, 900–1024* (Munich, 1941); H. Lintzel, "Heinrich I und das Herzogtum Schwaben," *Hist. Vierteljahrsschr.* 24 (1929); G. Waitz, *Jb. des dtsch. Reiches unter König Heinrich I* (Leipzig, 1885); Widukind, *Res Gestae Saxonicarum*, G. Waitz, ed., *MGH SS.*, 3 (Berlin, 1882).   D. S. Devlin

See CONRAD I; OTTO I.

HENRY II, THE SAINT (973–1024), duke of Bavaria, German king from 1002 to 1024, and Holy Roman emperor from 1014 to 1024, was the last of the Saxon line of German rulers. When Otto III died without an heir, the choice of succession fell on his third cousin, Henry, a direct lineal descendant of Henry I. The ancient principle of election was exercised by Henry's supporters, and after a brief civil war and negotiated concessions he was generally accepted as king. Such circumstances, however, encouraged the tribal and particularist tendencies of the German nobility, and Henry was faced throughout his reign with the task of maintaining a unified Germany and suppressing minor rebellions. He attempted, usually successfully, to follow the Ottonian policy of controlling Germany through the appointment of the dukes and the continuation of the alliance between the monarchy and the Church. In effect, he actually strengthened this latter alliance through further grants to the Church and the personal appointment and investment of virtually all important bishops and abbots during his reign. He perhaps relied more heavily on ecclesiastic support than any other emperor had.

Henry faced the usual problem of the German kings in controlling the turbulent German nobility, but his greatest problem was maintaining the border frontiers against incursions by ambitious foreign princes. In 1002 Henry was faced with war from every quarter. The Wends were in revolt, Boleslav the Great of Poland had seized some eastern territories and was attacking Bohemia, Ardvin of Ivrea had gained much of northern Italy, the count of Flanders had gained a foothold in Lorraine, and Burgundy was being dismembered by outside attacks. Henry dealt with these difficulties energetically but made little progress in most areas. He was able to reclaim Bohemia but otherwise bought peace from the count of Flanders and Boleslav only by the cession of minor territories. The Wends were essentially left to their own devices, and German control of Burgundy continued to wane. Henry met with moderate success in Italy, which he visited three times, mostly through the extension of the crown's alliance with the Church. By supporting the prelates against the lower clergy and the rapacious magnates and by awarding loyal bishoprics and abbeys with new grants and powers, he was able to maintain solid Italian ecclesiastical support for his projects. One of his strongest allies, Pope Benedict VIII (1012–1024) who crowned him emperor in 1014, maintained order in Rome, while Bishop Leo of Vercelli was instrumental in defeating Ardvin (d. 1015) and controlling northern Italy. Henry himself actually accomplished little in Italy and was constantly hindered by general hostility between his German and Italian citizens, whose rioting in 1004 resulted in the destruction of Pavia.

Compared with his immediate predecessors, Henry concentrated most of his resources on Germany itself. His activities in Italy and on the frontiers clearly indicate that he did not reject the concept of universality on which the Empire was based, but he expended energy in these directions only when forced by circumstances to do so. His seal was inscribed, "The Renewal of the Kingdom of the Franks."

Henry viewed his role as king, and as emperor as well, in a theocratic light. He thus expected ecclesiastical support for his policies, but at the same time increased the Church's power and wealth. He took seriously the idea that he was the head of the Church and spent great effort to encourage and initiate reforms of clergy and monks. Indeed his ardent concern for Church reform won for him enthusiastic support from the reform factions in Germany and Italy. He called and presided over synods concerned with everything from clerical discipline to ritual and theology; the men he appointed to high ecclesiastical positions were not only able administrators but conscientious and spiritually minded churchmen as well who attended equally to both their secular and sacred duties. Henry essentially made religion a department of the state and included higher Church leaders among the chief officials of the government.

On Henry's death in 1024, Germany itself was in a more ordered state of affairs than it was at his accession, the German Church had been invigorated and reformed, and the economic situation had improved. His strict attention to Germany, however, weakened imperial authority on the frontiers and in other areas of Europe, a situation with which his successors had to contend. He died without any male heirs, extinguishing the Saxon line. The dukes reverted to the elective principle in selecting his successor, Conrad, duke of Franconia, a distaff descendant of Otto I. Henry II was highly respected in his day and widely renowned for his ardent personal piety and religious conviction, being one of the few medieval monarchs to combine successfully administrative ability with sanctity. He was canonized a saint of the Catholic Church in 1146.

Works About: S. Hirsch, *Jb. des dtsch. Reichs unter Heinrich II.*, 3 vols. (Berlin, 1862–1875); R. Holtzmann, *Gesch. der sachsischen Kaizerzeit, 900–1024*, 4th ed. (Munich, 1961); *MGH Const.* (Berlin, 1893), vol. 1; *MGH Dip.* (Berlin, 1903), vol. 3; H. L. Mikoletsky, *Kaiser Heinrich II. und die Kirche* (Vienna, 1946); C. Pfaff, *Kaiser Heinrich II: Sein Nachleben und sein Kult im mittelalterl. Basel* (Basel, 1963); C. M. Ryley, *Cambridge Medieval Hist.* (Cambridge, England, 1964), vol. 3:272–308; T. Schieffer, "Heinrich II. und Konrad II.," *Dtsch. Archiv* 8 (1951) 384–437; H. Vogt, *Konrad II im Vergleich zu Heinrich II. und Heinrich III.* (Frankfurt am Main, 1957).   *D. S. Devlin*

See CONRAD II; OTTO III.

HENRY III (1017–1056), German king from 1039 to 1056, and Holy Roman emperor from 1046 to 1056, was the son and successor of Conrad II, with whom he was joint king from 1028 until the latter's death. Henry succeeded to the throne unchallenged, though his reign was periodically troubled by civil wars and rebellions led by the duke of Upper Lorraine, Godfrey the Bearded, and by moderate unrest among the nobility of Bavaria and Saxony. The king was quite successful in these wars and is counted among the most successful of all German monarchs in controlling the strong particularist tendencies among the higher nobility. Henry was also victorious in wars against his northern and eastern neighbors, extending the boundary of the Empire in the east to Hungary where it remained for nine-hundred years.

In many ways, the reign of Henry III is an enigma. Most historians consider his reign to mark the apogee of the medieval Empire, not only in regard to territorial expansion but in regard to the stable conditions within the Empire as well. On the other hand, Henry sowed the seeds of the Empire's later political enfeeblement through his reliance on the great prelates for governmental and military support—thus reversing his father's trend toward secularizing the government—and through his ardent advocacy of Church reform, especially the reform of the papacy, which he himself sponsored. His partnership with the Church was basic to his control of the restive German nobility and his attempts to keep order in the Empire and limit private warfare. The archbishop of Hamburg-Bremen, Adalbert, was instrumental in enabling Henry to defuse potential problems in Saxony and on the northern borders, and the king's prompt acceptance and encouragement of the Cluniac-sponsored Peace and Truce of God in 1043 provided him considerable ecclesiastical support in combating particularism and private warfare among the nobility.

Henry, a devoutly religious man, was more than merely sympathetic to the major reform movement underway in Christendom since the previous century. He took a substantial cut in imperial revenues by declaring that the customary payment made by a bishop or abbot to the crown following his ecclesiastical appointment was simony, and he discontinued the practice. He reformed many monasteries and bishoprics and established the Peace and Truce of God in Germany by publicly forgiving all of his enemies, including his nemesis, Duke Godfrey. Henry took seriously his position as the head of the Christian republic, based on the old imperial claims that the emperor was responsible for the welfare of the Church and ought to provide it both protection and guidance. Thus as a result of a disputed papal election, Henry seized on the opportunity to contribute to Church reform by reforming the head of the Church, the pope. At synods in Rome and Sutri in 1046, he declared the three rival papal claimants deposed and appointed in their stead a respectable German prelate, Clement II, by whom he was crowned emperor. In 1048, after Clement and his successor had died, Henry appointed as Leo IX his cousin who set about the complicated business of reforming the curia and the papal office and of directing further reform of the whole Church from Rome. Leo surrounded himself with the most capable reformers available, including Cardinal Humbert and the monk Hildebrand, who were to prepare the machinery for the eventual destruction of the emperor's political position two centuries later. Henry used wisely his powers of appointment to ecclesiastical posts and of calling synods to further his ideals of Church reform, and for the last ten years of his life the reform movement had no stronger lay champion than the emperor. It was ironic that immediately after his death, the ecclesiastical reformers, now led by a reinvigorated papacy, attacked the notion of imperial—or any lay—appointment to ecclesiastical office as simony and began the process of withdrawing the German Church from the control of future emperors, leaving them isolated in their continual struggle with the particularist higher nobility. From the time of Henry's death, the Church reform movement was in the hands of the papal curia, and not those of the emperor.

Henry III was noted in his lifetime for his love of peace, justice, and religious idealism. He was a strong and energetic ruler who attempted to maintain his ideals and to implement an imperial policy derived from them. While not totally successful in controlling the turbulent German nobility, he was more successful than most other emperors. He extended the Empire's borders and influence to their greatest limits, though he was blind to the threat of the growing Norman menace in southern Italy and generally ignored it, much to the detriment of his successors. His reforms of the German Church and of the papacy were eminently successful, also to the great detriment of his successors. With Henry III's death, the secular Empire began to deteriorate, though the state of affairs in 1056 was so bright due to his firm leadership that few contemporaries could have realized what dark days lay ahead. He was succeeded by his six-year-old son, Henry IV, under the regency of the Empress Agnes.

Works About: H. Bresslau and P. Kehr, eds. *Die Urkunden Heinrichs III., MGH, Dip.* (Berlin, 1931), vol. 5; P. F. Kehr, *Vier Kapital aus der Gesch. Kaiser Heinrichs III.* (Berlin, 1931); G. Ladner, *Theologie und Politik vor dem Investiturstreit* (Baden, 1936); C. M. Ryley, *Cambridge Medieval History* (Cambridge, England, 1964), 3:272–308; E. L. H. Steindorff, *Jb. des dtsch. Reichs unter Heinrich III.* 2 vols. (Leipzig, 1874–81).   D. S. Devlin

See CONRAD II; GREGORY VII; HENRY IV; INVESTITURE CONTROVERSY; LEO IX.

HENRY IV (1050–1106), German king from 1056 to 1106 and Holy Roman emperor from 1084 to 1106, was the son and successor of Henry III, whom he succeeded at age six. A regent ruled Germany until the young king attained his majority in 1065. His was one of the longer and more turbulent reigns in the Empire's history. It was during Henry IV's rule that the fifty-year-long investiture contest between the Empire and the papacy broke out; the first thirty years of the contest occurred while Henry was king, with his being the central figure in the dispute. His reign marks one of the most significant turning points in the Empire's history.

The ten years of regency visited upon the Empire while the young Henry grew up were disastrous for Germany, as well as for the position of king. The first regent was his mother, Agnes of Poitou, who lacked the ability and forcefulness to take firm command of the situation. She was beset on all sides by greedy nobles and churchmen who desired to enhance their wealth and power at the expense of the monarchy. The greater nobility, always resenting the limitations on their own particularist objectives required by the discipline of a centralized government, took advantage of the weak regency to pursue their own territorial and personal goals with complete insensitivity toward the potential damage they were causing Germany. The great prelates, traditionally allied with the royal power since the days of Otto I, also followed their own course because there was no leadership supplied behind which they could rally. By 1062 Agnes was forced aside by the archbishop of Cologne, Anno, who carried off young Henry from Kaiserswerth and proceeded to rule in his name together with the archbishop of Bremen, Adalbert. The young king's life was virtually unsupervised, and he was permitted to run wild in pursuit of the various pleasures and frivolities attractive to boys of his age while the two archbishops plundered the royal demesne and treasury to build up their sees and enrich their friends. Management of the royal estates, especially in Saxony, was lax and incompetent, with ecclesiastic and noble alike usurping whatever power and wealth could be taken from the crown. Anno was squeezed out of the regency in 1064, though Adalbert was not dismissed until 1066 when a group of jealous magnates secured his ouster through court intrigue.

The ten years of regency were costly not only in Germany, where the result was a vast reduction in the power and authority of the monarchy and an aggrandizement of particularist and personal ambitions, but in Italy as well. The period of Henry IV's minority saw the further development of the reformed papacy, which, led now by Peter Damiani, Humbert of Silva, Candida and Hildebrand, pursued its own goal of freeing itself of all lay and imperial control. Under the tutelage of Hildebrand in particular, the cardinals had altered and reformed the procedure for selecting the pope, who was henceforth to be elected by the cardinals and merely approved by the emperor. Not only did this new procedure of papal selection eliminate the emperor's earlier claims to have a strong hand in the selection of a new pope, almost to the point of personal appointment which had been exercised as recently as the reign of Henry III, it also eliminated the Roman nobility and greater prelates from having any voice in the selection of the pope. Taking advantage of the disorganization and weakness in Germany resulting from the incompetence of the regency government, the reform cardinals in Rome elected three popes on their own, allowing the German king, through his regency, only the right of approval. The last of these popes, Alexander II, was opposed by an imperial antipope set up primarily by the Roman nobility and the Lombard bishops but later tacitly supported by Henry IV, who failed to make good his claims, thus becoming the first imperially appointed pope not to be victorious in a dispute over the papal chair. Alexander II's success against his imperial opponent was therefore remarkable enough in the light of past history, but it also represented a significant turning point, for never again did the emperor appoint a successful papal candidate. From this point onward, the cardinals' choice always prevailed against the emperor's. Further damage was done in Italy during the regency, for Hildebrand succeeded in finding strong anti-imperial allies for the reformed papacy in the revolutionary Patarini of Milan and the Norman conquerors of southern Italy. By the time Henry IV was able to rule in his own right, he had powerful particularist forces ranged against him in Germany and a reinvigorated papacy in Italy daily becoming more independent of lay control. For the next forty years he struggled to overcome these forces, and although he had many successes, he failed in the end.

Henry IV's first task upon coming into his inheritance was to attempt the recovery of the royal demesne and revenues, which had been alienated over the previous ten years, and to begin the restoration of the power and authority of the centralized monarchy. Actually, these two objectives were the same, since the position of the monarchy in Germany could be restored only if the king had control over enough royal and ecclesiastical estates to make his power felt politically. The most dangerous situation existed in Saxony where the Saxons' usual particularist tendencies had been exacerbated by the fears of the Saxon bishops and magnates concerning the dominance of south Germans in the royal government. Moreover Saxony contained numerous lands and revenues, which had become part of the royal demesne in the days of Henry I and Otto I, themselves dukes of Saxony, and which had formed the power base of most German kings ever since.

Henry was at first very successful in Saxony where he covered the land with castles and through harsh methods extracted all of the monarchy's ancient rights, plus more. A brief revolt over Henry's excesses, fueled by the presence of numerous South German *ministeriales* as garrison troops in the royal castles, broke out in 1070 when he deprived the Saxon duke of Bavaria, Otto of Nordheim, not only of his duchy but of much of his Saxony lands as well. Although easily contained, this revolt merely prepared the way for the great Saxon revolt of 1073 in which Henry found himself deserted by the south German nobility who feared his power in a growing centralized government, and supported only by the rising industrial towns of the Rhineland, which favored strong centralized monarchy as a means of keeping the peace and protecting them against the rapacious German nobility. Though in serious danger at first, Henry was eventually saved by Saxon excesses, which alarmed the German churchmen and nobility. By the summer of 1075, Henry, aided greatly by the duke of Swabia, Rudolf, had succeeded in bringing Saxony under firm control. Believing himself in complete command of the situation, he recklessly punished the Saxons severely, attempted vigorously to increase the power of the monarchy, and ruptured his relations with Pope Gregory VII, the former Hildebrand, thus beginning the fifty-year investiture contest.

At first the new pope and the young German king had followed somewhat parallel paths in attempting to control their own domestic situations, their interests crossing only rarely. Henry was busy with the Saxons, while Gregory was occupied with extending his program of clerical reform and keeping his unruly Norman allies in line. By 1075, however, both had met with sufficient success to attempt an extension of their program into the other's domain. Henry's interests in Italy were his imperial coronation and the reestablishment of his authority in troubled Lombardy. Gregory's interests were the reinvigoration of the clerical reform movement in Germany under the pope's leadership and the extraction of the Church from lay control. Gregory's latter objective was especially significant in Germany where royal appointment of bishops and abbots had been the cornerstone of the king's power since the days of Otto I. The pope's desire to eliminate the German king's hand in the selection of prelates struck at the foundation of royal authority in two ways: it deprived the king of the right to select what were in essence the chief administrative officials of his government, and it potentially deprived the king of the use of the considerable wealth of the German Church, which made up a large portion of the resources available to him in attempts to centralize royal power in Germany. Thus Gregory VII's prohibition of lay investiture in the investiture decree of 1075 was a direct challenge to King Henry to defend the rights and needs of the German monarchy or to surrender any attempts to establish an effective independent royal power in Germany.

The point where the paths of pope and king crossed and their interests diverged was Milan, where Henry appointed and invested in late 1075 a new archbishop, Tedald, in opposition to the one recently appointed by the revolutionary Patarini reformers who had been confirmed by the pope. When Gregory sternly warned Henry of further violations of papal decrees and threatened to depose him, Henry responded by calling a synod at Worms in January 1076 where the German bishops, supported by the Lombards, declared Gregory deposed in a letter addressed to "Hildebrand, not the pope but a false monk." Henry had miscalculated his power, however, for the pope had strong support in Rome, and it was virtually impossible for a German king to depose a pope unless he was present in Italy with an army to do so. Gregory proved to have a more realistic grasp of the situation and in February deposed and excommunicated the king and his rebellious bishops. Henry suddenly found himself in a dangerous situation; his German bishops deserted him to retain the pope's favor, and the particularist German nobility joined forces with the Saxons in declaring Henry deposed unless he obtained absolution from the pope by February 1077, an act that they then proceeded to frustrate by attempting to block all the routes to Italy. The king did manage to get to Italy by January 1077, however; he appeared before the castle of Canossa where Gregory was staying and after standing barefoot in the snow for three days received the pope's absolution.

Henry's humiliation before the pope should have restored him to good standing with his subjects and forestalled any further attempts at revolt, but such was not the case; the rebel dukes and the Saxons remained consistent in their course and determined to depose him. They declared the king deposed in March 1077, elected Duke Rudolf of Swabia as antiking, and thereby precipitated a civil war. Henry had the support of most of the German Church, the Rhenish towns, and the lower nobility, and he continued to attract support from other magnates through clever diplomacy. The pope delayed in supporting either candidate, largely since he had no force with which to intervene. By 1080 Henry had gained the upper hand and, when he demanded that Gregory excommunicate the rebels, the pope miscalculated; he excommunicated and deposed Henry instead, prophesying that Henry would be dead in three months time. Gregory was wrong; it was Rudolf who was dead by autumn and Henry who had complete control of the situation, even to the extent of making Gregory appear to be a grasping, autocratic aggressor bent on destroying German and imperial rights. The German prelates, becoming fearful that the final objective of the pope's reforms was to transfer their obedience and appointment from emperor to pope, came to the aid of Henry and at the synod of Brixen in late 1080 deposed Gregory and set up an antipope, the saintly Guibert of Ravenna, as Clement III. By the following spring, the revolt in Germany was of so little danger to Henry that he invaded Italy in force, planning to depose Gregory with his army. Gregory's only support came from Countess Matilda of Tuscany, who was soon neutralized, and his popularity with the Roman people who held out for him during three years of siege before abandoning him. With Gregory still holding out in Castle Sant' Angelo, Henry gained control of Rome and was crowned emperor by Clement III. When the pope's Norman allies, led by Duke Robert Guiscard, finally arrived in Rome, Henry withdrew, leaving the Normans to sack the city viciously before carrying Gregory off to safety in Spoleto, where he died a year later.

Upon the emperor's return to Germany following his victorious sojourn in Italy, he still had a minor rebellion with which to contend, as well as the disaffection of some German bishops favorable to the Gregorian reforms. By 1088, however, he had come to terms with or defeated his political enemies, including the Saxons, and gained recognition of his imperial coronation from the bishops although many of the latter refused to recognize Clement as the pope, preferring instead the cardinals' choice, Urban II (1088–1099). Henry was secure enough at home to have his son, Conrad, crowned as joint king and to begin his program of restoring, consolidating, and expanding the royal power in Germany.

There was new trouble on the horizon, however; Urban II was just as formidable a foe as Gregory had been and had no intention of backing down on the issue of lay investiture, the contours of which had been so clearly delineated by Gregory. In 1089 the new pope arranged a potential marriage alliance between Matilda of Tuscany and the son of the rebellious Welf, duke of Bavaria, Welf V. Such an alliance posed a dangerous threat to Henry who could not allow this consolidation of hostile blocks of territory like Tuscany and southern Germany, and he was forced to invade Italy for a second time. Quite successful at first, the imperial cause was hurt by the desertion of Conrad to the papal party and by the growth of the communal movement in the towns of Lombardy, which deprived the emperor of some of his previously staunchest support. Henry's position was further weakened by more defections, including that of his second wife, the Russian princess, Adelaide, in 1094. By 1095 the emperor found himself trapped in Verona from which he was able to escape only in 1097 when the Welfs broke with Matilda and reconciled with him while Pope Urban was occupied in organizing the first crusade. Henry soon agreed to compromise with his most powerful magnate opponents, the result of which was their coronation of his second son, Henry, as joint king in 1099 and the monarchy's tacit abandonment of any plans to reestablish a powerful centralized government in Germany. Even the death of Pope Urban in 1099 did not alleviate Henry's problems with the Church because the new pope, Paschal II, continued the same policies regarding lay investiture. Moreover the reform party was fast winning fresh adherents in Germany, further undermining the king's position at home.

Henry's last attempt to restore his position as king of a united German nation was his proclamation of a four-year land peace in 1103, complete with serious penalties for breach of the peace. In theory the territorial nobility was to help the king enforce the peace, but in fact the nobility chafed against a peace that limited their cherished rights to pursue their private feuds. The peace, favored by the lower classes and burghers of the Rhenish cities, was designed to protect them from the rapacious nobles and enlist their aid in strengthening the central government. Increased disaffection among the nobility disturbed the emperor's son, the younger Henry, who feared the eventual destruction of the Salian monarchy, and he took advantage of the situation to rebel against his father by forming a coalition of nobility and reformed churchmen. Through treachery and cunning, he captured his father, imprisoned him in Ingelheim castle, and forced his abdication. The emperor escaped, however, and established a power base at Liège to oppose his son's usurpation. He died following a short illness in 1106.

Henry IV is generally listed among the greatest rulers of the medieval Empire despite his tragic life, ill fortune, and the failure of most of his projects. The very fact that he held his own against the various forces arrayed against him during his reign marks him as a king of unusual ability, vigor, and resourcefulness. It was his misfortune to rule at a time when the emperor was caught between the reforming demands of a reinvigorated, expanding papal power and the rising particularism and distrust of central government among the nobility. Against such odds, Henry IV probably succeeded better than most others could have. He had attempted to consolidate and extend the royal power against the particularist dukes but had been prevented from doing so when he ran afoul of the rising papal power whose interests were antithetical to his own. In the end he managed in difficult times to retain enough of the imperial legacy to allow future German kings to restore somewhat the glories of the Ottos by seeking new allies in the *ministeriales* and townsmen of the Rhineland. He was succeeded by his son, Henry V, who had forced his abdication in 1105 but to whom he sent the royal insignia from his deathbed.

Works By: *The Letters of Henry IV* in *Imperial Lives and Letters of the Eleventh Century*, ed. R. L. Benson (New York, 1962). **Works About:** Bruno of Meresburg, *De Bello Saxonico*, ed. H. E. Lohmann (Leipzig, 1937); Peter Crassus, *Defensio Heinrici Regis, MGH, Libelli de lite* (Hanover, 1892), vol. 1; A. Fliche, *La reforme grégorienne et la reconquête chrétienne (1059–1123)* (Paris, 1940); K. Hampe, *Germany under the Salian and Hohenstaufen Emperors*, tr. R. Bennett (Totowa, N.J., 1973); S. Hellmann, "De Vita Heinrici IV und die kaiserliche Kanzlei," Hist. Vierteljahrschrift 28 (1934): 213–334; G. Meyer von Knonau, *Jb. des Dtsch. Reiches unter Heinrich IV und Heinrich V*, 7 vols. (Leipzig, 1890–1909); T. Lindner, *Kaiser Heinrich IV* (Berlin, 1881); K. F. Morrison, "Introduction," *Imperial Lives and Letters of the Eleventh Century*, ed. R. L. Benson (New York, 1962); P. Rassow, "Der Kampf Kaiser Heinrichs IV mit Heinrich V," *Z. für Kir-*

chengeschichte 47 (1928:451–65; G. Tellenbach, *Church, State and Christian Society at the Time of the Investiture Contest,* tr. R. Bennett (Oxford, 1948).   *D. S. Devlin*

See AGNES OF POITOU; GREGORY VII; HENRY III; HENRY V; INVESTITURE CONTROVERSY; MATILDA OF TUSCANY; OTTO I.

HENRY V (1081–1125), German king from 1106 to 1125 and Holy Roman emperor from 1111 to 1125, the son and successor of Henry IV, was crowned joint king with his father in 1099. After Henry IV had proclaimed a general land peace in 1107, the younger Henry soon found himself at the head of a group of powerful nobles who opposed the four-year cessation of all warfare in Germany. While the purpose of the peace was to end the chaotic situation in certain regions of the Empire and to bring the nobility directly under the king's control in the enforcement of the peace, the younger Henry feared that the mounting discontent among the nobility would encourage their alliance with the papacy, whose objective would be the debilitation of the German monarchy and possibly the end of Salian rule. He therefore forged his own alliance with the nobility and Pope Paschal II and rebelled against his father in 1104. Through guile and treachery, young Henry captured the old emperor, imprisoned him in Ingelheim castle, and forced him to abdicate in 1105. The emperor escaped, however, and was in the process of gathering an army at Liège when he died in August 1106, thus leaving his son as the reigning king in Germany.

Henry V proved to be a clever, calculating, and politically astute monarch whose chief objective was maintaining the integrity of the Empire and the royal power so painstakingly constructed over the previous two centuries. His early alliance with the territorial nobility and the papacy were simply convenient political moves; he had no intention of surrendering any of the monarchy's claims in either the secular or religious spheres. Yet this alliance of 1104 worked to his advantage; it deceived pope and noble alike as to the young king's ability and interests. Formally reconciled with the Church, Henry V entered negotiations with the papacy concerning investiture of bishops while continuing from the very first to practice lay investiture in direct violation of papal directives, disregarding Pope Paschal's protests. His continued alliance with the German Church and nobility temporarily unified Germany, and his power was increased all the more through a marriage alliance in 1110 with Henry I of England.

By 1110 Henry felt secure enough in Germany to take a large army to Italy where the northern towns promptly offered their submission. Countess Matilda of Tuscany dared not oppose him, and the Normans were busy in the south. Pope Paschal, partly because of the presence of the imperial army and partly out of personal idealism as an ardent reformer, proposed a radical solution to the problem of lay investiture: if the emperor would agree to free clerical election and to cease investment of bishops and abbots, the German Church would cede back to the crown the *regalia*, the land, wealth, and ecclesiastic endowments of the Church, which had been the basis for the emperor's concern over investment in the first place. When the treaty was publicly announced in February 1111, the German clergy, backed by much of the nobility, set up a great outcry at the prospect of all their wealth, endowments, and power being given away. In the ensuing confusion the king's party kidnapped the pope and cardinals and removed them from Rome. Two months of captivity induced Paschal to submit to all Henry's demands, including lay investiture as traditionally practiced, his coronation as Holy Roman emperor, and a promise never to excommunicate him. This Treaty of Ponte Mammolo thus represented the greatest victory of the Empire over the reformed papacy, being a complete acknowledgment of all that Henry IV had striven to attain.

Great clerical indignation, especially from reformers, was immediately expressed, and by 1112 Pope Paschal had withdrawn his so-called privilege from the emperor, claiming that it had been extracted by force. Henry's true colors now quite apparent, he suddenly found himself opposed in Germany by a dangerous coalition of powerful churchmen, Saxons, and particularist nobles led by the duke of Saxony and the archbishop of Mainz. The revolt against Henry was caused by several factors, not the least of which was his increasing reliance on the lower nobility and *ministeriales* in the government and his friendship with the wealthy towns of the Rhineland. Other factors were the great magnates' fear of a renewed, more powerfully centralized monarchy, some clerical fear of losing a privileged position in the Empire, some clerical support for the principles of the papal reform program, and the seemingly natural particularism of the Saxons. This formidable alliance kept the emperor off balance for the rest of his reign, and he was never able to restore to Germany the peaceful situation that he desired.

Henry's policy for the implementation of royal power in Germany generally followed the practices of his predecessors in that he attempted to place as much land under his direct control as possible. For this reason, he left a precariously controlled Germany for Italy in 1116 to take possession of the rich lands of the late Countess Matilda of Tuscany who had been forced to name him her heir during his earlier visit and to reclaim as king her fiefs held of the Empire. Unable to arrange a meeting with Pope Paschal, who feared a repetition of earlier events, Henry was nonetheless able to increase imperial power and prestige in northern Italy, much of it at the expense of the papacy. Paschal died in 1118, shortly after the emperor's return to Germany to deal with more pressing problems at home. The election of a new pope, Gelasius II, however, intensified the already protracted investiture contest since Henry promptly set up an antipope, and Gelasius excommunicated the emperor. By this time the situation on both sides of the Alps appeared totally chaotic; half of Germany was in rebellion against Henry, and the Roman nobility and much of northern Italy opposed the new pope, who was forced to flee to France for safety.

It was soon clear to the leaders of both sides that the restoration of peace, together with the reconciliation of Empire and papacy, had become a necessity. The early death of Gelasius in 1119 and the election of Calixtus II opened the way for a compromise solution to the problem of investiture. Henry had several times claimed that his primary concern in investiture was with conferring the *regalia,* a position that probably would have been acceptable to Pope Gregory VII. Consequently the emperor and pope entered into negotiations in late 1119. They reached a compromise by 1122 that followed closely the arrangement worked out in 1107 by the papacy and the English crown. According to the Concordat of Worms the emperor retained the right to invest bishops and abbots with their secular powers and rights—the *regalia*—and to receive homage from them as vassals. The emperor surrendered the right to invest with ring and staff—the symbols of spiritual authority—and to appoint prelates who were now to be elected according to canonical tradition, although he was allowed to be present at the election as the representative of the people whom he ruled and to decide disputed election for the more qualified candidate. In sum, the Concordat of Worms forced both parties to compromise their claims. The agreement was not something that would have met with the clear approval of either Henry IV or Gregory VII, but it did give both sides much of what they wanted. The emperor was left with not inconsiderable powers, as Frederick Barbarossa later proved, nor was the papacy left without a clear confirmation of its spiritual authority over Christendom and its autonomy.

Henry's negotiations with the papacy had somewhat defused the strong opposition to him in Germany, especially since a solution to the investiture question that satisfied his interests tended also to satisfy and protect the interests of the German Church and the greater nobility. Indeed the investiture contest had demonstrated to both prelate and magnate the similarity of their interests and conditions. The result was a closer alliance between the two groups. The churchmen were now more independent of the king, and the nobility had increased its property, rights, and share in government. Even before the Concordat of Worms was officially agreed to, Henry had made peace with most of his German antagonists at the diet of Würzburg in 1121. Trouble with the Saxons remained unresolved, and Henry's invasion of that duchy was repulsed by Duke Lothar. The situation in Germany was stable enough, however, to allow the emperor to participate with his father-in-law, Henry I of England, in a joint invasion of France, though it proved to be a failure. His energetic attempt to create a strong monarchy in Germany had, however, alarmed his old particularist opponents who, led by the duke of Saxony, were again on the verge of rebellion when Henry died in May 1125, probably of cancer.

Henry V was an energetic and politically astute monarch in a troubled time. His personality tended to be abrasive, which made diplomacy and compromise difficult at times. He was one of the more cunning and treacherous emperors, using his abilities toward his one goal of maintaining the integrity of the Empire and the power of the emperor. To his credit, he succeeded in satisfactorily ending the debilitating investiture contest, which had wracked the Empire for half a century. He left the Empire in a better state than he had received it, and though it was weaker and less centralized in 1125 than it had been in the days of Henry III, it certainly was far from disintegrating. Henry died leaving no heir, and with his death the Salian dynasty ended. He was succeeded by the duke of Saxony, Lothar II, who was elected by the nobles.

Works About: W. Arndt, "Heinrich V," *ADB,* 11:411–19; G. Meyer von Knonau, *Jb. des Dtsch. Reiches unter Heinrich IV und Heinrich V,* 7 vols. (Leipzig, 1890–1909); K. Leyser, "England and the Empire in the Early Twelfth Century," *Transactions of the Royal Hist. Society* 5, series 10 (1960): 561–83; T. Schieffer, "Heinrich V," T. Schieffer, *NDB,* 8:320–23.   *D. S. Devlin*

See CONCORDAT OF WORMS; HENRY III; HENRY IV; INVESTITURE CONTROVERSY; LOTHAR II; MATILDA OF TUSCANY.

HENRY VI (1165–1197), emperor, was born at Nimwegen, the eldest son of Frederick I and Beatrice of Burgundy. The princes elected him king of the Romans in 1169; on August 15 he was crowned at Aachen. Henry received a good education and developed literary and cultural tastes along with the chivalric virtues of the day. On January 27, 1186, at Milan he married Constance, niece and heiress of William II of Sicily. He became regent when his father departed on crusade in 1189. William II's death in the same year brought the Norman kingdom into Hohenstaufen hands, while Barbarossa's death in 1190 gave Henry the German kingdom as well.

Having concluded a hasty treaty with Henry the Lion of Saxony to preserve peace in Germany, Henry set out for Italy. Pope Celestine III's opposition to Henry's move across the Alps was partly allayed by his recognition of papal territorial claims. On April 15, 1191, at Rome the pope bestowed the imperial crown on Henry VI. Next Henry proposed to enter the Norman kingdom and enforce his and his wife's rights there. An opposition party had developed, however, headed by Tancred of Lecce, an illegitimate grandson of Roger II, who united the anti-German factions and secured recognition as king. Henry VI's forces were not strong enough to deal with this nationalistic resistance; after a futile siege of Naples, he retreated across the Alps.

From late 1191 to spring 1194, Henry remained in Germany. His forceful assertion of control over the Church culminated in the assassination of bishop-elect Albert of Liège (November 24, 1192), brother of Duke Henry of Brabant. Popular rumor implicated the emperor in the murder, which he at least condoned but probably did not directly instigate. This crime became the pretext for a princely rebellion of considerable proportions involving most of the magnates of the Rhineland, Bohemia, and the adherents of the Welf party in northern Germany. From this precarious situation Henry was unexpectedly saved by a stroke of luck: the capture of King Richard of England by Duke Leopold of Austria in December 1192 while Richard was returning from the Third Crusade. Since Richard had recognized Tancred as king of Sicily and because of the traditional close ties between the English monarchy and the Welfs of Saxony, Henry VI considered Richard one of his foremost foes on the international scene. In exchange for a promise of a share in the ransom, Duke Leopold surrendered his prisoner the emperor. Richard in effect became a hostage for the good behavior of the anti-Hohenstaufen partisans. Their feud with Henry VI collapsed quietly. Not until February 4, 1194, did Henry release Richard after the latter agreed to pay a ransom of 150,000 marks and to surrender his kingdom to the emperor, who returned it to Richard in exchange for an oath of fealty. Henry made peace with the Welfs by coming to terms with Henry the Lion at Tilleda in March and by permitting the latter's son, Henry of Brunswick, to marry the emperor's niece, Agnes, daughter of Conrad of Staufen who held the county Palatine of the Rhine.

With Germany securely under control and with the English ransom to meet expenses, Henry VI turned his attention once again to Sicily. Tancred died on February 20, 1194, leaving only a minor son, William III, to carry on the struggle against the Hohenstaufens. In May 1194 the emperor crossed the Alps. After a short delay to recruit troops in northern Italy, he advanced on the Sicilian kingdom. Both the mainland and the island fell into his hands easily. Henry entered Palermo on November 20 and on December 25 was crowned king. The discovery of a plot against him induced Henry to send the child William and his mother, Sibylle, with other prominent supporters, to confinement in Germany, where the Norman treasure was also transported. At a large diet at Bari in March 1195, Henry laid the administrative foundation of his government in the peninsula. His wife, Constance, who had borne her first and only son, Frederick Roger, on December 26, 1194, became regent of the kingdom, assisted by Conrad of Urslingen as duke of Spoleto. Henry appointed his brother Philip duke of Tuscany and ruler of the Matildine lands. Markward of Anweiler, who held the margravate of Ancona and the duchy of Ravenna, was the foremost of several *ministeriales* who also received lands and duties in north central Italy.

Having acquired the Norman kingdom, Henry VI quickly revealed that he also espoused the Norman expansionist tendencies in the Mediterranean, reenforced by his own prerogatives as Holy Roman emperor. He revived Norman claims to Tunis and Tripoli in North Africa. He commissioned ambassadors to enfeoff Leo of Armenia as his vassal and to receive feudal homage from King Amalric of Cyprus. He let it be known that he intended to renew the Norman hostility against Byzantium. When he had conquered Palermo, he found there Irene, daughter of the Byzantine emperor Isaac Angelus, the betrothed of a deceased son of Tancred of Lecce. Henry arranged for her to marry his brother Philip (Pentecost, 1197), thus establishing a hereditary claim to the eastern empire. After Isaac Angelus's brother Alexius deposed that ruler and assumed the Byzantine imperial title, Henry VI took the stance of protector of the rights of his proposed sister-in-law. Eventually Henry forced Alexius III to pay him tribute. On March 31, 1195, Henry took the cross; there is reason to suspect that he was planning to move eventually against Constantinople, and he may have envisioned the crusade as the ideal opportunity for such an adventure.

From July 1195 to June 1196, Henry was again in Germany preparing for his crusade. To secure his government in his absence, he proposed a revolutionary scheme: in return for the princes' recognition of the hereditary character of the Empire, thus guaranteeing the succession of the infant prince, Frederick, the emperor promised to recognize the heritability of their fiefs in both male and female lines and to renounce the *jus spolii* in favor of the ecclesiastical princes. At a diet at Würzburg in April 1196, a majority of the princes present signified their willingness to accept this constitutional reform, but a determined group led by Archbishop Adolf of Cologne brought about its defeat later. They did compromise, however, by electing the infant Frederick king, thus assuring another generation of Hohenstaufen rule. The emperor tried to outflank the princes by persuading Pope Celestine III to endorse his scheme for a hereditary Empire. As an inducement, he offered to assign to the curia a number of lucrative prebends in each diocese of the German Church, thereby establishing the pope's and the cardinals' financial security. Celestine, however, disturbed by the encroachments of some of the German administrators on the papal state and aware of the inevitable loss of papal influence on imperial policy if the Empire became hereditary, rejected the emperor's proposal.

Meanwhile preparations for the crusade were going forward, interrupted only briefly by a plot against Henry on the part of some discontented Sicilians; possibly the Curia and even the Queen regent Constance were involved or at least aware of the scheme. The revolt erupted while Henry was in Messina in May 1197. Forewarned, he escaped and took fearful vengeance on the ringleaders. Early in September the first of the crusaders set sail, led by the chancellor Bishop Conrad of Hildesheim and the imperial Marshal Henry of Kalden. But the thirty-two-year-old emperor died at Messina, September 28, 1197, of an attack of malaria. He was buried in the cathedral at Palermo.

Works About: Hermann Bloch, *Forsch. zur politik Kaiser Heinrichs VI.in den Jahren 1191–1194* (Berlin, 1892) and "Some Unnoticed Aspects of the Emperor Henry VI's Conquest of the Norman Kingdom of Sicily," *Bulletin of the John Rylands Library* 36 (1953–1954):328–59; J. F. Böhmer, *Regesta Imperii*, 4 pt. 3, ed. by Gerhard Baaken (Vienna, 1972); D. Clementi, "Calendar of the Diplomas of the Hohenstaufen Emperor Henry VI concerning the Kingdom of Sicily," *Quel. und Forsch. aus ital. Arch. und Bibl.*, 35 (1955): 86–225; J. Haller, "Heinrich VI. und die römische Kirche, *MIÖG* 35 (1914):385–454, 545–669; J. Heinrich, "Kaiser Heinrich VI. und die Besetzung der dtsch. Bistümer von seiner Kaiserkrönung bis zur Eroberung Siziliens (April 1191 bis Ende 1194)," *Römische Quartalschrift für chrisliche Altertumskunde und Kirchengesch* 51 (1956): 189–227; Volkert Pfaff, *Kaiser Heinrichs VI. höchstes Angebot an die römische Kurie 1196* (Heidelberg,

1927); R. Schmandt, "The Election and Assassination of Albert of Louvain, Bishop of Liège, 1191–92," *Spec.* 42 (1967): 639–60; Theodor Toeche, *Kaiser Heinrich VI* (Leipzig, 1867, rpr. 1965). Werner Wohlfarth, *Kaiser Heinrich VI. und die oberitalischen. Städte* (Heidelberg, 1939); P. Zerbi, *Papato, impero e "Republica Christiana" dal 1187 al 1198* (Rome, 1955).   R. H. Schmandt

See FREDERICK I; HENRY THE LION.

HENRY VII (1274–1313), Dante's imperial savior of Italy, who ruled the Empire from 1308 to 1313, was the eldest son of Count Henry III of Luxembourg and Beatrice, the daughter of Baldwin of Beaumont and Avesnes. His brother was Archbishop Baldwin of Trier, the most politically acute and influential of the German electors and kingmaker of his day. With holdings on both sides of the Empire, Henry married his daughter Marie to King Charles VI of France and his daughter Beatrice to King Charles of Hungary. His son John became king of Bohemia and was the father of Charles IV, emperor from 1347 to 1378.

A vassal of both the king of France and the count of Flanders, Henry played an independent role in French and imperial politics. The accession of Baldwin to the archbishopric of Trier in 1308 and his own marriage to Margaret, the daughter of John I of Brabant, put Henry in a position to offer himself as an alternative to Charles V of Valois during the imperial election of 1308. Led by Baldwin and the archbishop of Mainz, Peter von Aspelt, his party sought to avoid a Habsburg succession to Frederick IV. They convinced the electors of Cologne, Saxony, and Brandenburg, and, with the support of Clement V, they elected Henry at Frankfurt on November 27, 1308. He was crowned on January 6 at Aachen.

Impoverished by the expenses of the election and determined to receive the full benefits of the imperial title, Henry sought to pacify Germany before traveling to Rome for his coronation as emperor. He established the public peace in southwest Germany and reorganized the royal domains. He made peace with the Habsburgs, indemnifying them for the loss of Moravia and transfering the lands and titles of Albert I's assassins to them. And he managed to secure the succession in Bohemia for his son John when the Bohemian nobility revolted against Duke Henry V of Carinthia in 1310.

His efforts to ensure imperial peace were successful, but both required more resources than Henry could spare. In the case of the southwest, he was unable to force Count Eberhard of Württemberg to drop local feuds and acquisitive ventures in the region and finally placed him under the ban of the Empire, diverting some of his imperial troops to enforce the edict. In Bohemia, he had to establish a regency government under Count Berthold VII of Henneberg-Schleusingen, which became more of an army of occupation when Henry V of Carinthia continued to resist efforts to seize the throne vacated by the last of the Premyslid dynasty in 1306. Although Henry strengthened his claim by marrying

John to Wenceslaus II's daughter Elizabeth, their joint coronation at Prague in 1311 was achieved at great cost. Thus the Bohemian venture too diverted resources from the Italian expedition.

Responding to imperial envoys, Pope Clement V recognized Henry as king of the Romans on July 26, 1309, but with some reservations. He refused to receive him in Rome for coronation until February 2, 1312. Worse, seven days later he crowned Robert of Anjou king of Naples and supported his efforts to mobilize an anti-imperial party in Lombardy and Tuscany. Later he made him papal rector of the Romagna and imperial vicar of Italy.

Despite assurances by Henry that he would protect the Church and its possesions in central Italy, which he delivered to Clement on October 11, 1310, the pope was unwilling to advance the coronation date. Henry was just as determined, although penniless and short of troops, to become emperor without delay. Knowing little about Italian politics, he crossed the Alps through Savoy to the upper Po Valley in late October. On January 6, 1311, he received the crown of the Lombards in Milan. With pacification of Italy and the reestablishment of imperial government as his objectives, Henry was less concerned with rapid transit to Rome than with territorial conquest. This error, which sank him into the mire of Italian politics, was probably made necessary by his penury and the consequent danger that he would lose the few German lords and retainers present in Italy with him. Impolitic choices of imperial vicars, the imposition of imperial levys, taxes, and tolls, and occasional brutality marred his progress to Rome. Much of Italy joined with Florence in a Guelph league. The siege of Brescia, from May 19 to September 19, 1311, was especially costly in time and troops lost, and more importantly in loss of reputation.

Because the pope forbad passage through the territories of Bologna, Henry was forced to travel down the western coast of Italy, wintering in Genoa, where he lost his queen, Margaret, on December 13, 1311. He left by sea for Pisa in mid-February, remained there for another two months, and arrived before Rome on May 7, 1312. Opposed by the troops of Robert of Naples, led by his brother John of Gravina, and by the Orsini family with their considerable number of supporters, Henry had to fight his way to the palace. There, and not in St. Peter's, he was crowned emperor on June 29, 1312, by Cardinal Nicholas of Ostia, who later repudiated the act.

Now turning to Florence, Henry sought to end the resistance of this focus of Guelph sympathy, which constantly threatened the imperial administration he had just established. Further he had charged Robert of Naples with treason at Arezzo on September 12, 1312. He preferred to attempt to pacify Florence and its Guelph allies before sentencing and attacking him. He invested Florence in mid-September; the siege was a fiasco and had to be lifted late in October, although fighting went on in the countryside through March 1313. Returning to Pisa, Henry declared Robert of Naples guilty and sought legal justification for his claims to the crown and his proceedings against Robert in Roman law. Meanwhile he tried to gather his supporters together for one more campaign to enforce his ban. He fell victim to malaria while moving his army south through Tuscany and died on August 25, 1313 at Buonconvento near Siena.

Works About: J. F. Böhmer, *Regesta imperii* (Frankfurt, 1844); William Bowsky, "Florence and Henry of Luxemburg," *Spec.* 33 (1958):177–203 and *Henry VII in Italy* (New York, 1960); Otto Herding, *Das römisch–dtsch. Reiche in deutscher und italiensicher Beurteiling von Rudolf von Habsburg zu Heinrich VII* (Erlangen, 1937); *MGH Legum Sectio IV Const. et Acta,* ed. Jacob Schwalm (Hanover, 1906), vol. 4; Friedrich Schneider, *Kaiser Heinrich VII, Dantes Kaiser* (Stuttgart, 1943); Camillus Wampach, *Urkunden–und Quellenbuch zur Gesch. der Altluxemburg Territorien bis zur burgundischen Zeit* (Stuttgart, 1949), vol. 7.   *S. A. Garretson*

See ALBERT I; CHARLES IV; DANTE.

HENRY THE LION (c. 1129–1195) was the greatest of the Welf dukes of Saxony and Bavaria. Son of Henry X, the Proud, of Bavaria (d. 1139) and Gertrude of Supplinburg, daughter of Emperor Lothar, he married in 1150 Clementia of Zähringen (the marriage was annulled in 1162) and then in 1168 Matilda, daughter of Henry II of England (d. 1189). The first marriage produced a daughter, Gertrude; the second, three sons who survived their father: Henry, count Palatine of the Rhine, Otto IV of Brunswick, and William, duke of Brunswick-Lüneburg. Henry also had one illegitimate daughter.

About ten years old when his father died, Henry the Lion inherited a bitter feud with Conrad III of Hohenstaufen who had just confiscated both Saxony and Bavaria from the Welfs. Henry's uncle Welf IV and his mother continued the struggle until a compromise was achieved in 1143: Henry recovered the Saxon duchy but resigned Bavaria to Henry Jasomirgott of the Babenberg family, whom Henry's mother married. As he matured, Henry the Lion determined to recover Bavaria. The accession in 1152 of Frederick I, anxious for princely support for his imperial schemes, offered the opportunity for renewed negotiations. In June 1154 at the diet of Goslar, Frederick yielded to Henry's importunities, but the investiture did not take place until 1156. At that time Henry agreed to the compensation of Henry Jasomirgott by detaching for him the Bavarian East March, which Barbarossa raised to the rank of the duchy of Austria.

For the next twenty years Welf-Hohenstaufen relations remained good. Henry accompanied Barbarossa to Italy in 1154–1155 and 1158–1162, and supported the emperor against Pope Alexander III. Barbarossa excused him from participation in the expeditions of 1167 and 1174, but early in 1176, at a crisis with the Lombard League, Barbarossa begged the Bavarian-Saxon duke, in an interview at Chiavenna, to supply reinforcements. Henry the Lion refused, as he was legally free to do, but morally and politically he was under obligations to the emperor for territorial grants and general support in internal Saxon affairs. Barbarossa's defeat at Legnano in 1176 followed, and the duke paid the price in the emperor's undying enmity.

Summoned to present himself before the diet in January 1179 to justify his conduct in several petty Saxon feuds, Henry repeatedly refused to appear. After a careful, correct legal process, he was placed under the imperial ban in 1180, and his fiefs were declared forfeited. The diet of Gelnhausen disposed of his duchies, dividing Saxony between the archbishop of Cologne and Bernard of Anhalt, and assigning Bavaria to Otto of Wittelsbach. After eighteen months of resistance, Henry surrendered. Allowed to retain his allodial possessions at Brunswick and Lüneburg, he lost all else and was sent into exile until 1185. Exiled again in 1189 when Frederick departed on crusade, Henry returned six months later to confront Henry VI. The new king, always anxious for peace in northern Germany to permit him to concentrate on his Norman kingdom in Italy, made small concessions to the duke in July 1190 at Fulda and again at Tilleda in March 1194, seventeen months before the duke's death.

Constructively more significant than his imperial relations were Henry the Lion's enduring achievements within his duchies, especially Saxony. He understood contemporary economic currents and encouraged the growth of cities and commerce. His foundation of Munich (1158) and restoration of Lübeck created two of Germany's great mercantile centers. In the spirit of the *Drang nach Osten* (Drive to the East), he encouraged merchants to venture into the Baltic and secured privileges for them at Wisby. His crusade against the Wends (1147) was only one aspect of his continued pressure against the Slavs of Holstein and Mecklenburg. He founded or restored the bishoprics of Oldenburg-Lübeck, Ratzeburg, and Mecklenburg-Schwerin as instruments for the Germanization and Christianization of the colonial lands, from which he also excluded the Danes.

Within his territories Henry ruled with an iron hand; even faithful collaborators such as Count Adolf of Holstein had to bend to his ruthless will. He invested his own bishops and exploited feudal practice in the construction of a centralized territorial administration. He shared Barbarossa's hierarchic view of political life, but it was his personal tragedy that he was stubbornly unwilling to give to the emperor the same degree of loyalty that he demanded from his own subordinates.

Works About: Paul Barg, *Heinrich der Löwe: einer Welfe bewegt die Gesch.* (Bonn, 1977); E. Joranson, "The Palestine Pilgrimage of Henry the Lion," in *Mediaeval and Historiographical Essays in Honor of James Westfall Thompson*, ed. James L. Cate and Eugene N. Anderson (Chicago, 1938), 146–225; K. Jordan, *Die Bistumsgründungen Heinrichs des Löwen* (Stuttgart, 1939; rp. 1962) and "Die Städtepolitik Heinrichs des Löwen, eine Forschungsbilanz," *Hansische Geschichtsblätter* 78 (1960):1–36; Karl Jordan, ed., *Die Urkunden Heinrichs des Löwen, Herzogs von Sachsen und Bayern* (Weimar, 1963); Theodore Mayer, *Friedrich I. und Heinrich der Löwe* (Darmstadt, 1958); Austin L. Poole, *Henry the Lion* (Oxford, 1912).   *R. H. Schmandt*

See CONRAD III; FREDERICK I; HENRY VI.

HENRY THE PROUD (c. 1108–1138), duke of Bavaria, was the son of Duke Henry IX of Bavaria, called the Black, of the Welf family, and of Wulfhild, daughter of Duke Magnus Billung, one of the great Saxon magnates. In 1127 Henry X, the Proud, married Gertrude of Supplinburg whose father Lothar was duke of Saxony, as well as German king. The marriage was an expression of Lothar's gratitude to Henry IX whose unexpected support had proved decisive in the royal election in 1125 when it had been anticipated that Frederick of Staufen, duke of Swabia, would win the royal throne as the Salian dynasty died out. Even though this Frederick (d. 1147) was married to Henry the Proud's sister Judith (d. 1126), the long Welf-Hohenstaufen feud stemmed from the election contest of 1125.

Inevitably Henry the Proud's lot was cast with that of his father-in-law. He fought alongside King Lothar in the civil war waged by Frederick of Staufen and his antiking brother, Conrad. Henry served Lothar well in fighting at Nuremberg, Speyer, and Zweifalten (1127–1129), and his capture of Ulm in 1134 was one of the final Welf victories that convinced the Staufen brothers to end their opposition. When Lothar journeyed to Italy in 1132, he left Henry as regent. The Bavarian duke accompanied the king on the Italian expedition of 1136–1137, leading one of the two divisions of the royal army and fighting all through the peninsula. From this campaign Henry acquired the margravate of Tuscany and the Matildan lands as papal fiefs.

Lothar of Supplinburg died in Reutte in the Tyrol on December 3, 1137; at his bedside stood his son-in-law, Henry of Bavaria, husband of his only child. From Lothar's dying hand Henry received the imperial insignia and his designation as successor to the German throne. But Henry of Bavaria was not popular with his fellow princes, who moreover had cause to fear his great power since he inherited Lothar's private domains along with, possibly, his Saxon duchy and added these to his vast Bavarian and Italian holdings, while his brother Welf VI held the family allods in Swabia. Archbishop Albero of Trier manipulated the electoral assembly in 1138 through unusual procedures that assured the election of Conrad of Staufen. After some hesitation, Henry of Bavaria surrendered the royal insignia, but when Conrad demanded that he give up one of his two duchies, Henry rebelled. Conrad proclaimed the royal ban against him and declared his fiefs forfeited; Saxony was given to Albert the Bear of Brandenburg, Bavaria to Margrave Luitpold IV of Babenberg of the Bavarian East Mark. Resisting, Duke Henry concentrated his efforts against Albert but death intervened at Quedlinburg on October 20, 1139. He left a ten-year-old son Henry the Lion, his widow Gertrude, and his brother Welf.

Works About: W. Bernhardi, *Lothar von Supplinburg* (Leipzig, 1879); Otto of Freising, *The Deeds of Frederick Barbarossa*, tr. C. C. Mierow (New York, 1953); Kurt Reindel, "Heinrich X. der Stolze," *NDB* 8:343–44, and "Das welfisches Jahrhundert in Bayern," in Max Spindler, ed., *Handbuch der bayerische Gesch.* (Munich, 1971), 1:246–67; S. Riezler, *Gesch. Baierns*, 2d ed. (Stuttgart, 1927, rpr. 1964), vol. 1.   *R. H. Schmandt*

See CONRAD III; HENRY THE LION; LOTHAR II.

HERDER, JOHN GOTTFRIED (1744–1803), philosopher and critic, was born in Mohrungen, a small town in East Prussia. His father made only a meager living as a schoolmaster, sexton, and cantor. During his early schooling, Herder mastered Latin and some Greek. For a while he worked for his father's religious superior in the production of turgid books on piety. This occupation gave him access to the deacon's fine library in which he read widely.

Herder began his university career in 1762 as a medical student at Königsberg. His tendency to faint during dissections forced him to turn to theology, where he became a student of Immanuel Kant, who helped the impoverished Herder by remitting his customary lecture fees. Herder was also greatly influenced by the antirationalist philosopher, J. G. Hamann.

Herder left Königsberg late in 1764 to take a teaching post at the cathedral school in Riga in the Russian empire of Catherine II. In Riga he launched his writing career as a critic of literature and philosophy. In May 1769 the critic left Riga on a series of travels before accepting the post of tutor to the prince of Holstein-Gottorp. While convalescing in Strasbourg from an eye operation, Herder met and greatly impressed the young Goethe. In 1771 Herder became court preacher to the count of Schaumburg-Lippe at Bückeburg, where he married Caroline Flachsland (1750–1809). Despite the press of his duties, Herder managed to continue his literary career, emerging as the theorist and leader of the storm and stress movement.

After the death of Countess Sophie, his pietistic friend and benefactor at Bückeburg, Herder obtained in 1776 the post of general superintendent and court chaplain at Weimar, where he remained for the rest of his life. Although it was Goethe's influence with the court that secured the appointment, Herder later broke with the great poet. His career at Weimar was burdened with heavy administrative responsibilities and financial anxiety because of his large family of seven children. Nevertheless, he continued his research and writing, including his famous *Ideas for the Philosophy of the History of Mankind* (1784–1791) and his liberal *Letters for the Advancement of Mankind* (1793–1797). Herder also wrote several works attacking the philosophy of his former teacher, Immanuel Kant, whose ideas he found muddled and perverse. Herder's influence on many fields, especially subsequent historiography, has been enormous.

Works By: *Herders Sämtliche Werke,* ed. Bernard Suphan et al., 33 vols. (Berlin, 1877–1913).
Works About: F. M. Barnard, *Herder's Social and Political Thought* (Oxford, 1965); R. T. Clark, *Herder, His Life and Thought* (Berkeley, 1969); R. F. Ergang, *Herder and the Foundations of German Nationalism* (New York, 1966); Alexander Gillies, *Herder* (Oxford, 1945).   *J. W. Zophy*

See GOETHE; KANT.

HERMAN V (1477–1552), count of Wied and archbishop-elect/elector of Cologne from 1515 to 1547, has been viewed by modern historians as a typical representative of the German nobility's interference in the holding of Church positions in the sixteenth century. In addition to being the seat of an influential archbishopric, Cologne offered a German noble the prestigious office of imperial elector. Moreover Cologne's importance extended beyond its jurisdictional borders. As an episcopal seat, Cologne could influence the affairs of such territories as the United Duchies, Paderborn, Münster, Osnabück, and Minden. It offered an ambitious man like Herman of Wied tremendous political possibilities.

Herman of Wied was not a particularly religious man. Life, for him as for other similar churchmen, differed little from that of any secular lord. While Wied's thought was seriously influenced by Christian humanism, his education was not thorough and, above all, his theological preparation for the important position he was to hold was insufficient.

Some historians credit Herman of Wied with an "earnest desire to live up to his Christian principles" in his efforts to reform his territory. Curiously groundwork for the Catholic reform in Cologne was laid under his leadership. In March 1536 the provincial council, one of the most important pre-Tridentine synods in Germany, was held in Cologne, where later in 1544 the first permanent Jesuit settlement was established by Peter Faber. Wied also attempted to carry out Church reform in other territories influenced by Cologne, especially the united duchies of Jülich-Cleves-Berg and Mark. From December 29, 1535, to January 7, 1536, a series of negotiations took place in the town of Neuss between the representatives of the archbishop and the minister of Duke John III of the united duchies. While the duke's representatives agreed with Wied's arguments for reform, they refused to permit the archbishop to have spiritual jurisdiction within the ducal territories. John III believed that he could control the religious situation in his lands without interference from Cologne.

Yet Herman of Wied's religious zeal was more driven by necessity than genuine desire. In addition, much of the responsibility for the actual work of reform in Cologne belonged to the Erasmian theologian John Gropper (1503–1559) rather than Wied. For Wied, religion was merely an annex to his secular policy. Nowhere can this fact be more clearly seen than in his attempt to Protestantize the archbishopric in the years 1542 to 1547. Known as the Cologne crisis of 1547, Herman's plan failed, and he was formally excommunicated and deposed from his episcopal seat. For the next several years, Wied maneuvered to win back Cologne, but he had little chance of success. He died in his home territory of Wied in 1552 as a converted Lutheran.

Works About: R. Braunisch, *Zur Gesch. der Katholischen Unions–und Reformsbestrebungen von 1538 bis 1542* (Rome, 1910); G. Drouven, *Die Reformation in der Cölnischen Kirchenprovinz zur Zeit des Erzbischofes und Kurfürsten Hermann V, Graf zu Wied* (Neuss and Cologne, 1876); Leonard Ennen, *Gesch. der Stadt Köln*, 5 vols. (Cologne, 1869–1880); August Franzen, *Bischof und Reformation* (Münster, 1971), and "Innerdiözesane Hemmungen und Hindernisse der kirchlichen Reform im. 16 under 17. Jahrhunderts," in *Colonia Sacra* ed. Eduard Hegel (Cologne, 1947), vol. 1; Hermann Kelm, "Zum Begriff 'Kölner Reformation,' " *Monatshefte für Evangelische Kirchengeschichte des Rheinlandes 20–21* (1971–1972).   C. T. Eby

See COLOGNE, CRISES OF.

HOHENFRIEDBERG is a village in Silesia where the Prussians defeated an Austro-Saxon army on June 4, 1745, also known as the Battle of Striegau, during the War of the Austrian Succession. As Empress Maria Theresa still hoped to recover Silesia from the Prussian king Frederick II, an Austrian army under her brother-in-law, Prince Charles of Lorraine (1712–1780), combined with a Saxon army under the duke of Weissenfels, crossed the Riesengebirge range to advance on Breslau. Frederick advanced from Schweidnitz to attack his opponents as they debouched from the foothills at Hohenfriedberg. The bluecoats approached the laxly encamped Austro-Saxon army, itself divided by a marshy stream, in an expertly conducted night march. At 4 A.M. on June 4, the right wing overran the Spitzberg, mounting cannon on its slopes, and drove the Saxons through Pilgramshain and off to the north. Frederick then marched the left wing across the bridge at Teichau against the Austrians. Prussian cuirassiers charged the Austrian right-wing calvary, but as the cavalry engagement receded to the southwest, Frederick's army was becoming divided, and Prince Charles' infantry in the center formed up intact. But General von Gessler now sent the large Fifth Bayreuth Dragoon Regiment, fifteen hundred sabers, directly against the Austrian center. The ten squadrons slashed their way into the white-coats, riding down twenty battalions in the process, and sent the rest of the Austrian army fleeing back into the mountains. Frederick's 50,000 had taken on 66,000 enemy, and routed them with 13,176 casualties to his own 4,737.

Works About: Austrian official, *Die Kriege unter der Regierung Kaiserin Marie Theresia* (Vienna, from 1895); Prussian official, *Die Kriege Friedrichs des Grossen*, 20 vols. (Berlin, 1890–1913), esp. *Der Zweite Schlesische Krieg*, vol. 13.   *A. H. Ganz*

See AUSTRIAN SUCCESSION; FREDERICK II, THE GREAT; MARIA THERESA.

HOLBEIN, HANS THE YOUNGER (1497–1543), painter, was born in Augsburg, the son of the well-known artist, Hans Holbein the Elder (c. 1460–1524). Following his studies with his father, Holbein journeyed to Italy in 1518. In Basel where he lived for the most part from 1515 to 1526, he established excellent connections among the humanists and did book illustrations for John Froben, the publisher of Erasmus. In addition, Holbein became the favorite artist of a number of wealthy merchants and nobles. In 1526 he traveled to England and completed a number of well-received portraits, including that of Erasmus and Thomas More. Holbein returned to Basel in 1528 but left permanently for London four years later, driven out by the iconoclasm induced by the Reformation. In England he concluded his career as the court painter for King Henry VIII.

Works About: A. B. Chamberlain, *Hans Holbein the Younger* (London, 1913); Ulrich Christoffel, "Hans Holbein," *DGD*, 1:471–86; Fritz Grossman, "Holbein," *EWA*, 7:586–97; H. A. Schmid, *Hans Holbein der Jüngere*, 3 vols. (Basel, 1945–1948).   *J. W. Zophy*

See ERASMUS.

THE HOMBERG SYNOD OF 1526 was an extraordinary assembly of the estates of Hesse, which laid the groundwork for a new church-state settlement in Hesse and the establishment of an evangelical territorial church. Landgrave Philip the Magnanimous invited clergy and laymen, nobles and townsmen to the synod to resolve finally and legally religious issues and instructed them to make all decisions in accordance with Scripture.

The landgrave employed Francis Lambert of Avignon to prepare a list of propositions for discussion at the meeting and to lead the discussion. Lambert's list, called the *Paradoxa,* combined Lutheran teachings with Philip's political plans to establish a sovereign state. When the synod met (October 21–23, 1526), Lambert read his *Paradoxa* to the delegates. Adam Krafft served as translator for the reading and later discussion. Nicholas Ferber, Franciscan guardian at Marburg, led the opposition, emphasizing that the synod was illegal in the eyes of the old Church.

At the conclusion of the meeting, a committee was elected to draw up a territorial order or law: this was the *Reformation of the Hessian Church.* Above all, Hesse would have an evangelical church with all things in accordance with Scripture. The document called for an elaborate church superstructure with a powerful synod in which laymen, including the landgrave, actively participated. On the other hand, the *Reformation* also laid plans for responsibility at the congregational level. The purely religious ban was assigned to the local congregations to maintain discipline. Responsibility for school and poor relief systems of remarkable proportions was assigned to the state. The plan for implementing the new church was utopian. On a given date, following a period of preaching the pure Word, the congregations of the faithful everywhere were simply to meet and establish the church.

The *Reformation* was not implemented in that year because Martin Luther recommended against such an action. Luther's reasons are important for the history of the Empire because Hesse was the first territorial state to undertake reformation according to his teachings, and hence was exemplary. Significantly the reformer expressed no theological reservations about any particulars of the *Reformation,* the particulars were in keeping with his teachings. Rather Luther objected to the *Reformation* because the plan for the implementation of the visible church on a territorial scale was too impractical, and the whole document was too legalistic. It would be preferable to proceed gradually, with one place at a time.

Philip followed Luther's advice. The *Reformation* document was not enacted as law, and the rapid establishment of the church on a territorial scale was abandoned. The church-state settlement and most of the major particulars set forth in the *Reformation,* nevertheless, were implemented by 1532 through a series of orders executed by the princely visitations. The synodal concept remained strong and was employed in Hesse until the ultimate breakdown of relations between Philip's four heirs around 1580. Moreover it was clear to all that this was a valid, workable evangelical idea.

Works About: Günther Franz, ed., *Urkundlichen Quel. zur hess. Reformationsgesch.* (Marburg, 1954), vol. 2; Francis Lambert, "paradoxa," in Wilhelm Schmitt, *Die Synode zu Homberg und ihre Vorgeschichte* (Homberg, 1926), pp. 52–67, and "Reformatio Ecclesiarum Hassiae," in Emil Sehling, ed., *Die ev. Kirchenordnungen des XVI. Jahrhunderts,* (Tübingen, 1965), 8:45–65; Wilhelm Maurer, "Franz Lambert von Avignon und das Verfassungsideal der Reformatio ecclesiarum hassiae von 1526," *Z. für Kirchen Gesch.* 8:209–260; Gerhard Müller, "Die Synode als Fundament der ev. Kirche in Hessen," *Jb. der hess. kirchengeschichtlichen Ver.,* 27:129–46; William J. Wright, "The Homberg Synod and Philip of Hesse's Plan for a New Church-State Settlement," *SCJ* (1973) 4:23–46.   *W. J. Wright*

See KRAFFT; LAMBERT; LUTHER; PHILIP OF HESSE.

HONORIUS III (c. 1150–1227), born Cencius Savelli, became a cardinal in 1193, edited the *Liber censuum,* the Roman Church's tax register, and was elected pope on July 18, 1216. Honorius' dealings with Frederick II concerned three issues: the crusade, the relationship between the Empire and the Norman kingdom, and the rights of the Church in the Norman state.

Until the Fifth Crusade was actually underway, Honorius exerted no pressure on Frederick II to fulfill his vow on July 25, 1215, to undertake a crusade. Thereafter, at various times and with increasing impatience he accepted Frederick's excuses and then assurances that he would set out on June 24, 1219, September 29, 1219, March 21, 1220, May 1, 1220, and August 1221. By the last date, the Fifth Crusade had come to grief and Frederick had not yet participated. In continued efforts to stir him to action, Honorius confronted Frederick at conferences at Veroli (April 1222), Ferentino (March 1223), and finally San Germano (July 1225). There Honorius bound him to precise, mutually acceptable terms, enunciated in a solemn pact and sanctioned by the penalty of automatic excommunication in case of failure for any reason. Frederick promised to depart on August 15, 1227, sustain one thousand knights in the Holy Land for two years, provide transportation, and advance one hundred thousand ounces of gold to be deposited in the East. Thus Honorius made it very difficult for Frederick to postpone his obligations again.

Papal interests demanded that the two Hohenstaufen kingdoms, Sicily and the Empire, held by Frederick under different laws of succession, be kept permanently distinct. At the very start of Honorius' pontificate, he became aware of Frederick's intention to change guarantees previously made to Innocent III. Originally Frederick had assigned the Norman kingdom to his infant son, Henry, as the price of Innocent's aid in the acquisition of the German kingship and the Empire. In 1216 Frederick brought Henry to Germany. Honorius protested strenuously because this step pointed to Henry's election as German king and thus to the eventual union in his person of the two states. Although Honorius failed to prevent that election in 1220, he accepted Frederick's avowal that the two governments would be kept separate. On that basis and with Frederick's acknowledgment that Sicily was a papal fief, Honorius bestowed the imperial crown on him on November 22, 1220. Since Frederick concentrated his own political activity on Sicily for the next decade, the pope, though uneasy, could not justly complain.

Honorius was determined to preserve the freedom of episcopal elections and appeals within the Sicilian kingdom as conceded by Empress Constance to Innocent III. As soon as he became aware of Frederick's tendency to violate those concessions, Honorius protested. Frederick yielded; in 1222 he instructed his officials to respect traditional clerical rights. Honorius' patient, honest, and conciliatory attitude toward Frederick II prevented any serious rupture of their relationships. By the time of his death on March 18, 1227, Honorius understood that Frederick could not be trusted, but he himself had rather successfully maintained the Church's interests vis-à-vis the emperor.

Works About: J. Clausen, *Papst Honorius III, 1216–1227* (Bonn, 1895); H. K. Mann, *Lives of the Popes in the Early Middle Ages* (London, 1925), vol. 13; A. Keutner, *Papsttum und Krieg unter dem Pontifikat des Papstes Honorius III, 1216–1227* (Münster, 1935); W. Knabel, *Kaiser Friedrich II. und Papst Honorius III. in ihren gegenseitigen Beziehungen von der Kaiserkrönung Friedrichs bis zum Tode des Papstes, 1220–1227* (Münster, 1905); P. Pressutti, *Regesta Honorii Papae III.* 2 vols. (Rome, 1888–1895). *R. H. Schmandt*

See FREDERICK II; INNOCENT III.

HROSWITHA OF GANDERSHEIM (Roswitha) (c. 935–c. 1002), poet, dramatist, and chronicler, was a canoness at Gandersheim, one of the richest and most distinguished convents founded by the Ottonian dynasty. As a free abbey, Gandersheim was responsible to the king rather than to the pope or a bishop. The abbess had privileges that permitted her to sit in the imperial diet, administer justice in her territory, deploy troops, and coin money. Canonesses came from noble families and took vows of chastity and obedience but not poverty. The cloister had close ties with the imperial court. Hroswitha's friend and abbess, Gerberga II (c. 940–1001), was the daughter of Emperor Otto I's brother, Henry I, duke of Bavaria (c. 920–955). Bruno, archbishop of Cologne (?–965), the youngest brother of Otto I, brought many scholars to the convent. Gandersheim also benefited from the influence of Theophano (956–991), the Greek princess who married Otto II in 973 and brought the refinements and learning of the Eastern imperial court into the royal household.

Hroswitha's origins are obscure, and a number of theories about her background have been put forth. It is most probable that she came from a noble Saxon family and was placed in the convent at an early age. She was well schooled in Scripture, the legends of the saints, and early Christian writers such as Prudentius, Venantius, Fortunatus, and Boethius. Classical Latin authors, Horace, Ovid, Terence, and especially Virgil, were the models for her Latin writings.

The works of Hroswitha include eight sacred legends, six plays, two historical epics, and several shorter poems and prefaces. Above all Hroswitha's writings were Christian literature, whose purpose was to inspire and teach the reader or listener. One of the legends, *The Fall and Conversion of Theophilus*, tells of a man who enters a covenant with the devil. It is the earliest example of the Faustian theme in medieval literature. Only the chronicle of the reign of Otto I gave Hroswitha a different task from her other works. The work was commissioned by Henry I, duke of Bavaria, and Hroswitha found that sorting testimony about contemporary events was a difficult and politically sensitive task. Henry I of Bavaria had been the favorite of his mother, Matilda, who had hoped that Henry rather than his older brother, Otto I, would become emperor. The brothers were not always on good terms, and Hroswitha ends her account fairly early in the reign with the marriage of Otto I's son, Liudolf (948). In that same year Otto I, reconciled with his brother, enfeoffed Henry I with the dukedom of Bavaria.

Renaissance humanist Conrad Celtis published the first edition of Hroswitha's works in Nuremberg (1501) based on the tenth- and eleventh-century manuscripts he discovered at the monastery of St. Emmeram in Regensburg. The plays have been translated from Latin into German, English, French, Italian, and Dutch and have been performed before modern audiences.

Works By: J. Bendixen, tr., *Das älteste Drama in Deutschland: Die Comödien der Nonne Hrotswitha von Gandersheim* (Altona, 1850, 1853); Charles Mognan, tr., *Théâtre de Hrotsvitha* (Paris, 1845); O. Piltz, tr., *Die Dramen* (Leipzig, 1889); Karl Strecker, ed., *Opera*, in *Bibliotheca Teubneriana* (Leipzig, 1930); H. J. W. Tillyard, tr. *The Plays of Roswitha* (London, 1923); Paul von Winterfeld, ed., *Opera*, in *MGH, SS* (Berlin, 1902). **Works About:** Sister Mary Marguerite Butler, R.S.M., *Hrotsvitha: The Theatricality of Her Plays* (New York, 1960); Robert H. Fife, *Hroswitha of Gandersheim* (New York, 1947); Anne Lyon Haight, ed., *Hroswitha of Gandersheim: Her Life, Times, and Works, and a Comprehensive Bibliography* (New York, 1965); Bert Nagel, *Hrotsvit von Gandersheim* (Stuttgart, 1965); Rhoda-Gale Polack, "Hroswitha, A Light in the Dark Ages," *Mills Quarterly* 58 (1976);11–15.   *J. W. Gates*

See CELTIS; OTTO I; OTTO II.

HUBMAIER, BALTHASAR (1485–1528), is particularly noted for his leadership of the early Anabaptist movement in Moravia and his involvement in the early phase of the Peasants' War in the Holy Roman Empire. Born in the 1480s, Hubmaier's native town was Friedburg near Augsburg. He began his university career at Freiburg in 1503, but his education was interrupted when he left to become a schoolmaster. In 1510 he returned to Freiburg where he received his baccalaureate and was ordained a priest. It was at Freiburg that Hubmaier became an ardent admirer of John Eck, the famous opponent of Luther at the Leipzig debate. Following Eck to the University of Ingolstadt, he received his doctorate in theology and took the position of corrector at the university. Soon after he was appointed chaplain at Regensburg, where he participated actively in the expulsion of the Jews from that town. Perhaps embarrassed by his role in this incident, he left Regensburg and became pastor at Waldshut in 1521.

At Waldshut his popularity rose. Although still a loyal Catholic, Hubmaier began to question certain religious ideas in correspondence with Erasmus and through contact with the writings of Luther. Yet it was the Swiss reform under Ulrich Zwingli that influenced him. By 1523 Hubmaier had successfully reformed Waldshut. The venacular mass was introduced, fasting was abolished, and Hubmaier himself married.

In 1524 the beginnings of the Peasants' War affected him. Nearby peasants in Stühlingen revolted against their lord and marched on Waldshut for support. Hubmaier encouraged them and urged that they resist their Austrian overlords. Pressures from authorities forced him to seek temporary refuge in Schaffhausen in Switzerland, but he soon returned and helped to revise the famous Twelve Articles of Memmingen on March 1, 1525. These articles contained not only the religious grievances of the peasants but also social, political, and economic demands. Hubmaier remained in Waldshut until its capture by Austrian forces in December 1525.

Escaping to Zurich, he soon was confined in the city prison for his religious views. Although earlier he had been a supporter of Zwingli, Hubmaier had broken with him concerning the question of infant baptism. In fact Hubmaier had become an Anabaptist in April 1525. Zurich officials permitted him to debate baptism but finally refused to accept his position. Hubmaier was forced after a period of torture to recant on April 15, 1526.

Yet he persisted. In the summer of 1526 he left Zurich and traveled to Nikolsburg in Moravia where a large Anabaptist community was thriving under the protection of the lords of Liechtenstein. There he assumed leadership of the moderate wing of the Anabaptists. Unlike his opponents, such as Hans Hut, Hubmaier advocated that a true Christian must support the state and that government has a right to punish criminals and collect taxes. When Moravia passed into the hands of Ferdinand I in 1526, toleration for the Anabaptists was over. Hubmaier was turned over to the Austrian officials on charges of sedition and heresy. After enduring a heroic torture, Hubmaier was burned at the stake in Vienna on March 10, 1528.

Works By: ed. G. Westin and T. Bergsten, *Schriften* (Gütersloh, 1962). **Works About:** Josef Beck, *Die Geschichtsbücher der Wiederstaufer in Österreich-Ungarn* (Nieuwkoop, 1967); Harold S. Bender, ed., *The Mennonite Encyclopedia* (Scottdale, Pa., 1955–1959); T. Bergsten, *Balthasar Hubmaier: Seine Stellung zu Reformation und Täufertum, 1521–1528* (Cassel, 1961); William Klassen, "Speaking in Simplicity: Balthasar Hubmaier," *MQR* (1966), pp.139–47; R. A. Macoskey, "The Contemporary Relevance of Balthasar Hubmaier's Concept of the Church," *Foundations* 6 (1963); Henry C. Vedder, *Balthasar Hubmaier* (New York, 1905); George H. Williams, *The Radical Reformation* (Philadelphia, 1962).   *C. T. Eby*

See ANABAPTISM; PEASANTS' WAR; ZWINGLI.

HUMANISM was a literary movement in the Empire. Just about every aspect of it is open to contention. Considerable debate exists, for example, on its origins, characteristics, and demise. In general, it appears that its practitioners were self-defined, if they felt themselves to be humanists, they were. The advantage of an open definition is that it includes writers and others who did not write extensively but were knowledgeable and often wealthy and rather served as stimuli and patrons of humanism. In many cases these people met in a circle, or *sodalitas,* to discuss recent and ongoing literary endeavors.

Lacking a clear-cut definition of humanism, its origins are problematic. Although some scholars push the foundations back to the fourteenth century and others look to the middle of the fifteenth, there seems little dispute that there were relatively numerous humanists emerging at the end of the fifteenth and early decades of the sixteenth century. The humanists attempted to do for the Germans in the Empire what the Italian humanists had done in Italy: evoke a sense of pride in German letters and scholarship by introducing classical style and form into their compositions. Thus humanists studied classical and Christian antiquities and set about to waken German literary consciousness.

As a result of their interest in the past and probably also as a reaction to the inferiority of German scholarship vis-à-vis that associated with the Italian Renaissance, humanists began to espouse the uniqueness of the German peoples. Many felt this uniqueness had been perverted by other nationalities, particularly Latins. This perversion, they thought, had denigrated native Germanic institutions, exploited the German peoples, and kept the Empire politically divided. Popularization of these views tended to make people more conscious of their national identity and, coupled with other manifestations of social, economic, and political discontent, prepared the backdrop against which the successful drama of the Protestant Reformation was played.

Because of the existence of so many political entities within the territorial boundaries of the Empire, humanist activity never acquired a uniform character or expression. As a result of the travels of Conrad Celtis (1459–1508) and his contemporaries, humanist groups tended to spring up wherever they touched base. These associates appeared in free imperial cities, university towns, and territorial capitals. Each of these had concerns of its own, but most evinced an interest in moral philosophy, history, rhetoric, and poetry.

Much has been written about the relationship of humanism to the Reformation in the Empire, and this stemmed from the fact that many younger humanists accepted and defended Protestantism, while their older counterparts, partial at first to Luther's views, remained in the Catholic camp. Two generalizations may be suggested to explain this phenomenon. First, the views of humanists and reformers were largely dissimilar, although there remained points of contact. Humanists were skeptical, stressed ethics and education, and tended to accept the particular rather than the universal. Older humanists were not as willing as their younger associates to forgo their pursuit of letters in order to build new institutions. Second, humanists who accepted and worked to advance the Protestant Reformation harmonized their humanist views with the new religious teachings. Thus some humanist themes persisted during the Reformation. Others did not, and from this point of view the Reformation brought about the demise of humanism.

Works About: Frank L. Borchardt, *German Antiquity in Renaissance Myth* (Baltimore and London, 1971); James M. Kittelson, "Humanism and the Reformation in Germany," *CEH* 9 (1976); 303–22; Bernd Moeller, "The German Humanists and the Beginnings of the Reformation," *Imperial Cities and the Reformation: Three Essays,* tr. H. C. Erik Midelfort and Mark U. Edwards (Philadelphia, 1972), pp. 19–38; Lewis W. Spitz, *Conrad Celtics, the German Arch-Humanist* (Cambridge, 1957), and *The Religious Renaissance of the German Humanists* (Cambridge, 1963).   *P. N. Bebb*

See CELTIS; ERASMUS; HUTTEN; LUTHER; MELANCHTHON; REUCHLIN; SCHEURL; SPENGLER; WIMPFELING.

HUS, JOHN (c. 1372–1415), Church reformer, was born in the hamlet of Husinec in southern Bohemia to a family of modest circumstances. In 1390 he entered the University of Prague founded by Emperor Charles IV. Hus stayed on at the Charles University as a lecturer and popular preacher. After 1402 he became the regular preacher at the Bethlehem chapel and was so eloquent and moving that even Queen Sophia of Bohemia, sister-in-law of the emperor, came frequently to hear him.

Many in the university community were concerned about corruption in the Church, and there was a growing movement for reform even before Jerome of Prague introduced the ideas of the English reformer John Wycliffe. Hus was sympathetic to much that he found in Wycliffe and added his own concerns about the nature of the Church and the need for reform. However, many of the German professors at the university were appalled by the ideas of Wycliffe and the other reformers. The dispute threatened to tear the university apart, particularly as it moved from purely academic concerns to matters of who was to control the university and the Church in Bohemia.

Finally in January 1409 King Wenceslaus, the emperor's brother and a supporter of moderate Church reform, issued a decree that gave the Czech student "nation" at the university three votes to the German one, a complete reversal of the prevailing situation. Several thousand students and professors, mostly Germans, left Prague and founded a new university in Leipzig, Saxony. The popular Hus was elected rector of the university on October 17, 1409.

Hus still had many enemies among the local clergy, and they urged Archbishop Zbynek of Prague to proceed against him as a dangerous heretic in the Wycliffite mold. In July 1410 Zbynek ordered Wycliffe's books burned and excommunicated Hus. The Czech persisted in preaching at the Bethlehem chapel until an interdict of June 20, 1411, stopped all religious services in Prague. At the suggestion of King Wenceslaus, Hus left the city in October 1412 in order to provide relief for the people of Prague from the effects of the decree. For the next year and a half, he preached and wrote in southern Bohemia, winning many new followers to the cause of Church reform.

Meanwhile his opponents pressed charges of heresy and contumacy against Hus at the papal court. Hus appealed the charges to a council of the Church meeting at Constance. Despite the promise of a safe conduct from Emperor

Sigismund, Hus had a foreboding of evil as he set for Constance in October, 1414. When he arrived at Constance, Hus found himself confined by order of the bishop of Constance, and his case was not formally heard until June 1415. Among his prosecutors were two eminent French prelates, Pierre d'Ailly and John Gerson. Basically the Church hierarchy feared Hus' conception of the Church as the congregation of the faithful, those predestined by God to be saved. This view rendered the pope and the cardinals superfluous in connection with salvation, and they could even be a hindrance to the Gospel. When Hus tried to speak in his own defense, outraged churchmen shouted him down. He concluded his remarks by observing, "In such a council as this I had expected to find more propriety, piety, and order." Emperor Sigismund privately advised the council not to let Hus go, and he was overheard by several Bohemians, who reported the emperor's treachery.

Pierre d'Ailly presented the council's final decisions on Hus. The Bohemian was ordered to confess his errors, promise never to hold them or teach them again, and make a public recantation. When Hus refused to buckle under enormous pressure applied over a four-week period, he was committed to the devil and turned over to the secular arm to be burned at the stake. Shortly before his death, Hus said, "In the truth of that Gospel which before now I have written, taught, and preached, I now joyfully die."

The trial and death of the man who had become a national hero and the perfidy of the emperor caused an enormous outrage in Bohemia; 452 nobles and knights sent an indignant protest to the council. Emperor Sigismund foolishly replied that they would very soon "drown all Wycliffites and Hussites." Rebellion now spread throughout Bohemia, and Wenceslaus was powerless to calm the storm.

A crusade against the Hussites was proclaimed in March 1520 by Pope Martin V and Emperor Sigismund. The Czechs found a skilled military leader in John Zizka (1376–1424) and managed to repel the invaders led by Sigismund. Three more invasions were launched as the emperor became obsessed with reasserting his authority over Bohemia. Despite fierce fighting and the differences between the Hussites, Sigismund failed to destroy the Hussites militarily. The Hussites had divided into two major groups: the Utraquists, a moderate group who believed in communion in both kinds, and the Taborites, who took their name from the city of Tabor, which became their center. The Taborites recognized only two sacraments and wanted simple ceremonies. They were less inclined to compromise with the Hussite opponents and for a time under Zizka's leadership had the upper hand in the civil war. Ten years after the death of Zizka, the Utraquists scored a decisive victory over the Taborites at the Battle of Lipan in 1434.

Once in control of Bohemia and having beaten the forces of Sigismund on four occasions, the Utraquists moved to achieve peace and official recognition from the Church. This was accomplished at the Council of Basel in 1436. Although Emperor Sigismund was finally allowed to enter Prague, which had been denied him for sixteen bloody years, the Utraquists remained the official church of Bohemia until after the Battle of the White Mountain in 1620 during the Thirty Years War. Bohemian church groups tracing their origins back to John Hus have survived to the present day. Hus inspired many, including Martin Luther, who at Leipzig in 1519 proclaimed, "We are all Hussites!"

Works By: *John Hus, The Church,* tr. David Schaff (New York, 1915); *The Letters of John Hus,* tr. H. B. Workman and R. M. Pope (London, 1904). **Works About:** Frederick G. Heymann, *John Ziška and the Hussite Revolution* (Princeton, 1955); *John Hus at the Council of Constance,* ed. and tr. Matthew Spinka (New York, 1965); Howard Kaminsky, *A Hist. of the Hussite Revolution* (Berkeley, 1967); Josef Macek, *The Hussite Movement in Bohemia* (Prague, 1958); Franz Machilek, "Böhmen, Polen und die hussitische Revolution," *Z. für Ostforschung* 23 (1973):401–30; O. Od-ložolik, *John Hus* (Chicago, 1953); M. Spinka, *John Hus* (Princeton, 1968); Melchior Vischer, *Jan Hus, sein Leben und seine Zeit,* 2 vols. (Frankfurt am Main, 1958); P. de Vooght, *L'herésie de Jean Huss* (Louvain, 1960); J. K. Zeman, *The Hussite Movement and the Reformation: A Biblio-graphical Study Guide* (Ann Arbor, 1977).   *J. W. Zophy*

See CHARLES IV; CONCILIARISM; LUTHER; SIGISMUND; THIRTY YEARS WAR.

HUT, HANS (c. 1495–1527), was the most successful and one of the most radical Anabaptist evangelists in south and central Germany. Revolutionary teachings attributed to Hut were largely responsible for the fierce repression of Anabaptism throughout Europe, with rebaptism being condemned by the diets of Speyer and Augsburg in 1529 and 1530, with punishment by death. Much controversy remains as to the exact nature of Hut's teachings, but their chiliastic bent is certain.

By trade a bookseller from Bibra in Franconia, Hut had early contact with the revolutionary peasant leader and theologian Thomas Müntzer. In 1525, Müntzer entrusted Hut with the task of seeing to print in Nuremberg a radical treatise he had written. Later Hut appeared in the area of Frankenhausen where the peasant armies were assembled and seems to have preached revolutionary sermons in the vicinity, urging peasants to rise up and kill their rulers. Little is known of Hut's career between the defeat of the peasants in the spring of 1525 and his appearance in Augsburg in May 1527. There he was reportedly rebap-tized by the theologian Hans Denck. From that point until his death in 1527, Hut embarked upon a remarkably successful preaching career, which established him as a major Anabaptist leader.

The distinctive features of Hut's teachings, which created great controversy among his fellow Anabaptists and which caused the secular authorities to react so harshly, included the views that all true Christians must share in Christ's suffering and martyrdom through baptism by spirt, water, and blood and that all property should be forsaken and shared equally by true believers. In addition, Hut taught that the end of the world and Day of Judgment were imminent; they would come three and one-half years after the Peasants' Revolt of 1525 and be initiated by the slaying of the godless by those truly baptized as children of God. Whether Hut actually intended to incite his followers to rebellion is questionable, and the evidence suggests that Denck had an ameliorating influence on Hut, causing him to spiritualize his eschatological views.

Nevertheless followers of Hut confessed, albeit under torture, that total social and political revolution was the ultimate aim of the movement. The alarm caused by such views among secular authorities was immediate and widespread. In turn, a split among Anabaptist leaders occurred over Hut's extreme views, leading to a famous dispute between Hut and Balthasar Hubmaier, the acknowledged father of south German Anabaptism, in Nikolsburg, Moravia.

Finally in August 1527, numerous Anabaptist leaders assembled in Augsburg at the so-called Martyrs' Synod to attempt to iron out differences. The meeting ended with the mass arrest of many participants by the Augsburg authorities. According to authorities, Hut was killed while attempting to escape, but his teachings continued to influence certain of the Anabaptist sects.

Works About: Herbert Klassen, "The Life and Teachings of Hans Hut," *MQR*, 33 (1959); Christian Meyer, "Zur Gesch. der Wiedertäufer in Oberschwaben. I. Die Anfänge des Wiedertäufertums in Augsburg," *Z. des Hist. ver. für Schwaben und Neuburg 1* (1874); Karl Schornbaum, ed., *Quel. zur Gesch. der Taüfer*, vol. 5: *Bayern* (Gütersloh, 1951) and *Quel. zur Gesch. der Wiedertäufer*, vol. 2: *Markgraftum Brandenburg*, pt. 1, *Bayern* (Leipzig, 1934); Gottfried Seebass, *Müntzers Erbe: Werke, Leben und Theologie des Hans Hut* (Gütersloh, 1974); Paul Wappler, ed., *Die Täuferbewegung in Thuringen von 1526–1584* (Jena, 1913).   *D. M. Hockenbery*

See ANABAPTISM; DENCK; HUBMAIER; MÜNTZER.

HUTTEN, ULRICH VON (1488–1523), humanist, author, knight, and supporter of the Reformation, began life as a member of an ancient but impoverished family of the Franconian lesser nobility. When Ulrich was eleven his parents placed him in the monastery school at Fulda apparently convinced that he was not strong enough to have a career as a knight. Six years later he left the cloister before taking his vows to begin a career as an itinerant scholar, much to the displeasure of his family. Between 1505 and 1511, Hutten studied at the universities of Cologne, Erfurt, Frankfurt, Greifswald, Wittenberg, and Vienna, becoming enthused by the new learning of the humanists. He also began writing poetry and made a good friend of the humanist Crotus Rubeanus.

From Vienna he traveled to Italy, his poverty forcing him for a while into service as a mercenary. By 1513 he had returned to Germany in the service of Eitelwolf von Stein and Albert, bishop of Magdeburg and Mainz. Embittered by the murder of his cousin Hans by Duke Ulrich of Württemberg, who coveted the victim's wife, Hutten launched a series of devastating literary attacks, *Exposures of Ulrich* in May 1515. He also wrote a well-received dialogue, *Phalarismus*, against tyranny. Now reconciled to his family, Ulrich returned to Italy, where he studied law and became proficient in Greek.

His growing literary reputation won him praise from Erasmus and the designation poet laureate from Emperor Maximilian in August 1517. Although strongly Germanic, Hutten was intrigued by the idea of a universal Roman Empire. He saw the office of the emperor as the embodiment of the virtues of the German people, who were the heirs of the ancient Romans. He was hopeful that the Empire would renew the virility of the German people. His hopes for a revived, universal Empire were dashed by the failure of Maximilian's Italian policy. By 1518 Hutten's emphasis in politics had shifted to a more nationally based Empire.

In late 1517 he entered the service of Archbishop Albert of Mainz as a councillor, which gave him the chance to study and write while meeting important personalities on court business. The pen was exchanged for the sword in March 1519 as Hutten gladly joined the successful campaign against his old enemy Duke Ulrich of Württemberg.

During the preparations for the campaign, Hutten became intrigued by the knight Franz von Sickingen, who promised to help his embattled hero, John Reuchlin. Hutten, who felt a strong sense of humanist solidarity, had been one of the anonymous authors of the biting satire, *Letters of the Obscure Men,* which had so thoroughly ridiculed the scholastic opponents of Reuchlin and Hebrew studies and had set many to laughing on the eve of the Reformation. Hutten later broke with Reuchlin when the latter publicly condemned Martin Luther's teachings.

The humanist knight had begun to see in Luther a fellow fighter for German freedom from the yoke of papal exploitation. He eagerly seized upon Luther's conception of the priesthood of all believers. In his pamphlet *The Roman Trinity,* Hutten called for the subordination of the papacy to the Empire. His pro-Luther writings and condemnations of the Church earned him a spot on the bulls against Luther. Hutten then withdrew to the safety of Sickingen's castle at Ebernburg, where he continued his polemics and converted his host to Luther's cause.

Disappointed by Emperor Charles's condemnation of Luther at the diet of Worms (1521), Hutten made several raids against Church property and hoped to join Sickingen in his campaign against the archbishop of Trier, Richard von Greiffenklau, but was prevented by recurring illness induced by syphilis, which had troubled him throughout much of his adult life. Following Sickingen's disastrous and fatal defeat, Hutten fled to Basel, then to Mühlhausen, and finally found refuge from his enemies in Zwingli's Zurich. There he died at age thirty-five seeking medical help from a doctor on Lake Zurich.

Works By: Ulrich von Hutten, *Dtsch. Schriften,* ed. H. Mettke (Leipzig, 1972); *Dtsch. Schriften,* ed. Peter Ukena (Munich, 1970); *Opera,* ed. Eduard Böcking, 5 vols. (Leipzig, 1859–1861); *Werke,* 2 vols. (Berlin, 1970). **Works About:** Joseph Benzing, *Ulrich von Hutten und seine Drucker* (Wiesbaden, 1956); Thomas Best, *The Humanist Ulrich von Hutten: A Reappraisal of His Humor* (Chapel Hill, 1969); Otto Flake, *Ulrich von Hutten* (Berlin, 1929); Hajo Holborn, *Ulrich von Hutten and the German Reformation* (New York, 1965); Paul Kalkoff, *Ulrich von Hutten* (Leipzig, 1920); L. W. Spitz, *The Religious Renaissance of the German Humanists* (Cambridge, Mass., 1963); D. F. Strauss, *Ulrich von Hutten: His Life and Times* (London, 1874); Fritz Walser, *Die politsche Entwicklung Ulrich von Huttens* (Berlin, 1928); Sam Wheelis, "Ulrich von Hutten: Representative of Patriotic Humanism," in Gerhart Hoffmeister, ed., *The Renaissance and Reformation in Germany* (New York, 1977). *J. W. Zophy*

See CHARLES V; HUMANISM; LUTHER; MAXIMILLIAN I; REUCHLIN; SICKINGEN; ULRICH OF WÜRTTEMBERG; ZWINGLI.

i

ILGEN, HENRY RÜDIGER VON (d. 1728), served Frederick William, the Great Elector, Frederick III, elector of Brandenburg (later Frederick I, king in Prussia), and Frederick William I. He came from an obscure family in Minden, Westphalia. After training for the diplomatic service by studying law and political science and by traveling throughout Europe, he served as secretary to Franz von Meinders during the peace negotiations with France in 1678. The Great Elector appointed him privy secretary in the privy council chancery (1679) and privy chamber secretary (1683). A brilliant and indefatigable worker, Ilgen wrote all of his own letters. He was gifted with a rare intelligence that is reflected in his writings. His accomplishments and drive made him by 1699 one of the most influential ministers at court. Although never a member of Frederick I's Council of State, he directed the formulation of Brandenburg foreign policy and carried on all correspondence and negotiations with foreign powers and ambassadors. He was instrumental in obtaining the royal title of king in Prussia for Frederick, who recognized his services by appointing him a privy councillor and admitting him to the cabinet. After Wartenberg's fall in 1711, Ilgen rose to first position in the cabinet. With the aid of Ernest von Kameke and Ludwig von Printzen and the support of the crown prince, he laid the groundwork for some of the later reorganization of the state administration under Frederick William I. He began his career as a cabinet secretary and ended it as principal minister of state under Frederick William I.

Works About: Charles-Lewis, baron de Poellnitz, *Mémoires* (London, 1745); Christophe, count von Dohna, *Mémoires originaux sur la règne et la cour de Frederic I, Roi de Prusse* (Berlin, 1833). Reinhold August Dorwart, *The Administrative Reforms of Frederick William I of Prussia* (Cambridge, 1953): Linda Frey and Marsha Frey, "The Foreign Policy of Frederick I: A Fatal Vacillation?" *East European Quarterly* (1975): 259–69: Walter Koch, *Hof-und Regierungsverfassung König Friedrick I von Preussen* (1699–1710) (Breslau, 1926): Carl von Noorden, *Europäische Gesch, im achtzehnten Jahrhundert* (Dusseldorf, 1894): Albert Waddington, *Histoire de Prusse* (Paris, 1911). *L. S. Frey and M. L. Frey*

See FREDERICK III, ELECTOR; FREDERICK WILLIAM, ELECTOR: FREDERICK WILLIAM I: WARTENBERG.

IMPERIAL CAMERAL COURT (Reichskammergericht), a supreme court for the Empire, was created by an act of the diet of Worms in 1495 as part of the imperial reform movement, whose leader was Archbishop Berthold von Henneberg of Mainz (1484–1504), archchancellor of the Empire. This court was distinguished from its predecessors in that it was a court of the Empire, not one of the emperor's attached to his person. The diet that created the court established the procedure for staffing and housing it and the financial means for maintaining it. Since one-half of the associate judges nominated to sit on the court were to be trained in Roman law, the court became a significant element in the reception of Roman law in Germany. Although subject to the vicissitudes of imperial politics, the court continued to function with a few exceptions (for example from 1519 to 1521 and from 1544 to 1548) until the end of the Empire in 1806.

The imperial reform movement resulted from the inefficiency, if not ineptitude, of the Empire's sovereigns in the fifteenth century. Foremost among these was Emperor Frederick III (1440–1493) whose virtual abdication of imperial responsibilities led to a loss of respect for the emperor and a loss of confidence in imperial organs. The emperor's personal court of justice *(Hofgericht)*, staffed by his own nominees and dependent on him, suffered from this loss and fell into disuse; later, toward the end of the sixteenth century, it reappeared in the form of the Imperial Aulic Council *(Reichshofrat)*. From this time on competition existed between the Imperial Cameral Court and the Aulic Council, with the latter gradually superseding the former in importance.

The diet that voted the supreme court into existence provided for the estates' control of it, and because Emperor Maximilian I (1493–1519) needed the support of the diet for his own programs, he assented to the estates' provisions. These allowed the emperor to appoint the chief justice—who had to be a prince and belong to the higher nobility—and two presidents who watched over the business of the senates. Associate justices were nominated by two categories of imperial estates, the electoral college and the imperial circles *(Reichskreise)*, the latter of which included the Habsburgs. Originally fixed at sixteen, these associate judges increased in number during the sixteenth century and finally reached as many as fifty in 1648. The estates also provided for a chancellory under the supervision of the elector of Mainz and for the various court officials, such as procurators and advocates, concerned with litigation.

With regard to residence and maintenance, the first years of the court's existence were tenuous. In the reconstitution of the court at the diet of Worms in 1521, it was tied closely to the Imperial Council of Regency *(Reichsregiment)*, resident in Nuremberg. Subsequently both organs were transferred to Esslingen. It was not until the demise of the Council of Regency, however, and the removal of the court to Speyer in 1526 that it assumed independent action. It remained in Speyer until 1693 and then moved to Wetzlar, where it stayed until 1806. In respect to finances the estates at Worms in 1495 voted the Common Penny tax, part of the income from which was to defray the court's expenses. With the discontinuation of this tax in 1499, diets proposed subsidies for its maintenance, and the princes who had the most to gain by its existence began to dominate the court. In some regards the Imperial Cameral Court became the princes' superior court of justice.

At its inception the estates voted that half of the judges had to be trained in Roman law. The remainder had to be knights. By 1555 the diet decided that all of the judges had to be knowledgeable in this law. Such a shift indicated a growing juridical reliance on Roman legal techniques, which were regarded not as an alien importation but as a complement to native Germanic law. Roman law as evinced by this court had its greatest impact in the area of procedure, and this became one of the reasons for the decline of the court's effectiveness. Complaints and evidence had to be written, and this led to indeterminable delays. Almost from the beginning, litigation overburdened court personnel. As a consequence litigious parties sought remedies outside the court. In some cases this resulted in supplications and appeals made directly to diets in an attempt to bypass the supreme court. In others this led to stricter enforcement in territories that had received privileges of *de non appellando* and *de non evocando,* that is, privileges that prohibited appeals to a superior court and prohibited subjects from appearing before a foreign court. Gradually, however, local and territorial courts adopted the principles and procedures of the Imperial Cameral Court.

Works About: Hermann Conrad, *Dtsch. Rechtsgesch.* (Kárlsruhe, 1966), vol. 2; Hist. Kommission bei der Bayerischen Akademie der Wissenschaften, ed., *DRTA jüngere Reihe: DRTA unter Karl V* (Munich, 1893–, rpr.1962–), vols. 1–4, 7, 8; Hajo Holborn, *A Hist. of Modern Germany*, vol. 1: *The Reformation* (New York. 1959); Otto Koser, ed., *Repertorium der Akten des Reichskammergericht,* 2 vols. (Heppenhaim, 1933–1936); Wolfgang Sellert, *Über zie Zuständigkeitsabgrenzung von Reichshofrat und Reichskammergericht* "Üntersuchungen zur dtsch. Staatsund Rechtsgeschichte," n. F., vol. 4 (Aalen, 1965); Rudolf Smend, *Das Reichskammergericht, Gesch, und Verfassung* (Weimar, 1911, rpr. 1965).   P. N. Bebb

See BERTHOLD; COMMON PENNY; ESSLINGEN; FREDERICK III; IMPERIAL COUNCIL OF REGENCY; MAXIMILIAN I; ROMAN LAW.

IMPERIAL CITIES (Frei-und Reichsstädte) received charters of freedom that made them subject directly to the emperor but independent of any other political power. Emperors granted these charters to certain important cities to ensure their continual support in times of difficulty. Thus their freedom was dependent upon faithful adherence to the emperor (*Kaisertreu*). The golden age of these cities was the thirteenth and fourteenth centuries, some remained important in the fifteenth and sixteenth centuries, and a few were significant after the Peace of Westphalia in 1648. From the fifteenth century on, however, they encountered increasing hostility from surrounding territorial princes who were jealous of the communes' independence and wealth. The princes used their support of the emperor's policies as a fulcrum by which they gained his assent to expand at the expense of the cities.

In 1489 the cities acquired the right to sit as the third college of the *Reichstag,* or diet. Here they were divided into two "banks," Rhenish and Swabian. From this time on, their power waned in contrast to that of the other two colleges. Nevertheless many of the cities played a major role in the Reformation by introducing Protestantism, and a few including Nuremberg, Strasbourg, and

Frankfurt am Main, were harbingers of the future. Like almost every other institution of the Holy Roman Empire, however, the constitutional status of the cities remained problematic.

Works About: M. M. Postan, E. E. Rich, and Edward Miller, eds., *Economic Organization and Policies in the Middle Ages,* vol. 3 of *The Cambridge Economic Hist. of Europe,* eds. M. M. Postan and H. J. Hagakkuk, (Cambridge, England, 1963); Richard Schmidt, *Dtsch. Reichsstädte* (Munich, 1957); Bernd Moeller, *Imperial Cities and the Reformation: Three Essays,* tr. H. C. Erik Midelfort and Mark U. Edwards (Philadelphia, 1972).   *P. N. Bebb*

See AUGSBURG: COLOGNE: FRANKFURT: NÖRDLINGEN; NUREMBERG: STRASBOURG; ULM.

IMPERIAL COUNCIL OF REGENCY (Reichsregiment), an executive organ, was created in 1500 and re-created in 1521 as part of the imperial reform movement to rule in conjunction with the emperor. If successful in its first installation, conciliar regency government would probably have brought about the demise of the emperor's power and begun a new epoch in German constitutional history. Sharing power, however, was neither the emperor's desire nor, apparently, the estates'. In both cases the Imperial Council of Regency collapsed, the first time in 1502 and the second in 1531. The causes for the lack of success were similar: lack of money, no independent source of authority, and disinterest.

The first Council of Regency was the creation of the diet of Augsburg in 1500, although the plan for it had been put forth at Worms in 1495; at Worms, however, the recalcitrance of Emperor Maximilian I (1493–1519) delayed its institutionalization. By an act of July 1500, the diet formed the council, which was to act as coruler of the Empire. Maximilian assented to the act because he needed the estates' support for his foreign policies. The ensuing council consisted of twenty members, including an elector and representatives of the other estates and imperial circles (*Reichskreise*), which functioned under the presidency of the emperor or his representative. From the onset the council, resident at Nuremberg, tended to act without the consent of the emperor, whose own role was limited. Due to the problematic constitutional structure of the Empire, which among other things raised the question of a diet's binding authority on the emperor, Maximilian declared this experiment in conciliar government at an end early in 1502 and ordered the return of the council's seal.

Following the death of Maximilian the electors extracted from Charles V (1519–1556) a capitulation of election by which Charles promised to re-create the council. This he did at his first diet held at Worms in 1521. The model of the renewed Council of Regency was that of 1500, although there were some adjustments, which better ensured the emperor's control of this organ. Charles specified that the council had authority only during his absence from the Empire, that there were to be two additional appointees nominated by him, and that his brother Ferdinand was to be governor of this body. Nuremberg again became the seat of the council, which remained there until the third diet of Nuremberg in 1524 transferred it to Esslingen, and then the diet of Speyer in 1526 moved it to Speyer. The impotence of the council became manifest during the great struggles of the early 1520s—the Reformation, the Peasants' War, and internal feuds—and by 1524 it was virtually devoid of power. When Charles returned to the Empire in 1530 and Ferdinand was elected king in 1531, the council passed into oblivion.

Works About: Adolph Grabner, *Zur Gesch. des zweiten Nürnberger Reichsregimentes 1521–1523,* Hist. Studien, no. 41 (Berlin, 1903, rpr. 1965); Hist. Kommission bei der Bayerischen Akademie der Wissenschaften, ed., *DRTA jüngere Reihe: DRTA unter Karl V,* (Munich, 1893–, rpr. 1962–), vols. 1–4, 7, 8; Viktor Kraus, *Das Nürnberger Reichsregiment, Grundung und Verfall 1500–1502* (Innsbruck, 1883, rpr. 1969); Julius Volk, *Die Kirchenpolitik des zweiten Nürnberger Reichsregiments von seinen ersten Anfängen an bis zu seiner Verlegung nach Esslingen 1521–1524* (Weida in Thuringia, 1910).   *P. N. Bebb*

See BERTHOLD; CHARLES VI; ESSLINGEN; FERDINAND I; MAXIMILIAN I; NUREMBERG; SPEYER, DIET OF 1526; WORMS.

The **IMPERIAL POSTAL SERVICE** was established in the late fifteenth century by Maximilian I who appointed John von Taxis as the first imperial master of posts as early as 1489 or possibly before. Although there had been other postal services in the Germanies and other lands under the Empire before this, the necessity of an imperial service became paramount for two reasons: the emperor's domestic control and more important, the fact that the Turks seemed bent on the destruction of Christendom. Thus regular diplomatic communications with the various princes of the Christian West became vital.

The fortunes of the Taxis family as postmasters of Empire rose and fell with the fortunes of the Habsburgs over the centuries. Of Lombard origin, various members of the family had seen royal service and had experience in laying posts in northern Italy and the Tyrol. Franz von Taxis was appointed Captain and Master of Our Posts at Ghent by Philip the Fair in 1505, and as the Habsburg influence spread, so routes for imperial posts were established on a regular basis to the courts of the French and Spanish kings, and to the pope in Rome.

The following timetable gives an idea of the desired speed of delivery of information from Brussels, which became the headquarters of the imperial postal system when John Baptista von Taxis was made general master of posts of the Low Countries under Charles V: Brussels to Innsbruck, five and a half days in summer and six and a half days in winter; Brussels to Paris, forty-four hours; and Brussels to Granada, fifteen days.

The imperial system may have been a diplomatic success, but it was a financial failure. The emperor, therefore, gave the family the right to open the post to all, with the reservation that imperial orders and wishes had priority. Thus, what had been solely a royal communications service became a public postal system.

It is remarkable how much of a family affair the imperial postal service was. John Baptista von Taxis was Charles V's master of posts, while his son Leonard managed the office for Ferdinand I; Gabriel, uncle of Franz, was postmaster in Innsbruck for seven years, John was at Augsburg, Simon was correo mayor in Spain, and his sister was also named in the contract. The list could be extended. In 1608 they were titled. Seven years later the postal system of the Empire was given to the family as a hereditary fief, and in 1624 they were raised to the status of counts of Thurn and Taxis.

The virtual monopoly of the Taxis family of the imperial posts was challenged most successfully by the Dutch during their revolt in the sixteenth century. In the seventeenth century the emperors supported the Taxis who came to run a service involving some twenty thousand men with their horses, and a communications network spread throughout Europe. The emperors recognized the worth of the Taxis family, and members of the family were raised to princes of the Empire at the end of the century. Postal routes that had previously been contracted for over a period of years were granted as a fief from the throne after 1700. It is true, however, that in spite of the imperial system's being closely controlled by the family, the other princes of the Empire, ever jealous of their perquisites, questioned the right of the Taxis family to lay posts through their lands, especially when it became clear how lucrative the imperial postal monopoly was. However, Leopold I in 1698 gave out regulations that supported the Taxis-run imperial system. These *Reichspostordnung* were confirmed by Joseph I, and further details were included under Charles VI.

Wars, too, disrupted the imperial system, but, in spite of a move of the headquarters from Brussels to Frankfurt during the War of the Spanish Succession, the Taxis' monopoly of the imperial posts in the Low Countries was regained in 1714. Further disruptions in the imperial service occurred in the midcentury wars, although Maria Theresa's very difficult position in Mitteleuropa forced her to increase the imperial posts to Trieste and Prague.

At the end of the eighteenth century as the revolutionary wars cut into the power of the Holy Roman emperor, so local posts replaced the Taxis' imperial system. When the Rhine became the new border between France and Germany in 1801 by the Treaty of Luneville, the Taxis family lost the lucrative monopoly west of the Rhine. In spite of a number of postal agreements, members of the family made with different German states, the imperial postal system fell with the 1806 abdication of the Holy Roman Emperor and the creation of the Confederation of the Rhine.

Works About: W. Beck, "Ein Postmonopol der Taxis im früheren Kirchenstaat 1522/23," *L'Union Postale* 85 (1960): 78–82; E. F. Hurt, "Pioneers of the Post," *American Philatelist* 65 (1951): 141–47, and "Thurn and Taxis," in *Billig's Philatelic Handbook,* 8:88–108; C. F. Müller, *Die Fürstlich Thurn und Taxis' schen Posten und Posttaxen* (Jena, 1845); F. Ohmann, *Die Anfänge des Postwesens und die Taxis* (Leipzig, 1909); J. Rübsam, "Francis von Taxis, the Founder of the Modern Post, and Johann Baptista von Taxis, His Nephew, 1491–1541," *L'Union Postale* 17 (1892): 122–26, and *Johann Baptista von Taxis: Ein Staatsmann und Militär unter Philipp II. und Philipp III., 1530–1610* (Freiburg im Bresgau, 1889); A. D. Smith, *The Development of Rates of Postage* (London, 1917).   *E. J. B. Allen*

See CHARLES V; CHARLES VI; JOSEPH I; LEOPOLD I; MARIA THERESA.

IMPERIAL REGALIA (**Reichskleinodien**) by the fifteenth century consisted of the octagonal imperial crown of Otto I; the sword and ring of Charlemagne; a scepter; an orb; a star-strewn mantle; and such religious relics as thorns from the crown of Christ, a chip from the cross of Christ, and the holy lance that had pierced Christ's side. These items plus other treasures were placed in Nuremberg in 1424 for safekeeping and remained there until 1796 when they eventually found their way to Vienna. The imperial regalia were utilized for important imperial ceremonies, such as the crowning of the emperor designate as king of the Romans or for an imperial coronation. At such events, a throne from Goslar was often used; it had been used by Henry IV, Philip of Swabia, Otto IV, and Frederick I.

The imperial regalia had enormous symbolic value and did a great deal to keep the imperial traditions alive. For example, the imperial crown of the Holy Roman Empire had an octagonal form which related to the Heavenly Jerusalem, a bow suggesting world dominion, and a cross of Christ emblematic of the emperor of heaven. The imperial crown of Otto I, therefore, embodied the Empire in itself; to possess the crown was to be in possession of the Empire.

In addition to this heavenly hat or crown, the emperor's orb or sphere was of great symbolic importance. When the orb was placed in the emperor's hands as a globe, some of the attributes of the Roman god Jupiter were said to be his. However, for the most part, pagan traditions gave way to Christian as was indicated in the emperor's vestments, which were those of a high priest. If his star-covered mantle suggests that he ruled over the cosmos, the emperor did so as Christ's vicar. The sword of Charlemagne reminded the emperor that he too must defend the faith, and the faith's relics and traditions. All of the items in the imperial regalia helped unite symbolically the many traditions embodied in the Holy Roman Empire.

Works About: H. Fillitz, *Die Insignien und Kleinodien des Heiligen Romisches Reiches* (Vienna, 1954); F. Heer, *The Holy Roman Empire,* tr. Janet Sondheimer (New York, 1968); P. E. Schramm, *Sphaira, Globus und Reichsapfel* (Stuttgart, 1958); Julia Schnelbögl, "Die Reichskleinodien in Nürnberg, 1424–1523," *MVGN* 47 (1956): 446–51.   *J. W. Zophy*

See AACHEN; CHARLEMAGNE; NUREMBERG; OTTO I; TITLES; VIENNA.

INNOCENT III (1161–1261), Lothario de Segni, became pope on January 8, 1198. Educated in theology at Paris and law at Bologna, he was made a cardinal in 1189. Innocent's pontificate coincided with a period of weakness in the Empire and in the Hohenstaufen dynasty, a situation that allowed him to exert great influence on German affairs in the advancement of papal policies on both sides of the Alps.

Innocent III's first concern was the late emperor Henry VI's three-year-old son, Frederick of Sicily, whose mother Constance severed all relations with the Empire as soon as her husband died. In the few months before her own death, she acknowledged the feudal dependence of Sicily on the pope and granted to Innocent control of the Sicilian Church, all in order to safeguard her son's throne. When she died (1199), Innocent became guardian of the child king by the terms of her testament as well as by feudal law. Until December 26, 1208, when Frederick came of age, Innocent struggled successfully to preserve royal authority against Walter of Palear's governing council of local barons and, on the other hand, various German captains, Markward of Anweiler the foremost, whose authority derived from Henry VI or Philip of Swabia.

In the Empire Innocent was initially a passive witness to the disputed election of 1198. The civil war there brought the Hohenstaufen faction supporting Philip of Swabia into conflict with the Welf party that promoted Otto of Brunswick. Quickly made aware of the controversy, Innocent ignored requests from several quarters for his intervention as judge between the candidates. Meanwhile he used the opportunity and took advantage of the anti-German sentiment in north-central Italy to consolidate papal control over many areas that had been disputed between papacy and Empire: the exarchate of Ravenna, the Pentapolis, the march of Ancona, the duchy of Spoleto, the lands of the Countess Matilda, and the county of Bertinoro. Thereafter it was one of Innocent's main goals to retain the rule of these provinces. This consideration shaped his attitude toward the German election dispute, which elicited from him eventually a number of statements revealing his theory of the relationship of the *sacerdotium* with the *imperium*. Not until late 1200 or early 1201 did he take a position. Then he reasoned that his uncontested right to bestow the imperial crown implied a right to pass judgment on the man to whom the crown would legally be due, the German king or king of the Romans as he was called.

Innocent formulated his assessment of the candidates in the *Deliberatio super negotio imperii* and confirmed his claims in the decretal *Venerabilem*. These documents show that he based his decision on the historical relationships between the papacy and the two dynasties concerned rather than on the facts of 1198. He decided for Otto since the Welfs had traditionally been more cooperative toward the papacy than had the Hohenstaufens. Hence Innocent excommunicated Philip and ordered the Germans to follow his direction. From Otto Innocent exacted a high price: the promises made at Neuss, June 8, 1201, wherein Otto swore to uphold the pope's recent territorial consolidations in Italy. Innocent's support, however, failed to produce victory for Otto, and in 1206 Innocent opened negotiations with Philip, whose legate in Italy the pope had by now repulsed. Secret discussions led to Innocent's lifting the excommunication against Philip, but before final agreement was reached, Philip was assassinated on June 21, 1208.

Again Innocent threw his support to Otto and helped persuade the Hohenstaufen faction to do the same. On March 22, 1209, at Speyer, Otto renewed the Neuss promises, but when Innocent met him at Viterbo in September, he became aware that Otto was beginning to waver in his concessions. Nonetheless Innocent crowned him emperor in Rome on October 4, 1209, and then watched in dismay as Otto IV seized the Italian jurisdictions he had sworn to yield to the pope. When Otto invaded Frederick of Hohenstaufen's Norman kingdom, Innocent excommunicated him (November 18, 1210). Four months later, on March 31, 1211, the pope published the excommunication. Now Innocent began to incite the already discontented princes in Germany to revolt. He easily persuaded Philip II of France to second his efforts against Otto, who was allied with John of England, Philip's foe. In September 1211 the German princes voted to depose Otto and promote Frederick of Sicily as their sovereign, and they dispatched legates to coordinate their decisions with the pope's plans.

In promoting Frederick of Sicily, the only available candidate for the German throne, Innocent faced two problems: how to avoid the union of the Norman kingdom with the Empire, which would jeopardize the Roman Church's territorial security and hence spiritual freedom while possibly also obliterating the feudal dependence of Sicily on the papacy, and, second, how to protect his own recent Italian acquisitions. On the first point, Innocent insisted on the immediate coronation of Frederick's infant son, Henry, as king of Sicily, implying the separation of the son's from the father's future realm. To allay Innocent's fears on the second point, Frederick in February 1212 guaranteed in writing the security and extent of the papal state. Satisfied for the moment, Innocent extended financial help and protection as Frederick journeyed north. On December 5 at Frankfurt, the princes elected him king; they crowned him in Mainz four days later, in the presence of Innocent's legate.

Innocent's efforts on Frederick's behalf were gratefully acknowledged in the Golden Bull of Eger, which the king formulated and swore to uphold on July 12, 1213. Frederick therein promised complete obedience to the Roman Church, guaranteed ecclesiastical freedom in elections and appeals to Roman tribunals, renounced the *jus spolii,* and acknowledged the permanency of the borders of the papal state as established by Innocent and previously recognized by Otto IV. On the battlefield of Bouvines in 1214, the German dispute was finally resolved in Frederick's favor. At the Fourth Lateran Council in 1215, Innocent engineered the confirmation by the assembled prelates of his measures against Otto and on behalf of Frederick.

During the final months of his pontificate, Innocent again became concerned about the relationship between Sicily and the Empire when Frederick requested, as part of his negotiations for his impending imperial coronation, that his son be allowed to come to Germany. The petition seemed to hint at the child's eventual election as king of the Romans. Because of Innocent's hesitation, Frederick prepared a document solemnly assuring the pope of his own intention to exercise no authority in Sicily and of his desire to avoid even the appearance of the dreaded union of kingdom and Empire. But Innocent died before this deposition reached Rome. He had supplied guidance and direction to the German princes through very difficult crises and in so doing had also advanced the Church's interests.

Works About: E. Engelmann, *Philipp von Schwaben und Papst Innocenz III während des dtsch. Thronstreites, 1198–1208* (Berlin, 1896); F. Kempf, *Papsttum und Kaisertum bei Innocenz III.* (Rome, 1954); A. Luchaire, *Innocent III,* 6 vols. (Paris, 1905–1908, rpr. in 3 vols., 1969); F. Kempf, ed., *Regestum Innocentii III papae super negotio Romani imperii* (Rome, 1947); Michele Maccarone, *Studi su Innocenzo III* (Padova, 1972); A. Potthast et al., *Regesta Pontificum Romanorum inde ab annum post Christum natum MCXCVIII ad annum MCCCIV,* 2 vols. (Berlin, 1874–1875, rpr. 1957); R. Schwemer, *Innocenz III. und die dtsch. Kirche Während des Thronstreites, 1198–1208* (Strasbourg, 1882); Helen Tillmann, *Papst Innocenz III* (Bonn, 1954); Thomas C. Van Cleve, *Markward of Anweiler and the Sicilian Regency* (Princeton, 1937); Daniel Waley, *The Papal State in the Thirteenth Century* (London, 1961).   R. H. Schmandt

See DISPUTED ELECTION; FREDERICK II; HENRY VI; OTTO IV; PHILIP OF SWABIA-HOHENSTAUFEN.

INTERREGNUM (1254–1273) was a period in the Holy Roman Empire when no single ruler could claim undisputed succession to the imperial throne. It was a time of great turmoil, dissolution, and brigandage. The underlying causes of the Interregnum can be traced to the many concessions Emperor Frederick II made to the German bishops and nobles in his Pragmatic Sanctions of 1220 and 1232. These concessions gave the German nobility a great deal of practical sovereignty in their towns and territories, except when the emperor was present in person. While Frederick and his son Conrad IV were preoccupied with Italian affairs, the German princes got used to exercising a great deal of authority. Unfortunately, no one lord was strong enough to assure peace throughout the German-speaking parts of the Empire.

The situation was further complicated by the early death of Conrad IV in 1254, who left behind only a two-year-old son Conradin as the last of the legitimate Hohenstaufens. Conradin was eventually murdered in 1268 in Italy and never had a chance to rule in Germany. The succession to Conrad IV was claimed by William of Holland, but was resisted by the Swabians. When he died in 1256 a new election was called for. This resulted in the misery of a double election in which both Richard of Cornwall, brother of the English king Henry III, and Alphonse of Castile, grandson of Philip of Swabia, were named emperor. Neither showed much inclination to come to Germany to claim his crown. This opened the floodgates to anarchy, which even protective associations like the Rhine League of Cities were unable to prevent. Petty warfare broke out among the nobles; brigands seemed to be everywhere. Although Richard of Cornwall was crowned at Aachen in 1257, he did not stay long in the

Empire or check the growing disruptions. Alphonse stayed in Toledo, but did not renounce his claim to the imperial dignity. Finally the farce ended when Richard of Cornwall died in 1272 and Pope Gregory X threatened the electors that if they did not name a new emperor he would. The electors finally named Rudolf, count of Habsburg, emperor in 1273.

Works About: James Bryce, *The Holy Roman Empire* (New York, 1961); F. Heer, *The Holy Roman Empire*, tr. J. Sondheimer (New York, 1968); O. Redlich, *Rudolf von Habsburg* (Aalen, 1965).   *J. W. Zophy*

See CONRAD IV; FREDERICK II; RHINE LEAGUE OF CITIES; RUDOLF I.

INVESTITURE CONTROVERSY is the name given to the dispute between the papacy and the imperial government over the appointment of bishops in the Empire. The controversy began in 1075 when Pope Gregory VII forbade the investiture, or appointment, of bishops by laymen and ended in 1122 with a compromise agreement, the Concordat of Worms.

The controversy derives its name from the feudal ceremony of investiture in which a lord conferred a fief or benefice on his vassal. After the vassal swore an oath of fealty and homage to obey and support his lord, the vassal received from the Lord some symbol or token of the land or office with which he was invested. In the case of a bishop vassal, the lord gave his vassal as symbols of office the episcopal ring and staff, items that for centuries had been symbolic of the pastoral office. In theory, the lay lord did not appoint the bishop vassal to his ecclesiastical office and the spiritual duties associated with it; rather he conferred upon him the land and property controlled by whomever held the episcopal office. The ring and staff were symbols of the land conferred upon the bishop as the lord's vassal, the office of bishop supposedly having been conferred as a result of an election by the clergy of the diocese.

The investiture controversy was one of the major struggles between the powers of Church and state in the Middle Ages. The basic difficulty arose as a result of the dual nature of the role of most medieval bishops and abbots. Since the early Middle Ages, prelates had served not only their obvious ecclesiastical function as spiritual leaders but also as temporal lords as a result of the vast amount of land attached to their church or monastery. Indeed many bishops and abbots had vassals of their own to whom they parceled out land under their control as fiefs. Thus bishops and abbots had both temporal and spiritual powers: the former a result of their being invested as vassals by lay lords, the latter a result of their election to high clerical office. In essence, however, a prelate could not function in his ecclesiastical office without being installed through investment as a vassal since he otherwise had no funds or temporal authority at his disposal. Clearly from the earliest period of the Middle Ages, both kings and popes were seriously concerned about the person who held the position of bishop or abbot.

As late as the middle of the eleventh century, there was no general agreement among churchmen and imperial advisers as to the respective powers of pope and king regarding the selection and installation of German prelates. All agreed that both parties had rights in the matter, but not of what these rights consisted. The confusion was further compounded by the obvious papal concern for the proper performance by a bishop or abbot of his spiritual duties and by the king's concern for the prelate's proper performance of various temporal and administrative duties related to the duties of a major vassal. The pope preferred that bishops and abbots give first loyalty to their spiritual functions, the king that they give it to their administrative and bureaucratic functions. It was the rare man who could satisfactorily serve both masters, even if he desired to do so. Especially since Otto I had created a powerful alliance between the emperor and German Church in the mid-tenth century in order to bolster the power of the emperor against the particularist dukes, the Holy Roman emperors had virtually appointed the important German bishops and abbots to ensure their support as vassals in the continual struggle with the turbulent German nobility.

Until Emperor Henry III reformed the corrupt papacy in 1046 as an extension of the clerical reform movement begun in the previous century, there was no major opposition to imperial policy concerning the investment and installment of prelates. With the reform of the papacy, however, papal reformers came to believe that the general reform of the Church and elimination of clerical abuses depended on the imposition of strict clerical discipline. The only men in a position to enforce such discipline were the bishops who, the papal reformers felt, could be relied upon only if their first allegiance was to the pope. Imperial authorities felt, however, that to permit such an allegiance would be to undermine the prelates' loyalty to the emperor and distract them from their administrative duties, thus opening the way for a resurgence of ducal and local resistance to imperial pacification and unification attempts in Germany. While only a very few imperial extremists contended that the king had the power to appoint bishops to their spiritual position, the vast majority of the imperial party did insist on the king's right and need to ensure the appointment of able and loyal administrators as bishops or abbots in Germany. On the other hand, papal reformers maintained that the pope must be able to select his own bishops if he were to effectively reform clerical abuse, and they advocated the abolition of lay investiture of clerics.

The dispute became an open struggle in 1075 when Pope Gregory VII forbade lay investiture and Emperor Henry IV ignored him in appointing and investing the archbishop of the key Italian city of Milan. When the pope issued threats against the king and his bishops, Henry called a synod at Worms in January 1076 and, as Henry III had done thirty years before, declared the pope deposed. Gregory responded in February by deposing and excommunicating Henry. The step was a severe blow since by making the king a spiritual pariah, it released the German nobility from feudal loyalty to him. Most German churchmen, caught in the middle and uncertain of their loyalties, remained neutral, while the greater nobility, led by the particularist dukes who, as usual, resented an increasingly centralized state, took Henry's excommunication as a signal for revolt. Henry was able to forestall disaster by visiting the pope in January 1077 at Canossa, Italy, where he begged forgiveness and was restored to the Church. The rebellious dukes were unwilling to submit and, electing Rudolf of Swabia as antiking, began a civil war in Germany. Henry's continued investment of bishops and his reliance on their support in the civil war eventually led Gregory to renew the excommunication in 1080 and throw his support to Rudolf. Henry, however, soon was victorious, and with the support of most German and Italian prelates deposed Gregory, appointed an antipope, and invaded Italy in 1081. With Gregory's death in Norman captivity in 1085, the dispute somewhat altered in focus, though the papal reformers held their ground. With Henry's death in 1106, the strained relations abated, and Pope Pascal II attempted negotiations with Henry V. After making some vague concessions to obtain his coronation as emperor, Henry captured the pope, releasing him only after Pascal had renounced all papal claims. Henry then proceeded ruthlessly to uphold and extend the claims of his father despite the pope's repudiation of the forced renunciation. Internal difficulties in Germany eventually required the emperor to open serious negotiation, and the dispute was settled in a compromise agreement in 1122 in the Concordat of Worms between Henry V and Pope Calixtus II. By the terms of the settlement, the emperor lost the right to invest with ring and staff but retained the power to invest bishops and abbots with the land and endowments associated with their ecclesiastical post.

The investiture controversy ended in a papal victory that, though far from complete at the time, paved the way for further papal advances in later gaining control of the German Church and reforming clerical abuses in it. While the emperor retained considerable power over the selection of the German bishops and abbots, the loyalty of the German Church to the imperial cause was henceforth questionable and the ability of the emperors to control the independence of the dukes and restrain the nobility was eroded. Powerful monarchs such as Frederick I could maintain their positions and even renew the old royal alliance with the German Church, but weaker kings such as Conrad II could not. Over the longer term, the investiture controversy and its results marked the beginning of the disintegration of the emperor's power. The issues involved in the controversy also sparked troubles between the papacy and other secular rulers, especially the kings of England and France.

Works About: A. Becker, *Studien zum Investiturproblem in Frankreich* (Saarbrücken, 1955); Z. N. Brooke, *Lay Investiture and Its Relation to the Conflict of the Empire and Papacy* (London, 1939); A. B. Cavanaugh, *Pope Gregory VII and the Theocratic State* (Washington, D.C., 1934); S. Z. Ehler and J. B. Morrall, eds. and trs., *Church and State through the Centuries* (London, 1954); A. Fliche, *La Réforme grégorienne et la Reconquête chrétienne, 1057–1123* (Paris, 1940), and *La Querelle des Investitures* (Paris, 1946); K. Hampe, *Germany under the Salian and Hoh-*

enstaufen Emperors, tr. R. Bennett (Totowa, N. J., 1973); P. Joachimson, "The Investiture Contest and the German Constitution," in *Medieval Germany, 911–1250,* ed. and tr. G. Barraclough (Oxford, 1938): 2:95–130: *The Life of Emperor Henry IV,* ed. and tr. T. E. Mommsen and K. F. Morrison, in *Imperial Lives and Letters of the Eleventh Century* (New York, 1962): K. F. Morrison, ed., *The Investiture Controversy: Issues, Ideas, and Results* (New York, 1971), and "Canossa, A Revision," *Traditio* 18 (1912): 121–48: G. Tellenbach, *Church, State and Christian Society at the Time of the Investiture Contest,* tr. R. F. Bennett (Oxford, 1940): B. Tierney, ed. and tr., *The Crisis of Church and State, 1050–1300* (Englewood Cliffs, N. J., 1964), W. Ullmann, *The Growth of Papal Government in the Middle Ages* (London, 1962); J. P. Whitney, *Hildebrandine Essays* (Cambridge, 1932).   *D. S. Devlin*

See CONCORDAT OF WORMS; CONRAD III; FREDERICK I; GREGORY VII: HENRY III; HENRY IV; HENRY V.

J

JEWS in the Holy Roman Empire had an experience that is often difficult to determine. Jews, a minority, encountered mass slaughters, large-scale expulsions, and destruction of many of their resources. Although the major outline of their development is rather well known, critical research in local areas tends to question too summary a conclusion.

From the time of the Diaspora, Jews migrated to parts of the Roman Empire where they became directly subject to the emperor. With the rise of the Holy Roman Empire, Jews were found in many Rhineland cities where extensive commercial activity occurred. During the Middle Ages tensions developed between pope and emperor with regard to supremacy over the Jews; in the Empire, the emperor successfully proclaimed his sovereignty. At the beginning of the thirteenth century, Emperor Frederick II (1211–1250) officially declared the Jews to be *servi camerae imperialis specialis* or *Reichskammerknecht* (chamber serfs attached to the imperial dignity). The emperor thus served as protector of Jews in return for which they supported him by special taxes and services. Although chronic need for increased monies often forced an emperor into alienating his direct authority over Jews, he still reserved to himself superior jurisdiction. He remained the final court of appeal in judicial contents between Jews and Christians. In short, no action might be taken legally against the Jews without the emperor's consent, and, because of this, Jews became a bulwark behind the maintenance of public order in the Empire since in times of lawlessness they often became the first victims.

In most senses Jews were separate from European Christian society. Forced in many places to live in ghettos and to wear distinctive apparel to indicate to Christians their differences, some Jews nevertheless received special charters that allowed them to live in Christian communities. These privileges gave to Jews a sense of separateness. They also tied Jews to the political authorities that granted the charters; Jews thus tended to support local peace as well as imperial public peace. Special taxes and oaths constituted part of their obligations, and the oaths—known as the *Juramentum Judaeorum* or *More Judaico*—became an especially important means of supervising Jewish communal activities.

When economic life became more diversified in the Empire during the later Middle Ages, outlets for Jewish economic activity tended to contract. This is largely explained by the fact that imperial estates feared competition between their Christian and Jewish subjects. Increased competition in many cases led Christian majorities into acts of violence against Jewish minorities. Governments placed new restrictions on Jewish economic activities, and as a consequence Jews were forced to migrate to other imperial territories or to leave the Empire.

While Jews occupied such occupations as butchers, scribes, notaries, bookbinders, and became particularly prominent as physicians, Christians associated their economic functions normally with money lending and pawnbroking. Because they loaned money, Jews incurred the hostility of their clients who became indebted. Until the sixteenth century, when the canonical prohibitions against charging interest on loans were somewhat relaxed, Christians borrowed money from Jews and Lombards at rather high interest rates. Generally these rates were fixed by law, although practice sometime exceeded the legal limit. In the Rhineland and southern Germany in the fourteenth century, for example, it was permissible for Jews to charge 43⅓ percent interest on loans to native residents, while loans to foreigners reached as high as 86⅔ percent. People borrowed at these and similar rates, although they resented their consequent indebtedness. This resentment expressed itself in attacks on the Jews.

Much of the history of the Jews in the Empire indicates the anomaly of this position. They were protected but rejected, functional yet expendable. This untenable situation explains both the anti-Jewish activities taken against them and, conversely, their tenacity. Christians always had at their disposal religious arguments against Judaism; and wherever anti-Jewish violence occurred these arguments—such as host desecrations and ritual murders—regularly appeared. Forced conversion, mass slaughter, and expulsions were often the result. The worst periods in the history of the Empire for the Jews were the first crusades, the Black Death in the middle of the fourteenth century, and the expulsions from the middle of the fifteenth to the middle of the sixteenth centuries. Due to the complex political structure of the Empire, however, it is probable that the Jews received better treatment here than in the more politically centralized states of western Europe.

Beginning in the seventeenth century and lasting until the end of the Empire, Jews began to receive more favorable treatment, and this finally led to emancipation. The most obvious cause for this change was the belief in toleration spawned by reactions to religious conflict. During the Enlightenment, emphases on reason and rationality denigrated religious differences and stressed the commonality of mankind. On the Jewish side, Moses Mendelssohn (1729–1786) advanced the Jewish Enlightenment.

Works About: Bernard S. Bachrach, *Jews in Barbarian Europe* (Kansas, 1977); Salo W. Baron, *A Social and Religious Hist. of the Jews*, 2d ed., 14 vols. (New York, 1952–1969); Phillip N. Bebb, "Jewish Policy in Sixteenth Century Nürnberg," *Occasional Papers of the American Society for Reformation Research* 1 (1977): 125–36; *Encyclopaedia Judaica*, 16 vols. (New York and Jerusalem, 1972); Jacob Katz, *Exclusiveness and Tolerance: Studies in Jewish-Gentile Relations in Medieval and Modern Times* (London, 1961); Guido Kisch, *Jewry-Law in Medieval Germany: Laws and Court Decisions Concerning Jews*, Texts and Studies, Vol. 3 (New York, 1949); Selma Stern, *Commander of Jewry, Josel of Rosheim in the Holy Roman Empire of the German Nation*, tr.

Gertrude Hirschler (New York, 1965); Raphael Straus, *Regensburg and Augsburg,* tr. Felix N. Gerson (Philadelphia, 1939).   *P. N. Bebb*

See FREDERICK II; NUREMBERG.

JOHN FREDERICK, called the Magnanimous (1503–1554), elector of Saxony, was the eldest son of Elector John the Constant and the nephew of Elector Frederick the Wise. He succeeded to the electoral title on the death of his father in 1532. He was the last Saxon elector from the Ernestine branch of the Wettin dynasty. As a youth he received a careful education but showed more inclination for jousting and the hunt than for academic matters.

Like his father, John Frederick early became an enthusiastic supporter of Martin Luther. His intercessions on behalf of the reformer helped to influence the policies of Frederick the Wise during the critical opening years of the Reformation. But it was his father's accession to the electoral office in 1525 that made possible John Frederick's assumption of an important role in evangelical politics and diplomacy. In 1525–1526 he played a leading part in the Saxon negotiations with Landgrave Philip of Hesse, which led to the first of a series of Protestant defensive alliances. Along with his father, he signed the Augsburg Confession presented to the Catholic emperor, Charles V, at the diet of 1530. He frequently represented Elector John at meetings of Schmalkaldic League members. And he was a central figure in the discussions with the Habsburgs, which preceded the religious Peace of Nuremberg (1532), signed shortly before his father's death.

Upon his own accession to power, John Frederick attempted to continue the policy of moderation in imperial politics pursued by his father. This involved an effort to preserve the peace in Germany through a demonstration of continued loyalty in temporal affairs to the emperor, Charles. It was the tragedy of John Frederick's career that a lasting reconciliation with the Habsburgs could not be attained. Negotiated settlements, such as those achieved in the 1539 Treaty of Frankfurt and the 1544 Speyer agreement, proved to be only temporary.

John Frederick's willingness to compromise on political matters did not extend to the realm of religious doctrine, where he strove to uphold Lutheran teachings. This Saxon confessionalism strongly influenced his relations with Protestant allies, as well as with the emperor. He successfully prevailed on fellow members of the Schmalkaldic League to reject a political coalition with Henry VIII of England unless it was preceded by a religious agreement. He was not able to have Luther's Schmalkaldic articles—drawn up at the elector's request—adopted as the official creed of the league but did secure his confederates' consent to repudiate the Church council called by Pope Paul III in the previous year (1536). His measures to ensure that Lutheran doctrine not be diluted contributed to the failure of the theological discussions sponsored by Charles V at Regensburg in 1541. It apparently was this turn of events that convinced Charles of the futility of further religious negotiations with the Protestants and the necessity of an eventual military showdown.

Unfortunately for John Frederick, when the critical moment came, electoral Saxony's relations with neighboring ducal (Albertine) Saxony were no better than those with the imperial government. A long-standing family feud between the two branches of the Wettin house (Ernestine and Albertine) had culminated in an intense political rivalry between John Frederick and his ambitious cousin, Maurice. It was Duke Maurice's decision to throw in his lot with the emperor in the Schmalkaldic War that sealed the fate of John Frederick. Electoral Saxony was defeated and the elector himself captured at the Battle of Mühlberg (April 1547). Charles condemned him to death as a rebel but then commuted the sentence to life imprisonment. John Frederick lost his electoral title and lands, as well as other claims, to his cousin Maurice and was left with a much-reduced state consisting largely of Ernestine possessions in Thuringia.

The time of John Frederick's imprisonment, however, proved to be his finest hour. He firmly refused to make any concessions on matters of religion, rejecting the Augsburg Interim proclaimed by Charles V in 1548. When in 1552 the emperor found it politically expedient to release John Frederick, the latter returned in triumph to Thuringia where he was welcomed by the Lutheran population as a martyr and hero of the faith.

It has been suggested that John Frederick lacked the ability to play a leading role in the dangerous power politics of the Reformation era. Whatever the final verdict on this question, it must be acknowledged that his steadfastness in adversity served at least partially to redeem his historical reputation.

Works About: *Die Schmalkaldischen Bundesabschiede 1533–1536* (Tübingen, 1958); Flathe, "Johann Friedrich der Grossmüthige," *ADB*, 4326–30; Thomas Klein, "Johann Friedrich (I.) der Grossmütige," NDB, 10: 524–5; Theodor Kolde, "Johann Friedrich der Grossmütige," *Realencyklopädie für prot. Theologie und Kirche* 9 (1901): 244–49; Georg Mentz, *Johann Friedrich der Grossmütige 1503–1554,* 3 vols. (Jena, 1903–1908); Hans Patze and Walter Schlesinger, *Gesch. Thüringens* (Cologne, 1967), vol. 3: Bernhard Rogge, *Johann Friedrich, Kurfürst von Sachsen* (Halle, 1902).   *C. C. Christensen*

See CHARLES V; FREDERICK III, THE WISE; JOHN OF SAXONY; LUTHER; MAURICE; PHILIP OF HESSE; SCHMALKALDIC LEAGUE.

JOHN GEORGE I (1585–1656), elector of Saxony, was born and died at Dresden. The second son of Elector Christian I, he succeeded his older brother, Christian II, in 1611, after having previously served as secular administrator of Merseburg (since 1603). John George was the leading Lutheran prince in the Empire; however, both as a ruler and as a public figure, he was a man of small stature. He was a devoted family man and honest politician but rather boring and not overly bright. Instead of shaping events, he permitted them to dominate him. John George continued the traditional Saxon policy of defending the constitution of the Empire. He talked a great deal about princely rights and German liberties but generally remained subservient to the emperor.

His resentment of Calvinism, nurtured by his fanatical court chaplain, Matthias Hoë von Hoënegg, who was one of the most powerful men at the Saxon court, and envy of the political influence of Frederick V of the Palatinate led John George to side with Emperor Ferdinand II during the Bohemian revolt (that sparked the Thirty Years War in 1618). As a reward Ferdinand permitted him to keep Lusatia, a neighboring province that had joined the rebellion and that the Saxon army had pacified. In addition the elector received some vague promises about the rights of Lutherans in Bohemia. John George's behavior during the revolt and in subsequent years was a reflection of the complete inadequacy of Saxon policy during the Thirty Years War. As Germany's foremost Lutheran, he lost the respect of many fellow Protestants, but in exchange he did not gain the support of the emperor and his allies. In spite of the elector's repeated appeals, Lutheranism was suppressed in Bohemia; John George's rights were even challenged in Lusatia. Over Saxony's objections Ferdinand II imposed the imperial ban on Frederick of the Palatinate, Bohemia's Winter King, and gave his land and electoral title to Maximilian of Bavaria. Then the emperor insulted John George personally by forcing the Magdeburg chapter to elect his son, Archduke Leopold William, after it had already chosen the elector's son, Prince August, as its administrator. Finally Ferdinand threatened him directly with the Edict of Restitution (1629), which ordered the immediate re-Catholization of all illegally secularized Church properties.

John George, who thus far had been unwilling to do little more than issue verbal protests, became alarmed. Urged on by Germany's more militant Protestant princes, particularly the Calvinists of neighboring Brandenburg, he agreed in 1631, at the Leipzig Convention, to head a defensive association of Protestant estates. This alliance was to stand as a neutral third block between the imperial and foreign armies; its goal was to protect the constitution of the Empire and the religious and political liberties of the evangelical princes. But the alliance failed, partly because John George again refused to provide the energetic leadership that the Protestants needed to succeed.

Such leadership at long last came from King Gustavus Adolphus of Sweden who had joined the war in the summer of 1630. John George, like other Protestant princes, initially refused to cooperate with the Swedes but concluded a military alliance with Gustavus when the league army threatened his lands (September 1631). Shortly afterward, the allies won an overwhelming victory over the Catholic forces at Breitenfeld. The Saxon army, well trained but inexperienced in combat, made a rather poor showing; nevertheless Gustavus entrusted it with the liberation of Silesia and Bohemia while his own forces pursued the fleeing league troops into southern Germany.

John George had never been an enthusiastic and reliable follower of the Swedes. Gustavus' death at Lützen (1632) provided him with an opportunity to assert greater independence for himself once again. He refused to support the Swedish-dominated Heilbronn League. At the same time he entered into secret peace negotiations with Wallenstein, commander-in-chief of the imperial forces. After the Austrian victory at Nördlingen (1634) he abandoned his former ally completely and signed the Peace of Prague (1635) with the emperor. But the treaty, which guaranteed John George's interests in Lusatia and Magdeburg, did not bring peace to the Empire. The Swedish army, still powerful in Germany, took bitter revenge on the elector's lands. It won major victories over the imperial and Saxon forces at Wittstock (1636) and Chemnitz (1639). In 1642 the allies suffered a drastic defeat at Breitenfeld, and Leipzig was occupied by the Swedes. The suffering and devastation continued until 1645 when John George signed the truce of Kötzschenbroda with the Swedes; three years later the war ended.

The elector remained loyal to the emperor even at the Westphalian peace congress but again received little in return. He was allowed to keep Lusatia; however, Magdeburg was given to his rival, the Calvinist elector of Brandenburg. To the end, John George opposed the recognition of Calvinism in the peace treaty; but here too the Brandenburger had his way. Saxony clearly had ceased to be the foremost Protestant power in the Empire; that place now belonged to neighboring Brandenburg. John George's dislike of Calvinism continued even after the war. At the imperial diet of 1653, he first declined the presidency of the *Corpus Evangelicorum* (the diet's Protestant members) but then accepted the post for fear that the Reformed elector of Brandenburg might be selected in his stead. Saxony's demise as a Protestant power was completed when John George, ignoring past family practice and primogeniture, decided to divide his inheritance among his four sons.

Works About: Karlheinz Blaschke, "Johann Georg I," *NDB*, 10:525ff; *Documenta Bohemica Bellum Tricennale Illustrantia*, 7 vols. (Prague, 1971–); Georg Irmer, ed., *Die Verhandlungen Schwedens und seiner Verbündeten mit Wallenstein und dem Kaiser von 1631 bis 1634*, 3 vols. (Leipzig, 1888–1891); Flathe, "Johann Georg I," *ADB*, 14:376–81; Rudolf Kötzschke and Hellmut Kretzschmar, *Sächsische Gesch.* (Dresden, 1935), vol. 2; Karl A. Müller, *Kurfürst Johann Georg der Erste, seine Familie und sein Hof* (Dresden and Leipzig, 1838); Michael Caspar Lundorp, ed., *Der Römischen Kayserlichen Majestät und dess Heiligen Römischen Reichs...Acta Publica* (Frankfurt am Main, 1668), vols. 1–5: Bodo Nischan, "Propaganda and Politics in an Age of Ideological Division: The Case of Saxony in the Thirty Years War," *Journalism Hist. 4* (1977):23–29.   *Bodo Nischan*

See EDICT OF RESTITUTION: FERDINAND II: MAXIMILIAN I, DUKE: THIRTY YEARS WAR.

JOHN OF SAXONY (1468–1532), elector of Saxony (also referred to as John the Constant), was the fourth son of Elector Ernest of Saxony and the younger brother of Elector Frederick the Wise. He succeeded to the electoral title and leadership of the Ernestine branch of the Wettin dynasty in 1525 upon the death of Frederick, who was unmarried. John appears to have had a relatively good education, although he probably did not develop as deep an interest in either scholarship or art as did Frederick. He also perhaps lacked the breadth of political vision attributed to his older brother.

On the death of their father in 1486, Frederick and John had entered into a joint rule of all the Ernestine lands except the electoral circle around Wittenberg, which accrued to Frederick alone. Their close partnership, which generally worked very well, makes it somewhat difficult to establish a distinct political identity for John in the early years of their long reign. This situation was not significantly altered in 1513 when there was a temporary division of power in the Ernestine lands, with the Thuringian portion being assigned to Duke John. Although two separate territorial administrations were created, there continued to be close ties between them, and each brother was inclined to employ the councillors of the other when the need arose.

John's early and enthusiastic commitment to Luther, however, set him somewhat apart from his brother, whose response to the Reformation was more cautious and restrained. It is reported that John liked to take notes on Luther's sermons, and the reformer gratefully acknowledged the duke's interest by dedicating important theological writings to him. Duke John did not share Frederick's reluctance to use the authority of the state to promote evangelical religious reform. Even before his brother's death, John had authorized an inspection of churches in western Thuringia. Many of the procedures developed then were incorporated into the visitations that later, after John became elector, were commissioned to regulate ecclesiastical affairs throughout the Ernestine lands. The territorial church organization that resulted became a model for much of Protestant Germany.

Perhaps it was John's diplomatic activity on behalf of the Reformation that constitutes his greatest claim to enduring historical significance. Although Frederick the Wise showed little interest in the formation of Protestant defensive alliances, Duke John is known to have taken up consideration of the matter already during his brother's lifetime. In March 1525, he entered into discussions with Landgrave Philip of Hesse, and there thus began a series of negotiations that led finally to the establishment of the first political alliance dedicated to the protection of the evangelical faith, the League of Torgau (May 1526). The formation of this union helps account for the firmness demonstrated by Saxony and Hesse at the imperial diet of Speyer (June 1526), where a temporary decision favorable to the Protestant cause was achieved. It was in these encouraging circumstances that John, as elector, began aggressively to promote reform of the churches throughout his territories.

Saxon diplomacy from this point until John's death presents a somewhat more complicated picture. In 1528 the elector, misled by false reports, became involved in a dangerous adventure (the Pack conspiracy) that almost led to Saxony and Hesse's launching a preemptive military strike against neighboring Catholic states. Fortunately Saxony withdrew from this ill conceived enterprise in good time, and the peace was preserved. But John received a rude shock from the experience, which influenced all of his subsequent actions. Henceforth Saxon policy was characterized by greater restraint, a preference for legal rather than military solutions, and an inclination to seek accommodation with Catholic rivals—where this was possible without compromising on essential matters of faith. The adoption of this more cautious approach frequently led to friction with John's venturesome ally, Philip of Hesse.

The circumstances of the Reformation, however, made it impossible for Saxony to avoid further confrontations. The antievangelical measures of the 1529 diet of Speyer prompted the elector, in conjunction with other reformed leaders, to issue a famous protest (hence "Protestant"). A similar outcome attended the 1530 diet of Augsburg, where John worked hard to attain an acceptable settlement with the Catholic emperor, Charles V. When Charles rejected the moderate statement of faith presented by Saxony and the other Lutheran estates (Augsburg Confession), the elector felt obliged to enter into negotiations leading to a new Protestant alliance, the Schmalkaldic League. Along with Philip of Hesse, he assumed leadership of this body, which remained for years the chief instrument of Protestant politics within the German Empire.

Works About: Johannes Becker, *Kurfürst Johann von Sachsen und seine Beziehungen zu Luther,* vol. 1: 1520–1528 (Leipzig, 1890); Ekkehart Fabian, *Die Entstehung des Schmalkaldischen Bundes und seiner Verfassung* (Tübingen, 1962); Flathe, "Johann der Beständige," *ADB,* 14:322–26; Thomas Klein, "Johann der Beständige," *NDB,* 10:522–24; Theodor Kolde, "Johann der Beständige," *Realencyklopädie für prot. Theologie und Kirche* 9 (1901): 237–44; Hans-Walter Krumwiede, *Zur Entstehung des landesherrlichen Kirchenregimentes in Kursachsen und Braunschweig-Wolfenbüttel* (Göttingen, 1967); Hans Patze and Walter Schlesinger, *Gesch. Thüringens* (Cologne., 1967), vol. 3.   *C. C. Christensen*

See BRÜCK; CHARLES VI; FREDERICK III, THE WISE; LUTHER; PHILIP OF HESSE; SCHMALKALDIC LEAGUE.

JOSEPH I (1678–1711), Holy Roman emperor from 1705 to 1711 was the eldest son of Leopold I and his third wife, Eleanor. He was crowned king of Hungary in 1687 and elected king of the Romans in 1688. Young, energetic, and handsome, Joseph had the family's blue eyes and blond hair but lacked the Habsburg lip. He shared his father's talents as a musician and lavishly patronized the arts during his reign. Unlike Leopold, he enjoyed the hunt and, although he avoided open confrontation with his wife, kept several mistresses. Like his father, he was very conscious of his duty toward God and Empire. In 1703, Joseph agreed to a mutual succession pact, which provided that if Joseph's line should become extinct, his younger brother, Archduke Charles, would succeed him. This compact, which recognized the right of both male and female succession, stipulated that Joseph's daughters were to have precedence over Charles'.

During the latter part of Leopold's reign, both Joseph and Charles had more influence than their father. Joseph, along with his younger brother, urged his father to fight Louis XIV of France for the Spanish inheritance in 1701. He was much more favorable to reform than was his father and supported the younger reform-minded ministers at court, Prince Eugene of Savoy (1663–1736), Count

John Wenzel Wratislaw (1669–1712), and Count Gundaker Thomas von Stahremberg (1663–1745).

He succeeded his father as Holy Roman emperor in 1705 in the midst of the War of the Spanish Succession (1701–1714) and a rebellion in Hungary, led by Francis II Rákóczi. Joseph defeated the rebels and began the negotiations which eventually led to the peace of Szatmár (1711). Rákóczi, who refused to accept the settlement, fled to France. During Joseph's brief six-year reign, Prince Eugene of Savoy ably led the imperial forces and worked closely with the commander of the allied armies, John Churchill, duke of Marlborough, to defeat Louis XIV. Joseph aimed for a greater centralization of government, an extension of imperial authority, an increase of imperial revenues, and reform of the governmental administration. In essence, Joseph followed his father's policies in trying to increase Austria's (the hereditary lands') power and prestige rather than that of the Holy Roman Empire. As emperor, Joseph made very few changes in governmental administration. Although he did reduce the privy council from 160 members to 34, he kept most of his father's ministers in office. Under Joseph, the influence of the younger ministers such as Wratislaw, Prince Eugene, and Baron Frederick von Seilern increased. The most influential men under Joseph were the Prince of Salms, Prince Eugene of Savoy, Count Frederick Paul Schonborn, Count Leopold Trautson, and Baron Frederick von Seilern. Joseph contracted smallpox and died on April 17, 1711. Because he had no male heirs, he was succeeded by his younger brother Archduke Charles.

Works About: K. O. Aretin, "Kaiser Joseph I zwischen Kaisertradition und Oesterr. Grossmachtpolitik," *HZ* 215:(1972): 533ff; K. O. Aretin and W. Bauer, "Joseph I," *Mitt. des Oberoesterr. Landesarchives* 4 (1955); Max Braubach, *Prinz Eugen von Savoyen,* 5 vols. (Vienna, 1963–1965): 2:130–34 and "Joseph I," *DNB.* 10:613–17; Johann Herchenhahn, *Gesch. der Regierung Kaiser Joseph des Ersten* (Leipzig, 1796); C. W. Ingrao, *In Quest and Crisis: Emperor Joseph I and the Habsburg Monarchy* (West Lafayette, Ind., 1979); Krones, "Joseph I," *ADB,* 14:534–42; Oswald Redlich, *Das Werden einer Grossmacht, Oesterreich von 1700 bis 1740* (Vienna, 1942); John P. Spielman, *Leopold I of Austria* (New Brunswick, N.J., 1977).   *L. S. Frey and M. L. Frey*

See CHARLES VI: EUGENE OF SAVOY: LEOPOLD I: SPANISH SUCCESSION: STAHRENBERG.

JOSEPH II (1741–1790), Holy Roman emperor from 1765 to 1790 was the eldest son of Maria Theresa and Emperor Francis I. As coregent with his mother, Joseph had developed an acute sense of frustration; he chafed at his political impotence and continually quarreled with his mother about her moderate policies. A solemn, earnest, sincere man, he was also dogmatic, single-minded, and unrealistic. Cold and unmagnetic, Joseph was unable to create a following or inspire confidence. Convinced of his infallibility, he completely ignored or disregarded any opposition. When he became ruler in 1780, he tried to implement the ideas of the *philosophes,* to make "philosophy the legislator of (his) empire." The Enlightenment's aptest pupil, he was also its most spectacular failure. Energetic and sincere, his reforms failed because of his own excesses and inflexibility. He saw himself as "the incarnation of reason and virtue, selflessly burning himself out in a war against error, vice, traditionalists and the enemies of human progress." He has been described as "a Caesar possessed by demons" and a latter-day Don Quixote "who spent the better part of his life tilting at windmills." Joseph could not have worked harder at reforming the state had he known that he only had ten years to live.

Joseph tried to reform his state following the cold-blooded dictates of reason. Joseph's ideal was the formation of a perfectly rational government and administration. Disregarding regional differences and traditions, Joseph divided his realm into governments relatively equal in population. In order to strengthen the unity of the state, he decreed that German would serve as the single language for government and education. Fierce resistance, particularly by the Magyars, who had resented Joseph's refusal to be specially crowned king of Hungary and his removal of the crown of St. Stephen's to Vienna, ensued. The struggle against Germanization came to symbolize resistance to the emperor.

Joseph also aroused opposition from the nobility when he granted the serfs personal liberty in 1781 (they could move, marry and choose their own professions), restricted the obligatory labor required of serfs and limited the lord's jurisdiction over the serfs. Unfortunately the peasants, believing that the emperor had abolished all of their obligations, refused to pay their customary dues or to perform any labor service. When the nobles tried to enforce their rights, the peasants revolted and Joseph had to send in troops. Joseph had also angered the nobility when he stipulated that noble and peasant land be taxed equally. Many of Joseph's social and economic reforms were aimed at ameliorating the lot of the peasantry, thus earning Joseph the sobriquet, "the peasant Emperor."

Although popular with the serfs, Joseph was feared and distrusted by the Church. Following Maria Theresa's lead, he tried to increase state control over the Church; he suppressed monasteries, required church officials to swear allegiance to the state, made marriage a civil contract, freed education from the control of the Church, and forbade the Church to publish bulls without the consent of the state or correspond directly with the papacy. Joseph, who had "an infinite capacity for taking pains," even regulated Church music and burial ceremonies. Unlike his mother, he espoused toleration. Although granting Catholicism the status of dominant religion, Joseph allowed Protestants to worship in their own homes and abolished most of the discrimination against religious dissenters. This policy was but part of Joseph's attempt to establish equality under the law for all groups in the state. He also decreed equal punishment for equal crimes regardless of class, limited the severity of punishments, abolished torture, and restricted the use of the death penalty.

Besides being influenced by the ideas of the *philosophes* like Beccaria, he was also swayed by the advocates of free trade. Accordingly he relaxed governmental supervision and regulation in the state. He had a passion for thrift and was, according to Frederick II, always "saving and scrimping." In spite of all his economies, Joseph left his successor a huge national debt.

One of the reasons for this deficit was Joseph's disastrous foreign policy. He attempted to annex Bavaria to the Habsburg lands, but was balked by Frederick II of Prussia in the War of the Bavarian Succession (the so-called Potato War, 1778–1779) and later in 1785 by the League of Princes. Joseph, however, did obtain a small section of Bavaria known as the Inn Quarter. Still later, he allied with Russia and declared war on Turkey (1778–1791). This too was a debacle. Joseph died in the midst of the conflict. His successor Leopold II extricated Austria in 1791 (Peace of Sistova) from a conflict that had cost it prestige and manpower and gained it nothing. Joseph's foreign policy was no more successful than his domestic policy.

A harsh, lonely man, Joseph's personal life was as unhappy as his reign was disastrous. Joseph quarreled frequently with his mother and despised his brother and sisters. He never recovered from the death of his beloved first wife, Isabel of Parma, who died three years after their marriage. "I have lost everything. The wife I have worshipped, the object of all my love." He predicted that he would be unhappy for the rest of his life. This unfortunately was only too prophetic. Joseph did marry again, but he had no affection for his second wife, Josepha of Bavaria, who died unlamented in 1767. His public life mirrored his desperately unhappy personal one. He distrusted his ministers and refused to listen to other opinions. He died a heartbroken and disillusioned man. On his epitaph he had written: "Here lies a prince whose intentions were pure, but who had the misfortune to see all his plans miscarry." When he died, Hungary and the Austrian Netherlands were in revolt, the nobles outraged, and the Church alienated. His brother Leopold II (1790–1792) a very able man, succeeded him and was forced to abrogate most of his reforms.

Works By: Alfred von Arneth, ed., *Joseph II and Leopold von Toscana, Ihr Briefwechsel* (Vienna, 1872), and *Maria Theresia und Joseph II, Ihre Correspondenz* (Vienna, 1867). **Works About:** Paul Bernard, *Joseph II* (New York, 1968); T. C. W. Blanning, *Joseph II and Enlightened Despotism* (New York, 1971); Francois Fejtö, *Un Habsburg revolutionaire, Joseph II: An Imperial Reformer for the Austrian Netherlands* (The Hague, 1974); Ferdinand Maas, ed., *Der Josephinismus. Quellen zu seiner Gesch. in Österreich 1760–1790. Amtliche Dokumente aus dem Wiener Haus-Hof-und Staatsarchiv,* vol. 2: *Entfaltung und Krise des Josephinismus 1770–1790* (Vienna, 1953) Paul von Mitrofanov, *Joseph II: Seine politische und kulturelle Tätigkeit,* 2 vols. (Vienna, 1910); Charles H. O'Brien, *Ideas of Religious Toleration of Joseph II* (Philadelphia, 1969); Saul Padover, *The Revolutionary Emperor* (New York, 1937); D. Silagi, *Jakobiner in der Habsburger Monarchie* (Vienna, 1962). F. Walter, *Maria Theresia: Briefe und Aktenstücke in Auswahl* (Darmstadt, 1968).   *L. S. Frey and M. L. Frey*

See BAVARIAN SUCCESSION; FRANCIS I; FREDERICK II, THE GREAT; LEOPOLD II; MARIA THERESA.

k

KANT, IMMANUEL (1724–1804), philosopher, was born in Königsberg, East Prussia, and spent his entire life there except for occasional journeys into the immediate vicinity. His father, John George, was a poor harness maker; his mother, Anna Reuter, was steeped in pietism, the Protestant religious movement that stressed emotional religiosity and the development of the inner life. During his early schooling, Immanuel acquired a strong foundation in mathematics, physics, geography, and Latin. The quality of his mind was quickly evident, and he was allowed to enter the University of Königsberg in 1740.

After spending nine years as a private tutor, Kant was granted the right to lecture in 1755. His lectures, on a variety of subjects including logic, ethics, metaphysics, law, and geography, were popular so he managed to eke out a modest living. Kant also began to make a reputation for himself with his writings. In his *General History of the Nature and Theory of the Heavens* (1755), Kant advanced a highly original account of the origin of the universe. Although he had successfully defended his doctoral dissertation "About Fire," he was forced to remain a lecturer for fifteen years. Twice his application for a professorship at Königsberg was rejected, and twice he turned down outside offers because of his reluctance to leave his home town, a thriving intellectual center.

Finally in 1770, Kant received an appointment as professor of logic and metaphysics at the university on the basis of his essay *On the Form and Principles of the Sensible and Intelligible Worlds*. A prolific author, his masterpiece was *The Critique of Pure Reason* (1781). In it Kant investigated the legitimacy of the claims to objective validity made by pure reason and by the concepts to which it gives rise. He assumed that the primary concepts have their origins in the mind itelf and are created a priori. Arguing that true knowledge cannot transcend or go beyond experience (we never know the thing-in-itself), he maintained that we know only appearances, sounds, colors, and the like. His other works followed in rapid succession including the *Critique of Judgment* (1788). Kant applied his critical philosophy to ethics, aesthetics, religion, theology, politics, and law. He also formulated categorical imperatives, basic ethical laws designed to instruct people in their moral duty. His fame spread throughout Europe, and his philosophy began to be taught at all the German universities and some in England and the Low Countries as well.

At home Kant got in trouble with the king of Prussia, Frederick William II, with the publication of his *Religion within the Limits of Reason Alone* (1793). Unlike his predecessor Frederick the Great, Frederick William had little sympathy for ideas of religious toleration. The king ordered his obscurantist minister of education, Wöllner, to extract from Kant a promise that he would not write again on religion. Kant's open admiration for the French Revolution also offended the Prussian court.

Vexed by increasing ill health, the lifelong bachelor was gradually forced to reduce his teaching commitments and finally retired in 1799. In his last years the once-scintillating intellect declined into a childlike senility. However, Immanuel Kant left behind a profound intellectual legacy, which reflects the deep piety and strong bent of his nature.

Works By: *Akademieausgabe,* 22 vols. (Berlin, 1900-1942), *Kant's Political Writings,* ed. Hans Reiss (Cambridge, England, 1970); *The Philosophy of Kant,* ed. Carl J. Friedrich (New York, 1949); *Critique of Pure Reason,* tr. N. K. Smith (New York, 1933). **Works About:** Ernst Cassirer, *Kants Leben und Lehre* (Berlin 1921); Lucien Goldmann, *Immanuel Kant* (London 1971); Martin Heidegger, *Kant and the Problem of Metaphysics,* tr. J. S. Churchill (Bloomington, Ind., 1962); S. Körner, *Kant* (London, 1955).   *J. W. Zophy*

See FREDERICK II, THE GREAT; SCHILLER.

KARLOWITZ, PEACE OF, 1699, ended Leopold I's war with the Porte, which began in 1683 when the Turks under Kara Mustapha, the grand vizier, broke the truce concluded at Vasvar in 1664 and invaded royal Hungary, then marched west to seize Vienna. The Turkish invasion of the Holy Roman Empire ignited the European crusading spirit and inspired the formation of a holy league composed of the Holy Roman Empire, Venice, the papacy, Poland, and Russia. The rebellion in Hungary led by Emerick Tököly had spurred the Turks to break the peace. With approximately two hundred thousand troops, the Turks endeavored to seize Vienna. Failing, they hastily and disastrously retreated. In 1686 Budapest fell to the Austrians as did Pécs, Szeged, and Arad. In 1687 Duke Charles V of Lorraine defeated the Turks at Mohács, and in 1688 Max Emmanuel, elector of Bavaria, seized the capital of Serbia, Belgrade. The Turks recouped their losses under the personal leadership of the sultan, Mustafa II, who reconquered Belgrade in 1690 and defeated the imperialists at Lugos in eastern Hungary. The Turks proved unwilling to sue for peace. In order to break this stalemate, Leopold appointed Prince Eugene of Savoy as commander-in-chief of the imperial forces in Hungary in 1697. With an army of fifty thousand, Eugene pursued the Turks and subsequently defeated them at Zenta (1697), totally destroying the Turkish infantry. Although skirmishing continued throughout 1698, Zenta effectually ended the Turkish war.

With the maritime powers acting as mediators, the Habsburgs began negotiating with the Turks in 1698 at Karlowitz near Peterwardein. By the treaty signed early in 1699, the Turks under Mustafa II recognized Leopold's sovereignty over most of Hungary, including Transylvania, except for one area, the banat of Temesvár, Polish acquisition of Podolia, and Venetian possession of

Dalmatia, the Morea, and Aegina. In 1699 Peter I would only agree to accept an armistice, but in 1700 he signed the Treaty of Constantinople, which confirmed Russia in its possession of Azov. For Leopold I, the treaty confirmed his recent conquests of the last sixteen years and marked the foundation of the Danubian empire. Never again could the Turks singlehandedly threaten the existence of the Holy Roman Empire. With his foe in the East conquered, Leopold could concentrate on challenging Louis XIV's bid for European hegemony and on fighting for the Spanish inheritance for his son (War of the Spanish Succession).

Works About: Max Braubach, *Prinz Eugen von Savoyen,* 5 vols. (Vienna, 1963–1965), and *Versailles und Wien von Ludwig XIV bis Kaunitz* (Bonn, 1952); William Coxe, *History of the House of Austria* (London, 1877); J. Dumont, *Corps Universel diplomatique* (Amsterdam, 1739); F. Heller, ed., *Prinz Eugen, militärische Correspondenz,* 2 vols. (Vienna, 1848); Helmut Oehler, *Prinz Eugen im Urteil Europas* (Munich, 1944); Oswald Redlich, *Weltmacht des Barock, Österr. in der Zeit Kaiser Leopolds I* (Vienna, 1961); John P. Spielman, *Leopold I of Austria* (New Brunswick, N. J., 1977).   *L. S. Frey and M. L. Frey*

See EUGENE OF SAVOY; LEOPOLD I; PETERWARDEIN; VIENNA, SIEGE OF; ZENTA.

KARLSTADT, ANDREAS BODENSTEIN VON (c. 1480–1541), was a colleague of Martin Luther at the University of Wittenberg, who became one of Luther's earliest and most vociferous supporters. However, his split with Luther in 1524 over the interpretation of the sacraments was to have far-reaching consequences for the Protestant Reformation. Many have argued that Karlstadt was largely responsible for converting the Swiss to an acceptance of his views of the sacraments. At the least, he was a major figure in the so-called sacramentarian controversy, which caused an irreparable split between Lutherans and the followers of Ulrich Zwingli. He also exercised considerable influence on the Anabaptists and other sectarians.

Born in Karlstadt am Main in Bavaria, Andreas studied philosophy and theology at the universities of Erfurt (1499–1502) and Cologne (1503). From 1505 to 1522, he served as professor of Thomistic philosophy and dean of the faculty at the new University of Wittenberg. He was heavily influenced by Augustine, German mysticism, particularly John Tauler and the *German Theology,* and by Martin Luther. His support of Luther against the attacks of John Eck led to the fateful Leipzig debates of 1519, after which Karlstadt wrote *Against the Dumb Ass and Stupid Little Doctor Eck.* He was condemned with Luther in the papal bull *Exsurge Domine.*

During Luther's exile following the diet of Worms in 1521, Karlstadt assumed a leadership role in the Reformation in Wittenberg. Preaching strongly against clerical celibacy, the Mass, and the ceremonies of the Roman Church, he, with Gabriel Zwilling, pushed impatiently for reforms more quickly than the elector of Saxony, or his fellow reformers Philip Melanchthon and Nicholas von Amsdorf wished. In December 1521, he served both bread and wine to the laity at

Holy Communion in the Church of All Saints. In January 1522, he married and urged that all clergy should be compelled to do so.

Although Karlstadt's reforms were accepted in essence by the Wittenberg city council, incidences of violence against the clergy, churches, and monasteries, capped by the appearance in Wittenberg of the Zwickau prophets, caused Frederick the Wise to command the restoration of the old order. Under these circumstances, Luther returned to Wittenberg on March 6, 1522. Through moderate reforms and a series of Invocavit sermons denouncing the use of violence in matters of religion, Luther was able to restore order. Karlstadt, however, did not willingly accept Luther's moderation and left Wittenberg for a pastorate at Orlamünde. There he continued with his own program of reform.

To this point, Karlstadt's views were considered extreme only in degree, not in substance. He extended Luther's concept of the priesthood of all believers to the extreme of not wearing vestments and asking the laity to address him as Brother Andrew, and he appeared to be a stronger advocate of social equality than was Luther. But his real problems began when he accepted a spiritual and symbolic interpretation of the sacrament of the Last Supper and questioned the necessity of both baptism and the Eucharist. Against Karlstadt's position, Luther wrote *Wider die himmlischen Propheten* ("Against the Heavenly Prophets"). In September 1524, Karlstadt was banished from Saxony.

For the next several years, Karlstadt was virtually without a homeland, traveling to south Germany, Switzerland, Rothenberg, Holstein, East Friesland, and back to Switzerland. In the sacramentarian controversy, he sided with the Zwinglians against Luther and, in turn, was defended by them. In 1534, he accepted a pastorate in Basel and professorship of theology at the university. He died in Basel of the plague on December 24, 1541.

Works By: Erich Hertzsch, ed., *Karlstadts Schriften aus den Jahren 1523–1525,* 2 vols. (Halle, 1956); R. Sider, ed., *Karlstadt's Battle with Luther* (Philadelphia, 1978).
Works About: Hermann Barge, *Andreas Bodenstein von Karlstadt,* 2 vols. (Leipzig, 1905); Erich Hertzsch, *Karlstadt und seine Bedeutung für das Luthertum* (Gotha, 1932); Karl Müller, *Luther und Karlstadt* (Tübingen, 1907); E. Gordon Rupp, *Patterns of the Reformation* (Philadelphia, 1969); R. J. Sider, *Andreas Bodenstein von Karlstadt* (Leiden, 1974).   *D. M. Hockenbery*

See AMSDORF; ECK; FREDERICK III, THE WISE; LUTHER; MELANCHTHON; ZWINGLI.

KAUNITZ, WENCESLAUS ANTHONY VON (1711–1794), diplomat and statesman, was born in Vienna to a noble family. After studying imperial law at Leipzig and traveling widely, Kaunitz entered into governmental service in 1730. A brilliant diplomat, he served as the representative of Emperor Charles VII to the diet at Regensburg, as envoy at several Italian courts including Turin, as chief minister to the Archduchess Maria Anna in the Netherlands, as ambassador at the court of St. James, and as a plenipotentiary at the conference at Aix-la-Chapelle (Aachen) of 1748. At that conference, Kaunitz came to realize that Austria's position in Europe depended largely on its position in the Holy Roman Empire and its ability to contain Prussia.

From 1750 to 1753 this cosmopolitan and sophisticated diplomat, who loved literature and the arts served as the ambassador to the court of Versailles, where he helped to lay the foundations for the Franco-Austrian reconciliation. Maria Theresa named him state chancellor in 1753, a post he held until his resignation in August 1792. Considered one of the finest statesmen of his century, Kaunitz transformed the state chancery into the Ministry of Foreign Affairs to which was entrusted also the control of Lombardy and the Netherlands. Perhaps his principal achievement was the engineering of the diplomatic revolution of 1756 by which Austria reversed centuries of tradition and allied with France.

Works By: S. K. Padover, "Prince Kaunitz' Résumé of His Eastern Policy, 1763–71," *JMH* 5 (1933): 352–65. **Works About:** K. O. von Aretin, "Kaunitz," *NDB*, ll:363–69; Alfred von Arneth, "Biographie des Fursten Kaunitz. Ein Fragment," *Archiv für Osterreichen Gesch.* 88 (1900): 5–201, and *ADB*, 15:487–505; William J. McGill, "The Roots of Policy: Kaunitz in Versailles and Vienna, 1749," *JMH* 43 (1971): 228–44.   *J. W. Zophy*

See CHARLES VII; FRANCIS I; MARIA THERESA; SEVEN YEARS WAR.

KAYSERSBERG, JOHN GEILER VON (1445–1510), influential preacher, was raised by his grandfather in the town of Kaysersberg in Alsace after the death of his father, a city clerk, in a hunting accident. Following a brilliant student career at the University of Freiburg, he was invited to stay on as a professor. After five years of teaching, he left to attend the University of Basel, where he obtained his doctorate in theology. Brought back to Freiburg by popular demand of the students, he was elected rector of the university in 1476.

Despite his successful academic career, Geiler yearned for the pulpit rather than the lectern. When the city of Würzburg invited him to preach a trial sermon, he jumped at the chance. Before he could accept a permanent pulpit there, he was persuaded to accept the position of people's priest and preacher at the cathedral in Strasbourg, where he served for thirty-two years. He became one of the most renowned preachers in the Empire, urging the moral reform of the clergy and laity alike.

Works By: *Geilers von Kaisersberg ausgewählte Schriften*, ed. Philipp de Lorenzi, 4 vols. (Trier, 1881–1883); *Die ältesten Schriften Geilers von Kaysersberg*, ed., L. Dacheux (Amsterdam, 1965). **Works About:** L. Dacheux, *Un reformateur Catholique a la fin du XV siècle, Jean Geiler de Kaysersberg* (Paris, 1876); E. Jane Dempsey Douglass, *Justification in Late Medieval Preaching: A Study of John Geiler of Keisersberg* (Leiden, 1966): D. C. Steinmetz, *Reformers in the Wings* (Philadelphia, 1971).   *J. W. Zophy*

See STRASBOURG: WIMPFELING.

KEPLER, JOHN (1571–1630), astronomer and mathematician, was born the son of a soldier at Weil in Württemberg. After attending several local schools, John went on in 1589 to study mathematics and theology at the University of Tübingen. There he was very much influenced by Michael Maestlin, a professor who knew Copernican astronomy well. In 1594 after taking his M.A., Kepler became provincial mathematician and a teacher of mathematics at a school in

Graz, Austria. He amazed the local residents by his calendars, which predicted future events with uncanny accuracy. On a more significant level, he began his mathematic calculations, which eventually led to his three famous laws of planetary motion.

Following the publication in 1597 of his pro-Copernican *Mysterium cosmographicum,* Kepler went to Prague to work with Tycho Brahe. When Brahe died in 1601, Kepler was named imperial mathematician and court astronomer by Emperor Rudolf II. In 1609 he published his *The New Astronomy,* which contained, among other things, his most famous discovery that planetary orbits are ellipses. After Rudolf's abdication in 1612, Kepler continued as imperial mathematician, but he also moved to Linz as a professor of mathematics. He remained in Linz for fourteen years despite periodic persecutions because of his Lutheranism.

A devoted son, Kepler made several trips to Swabia in 1620 and 1621 in order to help defend his mother from accusations of witchcraft. Because he often found his imperial pay in arrears, Kepler in 1628 went to work for Albert von Wallenstein, who was very much interested in astrology. After Wallenstein's fall, he left Sagan for Regensburg, where he died still seeking his imperial back pay. In his search for cosmic harmonies, John Kepler made many great contributions to the growth of modern science.

Works By: *Joannis Kepleri astronomi opera omnia,* ed. Christian Frisch, 8 vols. (Frankfurt, 1858– 1871 rpr. 1971–). **Works About:** Max Caspar, *Johannes Kepler,* tr. Doris Hellmans (New York, 1959); Walther Gerlach and Martha List, *Johannes Kepler* (Munich, 1971); Owen Gingerich, "Kepler," *DSB,* 7:289–312.   *J. W. Zophy*

See MATTHIAS; RUDOLF II; WALLENSTEIN, ALBERT.

KRAFFT, ADAM (1493–1558), of Fulda, Hessian reformer, was the son of a Fulda mayor. He took the B.A. and M.A. degrees at the University of Erfurt in 1514 and 1519, respectively, remaining there until 1521. At Erfurt, two influences left their marks on the young Krafft: Erasmian humanism and Lutheran teachings. Krafft left Erfurt in the summer of 1521 when the bubonic plague struck the city and returned to his native Fulda to asume a teaching and preaching post as vicar. Apparently motivated by a desire to prove to Landgrave Philip of Hesse that his preaching was not conducive to revolt during the Peasants' Revolt and by a genuine desire to quell unrest, the peacher devoted his attention to pacifying the agitated peasantry. He soon became known for the ironical nature of his sermons. After hearing him preach, the landgrave took Krafft into his service, first as a field preacher and then as a court preacher.

Krafft became a commanding figure in the new Hessian church and a professor at the new University of Marburg. Although Francis Lambert of Avignon was the main engineer of the Homberg synod—an extraordinary assembly of lay and spiritual representatives called by the landgrave to forge a new church-state settlement—and the chief author of the document resulting therefrom, the *Reformation of the Hessian Church* (1526), Krafft's position was in no way diminished thereby. It was Krafft, backed by the Hessian chancellor, John Feige, who induced Philip to send the *Reformation* to Wittenberg before enacting it as law, which was Lambert's intent. When Luther advised against such enactment, Krafft's position as the leading Hessian theologian was undoubtedly strengthened. Krafft was the major administrator of the new church-state settlement as chief visitor or superintendent. He assumed the major responsibility for the appointment of capable preachers and maintenance of orthodox doctrines, as well as the secularization of Church properties and their disposal according to Lutheran precepts. He took charge of establishing a common chest system, hospitals for the poor, and a state school system. He was the highest official in marital disputes, adjudicating as a member of the palace court at Marburg. Krafft's authority as chief superintendent was so extensive that one contemporary described him as archbishop of the Hessian church.

Perhaps his role as adviser to the landgrave at the time of the Marburg colloquy of 1529 was of the greatest importance for the history of the Empire. Many at the Hessian court, including the landgrave, most scholars agree, were leaning toward the Zwinglian position at that time, but Krafft remained unmoved. Zwingli encouraged the landgrave to diminish Krafft's authority, a move that surely would have led to the elimination of Lutheran teaching in Hesse. Krafft, backed by another Lutheran court faithful, Eberhard Schnepf, however, prevailed. As a result, Philip allowed both Lutherans and Zwinglians to preach and took advice from both. Krafft's failure to prevail in the landgrave's bigamy was equally important. He was almost alone in his refusal to recommend this act.

In addition to his social engineering in Hesse, Krafft is known for his connection with the Protestant reform of Wittgenstein, Höxter, and Göttingen.

Works About: C. Mirbt, "Adam Krafft,"*Herzogs Realenzyclopädie für Protestantische Theologie u. Kirche* (Leipzig, 1896) 11:57; Friedrich Wilhelm Schaefer, *Adam Krafft, der Reformator Hessens* (Darmstadt, 1911). *Urkundlichen Quel. zur hessischen Reformationsgesch.*, ed. Günther Franz, 4 vols. (Marburg, 1954).   *W. J. Wright*

See LAMBERT; MARBURG COLLOQUY; PEASANTS' WAR; PHILIP OF HESSE; ZWINGLI.

KRESS, CHRISTOPH (1484–1535), statesman, was born in Nuremberg, the scion of a wealthy patrician family. Educated in Italy, England, and the Netherlands, Christoph also attended the University of Ingolstadt. In his early life, Kress received military training such as during his service in the Bavarian War of Succession in 1504.

In 1513 Kress married and began a public career that was to make one of Nuremberg's most influential statesmen. He became one of the elite seven elders, Nuremberg's highest level of civic authority, as well as representing the city at numerous political and military meetings. Although initially somewhat

L

LAMBERT, FRANCIS, OF AVIGNON (1486/87–1530), evangelical theologian, was the son of a papal secretary. He joined the Observant Franciscans around 1501 but was unable to get along well with his fellows. When he began to preach Lutheran teachings, much to the chagrin of the brothers, he was given leave to travel north. Lambert studied briefly in Wittenberg (1522–1523) and began writing evangelical tracts. He was one of the first monks to marry, taking a baker's daughter as his wife in 1523. He traveled through the upper German cities looking for employment and stayed for a while at Strasbourg. His troublesome character and lack of proficiency in German were major deterrents, however.

Lambert emerged from obscurity and penury in 1526 when he was invited to serve Landgrave Philip of Hesse. Lambert's *Paradoxa* was the basis for discussion at the Homberg synod of 1526, at which he also led the argument for the evangelical cause. A committee, whose leader was surely Lambert, was elected from the synod to draw up a total plan for a new church-state settlement. The resulting document, *Reformation of the Hessian Church (1526),* combined plans for an elaborate synodal church structure and strong congregational discipline (ideas usually associated with the later Reformed churches) with a princely office that played an active and powerful role in church affairs. Basically it represented the Lutheran conception of the proper roles and relationships of the church and state, with the exception of the emphasis on the prince's role, which fit into Philip's political plans. Furthermore both the *Paradoxa* and *Reformation* were marked by the strict biblicism characteristic of Lambert.

For the remaining years of his life, Lambert served as a professor at the new University of Marburg, influencing students from as far away as Scotland. He is credited with authoring twenty three writings, many of which deal with the issue of monasticism. In his last years he conducted a veritable war in print with his chief opponent from the Homberg synod, Nicholas Ferber of Herborn, once Franciscan guardian at Marburg. Lambert succumbed to the English sweating sickness.

Works By: Francis Lambert, "Paradoxa," in Wilhelm Schmitt, *Die Synode zu Homberg und ihre Vorgesch.* (Homberg, 1926), pp. 52–67; "Reformatio Ecclesiarum Hassiae," in Emil Sehling, ed., *Die ev. Kirchenordnungen des XVI. Jahrhunderts,* 14 vols. (Tübingen, 1965), 8:43–65. **Works About:** Edmund Kurten, *Franz Lambert von Avignon und Nikolaus Herborn in ihrer Stellung zum Ordensgedanken und zum Franziskanertum im Besonderen* (Münster, 1950); Wilhelm Maurer, "Franz Lambert von Avignon und das Verfassungs-ideal der Reformatio ecclesiarum hassiae von

1526," *ZKG* 48 (1929): 209–60; Gerhard Müller, *Franz Lambert von Avignon und die Reformation in Hessen* (Marburg, 1958); Roy Lutz Winters, *Francis Lambert of Avignon: A Study in Reformation Origins* (Philadelphia, 1928).   W. J. Wright

See HOMBERG SYNOD; PHILIP OF HESSE.

LANG, MATTHEW (1468–1540), imperial chancellor during the reign of Emperor Maximilian I (1493–1519), cardinal, and archbishop of Salzburg, was born in Augsburg. He studied law and letters at Tübingen, Ingolstadt, and Vienna and obtained a position in the chancery of the imperial reformer Berthold von Henneberg, archbishop of Mainz. In 1494, the year he received his doctorate in law, he became secretary to Maximilian. Lang rose rapidly in the ranks of secular administration, becoming imperial councillor in 1501 and chancellor in 1508. As a result of imperial influence, he also acquired a large number of ecclesiastical offices: cathedral provost of Augsburg in 1500 and shortly thereafter in Constance, bishop of Gurk from 1505 to 1522 (although ordained and consecrated only in 1519), cardinal in 1513, coadjutor of the see of Salzburg in 1514, archbishop of Salzburg in 1519, and primate of Germany in 1529.

An ambitious man, Lang alienated many people, some of whom regarded him as an upstart because of his burgher origins, despite the patent of nobility bestowed on him in 1498. Yet his influence on imperial affairs, especially during the latter years of Maximilian's reign, was enormous. He served as the emperor's chief negotiator in the diplomatic meetings leading to the League of Cambrai, he effected the alliance of emperor and pope in 1512, and he played a key role at the Congress of Vienna in 1515.

With the death of Maximilian in 1519, Lang's diplomatic service in the Empire began to wane in spite of his successful lobby for the election of Charles V (1519–1556). He now turned his considerable talents to administering the extensive lands that belonged to Salzburg. In these territories he confronted powerful demands for religious and social change. He invoked the aid of the Swabian League in defeating peasant unrest, joined the Regensburg Union brought forth by Cardinal Campeggio in 1524, appeared at the second diet of Speyer in 1529, and held long conversations with Melanchthon at Augsburg in 1530.

Humanistically inclined, Lang numbered among his friends and associates moderate reformers and evangelical Catholics. These included John von Staupitz, Christoph Scheurl, and, for a time, Luther. He supported an Erasmian reform program, especially in the areas of religious and theological education for the laity and clergy. When Staupitz resigned as vicar general of the Augustinian Hermits in 1520, Lang acquired permission from Rome for Staupitz to enter the Benedictine order, and he successfully influenced Staupitz's election as abbot of St. Peter's in Salzburg. At synods he convened at Mühldorf in 1522 and 1537, he advocated Church reform and consulted with the laity. In his religious policies Lang gave expression to one of the first instances of Catholic reform in Germany.

Works About: Willibald Hauthaler, *Kardinal Matthäus Lang und die religiössoziale Bewegung seiner Zeit 1517–1540* (Salzburg, 1896); Michael Ott, "Lang," *The Catholic Encyclopedia,* 8:787 (New York, 1913); Alois Schopf, *Ein Diplomat Kaiser Maximilians* (Vienna, 1882); W. B. Slottman "Lang," *New Catholic Encyclopedia,* 8:363 (New York, 1967).   *P. N. Bebb*

See BERTHOLD; CHARLES V; HUMANISM; MAXIMILIAN I; SCHEURL; STAUPITZ.

LEIBNIZ, GOTTFRIED WILLIAM (1646–1716), mathematician, philosopher, diplomat, was born in Leipzig. His father, Frederick, was a professor of moral philosophy and administrator at the university, as well as a successful notary. His mother, Katherine Schmuck, came from an academic family. Gottfried attended the Nicholai school, where his precocity led his teachers to attempt to confine him to materials they considered suitable to his age. Upon the advice of a relative, at age ten he was given full access to his father's considerable library, where he read voraciously in a wide range of classical, patristic, and scholastic literature.

Leibniz entered the University of Leipzig in 1661 intending to be a lawyer. Five years and one brief stint at Jena later, he submitted a legal thesis for a doctor's degree at Leipzig. The degree was not granted, probably because Leibniz was only a youth of twenty. However, Altdorf did accept the dissertation and also offered Leibniz a post on the faculty. Instead he went to Holland and then to Nuremberg, where he studied alchemy and magic.

Through the intercession of J. C. von Boyneburg, Leibniz was introduced to the elector of Mainz, John Philip von Schönborn, who invited the young scholar to join his service. Leibniz worked on such legal problems as simplifying the laws of the Empire and began an extensive correspondence. He also began working on a calculating machine, which he was asked to send to Colbert, Louis XIV's great minister. Leibniz did go to France in the winter of 1671–1672 on a diplomatic mission. He wanted to forestall French attacks on the Rhineland by suggesting that they divert their ambitions to Egypt and North Africa and establish an empire there. Although little came of his plan, Leibniz made the most of the trip by immersing himself in the intellectual life of Paris, including the work of René Descartes. He also studied with and made a lifelong friend of the mathematician Christian Huygens.

The diplomat-scholar journeyed to London in January 1673 to encourage peace negotiations between England and the Netherlands; while there he became acquainted with such leading scientists as Robert Boyle and was elected to the Royal Society of London. During this mission, Elector John Philip died, and his successor showed little interest in continuing Leibniz' salary. Leibniz' pecuniary difficulties were alleviated by the offer of a post as librarian and adviser to Duke John Frederick of Brunswick-Lüneburg. Enroute, he stopped in Amsterdam for scientific discussions with Anton Leewenhoek and Jan Huddle and philosophical interviews with Spinoza.

Leibniz worked for the dukes of Brunswick-Lüneberg for forty years. He found a great patron and friend in Sophie Charlotte, a woman of charm and intellect, wife of John Frederick's successor, Ernest August. His major responsibility proved to be the writing of a genealogy of the house of Brunswick in order to support the imperial and dynastic ambitions of that family. While researching the genealogy, Leibniz was able to travel throughout Europe and discuss his ideas with a large number of eminent scientific thinkers. In October 1688 he had an audience with Emperor Leopold I, to whom he revealed a number of plans for economic and scientific reforms. The results of his genealogical inquiries were instrumental in the elevation of Hanover to electoral status in 1692.

When Elector Ernest August died in January 1698, he was succeeded by George Ludwig, an ignorant boor who resented Leibniz' contacts with foreign monarchs and his efforts to establish scientific academies. George placed restrictions on the scope of Leibniz' activities and travels. Relief was offered by George's sister, Sophie Charlotte, electress of Brandenburg, who like her namesake mother appreciated Leibniz' intellect and personality. She invited him to Berlin, where he founded and served as first president of the Berlin Academy.

Leibniz persisted in his efforts toward promoting religious, political, and cultural reforms such as his concern for religious toleration. His ideas won for him an appointment as privy councillor by Peter the Great of Russia. Not to be outdone by Peter, Emperor Leopold I invited him to Vienna, where he served as an imperial privy councillor from 1712 to 1714. His hopes for the post of court historian in London were dashed by George Ludwig, now King George I of England, who told him he must first complete his history of the house of Brunswick. A bachelor, Leibniz spent the last two years of his life plagued by gout trying to finish that monumental history. Shamefully neglected by those he had served so faithfully (the two Sophies were already deceased), only his secretary attended his funeral.

Perhaps his most famous discovery had been that of differential calculus in 1676, although he did not publish it until 1684, nine years before Isaac Newton, the English scientist. Despite the acrimonious controversy over the discovery, there is little doubt that the two men made it independently of one another. Characteristically George I was supportive of the Newtonian claims. Leibniz also invented the binary number system, a general method of integrating rational functions and the signs for similarity and congruence. Leibniz laid the foundations for linguistics and wrote a number of philosophical works, such as his *Theodicy* (1710), which argued that evil is necessary for the greatest moral good.

Works By: *Philosophical Papers and Letters*, ed. L. R. Loemker, 2 vols. (Dordrecht, 1969); *Samtliche Schriften und Briefe* (Hildesheim, 1923–). **Works About:** C. D. Broad, *Leibniz* (London, 1975); Ernst Cassirer, *Leibniz' System in seinem wissenschaftlichen Grundlagen* (Darmstadt, 1962); K. Fischer, *G. W. Leibniz* (Heidelberg, 1920); Frederick Kreiling et al., "Leibniz," *DSB* 7:149–68; R. W. Meyer, *Leibniz and the Seventeenth Century Revolution* (Glasgow, 1957); K. Müller *Leibniz-Bibliographie* (Frankfurt, 1967); B. Russell, *A Critical Exposition of the Philosophy of Leibniz* (London, 1937).   *J. W. Zophy*

See LEOPOLD I; SOPHIE CHARLOTTE.

LEIPZIG, CONVENTION OF (1631), a meeting of the Protestant estates, was held at the height of the Thirty Years War in the Saxon city of Leipzig. The meeting was called on January 8, 1631, by Elector John George of Saxony to deal with the religious and political crisis in which Germany's Protestants found themselves as a result of recent imperial victories, Sweden's intervention in the war, and Emperor Ferdinand II's Edict of Restitution. With the exception of the rulers of Hesse-Darmstadt and Pomerania, every major Protestant prince attended. Several imperial cities (including Nuremberg, Strasbourg, Ulm, and Mühlhausen) also sent representatives. The convention began on February 20 and lasted for two months. While the princes deliberated, their pastors, three Lutherans from Saxony and three Calvinists from Hesse-Cassel and Brandenburg, held a religious colloquy. Even though these six theologians were unable to resolve the major differences that separated the two Protestant communions, they showed an almost unprecedented harmony and thereby helped create an atmosphere of goodwill and cooperation that spilled over into the political deliberations at Leipzig.

The most important result of the convention was the Leipzig manifesto, which the assembled estates issued, largely on the initiative of Brandenburg's Calvinist councillors, at the conclusion of the conference on April 12. The manifesto created a Protestant defensive alliance for which the princes pledged to raise an army of forty thousand troops. Their recruitment and financing was left to individual imperial circles whose defensive efforts were to be coordinated by a committee headed by John George of Saxony. The alliance was designed to uphold the imperial constitution and to protect the political and religious interests of the Protestant estates (both Lutheran and Calvinist) by standing as a neutral third force among the imperial, league, and foreign armies whose fighting had turned the war in central Europe into a major international conflict. This Protestant third-party effort failed because of the military superiority of the Swedes and the emperor.

Works About: Michael Caspar Lundorp, ed., *Der Römischen Kayserlichen Majestät und dess Heiligen Römischen Reichs . . . Acta Publica,* (Frankfurt am Main, 1668), 4:144–46; Bodo Nischan, "Brandenburg's Reformed Räte and the Leipzig Manifesto of 1631," *Journal of Religious Hist.* (in press), and "Reformed Irenicism and the Leipzig Colloquy of 1631," *CEH* 9 (1976):3–26; *The Swedish Intelligencer* (London, 1632), 1:20–38.   *Bodo Nischan*

See EDICT OF RESTITUTION; FERDINAND II; JOHN GEORGE; THIRTY YEARS WAR.

LEO IX (1002–1054, pope from 1048), an Alsatian pope who was one of the founders of the Gregorian reform movement, was born as Bruno, son of count Hugo II of Eguisheim (Egisheim) near Colmar in Alsace. He was sent to Toul for his education, though he returned home during summers. After his cousin became King Conrad II in 1024, Bruno went to the royal court to continue his education. He commanded the Toul levy in the army that accompanied Conrad to Italy in 1026, and when the prior incumbent died, the young deacon Bruno was elected bishop of Toul in absentia. Bruno gained a high reputation both as a reformer of clerical life and as an able defender of the imperial frontier against the kings of France and the counts of Champagne.

When Pope Damasus II died in August 1048, an imperial assembly called by Emperor Henry III at Worms elected Bruno as pope, but he accepted only on the condition that he should also be elected in canonical form in Rome. As Pope Leo IX, he introduced many of the future leaders of the reform movement into the papal administration, and he effectively internationalized the cardinalate. His primary concern was to combat the sale of clerical office (simony) as well as clerical noncelibacy (Nicolaism), and he took the unprecedented step of touring outside of Italy and confronting clerics in regional synods to force them to reform. He made three journeys north of the Alps, and he was in Rome during the year only at Easter. In 1050 he condemned the heresy of Berengar of Tours, who was thought to have denied the real presence in the Eucharist. In late 1052 Leo arbitrated a dispute between Henry III and King Andreeas of Hungary at Bratislava.

In 1052 Leo had become alarmed at the takeover of southern Italy by Norman adventurers, and he organized an army of German and Italian warriors to attack the Normans in alliance with the Byzantines. The pope's protocrusade was utterly defeated by the Normans at Civitate on June 18, 1053. Leo was held in honorable captivity at Benevento, and it was from here in January 1054 that he dispatched an embassy to negotiate differences with the Church of Constantinople. This embassy ended with what was to become the definitive schism between the Eastern and Western churches on July 15, 1054. Leo had already died in April, shortly after his release from Norman captivity.

Leo was the first pope in over two centuries to be venerated as a saint. His memory was also cultivated by the Gregorian leaders, who saw him as a man who had helped set the great reform in motion.

Works By: Ernestus Sackur, ed., "Brunonis episcopi Signini libellus de symoniacis," *MGH, Libelli de lite* (Hanover, 1892), 2:543–62. **Works About:** Josef Deér, *Papsttum und Normannen* (Cologne, 1972); Augustin Fliche, *La réforme grégorienne* (Paris, 1924), vol. 1; Rudolf Huls, *Kardinale, Klerus und Kirchen Roms, 1049–1130,* Bibliothek des dtschen. hist. Inst. in Rom (Tübingen, 1977), vol. 48; Hubert Jedin and J. P. Dolan, eds., *Handbook of Church Hist.* (London, 1969), vol. 1; Jacques Paul Migne, *Patrologia latina* (Paris, 1853), 143: cols. 457–798; Albert Poncelet, "Vie et miracles du pape S. Léon IX," *Analecta bollandiana* 25 (1906):258–97; Sir Steven Runciman, *The Eastern Schism* (Oxford, 1965); Heinrich Tritz, "Die hagiographische Quell. zur Gesch. Papst Leos IX.," *Studi gregoriani* 4 (1952):191–364.   *S. W. Rowan*

See CONRAD II; HENRY III; STEPHEN IX.

LEOPOLD I (1640–1705), one of the most successful and conscientious of the Holy Roman emperors, was the second son of Ferdinand III and the Infanta Maria Anna of Spain. He was destined for the priesthood until the death of his elder brother, Ferdinand, of smallpox made him heir to the Habsburg dominions. Named king of Hungary in 1655 and king of Bohemia in 1656, Leopold was elected Holy Roman emperor in 1658. Leopold was married three times: to the infanta Margaret Theresa (1651–1673) in 1666, who bore him a daughter, Maria Antonia; to Claudia Felicitias of Tyrol (1653–1676) in 1673; and to Eleanor of Pfalz-Neuburg (1655–1720) in 1676, who bore him the future Joseph I (1678–1711) and Charles VI (1685–1740). Son of an Austrian and a Spanish Habsburg, Leopold had the typical Habsburg physical attributes: a long narrow face, blond hair, large light eyes, hollow cheeks, a prominent nose, a long, pointed chin, and a protruding lower lip. He was short, thin, pale, and walked with a tottering gait. Many of his contemporaries described him as "repulsively ugly." A silent, reserved man, he had grace in neither manners nor address. He excelled, however, in music. Leopold patronized musicians and encouraged building in the baroque style throughout his realm.

Contemporaries often compared Leopold to a clock that constantly needs rewinding because of his inveterate irresolution and vacillation. Leopold's indecisiveness stemmed in part from the inefficiency of early modern European government in central Europe and in part from his own lack of confidence. Leopold suffered from a mistrust of his own judgment and never felt equal to the task of governing the Danubian monarchy. Trained for the clergy, he always placed his faith in God before his faith in self. In many cases, Leopold's vacillation resulted not from his personality but from conscious policy. For example, during the War of the Spanish Succession (1701–1713), the unmistakable superiority of his allies, the maritime powers of England and the United Provinces, made the emperor financially and militarily dependent on them and unable to influence allied policy decisions. By using delaying tactics, the emperor could at least defer accepting the unpalatable decisions that were forced on him. When he believed that a certain policy was the correct one, he adhered tenaciously to it. He refused, for example, to give up what he regarded as the Habsburgs' inalienable right to the Spanish empire or to accede to the demands of the Hungarians who had revolted in 1703.

Under Leopold's guidance, the Habsburgs concentrated on building up their power in the hereditary countries rather than in the Holy Roman Empire. For most of his reign, Leopold was at war with either the Turks, who actually besieged the capital at Vienna in 1683, or the French under his cousin Louis XIV. Leopold battled the Turks intermittently until the conclusion of the Treaty of Karlowitz (1699), which gave Leopold almost all of Hungary, including Transylvania, except for one district, the banat of Temesvár. Besides warring with the Turks, Leopold also contested French hegemony in Europe (the Dutch war, 1672–1678, the Reunions, 1682–1684, the War of the League of Augsburg, 1689–1697) and the French claim to the Spanish Empire (the War of the Spanish Succession). Leopold also tried to repress Protestantism and extend royal absolutism in his dominions. In Hungary, the nobles lost their traditional right to elect their ruler and their ancient right to resist the king. The diet of Pressburg (1687) made the crown hereditary in the house of Habsburg. Leopold's conquest of Hungary did not end the unrest. The Hungarians wanted restoration of their traditional liberties. Revolt under Francis II Rákóczi broke out in 1703 and was not suppressed until the end of Joseph I.

Even on his deathbed in 1705 with his dominions endangered by war in the west with France and rebellion in the east with Hungary, Leopold still clung to his unshakable conviction that God was on the side of the house of Habsburg. When Leopold became emperor in 1658, the Holy Roman Empire was war ravaged, administratively chaotic, financially unstable, and threatened by both the Turks and France. Leopold attributed to God his success in raising the Turkish siege from Vienna (1683), challenging French hegemony, reconquering Hungary, incorporating Transylvania, and ending the Turkish threat to the Empire. In spite of his limitations as a ruler, Leopold was able to increase and consolidate Habsburg power during his reign.

Works About: Max Braubach, *Versailles und Wien von Ludwig bis Kaunitz* (Bonn, 1952), and *Prinz Eugen von Savoyen* 5 vols. (Munich, 1965); Hugo Hantsch, *Die Gesch. Österreichs* (Vienna, 1947), and *Die Entwicklung Österreichs-Ungarns zur Grossmacht* (Freiburg im Bresgau, 1933); Oswald Redlich, *Das Werden einer Grossmacht, Österreich von 1700 bis 1740* (Vienna, 1942); John P. Spielman, *Leopold I of Austria* (New Brunswick, N.J., 1977); Roger Wines, "The Imperial Circles, Princely Diplomacy and Imperial Reform, 1681–1714," *JMH* 39 (1967):1–29; A. Wolf, "Leopold I," *ADB*, 18:316–22.   *L. S. Frey and M. L. Frey*

See CHARLES VI; HARRACH; JOSEPH I; KARLOWITZ; SPANISH SUCCESSION; VIENNA, SIEGE OF; WAR OF THE LEAGUE OF AUGSBURG.

LEOPOLD II (1747–1792), Holy Roman emperor for eighteen months (1790–1792), was born in Vienna on May 5, 1747, the third son of Austrian Empress Maria Theresa (1717–1780) and her husband, Francis I (1708–1765), Holy Roman emperor. Originally educated for the priesthood, Leopold instead became imbued with the liberal principles of the Enlightenment, especially under the tutelage of the political philosopher Karl Anton von Martini. When his older brother, Charles Joseph, died in 1761, it was decided that Leopold should succeed to his father's grand duchy of Tuscany, as a "secundogeniture" or apanage for a second son. That his rule be an independent one was a condition of his marriage to the Spanish infanta Maria Luisa, daughter of Charles III (1716–1788), at Innsbruck, August 5, 1765. The marriage was a happy one and produced sixteen children, just as Leopold's parents' marriage had.

The marriage festivities were marred by the sudden death of his father, Francis I, on August 18, 1765. Leopold's eldest brother became emperor as Joseph II (1741–1790), and he became grand duke of Tuscany. For the next twenty-five years (1765–1790), Leopold brought that small state a prosperity and enlightenment it had not experienced under the last of the Medicis, and he was known by his full name, Peter Leopold, after the progressive Russian czar, Peter the Great. He reformed the tax structure, established free trade in corn, repressed the restrictive industrial guilds, lessened serfdom, and initiated public works, including road and canal construction and the draining of the Val di Chiana. He also eliminated military expenditure by disbanding the Tuscan fleet and replacing the armed forces with a civilian militia. His progressive views were stimulated in Florence by contact with Italian Enlightenment figures; and his association with Cesare Beccaria resulted in the abolition of torture, of the death penalty, and of the confiscation of property, in the penal code of 1768. Going beyond the enlightened despots of the age, Leopold accepted the political principles of Montesquieu and desired to turn the state into a constitutional monarchy. Nonetheless he was never popular with his Italian subjects. As an individual, he was cold and retiring, his reforms antagonized the interests that had prospered under the Medicean regime, and his clashes with the Church over the secularization of religious property and lay control of the clergy offended the sensibilities of the Catholic population.

Although Leopold's progressive ideas were in common with his older brother's, he was unwilling to inherit the unpopularity of Joseph II, caused by the haste with which numerous reforms had been improvised. Hence when the dying and childless emperor requested that Leopold come to Vienna as coregent in 1789, he evaded his brother's call. And when Joseph died on February 20, 1790, Leopold only reluctantly left the "garden of Italy" to become Austrian ruler. His new realm was at war with the Ottoman Turks, threatened by a rising Prussia, in an uneasy alliance with Russia, and experiencing the opposition of the Hungarians and the insurrection of the Belgians. In addition the revolution in France, which he had initially hailed as a "regeneration" that would result in "infinite happiness," was rapidly radicalizing, threatening his sister, Queen Marie Antoinette (1755–1793), and the stability of his own dominions.

Leopold skillfully handled a complex situation, over the objections of foreign minister Prince von Kaunitz (1711–1794). He pressured England by threatening to cede part of the Low Countries to France and renouncing territorial gains from the Turks, which forestalled the intrigues of Prussia, and he achieved a standoff with Frederick William II (1744–1797) at Reichenbach on July 27, 1790. By thus discouraging English aid to the Belgian insurgents and by a combination of concessions (amnesties and restoring the former constitution), the restoration of the historic franchises of the Flemings, and military threat, he quieted the Austrian Netherlands. He divided the nationalistic Hungarian diet by favoring the Illyrians (Serbs) and by detaching Transylvania, yet recognizing the dominance of the Magyars, and secured coronation as king of Hungary on November 15, 1790. He had also achieved coronation as Holy Roman emperor on October 9 in Frankfurt. He risked antagonizing Russia by negotiating a truce with the Porte, which resulted in the Treaty of Sistova on August 4, 1791. Domestically he placated aristocratic and clerical elements by repealing Joseph's most controversial reforms and reaffirming the position of the estates, yet qualified their reascendance by encouraging the middle class and peasantry. He was crowned king of Bohemia in Prague on August 12, 1791.

The French Revolution overshadowed Leopold's brief reign. While concerned with the plight of his sister, he nonetheless was not displeased to see Austria's traditional enemy weakened. After Louis XVI's arrested "flight to Varennes" in June 1791, he met with the king of Prussia at Pillnitz (August 27) to issue a declaration of possible intervention; yet he refused to treat with French émigrés, hoped not to intervene, if only because he distrusted the ambitions of Czarina Catherine II (1729–1796), and was greatly relieved when Louis accepted the Constitution of 1791 in September. Nonetheless he signed a defensive alliance with Prussia on February 7, 1792, that was oriented against revolutionary France. A skillful ruler of great promise, Leopold died suddenly on March 1, 1792. He passed on to his less-capable son, Francis, a reinvigorated Habsburg Empire.

Works By: A. von Arneth, ed., *Joseph II und Leopold von Toskana. Ihr Briefwechsel 1781–1790* (Vienna, 1872), and *Marie Antoinette, Joseph II und Leopold II. Ihr Briefwechsel* (Vienna, 1866); A. Beer, ed., *Joseph II, Leopold II und Kaunitz. Ihr Briefwechsel* (Vienna, 1873), and *Leopold II, Franz II und Catharina. Ihre Correspondenz* (Leipzig, 1874); A. Wolf, ed., *Leopold II und Marie Christine. Ihr Briefwechsel 1781–1792* (Vienna, 1867). **Works About:** A. Schultze, *Kaiser Leopold II und die französische Revolution* (Leipzig, 1899); H. von Sybel, *Ueber die Regierung Kaiser Leopolds II* (Munich, 1860); A. Wandruschka, *Leopold II,* 2 vols. (Vienna, 1963–1965); E. Wangermann, *From Joseph II to the Jacobin Trials* (Oxford, 1959).   A. H. Ganz

See FRANCIS I; FRANCIS II; JOSEPH II; MARIA THERESA; FRENCH REVOLUTIONARY WARS.

LESSING, GOTTHOLD EPHRAIM (1729–1781), critic and dramatist, was born the son of a Protestant minister in the town of Kamenz in Saxony. After attending school at Meissen, Gotthold entered the University of Leipzig in 1746. At Leipzig he became involved in the world of journalism and theater, making a valuable friend of Karoline Neuber and her company of players, who successfully performed one of his early plays.

Lessing settled in Berlin in 1749, where he worked as a journalist except for a year spent at Wittenberg acquiring his master's degree. During his stay in Berlin, he wrote a number of comedies, met Voltaire, and developed an enduring friendship with the Jewish philosopher, Moses Mendelssohn. A turning point in his life and that of German theater was reached in 1755 with his completion of *Miss Sarah Sampson,* which introduced domestic tragedy in the English style into the German theater.

From 1760 to 1765, the dramatist served as a military secretary to General B. F. von Tauentzien, governor of Breslau, and devoted himself to classical studies. In 1767 Lessing completed his greatest drama, *Minna von Barnhelm,* which was the first German national drama and marked Lessing's attempt to counteract the hostility between Prussia and Saxony following the Seven Years War. That same year he was appointed critic and literary adviser of the German National Theatre in Hamburg. His *Hamburg Dramaturgie* became the first handbook of dramatic technique. Following the financial failure of the Hamburg theater, Lessing became court librarian at Wolfenbüttel. His tragedy *Emilia Galotti* (1772) sharply criticized absolute government and was set in Italy rather than in Germany as a precaution. After a trip to Italy in 1776, he married Eva König, the widow of a friend, and found great happiness with her until her death only two years later. His drama *Nathan the Wise* (1778) was a stirring plea for toleration. Lessing was an author of European stature and one of the finest representatives of the ideals of the Enlightenment in the Empire.

Works By: *Samtliche Schriften,* ed. Karl Lachmann, 23 vols. (Stuttgart, 1886–1924); *The Dramatic Works of G. E. Lessing,* ed. Ernest Bell, 2 vols. (London, 1895). **Works About:** F. Andrew Brown. *Gotthold Ephraim Lessing* (New York, 1971); H. B. Garland, *Lessing* (London, 1937); Karl S. Guthke and Heinrich Schneider, *Gotthold Ephraim Lessing* (Stuttgart, 1967); Erich Schmidt, *Lessing,* 2 vols. (Berlin, 1923).   *J. W. Zophy*

See SEVEN YEARS WAR.

LEUTHEN (Polish Lutynia), village of Silesia, ten miles west of Breslau, is memorable as the site of Frederick the Great's greatest victory: that over the Austrians on December 5, 1757, during the Seven Years War. Having defeated the French at Rossbach in Saxony, Frederick II of Prussia force marched his bluecoats at fourteen miles a day to Silesia, where the Austrian prince Charles of Lorraine (1712–1780) had captured Breslau on November 25. Surprising the Austrian bakeries at Neumarkt, Frederick's 33,000 then advanced west on the Breslau road to Leuthen, where Prince Charles had drawn up his 65,000. Early on the fifth, Frederick drove in the Saxon outposts at Borne and feinted toward the Austrian right (northern) wing, causing General Lucchese to barrage Prince Charles with demands for reinforcement. Instead Frederick's columns turned south, smoothly converting from wings into lines and, concealed by the snow-dusted hills, marched to attack the Austrian left flank. From their parallel lines the Prussians then faced left into line of battle and advanced in oblique order, the battalions in echelons from the right, covered by Hans Joachim von Zieten's (1699–1786) cavalry. The Prussian grenadiers routed the Württembergers and Bavarians and rolled up the Austrian left flank at Sagschütz, while General Franz Nádasti (1708–1783) frantically realigned his wing. As the Prussians fought their way through Leuthen, General Lucchese brought seventy squadrons down to reinforce the Austrian line. But alert General von Driesen charged them with thirty-five cuirassier squadrons of the Prussian left wing cavalry, driving them into the white-coated masses who broke and fled, leaving behind casualties of 22,000, including 12,000 prisoners. Frederick had suffered 11,589 casualties. As night fell, Frederick pushed on to the bridge at Lissa, forcing Prince Charles to retreat to the border mountains, losing another 17,000 when Breslau capitulated to the Prussians again on December 21. Charles, brother of Emperor Francis I, defeated by Frederick for the fifth time in two wars, was relieved of his command.

Works About: Austrian official, *Die Kriege unter der Regierung der Kaiserin Marie Theresia,* 9 vols. (Vienna, 1896–1924); Prussian official, *Die Kriege Friedrichs des Grossen,* 20 vols. (Berlin, 1890–1913), esp. *Der Siebenjährige Krieg,* vol. 13.   *A. H. Ganz*

See FREDERICK II, THE GREAT; ROSSBACH; SEVEN YEARS WAR.

LIUTBERGA, SAINT (?–c. 870), a nun, whose learning and piety made her a model of Christian vocation, lived in the Harzgau during the first century after the introduction of Christianity to the area. She came from Salzburg and was being raised in a convent when she attracted the attention of a visiting noble woman, Gisla, daughter of Duke Hessi of Saxony and wife of Count Unwan. Gisla invited Liutberga to come to her household and assured her that she would be treated like a daughter. Liutberga established a reputation as a pious, earnest young woman, well versed in Scripture and skilled at weaving.

After the death of Gisla, Liutberga was welcomed into the household of Gisla's son, Bernhard. Liutberga often accompanied Bernhard as he visited his estates. She attended church wherever she traveled, even if she had to go long distances to hear Mass or night vigils. After a time Liutberga asked Bernhard to build a cell for her where she could spend her life doing penance. Bernhard and Bishop Theotgrim agreed. In the presence of her adopted brother, the bishop, and a number of priests and presbyters, Liutberga entered the cell. Bishop Theotgrim tearfully commanded that the door to the cell be walled up. Nevertheless Liutberga's biographer reports that she heard Mass daily, sang psalms with the nuns, and taught the art of weaving. Her good works and spiritual temptations are preserved in her biography. She died in the reign of Louis the German (866–876).

Works About: Ottokar Menzel, ed., "Das Leben der Liutbirg: Eine Quel. zur Gesch. der Sachsen in karolingischer Zeit," *Dtsch. Mittelalter* 3 (1937):1–54. Albert Reinecke, "Das Leben der heiligen Liutberg," *Z. des Harz-Vereins für Gesch. und Altertumskunde* 30 (1897):1–34.   *J. W. Gates*

See LOUIS II.

LOTHAR II, sometimes III (1075–1137), duke of Saxony, was German king from 1125 to 1137 and Holy Roman emperor from 1133 to 1137. He is also known as Lothar of Supplinburg. On the death of his predecessor, Henry V, the higher nobility and great prelates insisted on implementing the elective principle for the selection of the next king because Henry's nearest male relative was distaff nephew, Frederick of Hohenstaufen, the duke of Swabia. While the elective principle had been exercised in theory for over two centuries, in fact the power of the Saxon and Salian rulers had made it meaningless, and the principle of hereditary succession had essentially determined the choice of the new king. By 1025, however, the growth of particularism among the higher nobility and the increased power of the Church as a result of the investiture controversy made a free election a possibility. Lothar was an ideal choice. Fifty years old, sonless, a supporter of the Church, and a leader of several rebellions against Henry V, he was seen as the type of ruler likely to favor Church and local interests. His election over the more powerful Frederick led the latter to revolt, and in 1027 his able young brother, Conrad, the duke of Franconia, was elected antiking. Conrad at first made much progress, but opposed by the German Church, Pope Honorius II, and Lothar's new son-in-law, Henry the Proud, duke of Bavaria, and head of the powerful Welf family, the Hohenstaufen cause became stalemated. Both Conrad and Frederick submitted to Lothar by 1135.

As emperor, Lothar proved to be an effective but weak ruler. He was of no mind to deny his origins and in fact probably could not have done so. He owed his position to local particularism and the Church, having championed the former all his life and being sincerely devoted to the latter's spiritual interests. Those things he accomplished during his reign were in most respects achieved through the aegis of the Church and the higher nobility. Lothar has been much criticized as a creature of the Church who submitted to most of the ecclesiastical demands made of him, thereby putting his successor at great disadvantage when dealing with the Church. He was particularly ineffective in implementing the rights granted to the emperor by the Concordat of Worms in 1122 regarding the election and confirmation of bishops. Lothar was, however, at a great handicap in dealing with ecclesiastical affairs because of the power and influence of one of the greatest churchmen of the Middle Ages, the adroit and saintly Bernard of Clairvaux, the head of the Cistercian order of monks.

As a result of the disputed papal election of 1130, Lothar was drawn increasingly into Church politics by lending his support to Bernard's candidate, Innocent II. He entered Italy in a show of support for Innocent and received the imperial crown in 1133 at Rome, simultaneously having the pope ratify the imperial claims to important territories in Lombardy. Innocent, however, immediately portrayed this incident as Lothar's doing him homage in return for the fief of the Empire. Lothar was back in Italy in 1136 to campaign successfully aganst the Norman king, Roger II of Sicily, who supported the antipope, Anacletus, against Innocent. The emperor died on his way home in December 1137.

Lothar II had some success in pacifying Germany and reviving the Saxon dynasty's *Drang nach Osten* (Drive to the East) through political expansion, colonization, and missionary activity. Through Bernard of Clairvaux and Norbert of Xanten, he furthered reform of the German Church. On his death, he left a relatively prosperous and peaceful Germany, a more independent German Church, strong particularist dukes, and a weakened monarchical position.

Works About: *Die Urkunden Lothars II. und der Kaiserin Richenza,* ed. E. von Ottenthal and H. Hirsch, *MGH Dip.,* 4 (Berlin, 1889); K. Hampe, *Germany under the Salian and Hohenstaufen Emperors,* tr. R. Bennett (Totowa, N.J., 1973); *Historia Welforum Weingartensis,* ed. E. König (Stuttgart, 1938); A. L. Poole, "Germany, 1125–1152," *Cambridge Medieval Hist.* (Cambridge, 1926), 5:334–59; F. J. Schmale, "Lothar III und Friedrich I als Könige und Kaiser," *Vörtrage und Forsch. Herausgegeben vom Konstanzer Arbeits kreis* 12 (1968):33–52; H. Vogt, *Das Herzogtum Lothars von Supplingburg* (Hildesheim, 1959).   *D. S. Devlin*

See CONCORDAT OF WORMS; CONRAD III; HENRY V; INVESTITURE CONTROVERSY.

LOUIS I, THE PIOUS (788–840), only surviving son of Charlemagne, was crowned emperor by his father in 813 without benefit of clergy. He was anointed by the pope in 816, thus implying that papal sanctification alone gave substance to the imperial crown. One year later, Louis issued the *Ordinatio Imperii*. This document, in which Lothar, the eldest son, was associated with his father as emperor and the two younger sons were given subkingdoms within the Empire, has been viewed as an attempt by Louis to reconcile the Frankish custom of divided inheritance with the imperial ideal of unity.

Although Louis' reign has often been identified with the collapse of the Carolingian empire, the forces of disintegration were well advanced when he took office. In the last years of his long reign, Charlemagne had been unable and/or unwilling to keep close personal control over the strong-willed and powerful men he had appointed to office. Many high offices were becoming hereditary and thus less subject to the power of the emperor. Also the raids of the Northmen, or Vikings, were becoming more frequent and penetrating farther into the Empire year by year.

In addition to the problems that he inherited, Louis' personality and education contributed to the weakness and problems of his reign. The coronation of Charlemagne as emperor in 800 had led to much discussion regarding the nature of imperial power in the West. The educated clerics of the Palace School came to the conclusion that there were sharp distinctions between the spiritual and temporal power and that the spiritual was superior. Louis received his education from these men, so it is not surprising that, unlike Charlemagne, who was fundamentally a Frankish warrior king who controlled both his nobles and the Church, Louis saw himself as a servant of the Church. The growing influence of the Church in the Empire and the subsequent change in imperial-papal relations began in 816 when Leo III died and Stephen IV was elected pope. Stephen ruled without imperial ratification and went to Germany to renew the coronation ceremony of Louis the Pious. When Stephen died in 817, Pascal I was freely elected, and no imperial confirmation was sought or required. Although Louis still summoned Church councils, he did not interfere in doctrinal disputes.

Louis' perception of his role as a Christian emperor served not only to strengthen the position of the Church but also added to his difficulties with the Frankish nobility. After brutally suppressing a revolt by his nephew Bernard of Italy in 817, Louis began to have strong feelings of guilt over the incident. In 821 he pardoned those involved in the uprising and in 822 made a public confession, which was interpreted by the Frankish nobles as a further sign of Louis' weakness.

In addition to losing control of the Church and the nobility, Louis found himself plagued by dynastic problems. A widower, Louis married Judith, the daughter of the duke of the Alamans, in 819, and in 823 a fourth son, Charles, was born. Determined to assure her child the largest share of the inheritance, Judith soon persuaded Lothar's younger brothers, Louis the German and Pepin, to join her against Lothar who had been granted the imperial office in the settlement of 817. Thus two factions developed within the Empire: one demanded a sharing of the succession among all the brothers and another held firmly to the idea of imperial unity.

By 829 the forceful Judith had persuaded Louis to set aside the settlement of 817 and include Charles in the partition of the Empire. Louis called an assembly of notables at Worms and announced that Lothar's name would be erased as emperor and that Charles would receive a portion of the realm. Louis the German and Pepin were not satisfied with the division, believing that Charles' portion was far too generous. They reconciled with Lothar and rebelled against their father in 830. The rebellion continued in 832–833 when the three oldest sons, accompanied by Pope Gregory IV, defeated the forces of Louis the Pious. Lothar was restored to his imperial dignity and Louis was required to perform a humiliating penance. Still dissatisfied, Louis the German and Pepin again took up arms. Neither the death of Pepin in 838 nor that of Louis in 840 settled the problem. Finally in 843 at Verdun the old Frankish custom of divided inheritance triumphed over Louis' dream of a unified Christian Empire and the Empire was divided into three parts.

Works About: *Annales Fuldenses,* ed. F. Kurze, *SRG* (Hanover, 1891); J. F. Böhmer and E. Mühlbacher, *Regesta Imperii I,* ed. C. Brühl and H. H. Kaminsky (Hildesheim, 1966); *Carolingian Chronicles: Royal Frankish Annals and Nithard's Histories,* tr. B. W. Scholz and B. Rogers (Ann Arbor, 1970); E. S. Duckett, "Louis the Pious, King and Emperor," in *Carolingian Portraits* (Ann Arbor, 1962), pp. 20–57; F. L. Ganshof, *The Carolingians and the Frankish Monarchy* (Ithaca, N.Y., 1971); H. Fichtenau, *The Carolingian Empire,* tr. Peter Munz (Oxford, 1957); K. Heldmann, *Das Kaisertum Karls des Grossen* (Weimar, 1928); R. E. Sullivan, *Heirs of the Romans* (Ithaca, N.Y., 1960); G. Wolf, ed., *Zum Kaisertums Karls des Grossen* (Darmstadt, 1972).   *D. B. Mapes*

See CHARLEMAGNE; LOUIS II; VERDUN.

LOUIS II, THE GERMAN (805–876), was the third son born to Louis the Pious and his first wife, Ermengarde. He spent his early years at the court of Charlemagne, who is said to have recognized greatness even in the child. In the *divisio imperii* of 817, he received Bavaria but did not go there until late in 825. His realm included Carinthians, Bohemians, Avars, and, in the eastern part, Slavs. In 827 he returned to marry Emma, the daughter of Count Welf and sister of Judith, his stepmother. Emma bore her husband a number of children, of whom three sons survived him. She is praised by a chronicler for her aristocratic birth and intelligence; an inscription describes her as very beautiful. They set up a royal court in Regensburg that was virtually a miniature of the imperial court at Aachen. The following year Louis undertook a campaign against the Bulgars, but it had no lasting results.

His marriage to Emma could not but involve him in Judith's machinations in behalf of Charles the Bald, and they did not necessarily work to Louis' advantage. At the assembly of Worms in 829, the emperor, Louis the Pious, announced the granting of Swabia, as well as Alsace, Rhaetia, and part of Burgundy, to Charles. The disaffected elements, primarily Louis' brothers, Pepin and Lothar, led a rebellion that deposed their father in April 830. Louis probably took part in the coup, but his role is uncertain (one source says he tried to impede it). The emperor was restored (October 830) when he agreed to give additional territory to Pepin and Louis. Louis also gained greater independence in running the affairs of his kingdom. In 832 Louis was again in revolt against the emperor. Leading an army of Bavarians (both slave and free) and Slavs, he invaded Swabia—now allotted to Charles the Bald—in hope of adding it to his kingdom. The emperor responded with a superior force of Franks and Saxons and forced Louis' submission at Augsburg. There he swore not to perpetrate such actions or to conspire with others to that end. This happened in May 832; he then was allowed to return to Bavaria.

Probably in May 833, Louis left Bavaria to join forces with his brother, Lothar, coming from Italy and bringing Pope Gregory IV, and his brother, Pepin, coming from Aquitaine. They met in Alsace and marched against the emperor; both sides encamped near Colmar at a place called *rotfelth* ("red field"). By the end of June, the defection from the emperor's camp had increased to the point that the sons were victorious without a battle. The place subsequently merited the title *campus-mentitus* ("field of lies"). Lothar became emperor, and Louis gained Swabia, Alsace, and Franconia and possibly Saxony and Thuringia. Bad feeling between the new emperor and his brothers grew over Lothar's treatment of their father and his desire to claim the whole Empire. Thus Louis and Pepin marched toward Paris in February 834 to free their father. One chronicler attributes the journey to Louis alone. By August Lothar had surrendered without a battle and returned to Italy.

Still Louis' relations with his father did not improve. At an assembly at Aachen late in 837, the emperor gave Charles the Bald most of Belgium (which ran through the borders of Saxony) and an area between the Meuse and the Seine up to Burgundy. Louis reacted by meeting with Lothar early the next year. Despite Louis' oath that they had not plotted against the emperor, an exchange of words took place between father and son that resulted at the assembly at Nimwegen (June 838) in the emperor's stripping Louis of his domains except for Bavaria. In November Louis again rebelled to recover the lost territories; the emperor crossed the Rhine and Louis retreated. When his brother Pepin died in December 838, a partition of his domains took place at the assembly at Worms (May 30, 839) between Lothar and Charles; Louis, who probably had submitted in April, was allowed only Bavaria. Negotiations between the emperor and Louis proved fruitless, and the struggle continued. However, the campaign in 840 ended in the death of the emperor, and the civil war began that was ended by the Treaty of Verdun. After Louis crushed the revolt of a league of freed slaves (or perhaps peasants) in Saxony called the *Stellinga* in 842 and accepted the treaty, for all practical purposes his kingdom east of the Rhine was never seriously jeopardized. There were frequent campaigns on the eastern front against the Slavs, Moravians, Bulgars and others. The Danes were occasionally a problem—in 845 they raided and plundered Hamburg virtually without opposition—but generally were controlled. Conferences with his brothers and synods were held with regularity. In 850 he had to deal with a severe famine that hit hardest near the Rhine.

The intrigues between brothers gained fresh impetus in 853 when envoys from Aquitaine came to ask him to release them from their lord, Charles the Bald. He responded by sending his son, Louis the Younger, the following year to see whether they spoke the truth. This drew Charles and Lothar closer together, and they encouraged raids by Bulgars and Slavs on Louis' eastern frontier. Late in 854 Louis the Younger returned from Aquitaine as Charles recovered his control. Lothar died in 855, and Louis looked with favor on the elevation of his son, Lothar II. Involvement in Aquitaine began again in 856, and matters progressed to the point that by the end of 858 Louis had won over most of the vassals of Charles, who had since fled to Burgundy. On December 7, 858, Louis issued a charter at Attigny dated in the first year of his reign in west France (*Francia occidentalis*). Nevertheless the clergy would not legitimate his position, which then deteriorated, replete with the now customary desertions, until Louis renounced his intentions there at Koblenz (June 7, 860). Revolts by his sons followed. Carloman revolted in 861, was suppressed the next year, and revolted again in 863. Louis III revolted in 866.

At Tusey (February 19, 865) Louis and Charles reaffirmed the agreement made at Koblenz and undoubtedly prepared to divide the kingdom of Lothar II, whose wife was childless and any hope of remarriage denied by Pope Nicholas I. A partition was agreed upon at Metz (probably 867). Floods, famine, and plague then afflicted both Germany and France for a two-year period. When Lothar died on August 8, 869, Charles seized his kingdom; Louis was seriously ill. After Louis recovered, he asserted his claims, and at Meersen (August 870) a nearly equal division of Lothar's kingdom (greater Lorraine) was effected. The Meuse and part of the Moselle were its rough boundaries.

The year 871 began with the revolt of his younger sons, Louis and Charles, who complained that lands designed for them were being given to Carloman, their mother's favorite, through her influence. A truce was arranged until the meeting of the assembly; in June kind words and promises of fiefs pacified them.

His remaining years were spent intriguing in Italy. He met with Engelberga, the wife of the Emperor Louis II—who had no sons—at Trent in 872 to form an alliance against Charles the Bald and have Carloman named as the emperor's successor. He visited Italy again in 874 to meet with the emperor and Pope John VIII. Louis II died in 875, Carloman was named his successor, and Charles was crowned emperor. While mobilizing his army, Louis the German died on August 28, 876, at Frankfurt and was buried at Lorsch. Emma had died earlier in the year.

Despite his frequent campaigns against the Slavs and others on the eastern frontier, the rest of his kingdom had been relatively stable. The majority of his *acta* deal with the Church. He endowed a number of churches and monasteries; he also was eager to convert his neighbors. He is known to have been responsible for the baptism of fourteen Bohemian chiefs (845) and a Dane (952); he sent Bishop Ermenrich to convert the Bulgars to the Catholic faith (867). He seems to have been a just ruler for the time; a legal reform in 852, for example, forbade nobles from being both judge and party in the same suit.

Works About: *Annales de Saint–Bertin,* ed. F. Grat, J. Vielliard, S. Clémencet, and L. Levillain (Paris, 1964); *Annales Fuldenses,* ed. F. Kurze, SRG (Hanover, 1891); G. Barraclough, *The Crucible of Europe* (Berkeley, 1976); J. Böhmer and E. Mühlbacher, *Regesta Imperii I,* rev. ed. C. Bruhl and H. Kaminsky (Hildesheim, 1966); J. Calmette, *La diplomatie Carolingienne du traité de Verdun à la mort de Charles le Chauve,* Bibliothèque de l'École des Hautes Études, 135 (Paris, 1901); E. Dümmler, *Gesch. des Ostfranken Reiches* (Darmstadt, 1960); E. Muller–Mertens, *Regnum Teutonicum* (Vienna, 1970); J. W. Thompson, *The Dissolution of the Carolingian Fisc* (Berkeley, 1935).   C. J. Dull

See AACHEN; CHARLEMAGNE; CARLOMAN; CHARLES II; LOUIS I; VERDUN.

LOUIS III, THE CHILD (893–911) was the last Carolingian king of the East Franks. He was declared king on February 4, 900, at Forcheim on the river Regnitz. Louis was only six years old, so the actual functioning of the government was placed in the hands of his brother-in-law Otto of Saxony and the archbishops of Mainz, Cologne, and Trier.

The child king was faced with two overwhelming and related problems: an increasingly independent nobility and repeated invasions by the Hungarians. Support for the king came from the Church, which had always found it much easier to deal with one monarch than with many local leaders. In addition, Louis benefited in a less tangible way from the fact that he was a descendant of Charlemagne, whose legend had grown tremendously in the century since his death.

The German kingdom of Louis the Child was composed of five relatively independent duchies. Although some historians have suggested that the growing independence of these duchies was due to to a reemergence of older tribal allegiances, it seems more likely that the rise of local or ducal power was the result of current conditions. Since the time of Louis the Pious (d. 840), the power of the Carolingian dynasty had been slowly eroded by a series of forces from within and without. The later Carolingians had allowed the highest offices to become hereditary and thus were out of their control to a large extent. Much of the royal land from which they should have been able to draw men and supplies had been allowed to slip away. From without, the repeated assaults by the Magyars (Hungarians) had forced people to rely upon the local military leaders for protection. This process of decentralization was well underway when Louis the Child became king of the Germans in the year 900.

Louis' kingdom included the five territories or duchies of Saxony, Bavaria, Franconia, Swabia, and Lotharingia. In the early tenth century, the dukes of Saxony and Bavaria were the successors of frontier commanders. In Saxony power was exercised by Otto the Younger, son of Count Liudolf, who had founded the territory in the ninth century. Bavaria was led by Liutpold who was killed in battle in 907. His son, Arnulf, inherited Bavaria as duke by divine providence. The hereditary claims of both Otto and Arnulf met no opposition in Saxony or Bavaria.

In Swabia the power and authority of Salamo III, bishop of Constance and abbot of St. Gall, was challenged by several families. Among the laymen contending for power, Burchard of Rhaetia (Burchard I) was the strongest.

In the western part of Louis' kingdom, in Franconia, two rival families vied for power. The house of Babenberg, led by Adalbert, fought the house of the Conradins headed by Conrad the Old at Fritzlar on the bank of the River Eder in Hessen in 906. Adalbert won the battle, and Conrad the Old was killed. The victory proved to be of short duration for the house of Babenberg. Several months later Adalbert was accused of treason and put to death. The death warrant was signed by the thirteen-year-old King Louis. Leadership of Franconia passed to Conrad the Younger, later known as Conrad of Franconia, who became the first non-Carolingian king of the Germans in 911.

Lotharingia, comprised basically of the old middle kingdom of Lothar, was given by Arnulf of Germany to his favorite son, Zwentibold, in 895. Within a few months Lotharingian nobles complained of "the insolence of his ways." They declared that he ordered the business of the realm in company with women and vulgar folk and that he stripped those high in dignity of their due and valid rights. On August 13, 900, Zwentibold was killed in battle against his rebel subjects on the bank of the Meuse, and the Lotharingians recognized Louis the Child as king. Still the power of the nobles remained strong, and Louis decided to allow Lotharingia independent administration under his crown. He appointed Gebhard to govern and protect it as duke. But Gebhard was a Conradian from Franconia and as such was resented by the Lotharingian nobles. Soon Count Matfrid rose in rebellion and war broke out. In 906 Matfrid was driven to exile. Duke Gebhard died in 910 and control of Lotharingia was seized by Reginar the Long-Neck. When Louis the Child died in 911, Lotharingia placed itself under the crown of France where Charles the Simple, a Carolingian, ruled.

Works About: G. Barraclough, *The Crucible of Europe* (Berkeley, 1976); J. F. Böhmer and E. Mühlbacher, *Regesta Imperii I*, ed. C. Brühl and H. H. Kaminsky (Hildesheim, 1966); E. Duckett, *Death and Life in the Tenth Century* (Ann Arbor, 1967); E. Dümmler, *Gesch. des Ostfranken Reiches* (Darmstadt, 1960); F. L. Ganshof, *Feudalism* (New York, 1964).   D. B. Mapes

See ARNULF; CHARLEMAGNE; CONRAD OF FRANCONIA; LOUIS I.

LOUIS IV, THE BAVARIAN (1283–1347), one of the most controversial of the kings of Germany (he ruled from 1314 to 1347), was the son of Louis II of

Upper Bavaria and count Palatine, and Mechtild, the daughter of the Habsburg king Rudolf I. He was married twice: to Beatrice of Silesia-Glogau in 1309 and to Margaret of Holland in 1324. Among his many sons were Louis, margrave of Brandenburg, duke of Upper Bavaria, and duke of Tyrol and Carinthia; Stephen II, duke of Lower Bavaria-Landshut; Louis II, margrave of Brandenburg; and Otto V, margrave of Brandenburg.

On the death of his father in 1394, Louis, at age seven, shared Upper Bavaria and the Rhenish palatinate with his brother Rudolf. He spent most of his time at the Habsburg court in Vienna with his mother and was thus associated with the Habsburg imperial party early in his life. By 1301, Louis was claiming his rights to govern in his territories and Rudolf, bowing to pressure from the Habsburg emperor Albert I, was promising but failing to deliver a share in the government of their holdings. Albert's death in May 1308 and the election of the Luxembourg, Henry VII, who was not favorably disposed toward Louis, ended this incentive. In 1310, Louis demanded partition of their holdings and received the northwest portion of Upper Bavaria, but Rudolf refused to partition the Palatinate. The situation was further complicated by the wardship of the two sons of Stephen I, duke of Lower Bavaria, who died in December 1310 and who was succeeded in September 1312 by Duke Otto III, leaving Louis regent. When Rudolf objected, Louis drew upon his Habsburg allies, while the Lower Bavarian cities and nobles, fearing such an arrangement, formed a defensive alliance with his brother in May 1313. Hostilities were ended with the Peace of Munich on June 21, 1313, by which an uncomfortable dual government was established. Meanwhile Frederick I, duke of Austria, intervened and was defeated by Louis at the Battle of Gammelsdorf on November 9, 1313, before he could link his troops with a Habsburg contingent assembled in Swabia and the mediation of the archbishop of Salzburg finally established peace on April 17, 1314.

Peace with Frederick simply cleared the way for a more tragic conflict. When Henry VII died in Italy on August 24, 1313, the Wittelsbach-Luxembourg faction found itself arrayed against the Habsburgs in a double election. While the Habsburgs, along with Louis' brother Rudolf of the Palatinate, elected Frederick I at Sachsenhausen on October 9, 1314, their opponents, led by archbishops Peter of Mainz and Baldwin of Trier, elected Louis at Frankfurt on October 20. He was crowned at Aachen not, as was customary, by the archbishop of Cologne, but by Mainz on December 25. Seven years of intermittent warfare followed before Frederick was defeated and captured at Mühldorf on November 15, 1322, and imprisoned at Trausnitz in the upper Palatinate. He was released in 1325 and made joint king, although in a purely honorific capacity, and confirmed in all his lands and titles.

With his crown secured, Louis turned to dynastic politics. The death of the last Askanian prince of Brandenburg in 1320 allowed him to acquire the Mark Brandenburg for his eldest son in 1328, despite a prior Bohemian Luxembourg claim. And in the dynastic agreement of Pavia in 1329, Louis put the affairs of the Wittelsbach house in order. He was to retain possession of Upper and Lower Bavaria, which were formally united in 1341. More importantly, the electoral vote was to be exercised alternately by both lines, an arrangement that remained in effect until Charles IV reassigned the vote to the Palatinate.

With the support of Philip V of France, Pope John XXII claimed the right to govern Germany during an interim and, setting aside both the election of Frederick and of Louis, called for abdication within three months under threat of excommunication. His antagonism could hardly have been mollified by the appearance of Louis' troops before Milan under Berthold von Neifern in 1322, where papal forces were besieging the city. In response, Louis appealed to a general council to hear the pope's claims; on March 23, 1324, he was excommunicated. On May 22, the king published a more far-ranging indictment of papal abuses, the appeal of Sachsenhausen. He may or may not have felt comfortable with the more radical criticism of the Church presented in his defense by the Franciscan Minorites, whose arguments for Church reform revolved around the ideal of Christian poverty. In the course of this largely ideological conflict, Louis quickly drew to his cause leading intellectuals such as Marsiglio of Padua, whose *Defensor pacis* presented a rigorous argument for imperial supremacy.

The military side of Louis' struggle with the papacy was bound to be inconclusive, rooted as it was in the constantly shifting facts of Italian political life, where strategic alliances of smaller or larger peninsular powers were glossed in terms of pro-imperial or anti-imperial parties. Briefly, Louis crossed the Alps and linked up with his allies at Trent, arriving in May 1327 in Milan to receive the Lombard crown. He took Pisa and from there marched on Rome, where he was crowned emperor at St. Peter's by Sciarra Colonna, leader of the ruling clique of Roman nobles, on January 17, 1328. He deposed John XXII and replaced him with Peter of Corvara, Nicholas V. A desultory expedition against Robert of Naples was crippled by disorganization and poor provisioning, while the taxation necessary to continue it eroded Louis' support in Rome. Retiring to Pisa, Louis waited for more imperial allies and more propitious diplomatic advantages, neither of which came. Upon hearing of Frederick's death in January 1330, he left for Germany, and Nicholas V soon abdicated. He set up residence in Munich, turning the city into an intellectual garrison, the source of a pamphlet war against the pretensions of the papacy, staffed not only by Marsiglio but by other intellectuals such as William of Occam, Bonagratia of Bergamo, and Michael of Cesena, the general of the Franciscan Minorites.

Pope John XXII died in 1334, but his successor, Benedict XII, was a creature of Philip VI of France, and there was still no likelihood of resolution despite major concessions offered by the emperor. Louis' position in Germany seemed precarious, although the general pandemonium that was supposed to have occurred when he was excommunicated never came about. The pope organized a league of princely opponents, but its members were more concerned with local feuds and acquisitions than with confrontation with the emperor, and they were readily detached from the papacy. Of more consequence was King John of Bohemia's attempt to offer himself as an alternative to Louis and his agreement with the pope to act as papal overlord in Italy in April 1331. Fortunately John was pulled away from his Italian campaigns by Polish and Hungarian incursions into Bohemia, and he remained obedient to the emperor even while Louis retrieved Tyrol from his son John Henry and arranged for its succession to his eldest son, Louis of Brandenburg, in 1342. And an alliance between Edward III of England, once again at war with Philip VI, and Louis was concluded on July 23, 1337, in which Louis agreed to open an eastern front with France in exchange for a considerable subsidy.

Louis could expect support from the German princes because he was defending not only his crown but their right to elect him. The electoral union at Rhense in July 1338 made that expectation a reality when the princes asserted that their electoral rights superseded papal approbation. And the imperial diet at Frankfurt in August 1338 confirmed Louis' election, forbad all subjects to observe his excommunication, and, in the ordinance *Licet iuris,* denounced any pretension that the pope might have to confirm the election of a German king.

This mood continued into the early 1440s, with most of Louis' princely opponents resolving upon coexistence with, if not support of, the crown. John of Bohemia agreed to accept the Tyrol as an imperial fief and promised to ignore his French alliance in March 1339. Henry of Lower Bavaria acquiesced to pressure from Louis and the Habsburgs and settled upon a marriage alliance with the emperor in February 1339, a settlement that quickly brought both Upper and Lower Bavaria to Louis when Henry and his son died in 1341. And Rudolf, the elector Palatine, was finally forced to turn over long-disputed territories in July.

Louis' alliance with Edward III broke down, however, when Philip VI sued for peace after the Battle of Sluys, asking the emperor to mediate with Edward in exchange for his own mediation with the pope. Louis had been less than wholehearted in his support of Edward's campaigns and had sent only his son Louis of Brandenburg with nominal imperial forces to Cambrésis. In the process of negotiating the peace, Louis deprived Edward of the "vicariate of the empire," a practically empty title but a diplomatically sound gesture, which he had made with great pomp and circumstance at the diet of Frankfurt. Further the seizure of the Tyrol, along with Carinthia, from the Luxembourg John Henry in 1342 outraged John of Bohemia, while the emperor's cavalier annulment of Margaret Maultasch's marriage to John Henry and her subsequent marriage to Louis of Brandenburg incensed the rest of Germany.

Worse, the new pope, Clement VI, was much more cautious in his handling of the German princes, and he knew by now that they would not listen to attempts to deprive them of their own electoral rights. They did listen to new proceedings against Louis in April 1443, which wisely skirted that issue. Worried by the growing dynastic power of a newly united Bavaria, most recently augmented in 1445 by the addition of Holland, Zeeland, and Friesland through Louis' second wife, Margaret of Holland, they began to look for a rival candidate. John of Bohemia, negotiating for his son Charles with Clement VI, soon convinced the king-making Archbishop Baldwin of Trier and the other Rhenish ecclesiastical electors. They, along with Saxony-Wittenberg, elected Charles king at Rhense on July 11, 1347. Louis' death on a bear hunt near Munich on October 11 ended the possibility of serious opposition.

Works About: H. Bansa, *Studien zur Kanzlei Kaiser Ludwigs des Bayern,* 1314–1329 (Kallmünz, 1968); J. F. Böhmer, *Regesta imperii:1313–1347* (Frankfurt, 1839); Karl Bosl, *Der geistige Widerstand am Hofe Ludwigs der Bayer gegen die Kurie,* Vorträge und Forschungen (Stuttgart, 1965); *MGH Legum Sectio IV const. et Acta,* vols. 5–7, ed. J. Schwalm (Hanover, 1909/1913); C. Muller, *Der Kampf Ludwigs der Baier mit der römischen Curie* (Munich, 1879–1880); H. S. Offler, *Empire and Papacy: The Last Struggle,* Transactions of the Royal Historical Society, Series 5, vol. 6 (1965); Sigmund Riezler, *Die literarischen Widersacher der Päpste zur Zeit Ludwig des Baiers* (Leipzig, 1874); Sigmund von Riezler, *Vatikanische Akten zur dtsch. Gesch. in der Zeit Kaiser Ludwigs des Bayern* (Innsbruck, 1891); Edmund Ernst Stengel, *Avignon und Rhens, Figuren zur Gesch. des Kampfes um das Recht am Reich in der ersten Hälfte des 14. Jahrhunderts* (Weimar, 1930); Richard Scholz, *Unbekannte Kirchenpolitische Streitschriften aus der Zeit Kaiser Ludwigs des Bayern* (Rome, 1911–1914).   *S. A. Garretson*

See ALBERT I; FRANKFURT; HENRY VII; MARSIGLIO; VIENNA.

LÜDER, HEINZ VON (?–1559), governor of the fortress of Ziegenhain and supreme administrator of the territorial hospitals of Hesse, rose from obscure beginnings to an outstanding dual career. Lüder began his military service under Philip of Hesse around 1520, serving as a captain. He soon became involved in the Hessian reformation. Lüder demonstrated considerable versatility by taking on additional responsibilities as an administrator in the new Hessian church. He worked closely with Adam Krafft, a preacher and reformer in the court. Together they conducted visitations, beginning in 1527, and established the first territorial hospitals at Haina and Merxhausen around 1533. Lüder gained primary responsibility for the hospitals and issued detailed plans for the spiritual, mental, and bodily care of the inmates.

The landgrave also sent Lüder on diplomatic missions. He served as a Hessian representative to France in some of the negotiations leading to the restoration of Duke Ulrich of Württemberg. Lüder is credited with extensive work of the same dual nature in Württemberg from 1534 until 1537, following the successful restoration of the duke. Lüder's success as an administrator of fortifications and hospitals may be seen in his almost simultaneous appointments in 1537 as governor of Ziegenhain and commander of the territorial hospitals. After 1543, he bore the title of supreme commander of the Hessian hospitals.

Works About: Heinz Brandt, *Das Kloster Haina* (Frankenberg, 1976); Karl Knetsch, "Heinz von Lüder," in *Hessenkunst* (Marburg, 1922), pp. 1–7, and "Neues von Heinz von Lüder," *Hessen-*

kunst (Marburg, 1925), pp. 1–4; Julius Paulus, "Heinz von Lüder," *Ziegenhainer Zeitung* 26 (1932); *Urkundlichen Quel. zur hessischen Reformationsgesch.* 4 vols., Günther Franz, ed. (Marburg, 1954).   *W. J. Wright*

See KRAFFT; PHILIP OF HESSE; ULRICH OF WÜRTTEMBERG.

LUDWIG III (1554–1593), duke of Württemberg and promoter of Luthern unity, was born in Stuttgart to Duke Christopher of Württemberg and Duchess Anna Maria of Brandenburg-Ansbach. Educated in his own separate court in Tübingen to prevent a repetition of his elder brother Eberhard's disastrous educational program in Stuttgart, Ludwig was brought to that city following his father's death in 1568, to be instructed there together with his younger cousin and eventual successor, Frederick. His education was supervised by Count Henry of Castell under the watchful eyes of his mother and a three-member council until he was declared to be of age in 1578.

It was during Ludwig's minority that the Swabian theologians, under the leadership of Jacob Andreae, the chancellor of Tübingen University, concluded a series of successful conferences that laid the groundwork for the final formulation and formal adoption of the Lutheran Formula of Concord in 1577. Ludwig was to be noted for his zealous opposition to Catholicism and Calvinism alike, and, like his father, he took care to cultivate good relations with the Holy Roman Empire and its rulers, as was evidenced in 1577 and again in 1585 by his spurning of Queen Elizabeth of England's efforts to establish an alliance of Protestant states. Ludwig similarly displayed a particular interest in the *Collegium illustre* in Tübingen, the unique institution founded by his father to educate secular officials from all social classes; eventually it was transformed into Germany's first academy for the education of princes (*Ritterakademie*).

Although he was universally regarded as a good-intentioned, well-meaning man, Ludwig turned out to be a rather mediocre ruler. He married twice, both times without offspring. His first wife, Dorothea Ursula of Baden, whom he married in 1575, died in 1583. A year later, in accord with the fervent request of his estates, who desired princely issue, he married Ursula, the daughter of Count Palatine John George of Lützelstein. Ludwig's religiosity did not prevent him from indulging in the earthier joys of life, such as excessive drinking, hunting wild game, riding as a knight in tourneys, and participating in theological disputations. The duke's impressive tomb in the Tübingen Collegiate Church appropriately documents these reigning passions in the form of a large stag at his feet, wild grapevines at his head, and biblical scenes from Old Testament battles on the side panels.

On the basis of the existing evidence, later Swabian historians were moved to conclude, reluctantly, that Ludwig was at best "a good but weak prince who failed to inherit his father's spirit . . . he proved unable to make his people as happy as his good heart undoubtedly desired."

Works About: Alberti, "Ludwig, Herzog von Württemberg," *ADB*, 19:597–98; Karl Pfaff, *Gesch. Wirtenbergs*, (Stuttgart, 1819), vol. 1; C. F. Sattler, *Gesch. des Herzogthums Würtenberg unter der Regierung der Herzogen* (Ulm, 1772), vol. 5; Theodor Schott, "Herzog Ludwig von Württemberg und die französischen Protestanten während des dritten Religionskriegs 1568–1570," *Festschr. zur vierten Säcular-Feier der Universität zu Tübingen* (Stuttgart, 1877), pp. 53–68; C. F. von Stälin, *Wirtembergische Gesch.* (Stuttgart, 1873); Karl Weller and Arnold Weller, *Württembergische Gesch. im südwestdtsch. Raum*, 6th. ed. (Stuttgart and Aalen, 1971).   *L. J. Reith*

See ANDREAE; CHRISTOPHER.

LUDWIG WILLIAM (1655–1707), margrave of Baden, famous imperial field marshal and knight of the Golden Fleece, acquired his reputation as a forceful, obstinate, quick-tempered, courageous military leader in the Turkish war (1683–1699). The son of Ferdinand Maximilian of Baden-Baden and Princess Louisa Christina of Savoy-Carignan, he was born in Paris in 1655. He assumed the title of margrave on the death of his grandfather in 1677 and married Princess Sybil of Saxe-Lauenberg in 1690. He served his military apprenticeship in the 1670s under Montecuccoli and Duke Charles V of Lorraine in the war against France. He was particularly noted for his valor at Philippsburg (1676), Freiburg (1677), and Stäffen (1678). During the Turkish wars, he quarreled with but fought bravely under Charles of Lorraine. He aided in the relief of Vienna (1683), led raids into southern Hungary (1686), and took part in the unsuccessful siege of Peterwardein and the subsequent victory against the Turks at Mohács (1687). He acquired his military reputation and nickname, the "Turkenlouis," because of his victories over the Turks, particularly in the bloody battle of Slankhamen in which the grand vizier, Mustafa Köprülü, was killed. This victory enabled the Habsburgs to hold the Save-Danube frontier.

Soon after his victory at Slankhamen (1691), Leopold I appointed Ludwig commander-in-chief on the Rhine to succeed the superb tactician Charles of Lorraine who died in 1690. During the rest of the War of the League of Augsburg (1688), Louis conducted a campaign of maneuvering and position. Although unable to take the offensive because of extremely limited manpower, he did succeed in restoring the military balance on the upper Rhine.

During the War of the Spanish Succession (1701–1714), Leopold appointed the popular margrave imperial commander on the Rhine. Early in the war, he captured Landau (1702), the gateway to Alsace, but could not stop the French advance across the Rhine because of a chronic shortage of men and arms. Old, grumpy, overcautious, touchy, and methodical, he blamed the imperial ministers for his inaction and continued to conduct the same type of static warfare that had brought him so much success during the War of the League of Augsburg. He questioned the loyalty of Count Henry Mansfeld, prince of Fondi and president of the Council of War (1701–1703); he accused him "not only of Negligence, but of Treachery" in failing to send desperately needed men and supplies to the Rhine front. He did convince Leopold to grant him full powers to act offensively. He advocated a purely defensive strategy against the elector of Bavaria, Maximilian Emmanuel, an old friend and colleague, who had allied with France early in the war. Ludwig proposed an offensive thrust into France from the Moselle, which Leopold I would not support. During 1704, he garrisoned troops along the lines of Stollhofen, a twenty-five mile stretch of fortresses designed to protect the central Holy Roman Empire. Throughout 1705 and 1706, he repeatedly refused to take the offensive because he felt that his troops were ill prepared to move against the French. Sick with gout and angry because of lack of support, he retired his command in the fall of 1706 and died a few months later (January 1707).

Tenacious, stubborn, self-reliant, and trustworthy, the Turkenlouis was one of Leopold's most illustrious generals. Prince Eugene of Savoy, his cousin and colleague whom he had befriended early in his career, conducted the later peace negotiations with Claude Louis Hector, duke of Villars, the representative of Louis XIV at the palace which Ludwig had spent his last years patterning after Versailles. These negotiations eventually resulted in the conclusion of the treaties of Rastatt and Baden (1714), which ended the War of the Spanish Succession for the Habsburgs and the Empire—a fitting tribute to a great soldier.

Works: Philip Roder von Diersberg, ed., *Kriegs-und-Staatschriften über der spanischen Erbfolgekrieg, 1700–1707* (Karlsruhe, 1850); F. Heller, ed., *Prinz Eugen: militarische Correspondenz,* 2 vols. (Vienna, 1848). **Works About:** "Ludwig Wilhelm I," *ADB,* 19:485–91; Max Braubach, *Prinz Eugen von Savoyen,* 5 vols. (Vienna, 1963–65); Winston S. Churchill, *Marlborough, His Life and Times* (London, 1947); Eugene–Francois, Prince of Savoy, *Feldzüge* (Vienna, 1876–92); Otto Flake, *Der Turkenlouis, Margraf Ludwig von Baden, 1655–1707* (Karlsruhe, 1850); Oswald Redlich, *Weltmacht des Barock, Oster. in der Zeit Kaiser Leopolds I* (Vienna, 1961); John P. Spielman, *Leopold I of Austria* (New Brunswick N.J., 1977). *L. S. Frey and M. L. Frey*

See LEOPOLD I; PETERWARDEIN; SPANISH SUCCESSION; VIENNA, SIEGE OF; WAR OF THE LEAGUE OF AUGSBURG.

LUTHER, MARTIN (1483–1546), the initiator of the Protestant Reformation and father of Lutheranism, was born in Eisleben, Germany. His parents, Hans and Margaret, were of peasant stock. Because Hans was an eldest son and therefore without inheritance, he turned to mining. His ambition and diligence eventually enabled him to become the owner of a number of foundries.

Hans Luther had even greater expectations for his son. He wanted him to be a lawyer, a profession that would assure both financial security and social status. Luther was therefore sent to three preparatory schools in Mansfeld, where the family had moved in 1484, Magdeburg, and Eisenach. He matriculated at the University of Erfurt in 1501 and received his B.A. and M.A. degrees in 1502 and 1505, respectively. Erfurt enjoyed an excellent academic reputation, especially in the liberal arts and law. The philosophical faculty under which Luther studied espoused the *via moderna* (nominalism) of William of Occam (c. 1280–1349) and Gabriel Biel (c. 1420–1495).

According to his father's wishes, Luther commenced his legal studies in May 1505. However, in July of the same year he abruptly entered the Black cloister of the Augustinian Hermits in Erfurt. Luther cited his confrontation with death during a severe thunderstorm on July 2, 1505, as the immediate impetus for his crucial decision. The thunderstorm, however, had merely brought to focus his spiritual struggles.

Those struggles—he called them *Anfechtungen*—revolved around a crucial question, How can I be saved? Deeply spiritual, Luther was profoundly aware of God's holiness and righteousness and of his own sinfulness. He therefore desperately sought a way whereby he could become acceptable to God. Monasticism, long espoused by the Church as the ideal form of Christian life, seemed to be the way, and Luther pursued the monastic discipline with diligence. He also took advantage of the sacramental system of the Church, was ordained a priest in 1507, and faithfully practiced the piety of his day. However, the Church's answers to his question did not satisfy him. His spiritual struggles persisted, for his perceptions of God and of himself did not change. He could not be assured that he was justified because he could not be certain that he was fulfilling his responsibilities in the justificatory process.

Luther's spiritual counselor during much of his monastic period was John von Staupitz, his ecclesiastical superior. When Staupitz recognized that neither the monastic life nor the Church's sacramental system effectively addressed Luther's spiritual concerns, he sought other remedies. He determined that Luther should preach regularly, study for the doctorate of theology, and teach at the universities of Erfurt and Wittenberg, endeavors that had the desired effect of focusing Luther's attention on the Bible. It was through the careful and persistent study of Scripture that Luther achieved his evangelical insight: a full understanding of the Pauline doctrine of justification by grace through faith. Luther now affirmed that God is a gracious God who justifies the sinner freely for the sake of Jesus Christ. The individual cannot and does not contribute anything to his salvation, which is solely God's work. That understanding was achieved during the teens of the sixteenth century. Scholars have been unable to agree on the exact date of Luther's tower experience. It is clear, however, that his evangelical insight answered his persistent spiritual question. He had discovered the Gospel. It was on the basis of this discovery that he articulated his own theology and addressed the theology, life, and practices of the Church.

Luther's ideas first attracted attention with the publication of the Ninety-five Theses in October 1517, and they have been evaluated, criticized, and rejected or affirmed ever since. Luther had not expected the uproar that resulted from the indulgence controversy, nor had he sought publicity. He did not shrink from controversy, however, and was prepared to devote his considerable energies and talents to the defense of the evangelical understanding of God's word. He did so from the pulpit, the professor's podium, and the writer's desk. His literary output was voluminous and persisted throughout his life.

Luther's attitudes and actions became more radical as the early years of the Reformation progressed. The theological insights he articulated struck at the very heart of the sacramental and sacerdotal systems of the Church. In 1520 he produced two revolutionary works, *The Address to the Christian Nobility* and *The Babylonian Captivity of the Church,* in which he severely limited papal claims of power and radically reinterpreted the Church's sacramental theology. He also defended himself and his thought against the attacks of his opponents. He argued that he was and intended to remain a faithful and obedient son of the Church, and he expressed a willingness to be corrected. However, he demanded that he be shown his errors on the basis of Scripture. Scripture, not the Church, was now Luther's final authority.

Opposition to his ideas was quickly forthcoming. Although Leo X (1513–1521) initially dismissed the indulgence conflict as a squabble between the Dominicans and the Augustinians, the papacy and its advisers soon recognized the challenge Luther presented. Charges of heresy surfaced. When his own order did not respond to papal demands that Luther be disciplined, proceedings against him were initiated in the curia, which ultimately resulted in his excommunication in 1521. Even before that excommunication was announced, however, Luther had come to the conclusion that a fair hearing before the curia would be unlikely. He therefore, called for a general council to decide his case, and in August of that pivotal year, 1520, he appealed to the emperor.

Charles V had been elevated to the imperial throne in 1519. He was a pious Catholic who swore to defend the Church in his coronation oath, a promise that he never repudiated or forgot. His attitude toward Luther, therefore, was not favorable. He answered Luther's appeal by summoning him to appear before the diet of Worms. Although he granted the reformer a safe conduct, Charles did not intend to preside over a hearing. He sought a recantation. Luther appeared before the diet on April 17 and 18, 1521. He did not receive a hearing, and he did not recant. He again expressed his willingness to be corrected but only on the basis of God's word. In response to Luther's unflinching stand before the emperor and the estates of Germany, a rump session of the diet passed the Edict of Worms, which declared Luther to be a heretic and an outlaw. Both the ecclesiastical and the secular authorities had rejected Luther and his message by the end of 1521.

That message was not silenced, however, nor did Luther's activity cease. Although he was taken to the Wartburg for protection and did not return to Wittenberg until March 1522, he did not spend his exile idly. His most important accomplishment during the Wartburg stay was the translation of the New Testament into German. It was published in 1522, and the whole Bible followed in 1534. The German Bible stands as one of Luther's most significant contributions to the Reformation and to German culture.

Until 1522 the Lutheran Reformation was a growing and unified movement; nevertheless, internal difficulties and disagreements also surfaced. This was a new experience for Luther who had only faced opposition from the defenders of the Church. Now he discoverd that not all of his followers interpreted Scripture or his theology as he did. Furthermore individuals and groups began to join the Reformation movement for economic and social as well as religious reasons. Diversity was inevitable. Thus Luther confronted the enthusiasts in Wittenberg who sought radical and immediate reform. He chastised the peasants for what he considered to be false priorities and for taking up arms. He clashed with Erasmus over a crucial theological issue: the freedom or bondage of the will. He could not accept Ulrich Zwingli's eucharistic theology. When the Marburg colloquy (1529) did not result in theological agreement, attempts to unify the Swiss and German reform groups also failed.

Despite such difficulties and divisions during the 1520s the Luthern movement continued to grow, to change, and to mature into the Lutheran church. Luther was sincere in his desire to avoid a schism. His fervent and uncompromising defense of his position, however, and the Roman Church's unwillingness and inability to tolerate his theology resulted in conflict and, ultimately, division. That division was clearly apparent by 1530. Luther himself remained the dominant personality within Lutheranism until his death on February 18, 1546. He was recognized and affirmed as the theological authority for the evangelical movement, and his stature and personality constituted a powerful unifying force within Lutheranism, though some defections occurred.

Throughout the last two decades of his life, he continued to devote his energies to the promotion of the movement he had initiated. He continued to explicate and refine his theology in lectures, theological treatises, sermons, and letters. Not all of his time was spent at the writer's desk. He taught at the University of Wittenberg, preached regularly as the assistant pastor of the city church, and served as a spiritual and political counselor. It is difficult to overemphasize his impact on Lutheranism specifically and on the Protestant Reformation in general.

Luther's significance for the reign of Charles V and for the Holy Roman Empire is profound. Luther and Charles met face to face only at Worms. That single meeting, however, is not indicative of the effects they had upon one another. Luther deeply respected secular authority, including the Holy Roman emperor. On the basis of Romans 13, he was convinced that magistrates receive their authority from God and that God works through them. He therefore demanded that rulers be respected and obeyed, and he refused to condone revolution and insurrection. He did, however, allow for the possibility and even necessity of civil disobedience if the ruler's demands contradicted God's will. His own challenge of ecclesiastical and secular authority was justified on this basis. Thus although Luther faithfully urged his fellow Germans to obey their rulers and to respond to the emperor's pleas for assistance against the Turks, he refused to heed the emperor's demand to recant. For Luther, obeying God took precedence over obeying the emperor.

The reformer and the movement he inspired were clearly a major challenge of Charles' reign. Although dynastic priorities, the Habsburg-Valois conflicts, and the Turks frequently diverted his attention, he attempted to deal with the

Lutherans whenever possible. The Lutheran problem was repeatedly on the agenda of the diets that met throughout the 1520s and 1530s. Charles himself attended the diet of Augsburg in 1530, intent upon resolving the schism. He therefore demanded that the Lutheran estates submit to the authority of the Roman Church. The Lutherans, in turn, defended their position and presented the Augsburg Confession as a summary of their faith and a vindication of their stand. Although it was a nonpolemical, conciliatory statement, the Augsburg Confession did not compromise the essentials of the evangelical faith. Luther, who could not be present at Augsburg because of the Edict of Worms, was pleased. He had feared that Melanchthon, the main author of the confession, might be too irenic. This was not the case, nor was the Catholic party prepared to negotiate. Charles finally threatened the use of force if the Lutherans did not submit by April 1531. In response the evangelical estates organized the Schmal-kaldic League for defensive purposes. Luther was deeply troubled by these developments. Although he was determined to defend the evangelical faith with the spoken and written word, he could not justify the use of the sword. Military action against the emperor was repugnant to him because of his deep respect for authority. While he finally agreed to a defensive alliance, he did so reluctantly.

Charles was unable to carry out the threat he made at Augsburg until after Luther's death. Thus the reformer was spared the agony of experiencing actual military conflict between the emperor and the Lutherans. The decisive battle of that conflict, the Schmalkaldic War, was fought at Mühlberg in April 1547. Charles defeated the Lutheran forces, but the Lutheran movement did not die. Indeed in 1555 the emperor agreed to the religious Peace of Augsburg, which officially recognized Lutheranism. He had failed to accomplish a major goal of his lengthy but frustrating reign. Although Luther was basically a religious personality and his interests were essentially theological, his thoughts and actions clearly affected the political as well as the religious realm.

Works By: *D. Martin Luthers Werke* (Weimar, 1883–); *Luther's Works,* ed. Jaroslav Pelikan and Helmut T. Lehmann, 55 vols. (Philadelphia, 1955–1975). **Works About:** Paul Althaus, *The Theology of Martin Luther,* tr. R. C. Schultz (Philadelphia, 1966); R. H. Bainton, *Here I Stand* (New York, 1950); Heinrich Böhmer, *Martin Luther,* tr. J. W. Doberstein and T. G. Tappert (Philadelphia, 1946); Heinrich Bornkamm, *Luther's World of Thought,* tr. M. H. Bertram (St. Louis, 1965); Gerhard Ebeling, *Luther,* tr. R. A. Wilson (Philadelphia, 1970); Richard Friedenthal, *Luther,* tr. John Nowell (New York, 1970); G. W. Forell, *Faith Active in Love* (New York, 1954); H. J. Grimm, *The Reformation Era* (New York, 1973); Fritz Hartung, *Karl V. und die dtsch. Protestanten* (Halle, 1910); Gerhard Ritter, *Luther,* tr. John Riches (New York), 1963); Gordon Rupp, *Luther's Progress to the Diet of Worms* (New York, 1964); E. G. Schwiebert, *Luther and His Times* (St. Louis, 1950). *K. K. Hendel*

See CHARLES V; ECK; ERASMUS; FREDERICK III, THE WISE; KARLSTADT; MARBURG COLLOQUY; MELANCHTHON; STAUPITZ; WORMS; ZWINGLI.

M

MANSFELD, ERNEST VON (1580–1626), count and military condottiere, was born in Luxembourg and died at Rakowitzka near Sarajevo. He was the illegitimate son of Peter von Mansfeld, one-time governor of Luxembourg. Birth and education made Ernest an adventurer. He was the first of a number of successful soldiers of fortune, who believed that war should be financed through war. A Catholic, he lacked confessional and political convictions. As a military leader in the Thirty Years War, he became known for his ability to recruit and to keep soldiers.

Mansfeld began his career as a soldier in his brother's army in Hungary. He served the Spanish in the war against the Netherlands. During the Jülich-Cleves succession dispute (1609), he commanded the troops of Archduke Leopold. When the Habsburgs refused to grant him the recognition he yearned for, he joined the Protestant Union in 1610. He fought for the duke of Savoy in Italy against the Habsburgs. In the Bohemian revolt, which started the Thirty Years War, he aided the rebels as a general of the artillery. After the Bohemian debacle, he moved his army through southwestern Germany into the Palatinate and Hesse. Together with Duke George Frederick of Baden, he won a battle against the league forces at Wiesloch (1622) but thereafter was checked by Tilly's troops. Always a self-seeking individual, he offered his services to the Spanish, the French, the emperor, and even to Tilly. The Dutch finally took Mansfeld into their employ but became very disillusioned with him when he ruthlessly devastated East Frisia (1622–1624). In 1624 King James I of England agreed to equip Mansfeld with an army that was to operate against the emperor in central and northern Germany. But Mansfeld failed to coordinate his military activities with King Christian IV of Denmark, who joined the conflict in 1625. While trying to dislodge an imperial army under General Wallenstein from its position on the Elbe River, Mansfeld lost one-third of his troops at the Dessau Bridge (April 25, 1626). With French subsidies he was able to reorganize his forces and break through Silesia to join Bethlen Gabor in Transylvania (July, 1626). The Transylvanian prince, however, refused Mansfeld the support he had promised. On his way through Bosnia to Venice (in whose employ Mansfeld next hoped to fight the hated Habsburg), he was suddenly taken ill and died on November 29, 1626.

Works About: *Briefe und Akten zur Gesch. des Dreissigjährigen Krieges* (Munich, 1870–1909; new series, 1907–); *Documents Bohemica Bellum Tricennale Illustrantia*, vols. 2–4 (Prague, 1972–1976); "Mansfeld," *ADB*, 20:222–32; Ludwig W. S. Count Uetterodt zum Scharffenberg, *Ernest*

Graf zu Mansfeld, 1580–1626 (Gotha, 1867); Antoine C. Villermont, *Ernest de Mansfeldt,* 2 vols. (Brussels, 1865–1866).   Bodo Nischan

See THIRTY YEARS WAR; TILLY; WALLENSTEIN, ALBERT.

MANSFELD, HENRY FRANCIS (1640–1715), count, prince of Fondi, served as imperial ambassador to Spain (1682–1690), marshal of the court, president of the Council of War (succeeding Count Ernest Rüdiger von Stahremberg, 1638–1701), and grand chamberlain to Emperor Leopold I. Mansfeld was an important member of the old ministerial party at court, which had served Leopold since his early days as emperor and which blocked attempted reforms suggested by the younger ministers. This group opposed war with France over the Spanish inheritance in 1701 because they believed that the Habsburgs had neither the financial means nor the military ability to engage in a protracted conflict. After war broke out, they insisted that the success of the war effort depended upon the favorable outcome of the imperial campaign in Italy. Because of its proximity to the hereditary countries, Italy, they thought, should be the first line of defense.

At the imperial court, Mansfeld was supported by his nephew, Count Leopold William Auersberg, and by the president of the chamber, Count Gothard Henry Salaburg. Mansfeld, a conscientious minister devoted to the imperial family, resented Count Dominik Andreas Kaunitz (1655–1705), vice-chancellor of the Empire, who was trying to usurp his power. He also quarreled with Prince Eugene of Savoy, who denounced him for incompetence, and with Prince Louis, margrave of Baden, the imperial commander on the Rhine, who had accused him ''not only of Negligence, but of Treachery'' in failing to send desperately needed men and supplies. In June 1703, when the Empire faced almost certain military disaster, Leopold replaced Mansfeld as president of war with Prince Eugene of Savoy.

Works About: Max Braubach, *Prinz Eugen von Savoyen* 5 vols. (Vienna, 1963–55); Philip Roder von Diersberg, ed., *Kriegs–und Staatschriften über der spanischen Erbfolgekrieg,* 1700–1707 (Karlsruhe, 1850); Otto Flake, *Der Türkenlouis, Margraf Ludwig von Baden, 1655–1707* (Karlsruhe, 1955); Hugo Hantsch, *Die Gesch. Österreichs* (Vienna, 1947) and *Die Entwicklung Österreichs–Ungarns zur Grossmacht* (Freiburg im Breisgau, 1933); Oswald Redlich, *Das Werden einer Grossmacht, Österreich von 1700 bis 1740* (Vienna, 1942); John P. Spielman, *Leopold I of Austria* (Rutgers: New Brunswick, N.J., 1977).   *L. S. Frey and M. L. Frey*

See EUGENE OF SAVOY; LEOPOLD I.

MARBURG, COLLOQUY OF, was a theological discussion held from October 1 to 4, 1529, between the theologians of Wittenberg and Zurich in an attempt to settle the dispute over the presence of Christ in the Lord's Supper.

The theological point of contention between the Lutherans of Wittenberg and the Zwinglians of Zurich was that Luther held to a literal interpretation of the Words of Institution and hence the Real Presence of Christ in the Eucharist, whereas Zwingli insisted on a purely symbolic and figurative interpretation and understanding. This theological debate caused a rift between the Protestant princes and estates that supported one or the other theologian, dividing the Protestants into Lutherans and Zwinglians.

Both Zwingli and Landgrave Philip of Hesse found this division among the Protestants untenable. Both advocated a federation of all Protestant princes and estates to counterbalance the cluster of Roman Catholic powers around the Empire and the militantly Catholic Charles V, but this federation could not come about if the Protestants were divided over their eucharistic theology (a situation illustrative of the extreme seriousness with which theology was taken during the Reformation).

In 1526, the Zwinglian theologian Wolfgang Capito of Strasbourg met Philip of Hesse at the first diet of Speyer and initiated correspondence between the landgrave and Zwingli. A year later, Philip of Hesse wrote to Luther proposing a theological colloquy between the Wittenberg and Zurich reformers in the hopes of ironing out religious disagreements and thus paving the way for political alliance. Luther rejected the suggestion, saying that he opposed any sort of political alliance for religious reasons on the grounds that political force had no place in the matters of faith. Moreover, Luther argued, nothing would come of such a colloquy; both he and Zwingli had already set forth their positions in their respective writings and no reconciliation would be possible unless one simply capitulated to the other, which was not likely.

Zwingli, however, did not think the theological differences were insurmountable and was supported in this conviction by his close associate, Martin Bucer. Zwingli shared Philip of Hesse's concern for the safeguarding of Protestantism against the Empire and agreed that the only course open was a political alliance of all Protestants. Bucer added to this conviction his scholarly opinion that doctrinal compromise could be reached without sacrificing the tenets of the faith, and so the Lutheran Philip kept in close touch with Zwingli in continuing efforts to bring about a colloquy.

At the diet of Speyer (1529), Philip of Hesse led an organized protest of the evangelical princes against the stringent anti-Reformation measures set forth at the diet (hence, ''protestants''). With this united move, Philip believed the time was ripe for making broad political alliances among the German and Swiss Protestants and bringing about the federation for which he had worked so long. Philip thus sought a colloquy all the more vigorously. At the diet of Speyer, the landgrave approached Philip Melanchthon and suggested to him a colloquy between Luther and the Basel reformer and ally of Zwingli, John Oecolampadius. At the same time Philip of Hesse wrote to Zwingli proposing a meeting with Luther and Melanchthon to discuss religious differences. Philip also engaged in some politicking with Luther's prince, Elector John Frederick of Saxony, and convinced the elector of the necessity of political alliance and so of the importance of a colloquy between Luther and Zwingli. Thus at the prodding of his friend Melanchthon and his prince John Frederick, Luther halfheartedly agreed to meet with the Zwinglians.

Philip of Hesse's long-awaited colloquy was held at the landgrave's new university, the University of Marburg, which he had founded as the first Protestant university in 1527. The colloquy formally opened on October 2, 1529. On October 1, Melanchthon had met informally with Zwingli while Luther met with Oecolampadius in order to explore any areas of possible agreement beforehand. The theologians found themselves to be in essential agreement on everything except the Lord's Supper, and it was this issue that occupied nearly all the debates between Luther and Zwingli on October 2 and 3. The debates were conducted in German so that Philip of Hesse, Duke Ulrich of Württemberg, and other laity in attendance might understand what was said. At Luther's request, no official minutes or transcripts were kept. For the most part, the debate was scholarly and conducted with comparative politeness and courtesy for the sixteenth century.

True to Luther's prediction, no agreement was reached on the only issue dividing Luther and Zwingli, the Lord's Supper. Philip of Hesse was greatly disappointed and continued to try to find ways for a political federation between Lutherans and Zwinglians despite doctrinal differences. On October 4, Philip gathered the principal participants in the Marburg colloquy to discuss this possibility. The Lutherans declared that political alliance without doctrinal agreement was impossible. Philip thereupon asked Luther to draw up a list of articles of faith that both parties could sign in good conscience. Luther produced a list of fifteen. Zwingli agreed to fourteen of the fifteen, and five of the six points on the disputed article concerning the Lord's Supper, taking exception only to the insistence on the Real Presence. Even with this disagreement, however, Zwingli and his followers agreed to sign the Marburg articles (with an appended statement concerning the disagreement) in order to establish political solidarity with the Lutherans. Luther also agreed to sign such a document, and thus the Marburg articles resulted as the tangible product of the colloquy.

The Marburg colloquy heralded the final break between Luther and Zwingli over the Lord's Supper, a division that could not be rectified. Protestantism thus divided into two definable and mutually exclusive camps over the particular eucharistic theology one favored. This situation made a federation of all Protestants impossible. Many of the Protestants in the Empire opted for the Lutheran position in the Württemberg Concord of 1534 and the Wittenberg Concord of 1536, but not all of them, and no united front could be made with the German-speaking Swiss or the Protestants of Strasbourg. This division was to prove disastrous for the Protestants in the religious wars in the Empire during the next two decades.

Works About: Walther Koehler, ed., *Das Marburger Religionsgesprach: Versuch einer Rekonstruktion* (Leipzig, 1929); Walther Koehler, *Zwingli und Luther*, 2 vols. (Leipzig, 1924; Gütersloh,

1953); *D. Martin Luther Werks,* 303: 110–59; *Luther's Works,* 38:5–89; "Relatio Rodolphi Collini de Colloqio Marburgensi," in *Zwingli Opera,* ed. M. Schuler and J. Schulthess (Zurich, 1841) 4:173–182; Hermann Sasse, *This Is My Body* (Minneapolis, 1959).   *M. E. Chapman*

See BUCER; CAPITO; JOHN FREDERICK; LUTHER; MELANCHTHON; PHILIP OF HESSE; SPEYER; ZWINGLI.

MARENGO, a village in north Italy, was the scene of the battle of June 14, 1800, in which Napoleon Bonaparte defeated an Austrian army under Baron Michael Frederick von Melas (1730–1806) during the French Revolutionary Wars. On May 15, 1800, Napoleon began moving his forty thousand troops of the Army of the Reserve from Dijon across the Alps by the Great St. Bernard Pass to trap Melas, who was besieging André Masséna (1756–1817) in Genoa. Although delayed by Austrian resistance at Fort Bard, Napoleon entered Milan on June 2 and began crossing the Po on pontoon bridges to concentrate for expected battle at Stradella. On June 4, however, Masséna was forced to capitulate at Genoa. The terms were lenient: Masséna's troops were to be repatriated behind the River Var, whereupon they could resume combatant status; but Melas was freed to concentrate his forces at Alessandria, being supplied by the Royal Navy through Genoa if necessary.

Napoleon now had to strike before Melas completed his concentration. He marched for Allesandria, General Lannes' advance guard driving Lieutenant Field Marshal Karl Ott from Montebello on the ninth. Believing that Melas was not yet ready for battle, Napoleon dispatched several divisions to intercept any possible Austrian move. Hence when Melas marched out of Alessandria early on June 14 with thirty-one thousand troops in three columns, crossed the Bormida, and attacked Napoleon's forces camped on the field of Marengo, there were only twenty-four thousand French troops to meet him. Victor's corps was driven back, and Lannes' flanked on the north by Ott's column, which was storming through Castel Ceriolo. Convinced of victory, the exhausted and slightly wounded Melas left the pursuit of the beaten French to his chief of staff, General Zach.

But at 4 P.M. General Desaix arrived from Rivalta with Boudet's division, and Napoleon rallied his tired troops. Marmont massed eighteen guns to stop the Austrians, Desaix led a counterattack (in which he died), and then young Kellermann led four hundred dragoons slashing through the whitecoated masses. Zach and two thousand prisoners were taken, and the rest fled back to the walls of Alessandria. Austrian casualties were about ten thousand, the French six thousand; but so shaken was Melas that he requested an armistice that same night. By the Convention of Alessandria, signed the next day, the Austrians agreed to evacuate all of Lombardy (east to Mantua and the Mincio). Italy was not the decisive theater, however, and it was only with the French victory at Hohenlinden on December 3, 1800, that Austria agreed to peace.

Works About: D. Chandler, *Campaigns of Napoleon* (New York, 1966); G. de Cugnac, *La campagne de l'armée de réserve en 1800,* 2 vols. (Paris, 1900–1901); Emperor Napoleon I, *La Correspondance de Napoleon I^ier,* 32 vols. (Paris, 1858–1870).   *A. H. Ganz*

See FRENCH REVOLUTIONARY WARS.

MARIA THERESA (1717–1780), archduchess of Austria, queen of Hungary and Bohemia, was the eldest daughter of Charles VI and Elizabeth Christina of Brunswick—Wolfenbüttel and the wife of Emperor Francis I, grand duke of Tuscany. Maria Theresa was the only woman to rule in the 650-year history of the Habsburg dynasty; her father had been the last male Habsburg. Warm, spontaneous, gay, courageous, and one of the most beautiful women of her day, she was loved by her people and respected by her foes. Frederick the Great, who admired Maria Theresa, called her "a great man" and said that she was "a credit to her throne and her sex." Maria Theresa had a keen sense of duty toward her family and her state. Aware of the danger that her dynasty faced because of the paucity of heirs during her father's lifetime, Maria Theresa gave birth to five boys and eleven girls. Of her frequent pregnancies, she wrote, "I can never have enough children; in this I am insatiable." One of the few times that she ever resented being pregnant was when she wanted to ride a horse and lead the troops on the battlefield. She believed that her children should marry to further the family's interests. Marie Antoinette, for example, was married to the French dauphin, later Louis XVI, in order to cement Austria's alliance with France. Maria Theresa was deeply devoted to her children and her likable but incompetent husband.

Upon ascending the throne in 1740, the twenty-three-year-old empress found herself "without money, without credit, without an army, without experience and without advice." Within months of her father's death, the contingency that he had so struggled to avoid occurred: war broke out over the Habsburg lands. Although the Pragmatic Sanction had ensured that Maria Theresa would not meet with any opposition in the Habsburg territories, the foreign powers immediately took advantage of Austria's debilitated military and financial position. Frederick II invaded and occupied Silesia, the wealthiest of the Habsburg lands. Charles Albert of Bavaria, who had married one of Joseph I's daughters, contested Maria Theresa's right of succession and immediately went to war, as did Saxony, France, and Spain. With French support, Charles Albert of Bavaria was elected Holy Roman emperor in 1742. After his death three years later, Bavaria withdrew from the war (Treaty of Füssen), and Maria Theresa's husband was elected Holy Roman emperor. Meanwhile Maria Theresa was able to secure the alliance of Britain, Sardinia, and various German states, including Saxony. Frederick II finally withdrew from the war and agreed to the Peace of Dresden (1745); by this treaty he recognized Stephen Francis of Lorraine as Holy Roman emperor, and Maria Theresa accepted Prussian acquisition of Silesia. War dragged on with France until 1748. In the Treaty of Aachen, France recognized

Maria Theresa's succession and her husband's election as Holy Roman emperor. In turn Maria Theresa acknowledged the cession of Silesia to Prussia and the loss of Parma, Piacenza, and Gustalla to Spain, but did recover the Netherlands, Piedmont-Sardinia, and part of Lombardy. Maria Theresa never reconciled herself to the loss of Silesia. For years she cherished the hope of recovering that strategically important territory in the north from that "evil man in Potsdam."

Realizing that reform was imperative if she wanted to recover Silesia, Maria Theresa turned to her council of state and advisers such as Count Frederick William von Haugwitz and Count Wenceslaus von Kaunitz. Most of her reforms were concentrated in the Habsburg hereditary lands, Austria and Bohemia. She did not attempt to change the system of government in Italy, the Netherlands, or Hungary. Maria Theresa increased the authority of the government by reorganizing both the central and local administration. She separated the judicial and executive branches of government and made the chief offices of the state—defense, foreign affairs, justice, interior, and commerce—directly responsible to the monarch. She weakened the authority of the estates by restricting their power, limiting their approval of taxes to every ten years, and abolishing their right to collect taxes. A central board in Vienna now levied taxes, raised and paid troops, and nominated officials. On the provincial level, the government established representations and chambers and under them district offices.

Financially Maria Theresa aimed to improve the efficiency of the government. She strove to restrict expenses rather than raise taxes, but she did levy taxes on the previously exempt Church and nobility and erected a general tariff wall around the Bohemian and Austrian lands. By restricting patrimonial jurisdiction and releasing the peasants of many of their servile obligations, particularly labor service, on the crown lands, the empress hoped to improve rural conditions.

Maria Theresa also stressed the need for religious unity and was notably intolerant of Jews. She was a devout Catholic but was under no illusion about the abuses in the Church. She forbade flagellation, reduced the number of religious holidays and processions, and limited the number of monastic orders in the state. Following the advice of Gerhard von Sweiten, she removed education from Church control and began the establishment of a universal school system.

Besides instituting these much-needed reforms in her realm, Maria Theresa reoriented Habsburg foreign policy; she realized that Prussia, not France, was the real enemy. Following the advice of Kaunitz, Maria Theresa abandoned her traditional alliance with Britain and allied with her age-old foe, France. The diplomatic revolution of 1756 was a recognition of the danger that Prussia posed. Frederick's invasion and seizure of Silesia was neither forgiven nor forgotten. During the Seven Years War (1756–1763), Maria Theresa attempted, but failed to regain Silesia. Russia and Saxony joined the Austro-French coalition. In turn Great Britain allied with Prussia, as did some of the smaller German states. On the death of Elizabeth II of Russia, her successor, Peter III, withdrew from the war. Without Russian support, Maria Theresa was forced to sue for peace in

1763. The elector of Saxony recovered his lands and Prussia retained Silesia but agreed to vote for Archduke Joseph as king of the Romans.

Against her better judgment, Maria Theresa took part in the first partition of Poland (1772) and the War of the Bavarian Succession (1778–1779). The empress was reluctant to join Prussia and Russia in partitioning Poland, but she was unwilling to allow the expansion of these eastern neighbors without commensurate Austrian gains. In the 1772 partition Austria received Zips and Galicia. On the death of the elector of Bavaria, her coruler, Joseph, tried to claim Bavaria for the Habsburgs. Frederick II, fearing the growth of Austrian territory and prestige, went to war. The Potato War, so called because the soldiers spent more time digging potatoes than fighting, ensued. Maria Theresa, who disapproved of this conflict from the outset and had been anxious to avoid war with Prussia, agreed to a compromise peace (Teschen), which ceded a small part of Bavaria, the Inn Quarter, to Austria. The ratification of this treaty was the last significant act of her reign. When the warm, moderate, beloved empress died in 1780, her son and coruler, the cold, inflexible, unmagnetic Joseph II, succeeded her. His reign was as much a disaster for Austria as Maria Theresa's had been a success.

Works By: Josef Kallbrunner, ed., *Kaiserin Maria Theresias politisches Testament* (Vienna, 1952); Friedrich Walter, ed., *Maria Theresia: Briefe und Aktenstücke in Auswahl* (Darmstadt, 1968). **Works About:** Alfred von Arneth, *Gesch. Maria Theresias*, 10 vols. (Vienna, 1863–1879); George P. Gooch, *Maria Theresa and Other Studies* (London, 1951); Edward Crankshaw, *Maria Theresa* (London, 1969); Eugen Gaglia, *Maria Theresia: Ihr Leben und ihre Regierung*, 2 vols. (Munich, 1917); C. A. Macartney, *Maria Theresa and the House of Austria* (Mystic, Conn., 1969); William J. McGill, "The Roots of Policy: Kaunitz in Versailles and Vienna, 1749–1754," *JMH* 43 (1971): 228–44; Robert Pick, *Empress Maria Theresa: The Earlier Years, 1717–1757* (New York, 1966).   *L. S. Frey and M. L. Frey*

See AUSTRIAN SUCCESSION; CHARLES VI; FRANCIS I; FREDERICK II, THE GREAT; JOSEPH II; KAUNITZ; PRAGMATIC SANCTION; SEVEN YEARS WAR.

MARPECK, PILGRAM (c. 1495–1556), civil engineer and Anabaptist theologian, was born at Rattenberg in the Inn valley of Austria to a prosperous family. After attending Latin school, he entered the Rattenberg brotherhood of miners. In 1523 he became a member of the town council; two years later he became mining judge.

His religious conversion remains somewhat of a mystery, although it cost him his judgeship when he refused to assist in the persecution of Anabaptists in 1528. Marpeck fled to Strasbourg leaving his worldly goods behind. There he became one of the leaders of the Anabaptist community and a city engineer. After losing out to Martin Bucer in a theological debate over infant baptism, he was forced to leave in 1532.

After a period of wandering in which he established himself as an influential Anabaptist leader in the south of Germany, Marpeck settled in Augsburg in 1544, where he was once again hired as city engineer. His technical competence was such that despite warnings from the government, he was allowed to live out his life in Augsburg as a practicing Anabaptist elder.

Works About: H. S. Bender, "Pilgram Marpeck, Anabaptist Theologian and Civil Engineer," *MQR* 38 (1964): 231–65; Jan J. Kiwiet, *Pilgram Marbeck: Ein Führer der Täuferbewegung im suddeutschen Raum* (Cassel, 1957); William Klassen, *Convenant and Community: The Life, Writings and Hermeneutic of Pilgram Marpeck* (Grand Rapids, 1968).   *J. W. Zophy*

See ANABAPTISM; AUGSBURG; BUCER; STRASBOURG.

MARSIGLIO OF PADUA (c. 1275/80–1342), the most creative and revolutionary political theorist during the Middle Ages, was born in Padua. There is a lack of information concerning his early life. He apparently began his education at Padua and then studied medicine and philosophy at the University of Paris. He eventually taught at Paris and was rector in 1313. It was at Paris that he completed and published the *Defensor pacis* in 1324. Pope John XXII responded to this radical attack on the papacy by placing Marsiglio under papal condemnation in 1326, an action that forced Marsiglio to leave Paris. He sought and received refuge at the court of Emperor Louis of Bavaria who was embroiled in a bitter power struggle with the pope and had himself been excommunicated in 1324.

Marsiglio served as adviser and theoretician for Louis. When the pope refused to approve Louis' election or coronation, the emperor, influenced by Marsiglio's concept of popular sovereignty, determined to let the people of Rome elect and crown him. This was accomplished in January 1328 after Louis and his forces had occupied the city. Marsiglio accompanied the emperor to Italy and was appointed vicar of Rome. Within a few months, however, Louis and his entourage were forced to leave the city when the people turned against them. Marsiglio returned to Germany with Louis and remained in the imperial court until his death in 1342.

Marsiglio's reputation and significance rest on his one important publication, the *Defensor pacis*. The volume constitutes the most creative and profound statement of political thought formulated during the Middle Ages. While Marsiglio's precise impact on future political and ecclesiastical developments continues to be debated, it is clear that his theories anticipated those developments. His concept of sovereignty literally turned medieval views of hierarchical authority upside down and radically refocused the persistent conflict between Church and state. Indeed the debate between *regnum* and *sacerdotium* over which one exercises supreme authority became meaningless in the light of Marsiglio's concept of popular sovereignty.

Aristotle served as Marsiglio's major source and authority as he formulated his political theory. Like Aristotle, Marsiglio asserted that the state exists so that people may live a prosperous, complete life. Peace must prevail if this goal is to be achieved, but peace will be a reality only when all parts of the state fulfill their respective responsibilities and function together harmoniously. Because of the human proclivity for discord, Marsiglio maintained that regulation or coercion is necessary in order to resolve conflict, facilitate cooperation, and ensure peace. The secular government is the part of the state that regulates human actions and exercises coercive power, but it cannot act arbitrarily. It must carry out its coercive function according to law in order to ensure that its actions will be just and for the common good. Only then will the sufficient life be assured for all.

In its actions, the government merely functions as the representative and agent of the *legislator humanus*. Marsiglio is somewhat nebulous in his definition of this central concept. He identifies all the people as the legislator but allows that it may also be their "better part" (*pars valentior*). Quite obviously he takes into consideration quality as well as quantity. The legislator, the collective will of the people, constitutes the supreme authority in the community; it passes laws and is the source of coercive power. Therefore coercive power, which is the essence of political authority, is legitimate only if it is derived from the collective will of the people and is in agreement with the law that is an expression of that will. The legislator also chooses the government and may depose it if it violates the law. Marsiglio does not specify what form of government the people should choose. That decision is the legislator's. What is necessary, however, is that the collective will of the people reign supreme, for it alone works for the common good.

The most original aspect of Marsiglio's thought is his concept of the Church and its relationship to the state. In the Christian context, Marsiglio envisions a unified state and church, for both the state and the Church are ultimately composed of the people. The body politic and the community of the faithful are one and the same. Both also have the same ultimate authority: the people, the *legislator humanus*. The clericalism of the Middle Ages is clearly rejected by Marsiglio. The priesthood is designated part of the state. It has no privileged legal and social position and is subject to the laws and coercive power of the secular government. Like the secular leaders, the ecclesiastical leaders, the priests and bishops, are chosen by the people. The ecclesiastical hierarchy of the Church is not of divine but of human origin. Marsiglio also rejected the theory of Petrine supremacy and with it papal claims of *plenitudo potestatis*. The responsibilities and prerogatives of all priests, including the pope, are the preaching of God's word and the celebration of the sacraments. Those responsibilities and rights are given by God. The priests have no coercive power, however, for that power belongs to the legislator and is exercised by the secular authorities. In matters of faith, the general council, as the properly designated representative of the community, makes the appropriate decisions. All of the faithful, including the pope, must abide by these decisions. Marsiglio was one of the early articulators and defenders of the conciliar position, which asserted that the council is superior to the pope.

The sovereignty of the people and the superiority of the state in the Marsiglian state and church are dominant themes in Marsiglio's thought. Secular leaders, especially Louis of Bavaria, were particularly interested in his attack on papal *plenitudo potestatis*. They did not fully recognize the implications of his thought for monarchical sovereignty. It was the papacy that called those implications to the attention of the princes as it sought their support in its struggle to defeat the conciliar movement. Marsiglio cannot be viewed as an early proponent of democracy, but he was clearly a champion of the sovereignty of the people and of constitutional government. His ideas were ahead of their time. Although constitutionalism was slowly emerging, the major trend in the political realm was toward centralized, absolute monarchy. Marsiglio, therefore, did not significantly affect his contemporary political or ecclesiastical contexts, though his thought received considerable attention. He did, however, leave an important ideological legacy that had an impact on future developments.

Works By: *The Defender of Peace*, tr. Alan Gewirth (New York, 1956). **Works About:** Alexander Passerin D'Entreves, *The Medieval Contribution to Political Thought* (London, 1939); Alan Gewirth, "John of Jandun and the *Defensor Pacis*," *Spec.* 23 (1948): 267–72, and *Marsilius of Padua*, 2 vols. (New York, 1951–1956); E. Lewis, "The 'Positivism' of Marsiglio of Padua," *Spec.* 38 (1963): 541–82; Leopold Stieglitz, *Die Staatstheorie des Marsilius von Padua*, Beiträge zur Kulturgeschichte des Mittelalters und der Renaissance, ed. Walter Goetz (Hildesheim, 1971), vol. 19.   *K. K. Hendel*

See CONCILIARISM; LOUIS IV.

MARY OF BURGUNDY (1457–1482), first wife of Emperor Maximilian I, was born in Brussels on February 13, 1457, the daughter of Charles the Bold, duke of Burgundy, and his wife, Isabelle de Bourbon. Because of the Burgundian succession, Mary had numerous suitors for her hand but was promised in 1476 to Archduke Maximilian, the Austrian Habsburg heir. This alliance, from the viewpoint of Charles the Bold, could secure the assistance of the Holy Roman Empire against France. When Charles the Bold was killed at Nancy on January 5, 1477, Mary was faced with two problems. Revolts in the provinces of the Burgundian Netherlands occurred in which the Estates General sought to reestablish their old authority. Mary was forced to grant the *Grand Privilege* of February 11, 1477, by which the previous work of centralization of her predecessors was undone. Mary was also confronted by the invasions of the Burgundian lands by Louis XI of France. Louis demanded her marriage to his son, but Maximilian sent his proxy to marry Mary at Bruges on April 21 and married her in person at Ghent on August 19. Maximilian provided the military assistance to resist the French incursion successfully, although eventually losing ducal Burgundy to the French. After Mary's untimely death on March 27, 1482, as a result of a fall from her horse while hunting with her husband, Maximilian was eventually able to secure possession of Franche-Comté, Artois, and the Netherlands for his and Mary's son Philip and thus for the Habsburg dynasty.

Works About: Luc Hommel, *Marie de Bourgogne ou le grand héritage* (Brussels, 1951); Karl Rausch, *Die burgundische Heirat Maximilians I* (Vienna, 1880).   *J. J. Spielvogel*

See MAXIMILIAN I.

MATILDA (c. 895–968), daughter of Dietrich of Saxony and Reinhilde, in 909 became the second wife of Henry I, the Fowler, king of the Germans (c. 876–936). Five children were born to Matilda and Henry I: Emperor Otto I, the Great (912–973); Henry I, duke of Bavaria (c. 920–955); Bruno, archbishop of Cologne (?–965); Gerberga (c. 913–968), who married first the duke of Lotharingia and later the west frankish king, Louis IV; and Hedwide (c. 960–965), wife of Hugh, count of Paris, whose son, Hugh, founded the Capetian dynasty. Contemporary chronicles praise Matilda's intelligence, humility, and piety, reporting that she used her influence to temper Henry I's administration of government and to further the interests of the Church.

Matilda's political influence was felt in the reigns of her husband and her son Otto I. Henry I left the administration of all of his properties in Matilda's hands. When Otto I and Henry I accused her of being so generous in Church endowments and gifts that their father's realm was being impoverished, Matilda returned Henry I's holdings and withdrew to the inheritance she had received from her father. Otto I's wife, Edgitha, negotiated a reconciliation between Matilda and her sons. Henry I's gifts to Matilda of Quedlinburg, Pölde, Nordhausen, Gronau, and Duderstadt were returned to her.

Matilda favored her second son, Henry I, over Otto I and wanted him to be named Otto's successor. Failing in this Matilda worked to heal the breach between Otto I and Henry I. Otto I granted Henry the dukedom of Bavaria in 948. Henry's death before the age of forty deeply grieved Matilda.

Matilda spent her later years in service to the Church. Her husband, Emperor Henry I, endowed a convent at Quedlinburg shortly before his death. Matilda founded a monastery at Quedlinburg and convents at Nordhausen and Pölde. She outlived her husband, two sons, Henry and Bruno, and her daughter, Hedwide. She found great comfort in her friendship with Abbess Richburg of Nordhausen, however, and lived to see her young granddaughter, Matilda, dedicated as abbess at Quedlinburg. Matilda died at Quedlinburg and was buried there next to Emperor Henry I.

Works About: Albrecht Buesing, *Mathilde, Gemahlin Heinrichs I.* (Halle, 1910); E. Dümmler and R. Köpke, *Jb. der de tsch. Gesch. unter Kaiser Otto der Grosse* (1876); P. Jaffé, tr., "Das Leben des Königin Mathilde," *Geschichtschreiber der deutschen Vorzeit* (Leipzig, 1891), vol. 4; William Volk, *Die heilige Mathilde, ihr Gemahl Heinrich I. und ihre Söhne Otto I., Heinrich und Bruno* (Quedlinburg, 1867); G. Waitz, "Mathilde, deutsche Königin," *ADB*, 20:591–93, and *Jb. der dtsch. Gesch. unter König Heinrich I* (Darmstadt, 1963).   *J. W. Gates*

See HENRY I; MATILDA OF QUEDLINBURG; OTTO I.

MATILDA OF QUEDLINBURG (955–999), daughter of Otto I, the Great (912–973) and Adelheide of Burgundy (c. 931–999), became the first abbess of Quedlinburg. Her parents placed her in the care of the nuns at Quedlinburg at an early age. Matilda was still a young girl at the time of her consecration as abbess in 966. She was a gifted young woman whose intelligence and piety won high praise from the tenth-century chronicler, Widukind, and from Pope John XII. Quedlinburg was one of the richest and most renowned convents for noblewomen in the tenth century. The vow of chastity and obedience (but not poverty) permitted members of the community to move freely between court and cloister. Matilda chose the *vita activa* and played an influential role at the imperial court, expecially under Otto III.

When Adelheide left the court of her son, Otto II, in 978 and went to Italy, Matilda followed her. Matilda was present at Pavia in December 980 as Adelheide and Otto II reconciled the differences that had arisen between them. Otto II died in 983 leaving a three-year-old heir, Otto III, to the imperial throne. Henry II, the Quarrelsome, duke of Bavaria, challenged the regency of Adelheide and Otto III's mother, Theophano. Matilda accompanied her mother back to Germany in 984 to oppose Henry II's plan. Henry II was persuaded to abandon his claim to the regency and to support Adelheide and Theophano. Adelheide and Archbishop Willegis of Mainz administered the Empire after the death of Theophano in 991 until Otto III was declared of age in 995. Matilda lived at court after 991 and played an active role in imperial administration. When Otto III left for a military campaign in Italy in 996, he entrusted Matilda with the administration of the Empire. She defended the eastern border of the empire against the Slavs and presided over meetings of the court in his absence.

Otto II left one-quarter of his holdings to Adelheide and Matilda. He and Otto III both substantially enriched the endowments to Quedlinburg in honor of Matilda. Otto III granted the city of Quedlinburg the same market, coinage, and customs privileges held by Cologne, Mainz, and Magdeburg (994) and greatly enlarged the convent's church (997). Matilda died on February 9, 999, and was buried at the convent church near her grandparents, Emperor Henry I, the Fowler, and Matilda.

Works About: Janicke, "Mathilde, Aebtissin von Quedlinburg," *ADB* 20:593–94; K. Uhlirz, *Jb. des dtsch. Reichs unter Kaiser Otto II and Otto III*. (Berlin, 1967)   *J. W. Gates*

See ADELHEIDE; HENRY I; MATILDA; OTTO I; OTTO II; OTTO III.

MATILDA OF TUSCANY (Matilda of Canossa) (1046–1115), daughter of Beatrice of Bar and Boniface II of Tuscany, was the only living heir to her parents' extensive holdings in northern and central Italy. Although she was twice married, Matilda never relinquished her personal control of her inheritance after her mother's death in 1076. She had deep religious convictions and became a loyal supporter and representative of reform popes Gregory VII, Victor III, Urban II, and Paschal II. Her association with Gregory VII brought her in conflict with Emperor Henry IV. During his Italian campaigns, Henry IV formed alliances with some of Matilda's lay and ecclesiastical vassals. They fought openly between 1080 and 1085 and from 1090 to 1097, but Henry IV was never able to bring Matilda's territories permanently under his authority.

Matilda was well educated. She spoke Italian, German, and French and conducted her correspondence in Latin. Matilda acquired a large library and supported work on an edition of Justinian's *Pandects*. She had close friends among contemporary popes and scholars. Archbishop Anselm of Canterbury visited her in 1103, and Matilda interceded on his behalf with Pope Paschal II.

Matilda had two unhappy marriages. Her mother, Beatrice, married Gottfried II of Lower Lorraine in 1054, and the couple agreed (1057) that the young Matilda should marry Gottfried's son by a previous marriage, Gottfried III, the Hunchback. Matilda may have had reservations about the union. She was well beyond the legal age for marriage (fourteen years for women) when the wedding occurred in 1069. Matilda and Gottfried III did not get along well. Both were closely involved in the investiture controversy, Matilda as a staunch ally of Gregory VII and Gottfried III as a trusted friend of Emperor Henry IV. Gottfried III was, in fact, sent to Italy to represent the emperor in 1075, and Matilda's castle at Canossa was the setting for Henry IV's penitent audience with Gregory VII on January 28, 1077. In 1072 Matilda left Gottfried III and returned to Italy with her mother to govern their estates. Gottfried III was murdered by a servant of Count Dietrich of Holland in 1076.

Matilda's second marriage at the age of forty-four to the seventeen-year-old Welf II of Bavaria was negotiated at the request of Pope Urban II. Matilda and Welf II were married in 1089, but Welf II soon found that Matilda intended to share neither her bed nor the control of her lands with him. The marriage was dissolved in 1095 at Welf II's request.

Matilda had no heirs. Moreover she left the administration of her inheritance in question by willing her lands to the Church on one occasion (1079) and on another designating Emperor Henry V heir to her estate (1111). After the death of Henry V, twelfth-century popes and emperors asserted rival claims to "Matilda's inheritance." Not until Frederick II formally relinquished his claim to her territory in 1213 was the matter settled.

Works About: L. Bethmann, ed. *MGH, SS* 12:348–409; R. de Briey, *Mathilde, duchesse de Toscane* (Gembloux, 1934); F. Dieckmann, *Gottfried III. der Bucklige* (1885); A. Falce, "Matilde di Canossa," *Enciclopedia Italiano* (Rome, 1934): 22:568–69; and ed., *Documenti inediti dei duchi e marchesi di Tuscia* in *Archivie storico italiano* (1928); N. Grimaldi, *La Contessa Matilde e la sue stirpe feudale* (Florence, 1928); G. Meyer von Knonau, *Jb. des dtsch. Reiches unter Heinrich IV.* (Leipzig, 1890); "Matilda, Countess of Tuscany," *Encyclopaedia Britannica* (London, 1957): 15:91; Alfred Overmann, *Gräfin Mathilde von Tuscien* (Innsbruck, 1895); A. Pennenborg, *Studien zur Gesch. der Herzogin Matilde von Canossa* (Göttingen, 1872); L. Tondelli, *Matilda de Canossa* (Rome, 1925).   *J. W. Gates*

See BEATRICE OF TUSCANY; FREDERICK II; GREGORY VII; HENRY IV; HENRY V; IN-
VESTITURE CONTROVERSY; TUSCAN MARCH.

MATTHIAS (1557–1619), Holy Roman emperor from 1612, was born in Vi-
enna on February 24, 1557, the third son of fifteen children of the future
Maximilian II and Mary, daughter of Charles V. Educated in Spain, Matthias
went to Brussels in October 1577 at the invitation of the Catholic nobility of the
Netherlands to become regent, despite the disapproval of his uncle, King Philip
II of Spain (1527–1598), and to the discomfiture of his brother, Emperor Rudolf
II (1552–1612). He attempted to mediate between Spain and the Dutch Calvin-
ists, led by William the Silent, prince of Orange (1533–1584). But the Dutch,
who had been resisting since 1566 (the Compromise of Breda) the attempts of
Philip II to restore them to Catholicism with the Inquisition, end their self-
government with the armies of the duke of Alba (or Alva), and return their
prosperous mercantile territories to the kingdom, were not to be reconciled.
Holland and the other six northern provinces drew together in the Union of
Utrecht in 1579 and declared their independence as the United Provinces in
1581.

Matthias left the Netherlands for Germany in October of that year, but his
brother, the emperor, would not grant him a governorship until 1593 when he
received that of Austria. But he did represent Rudolf at the imperial diets and
gained some fame as a soldier in the Turkish war (1593–1606). As governor he
suppressed risings of the Protestant peasants (1594–1597), though personally
tolerant of that religion, and fought the Hungarians and Turks. The Hungarian
nobleman István (Stephen) Bocskay (c. 1557–1606) had initiated revolt in 1604
to secure the independence of Transylvania. The Peace of Vienna (June 23,
1606) guaranteed religious freedom and legalized the existing threefold partition
of Hungary (among Austria, Transylvania, and the Ottoman Turkish Empire).
The partition was confirmed at Zsitvatörök (Szitvatorok) on November 11, 1606,
by Matthias and the Turkish sultan, Ahmed I (1589–1617). This armistice was
broken in 1611 but reaffirmed in 1615, and peace between the Habsburgs and
the Turks lasted until 1663.

Emperor Rudolf was childless and perceived as mentally unbalanced and
incompetent, and because the second brother, Ernest, had died in 1595, the
Habsburg archdukes acknowledged Matthias as heir presumptive in April 1606.
His policies after 1598 reflected the increasing influence of his adviser, the
ecclesiastical statesman Melchior Klesl (Khlesl) (1552–1630), bishop of Vienna,
who sought religious conciliation and the enhancement of Matthias' imperial
position. Matthias, allied with the estates of Hungary, Austria, and Moravia,
forced Rudolf to cede him these lands in June 1608, whose estates in turn
compelled religious concessions from Matthias when he was crowned king of
Hungary in November.

Although Rudolf and Mattias were briefly reconciled in 1610, Rudolf's troops under the archduke Leopold (1586–1632) ravaged Protestant Bohemia, bringing its estates to force Rudolf to abdicate as king of Bohemia, and crowning Matthias on May 23, 1611. Rudolf died on January 20, 1612, still opposing his brother's succession, and having prevented his election as king of the Romans, or successor designate. Matthias was elected emperor on June 13, though the ecclesiastical electors favored his younger brother, the archduke Albert (1559–1621), and crowned him on June 24, 1612.

In December 1611 Matthias had married his twenty-six-year-old cousin, Anna of Tyrol, daughter of his uncle, the archduke Ferdinand (1529–1595). He was increasingly ill and indolent and devoted himself to his household and the patronage of the arts, leaving government affairs to Klesl. Although Klesl became a cardinal in 1615, he tried to reconcile the antagonistic religious groups with compositions (reciprocal concessions). But this conciliatory policy was hopeless, as demonstrated at the diet of Regensburg in 1613; it was opposed by the Catholic princes and the younger Habsburgs, led by Matthias' brother, the archduke Maximilian (1558–1618), and his cousin, the archduke Ferdinand of Styria (1578–1637), who would succeed him as Emperor Ferdinand II in 1619.

Klesl was also unable to revive the imperial institutions, and the emperor's instructions were flouted in Cologne and Aachen over the disputed succession to the duchies of Cleves and Jülich, which again threatened a European war. Matthias was now old, ill, and childless, and the Habsburg archdukes decided that Ferdinand should be his successor. They secured Ferdinand's election as king of Bohemia in June 1617 and as king of Hungary in July 1618.

But the Bohemian Protestants refused to accept the ardently Catholic Ferdinand as king, and disorders broke out, culminating in the defenestration of Prague, on May 23, 1618. Matthias and Klesl favored concessions, but Ferdinand and Maximilian forestalled this by seizing Klesl on July 20, 1618, and imprisoning him at Ambras fortress in Tyrol. Gregory XV (pope 1621–1623) secured Klesl's transfer to Rome in 1622, and Ferdinand allowed him to resume his episcopal duties in Vienna in 1627. By the spring of 1619, the imperial forces in Bohemia had been defeated, Pilsen was taken, and the Protestant revolt was spreading. When Matthias died at Vienna on March 20, 1619, at age sixty-two, the Thirty Years War had begun.

Works About: P. von Chlumecky, *Karl von Zierotin und seine Zeit* (Brünn, 1862–1879); A. Gindely, *Rudolf II. und seine Zeit* (Prague, 1862–1868); J. Heling, *Die Wahl des römischen Königs Matthias* (Belgrade, 1892); A. Kerschbaumer, *Kardinal Klesl* (Vienna, 1865; 2d ed. 1905); M. Ritter, *Dtsch. Gesch. im Zeitalter der Gegenreformation und der dreissigjährigen Krieges*, 3 vols. (Stuttgart, 1889–1908); *Quellenbeiträge zur Gesch. des Kaisers Rudolf II.* (Munich, 1872); F. Stieve, *Die Verhandlungen über die Nachfolge Kaisers Rudolf II.* (Munich, 1880); L. Wilz, *Die Wahl des Kaisers Matthias* (Munich, 1911).   A. H. Ganz

See FERDINAND II; MAXIMILIAN II; RUDOLF II; THIRTY YEARS WAR.

MAURICE (MORITZ) (1521–1553), duke of Albertine Saxony, and later elector of Ernestine Saxony, was born in Freiburg and raised at the court of his uncle, Duke George of Saxony, where he was exposed to both Roman Catholic and Lutheran influences. Duke George, who was hostile to Protestantism, died in 1539 and was succeeded by his brother Henry, who ruled as duke for only three years, dying in 1541 and leaving the office to his twenty-year-old son, Maurice.

Duke Henry had been openly friendly toward Protestantism, and especially the Lutherans of electoral Saxony; he had allied himself with the League of Schmalkalden and had arranged the marriage of his son, Maurice, to the daughter of the prominent Lutheran prince, Landgrave Philip of Hesse. Maurice, upon becoming duke of Saxony, continued his father's friendly policy toward the Lutherans, but more cautiously; he signed the Schmalkald Articles but refused to join in the League of Schmalkalden.

In 1546, at the diet of Regensburg, the emperor's counselor, Granvelle, convinced Maurice to enter into a neutrality agreement with Charles V. Later in that same year, Maurice was offered the lands and titles of electoral Saxony if he could overthrow the Lutheran elector, John Frederick, Maurice accepted the emperor's offer and marched on electoral Saxony. Elector John Frederick immediately withdrew his troops from the army of the Schmalkaldic League to defend his lands. This division of the Protestant army was instrumental in leading to the crushing defeat inflicted upon John Frederick, Philip of Hesse, and the army of the League of Schmalkalden at the battle of Mühlberg (April 24, 1547) by a combined Catholic force led by Charles V, the emperor's brother Archduke Ferdinand of Austria, and Duke Maurice of Saxony. Both John Frederick and Philip of Hesse were taken prisoner in the battle. On May 19, 1547, Wittenberg capitulated, and Maurice assumed control of electoral Saxony. Maurice was confirmed as elector of Saxony at the diet of Augsburg in 1548.

Having united Albertine and Ernestine Saxony under his rule, however, Duke Maurice began to drift away from his Catholic benefactor, Charles V. Maurice was annoyed by the emperor's continued imprisonment of Maurice's father-in-law, Philip of Hesse, despite the duke's repeated requests for the release of the landgrave. Maurice also found it difficult to rule electoral Saxony because his subjects there, as well as fellow princes of Protestant persuasion, considered him a traitor to the cause of the Gospel. Maurice thus saw more advantage in realigning himself with the Protestants than in remaining loyal to the Catholic emperor. The Saxon duke sought to placate the ire of the Lutherans by calling upon Philip Melanchthon to restore the University of Wittenberg, which had been disbanded during the Schmalkaldic Wars. Maurice instructed Melanchthon to restore the university along Lutheran lines, employing as many of the former faculty as possible. Maurice continued the restoration of the university in open defiance of the emperor's repeated demands for the arrest of Melanchthon, whom Maurice harbored and protected as his chief theologian.

Maurice's political position with the Empire became especially precarious when Charles V imposed the Augsburg Interim on May 15, 1548. The Interim conceded clerical marriage and communion in both kinds to the Protestants, but on all other theological issues—including that of justification—it called for an immediate return to Catholic practice until the Council of Trent reached a final decision. Charles V declared that he would use force of arms to ensure the observance of the Augsburg Interim in the Empire if need arose.

Maurice was put in a difficult position: to sign the Augsburg Interim meant losing the support of his subjects and neighboring princes; not to sign it meant bringing down the wrath of the emperor upon Saxony. Maurice tried to buy time by repeatedly asking the theologians of the University of Wittenberg for their opinion on the Augsburg Interim. Maurice's principal theologians—Melanchthon, Cruciger, Major, and Pfeffinger—diligently responded to these repeated requests and every time arrived at the same reply: it would be impossible for Lutherans to agree to the Augsburg Interim. In a further effort to stall the emperor, Maurice called a meeting of Protestant princes at Celle in December 1548. There, without the advice of the theologians, the princes drafted and published the Celle Interim on December 17, 1548, a document that virtually conceded the Augsburg Interim by merely couching it in ambiguous language. Melanchton convinced Maurice to amend the document, and Melanchthon's amended version appeared as the Leipzig Interim of 1549.

Maurice's adherence to the Leipzig Interim pacified Charles V, who in 1550 entrusted the siege of the Protestant city of Magdeburg to Duke Maurice. But Maurice proved to be an unreliable ally to the emperor; the duke had cast his lot with the Protestants and at Magdeburg came out in open opposition to the emperor, offering the besieged city extremely favorable terms and taking it for himself. With this act of defiance, Maurice gathered around him the forces of the Protestant princes in revolt against the Empire. In 1552 Maurice, at the head of the Protestant army, marched on Innsbruck, where Charles V was in residence keeping watch over the Council of Trent. The imperial forces were taken by surprise, and Charles V was forced to flee before Maurice. The Saxon duke's march on Innsbruck also caused the hasty suspension of the Council of Trent. With the Turks threatening to the east, Charles V found he could not afford another war with the Protestants and in August 1552 agreed to the Treaty of Passau with Maurice of Saxony, granting religious liberty to the Protestants until the next imperial diet. At the same time Maurice also procured the release of his father-in-law, Philip of Hesse, with complete amnesty.

The signing of the Treaty of Passau marked the high point in Maurice's career. He looked upon himself as the defender of Protestantism in the Empire and went to war against Margrave Albert Alcibiades of Brandenburg when the margrave refused to honor the Treaty of Passau. On July 9, 1553, Maurice went into battle against the margrave of Brandenburg at the Battle of Sievershausen and crushingly defeated the margrave. But Duke Maurice himself was severely wounded in the battle and died of his wounds two days later, ending his chameleon-like life in the role of the heroic general of the Protestant army and defender of the Gospel.

Works By: *Politische Korrespondenz des Herzogs und Kurfürsten Moritz,* ed. E. Brandenburg, 2 vols. (Leipzig, 1900–1904). **Works About:** Hildegard Jung, *Kurfürst Moritz von Sachsen* (Hagen, 1966); Clyde Manschreck, *Melanchthon, the Quiet Reformer* (New York, 1958); W. Maurenbrecher, "Moritz, Herzog und Kurfürst von Sachsen," *ADB*, 22: 293–305; *Nuntiaturberichte aus Deutschland nebst ergänzenden Aktenstücken,* sect. 1: *1533–1559,* 13 vols. (Gotha, 1892–1912; Tübingen, 1959); *Venetianische Despechen von Kaiserhof. Dispacci di Germania,* ed. E. Turba, 3 vols. (Vienna, 1889–1896).   *M. E. Chapman*

See ALBRECHT ALCIBIADES; CHARLES V; FERDINAND I; JOHN FREDERICK; MELANCHTHON; PHILIP OF HESSE; SCHMALKALDIC LEAGUE; SCHMALKALDIC WAR.

MAXIMILIAN I (1459–1519), Holy Roman emperor from 1493 to 1519, was born at Wiener Neustadt, Austria, on March 22, 1459, the oldest son of Emperor Frederick III and Eleanor of Portugal.

From infancy, Maximilian was looked upon as a "new Constantine" who would save Christendom from Islam. His childhood was marred by difficulties in communicating as the result of rather brutal treatment by his teacher, Peter Engelbrecht. As a young man Maximilian learned an enormous number of subjects: the seven liberal arts, astrology, carpentry, music, lute playing, mining, hunting, fishing, weaponry, painting, and drawing. He acquired a speaking knowledge of seven languages. He was an extremely congenial person with a very engaging manner that allowed him to be at ease with all groups of people. It is no wonder that contemporary Germans saw him as "the last knight," an ideal ruler to fulfill their hopes and aspirations.

The marriage of Maximilian to Mary, the daughter of Charles the Bold (who was killed in battle in January 1477), in 1477 marked the beginning of the rise of European preeminence of Maximilian and the Habsburg dynasty. Maximilian successfully defended the Burgundian inheritance against the French kings Louis XI and Charles VIII by defeating Louis at Guinegate in Artois in 1479 and Charles at Salins in Franche-Comté in 1493. The latter battle resulted in the Treaty of Senlis in 1493, which left the Netherlands and Franche-Comté in Maximilian's hands and ducal Burgundy with the French. Throughout this struggle with the French, Maximilian had also had difficulty in establishing control over the Netherlands. After Mary's death in 1482, the Estates General of the Netherlands insisted on acting as regent for Philip, the infant son of Maximilian and Mary. Maximilian managed to reacquire control of the regency for his son but only after much struggle, including an embarrassing imprisonment in Bruges for four months in 1488, which was ended only by making extensive concessions. In 1494, Maximilian formally handed over the government of the Netherlands to his son, Philip. Maximilian's successful acquisition of the Burgundian lands laid the foundation for the great struggle between the Habsburgs and the

French in the sixteenth century. After 1494, Maximilian would continue this struggle primarily by opposing French advances in Italy.

Meanwhile, in 1486, Maximilian was elected king of the Romans, thus joining his father in the administration of the Holy Roman Empire. When Frederick III died in August 1493, Maximilian became the sole ruler of the Empire and head of the house of Habsburg. As Holy Roman emperor, Maximilian faced three major problems: the French, especially in Italy; the Turks and the eastern frontiers; and the internal problems of the Empire.

King Charles VIII of France invaded Italy in 1494. Although Maximilian was originally not opposed to the invasion, Charles' rapid success induced him to join Spain, Pope Alexander VI, Milan, and Venice in a league to drive the French out of Italy. He also married Bianca Maria Sforza, niece of Ludovico il Moro, regent of Milan, to further his own interests in Italy. Maximilian played no role in the ensuing victory of the league due to lack of financial support from the Empire. In 1496, financed by Milan, he made an ineffective expedition to Italy and was forced into a hasty withdrawal. After Charles VIII's successor, Louis XII, invaded Italy and conquered the imperial fief of Milan in 1499, Maximilian tried again to get the support of Germany to eject the French king. Once again he was unsuccessful and concluded a treaty with Louis XII in 1504 that recognized his possession of Milan in return for the agreement of Louis not to interfere in the affairs of the Empire. After regaining considerable prestige in the Empire in the war of Landshut succession, Maximilian was voted a moderate force by the imperial diet to accompany him to Rome for his imperial coronation, following the customary procedure of being crowned as emperor by the pope. Because of the resistance of the Venetians, Maximilian was forced to stop at Trent in 1508, where, with the consent of Pope Julius II, he assumed the title of emperor elect. In order to recover long-lost imperial territory, he also began a war against Venice, which lasted intermittently for eight years. Since the diet would give him no support for a war so damaging to German trade, he was virtually reduced to poverty in pursuing it. To continue this war, Maximilian even went so far as to ally himself with his old enemy France, as well as Spain and the pope, in the League of Cambrai, whose purpose was to partition Venice. Only Maximilian, without funds and troops, failed to provide any real assistance in the attack on Venice. When the overwhelming success of this league, and especially France, frightened Pope Julius II into forming the Holy League against the French, Maximilian joined it, but again without providing any real material aid except serving as an adviser to Henry VIII's English army in Artois. At this time Maximilian also added to his endless array of grandiose schemes a rather bizarre one when he contemplated being a candidate for pope because of Julius II's severe illness. His final effort in Italy came in 1515. After the new French king, Francis I, reannexed Milan in September 1515, Maximilian borrowed more money, hired some troops, and entered Milan. Because his unpaid troops mutinied, the emperor hurried back to Germany. In 1516 he recognized the

French possession of Milan and a final end to all his vain efforts against the French in Italy.

The problem of the Turks and the eastern frontiers was another of Maxmilian's preoccupations. After the death of King Matthias Corvinus of Hungary in 1490, Maximilian was able to drive the Hungarians out of Austria and regain Vienna. Corvinus was succeded by Vladislav Jagiello, king of Bohemia since 1471, but Maximilian's expedition into Hungary in 1491 resulted in Vladislav's agreement that succession to both Hungary and Bohemia should pass to the Habsburgs if Vladislav had no male heir. Later, in 1515, succession agreements first arrived at in 1506 and 1507 were renewed in which Vladislav's son Louis was betrothed to Maximilian's granddaughter Mary and his daughter Anna to Maximilian's grandson Ferdinand. Although he did not live to see it, Maximilian's arrangement led to Ferdinand's succession to the thrones of Bohemia and Hungary when Louis Jagiello was killed by the Turks in 1526. In regard to the Turks, Maximilian had rather impressive schemes for expelling the Turks from eastern Europe and then taking the imperial crown of Byzantium, but little was done beyond local successes against the Turks in his Austrian possessions.

The problem of the Empire proved to be as intractable as foreign policy. Maximilian hoped for the unity of Germany under a strong Habsburg monarchy with the right of taxation and a standing army to provide defense, especially against the French and Turks. Maximilian appealed repeatedly to the diets to support him in his view of the Empire's needs but, despite his popularity among the German people, the ruling authorities, especially the princes, refused to accept his position and even strongly distrusted him at times. Some of that mistrust was well founded. Maximilian's policies, as seen in the case of the French in Italy, often lacked clear and realistic objectives. In addition, German leaders were never sure whether Maximilian's policies were meant to secure the welfare of the German nation, as he claimed, or to provide for the enlargement of Habsburg possessions. Indeed the latter often appeared to be the case. This gulf between emperor and Empire is evident throughout Maximilian's reign, especially in his dealings with the diets, which often failed to give him the money and troops he desired.

This separation was already evident at the diet of Worms of 1495, where a group of reformers, led by Berthold of Henneberg, archbishop of Mainz, wished to establish the Empire on a federal basis by instituting effective organs of central government with a leading role for the greater princes as councillors to the monarchy. To make possible the growth of the new institutions of government, they hoped to avoid foreign war. In 1495, the reformers accomplished some of their goals with the proclamation of the *ewiger Landfrieden*, the perpetual internal peace outlawing personal feuds, and the creation of the *Reichskammergericht*, an Imperial Chamber Court dominated by the princes. As a compromise with Maximilian, the diet also established the Common Penny, a general tax to be used for the support of an imperial army and expenses of government. Since many of the estates refused to pay, it was of little help to Maximilian, who was left then and throughout his reign to finance his wars and other projects by borrowing from banking families, such as the Fuggers.

As a result of his foreign policy failures and subsequent dire political straits, Maximilian acquiesced at the diet of Augsburg in 1500 in the formation of the *Reichsregiment,* an Imperial Council of Regency with claims to full authority in ruling the Empire. Maximilian was virtually reduced to a figurehead monarch. Unable to gain the assistance of either Maximilian or the estates, the *Reichsregiment* failed to govern. By 1502 it ceased to function and Maximilian quickly established his own *Hofrat,* or privy council, for the imperial administrative functions. The reform movement began to wane, and in 1504 the death of its leader, Berthold of Mainz, brought it to a standstill.

Maximilian was able to regain much prestige in the Empire as a result of his victories in the dynastic war between Bavaria and the Rhenish Palatinate in 1504. At the diet of Cologne in 1505, he arranged the final territorial settlement and achieved a moment of personal triumph. Venetian envoys reported home that "his imperial majesty is now a true emperor and ruler of Germany." The diet was tired of constitutional experiments and was content to continue with the existing constitutional confusion. It was even willing to grant the emperor's request for money for war, this time against Hungary although only in a moderate amount. In 1507, at the diet of Constance, the estates actually supported an expedition to Rome for the imperial coronation but did not grant enough for a serious war against Venice and France as Maximilian wanted. His war against Venice, begun in 1508, was unpopular with German merchants and resulted in his inability to gain any financial support from subsequent diets. In fact, after 1508 there was little hope of any real cooperation between Maximilian and the diets. At the diet of Augsburg in 1518, he was unable to secure the election of his grandson Charles as king of the Romans.

Maximilian's reign witnessed additional dissolution of the Empire when the Swiss Confederation went to war in 1499 against the emperor over some imperial legal decisions. By the Treaty of Basel, the Swiss were recognized as virtually independent of the Empire. Overall Maximilian left the Empire in greater anarchy than when he began ruling. He was more successful in his own Austrian lands where he laid the foundations for unified government over various provinces, earning him the title Founder of the Austrian State. And, although unsuccessful in war, his marriage arrangements produced the vast Habsburg empires of his grandsons Charles and Ferdinand.

Maximilian was well known for his patronage of the arts and literature. He employed artists such as Albrecht Dürer and Hans Burgkmair on numerous projects, including illustrations for his own literary efforts. He patronized humanists such as John Cuspinian and Conrad Peutinger. His support of artists and humanists, however, was often done for personal vanity since they could present him to the world in his greatness as a new Augustus. Also an author, his writings are marked by great self-esteem. The most famous are *Theuerdank* (1517), a political allegory describing his journey to claim Mary of Burgundy as his bride, and his unfinished autobiographical work of the young "white king," *Weisskunig* (1518).

Maximilian died at Wels in Upper Austria on January 12, 1519, and was buried at Wiener Neustadt.

Works By: Joseph Chmel, ed., *Urkunden, Briefe und Aktenstücke zur Gesch. Maximilians I und seiner Zeit* (Stuttgart, 1845), and *Monumenta Habsburgica. Sammlung von Aktenstücke und Briefe zur Gesch. des Hauses Habsburg in dem Zeitraum von 1473– 1576. Das Zeitalter Maximilians I.,* 3 vols. (Vienna, 1854–1858); Louis Gachard, ed. *Letters inédits de Maximilien, duc d'Autriche, roi des Romains et empereur, sur les affaires de Pays-Bas* (Brussels, 1851–1852). **Works About:** Erhard Breitner, *Maximilian I* (Bremen-Vienna, 1939); Rudolf Buchner, *Maximilian I, Kaiser an der Zeitenwende* (Göttingen, 1959); Christopher Hare, *Maximilian the Dreamer* (London, 1913); R. G. D. Laffan, "The Empire under Maximilian I," in *The New Cambridge Modern Hist.,* vol. 1: *The Renaissance* (Cambridge, 1957), pp. 194–223; Heinrich Ulmann, *Kaiser Maximilian I,* 2 vols. (Stuttgart, 1884–1891); Glenn E. Waas, *The Legendary Character of Kaiser Maximilian* (New York, 1941); Hermann Wiesflecker, *Kaiser Maximilian I. Das Reich, Österreich und Europa an der Wende zur Neuzeit,* 3 vols. (Munich, 1971–1977).   *J. J. Spielvogel*

See BERTHOLD; BURGKMAIR; CUSPINIAN; DÜRER; ENGELBRECHT; FREDERICK III; FUGGER; IMPERIAL CAMERAL COURT; IMPERIAL COUNCIL OF REGENCY; MARY OF BURGUNDY; PEUTINGER; SFORZA; VILLINGER.

MAXIMILIAN II (1527–1576), Holy Roman emperor from 1564 to 1576, was the eldest son of Emperor Ferdinand I and Anna of Bohemia and Hungary. An intelligent, cultivated, and tolerant man, Maximilian was frequently frustrated by the seething religious passions and political dilemmas of his day.

He spent his infancy and childhood in Innsbruck. One of his early tutors was Wolfgang Schiefer, a former student and table companion of the reformer Martin Luther. His uncle, Emperor Charles V, had a high opinion of the young Maximilian and brought him to his court in Spain in 1544. Charles V took him campaigning against the French and the evangelicals in the Empire. Maximilian was present with his uncle at the Battle of Mühlberg in 1547 and witnessed the Protestant defeat. Later he would make a careful study of the Lutheran Bible captured along with John Frederick of Saxony.

Against his will, Charles married Maximilian to his daughter Mary, and Maximilian became king of Bohemia in 1548. Although Mary remained a thoroughgoing Spaniard for the rest of her life, the marriage proved to be reasonably happy, and they had a large family. Maximilian, however, considered himself a German and disliked the pomp and severity of Spanish court life. In 1550 he eagerly left Spain for the Empire. He later became seriously ill after leaving Trent, the site of the great Church council and became convinced that he had been poisoned by agents of Cardinal Christoph Madruzzo, his host at Trent.

At home in Vienna at his father's court, Maximilian came under the influence of John Sebastian Pfauser, a court chaplain who claimed to be "neither Lutheran nor Papalist'' but was considered to favor an evangelical approach. Maximilian took a similar line, on one occasion informing a papal nuncio that he was ''neither Catholic nor Protestant, but a Christian.'' Nevertheless, he had many German Protestant friends, some of whom he wrote to in code and with invisible ink. The young king also seemed to be influenced by the Czech nobles, who were always in his retinue, and like them he favored Communion in both kinds.

Not only did Maximilian not trust the political maneuverings at Trent, he did not trust those shock troops of the Counter Reformation, the Jesuits. He complained of being spied upon at his father's court and refused to allow his children to be educated by Jesuits. Instead he turned them over to George Muschler, a professor at the University of Vienna. On one occasion he refused to take part in a Corpus Christi procession.

Matters came to a head when Pope Paul IV severely reprimanded Ferdinand for accepting the religious Peace of Augsburg, which made Lutheranism legal in the Empire in 1555, and for harboring a ''wicked heretic son.'' Ferdinand finally lashed out at Maximilian, ordering him to stop turning his subjects into heretics. Maximilian was offered the choice of submission to the Catholic faith or the loss of his inheritance. When Maximilian found that his Protestant allies in the Empire would not back him in any open break with Emperor Ferdinand, the disillusioned prince submitted to the parental yoke. On February 1562 at Prague before his brothers Charles and Ferdinand, Maximilian placed his hands between those of his father's and swore to live and die within the Catholic church. As a further sign of his submission, he reluctantly sent his sons Rudolf and Ernest to Spain to be educated in that traditionally pious atmosphere.

To ease the penitent Maximilian's burdens, Ferdinand divided the inheritance. Maximilian, since 1562 king of the Romans and of Hungary and Bohemia, received the Bohemian lands, the surviving fragment of Hungary, and Lower and Upper Austria. His brother, Archduke Charles (1564–1590), received Inner Austria (Styria, Carinthia, and Carniola), with Graz as his residence. Archduke Ferdinand (1564–1595) was given hereditary possessions in the Swabian Rhineland, Tyrol, and the Vorarlberg. Maximilian's position was further weakened when his cousin Philip II, born the same year, was named head of the house of Habsburg. Nevertheless, Maximilian was elected Holy Roman emperor at Frankfurt in 1564. He was also crowned there because of the sudden death of the archbishop of Cologne, who would have presided over the coronation at Aachen under normal circumstances. This set a precedent, and thereafter both ceremonies took place at Frankfurt.

Proficient in German, Latin, Italian, French, Spanish, Czech, and Hungarian, Emperor Maximilian II believed that his supreme duty as ruler was to keep peace and attempt to reconcile his diverse peoples. In agreements made in 1568 and 1571, he was able to secure religious freedom for Lutherans in Lower Austria. His brother Charles, although more in sympathy with the spirit of Trent, granted similar toleration in his territories. He talked about leading the bishop of Rome back to the apostolic path. His efforts to restrain the severity of his cousin Philip toward the Netherlands, then in revolt, failed. In general his efforts to promote peace through negotiations, compromises, treaties, and dynastic marriages were unsuccessful. The temper of the times was more in the spirit of the St. Bartholomew's massacre, which Maximilian deplored, than in his Erastian position of a state-controlled church with toleration for religious minorities.

Maximilian also failed as a warrior. Granted a large army for a war against the Turks in 1566, he proved an overly cautious general and after two years of inconclusive fighting had to continue paying an embarrassing tribute to the Turks. The plan of his adviser and general, Lazarus von Schwendi, for a change in the imperial military appropriations procedure was rejected by the princes at the diet of Regensburg in 1570. In dealing with the Turkish threat, Maximilian found himself once again at loggerheads with his cousin Philip of Spain. Maximilian wanted to ally with the Poles and in fact attempted to become their king in 1573; Philip looked instead to the Russians.

Maximilian was successful as a patron of the arts and sciences. Determined to make Vienna a center of European intellectual life, the cultured emperor brought to the city such distinguished scholars as the botanist Karl Clusius and the physician John Crato von Krafftsheim, both of them Protestants. The emperor himself experimented with plants: the lilac became his favorite. Like Erasmus he wanted Europe not to dissolve into ashes but to burst into flower. Musicians were brought to Vienna from all over Europe, and Maximilian even made an unsuccessful attempt to lure the great Palestrina from Rome.

As he lay dying at the diet of Regensburg, one last battle swirled around him as he refused to take the last sacrament from the court chaplain. Maximilian argued that his chaplain was in heaven. The news of his death on October 10, 1576, was greeted with genuine sorrow throughout the Empire by both Catholics and Protestants.

Works About: Victor Bibl, *Maximilian II, der rätselhafte Kaiser* (Vienna, 1929): R. J. W. Evans, *Rudolf II and His World* (Oxford, 1973); A. Gindely, *Gesch. der Böhmischen Brüder* (Prague, 1868) F. Heer, *The Holy Roman Empire* (New York, 1968); H. Holborn, *A Hist. of Modern Germany* (New York, 1959); vol. 1; M. Ritter, *Dtsch. Gesch. im Zeitalter der Gegenreformation und des dreissigjährigen Krieges* 3 vols. (Stuttgart, 1889–1905).   J. W. Zophy

See CHARLES V: FERDINAND I; FRANKFURT; MATTHIAS; RUDOLF II: SCHMALKALDIC WAR; VIENNA.

MAXIMILIAN I (1573–1651), duke (after 1623 elector) of Bavaria, the son of William V and Renata of Lorraine, was born in Munich and died at Ingolstadt. Educated at the Jesuit University of Ingolstadt (1587–1591), Maximilian became coregent in 1591 and took full charge of Bavaria's government in 1598. He spent the first ten years of his reign ordering the internal affairs of his country, which suffered under huge debts and an inefficient bureaucracy. He revised the law (the *Codex Maximilianeus* of 1616 remained in force until 1751), turned Bavaria into a centralized absolutistic state, and, most important of all, ordered the duchy's finances. The country's economic health, more than anything else, allowed Bavaria to enter the Thirty Years War with great strength. Maximilian was an ardent supporter of the Catholic Counter Reformation and was deeply influenced by his Jesuit advisers.

He pursued a very active foreign policy. Like his predecessors he sought to control the adjacent bishoprics of Salzburg, Freising, Passau, and Regensburg. In 1607, he enforced the imperial ban against Donauwörth: with the emperor's approval he took possession of the small imperial city and then re-Catholicized it. He placed himself at the head of the Catholic League, which he had organized in 1609 in defense against the Protestant Union under Frederick V of the Palatinate. But he prudently refrained from intervening militarily in the Jülich-Cleves succession dispute (1609–1610). At the same time, though, he ensured the survival of the old faith in Jülich by backing the Catholic claimant in the dispute, Wolfgang William of Neuburg, a convert from Lutheranism, who had married his sister (1614). Meanwhile, he valiantly opposed efforts by the emperor who, jealous of Maximilian's power, was trying to turn the league into an instrument of Habsburg family politics.

He regarded the political adventures of Frederick V of the Palatinate, particularly his intervention in the Bohemian revolt (which started the Thirty Years War), as a serious threat to the Empire's constitution and to peace generally. When the Palatinate elector clumsily offered him the imperial crown in order to split the Catholic group, Maximilian rejected the offer, thereby ensuring the election of his cousin, Ferdinand of Austria. In the Treaty of Munich (October 8, 1619), he pledged the league's military support to the new emperor, while Ferdinand promised to reimburse Maximilian for his expenses, allowing him to hold, as a guarantee of payment, all of the lands that he liberated. In addition, Ferdinand offered to transfer the Palatinate electoral title to Bavaria. Having ensured the neutrality of the Protestant Union by means of another treaty (Ulm, 1620), the league joined Ferdinand in Bohemia. Bavarian forces, led by Count Tilly, defeated the army of Frederick V at the White Mountain (near Prague) and occupied and devastated the Palatinate. Ferdinand awarded Maximilian for his services by granting him the promised electoral diginity (1623). The Bavarian also obtained the Palatinate territories on the right bank of the Rhine in exchange for the evacuation of Upper Austria (1628).

Like Ferdinand, Maximilian interpreted the Catholic victories in the war as a divine mandate to restore the old faith in Germany; he therefore supported the emperor's Edict of Restitution (1629). But the two rulers soon clashed over the edict's execution since both wanted to use it to further their own family interests in the Empire. Another divisive issue was Duke Albert von Wallenstein, the imperial commander-in-chief, whose army, Maximilian feared, not unjustly, was being used to turn the federal Empire into an absolute, centralized Habsburg monarchy. Together with the other League princes, he forced Ferdinand to dismiss his powerful general (1630), reduce the imperial army, and appoint

Tilly, head of the league forces, as his new commander-in-chief. In addition, Maximilian sought to guard his own interests by signing a treaty with France (1631).

None of these steps, however, could protect him against King Gustavus Adolphus of Sweden who had entered the war in July 1630. The Swedish forces beat Tilly's army decisively at Breitenfeld (September 1631) and then pushed deep into Germany. Maximilian asked for but received no support from the French (who were also allied with Sweden). Weakened and demoralized, the league army tried to stop the Swedes at Rain on the Lech (April 15, 1632) but was overwhelmed; Gustavus' forces poured into Bavaria, deliberately devastating its countryside. Wallenstein, whom Ferdinand had recalled from retirement, did little to aid Maximilian. By 1633 the elector again was urging the emperor to dismiss his recalcitrant general.

Wallenstein's assassination and the imperial victory over the Swedes at Nördlingen (1634) permitted Maximilian greater freedom of action. Very reluctantly he joined the Peace of Prague (1635), which the Saxons and Austrians had negotiated. But the war continued, and Maximilian now was also forced to fight the French, who had intervened on the side of the Swedes (1635). The Bavarian armies, ably commanded by Francis von Mercy and John von Werth, were too weak to push the invaders out of southern Germany. With the greater part of his states occupied, the elector finally agreed to a truce with the French (1647) but soon broke it to rejoin the emperor. At the Westphalian Peace Congress, which ended the war, Bavaria sided with France and therefore was partly responsible for Germany's loss of territories in Lorraine and Alsace. The French, in return, supported Maximilian, thereby enabling him to retain the electoral dignity and the Upper Palatinate; however he had to give up the Rhenish Palatinate, which was restored to Charles Louis, the eldest son of the disgraced Frederick V.

Maximilian was superior to most other princes of his age, not only morally but also as a statesman and administrator. Next to the Habsburg, he was the leading Catholic prince in the Empire. At the same time he was one of the foremost defenders of princely rights and German liberties. He, more than any other German prince, was responsible for stopping Ferdinand II in 1630 from turning the Holy Roman Empire into a centralized absolute Catholic monarchy.

Works About: Dieter Albrecht, *Die auswärtige Politik Maximilians von Bayern 1618–1635* (Göttingen, 1962); Robert Bireley, *Maximilian von Bayern, Adam Contzen S. J. und die Gegenreformation in Deutschland 1624–1635* (Göttingen, 1975); *Briefe und Akten zur Gesch. des Dreissigjährigen Krieges.* 11 vols. (Munich, 1870–1909; new series, 1907–): Heinz Dollinger, *Studien zur Finanzreform Maximilians I. von Bayern in den Jahren 1598–1619* (Göttingen, 1968); Hermann Hallwich, ed., *Briefe und Akten zur Gesch. Wallensteins*, 4 vols. (Vienna, 1912); Kurt Pfister, *Kurfürst Maximilian von Bayern und sein Jahrhundert* (Munich, 1948); Sigmund von Riezler, *Gesch. Bayerns* (Gotha, 1903) vols. 5, 6; Stieve, "Maximilian," *ADB*, 21:1–22. *Bodo Nischan*

See CATHOLIC LEAGUE; EDICT OF RESTITUTION; FERDINAND II; FREDERICK V, ELECTOR; THIRTY YEARS WAR; TILLY.

MELANCHTHON, PHILIP (1487–1560), the foremost Lutheran dogmatician of the early sixteenth century, is known also in history as the *Praeceptor Germaniae* ("teacher of Germany") for his achievements as an educator and humanist.

Born in Bretten near Karlsruhe (Baden) to George, a manufacturer of armour, and Barbara Reuter Schwartzerd, Philip enjoyed the privilege of a classical education. After the death of his father in 1507, the direction of his education was assumed by an uncle, the renowned humanist John Reuchlin, who was popularly called the "transalpine Greek." As a result of this association and of his own ability, he earned a reputation for his humanist learning; like his peers he soon used a classical form of his family name, Melanchthon, which is Greek for "Schwartzerd."

After studies at Heidelberg (B.A., 1511) and Tübingen (M.A., 1514), he was called to Wittenberg (1518) where he lectured on the classics and acquired a popularity second only to Luther. Of all the admiration and respect bestowed upon him, however, the most important for the development of his career came from Martin Luther himself. In return Melanchthon provided countless intellectual services in the interests of the Reformation. The earliest of these is the first edition of the *Loci Communes* (1521), a basic text for the teaching of theology. It reflected the attitudes of Martin Luther and his associates on the fundamental issues of Christian belief. Luther held this small book to be one of the most significant theological works ever written. In subsequent revised and expanded editions, Melanchthon gave the Lutheran community a systematic theology which has its parallel in classics such as Calvin's *Institutes of the Christian Religion*.

Equal in importance to his intellectual achievements were his services as a personal representative of Luther. Since the Edict of Worms had politically disabled the Great Reformer, Melanchthon became for all practical purposes the chief public spokeman for the Wittenberg community of theologians. It was in this capacity that he attended the diet of Augsburg (1530) and wrote, in consultation with others, the definitive Lutheran creed, the Augsburg Confession. Throughout the course of his life, he played a similar role on numerous occasions, including all important diets and gatherings at which religious issues were treated.

In these and other public activities, Melanchthon displayed the qualities of dispassionate scholar, teacher, and irenicist. In an age of heated debate, hyperbole, and slanderous name calling, he was one of the few who stood above the general combatants. Whether in discussion with Zwinglians, as at Marburg (1529), or in negotiations with traditional Catholic theologians, as at Augsburg (1530), Melanchthon brought a certain emotional detachment to his work, which allowed discussants to get to the most difficult issues. As a result, he was often able to treat complex issues with success and prepare consensus statements of Christian doctrine. His recognition and tolerance of the role of adiaphora (non-essential or traditional practices) in religious life was one of the more controversial elements of his approach to religious issues.

If his efforts to reach solid agreements failed, the fault usually rested with the partisanship of political leaders and the rigid religious idealism of his contemporaries. As close and as solid as was his friendship with Luther, strains developed between the two men. These are best explained by differences in their professional activities (one a fiery preacher, the other a mild humanist teacher) and their individual temperaments. On occasion Melanchthon was forced to admit frustration and disappointment at Luther's inflexibility and insensitivity, which made it almost impossible to resolve the issues that divided the Church. This phenomenon is mirrored further in the development of parties within the Lutheran community: the Philipists, who were flexible and open to the religious opinions of their counterparts, whether Catholic or Calvinist; and the Gnesio-Lutherans, who guarded the letter of the Lutheran experience and viewed Melanchthon's irenicism as weakness at best and apostasy at worst.

While the desire to reconcile was rejected by some contemporaries, it was honored by others as extraordinary statesmanship. For the humanist community in general, which had been alienated by Luther's immoderation, Melanchthon was the voice of reason and responsible change. He not only provided a respectability for the Lutheran leadership among the broad European intellectual circle, but he also served as a bridge to that same *honesta aristocratia* and forestalled the isolation of his colleagues. Among many men he was seen as the heir of Desiderius Erasmus.

Magistrates at all levels of political life recognized these same virtues in the *praeceptor* and required his services as a competent diplomat. He gave expression to the delicate positions of Protestant princes and of the Schmalkaldic League in their negotiations and communications with others. The measure of his success is seen in the degree to which all princes, Catholic and Protestant alike, courted his favor. Philip of Hesse, for example, proved to be one of his foremost admirers; from this relationship came one of the earliest official reformations in a principality of the Empire, the establishment of the first Protestant university, and the first attempts to reconcile north and south German theologians. Catholic princes, such as Francis I and Henry VIII, were quick to recognize his international reputation and his standing in the evangelical community and sought his advice and support for their personal and political objectives. Some of these contacts brought significant advantage to the Reformation; others, such as Melanchthon's role in the bigamous marriage of Philip of Hesse, were painful and embarassing.

There is no doubt that some of Melanchthon's most lasting achievements were made in the cause of education. His aid in the founding of the gymnasium at Nuremberg (1526) and his role in the establishment of the University of Marburg only begin to measure the extent of his accomplishments. He reformed curricula and set high standards for every level of education; his impact in this area lasted into the nineteenth century. He wrote textbooks on Latin and Greek grammar, dialectic, rhetoric, psychology, physics, ethics, history, and religion. And he created a circle of humanists, teachers, and students who gave Wittenberg an intellectual tradition and who provided the Empire with services and influence that its numbers would justify.

After a brief illness in April 1560, Philip Melanchthon died and was buried in Wittenberg near his colleague Martin Luther.

Works By: C. G. Bretschneider and H. E. Bindseil, eds., *Philippi Melanchthonis opera quae supersunt omnia*, vols. 1–28 of the *Corpus Reformatorum* (Halle and Braunsweig, 1834–1860); Hans Engelland et al., eds., *Werke in Auswahl* (Gütersloh, 1951–); C. L. Hill, ed. and tr., *Selected Writings* (Minneapolis, 1962). **Works About:** G. Ellinger, *Phillip Melanchthon* (Berlin, 1902); Willem Jan Kodiman, *Phillippus Melanchthon* (Amsterdam, 1963); Clyde Manschreck, *Melanchthon, the Quiet Reformer* (New York, 1958); Wilhelm Maurer, *Der junge Melanchthon*, 2 vols. (Göttingen, 1967–69); Robert Stupperich, *Melanchthon*, tr. Robert Fischer (Philadelphia, 1965). *J. P. Ryan, Jr.*

See AUGSBURG, DIET OF; ERASMUS; HUMANISM; LUTHER; MARBURG COLLOQUY; PHILIP OF HESSE; REUCHLIN; SCHMALKALDIC LEAGUE.

MOHÁCS, BATTLE OF, occurred in the spring of 1687 when the imperialists under Duke Charles V of Lorraine (1655–1729) defeated the Turks at the very place where their armies had been victorious a century and a half earlier (1526), where Louis of Hungary had lost his life and his kingdom. Mohács was but a part of a larger campaign that began in 1683 when the Turks, breaking the truce concluded at Vasvar in 1664, invaded the Holy Roman Empire and besieged the capital at Vienna. The rebellion in Hungary led by Emerick Tököly had spurred the Turks to break the peace. With approximately two hundred thousand troops, the Turks endeavored to seize the city. Failing, they hastily and disastrously retreated. In 1686, Budapest fell to the Austrians as did Pécs (Fünfkirchen), Szeged, and Arad. At the ensuing battle (Berg Harsan), close to Mohács, the sixty thousand imperialists defeated the Turks under the command of the grand vizier, Suleiman Pasha. Max Emmanuel, elector of Bavaria, Prince Louis, margrave of Baden, and Prince Eugene of Savoy, who later achieved fame as military commanders in their own right, acted courageously in this campaign. In particular, Prince Eugene of Savoy was noted for his bravery and given a jeweled portrait of the emperor. The victory at Mohács and the seizure of Buda permanently destroyed Turkish power in central Hungary. The Habsburgs were able to re-establish control over almost all of Hungary. The Hungarians subsequently lost the right to elect their ruler and to resist the king with arms. The war continued until 1699 (Treaty of Karlowitz).

Works About: Max Braubach, *Prinz Eugen von Savoyen* 5 vols. (Vienna, 1963–65); Otto Flake, *Der Türkenlouis, Margraf Ludwig von Baden, 1655–1707* (Karlsruhe, 1955); Nicholas Henderson, *Prince Eugene of Savoy* (London, 1964); Robert A. Kann, *A Hist. of the Habsburg Empire* (Berkeley, 1974), pp. 65–66: Derek McKay, *Prince Eugene of Savoy* (London, 1977), pp. 23–26; Helmut

Oehler, *Prinz Eugene im Urteil Europas* (Munich, 1944); Oswald Redlich, *Weltmacht des Barock, Österreich in der Zeit Leopolds I* (Vienna, 1961); John P. Spielman, *Leopold I of Austria* (New Brunswick, N.J., 1977).   *L. S. Frey and M. L. Frey*

See EUGENE OF SAVOY; KARLOWITZ; LEOPOLD I; VIENNA, SIEGE OF.

MOLLWITZ is a village in Silesia where the Prussian army defeated the Austrians (April 10, 1741) in the War of the Austrian Succession. Stung by Frederick II's seizure of Silesia upon her succession to the Habsburg lands, Maria Theresa (1717–1780) had a field army formed in Moravia under Count William von Neipperg (1684–1774) in February 1741. The Austrian army was ill trained and ill equipped; Austria had just been defeated by the Turks and was faced with the hostility of France, Bavaria, and other European powers. Nonetheless Neipperg advanced while the Prussian army was still in its winter cantonments and, though Glogau had been stormed by Prince Leopold (the Younger) of Anhalt-Dessau (1700–1751) on the night of March 9, he relieved the garrison at Neisse and marched to relieve that at Brieg. After a few days of maneuvering, Neipperg and Frederick met on the snowy fields of Mollwitz on April 10.

Before the Prussian army deployed, the Austrian cavalry routed the Prussian cavalry, General von der Schulenburg being killed, and Field Marshal Count Kurt Christoph von Schwerin (1684–1757) advised young Frederick to flee. After riding some fifteen miles, escaping capture by Austrian hussars, Frederick returned, mortified to learn that Schwerin in the meantime had rallied the Prussian infantry who, with their disciplined volleys of platoon fire, drove the Austrians from the field. The Prussians lost 4,850 men of the 22,000 engaged, the Austrians 4,551 of their 18,100.

The victory of the underestimated Prussians convinced the rest of Europe of Austria's weakness. France sent Marshal duke de Belle-Isle to negotiate an alliance with Prussia, resulting in the Treaty of Breslau (June 5, 1741), which acknowledged Prussian ownership of Lower (northern) Silesia.

Works About: Austrian official *Die Kriege der Kaiserin Marie Theresia* (Vienna, from 1895); Prussian official, *Die Kriege Friedrichs des Grossen,* 20 vols. (Berlin, 1890–1913), esp *Der Erste Schlesische Krieg.*   *A. H. Ganz*

See AUSTRIAN SUCCESSION; FREDERICK II, THE GREAT; MARIA THERESA.

MOZART, WOLFGANG AMADEUS (1756–1791), composer and musician, was a native of Salzburg, the son of Leopold Mozart, who was a composer and vice-chapel master of the archbishop of Salzburg. Showing an early proclivity for music, Wolfgang was taught at an early age by his father and at age five was beginning to compose music as well as demonstrating proficiency on the harpsichord and violin. Seeking to profit from the precocity of his son and daughter, Anna Maria, Leopold took them on a series of concert tours throughout Europe. The genius of young Wolfgang came to the attention of Emperor Joseph

II, who commissioned an Italian opera and invited Mozart to play it on the harpsichord. Although jealousy and court intrigue prevented the opera from being produced, Mozart did conduct a newly composed Mass and other works before the imperial court.

The Mozarts returned to Salzburg, where Archbishop Sigismund von Schrattenbach, an old friend and patron of the Mozart family, had one of Wolfgang's operas performed and made him his unsalaried concert master. Off and on from December 1769 to March 1773, Mozart toured and played concerts in Italy. He visited Vienna again in July 1773, hoping to obtain a court appointment. There he came under the influence of Joseph Haydn's music while writing a great deal of his own. Mozart lived in Salzburg for much of 1775 to 1777. Leaving Leopold behind, Wolfgang and his mother started a long journey through Germany to Paris with the hope of finding some sort of permanent situation. His mother died on the trip, and two years later he returned to Salzburg as a court organist. His hopes were raised when Archbishop Colloreda summoned Mozart to Vienna, but dashed when he found himself treated like a lower-echelon servant.

Emperor Joseph II finally engaged Mozart, after years of waiting without patronage, as a chamber composer in 1787 but at a meager wage. Mozart did get a commission to write a German opera for the National Singspiel, founded by the emperor in 1778. Despite the protests of his father, he married Constanze Weber in 1782, and she was a good wife to him for the most part. Mozart began giving subscription concerts of his own music, playing his own concerto for piano and also improvising on that instrument. Although never financially successful, Mozart's operas enjoyed great popularity with almost everyone. A notable exception was the wife of Emperor Leopold II, who referred to one of his operas as "German muck," even though it had been commissioned for the coronation of her husband. That concert tour proved to be Mozart's last, for he died in Vienna of rheumatic fever. His extraordinary contribution to music was not fully appreciated until after his death when he came to be recognized as one of the greatest figures in Western music.

Works By: *The Letters of Mozart and His Family*, ed. Emily Anderson 3 vols. (New York, 1966). **Works About:** O. E. Deutsch, *Mozart, A Documentary Biography* (Stanford, 1965); Alfred Einstein, *Mozart* (New York, 1965); *Grove's Dictionary of Music and Musicians*, ed. Eric Blom, 10 vols. (New York, 1960), 5:923–83; Erich Schenk, *Mozart and His Times* (New York, 1960).   *J. W. Zophy*

See HAYDN; JOSEPH II; LEOPOLD II; VIENNA.

MÜNSTER AFFAIR (February 1534–June 1535) was an attempt by a radical group of Anabaptists to establish the new Jerusalem in the city of Münster, located in Westphalia. It dramatically colored the opinion that Catholics and conservative Protestants alike maintained toward Anabaptism in the Holy Roman Empire in the sixteenth century. Anabaptism had been condemned as a religious heresy several years before the Münster rebellion at the second diet of Speyer in April 1529, but the events of 1534–1535 altered the view that Anabaptism was merely a religious problem. Instead it became commonly held that Anabaptism constituted a direct menace to the established civil order.

The causes of the Münster revolt are a complex series of interconnected religious, political, and social issues. For several years prior to 1534, Münster had been tottering on the brink of a sweeping revolution. This northwestern German city with a population of about fifteen thousand was torn in the 1520s by a struggle among three groups. The bishop and city council were engaged in the almost traditional battle to gain supremacy over each other, and the guilds were clamoring for a greater voice in city affairs. In 1531 this conflict, which had been basically political and social, also became religious. The bishop-prince of Münster, the worldly Franz of Waldeck, was not especially concerned about the spiritual fate of Catholicism in his diocese. In particular he made only meager efforts to halt the growing influence of Lutheran ministers in the city. So lax had been his concern that his major opponent, the city council, became predominantly Lutheran. On the other hand, the guilds and lower classes were not attracted to either the Catholic or Lutheran cause. Instead they came under the sway of the Anabaptist movement. Spearheaded by such men as Henry Rol, John Klopreis, Henry Staprade, and Dionysius Vinne, the Anabaptists, with guild support, slowly took control of Münster's political organization. The move gained further momentum when Bernhard Rothmann, who had earlier led the Lutheran movement, converted to the Anabaptist faith.

With the coming of the visionist, Jan Matthys, and his even more radical companion, John Beukelsz, in January 1534, the religious situation in Münster altered dramatically. Early in February 1534 the Anabaptists seized control of the city and elected their representative, Bernard Knipperdolling, a former patrician, as mayor. Shortly after, Matthys, who was the true power, ordered that only those people who adhered to Anabaptism were permitted to remain in the city. Under the threat of death, Catholics and Lutherans left the city by March. Franz of Waldeck, with aid from Catholic and Protestant princes, invested the town but could make little headway against fierce resistance.

Münster became the symbol of the promised life, the new Jerusalem for persecuted Anabaptists throughout northern Germany and the Netherlands. While many were stopped, refugees from these areas poured into Münster.

The rebellion gradually deteriorated. In an act of foolish inspiration, John Matthys tried to demonstrate God's support for their cause when he sallied out against the besieging mercenary army followed by about twenty compatriots. In meeting this useless death before the walls of Münster, Matthys succeeded only in proving his fanaticism. With the death of Matthys on April 4, 1534, power fell largely into the hands of John Beukelsz. It was the excesses with which Beukelsz carried out during his so-called reign in Münster that history best remembers. Whatever moderation might have existed in the Anabaptist ranks disappeared with Beukelsz. Cleverly maneuvering the twelve elders of the ruling council, Beukelsz, better known as John of Leiden, was appointed king, the new David who would lead God's chosen people. Yet John of Leiden ruled more like a secular prince than a religious leader. Opposition to his rule, such as the attempted overthrow by the moderate Anabaptist, Henry Mollenhecke, was ruthlessly suppressed, and his daily life was characterized by pompous ceremony and costly splendor. Radical social and economic changes, such as the introduction of primitive communism and polygamy, alarmed established authorities.

King John's reign proved to be short-lived. Relief from the outside was cut off, and finally on June 25, 1535, two Anabaptists, Hans Eck and Henry Gresbeck, were bribed to open the gates to Waldeck's mercenaries. King John and several of his leaders were brutally executed, and the dream of a new Jerusalem ended in repression and bloodshed.

Works About: Karl-Heinz Kirchhoff, *Die Täufer in Münster 1534–35* (Münster, 1973); Klemens Löffler, *Die Wiedertäufer zu Münster 1534/35* (Cologne 1923); John Oyer, *Lutheran Reformers Against the Anabaptists* (Hague, 1964). Ottheim Rammstedt, *Sekte und soziale Bewegung: Soziologische Analyse der Täufer in Münster 1534–35* (Cologne, 1966); James M. Stayer, *Anabaptists and the Sword* (Lawrence, Kan., 1971); George Huntston Williams, *The Radical Reformation* (Philadelphia, 1962).   *C. T. Eby*

See ANABAPTISM.

MÜNSTER, TREATY OF, the agreement between France and the Empire that became part of the Peace of Westphalia, was signed on October 24, 1648, ending the Thirty Years War.

Since 1644 peace negotiations had been conducted concurrently in the Westphalian cities of Münster and Osnabrück to end the fighting in central Europe. Münster was the site for talks among Emperor Ferdinand III, the French, and the German Catholic estates. At the same time Spain was holding peace negotiations with France and the United Provinces there. Thus most European powers involved in the Westphalian congress, except Sweden and Denmark, were represented at Münster. The chief negotiators were the imperial representative Count Maximilian von Trauttmansdorff and the French diplomats Abel Servien and the Marquis d'Avaux. The papal nuncio Fabio Chigi, later Pope Alexander VII, and the Venetian ambassador Aluise Contarini served as mediators. The leading German Catholic prince represented at Münster was Maximilian of Bavaria, who generally sided with France in the negotiations. The French in turn backed Maximilian's claim to the land and title of the disgraced Palatinate elector Frederick V.

The terms of the Treaty of Münster, or *Instrumentum Pacis Monasteriense*, were agreed upon on September 22, 1648. France obtained full sovereignty over upper and lower Alsace, except the imperial free city of Strasbourg, and the three Lorraine bishoprics of Metz, Toul, and Verdun. In addition it gained control of the Rhenish fortress cities of Breisach and Philippsburg. Besides greatly altering Germany's western frontier, the agreement contained important provisions, which, together with those of the Treaty of Osnabrück, affected the internal affairs of the Empire.

The negotiations, concurrently conducted at Münster between Spain and the Low Countries, led on January 30, 1648, to a peace treaty whereby the independence of the victorious United Provinces of the Netherlands was recognized. The talks between Spain and France remained fruitless and it was only with the Peace of the Pyrenees in 1659 that these two powers finally made peace.

Works: Ernst Hövel, ed., *Pax optima reum. Beiträge zur Gesch. des Westfälischen Friedens 1648* (Münster, 1948), pp. 9–61; Konrad Müller, ed., *Instrumenta Pacis Westphalicae. Die Westfälischen Friedensverträge 1648*, Quell. zur neueren Gesch. Nos. 12/13 (Bern, 1949), pp. 79–97, 153–166. **Works About:** Max Braubach, *Der Westfälische Friede* (Münster, 1948); Fritz Dickmann, *Der Westfälische Frieden*, 3d ed. (Münster, 1972); Hajo Holborn, *A History of Germany: The Reformation* (New York, 1959), pp. 361–74; Alfred Overmann, *Die Abtretung des Elsass an Frankreich im Westfälischen Frieden* (Karlsruhe, 1906). Henri Vast, ed., *Les grands traités du règne de Louis XIV*, vol. 1, *Collection de textes pour servir à l'étude et à l'enseignement de l'histoire* (Paris, 1893), pp. 1–64.   *Bodo Nischan*

See OSNABRÜCK TREATY; THIRTY YEARS WAR; WESTPHALIA.

MÜNTZER, THOMAS (c. 1490–1525), was the most famous of the leaders of the Peasants' War in Germany of 1524–1525. His notoriety stems in part from his literacy, making him an especially visible peasant leader, and because Martin Luther so vividly singled him out in his attacks upon the rebellious peasants of Saxony and Thuringia. Catholic contemporaries and historians cited him as an example of the excesses inherent in Protestantism; more recently, Marxist historians have pointed to him as the true revolutionary leader of the Reformation era.

A Saxon native, Müntzer studied at Leipzig, Frankfurt, and Mainz. As early as 1518 and certainly by the Leipzig debates of 1519, he became a partisan of Luther. Under the influence of German mysticism, however, he also began to develop a divergent theology centering on the concept of continuing revelation. With Luther's help, Müntzer secured a pastorate in the town of Zwickau, where he was directly influenced by Nicholas Storch, one of the "Zwickau prophets." Disturbances in Zwickau, prompted by Müntzer's sermons, caused his ouster in April 1521. He proceeded from Zwickau to Prague, where he came into conflict with the metropolitan, and appeared again in Saxony in the spring of 1523 at the town of Allstedt.

By the time of his Allstedt pastorate, Müntzer had fully developed his concept of continuing revelation and had begun to see himself as a prophet of God in the Old Testament tradition. He began openly to challenge Luther for being "slavishly bound to the Gospel" and not recognizing the continuing revelation of the Holy Spirit. His sermons became increasingly apocalyptic as he foresaw the destruction of the godless by the elect of God and the ushering in of Christ's reign on earth. On July 13, 1524, he preached before the Saxon duke John and his son, calling upon the princes to take up the sword and slay the godless. The sermon was ill received, and Müntzer fled Allstedt for Mühlhausen, where a sociopolitical revolution was already underway, led by an ex-priest named Henry Pfeiffer.

Rejected by the Saxon princes and under the influence of Pfeiffer and others, Müntzer now saw the peasants and, later, urban artisans as the elect of God who would take up the sword against the godless, a message he put forth in sermons and printed religious pamphlets. For a brief period, opposing forces regained control of Mühlhausen, sending Müntzer and Pfeiffer into exile. But as the peasant rebellion spread, Pfeiffer regained control of the city, Müntzer returning in January 1525. From that date until the defeat of the peasants and his own execution in May, Müntzer played the role of propagandist and public leader of the revolt in Saxony and Thuringia.

Controversy remains as to the exact nature of Müntzer's teachings and the extent of his influence after his death. He has often been viewed as a central figure in the development of Anabaptism after 1525. His printed works tend to suggest that he was more a radical theologian than a social or political revolutionary. But his support of the peasants, and his fiery sermons and pamphlets, must have served to incite the rebels further. As for the Anabaptists, many elements of Müntzer's theology appear in that of later Anabaptist leaders.In particular, his concept of continuing revelation and his apocalypticism appear most dramatically in the teachings of Hans Hut and his followers in south Germany.

Works By: Günter Franz, ed., *Thomas Müntzer: Schriften und Briefe: Kritische Gesamtausgabe* Quel. and Forsch. zur Reformationsgesch., vol. 33, (Gütersloh, 1968). **Works About:** Otto Brandt, *Thomas Müntzer: Sein Leben und seine Schriften* (Jena, 1933); Walter Elliger, *Aussenseiter der Reformation: Thomas Müntzer* and *Thomas Müntzer: Leben und Werk* (Göttingen, 1975); Eric W. Gritsch, *Reformer Without a Church: The Life and Thought of Thomas Müntzer, 1488–1525* (Philadelphia, 1967); Karl Hinrichs, ed., *Thomas Müntzer: Politische Schriften mit Kommentar* (Halle, 1950); Otto Merx, *Thomas Müntzer und Heinrich Pfeiffer, 1523–1525* (Göttingen, 1889); M. M. Smirin, *Die Volksreformation des Thomas Müntzer und der grosse Bauernkrieg* (Berlin, 1956). *D. M. Hockenbery*

See ANABAPTISM; HUT; LUTHER; PEASANTS' WAR.

MUTIAN or Conrad Mutianus Rufus (1471–1526), humanist philosopher, was born in Homberg, Hesse, of a prosperous patrician family. At age ten he entered the school of the Brethren of the Common Life at Deventer. In 1486 Mutian entered Erfurt University and received his B.A. in 1488 and his M.A. in 1492. After teaching at Erfurt for two years, he left for Italy, where he spent a year and a half studying law at Bologna. After brief stint as a councillor in Hesse, Mutian entered the Chapter of Mary in Gotha, where he became a canon and spent the remainder of his life. His home became the focal point for a large humanist circle. A neo-Platonist who argued for a moralistic view of Pauline Christianity, Mutian was one of the most learned and influential men of his day.

Works By: Karl Gillert, ed., *Der Briefwechsel des Conradus Mutianus* (Halle, 1890); Carl Krause, *Der Briefwechsel des Mutianus Rufus* (Cassel, 1885). **Works About:** Ludwig Geiger, "Mutian," *ADB*, 33:108; Maria Grossmann, *Humanism in Wittenberg* (Nieuwkoop, 1975); F. Halbauer, *Mutianus Rufus* (Leipzig, 1929); L. W. Spitz, *The Religious Renaissance of the German Humanists* (Cambridge, Mass., 1963).   *J. W. Zophy*

See HUMANISM; SPALATIN.

NAPOLEONIC WARS (1803–1815), the second half of a twenty-three-year European conflict triggered by the French Revolution, were resumed after the Treaty of Amiens and ended at Waterloo in 1815. Napoleon utilized the period of peace after 1802 to consolidate his political power in France and to initiate domestic reform. But France's power and the ferment of the Revolution, now combined with Napoleon's imperial ambition, was perceived by the other European states as a continuing threat. Claiming that Napoleon was not living up to the Treaty of Amiens, the British government itself broke the terms by retaining Malta and then declared war on France on May 13, 1803.

England began forming the Third Coalition against France with Sweden (December 1804) and Russia (April 11, 1805), offering a subsidy of £1,250,000 for every 100,000 troops put into the field. On August 9, 1805, Austria joined the coalition. The Holy Roman Empire was now almost nonexistent, Francis II (1768–1835) assuming the title of emperor of Austria as Francis I in August 1804. The south German states were joining Napoleon: Bavaria on August 25, 1805, Baden on September 5, and Württemberg on October 5.

Napoleon gathered an army to invade England, but the French navy failed to concentrate to cover the projected cross-Channel invasion. In September 1805 Napoleon marched La Grande Armée, 210,500 troops in nine army corps, across France to defeat Austria before the Russian armies could arrive. La Grande Armée reflected the refinements of the Napoleonic method. There was no new technology. The French infantry still carried the 1777 model muzzle-loading, smooth-bore, flintlock musket and bayonet; the cavalry were armed with flintlock pistols and sabres or swords; and the artillery employed muzzle-loading, smooth-bore cannon, four- to twelve-pounders, firing solid or round shot, grapeshot, and caseshot or canister, and six-inch (bore-diameter) howitzers firing explosive shell. The basic tactical units of the line infantry regiment (Revolutionary "demibrigade") were its four battalions, each with 800 soldiers in six companies (four fusilier, one elite grenadier, and one voltigeur or skirmisher company). The cavalry regiments had four or five squadrons of 250 troopers each. The heavy cavalry were breast-plated cuirassiers and carabiniers, the line or medium were dragoons, and the light (for scouting and harassing) included hussars and chasseurs, and, later, lancers. Napoleon massed his heavy cavalry and heavy artillery while distributing the light cavalry and artillery with the infantry divisions.

Napoleon's real innovations were in tactics and organization. The Revolution produced armies more numerous and more ardent but less trained than the small professional armies of the eighteenth century. Napoleon introduced the attack in battalion mass column, which covered ground more quickly though was subject to heavier casualties. He also introduced the army corps organization, each corps being a complete combined arms force under a marshal, numbering one light cavalry and several infantry divisions and its own artillery. The corps could be given independent missions or be concentrated for a culminating battle of decision, the Napoleonic goal. By 1809 most of the other nations had emulated Napoleon's organizations and methods.

In planning allied strategy, the Austrian Aulic Council determined to reconquer northern Italy with the 95,000 troops of the Archduke Charles (1771–1847) crossing the River Adige and advancing on Milan. Archduke John (1782–1859) was to secure the Tyrol with 23,000 troops, acting as a link to the 70,000 men under the third brother, the Archduke Ferdinand (1769–1824), who would advance into Bavaria and discourage the elector, Maximilian IV Joseph (1756–1825), from cooperating with the French. Czar Alexander I (1777–1825) promised the support of three Russian armies: 35,000 troops under General Michael Kutusov (1745–1813) to arrive in Bavaria by October 20, followed by General Count Frederick William Buxhöwden's 40,000 and 20,000 troops under General Levin August Benningsen (1745–1826), which would move on Franconia by way of Bohemia, guarding against an uncertainly neutral Prussia to the north. The combined Austro-Russian armies would then march on Strasbourg under the Emperor Francis. The Austrian main effort, however, was initially to be in Italy, whereas the decisive theater of operations would be southern Germany; Francis placed more reliance on Quartermaster General Mack von Leiberich (1752–1828), chief of staff to the Archduke Ferdinand, than on his brother, the nominal commander, which created command disagreements; and third, the Austrians simply forgot that the Russians dated by the Julian calendar, which was ten days behind the Gregorian calendar, completely confounding allied coordination.

Ordering Marshal André Masséna (1756–1817) to occupy the archduke Charles in Italy with 50,000 troops, Napoleon joined his main army, which crossed the middle Rhine between Mainz and Strasbourg on the night of September 24–25, 1805. The French corps marched thirty kilometers a day through southern Germany, bringing Napoleon the allegiance of the duke of Baden and the elector of Württemberg, to envelop Ferdinand's army, under Mack, now at Ulm. Using the Black Forest as a curtain of maneuver where Marshal Murat's cavalry screened his advance, Napoleon swung his army down and across the Danube by October 7, behind Mack, using the River Lech as a strategic barrier to prevent reinforcement from Austria. Demoralized by Napoleon's brilliant strategy, the archduke and some forces escaped the trap, leaving the unhappy

General Mack to request an armistice on October 17 and surrender his 30,000 men without a fight three days later.

Sending Marshal Ney's VI Corps toward Innsbruck and the Brenner Pass to protect his southern flank, Napoleon marched eastward to defeat the arriving Russians in detail. News of the decisive naval defeat off Trafalgar on October 21 did not slow the French advance; Murat entered Vienna on November 13, pursuing the retreating Austrians and Russians into Moravia, while Masséna chased the Archduke Charles out of Italy.

Nonetheless the retreating Austro-Russian forces finally halted at Olmütz (Czech Olomouc) where they were joined by Buxhöwden's 40,000; autumn rains and sleet slowed the French advance; Napoleon had had to detach many of his units to protect his extending lines of communication; and Prussia, led by King Frederick William III's (1770–1840) militant Queen Louise, threatened hostilities. Eager to bring the campaign to a successful conclusion before winter and before the coalition should be strengthened, Napoleon determined to lure the Austro-Russian force into battle. Feigning weakness, he initiated peace overtures, deliberately left his army dispersed, and had his advance forces fall back before any enemy forward movement.

The Austro-Russian army advanced, but at Austerlitz on December 2, 1805, Napoleon broke the allied center and shattered the allied force. The Russians withdrew under a truce, while the Austrians signed the Treaty of Pressburg (Bratislava) on December 26. Austria ceded Venetia, Istria, and Dalmatia to Napoleon (as king of Italy), the Tyrol and Voralberg to Bavaria, and Swabia to Württemberg and Baden. The elector of Bavaria was further rewarded by Napoleon with the title King Maximilian I and the leadership of the Confederation of the Rhine (Bavaria, Württenberg, Baden, and Hesse-Nassau, and later Saxony and Westphalia), created by Napoleon on July 12, 1806. The political reorganization of Germany effectively destroyed the Holy Roman Empire, and Francis II renounced his title as Holy Roman emperor on August 6, 1806, leaving him as Emperor Francis I of Austria.

The continuing Napoleonic Wars are beyond the limits of the Holy Roman Empire; nonetheless a brief summary may be in order. Napoleon destroyed the Third Coalition by routing its newest member, Prussia, at Jena-Auerstädt on October 14, 1806, and fighting the Russians at Eylau on February 8, 1807, and defeating them at Friedland (June 14, 1807), which led to the treaties of Tilsit, July 7 and 9, 1807, with Russia and Prussia, respectively.

As England once again stood defiantly alone, Napoleon initiated the Continental System to cripple England economically by coercing the rest of Europe into not trading with the nation. But England's maritime position remained secure, and it was the Continent that suffered and became restless. The failure of Napoleon to control Spain in the peninsular campaigns (1808–1814) encouraged Austria to take up arms again, only to be defeated at Wagram (July 5–6, 1809) and lose more territory in the Treaty of Vienna (Schönbrunn) on

October 14. When Russia defied Napoleon, he invaded that country on June 24, 1812; but though he won a bloody battle at Borodino (September 7, 1812) and entered Moscow a week later, Russia would not surrender.

Napoleon's Grande Armée was destroyed in the disastrous winter retreat from Moscow, and subject Europe rose up against him. England engineered yet another coalition (Prussia, Russia, Sweden, and, after August 1813, Austria), which defeated Napoleon at Leipzig on October 16–18, 1813, in the Battle of Nations, and pursued him into France. Napoleon abdicated on April 12, 1814, and was exiled to the island of Elba. The Congress of Vienna met to redraw the map of Europe (October 1814–June 1815) interrupted by Napoleon's return until his final defeat by Anglo-allied and Prussian forces at Waterloo, June 18, 1815, and his final exile to St. Helena.

Works By: Emperor Napoleon I, *La Correspondance de Napoléon Ier*, 32 vols. (Paris, 1858–1870). **Works About:** D. Chandler, *Campaigns of Napoleon* (New York, 1966); M. Dumolin, *Précis d'Histoire Militaire, Révolution et Empire*, 3 vols. (Paris, 1906): J. E. Woerl, *Gesch. der Kriege von 1792 bis 1815 mit Schlachten Atlas* (Freiburg, 1852).   *A. H. Ganz*

See AUSTERLITZ; FRANCIS II.

NICHOLAS OF CUSA (1401–1464), humanist scholar, was born at the village of Cues on the Moselle River. A boatman's son, Nicholas received his elementary education from the Brethren of the Common Life at Deventer in Holland. In 1406 he took his B.A. at Heidelberg and went on to Padua to study Church law. Six years later, Nicholas returned to Germany with his doctorate. He eventually took a position as a professor at the University of Cologne, where he also gave legal advice to the bishop.

Nicholas discovered the *Codex Carolinus*, which contained papal letters to the Frankish kings and official reports of provincial parliaments near Arles of 417–418. These documents helped support his belief that the *imperium romanum* (Roman rule) had passed from the ancient Romans to the Germanic peoples in the Holy Roman Empire. His fame was also enhanced by his discovery of a number of lost plays by the Roman playwright Plautus.

Nicholas of Cusa became the private secretary to Cardinal Orsini, papal legate to Germany. As such he was active at the Council of Basel (1431–1437), where he submitted his *Concerning Universal Harmony*, which offered an able defense of conciliarism as part of God's plan for order in the universe. Curiously enough, Nicholas reversed himself in 1437 and became a proponent of papal authority.

He spent ten years in the service of Pope Eugene IV, representing him on missions to German emperors and princes. Nicholas also had a highly important mission to the Greek emperor and the patriarch of the Eastern Church at Constantinople. He was able to bring them back to Italy in an effort at reconciliation. Eugene rewarded Nicholas for his labors by making him a cardinal in 1448 and then bishop of Brixen in the Tyrol in 1450. For some years, as virtual supervisor of the Church in Germany and the Low Countries, he held synods and worked on reforming the clergy, with some success. In his own diocese of Brixen, his reform efforts met with fierce resistance from a corrupt, entrenched clergy. To make matters worse, Nicholas got into a quarrel with Archduke Sigismund over episcopal revenues and land jurisdiction. The cardinal was even imprisoned for a while. Nicholas left the diocese in 1460 for Rome, where he continued his writings and served Pope Puis II, a fellow humanist. Among his numerous mathematical and philosophical writings was his famous *On Learned Ignorance* (1440).

Works By: Nicholas of Cues, *Briefwechsel*, ed. Josef Koch et al., 4 vols. (Heidelberg, 1944–1960); *On Learned Ignorance*, tr. G. Heron (New Haven, 1954); *Opera Omnia* (Leipzig, 1932–1959); *Unity and Reform, Selected Writings of Nicholas de Cusa*, ed. J. P. Dolan (Notre Dame, Ind., 1962). **Works About:** Henry Bett, *Nicholas of Cusa* (London, 1932); Robert Joda, "Nicholas of Cusa: Precursor of Humanism," in *Renaissance and Reformation in Germany*, ed. G. Hoffmeister, (New York, 1977); Erich Meuther, *Nikolaus von Kues* (Münster, 1964); Paul Sigmund, *Nicholas of Cusa and Medieval Political Thought* (Cambridge, Mass., 1963); Morimichi Watanabe, *The Political Ideas of Nicholas of Cusa* (Geneva, 1963).   *J. W. Zophy*

See CONCILIARISM; PIUS II.

NÖRDLINGEN, a town in south central Germany, was an imperial free city from the thirteenth century until 1803. It is located in the Ries, a fertile agricultural basin just north of the Danube. The existence of Nördlingen can be documented from a charter of 898 A.D., but thereafter the records remain silent until 1215, when possession of the city was transferred from the bishop of Regensburg to the emperor. Despite many subsequent threats to its liberties, notably from the neighboring counts of Oettingen, Nördlingen's status as an imperial city was preserved from that time onward. As early as 1219 there is evidence of the city's annual trade fair, which in later centuries became a major focus of commercial activity in southern Germany.

The fourteenth century was an era of physical growth and political tension in Nördlingen. Beginning in 1327, the community undertook construction of a new outer ring of walls, which continued to contain the entire community until the nineteenth century. Like many other German cities, Nördlingen experienced an antipatrician movement in the mid-fourteenth century. The resulting constitutional changes of 1348 guaranteed the guilds a share in the city government, which they continued to enjoy until 1552. In 1377 Nördlingen joined the short-lived league of Swabian cities; in 1488 it joined the longer-lived Swabian League, in whose affairs it was deeply involved until the league's dissolution in 1534.

The fifteenth century is rightly celebrated as Nördlingen's economic and cultural zenith. Nördlingen's products—particularly textiles—were widely exported, and the annual Pentecost fair attracted merchants from all over southern and central Germany. The imposing St. George's Church was constructed between 1427 and 1505, and the arts—above all, painting—flourished in Nördlingen as they never have since. A unique census of the year 1459 recorded the population of Nördlingen at precisely 5,295. By the end of the Middle Ages, the city had accumulated extensive land holdings in the surrounding region. But Nördlingen never developed a closed countryside, and most of the city's tenants continued to be subjects of the counts of Oettingen or other regional powers.

As in many other cities, the Reformation was received with considerable enthusiasm on the popular level in Nördlingen, although the city fathers took a more hesitant stance. Nördlingen was one of the fourteen protestant cities at the diet of Speyer in 1529, but the following year the magistrates declined to subscribe to the Augsburg Confession. The city did, however, offer assistance to the Protestant side in the Schmalkaldic War, suffering in consequence an imperial occupation in 1547. In 1552 Charles V ordained a new constitution for Nördlingen, which eliminated the guilds from participation in civic government. But there was no hope of restoring Catholicism, and from the time of the Peace of Augsburg (1555) onward, the city was unambiguously Protestant.

The later half of the sixteenth century was a prosperous epoch in Nördlingen, as reflected in the numerous building projects dating from that period. A witch craze in the early 1590s claimed the lives of thirty-five persons, including the widows of some of Nördlingen's leading citizens, yet this appears to have left no long-lasting repercussions.

The Thirty Years War, however, brought about a drastic reversal of Nördlingen's fortunes. Located as it was at the intersection of two major routes, the city suffered from both Protestant and Catholic occupations throughout the war. In 1634 the city was occupied by Swedish troops and was promptly besieged by an imperial army. A Swedish attempt to relieve the city resulted in the Battle of Nördlingen (September 6, 1634), a disastrous defeat for the Protestant cause. In the months that followed, the city was visited with a punitive imperial occupation and with a devastating outbreak of the plague, which claimed well over a thousand lives. A second battle of Nördlingen, which took place near the village of Alerheim in 1645, was less decisive, although the French retained the field.

The war left Nördlingen financially drained, and such recovery as the city managed to achieve was undermined by the French and Turkish wars of the later seventeenth and early eighteenth century. Although the campaigns themselves usually took place far from Nördlingen, the city felt their effects through the system of imperial war taxation, which was administered with great effectiveness by the Swabian circle. During the early phase of the War of the Spanish Succession, the theater of battle did move close to Nördlingen, culminating in the Battle of Blenheim (1704), which took place fifteen miles south of the city. Nördlingen's financial system never recovered from the strains it had experienced in the seventeenth and early eighteenth century. By the 1740s the city was nearly bankrupt, and it required the intervention of an imperial commission to reorganize the city treasury and save it from collapse.

The Revolutionary wars placed Nördlingen once again directly in the midst of military activity. The city was occupied by French troops in 1796 and again in 1800. Even more importantly, the upheavals of that period paved the way for the city's loss of its imperial status. In 1802 Nördlingen was taken over by Bavarian troops, and the following year it was peacefully incorporated into the kingdom of Bavaria.

Works About: Alfons Felber, "Unzucht und Kindsmord in der Rechtsprechung der freien Reichsstadt Nördlingen vom 15. bis 19. Jahrhundert" (Diss., Bonn, 1961); Christopher R. Friedrichs, *Urban Society in an Age of War: Nördlingen, 1580–1720* (Princeton, 1979); Dieter Kudorfer, *Nördlingen*, Hist. Atlas von Bayern, Teil Schwaben, no. 8 (Munich, 1974); *Jb. des historischen Vereins für Nördlingen und das Reis* (1912–1971), vols. 1–25; K. O. Müller, *Nördlinger Stadtrechte des Mittelalters*, vol. 2: *Bayerische Rechtsquellen* (Munich, 1933); Karl Puchner, Walter E. Vock, and Gustav Wulz, eds., *Die Urkunden der Städt Nördlingen, 1233–1449*, 4 vols. (Augsburg, 1952–1968); Heinrich Steinmeyer, "Die Entstehung und Entwicklung der Nördlinger Pfingstmesse im Spätmittelalter, mit einem Ausblick bis ins 19. Jahrhundert" (Diss., Munich, 1960); Gustav Wulz, "Hist. Einleitung," in Karl Grober and Adam Horn, *Die Kunstdenkmäler von Schwaben und Neuberg*, vol. 2: *Städt Nördlingen* (Munich, 1940), pp. 1–45.   *C. R. Friedrichs*

See IMPERIAL CITIES; SWABIAN LEAGUE; THIRTY YEARS WAR.

NORTHERN WAR (1700–1721) began when a coalition composed of Peter I, czar of Russia, Frederick IV, king of Denmark-Norway, and Augustus II, king of Poland (Frederick Augustus I, elector of Saxony) attacked Sweden. The triumvirate, masterminded by a Livonian squire, John Reinhold Patkul, was bent upon partitioning Sweden's empire; Frederick wanted Holstein-Gottorp, Augustus Livonia, and Peter Ingria and Estonia. Frederick was to attack Sweden's western provinces while Peter and Augustus attacked from the east. The conspirators underestimated the power and resilience of Sweden and the resolution of the young king, Charles XII. The Saxons invaded Livonia but were repulsed from Riga, defeated at Jungfernhof, and driven over the Dvina by the Swedish veteran Dahlberg. With the aid of the Anglo-Dutch fleet, the Swedes moved troops into Zeeland. Frederick was then forced to come to terms; he recognized the independence of the duchy of Holstein-Gottorp and withdrew from the coalition. Charles could now turn against Peter and Augustus.

The Czar had invaded Ingria, intending to take Narva, the key to that province. Charles garnered supplied and transported an army across the Baltic in October 1700. After reaching Pernau, he turned north to aid Narva. As the Swedish army approached the Russian lines, Peter fled, leaving his army in the command of an adventurer, Carl Eugene de Croy. In the midst of a blinding snowstorm, Charles launched his forces against the Russians entrenched before Narva. The Swedish assault carried, and the Russian cavalry fled in panic. In order to escape massacre by his own troops, the commander along with most of the foreign officers, surrendered. Eighty-four hundred Swedes had defeated forty thousand Russians (November 1700).

Charles now turned against the Saxons. He resolved to punish Augustus and invade Poland. In 1701, the Swedish army crossed the Dvina, routed the Russians and the Saxons at Dunamünde, and occupied Courland. In 1702, Charles crushed the Poles and Saxons at Klissow and later in that same year took Cracow. In 1703, the Swedes defeated the Saxons at Pultusk and took Thorn. Charles then put forward a pro-Swedish nominee for the Polish throne in place of the incalculable and treacherous Augustus. In January 1704, a Polish confederation under Swedish pressure deposed Augustus and in July 1704, elected the palatine of Posen, Stanislaus Leszczynski. Crowned in October 1705, he would keep that throne only as long as he was supported by Swedish arms. Augustus was not cut off from Poland.

After five years of campaigning in Poland, Charles struck at the elector's home base, Saxony. Augustus was then forced to sue for peace. By the Treaty of Altranstadt (1706), Augustus recognized Stanislaus as king of Poland, abandoned his alliance against Sweden, and agreed to support the Swedish troops during the winter and to turn over the traitor Patkul to the Swedes. Peter alone remained at war with Sweden.

Meanwhile the Russians had made repeated incursions into Ingria and Livonia, devastating the land. In 1704, they had seized Dorpat and Narva. While the Swedes were campaigning in Poland, the Russians had taken most of eastern Finland and Estonia. In order to dictate terms to the czar, Charles decided to invade Russia. He was counting on General Lewenhaupt to bring supplies and reinforcements and on Ivan Mazepa, the hetman of the Zaporogian Cossacks, to rally the Ukraine against Peter. Lewenhaupt, who had been overwhelmed by the Russians in a two-day battle, finally joined Charles with only the remnants of his army. He had been forced to burn his stores. Mazepa's treachery had been detected. He came to Charles as a ruined man with only his thirteen hundred personal adherents, not the projected thirty thousand men. The Russians progressively retreated before Charles' advance, destroying all in their wake. The Swedes began to suffer from a lack of bread and fodder. The winter of 1708–1709 was unusually severe, and the army became decimated and demoralized, dwindling from forty-one thousand to twenty thousand. Nevertheless they pushed on to Poltava, which they besieged in May 1709 in spite of a lack of artillery and ammunition. The main Russian army then arrived. The Swedes fought with unusual ferocity, but they were enveloped in a vast semicircle by the Russian forces. After a desperate struggle, the Swedish infantry was annihilated. The cavalry surrendered two days later at Perevolchna on the Dnieper. Charles managed to escape to Turkey with a small band. The battle of Poltava ensured Russian hegemony in northeastern Europe.

Peter, Augustus, and Frederick again joined forces against Charles. Russian armies occupied the Baltic provinces. The Poles repudiated Stanislaus, who retreated with Krassow's army to Swedish Pomerania. In November 1709 the

Danes invaded Sweden but were driven out in March 1710. In that same year the Russians took Riga and Viborg. The allies who were fighting the War of the Spanish Succession against France drew up a convention (March 1710) that neutralized Sweden's German possessions, thus denying Charles a German base, and, they hoped, isolating the northern conflict.

Charles was now living in Bender as the guest of the sultan, who had been at war with Peter since 1711. The czar, taking the initiative, had set out against the Porte. Arriving at the Pruth River in search of illusory supplies, the Russians found themselves trapped, in a desperate position, outmanuevered, outnumbered, and unable to escape. Surprisingly the Russian offer of peace was accepted by the grand vizier. The Russian army could retire in exchange for the cession of Azov, razing Taganrog and the other fortresses on the sea of Azov, and granting Charles passage to his lands. Charles' anger at the betrayal and "treason" of the vizier could not stop the conclusion of the final peace at Adrianople in 1713. Charles finally left Turkey reaching Stralsund in 1714.

Meanwhile Prussia and Hanover had joined the coalition against Charles. His death (December 1718) in the trenches before the Norwegian fortress of Fredrickssten deprived Sweden of its most able commander. Hostilities were ended by the treaties of Stockholm (1719), Frediksborg (1720), Copenhagen (1720), and Nystad (1721): Hanover received Bremen and Verden; Prussia, Stettin and part of Pomerania; Denmark, the Gottorp share of Schleswig; Augustus, recognition of his right to the Polish throne; Russia, Livonia, Estonia, Ingria, Karelia, and Viborg. The Swedish empire was destroyed. The war had established Russia as a European power.

Works About: H. Brulin, *Sverige och Frankrige under Nordiska Kriget och Spanska Siccésion–krisen Åren 1700–1701. Till Belysning of Sveriges Utrikespolitik under Karl* XII (Uppsala, 1905); Charles XII, *Egenhändiga bref* (Stockholm, 1893); F. de Fabrice, *Anecdotes du séjour du Roi de Suède à Bender* (Hamburg, 1760); R. Fåhraeus, *Sveriges Historia till våra Dagar*, vol. 7: *Karl XI och Karl XII* (Stockholm, 1923); G. J. Golovkin, *Corespondence, 1708–1712* (Kiev, 1852), vol. 2: Erich Hassinger, *Brandenburg-Preussen, Russland und Schweden, 1700–1713* (Munich, 1953); Ragnhild Hatton, *Charles XII* (London, 1968); John Joseph Murray, *George I, the Baltic and the Whig Split of 1717* (Chicago, 1969); B. H. Sumner, *Peter the Great and the Ottoman Empire* (Oxford, 1949).   *L. S. Frey and M. L. Frey*

See FREDERICK AUGUSTUS; SPANISH SUCCESSION.

NUREMBERG was an imperial city of great importance for the history of the Holy Roman Empire. Although the town's exact origins are still a matter of speculation, it may have had its beginnings in connection with an imperial fortress built by Emperor Henry III in about 1040. Henry wanted to ensure the protection of his holdings in eastern Franconia by constructing a castle on a commanding site. He selected a high hill overlooking the Pegnitz River. Around this imperial stronghold eventually clustered artisans and tradespersons to help service the needs of those who resided in the castle. Even though the sandy soil of the region limited its agricultural potential, when the town received market privileges from the emperor, its future was assured.

A succession of Holy Roman emperors found Nuremberg to be not only a good military and administrative center but also a good place for sport. The surrounding forests abounded in game, and the shrewd merchants who came to live near the castle knew how to please their imperial overlords. Furthermore the inhabitants of Nuremberg could be relied on in a crisis to support their benefactors. For example, in the conflict between Henry IV and his son, Henry, in 1106, Nuremberg stayed loyal to the old emperor even while being besieged by his heir. Indeed in less than a century, the town had established itself as a valuable imperial possession worth fighting for by a succession of princes until claimed with great firmness by Emperor Conrad III in 1138.

Extensive changes in the physical appearance of the imperial castle were made during the reign of Frederick I, Barbarossa (1152–1190). Not only was the castle renovated and enlarged, but Barbarossa made Conrad of Hohenzollern the town's burggrave, or imperial overlord. This meant that even when the emperor was not in residence, an important imperial official was on hand to guide the destiny of the growing community. This relationship was cemented in 1219 when Barbarossa's son, Frederick II, held a glittering imperial diet at Nuremberg and granted the commune its first charter, which declared the town to be free of any authority save the emperor and his burggrave. The town owed no outsider feudal dues and had the right to engage in commerce and collect tolls.

Given so many signs of imperial favor, the citizens of Nuremberg continued to prosper. In 1225 construction began on the town's first major church, St. Sebald, named after Nuremberg's patron saint. St. Sebald became the location of many important imperial weddings as the imperial families continued to enjoy staying in Nuremberg.

During the thirteenth century, the town established itself as a mercantile center of great significance. Located near twelve major trade routes and protected by strong walls, Nuremberg was in an ideal position to take advantage of expanding commercial opportunities. Textiles, metal wares, and other fine goods produced in the town's workshops were added to the growing stream of economic activity. To help protect that hard-won prosperity, Nuremberg joined the League of Rhenish cities and, later, the Swabian League. Such alliances were necessary in the Middle Ages to fight off predators such as the robber knight, Götz von Berlichingen, who repeatedly attacked the city's merchants in the early years of the sixteenth century.

To accommodate changes in the economic life of Nuremberg, changes in the town's political structure were inevitable. For many years an imperial baliff, or *Schultheiss*, was the chief magistrate inside the town itself as distinguished from the imperial castle. Gradually a council of leading burghers came to assume more and more of the functions of government. In 1313 in a new charter issued by Emperor Henry VII, the baliff was completely shorn of his powers, although the town council still had to share power with the burggrave and the religious superior, the neighboring bishop of Bamberg. It was an uneasy alliance, which at times became heated such as when the council wanted to improve the city's walls in 1367 and was opposed by the burggrave.

The pattern of late medieval urban development was on the side of the council of merchants, for even the most traditional of emperors could not resist the force of early capitalism. In 1422 Emperor Sigismund awarded the entire castle hill area to the town, and the remainder of the burggravial prerogatives were sold to the council in 1427 by Burggrave Frederick VI for 120,000 gulden. Frederick had recently become margrave of Brandenburg, and as his horizons widened, arguments with the Nurembergers over trivial matters of jurisdiction seemed hardly worth the trouble, especially when they were willing to pay so handsomely for their freedoms. The fact that Nuremburg could make such an offer shows how much the burghers had prospered by the city's commercial life. Although Nuremberg would still have to fight off the pretensions of some of Frederick's descendants, such as Albert Achilles in 1449–50, for the most part it had achieved a high degree of autonomy.

Nuremburg's ruling class was composed almost entirely of wealthy merchants. The right to rule of these "honorable ones" or patricians was challenged publicly in 1348 by a group of artisans, who demanded recognition as corporate groups and a share in the town's government. The artisans might have revolted earlier like their compeers in other communes in Italy and southern Germany, but they were somewhat overawed by the imperial presence of Emperor Louis IV and his troops, who lived in the city almost constantly from 1320 to 1347. When the emperor, Charles IV, appeared before the city gates with an army in September 1349, the artisans' revolt was put down, guilds were prohibited, and the leaders of the insurrection were banished with their families. The political monopoly of the patriciate became an enduring tradition, and the men of commerce ran their town almost as shrewdly as they ran their businesses.

The history of Nuremberg continued to be thoroughly intertwined with the larger history of the Empire. In 1356, for example, during an imperial diet in the city, Emperor Charles IV issued the famous Golden Bull, which fixed in law the method for electing the Holy Roman emperor, among other provisions. One of the provisions that especially delighted the Nurembergers was one allowing Nuremberg the honor of hosting the first diet of each newly elected emperor, a sign and symbol of the town's special place in the imperial scheme. Further recognition came in 1424 when Emperor Sigismund made Nuremberg the jewel box of the Empire by housing the imperial regalia there; they remained for the next three hundred years safe behind the city's elaborate system of fortifications.

During the reign of Emperor Maximilian I (1493–1519), Nuremberg achieved a commercial and artistic peak of Renaissance glory. Maximilian, who had lived in the city for nearly six months in 1491, had a special fondness for the people of Nuremberg, especially the wealthy who loaned him money, and the great artists such as Albrecht Dürer, Veit Stoss, and Peter Vischer, who produced beautiful works for him. Nuremberg had become one of the largest cities in the Empire with a population of perhaps fifty thousand inside its walls and another fifty thousand living in its extensive surrounding territories. Its trade was now international in scope. Nuremberg had joined the ranks of the new printing centers. Leading intellectuals and artists lived and worked in Nuremberg: the list includes Dürer, Stoss, Vischer, Adam Krafft, Michael Wolgemut, Hans Sachs, Willibald Pirckheimer, Christoph Scheurl, Lazarus Spengler, Martin Behaim, and Regiomontanus.

Yet there were a few signs of trouble lurking behind the facade of Renaissance splendor. Not everyone shared in the glory of Nuremberg. The city's Jews, for example, had been exiled in 1499 after having suffered severe persecutions in 1298 and 1349. Although many never got farther away than nearby Fürth, they were not allowed to return as residents until 1850. In addition, there were some among the working classes who wanted greater political and economic power. They would force the government to make modest concessions during the crisis of the Peasants' Revolt in 1525, along with the fear of rural dissidents.

The city fathers were also troubled by the pressures placed upon them by the Reformation movement. The preaching and talking of John von Staupitz in Nuremberg had helped pave the way for the evangelical theology of Martin Luther. Luther's ideas were eagerly received by many within the ranks of the Nuremberg humanists, whose circle included members of the ruling elite. Luther had visited Nuremberg twice in 1518 and made a firm friend of Lazarus Spengler, the highly repected first secretary to the city council. Support for Luther from other classes was also in evidence as literate cobblers, painters, and weavers wrote in his defense. Such was the popularity of the Lutheran movement that visiting dignitaries like Cardinal Campeggio complained of it as early as March 1524. The situation for Nuremberg was further complicated by the fact that not only had the diet at Worms in 1521 outlawed Luther, but it voted to locate both the Imperial Council of Regency and the Imperial Cameral Court in Nuremberg. Nuremberg was also the site of three imperial diets held between 1522 and 1524. The city was close to being regarded as the capital city of at least the German portion of Charles V's far-flung empire. Both Charles and Archduke Ferdinand, who lived in Nuremberg while the diets were in session, were staunch supporters of the old faith.

Nuremberg's political shrewdness was never more in evidence during the period of the early Reformation. Professing its continued loyalty to the emperor, Nuremberg's council hired Lutheran clergy to man the city's main pulpits. After a religious colloquy in March 1525, which skirted the imperial law, Nuremberg declared itself to be officially evangelical, and representatives of the Roman Catholic church had to convert or leave the city with angry mobs cursing them on their way. The Council of Regency and the Cameral Court conveniently moved to Esslingen a year earlier when Ferdinand shrewdly recognized that the prevailing theological currents were too strong to be resisted by even the staunchest defenders of the old faith on the city council. Why provoke further trouble by having too much imperial machinery in Nuremberg in the midst of the Reformation crisis? Ferdinand like many other imperial politicians found their powers of repression limited by marauding peasants, not to mention the threats posed by the Turks and the French.

Nuremberg and the Empire weathered the storm with their relations strained but relatively intact. Nuremberg did join the Speyer protest of 1529 and signed the Augsburg Confession of 1530, but most crucial, the Nurembergers did not join the Schmalkaldic League. The city also showed its loyalty to the Empire by sending large amounts of money and even troops for the campaigns against the Turks. Charles V was sufficiently impressed by these shows of goodwill that he visited the evangelical city in 1541. During the Schmalkaldic War, Nuremberg stayed neutral while paying money to both Charles and, secretly, to the Protestant powers. In June 1552, after having accepted the Augsburg Interim, Nuremberg was forced to join the Schmalkaldic League for a while by the threats of Albert Icibiades, margrave of Brandenburg. After his fall, Nuremberg placated the emperor by paying a fine and was allowed to keep its brand of Lutheranism.

The Reformation crisis left Nuremberg with some scars, but with little permanent damage, and most important for many, business continued to be relatively good. All of this was rudely shattered by the Thirty Years War (1618–1648). Prewar tensions had been sufficient to make Nuremberg join the Protestant Union in 1610. Frightened by the brutal destruction of Protestant Magdeburg in 1631, Nuremberg stopped sending money and aid to the Protestants and instead sent cash to Emperor Ferdinand II as a sign of good faith. As the fortunes of war continued to shift, so did the "gulden diplomacy" of Nuremberg. After the imperial defeat at Breitenfeld, the council reversed itself and stopped contributing to the imperial coffers. This was followed by an agreement in October 1631 to cooperate with King Gustavus Adolphus of Sweden, the Protestant champion. In March 1632 the Lion of the North entered Nuremberg to jubilant popular acclaim. Three months later Gustavus Adolphus returned to protect Nuremberg from the army of Wallenstein, which was encamped at nearby Fürth. Famine and disease hit not only the opposing armies but also the now-crowded cities of Nuremberg and Fürth. Finally both armies withdrew in mid-September.

Nuremberg's active participation in the Thirty Years War ended in September 1634 when it was taken by imperial troops. Although the city was granted full political equality with the princes of the Empire by the terms of the Peace of Westphalia, the war had shattered the commercial life of Nuremberg and imposed a crippling burden of debt. Death and disease had done their work in further undermining the confidence of the inhabitants of the city on the Pegnitz. By 1806 Nuremberg's population had shrunk to twenty-five thousand.

Matters were not helped by the shift in trade routes from the Mediterranean with overland routes to the Atlantic axis. Nuremberg's exaggerated system of protection and regulation of commerce along with exorbitant taxes levied on goods further hurt the chances of recovery. The pragmatic conservatism of the preceding century gave way to blind reaction as the patriciate made error after error in government and business. One example is afforded by the refusal of the Nurembergers to take in Protestant weavers exiled from France and Flanders. Many of those weavers settled elsewhere, including neighboring Erlangen, where they offered formidable competition.

Although no major battles were fought near declining Nuremberg, the city suffered from the French wars, the War of the Austrian Succession, and the Seven Years War. Various reform measures failed to stem the mounting tide of decline and mounting deficits. Further humiliation occurred in August 1796 when a French army entered the city. Later the city offered itself to the king of Prussia, who refused to take control because of the city's heavy load of debt, among other problems. Nuremberg's agony was finally ended for a time when it was united with Bavaria by a decree of the Emperor Napoleon in 1806, the year of the dissolution of the Holy Roman Empire.

Works About: Adolf Engelhardt, *Die Reformation in Nürnberg, MVGN*, 33–34 (1936–1937); Eugen Franz, *Nürnberg, Kaiser und Reich* (Munich, 1930); Harold J. Grimm, *Lazarus Spengler* (Columbus, Ohio, 1978); Cecil Headlem, *The Story of Nuremberg* (London, 1927); Albert Kirchner, *Dtsch. Kaiser in Nürnberg*, (Neustadt, 1955); G. Pfeiffer, *Quellen zur Nürnberger Reformationsgesch.* (Nuremberg, 1968) and *Nürnberg*, 2 vols. (Munich, 1970–1971); Emil Reicke, *Gesch. der Reichstadt Nürnberg* (Nuremberg, 1896); J. C. Siebenkees, *Materialien zur Nürnbergischen Gesch.* 4 vols. (Nuremberg, 1792–1795); Gerald Strauss, *Nuremberg in the Sixteenth Century* (Bloomington, Ind. 1976); *The Social Hist. of the Reformation*, ed. L. P. Buck and J. W. Zophy (Columbus, Ohio, 1972).   *J. W. Zophy*

See CHARLES IV; CHARLES V; DÜRER; GOLDEN BULL; HENRY VII; MAXIMILIAN I; NUREMBERG, DIETS OF; SACHS; SIGISMUND; SPENGLER; THIRTY YEARS WAR.

NUREMBERG, DIETS OF 1522–1524, were the immediate and rather unsuccessful successors to that of Worms in 1521; there were three such diets.

From the onset, estates at the diets were divided on issues, most pressing among which were regulation of imperial economic affairs, maintenance of the Imperial Council of Regency (*Reichsregiment*) and the Imperial Cameral Court (*Reichskammergericht*), support against the Turks, and enforcement of the Edict of Worms. Of these the first diet, which met from March to April 1522, dealt almost exclusively with the problem of the Turks who had invaded Austria and had just captured Belgrade and the island of Rhodes. Legislation to regulate the Empire's economic affairs and to support imperial institutions formed a major part of the second diet's deliberations during the winter of 1522–1523. The resulting decisions—such as the imposition of a customs toll and laws creating a ceiling on a company's capital and opposing monopolies—largely emerged by agreement from within the college of princes. Emperor Charles V (1519–1556) voided these decisions after hearing complaints from a cities' deputation.

In the third diet, which opened in January 1524, the estates encountered increasingly rigorous papal claims for the enforcement of the edict of Worms. These demands had been put forth at the second Nuremberg diet by Pope Adrian VI's nuncio, Francesco Chieregati, who admitted that there had existed abuses in the Church but that the edict must be enforced. Such utterances played into the hands both of evangelical and nationalistic estates. They decided to place Chieregati's demands in committee, and they called for a free, general council to meet on German soil to deal with the religious situation. Until such a meeting, nothing was to be preached except the pure Gospel. In a similar vein, the estates submitted their gravamens to the nuncio. By 1524, however, Pope Adrian had been succeeded by Clement VII and Chieregati by Lorenzo Campeggio.

When legate Campeggio appeared before the assembled estates at the third diet in March, he attempted to gain their support against the new teachings. The estates replied that they had already treated that question at the previous diet and now wished to know what had occurred with respect to their gravamens. Campeggio's innocuous response alienated them, and in their recess they issued a call for a general assembly of the German nation to meet before the end of the year at Speyer. The recess also included reference to the estates' enforcement of the edict "insofar as might be possible." Despite Charles' subsequent prohibition of the Speyer meeting, the estates' decision on the edict became a basis for the introduction of Lutheranism in the Empire.

Works About: Hist. Kommission bei der Bayerischen Akademie der Wissenschaften, ed., *DRTA, jüngere Reihe*, vols. 3–4: *DRTA unter Kaiser Karl V.*, ed. Adolf Wrede (Gotha, 1901–1905, rpr. 1963); Karl Hofmann, *Die Konzilsfrage auf den dtsch. Reichstagen von 1521 bis 1524* (Mannheim, 1932); B. J. Kidd, *Documents Illustrative of the Continental Reformation* (Oxford, 1911), pp. 106–21, 134–51; Otto Redlich, *Der Reichstag zu Nürnberg, 1522–1523* (Leipzig, 1887); Ernest Richter, *Der Reichstag zu Nürnberg 1524* (Leipzig, 1898); Ernst Wulcher and Hans Virck, eds., *Des Kürsächsischen Rathes Hans von der Planitz Berichte aus dem Reichsregiment in Nürnberg, 1521–1523* (Leipzig, 1899).   *P. N. Bebb*

See ADRIAN VI; CAMPEGGIO; CHARLES V; FERDINAND I; IMPERIAL CAMERAL COURT; IMPERIAL COUNCIL OF REGENCY; NUREMBERG; WORMS.

NUREMBERG *REFORMATION* is the civil code of Nuremberg published by Anton Koberger in 1484. Three new editions appeared before the final redaction in 1564. The 1564 code, reissued in 1595 and 1737, remained in effect until 1900. Not to be confused with the religious Reformation either in the Empire or the city, the word *reformation* in the title was commonly applied to legal codifications.

In content the various editions of the *Reformation* evinced a growing tendency to adopt Roman law principles and Roman canon law procedures. This is manifest by a comparison of the 1484 and 1564 editions. Each redaction contained customary laws insofar as they were not in opposition to imperial laws, upon which the city rested its strength. Moreover each edition maintained the same tripartite division: procedural laws, marriage and testamentary laws, and contractual and property laws. The extensive Jewish oath that occupied a prominent place in the first editions was absent from the 1564 one. After a constant reworking of the laws, the final edition was more rational in its organization and relied more on Roman law principles.

This was the first important city codification in the Empire, and, accordingly, it exerted an influence on the development of other city and territorial codes. Free imperial cities in Franconia felt its effects, but so also did such places as Dinkelsbühl, Tübingen, Worms, Frankfurt am Main, Bamberg, Ansbach, and Württemberg, to name a few. Because of its influence, it became a means to further the reception of Roman law.

Works: *Gesetze der neuen Reformation der Stat Nuremberg Nach crist gepurt Tausend vierhundert und in dem neun u. sibentzigsten Jare fürgenommen* (Nuremberg, 1484); *Der Stat Nürnberg verneute Reformation 1564* (Nuremberg, 1564). **Works About:** Hans Liermann, "Nürnberg als Mittelpunkt deutschen Rechtslebens," *Jb. für fränkische Landesforschung* 2 (1936): 1–17; Werner Schultheiss, "Die Einwirkung Nürnberger Stadtrechts auf Deutschland, besonders Franken, Böhmen und die Oberpfalz (Der nürnberger Stadtrechtskreis)," *Jb. für fränkische Landesforschung* 2 (1936): 18–54; Otto Stobbe, *Gesch. der dtsch. Rechtsquel.* 2 vols. (Leipzig, 1860–1864); Daniel Waldmann, "Die Entstehung der Nürnberger Reformation von 1479 (1484) und die Quel. ihrer prozessrechtlichen Vorschriften," *MVGN* 18 (1908): 1–98.   *P. N. Bebb*

See NUREMBERG; ROMAN LAW.

NÜTZEL, CASPAR (c. 1471–1529), a prominent Nuremberg patrician and a member of the Nuremberg city council for twenty-seven years, was a strong advocate of Lutheran religious reforms in the 1520s. He prepared a German translation of Luther's Ninety-five Theses in 1517 and was a member of the humanist-evangelical circle of patricians and clergymen that met at the Augustinian cloister in Nuremberg. Nützel represented Nuremberg at the diet of Worms (1521). The first Lutheran baptismal rite was performed in 1524 at Nützel's home. After 1514, Nützel served as trustee for the St. Clara convent, and in 1519 he placed one of his daughters in the cloister. Six years later, his convictions compelled him to remove her from the cloister, even though this was accomplished against her wishes. Nützel carried out a number of diplomatic missions for Nuremberg and was elected to the city council's second highest office, second assessor in 1524. His marriage to Clara Hagelsheimer in 1499 produced twenty children.

Works About: Gustav Bub, "Kaspar Nützel und die Reformation," *Fränkischer Kurier*, September 25, 1929; E. Mummenhoff, "Kaspar Nutzel," *ADB*, 24: 66–70; Gerhard Pfeiffer, "Entscheidung zur Reformation," in G. Pfeiffer, ed., *Nürnberg: Gesch. einer europäischen Stadt* (Munich, 1972); G. A. Will, "Kaspar Nützel," *Nbg. Gelehrten–Lexicon* (Nuremberg, 1755–1758) 3:46–47.   *J. W. Gates*

See LUTHER; NUREMBERG; WORMS.

O

OPITZ, MARTIN (1597–1639), poet and statesman, was born in the town of Bunzlau on the Bober River in Silesia, the son of a butcher. Educated by his uncle, a retired schoolteacher, Martin showed an early aptitude for poetry and had his first verses published in 1616. After several years of study and travel in various parts of the Empire and the Low Countries, Opitz attached himself to the court of Duke George Rudolf in Liegnitz. His *Book on German Poetry* published in 1624 was a major success. Further distinction came to him when Emperor Ferdinand II named him poet laureate in Vienna in 1625 and ennobled him two years later.

Martin Opitz also achieved notice for his translations of the writings of the jurist Hugo Grotius and of such classics as Seneca's *Trojan Women*. In addition to his literary activity, he continued to be active politically, especially as a diplomat. Opitz served for many years as secretary to the real power broker in Liegnitz, Karl Hannibal von Dohna. He ended his career at the court of the Polish king, Vladislaus IV, who made him his secretary and archivist. Opitz died of the plague in Danzig.

Works By: *Ausgewählte Dichtungen von Martin Opitz*, ed Julius Tittmann (Leipzig, 1869). **Works About:** Marian Szyrocki, *Martin Opitz* (Berlin, 1956); Bernhard Ulmer, *Martin Opitz* (New York, 1971).   *J. W. Zophy*

See FERDINAND II.

OSIANDER, ANDREAS (1498–1552), controversial Lutheran theologian, church organizer, and patron of the astronomer Copernicus, was born in Gunzenhausen in Franconian Brandenburg. As a student at Leipzig, Altenburg, and Ingolstadt, he became an accomplished linguist, publishing in 1522 a version of the Vulgate, *Biblia Sacra*, based on original texts. Ordained in 1520, Osiander served as priest at the Church of St. Lawrence and taught Hebrew at the Augustinian cloister in Nuremberg.

Attracted to the teachings of Martin Luther, Osiander became an important influence for the official acceptance of Lutheranism by the Nuremberg city council in 1525. He was married in the same year. As pastor of St. Lawrence, he was frequently called upon by the city council to give expert theological opinion on a variety of issues confronting the city. In this position, he was one of the first to urge the death penalty for Anabaptists, a policy the council never adopted.

In 1529, Osiander attended the Marburg colloquy, siding with Luther against Zwingli, and in 1530 was a participant at Augsburg. In subsequent years, he was a discussant at conferences in Schmalkalden (1537), Hagenau (1540), Worms (1540), and Regensburg (1541). As a church organizer, he drafted the Nuremberg-Brandenburg Church Ordinance of 1533 and introduced Lutheran reform to the Palatinate-Neuberg in 1544. He also became noted through the marriage of his niece to the English reformer and future archbishop of Canterbury, Thomas Cranmer. As a sponsor of Copernicus, Osiander edited and wrote the preface for *De revolutionibus orbium coelestium*, published in Nuremberg in 1543.

In later years, Osiander increasingly began to differ with Luther and other reformers on questions of church discipline, private confession, and the doctrine of justification. His criticism of Philip Melanchthon at Regensburg in 1541 had caused his recall from that conference, and his opposition to the Augsburg Interim of 1548 led to his leaving Nuremberg for Königsberg, Prussia. There he spent his remaining years as pastor and professor of theology at the new university of Königsberg. His last years were also marked by a bitter dispute with other Lutheran theologians over his view of justification. In contrast to Luther's doctrine of justification by faith alone, Osiander maintained that the individual was gradually justified through the work of the in-dwelling Christ, a position close to that of Catholic theologians. The dispute, known as the Osiandrian controversy, persisted for several years after his death in 1552.

Works By: Gerhard Müller, ed., *Andreas Osiander D. A. Gesamtausgabe*, 3 vols. (Gütersloh, 1975–). **Works About:** Wilhelm Möller, *Andreas Osiander: Leben und ausgewählte Schriften* (Elberfeld, 1870); Gottfried Seebass, *Bibliographia Osiandrica: Bibliographie der gedruckten Schriften Andreas Osianders d. A.* (Nieuwkoop, 1971), and *Das reformatorische Werk des Andreas Osiander* (Nuremberg, 1967); D. C. Steinmetz, *Reformers in the Wings* (Philadelphia, 1967); Martin Stupperich, *Osiander in Preussen, 1549–1552* (Berlin, 1973).   *D. M. Hockenbery*

See LUTHER; MELANCHTHON; NUREMBERG; ZWINGLI.

OSNABRÜCK, TREATY OF, was the agreement between Sweden and the Empire that became part of the Peace of Westphalia, signed on October 24, 1648, which ended the Thirty Years War.

Since 1644, peace negotiations had been conducted concurrently in the Westphalian cities of Münster and Osnabrück to end the fighting in central Europe. Osnabrück was the site for talks among Emperor Ferdinand III, the Swedes, and the German Protestants. At Osnabrück most of the inner-German questions were discussed and resolved. The chief negotiators were the imperial representative Count Maximilian von Trauttmandorff and the Swedish diplomats Adler Salvius and Axel Oxenstierna. There were no mediators at Osnabrück as there were at Münster. The leading German Protestant princes represented at Osnabrück were the electors of Brandenburg and Saxony. The main issue in the negotiations was Sweden's demand of the north German province of Pomerania, a duchy near the Baltic Sea to which Frederick William of Brandenburg had incontestable legal claim. The elector's fierce resistance to Sweden's claims in the end produced a compromise.

The Treaty of Osnabrück, or *Instrumentum Pacis Osnabrugense*, (August 6, 1648), divided Pomerania between Sweden and Brandenburg. Sweden took control of western Pomerania, including the mouth of the River Oder and Stettin, and the islands of Rügen, Usedom, and Wollin. In return for letting Brandenburg have eastern Pomerania, the Swedes obtained the Mecklenburg port city of Wismar and the secularized bishoprics of Bremen and Verden, giving them control over the estuaries of the Elbe and Weser rivers. Sweden also received a $5 million imperial indemnity for the demobilization and withdrawal of its army from Germany. In compensation for the loss of western Pomerania, Frederick William of Brandenburg gained the secularized bishoprics of Kammin, Halberstadt, and Minden and the archbishopric of Magdeburg, which, on the death of its Saxon administrator, was to revert to Brandenburg.

Besides normalizing relations between Sweden and the Empire, the Treaty of Osnabrück also contained important provisions that, together with those of the Treaty of Münster, affected the Empire's internal affairs, particularly the confessional and constitutional interests of the German princes.

Works: Konrad Müller, ed., *Instrumenta Pacis Westphalicae. Die Westfälischen Friedensverträge 1648*, vol. 12/13: *Quel. zur neueren Gesch.*, (Bern, 1949), pp. 9–78, 99–152; Karl Zeumer, ed., *Quellensammlung zur Gesch. der dtsch. Reichsverfassung in Mittelalter und Neuzeit*, 2d ed. (Tübingen, 1913), 2:395–434. **Works About:** Ludwig Bäte, ed., *Der Friede in Osnabrück 1648. Beiträge zu seiner Gesch.* (Oldenburg, 1948); Max Braubach, *Der Westfälische Friede* (Münster, 1948); Fritz Dickmann, *Der Westfälische Frieden*, 3d ed. (Münster, 1972); Hajo Holborn, *A Hist. of Germany: The Reformation* (New York, 1959), pp. 361–74.   *Bodo Nischan*

See FERDINAND III; MÜNSTER TREATY; THIRTY YEARS WAR; WESTPHALIA.

OTTO I, THE GREAT (912–973), duke of Saxony, German king from 936 to 973, and Holy Roman emperor from 962 to 973, was the son and successor of King Henry I. Most historians consider him the true founder of the Holy Roman Empire, although those few who accord this honor to Charlemagne consider Otto I to be the revitalizer of the Empire. His coronation as emperor in 962 revived a title that had been vacant for half a century.

As king and emperor, Otto built on firm foundations laid by his father. From Henry he inherited a powerful Saxony, and his election as king in 936 was not disputed by the other dukes, who essentially acknowledged his superiority as first among equals. Otto, however, was determined to be the real ruler of Germany rather than merely the chief duke, and he spent much of his reign pursuing a policy of German unification. Such a policy gained the opposition of the particularist tribal dukes, whose rebellious activities precipitated numerous civil wars, as well as attacks by the Carolingians to the west and the barbarian Wendish and Magyar tribes to the east. The first series of ducal rebellions led by Henry of Bavaria, the king's brother, ended in the 940s after an exhausting round of raids and sieges enabled Otto to replace the disloyal tribal dukes with his own nominees chosen from among his relatives in an attempt to end the hereditary autonomy previously enjoyed by the dukes. This system eventually proved unworkable as the new alien dukes were either unable to control their particularist nobility or joined in fresh revolts against the king. By 953 the situation was nearly out of hand when Conrad of Franconia and Liudolf of Swabia, the king's son, joined in open revolt, while the more loyal dukes encountered great difficulty in restraining their unruly hereditary nobility. From his power base in Saxony, Otto was more than able to hold his own, but he made most headway when a serious Magyar invasion from the east forced the nobility to unite under the king's leadership. Otto capitalized on the opportunity, inflicting a crushing defeat on the enemy at the Lechfield in 955, thus eliminating forever the Magyar threat to German security and pacifying the eastern marches.

With Germany temporarily at peace, Otto attempted to create a new system to unify and control the major territories of Germany. Realizing that hereditary feudalism was the greatest threat to a strong monarchy, Otto turned increasingly to the great prelates and abbots for support. Celibate churchmen were unable to bequeath property or position to heirs; as the only educated class in Germany they could provide much needed bureaucratic assistance; they could conceive of a unified German state with a strong central monarchy; and they were natural allies of the king against the turbulent, encroaching lay nobility. Land, privileges, and wealth granted to the Church remained forever outside the grasp of the hereditary nobility, yet they were available to the monarchy when such resources were needed. Beginning with the appointment of his brother, Bruno, the archbishop of Cologne, as duke of Lorraine in 953, Otto increasingly came to rely on an alliance with high ecclesiastical officials to govern Germany, thus replacing unreliable lay officials with loyal and competent churchmen. Such a policy was feasible, however, only if the crown controlled the German Church by appointing all important bishops and abbots and having first call on their loyalties and services. This step was accomplished essentially by assimilating an ecclesiastical position with a fief and requiring the nominee to a position to become a direct vassal of the king.

Although the system of Church-state alliance created by Otto functioned well under Saxon and early Salian emperors, there was a built-in danger that was overlooked at the time, becoming apparent only in the mid-eleventh century. There was a fundamental contradiction inherent in bishops' and abbots' serving in both a spiritual and secular capacity, a contradiction quite apparent to Church reformers of a later age who questioned the viability of an ecclesiastical official's serving two masters. But the necessity of bringing order to tenth-century Germany made Otto's system workable at the time, hiding for over a century the basic flaw involving the dual nature of German churchmen's functions. While this system worked well while it was operative, it nonetheless carried within it the seeds for the eventual erosion of the imperial power that Otto was then in the process of establishing. Most German ecclesiastical officials performed both their secular and spiritual duties adequately, yet there was always the unsolved problem concerning their first loyalty in certain situations, the resolution of which was not determined until the investiture controversy of the 1070s. By the early twelfth century, when the monarchy no longer controlled the German Church as Otto had and the crown's absolute right of appointment of high eccelsiastic officials had been eliminated by Church reformers, the German kings found themselves still opposed by the particularist nobility but now without the assured support of the resources of an increasingly independent German Church.

As king, Otto always had before him the general example of Charlemagne, whose Empire he attempted to rebuild, though in reality his primary model was Lothar I who had combined the imperial crown with rule over the old Middle Kingdom, which included Italy. Thus besides his concern for controlling a unified Germany, he also had ambitions toward extending his influence into France and restoring Italy to the Empire. He generally supported the weak, almost powerless, kings of France and Burgundy against their strong local magnates, sometimes through an adept diplomacy and sometimes by minor military expeditions. Although the latter were largely unsuccessful, they nonetheless enabled these kings to hold their own against their powerful subjects while at the same time making them dependent on Otto for continued support. In essence, Otto's influence in France remained strong since he held the balance of power there, a situation with which he was content as long as the weak kings were forced to rely on him for protection. He was, moreover, related by marriage as brother-in-law to both the French king, Louis IV, and the leader of the French magnates, Hugh the Great.

While he was satisfied with exercising the balance of power in France and Burgundy, Italy presented an altogether different situation. The land was wealthier than Germany, especially through its growing commercial contacts with the East by the sea route. The papacy was there, in Rome, the capital of Christendom, the control of which would facilitate Otto's dealings with the German Church. Tradition also mandated Otto's interference in Italian affairs; both Charlemagne and Lothar had included it in their dominions. What was more, the political turmoil in Italy had already attracted the attention of the dukes of Bavaria and Swabia who were already active in northern Italy. Thus from a purely practical political consideration, it was to Otto's advantage to enter the contest for the control of Italy. By 950 the conquest of Italy not only appeared to be a distinct possibility but highly desirous as well.

Otto had, in fact, been involved in Italian affairs since the beginning of his reign, though his involvement remained on a diplomatic level until 951. Through his control of Burgundy, he obtained a claim on the Italian crown previously held by Rudolf II of Burgundy. While unable to exercise this claim at first since the Italian throne had been held by Count Hugh of Arles since 926, he was able to intervene indirectly in Italy by throwing his support to the various factions of magnates who opposed King Hugh. Thus he prohibited the consolidation of power in the hands of any one person while he himself was occupied with the pacification and unification of Germany. The real power in Italy was held by the magnates in any case, and the only way King Hugh could extend his influence was through his control of them. A crafty statesman, Hugh eventually was able to gain control of most of the Italian magnates with the exception of Alberic of Spoleto, who held Rome and the papacy, and Berengar of Ivrea, who was forced in 945 to flee to Otto's court for protection. When Hugh died in 948, the way was opened for Berengar to be elected king in 950, though he never effectively controlled much of the kingdom since many magnates and bishops rallied around Adelheide of Jurane Burgundy, the widow of King Hugh's son, Lothar II (d. 950). His carefully constructed balance of power in Italy destroyed, Otto was forced to invade Italy in 951 lest the dukes of Swabia and Bavaria gained a foothold there.

Otto's invasion of Italy was immediately successful. The bishops and magnates rallied to him; the German dukes withdrew; he declared himself king of Italy and married Adelheide. Alberic, however, refused to allow the pope to crown Otto as emperor, and when a fresh revolt broke out in Germany, he was forced to return home to deal with his restive dukes. This serious rebellion, which broke out in 953, coupled with the Magyar invasion of 955 and Otto's reorganization of Germany, occupied most of his energies for the next several years. Otto's absence from Italy and the death of Alberic of Spoleto in 954 thus opened the way for Berengar of Ivrea to extend his position in Italy, an activity at which he was so successful that by 961 Alberic's son, Pope John XII, and the Italian magnates invited a return visit by Otto. This time the imperial crown was the promised prize for German intervention, and, after a quick expulsion of Berengar, Otto received from the pope in February 962 the coronation as Holy Roman emperor.

By 965 the emperor had captured Berengar and reduced northern Italy to complete submission. Problems remained, however, with the restive Roman populace and the Byzantine presence in southern Italy. After a series of depositions and reinstatements, the question of the papacy was settled with the election of Otto's candidate, John XIII in 966. Between 962 and 966 Otto had been plagued by Roman rebellions against the hated German rule, but after he severely crushed the rebellion of 965, no more trouble ensued from that quarter. Sporadic attempts to expand his power into southern Italy between 966 and 972 were unsuccessful, and that area remained in Byzantine and Saracen hands until the next century when the Normans conquered it. Otto's activities in southern Italy did, however, have an indirect result; a diplomatic victory of sorts was achieved in 972 when the Byzantine emperor, John Tzimiskes, permitted the marriage of his ward, Princess Theophano, to Otto's son and successor. Thus the Byzantine court, which to this point had viewed the upstart German emperors rather disdainfully, acknowledged in a sense the legitimacy of Otto's claim to be emperor of Rome and the West. Otto's rule in Italy was largely indirect. As king and emperor he was satisfied with the right to intervene in any serious affairs, but in general he made no significant changes or reforms in Italy and left the government of the country to the local magnates and prelates with whom he was allied. The value of Italy for Otto lay more in its imperial symbolism, the control of the papacy and Rome, and the potential as a commercial stimulus for Germany, than in its role as a source of further political power or revenue.

Although Otto concentrated most of his energy as king and emperor on the consolidation of the monarchy in Germany and the extension of his power and influence to France and Italy, he never completely ignored the situation on his eastern borders. Rightly remembered for his defeat of the Magyars in 955, he nonetheless accomplished still more in that quarter. Otto relentlessly continued his father's policy of the *Drang nach Osten* (Drive to the East), relying chiefly on the loyal Saxon nobility for the work. Bohemia was forced to recognize German hegemony, the Magyars were removed as a serious threat, and the Germans penetrated deeply into the territory of the Wends and Lyutitzi. Otto's policy was not merely conquest but also Christianization. Fortresses and colonies were established in the conquered territories, but so were monasteries and missionary bishoprics like Brandenburg, Havelberg, and Magdeburg. As king, Otto recognized the role of the Church in stabilizing and pacifying the eastern marches, but as the leader of Western Christendom he also recognized the importance of his duty in the Christianization of the heathen eastern tribes.

Otto's long reign as king and emperor is one of the most significant in the history of the Holy Roman Empire. His energy, aptitude, vision, and foresight enabled him to establish the German monarchy as the leading political force in Europe for three hundred years. He reformed and centralized the monarchy and government as well as was feasible in the tenth century, brought more unity to the Empire than it had previously known, pacified and extended the borders, and increased the imperial power and prestige to the extent of gaining tacit Byzantine recognition. Under his rule, the cities of Germany grew and prospered, and German commercial contacts with the rest of Europe broadened. He brought the imperial title to Germany, where it remained for several centuries, establishing himself in the medieval mind as a model monarch second only to the legendary Charlemagne. He left Germany and the Empire in an inestimably superior state than he had received them. Otto the Great was succeeded at his death in 972 by his surviving son by Adelheide, Otto II, who had been joint emperor since 967.

Works About: H. Aubin, *Otto der Grosse und die Erneuerung des abendländischen Kaisertums im Jahre 962* (Göttingen, 1962); H. Beumann and H. Buettner, *Das Kaisertum Ottos des Grossen* (Munich, 1963); J. F. Böhmer, *Regesta imperii*, ed. E. von Ottenthal (Innsbruck, 1893), vol. 1; J. A. Brundage, "Widukind of Corvey and the 'Non-Roman' Imperial Idea," *Medieval Studies* 22

(1960): 15–26; C. Erdmann, "Königs- und Kaiserkrönung im Ottonischen Pontifikale," in *Forsch. zur politischen Ideenwelt des Frühmittelalters* (Berlin, 1951); John F. Gallagher, *Church and State in Germany under Otto the Great* (New York, 1938); B. H. Hill, *Medieval Monarchy in Action* (New York, 1972) and *The Rise of the First Reich* (New York, 1969); R. Holtzmann, *Gesch. des sachsischen Kaiserzeit, 900–1024*, 4th ed. (Munich, 1961) R. Köpke and E. Dümmler, *Jb. der dtsch. Gesch.: Kaiser Otto der Grosse*, 2d ed. (Munich, 1962); K. Leyser, "The Battle on the Lech," *History* 50 (1965): 1–25; M. Lintzel, *Die Kaiserpolitik Ottos des Grossen* (Munich, 1943); Luidprand of Cremona, *The Works of Luidprand of Cremona*, ed. and tr. F. A. Wright (London, 1930); A. L. Poole, "Germany and the Western Empire," *Cambridge Medieval History*, ed. C. W. Previté-Orton (New York, 1964), 3:179–215; M. Uhlirz, "Die italienische Kirchenpolitik der Ottonen," *MIÖG* 48 (1934):201–31; Widukind of Corvey, *Res Gestae Saxonicae*, ed. P. Hirsch and H. E. Lohmann (Hanover, 1935).   *D. S. Devlin*

See ADELHEIDE; CHARLEMAGNE; HENRY I; INVESTITURE CONTROVERSY; OTTO II.

OTTO II (955–983), Holy Roman emperor from 973 to 983 and German king from 961 to 983, was the son and successor of Otto the Great with whom he was joint emperor after 967. His position as emperor was contested at his father's death by his cousin, Henry the Wrangler, duke of Bavaria. By 978 he had subdued Henry, deposed and replaced him with a more pliable duke, and reduced the size of Bavaria. Between 973 and 980, Otto also succeeded in securing his borders against the Wends, Poles, and Danes, though his attempts to reduce the independence of Lotharingia (Lorraine) led only to an inconclusive war with the king of France who had supporters among the Lotharingian nobility and had ambitions of annexing part of the territory.

In the last three years of his life, Otto turned his attention to Italy where the Byzantines were having difficulty checking Saracen advances in the south. Byzantine weakness, coupled with petty wars among the Lombard principalities, provided him the opportunity to interfere there. Following some initial successes in Lombardy where he forced the local nobility to become his vassals, Otto moved his army to Calabria to confront the Saracen army under Adu'l-Qasim. At Cortone in 982, the German army was disastrously defeated as a result of poor leadership, with Otto himself escaping only by swimming to a Byzantine ship offshore. The defeat at Cortone had serious repercussions for the Empire. It not only cost the Empire the best among its nobility but also presented a grand opportunity for uprisings and invasions along the northern borders. The Danes, Slavs, and Wends, revolted, thereby losing for the Empire all the territory so recently annexed by Otto the Great. It was not until the twelfth century that the Holy Roman Empire succeeded in reconquering and pacifying these areas.

Otto II considered his position as emperor of greater significance than his position as German king, seeing the Empire as a united realm of which Germany was a part as well as Italy. Although Germany was his base of power, he nonetheless felt very keenly his duty toward Italy and Rome as integral parts of his dominions as emperor. This view of the united Empire was, in most respects, identical to that held by Otto the Great, and Otto II in general continued his father's policies. His imperial ambitions were aided and fostered by his mother, Adelheide, and by his brilliant wife, the Byzantine princess Theophano. The reign of Otto II saw the commencement of a period of cultural flowering within the Empire where, under the leadership of Adelheide and Theophano, many Byzantine scholars and clergy were brought to Germany to serve the imperial government and to act within the government and strongly committed to general reform of the Church and the foundation of nunneries for women of the nobility.

At a diet in Verona in 983, Otto attempted to repair the damage caused to the Empire by the Cortone disaster by reorganizing some of the German duchies and having his infant son named the German king. Otto died suddenly in December 983, leaving behind him a weakened and more chaotic Empire than he had inherited, vastly reduced in prestige because of his failures in Italy. The government and regency eventually fell into the capable hands of Adelheide and Theophano.

Works About: J. F. Böhmer, *Die Regesten des Kaiserreiches unter Otto II.*, ed. H. L. Mikoletzky in *Regesta imperii* (Graz, 1950), vol. 2, pt. 2: M. Hellmann, "Die Ostpolitik Kaiser Otto II.," *Syntagma Friburgense* (Lindau, 1956); B. H. Hill, *Medieval Monarchy in Action* (New York, 1972); R. Holtzmann, *Gesch. der sachsischen Kaiserzeit*, 4th ed. (Munich, 1961); P. E. Schramm, *Kaiser, Rom und Renovatio*, 2d ed. (Darmstadt, 1957); Theitmar of Meresburg, *Chronicon*, ed. L. Schmidt (Dresden, 1905); K. Uhlirz, *Jb. des dtsch. Reiches unter Otto II. und Otto III.* (Berlin, 1967), vol. 1.   *D. S. Devlin*

See ADELHEIDE; OTTO I; OTTO III.

OTTO III (980–1002), German king from 983 to 1002, and Holy Roman emperor from 996 to 1002, was the son and successor of Otto II and his brilliant wife, the Byzantine princess Theophano. On his father's death, armed disputes erupted among the German nobility for control of the regency. One party supported the duke of Bavaria, Henry the Wrangler; another party supported Lothar, the king of France; the victorious party, led by the great ecclesiastics of the Empire, succeeded in naming Theophano and the infant king's grandmother, Adelheide, as guardian and regents. Theophano exercised power in the Empire until her death in 991; Adelheide then succeeded her until her death three years later, whereupon the fourteen-year-old king began to rule in his own stead until his death.

One of the most talented and well-educated individuals ever to hold the position of Holy Roman emperor, Otto III was torn between a life of extreme religious asceticism and the pursuit of grandiose schemes for the creation of a universal ecclesiastical Empire ruled by himself out of Rome. From his two immediate predecessors as emperor, he inherited the idea of a united Holy Roman Empire as conceived by Otto I; from his Byzantine background and tutors, he inherited the concept of a universal imperial power. He was also greatly influenced by the greatest scholar of the time, Gerbert of Aurillac, who encouraged his desire to forge a Christian empire centered at Rome and ruled by the pope and emperor in partnership. Otto hoped to reestablish a true Western Roman Empire, taking as his models Charlemagne and Constantine. He denounced the Donation of Constantine, strongly supported Church reform, and attempted to establish an imperial administration along Byzantine lines. Viewing the Church as the key to his imperial dreams, he generally supported the great ecclesiastics against the nobility and burghers in his attempt to create an imperial theocracy. His schemes were frustrated, however, by the fact that his base of power was Germany and that most of his real authority derived from his position as German king. He consequently had little direct control over the magnates and burghers of Italy, and relied, as had his predecessors, on an alliance with the powerful bishops and abbots. His more universal ambitions were frustrated by the activities of the very capable Byzantine emperor, Basil II.

By 996 Otto had established firm control over his German dominions, reduced the degree of danger on his borders posed by the Vikings, Wends, and Slavs, and was able to turn his attention to Italy where he received the imperial crown in Rome. In his attempt to establish a partnership between the emperor and pope, he appointed as pope his cousin, Bruno (Gregory V). When Otto returned to Italy, however, the Roman nobility deposed Gregory and appointed in his place John XVI. Otto returned to Rome in 998, restored his cousin as pope, and then set about implementing his ideas of imperial theocracy. When Bruno died the following year, Otto appointed his friend, Gerbert of Aurillac, as Sylvester II, and the two worked together closely over the following four years to transform and renovate the Empire. Otto's seal bore the inscription, "The renovation of the empire of the Romans." Otto and Sylvester made considerable progress in the Christianization of the Slavic peoples of eastern Europe and in implementing Church reform. Most of the emperor's chief advisers and counselors were non-German bishops and abbots. This coalition between the emperor and the great prelates was, however, increasingly ineffective, especially in Lombardy, because of the opposition directed toward them by the nobility and the growing merchant classes.

After 1000, the emperor's position began to deteriorate. The Italian cities grew more restive, opposition to his reforms mounted, and in 1001 he was expelled from Rome by the citizenry. Moreover the lack of a strong monarchical presence in Germany over the previous quarter century had encouraged the nobility there to pursue its local, particularistic designs, and the situation was just barely kept in hand by Otto's relatives led by Henry, the duke of Bavaria. Otto III died in January 1002 while preparing to besiege Rome, and his German army had to fight its way back home. With Pope Sylvester's death in the following year, Otto's dream of a centralized and renewed western Roman theocratic state also died. Otto was a skillful diplomat and an energetic and farsighted ruler, but he was unaware that his wide ambitions had little chance of success given his narrow power base and the forces ranged against him. The peace Otto I had brought to western Europe had opened the gates to prosperity and vast social and economic change; in the new Europe resulting from this development, Otto III's dream of a united theocratic Western Empire was anachronistic.

Works About: J. F. Böhmer, *Die Regesten des Kaiserreiches unter Otto III.*, ed. M. Uhlirz in *Regesta imperii* (Cologne, 1956), vol. 2, pt. 3; A. Brachmann, *Kaiser Otto III. und die staatliche Umgestaltun Polens und Ungarns* (Berlin, 1939); K. Hampe, "Kaiser Otto III. und Rom," *HZ* 140 (1929); *MGH Dip.*, ed. T. Sickel, 2d ed. (Berlin, 1957), vol. 2, pt. 2; M. Ter Braak, *Kaiser Otto III.* (Amsterdam, 1928); K. Uhlirz, *Jb. des dtsch. Reiches unter Otto II und Otto III* (Berlin, 1967), vol. 2.   *D. S. Devlin*

See ADELHEIDE; CHARLEMAGNE; OTTO II; SYLVESTER II.

OTTO IV OF BRUNSWICK-WELF (1182–1218), emperor, born probably in Normandy, second son of Henry the Lion and Matilda of England, was the only member of his dynasty to attain the imperial throne. Sharing his parents' exile Otto grew up at the English court; Richard I enfeoffed him with the county of Poitou. After his father's death in 1195, Otto inherited one-third of the Welf allods in Brunswick. Despite his youth and deficiencies of character, Otto was chosen by the anti-Hohenstaufen faction to lead their feud against Frederick of Sicily and Philip of Swabia after Henry VI's death in 1197. On June 9, 1198, a small number of princes, the chief of whom was Archbishop Adolf of Altena of Cologne, elected Otto king; on July 12 he was crowned in Aachen.

Of crucial importance to Otto in the ensuing civil war against Philip of Swabia was the financial and diplomatic support Otto received from his uncle, King Richard, whose death in 1199 created a crisis for the Welfs. Now in desperation, Otto begged Pope Innocent III for support. Innocent recognized Otto as king, March 1, 1201, but at the price of Otto's oath in support of the concessions of Neuss (June 8, 1201). The fortunes of war gradually shifted against him, but Otto was saved from defeat by the assassination of his rival in 1208. Philip's partisans gave up the struggle. Otto submitted to a second, unanimous election on November 11, 1208, which clearly marks the legal beginning of his reign. To reconcile former foes, he punished Philip's murderer and agreed to marry Philip's eleven-year-old daughter, Beatrice. She died shortly after the wedding in 1212, whereupon Otto married Maria of Brabant. Having renewed and even expanded his promises to the pope, Otto received the imperial crown on October 4, 1209.

Unexpectedly despite all his oaths and promises, Otto suddenly seized parts of the papal state and prepared to invade Sicily where German influence had declined under the papal-Hohenstaufen regime of Frederick, son of Henry VI. On November 18, 1210, Innocent III excommunicated Otto. At the urging of the pope and King Philip II of France, many of the already discontented German princes withdrew their allegiance from Otto and proposed to acknowledge Frederick as their king. Forced to hasten back to Germany, Otto narrowly missed intercepting Frederick at Constance in 1212, whom the princes elected and crowned in that same year. In renewed civil war, the Welfs and Hohenstaufens faced each other for two years. With promises of aid from John of England and from the lower Rhenish princes, Otto led his forces westward and encountered a Hohenstaufen-Capetian army at Bouvines, near Lille, on July 27, 1214. Defeated, he withdrew to Brunswick as his remaining partisans gradually dropped away. He lived there impregnable but helpless until his death at the Harzburg on May 19, 1218, leaving no direct heirs.

Works About: J. Haller, "Innocenz III. und Otto IV.," in *Papsttum und Kaisertum*, ed. Albert Brachmann (Munich, 1926), pp. 475–507; L. von Heinemann, *Die Welfischen Territorien seit dem Sturze Heinrichs des Löwen bis zur Gründung des Herzogthums Braunschweig-Lüneburg* (Leipzig, 1882); Friedrich Kempf, ed., *Regestrum Innocentii III super negotio Romani imperii* (Rome, 1947). F. Kempf, "Die zwei Versprechen Ottos IV. an die römische Kirche," *Festschrift für E. E. Stengel* (Münster-Cologne, 1952), pp. 359–384; E. Winkelmann, *Philipp von Schwaben und Otto IV. von Braunschweig* (Leipzig, 1878, rpr. 1963), vol. 2.   *R. H. Schmandt*

See DISPUTED ELECTION; HENRY VI; HENRY THE LION; INNOCENT III; PHILIP OF SWABIA-HOHENSTAUFEN.

OTTO OF FREISING (c. 1110–1158), one of the most significant and reliable historians of the medieval Empire, was a member of the very powerful Babenberg family. A younger son of Margrave Leopold III of Austria and Agnes, daughter of Emperor Henry IV, Otto was a half-brother of Emperor Conrad III and uncle of Frederick I Barbarossa. He studied at the University of Paris (1127–1133), joining the new Cistercian order of monks about 1133. He became bishop of Freising in 1137, holding that post until his death.

Otto is remembered for his two books of history: *Two Cities* (1146) and *The Deeds of Frederick Barbarossa* (1169). The former, considered to be his major work, is a chronicle of world history in the tradition of St. Augustine with particular emphasis on events in the Holy Roman Empire from approximately 1000. It thus provides valuable information about the Salian and early Hohenstaufen emperors, including the origins and course of the crucial investiture controversy between the Empire and papacy. *The Deeds of Frederick Barbarossa* covers the years 1075 to 1160, though most of the work is concerned with the years following Frederick's coronation in 1152. Only half of this book was written by Otto; the material for the years following his death was composed by his secretary, Rohewin, a far inferior historian.

Otto of Freising was perhaps the premier philosophical historian of the Middle Ages, the *Two Cities* being one of the foremost examples of medieval historiography. In this book, Otto sees the history of the world consisting of a struggle between good and evil, between the city of God and the worldly city. Faithfully adhering to the Augustinian concept of history, Otto presents his own time in an apocalyptic sense, seeing the Empire as the last of four great empires foretold by the prophet Daniel. The sorry state of affairs in the Empire during the early twelfth century was evidence enough to Otto that the collapse of the Empire, and thus the end of time, was relatively imminent. *Two Cities* strikes a profoundly pessimistic note, especially as Otto appears confused and distressed about the prevalent quarrel between papacy and Empire during the previous hundred years. It seems to him obvious that the two powers should cooperate, yet they are in the process of becoming enemies. Worse yet, the decline in power and prestige of the Empire was ironically accompanied by just the opposite on the part of the papacy. Both a bishop and imperial administrator, Otto felt himself torn between these two forces, a feeling reflected in his objective analysis of the situation.

The Deeds of Frederick Barbarossa shows an entirely different viewpoint. Written in the earliest, most successful, years of Frederick's reign, it presents a view of optimism and hope, emphasizing peace, prosperity, and stability as Otto sees the young emperor resolving the many complex problems plaguing the Empire. This transformation from pessimism to optimism in only a decade signals a change in Otto's view of history and the world and clearly indicates the great expectations in Germany that accompanied Frederick's early years as emperor. Otto of Freising's histories remain among the classics of medieval historiography, providing both valuable factual information and insight into a most crucial time in the Empire's history.

Works By: *The Two Cities*, tr. C. C. Mierow (New York, 1928): *The Deeds of Frederick Barbarossa* tr. C. C. Mierow (New York, 1953). **Works About:** A. Hofmeister, "Studien uber Otto von Freising," *Neues Arch. der Gesch. fur ältere dtsch. Geschichtskunde*, 37 (1911–12)1: 99–161, 633–768; C. C. Mierow, "Otto of Freising: A Medieval Historian at Work," *Philological Quarterly*, 14 (1935): 344–62; J. Schmidlin, *Die geschichtsphilosophische und Kirchenpolitische Weltanschauung Ottos von Freising* (Freiburg im Breisgau, 1906).   *D. S. Devlin*

See CONRAD III; FREDERICK I; HENRY IV.

P

PAPPENHEIM, GOTTFRIED HENRY (1594–1632), count and military leader during the Thirty Years War, was born at Pappenheim am der Altmühl and died at Leipzig. He studied at the celebrated Protestant universities of Altdorf and Tübingen. After the customary grand tour that took him through the Low Countries, France, and Italy, he converted to Roman Catholicism in 1614; he remained a devoted, often fanatical, follower of the old faith until the end of his life. His training as a lawyer, and especially his religious zeal, led Emperor Matthias to appoint him to the imperial privy council in Prague. Yet Pappenheim soon left this post again in order to pursue a military career.

He fought for King Sigismund of Poland against Sweden and Russia. When the Thirty Years War began in Bohemia, he joined the Catholic League and became a lieutenant colonel in the army of Count Tilly. He was severely injured in the Battle of the White Mountain near Prague (November 8, 1620). After recuperating, he followed Tilly into the Rhineland. Yearning for greater military glory, he decided to take a brief leave of absence from the league army to join the Spanish who were fighting the French in northern Italy (1623–1626). In 1626 he ruthlessly suppressed the peasants' revolt in Upper Austria. Then he returned to Germany, where the war meanwhile had spread into Lower Saxony. His horsemen, known as the Pappenheimer, a terror to Protestants, besieged and captured the city of Wolfenbüttel (1627). But Pappenheim could not persuade Emperor Ferdinand II to grant him the duchy of Brunswick-Wolfenbüttel as a hereditary fief. Early in 1631 he took charge of the siege of Magdeburg. Tilly, chief of the league forces, hoped to take the wealthy north German Lutheran citadel before King Gustavus Adolphus could come to its rescue. Pappenheim's forces stormed and seized the city (May 20, 1631) but were not responsible for its total destruction; the residents themselves had set fire to their city.

As Tilly's second in command, Pappenheim had become increasingly impatient with the aging general's cautious style and military leadership. His rashness was largely responsible for the Battle of Breitenfeld (September 17, 1631), which Tilly had sought to postpone; Gustavus' forces completely routed the league army. While Tilly fled and the Swedes penetrated deep into Germany, Pappenheim remained behind and kept the north German princes occupied to prevent them from aiding the king in the south. In the summer of 1632, his forces attempted to liberate Maestricht, which had been seized by the Dutch. His soldiers stormed the fortress on August 17 but were unable to dislodge its defenders; and in the end they found themselves abandoned even by the Spanish whom they had come to aid. On Wallenstein's orders, Pappenheim then moved his cavalry into Saxony. There he was to fight his last battle at Lützen (November 16, 1632); like his great antagonist, Gustavus Adolphus of Sweden, he was mortally wounded in the encounter.

Pappenheim became primarily known as a skillful and dashing cavalry officer. He was utterly without fear, very ambitious, and always eager to win fame on the battlefield. But he was also moody, arrogant, impatient, and often not very realistic in his political and military schemes. His rashness made him a poor commander-in-chief; yet his temperament did not qualify him for a subordinate post either. As a military leader in the Thirty Years War, Pappenheim ranks below Tilly and Wallenstein and significantly above the average soldier of fortune.

Works About: Hermann Hallwich, ed., *Briefe und Akten zur Gesch. Wallensteins,* 4 vols. (Vienna, 1912); Rudolf Herold, "General Graf Pappenheim" (Diss., University of Munich, 1906); Karl Wittich, "Pappenheim," *ADB,* 25:144–61, and *Pappenheim und Falkenberg* (Berlin, 1894).

Bodo Nischan

See FERDINAND II; MATTHIAS; THIRTY YEARS WAR; TILLY; WALLENSTEIN, ALBERT.

PARACELSUS or Philippus Aureolus Theophrastus Bombastus von Hohenheim (1493–1541), physician and theorist, was born at Einsiedeln in Switzerland. His physician father introduced him to the practice of medicine at an early age by taking the boy with him on his rounds. When Paracelsus was ten, the family moved to Villach, a mining community in the Tyrol, where with his customary curiosity he became interested in mining, minerals, and the occupational diseases of miners. Most of his education was informal and practical, although he did study with John Trithemius, abbot of Sponheim, and at a number of Italian universities. He may even have received a doctor of medicine degree from Ferrara.

For a number of years, Paracelsus traveled throughout Europe and maybe even to Arabia and Egypt. He seems to have spent some time as an army surgeon before setting up a medical practice in Salzburg in 1525. There he began a lifelong pattern of public controversy with the authorities followed by a hasty departure. The next year he surfaced at Basel as city physician and professor at the university, although the latter position was not approved by the faculty, many of whom were hostile to him. Although he achieved a number of practical successes such as winning the respect of Erasmus and saving the leg of the humanist publisher, John Froben, from amputation, Paracelsus became the center of controversy. Announcing that he alone would restore medicine from its barbarous state, Paracelsus threw copies of Galen and Avicenna, the ranking medical authorities of the Middle Ages, into a bonfire in order to symbolize his rejection of traditional medical theory and practice. He also began to lecture in

German rather than in the customary Latin. This plus his condemnation of his critics resulted in his expulsion from the city in 1528.

His wanderings as an itinerant lay preacher and physician took him to Nuremberg, Beretshausen, Regensburg, and St. Gall. During these times he continued to write works, including *Chirurgia Magna (Great Surgery)* of 1536 and his *Seven Defenses* (1538). Following an interview with Archduke Ferdinand, which gave him a greater measure of respectability, Archbishop Ernest invited him to return to Salzburg, where he died.

Controversy stalked Paracelsus in life and continues to swirl around him in death. Although he did not make any startling discoveries and his works contain numerous errors, his contributions to both science and theosophy are considerable. Paracelsus sought to learn the truth about life and nature—the living world in all its parts as created by God. His God was an eternal mind and an eternal center of power, from which all things flow. Paracelsus's thought blended alchemy, magic, and mysticism; his medicine utilized pain-killing drugs, natural healing, and causes of diseases and recognized the power of the mind on illnesses. His study of mercury and other substances made real advances in chemistry.

Works By: Paracelsus, *Die theologischen und religionswissenschaftlichen Schriften,* ed. Kurt Goldhammer, 6 vols. (Wiesbaden, 1955–1973); *Gesammelte Werke,* K. Sudhof and W. Matthiesson, eds., 14 vols. (Munich, 1920–1933); A. E. Waite, *The Hermetic and Alchemical Writings of Paracelsus the Great,* 2 vols. (London, 1966). **Works About:** Alexander Koyré "Paracelsus," in *The Reformation in Medieval Perspective,* ed. S. E. Ozment (Chicago, 1971), pp. 185–218; Walter Pagel, "Paracelsus" *DSB*, 10:304–13, and *Paracelsus: Introduction to Philosophical Medicine in the Era of the Renaissance* (New York, 1958); Karl Sudhoff, *Paracelsus* (Leipzig, 1936).   *J. W. Zophy*

See ERASMUS; FERDINAND I.

PASSAROWITZ (Požarevac), TREATY OF (1718), ended Charles VI's war with the Ottoman Porte, which had begun in 1716. During that conflict, Eugene of Savoy had won several notable victories at Peterwardein, Temesvár, and Belgrade. The Turks refused to initiate direct talks but finally accepted Anglo-Dutch mediation. With little aid from his Dutch colleague, Sir Robert Sutton, the representative of George I, brought about the final settlement of July 21, 1718. In that agreement, the Turks gave to Austria the banat of Temesvár, the northern part of Serbia, including Belgrade, sections of Wallachia and Bosnia, and important trading rights in the Turkish empire. The Porte retained the Morea, which the Turks had taken from Venice. The peace marked the end of the Turkish military threat to Hungary. Yet all of Austria's territorial gains, except the banat of Temesvár, were lost in the war that Austria waged with Russia against Turkey (1736–1739). Although the commercial agreement admitted imperial merchants on favorable terms into the Ottoman empire, the attempt to gain for the Habsburgs a share of the Far Eastern trade failed. Nevertheless the growth of the port of Trieste marked a beginning in the development of maritime commerce. The settlement of Passarowitz proved to be the high point of Habsburg expansion into the Balkans.

Works About: Max Braubach, *Prinz Eugen von Savoyen*, 5 vols. (Vienna, 1963–1965); *Feldzüge des Prinzen Eugen von Savoyen*, 20 vols. Vienna, 1876–1892). E. Odenthal, *Österreichs Türkenkrieg, 1716–1718* (Düsseldorf, 1938); Oswald Redlich, *Das Werden einer Grossmacht, Österreich von 1700 bis 1740* (Vienna, 1942).   L. S. Frey and M. L. Frey

See CHARLES VI; EUGENE OF SAVOY; PETERWARDEIN.

PASSAU, a strategically important city on the Danube, had served as the refuge for Leopold I and his court when the Turks invaded the Holy Roman Empire and besieged the capital at Vienna in 1683. Passau was easily taken by Max Emmanuel of Bavaria on January 11, 1704, during the War of the Spanish Succession (1701–1714). The elector's seizure of Passau in 1704 highlighted the ineffectiveness of the imperial military effort and spotlighted the weakness of the Empire. With a mere nineteen hundred men, the commander had been unable to withstand the ten thousand Bavarian troops. Most of the soldiers in Passau had earlier been sent to Lower Austria to stop the raiding of the Hungarian rebels. The easy capitulation of Passau seemed to prove the allied contention that the emperor could not maintain a war effort in the Empire and Italy and suppress the Hungarian rebellion at the same time.

After the seizure of Passau, the elector tried to force Leopold I to come to terms. Leopold, however, refused to negotiate with the elector and would not give up his demands for the kingship or for extensive territorial concessions in the Empire. The situation in 1704 was desperate; Vienna was trapped between the Hungarian rebels and the Franco-Bavarian troops. The enemy occupied the Danube valley from Ulm to Passau. Many feared that it was only a matter of time before the capital would fall. Because of Passau's importance as the key to the hereditary countries, its surrender impelled Leopold I to request military aid from his allies, particularly the maritime powers, England and the United Provinces. John Churchill, commander-in-chief of the English forces, with the greatest secrecy engineered the brilliant campaign at Blenheim (August 1704), which forced Bavaria out of the war and staved off imperial defeat.

Works About: Max Braubach, *Prinz Eugen von Savoyen*, 5 vols. (Vienna, 1963–1965); David Chandler, *Marlborough as Military Commander* (London, 1973); Philip Roder von Diersberg, ed., *Krieg-und Staatschriften über der spanischen Erbfolgekrieg 1700–1707* (Karlsrühe, 1850); B. Van T'Hoff, *The Correspondence of John Churchill, First Duke of Marlborough, and Anthonie Heinsius, Grand Pensionary of Holland* (The Hague, 1951); Onno Klopp, *Der Fall des Hauses Stuart* (Vienna, 1879); George Murray, ed., *The Letters and Dispatches of John Churchill, First Duke of Marlborough from 1702–1712* (London, 1845); Max Spindler, ed., *Handbuch der bayer. Gesch.*, 2 vols. (Munich, 1966).   L. S. Frey and M. L. Frey

See BLENHEIM; LEOPOLD I; SPANISH SUCCESSION; VIENNA, SIEGE OF.

The **PEASANTS' WAR** took place between 1524 and 1526. No single formulation can adequately explain why the war took place. In fact, there were a
number of causes. Numerous late medieval agrarian revolts (*Bundschuh* and
Arme Konrad movements) had established a tradition of peasant insurrection.
Clerical and petty noble landlords, hoping to build their territorial hegemony,
had exploited their peasants and had violated village rights and legal traditions.
The Protestant Reformation, in accordance with Luther's doctrine of the universal priesthood of believers, taught the sanctity of lay occupations and gave
a new importance to laymen in the affairs of the church. Propagandists for
reform, in turn, popularized the ideal of *Karsthans*, the evangelical peasant who
stood closer to God than a priest did. Moreover the Reformation seriously weakened the Catholic church, the basis of authority in medieval feudal society.
Under the influence of Reformation teachings, the peasants themselves began
to justify their demands not only in terms of traditional law but also in terms of
divine law and the Scriptures.

Serious financial and political grievances also motivated the rebels. Their
complaints treated the problems of hoarding, speculation, new taxes, and unfair
rents. The impact of early capitalism, in combination with a rise in population
and the emergence of the territorial state, often led to a struggle for control of
village affairs among lords, tenant farmers, and landless cottagers. Also from
1517 through 1524, much of Germany suffered from a series of bad harvests.

Finally in 1524 there was the widespread belief that a violent confrontation
between lords and subjects was inevitable. This idea, supported by the predic-
tions of astrologers, was well summed up in the popular saying, "He who does
not die in 1523, does not drown in 1524, and is not killed in 1525 can truly
speak of miracles."

In June 1524 the insurrection began at Stühlingen in the southern Black Forest.
The rebels elected as their leader the former lansquenet, Hans Müller of Bul-
genbach. They found ready allies among the burghers of Waldshut, led by the
reform-minded pastor, Balthasar Hubmaier. The revolt quickly spread throughout Hegau, Württemberg, Breisgau, and Klettgau. Both Archduke Ferdinand of
Austria and the Swabian League found it impossible to take immediate steps
against the rebels, for nearly all available military forces were committed to the
war with France in northern Italy. By the end of 1524, relative calm had returned, though the entire region encompassed by the Danube, the Rhine, and
the Lech had experienced revolt.

During February–March 1525 three major peasant armies developed in Upper
Swabia. The Baltringen army was the largest; it was headed by Ulrich Schmid,
a smith from Sulmingen, and gradually grew to a force of about seven thousand.
The Algau host developed out of a revolt against the prince-abbot of Kempten.
The leaders were Jörg Schmid (known as Knopf) and Jörg Täuber. The Lake
Constance force originated in the region between Lindau and Constance. The

dominant figures, Dietrich Hurlewagen of Lindau and Hans Jacob Humpis of Senftenau, were well-born city dwellers rather than peasants.

In search of support, Ulrich Schmid went to the imperial city of Memmingen. There he found an invaluable ally in the journeyman furrier, Sebastian Lotzer. Lotzer drafted the famous Twelve Articles, which the rebels adopted almost universally as a statement of their demands. He based his document upon the grievances of the Baltringen peasants, but he gave it supraregional significance by justifying the reforms in terms of divine law and the Scriptures. The Zwinglian preacher of Memmingen, Christoph Schappeler, contributed the introduction, which also helped generalize and justify the demands. The Twelve Articles called for congregational selection of pastors, abolition of the small tithe, elimination of serfdom, relaxation of hunting and fishing restrictions, provision of free firewood and timber, abrogation of new dues and services, adjustment of rents, reform of criminal jurisdiction in accordance with traditional law, restoration of the commons to community control, abolition of the heriot, and harmonization of all changes with the word of God.

At the parliament of Memmingen (March 6–7, 1525), the three Upper Swabian peasant forces joined together in the Christian Union. Just as this alliance was being arranged, a fourth rebel army came into being at Leipheim near Ulm. Meanwhile the Swabian League was preparing to take action against the rebels. After the Battle of Pavia (February 24, 1525), troops became available for the army of the league, commanded by George Truchsess. On April 4 Truchsess routed the Leipheim force. Next he moved against the Bildhausen army and easily dispersed it. After these two successes, he advanced on the Lake Constance group, which outnumbered his men almost two to one and which included many experienced lansquenets. He therefore negotiated the Treaty of Weingarten (April 17), according to which the peasants agreed to cease hostilities and to submit their demands to arbitration. The Algau rebels eventually also joined in the truce. The treaty blunted the impact of the revolt in Upper Swabia and freed the league to act against rebels elsewhere.

Truchsess set out from Weingarten to suppress a new rebellion in the Black Forest, but before he could do so, the league ordered him to proceed to Württemberg. In the Black Forest the renewed revolt lasted until the fall, for the league now directed its efforts to the north.

In March the peasant insurrection spread from Swabia to Franconia. There major armies developed in the Tauber valley, in the Oden Forest and Neckar valley and in the area around Bildhausen. Eventually all three joined in an unsuccessful siege of the fortress at Würzburg.

The Tauber valley force grew out of insurrections within the territory of the city of Rothenburg; the leaders were two minor clerics, Leinhart Denner and Hans Hollenpach. On April 4 the army left the Rothenburg territory, traveling down the Tauber valley, recruiting support from subjects of the Teutonic Knights, the margrave of Brandenburg, and the bishop of Würzburg. This larger, more diverse force drafted a reform program that reflected the demands of the entire Tauber valley. It called for nobles and clergy to become the legal equals of burghers and peasants; it ordered the destruction of castles and fortresses, the confiscation of ordnance, and the surrender of all cached goods of clerics and nobles who had opposed the peasant cause; and it postponed payment of rents, tithes, the heriot, and transfer fees until the completion of a religious reformation. Early in May the Tauber valley army moved to Heidingsfeld near Würzburg to begin the siege of the Unserfrauenberg.

The second Franconian rebel host came into being when peasants from the Oden Forest and the Neckar valley formed a league under the leadership of Wendel Hipler, a former secretary of the counts of Hohenlohe, and Jäcklein Rohrbach, a revolutionary serf from Böckingen. The insurgents adopted the Twelve Articles as their reform program and proceeded to Weinsberg, where occurred the infamous "murderous deed of Weinsberg." There Count Ludwig von Helfenstein, son-in-law of Emperor Maximilian, commanded a defensive force of about eighty men. On Easter Sunday (April 16) a troop of lansquenets and peasants captured the town, forced the count and his men to run a gauntlet of pikes, and then executed them. Until the vicious end of the war, this act of revolutionary terror was the most gruesome of the revolt. It sent a shudder of horror through the nobility and led numerous nobles and towns to surrender to the rebels without resistance. Shortly after the events of Weinsberg, the peasants chose the colorful knight, Götz von Berlichingen, as their new commander. To plan for the future, Wendel Hipler and Friedrich Weigandt, a former financial steward from Mainz, developed elaborate plans for a peasant parliament at Heilbronn. Peasant representatives from several regions met briefly at Heilbronn, but before the delegates could begin deliberations, the approach of the forces of the Swabian League dispersed them. Meanwhile the main body of the Oden Forest–Neckar valley army set up camp at Höchberg (near Würzburg) and joined in the siege of the Marienberg.

The third Franconian force was composed of insurgents from the area between the Main River and the Thuringian Forest. On April 12 insurgents occupied the monastery at Bildhausen and proceeded to plunder neighboring religious houses. Two men from Münnerstadt, Hans Schnabel and Hans Scharr, emerged as leaders. Only part of the Bildhausen group joined with the peasants at Würzburg, for a sudden attack by Landgrave Philip of Hesse diverted most of the insurgents to the north to defend their homes.

The combined armies at Würzburg amounted to about fifteen thousand men. The city itself put up no resistance, but the defenders of the Marienberg refused to surrender. The insurgents therefore decided to storm the fortress. Ater the first attempt failed, the rebels began an unsuccessful artillery siege, which lasted almost a month.

While this fruitless siege was going on, circumstances elsewhere were rapidly changing. After defeating the rebels in Württemberg at the Battle of Böblingen

(May 12), George Truchsess joined with Elector Louis of the Palatinate, the archbishop of Trier, and the bishop of Würzburg and began a march toward Würzburg. At word of the approaching troops, the Neckar valley force immediately left for home. The Oden Forest group retreated to the Tauber River, where, together with reinforcements, it faced the Swabian League on June 2, 1525, at the Battle of Königshofen. The rebels were completely routed. Two days later the remaining insurgents were defeated at the Battle of Ingolstadt. These two engagements ended the revolt in Franconia.

In Thuringia, the most important center for the revolt was the free imperial city of Mühlhausen. There in 1524 Thomas Müntzer and Henry Pfeiffer attempted to hasten reform through political pressure. They drafted the articles of Mühlhausen, which demanded a new council that would have salaried members with an unlimited term of office. The new regime was to govern justly according to the word of God, expose the crimes of the former council, and establish a new constitution. With a brief display of strength, the city council thwarted the attempted coup, rejected the articles, and expelled both Müntzer and Pfeiffer (September 27, 1524). However, through the winter the rebels again gained influence, and by February 1525 both Pfeiffer and Müntzer were back. They recruited supporters, and organized them in the "eternal league of God." In March 1525 the rebels succeeded in completely supplanting the old council with a new "eternal council." The plan was to establish a Christian democracy along the lines of the Mühlhausen articles.

In his sermons and writings, Müntzer taught that the elect, filled with spiritual enlightenment through the Holy Ghost, were obligated to remove political injustice and to establish the visible Kingdom of God on earth. If necessary, force was to be used. Encouraged by Müntzer's preaching, the Thuringian rebellion spread rapidly in the last week of April and the first week of May 1525. At its greatest extent, the insurrection stretched from the Hessian border in the west to the Saale River in the east, from the Thuringian Forest in the south to beyond the Harz Mountains in the north.

The army of Frankenhausen was the most important of the Thuringian rebel forces. It had well-articulated demands that called for the word of God to be preached freely; forests, streams, and meadows to be opened to all; princely titles and castles to be surrendered; and all pledged properties to be returned to the original owner. At first the princes were slow to respond to the peasants, but by mid-May Duke George of Saxony had joined forces with Landgrave Philip of Hesse to attack the rebels. Müntzer hurried to Frankenhausen with a force of three hundred men, but his reinforcements and his inspirational oratory could not save the day. The Battle of Frankenhausen (May 15, 1525) ended in a complete rout of the peasants. The victors arrested Müntzer, viciously tortured him, and later executed him, together with Henry Pfeiffer and fifty-two other rebel leaders. The defeat at Frankenhausen signaled the end of the Peasants' War in Thuringia.

Pacification came last to Austria. Open rebellion broke out in Brixen on May 9, 1525, and rapidly spread through the Etsch valley, the bishopric of Trent, and the area around Meran. The rebels plundered religious houses and noble residences and joined in opposition to tithe payments. The bishops of Brixen and Trent and the hated Salamanca (Archduke Ferdinand's Spanish favorite) had to flee the country. The peasants of Brixen elected Michael Gaismair as their leader. Formerly the secretary of the bishop of Brixen, Gaismair was a brilliant military leader, a progressive reformer, and a humanitarian. The Tyrolian rebels summarized their grievances in the articles of Meran. These sixty-two demands were moderate and evidenced Gaismair's influence. In negotiations with the rebels, Archduke Ferdinand whittled away at these points until the Tyrolian dissidents finally received only a few moderate concessions. Meanwhile Gaismair fled across the Italian border to return next year as a leader in the Salzburg revolt.

During February–March 1526 Gaismair drafted his famous *Landesordnung,* a utopian constitution based upon peasant demands and Reformation ideals. It called for an egalitarian Christian democratic republic that would care for the poor, ensure speedy justice for all, establish a new university, effect currency and tax reform, introduce sweeping agricultural innovations, expropriate mines and smelteries, and guarantee the free preaching of the word of God.

In April 1526 Gaismair made his plan public just as rebels at Salzburg were beginning a new disturbance. Gaismair became the leader of the Salzburg revolt. He attempted to put together an anti-Habsburg alliance with support from Venice, France, and various Swiss cities. However, with forces from the Swabian League, the archbishop of Salzburg, Cardinal Lang, was finally able to defeat the rebels by July 1526. Gaismair escaped to Italy, where Venice retained him as an adviser and anti-Habsburg agitator. In 1532 a henchman of the Habsburgs assassinated him. The defeat of the 1526 Salzburg uprising effectively ended the peasant disturbance in Austria.

Altogether the great revolt of 1524–1526 resulted in the deaths of approximately a hundred thousand peasants. Luther denounced the rebels, and thereby blunted the appeal of the Lutheran Reformation to much of the peasantry. Many former dissidents turned instead to the Anabaptist movement. Nevertheless the Protestant reformers and the peasant rebels together struck a serious blow against the remains of feudalism and against the feudalized Catholic church. The insurrection occasioned numerous reform programs, some utopian and some practical. But the defeat of the peasants showed that democratic social reforms stemming from popular impulses were not feasible in the Empire of the sixteenth century.

Works About: Janos Bak, ed., *The German Peasant War of 1525* (London, 1976); Peter Blickle, ed., *Revolte und Revolution in Europa, HZ,* Beiheft 4 (1975); Frederick Engels, *The Peasant War in Germany* (New York, 1966); Günther Franz, *Der dtsch. Bauernkrieg,* 10th ed. (Darmstadt, 1975) and *Quel. zur Gesch. des Bauernkrieges* (Munich, 1963); Abraham Friesen, *Reformation and Uto-*

pia: The Marxist Interpretation of the Reformation and its Antecedents (Mainz, 1974); Walther P. Fuchs, Günther Franz, and Otto Merx, eds., Akten zur Gesch. des Bauernkriegs in Mitteldeutschland, 2 vols. (Leipzig, Jena, 1923, 1934, 1942); Erich Gritsch, Reformer Without a Church (Philadelphia, 1967); Gerhard Heitz et al., eds., Der Bauer im Klassenkampf (Berlin, 1975); Walter Klaassen, Michael Gaismair: Revolutionary and Reformer (Leiden, 1978); Josef Macek, Der Tiroler Bauernkrieg (Berlin, 1965); David Sabean, "The Social Background to the Peasants' War of 1525 in Southern Upper Swabia" (Ph.D. diss., University of Wisconsin, 1969); B. Scribner and G. Benecke, eds., The German Peasant War, 1525; New Viewpoints (Winchester, Mass., 1979); Kyle C. Sessions, ed., Reformation and Authority: The Meaning of the Peasants' Revolt (Lexington, Mass., 1968); Hans–Ulrich Wehler, ed., Der dtsch. Bauernkrieg 1524–1526, Gesch. und Gesellschaft, Sonderheft 1 (1975); Rainer Wohlfeil, ed., Der Bauernkrieg 1524–1526 (Munich, 1975); Lowell Zuck, ed., Christianity and Revolution (Philadelphia, 1975).   L. P. Buck

See BERLICHINGEN; FERDINAND I; GAISMAIR; HUBMAIER; LUTHER; MÜNTZER; PHILIP OF HESSE; SWABIAN LEAGUE; TRUCHSESS.

PETERWARDEIN, BATTLE OF (1716), signaled the triumph of Charles VI, the Holy Roman emperor, over the Ottomans. The imperialists, especially Prince Eugene of Savoy, had long realized the growing danger from the Turks. The Ottoman Porte had declared war on Venice in 1714 and taken the Peloponnesus peninsula and the islands in the Aegean archipelago. Charles VI, fearing that the Turks intended to attack Hungary and undo the Karlowitz settlement, had allied with Venice in 1716. Eugene had begun to prepare the army and garrison the Hungarian forts as early as 1715 and to reorganize finances under the *Finanzconferenz* in 1716. When the Turks did not reply to the imperial demand to respect the Karlowitz settlement, war began (May 1716). Austria received only nominal support from the imperial princes and fought and won largely on her own resources. A large Turkish force under the grand vizier Silahdar Ali Pasha invaded Hungary, encountering the imperial forces at Peterwardein (Petrovaradin) in southern Hungary. Eugene with only seventy thousand troops annihilated the Ottoman army of one hundred twenty thousand. The Turkish cavalry fled toward Belgrade, leaving a dead grand vizier and the Janissaries on the field. Eugene then moved on and besieged Temesvár (Timisoara), which surrendered in mid-October; the last Ottoman enclave in Hungary, the Banat, was conquered. In 1717, Eugene crossed the Danube and forced Belgrade, the key to the Turkish invasion route, to capitulate. That city then became the outer bastion of imperial power.

Works About: A. von Arneth, Prinz Eugen von Savoyen, 3 vols. (Vienna, 1858); Max Braubach, Prinz Eugen von Savoyen, 5 vols. (Vienna, 1963–1965); Eugene-François, Feldzüge des Prinzen Eugen von Savoyen, 20 vols. (Vienna, 1876–1892); W. Hacker, "Das Regiment Hoch-und Deutschmeister, Prinz Eugen und der Türkenkrieg, 1716," Südostdeutsche Arch. 14 (1971); W. H. McNeill, Europe's Steppe Frontier, 1500–1800 (Chicago, 1964); E. Odenthal, Österreichs Türkenkrieg, 1716–1718 (Düsseldorf, 1938); Oswald Redlich, Das Werden einer Grossmacht, Österreich von 1700 bis 1740 (Vienna, 1942).   L. S. Frey and M. L. Frey

See CHARLES VI; EUGENE OF SAVOY; KARLOWITZ; PASSAROWITZ; PASSAU.

PETRARCH, FRANCESCO (1304–1374), poet and humanist imperial supporter, was born in Arezzo near Florence to a family of political exiles. His notary father was a White Guelph, who had been forced out of Florence by the Blacks at about the same time as Dante in the local variation of the larger pope versus emperor dispute. Life was not easy for the family of an exiled notary with imperial sympathies, but young Francesco managed to get four years of legal study at Montpellier in France and three years at Bologna. After his father's death in 1326, Petrarch, who had already developed a taste for classical literature, returned to Avignon, a lively intellectual center and the home of the papacy. There he made good friends of the influential Colonna family, who became generous patrons of the emerging poet and scholar. It was the Colonnas who underwrote his trip to the Netherlands and the Empire in 1333.

While in Avignon, Petrarch first saw the married woman whom he immortalized in his sonnets as Laura. She failed to return his passion, but she did provide sufficient inspiration for his poetry, which made him a seminal force in Italian literature. The poet also had a great passion for the city of Rome, which he eagerly visited in 1336. He was appalled by the Romans' seeming indifference to the glories of their heritage. His own love for the classics led him to search for ancient manuscripts, correspond with the ancient dead, and even write his own epic in the classic manner of Virgil, the *Africa*, about Scipio Africanus, the Roman victor over Hannibal. Petrarch has become known as one of the fathers of Italian humanism.

His fame as a poet and classical scholar was such that both the University of Paris and the Roman Senate offered him the laurel crown of the poet. Petrarch accepted the Roman offer and was crowned on April 8, 1341, in Rome, which also made him a citizen. His hopes for the revival of Rome led him to support the schemes of Cola di Rienzi. After the collapse of Rienzi's short-lived tribunate in 1347, Petrarch turned to the Holy Roman emperor, Charles IV, for the fulfillment of his political dream.

Petrarch, like Dante, wanted the emperor to restore Rome to its old greatness, to bring peace to all of Italy, and to impose the beneficent yoke of the *imperium* on all mankind. First the *imperium* must be transferred from the Germanic lands to its rightful home in Italy. In Petrarch's vision, it was the Roman people who had the right to elect the emperor. The emperor would be Italy's messiah, and a revived Italy would help renovate the entire Empire and recapture some of the lost grandeur of the days of Cicero and Virgil. More pragmatically, Charles seemed a reasonable alternative to the distressing political turmoil in Italy.

Petrarch initiated a correspondence in 1351 urging the emperor to intervene in Italy. Charles was skeptical about his chances for shifting the focal point of the Empire from the north to Italy; the city of Prague in Bohemia was his home. When the emperor finally made his appearance in Italy in 1354, he invited the poet to a personal interview. Traveling over icy roads, Petrarch arrived for his interview on December 15. Although refusing Charles' invitation to join his court at Prague, Petrarch did accompany him to Piacenza. It was clear that Charles IV was not ready to fulfill the poet's dream. Further disappointment came in 1355 when the emperor abruptly withdrew from Italy shortly after his coronation in Rome.

Petrarch continued to write Charles urging him to intervene in Italian affairs and finally visited the imperial court in Prague (June–July 1356). The emperor was still cautious, but the charming Italian made a great hit with the seventeen-year-old empress, Anna of Schweidniz, Chancellor John of Neumarkt, and others at court. The emperor rewarded Petrarch by making him a count of the Empire and a councillor. Charles later sent the poet a gold cup. Ironically when at long last the emperor did intervene militarily in Italian affairs, he did so in opposition to Petrarch's patrons, the Visconti of Milan. Petrarch did agree to serve as a mediator for the Visconti, but peace came through other channels. Despite the failure of his imperial hopes, the poet's last years were spent in relatively peaceful comfort on a little farm at Arqua, where he was tended by his daughter, Francesca.

Works By: *Letters from Petrarch*, tr. Morris Bishop (Bloomington, Ind., 1966); *Petrarch's Africa*, tr. T. C. Bergin and Alice S. Wilson (New Haven, 1977); *Petrarch: Selected Sonnets, Odes and Letters*, ed. T. C. Bergin (New York, 1966). **Works About:** C. C. Bayley, "Petrarch, Charles IV, and the 'Renovatio Imperii,' " *Spec.* 17 (1942): 323–41; T. C. Bergin, *Petrarch* (New York, 1970); Morris Bishop, *Petrarch and His World* (Bloomington, Ind., 1963); E. H. R. Tatham, *Francesco Petrarch*, 2 vols. (London, 1925–1926); E. H. Wilkins, *Life of Petrarch* (Chicago, 1961). *J. W. Zophy*

See BOCCACCIO; CHARLES IV; DANTE; WELF-WAIBLINGEN CONTROVERSY.

PEUTINGER, CONRAD (1465–1547), humanist statesman, was a native of Augsburg, a scion of an established family. A patrician, Conrad studied at Padua, Bologna, Florence, and Rome. In addition to obtaining a doctorate in law, Peutinger developed a passion for classical learning. Connected in business with the wealthy Fuggers and Welsers, he also began collecting coins, artwork, maps, and manuscripts. In the tradition of civic humanism, Peutinger in 1490 entered into the service of his home town and eventually became city secretary, an important administrative post. He also served Augsburg, the Swabian League, and Emperor Maximilian as a diplomat, making trips to Italy, Hungary, England, and the Low Countries, as well as to various imperial diets and other important political meetings. Peutinger also wrote speeches for Maximilian and advised him on cultural affairs. For his part, the emperor helped him with his collections from Roman and imperial history.

The leader of the Augsburg humanists, Peutinger supported Reuchlin in his controversy with Pfefferkorn. He was also initially sympathetic to Martin Luther and had him for dinner during his interviews with Cardinal Cajetan in 1518. Later he took a more Erasmian position and told Luther at Worms that he should retrace his steps and not leave the Church. Peutinger became increasingly concerned that the growing evangelical movement in Augsburg would hurt the city's political and economic position within the Empire.

Works By: Conrad Peutinger, *Briefwechsel*, ed. Erich König (Munich, 1923). **Works About:** H. M. Lier, "Peutinger," *ADB*, 25:561–68; Heinrich Lutz, *Conrad Peutinger: Beiträge zu einer Politischer Biographie* (Augsburg, 1958). *J. W. Zophy*

See AUGSBURG; CELTIS; FUGGER; HUMANISM; LUTHER; MAXIMILIAN I.

PHILIP OF HESSE (1504–1567), called the Magnanimous, lay counterpart to Martin Luther, and an antagonist of the Habsburgs, was born at Marburg, the son of William II, landgrave of Hesse, and Anna of Mecklenburg. Philip's youth was tumultuous. His father succumbed to syphilis when Philip was only four years old. His mother was barely able to hold the reins of government through a disputed regency in the face of a rebellious nobility. Little is known of his education. His parents' counselors surely taught him much, as may be seen in his continuing employment of these men until their deaths. Philip's first wife, Christine, daughter of Duke George of Saxony, bore him nine children, including his male heirs, William IV, Ludwig IV, Philip d. J., and George, among whom he divided his lands. Philip and his bigamous wife, Margaret von der Saale, had eight children.

Philip assumed his majority in 1518. He effectively met the challenges of the rebellious knights under Franz von Sickingen (culminating in 1522–1523) and the Peasants' Revolt (1524–1526), thus gaining security and prestige. Philip took a decisive step in July 1524 with the announcement of his conversion to the Lutheran teachings. His personal commitment became very important for imperial affairs. He played a leading role at the diet of Speyer (1526) and with its recess began in earnest to administer a new Church-state settlement. Hesse became a sovereign state with a separate Protestant territorial church, which from the beginning emphasized discipline and a synodal structure (phenomena usually associated with the later reformed churches). Lutheran educational and charitable promotions were administered, resulting in the establishment of state schools, hospitals, and common chests. Various former Church properties were secularized to support these and other activities. Philip's commitment was particularly significant because Hesse was one of the first princely states to take these steps, and it lay geographically between the Habsburgs' Austrian stronghold and their tightly controlled lowland holdings. The defense of Protestantism was also intimately tied to Hessian political objectives. Hesse was vulnerable to a growth of Habsburg power in the central Rhine area because of its insecure position in the recently acquired wealthy counties of Katzenelnbogen. These counties were also claimed by the rulers of Nassau-Dillenberg, who were traditionally supported by the Habsburgs, and had remained Catholic.

Philip recognized the need for a political mechanism to defend the Protestant position as early as 1526. He became the major driving force for a large European-wide alliance against any Habsburg-Catholic threat, culminating in the powerful Schmalkaldic League in 1531. Philip used the infamous Pack affair (a false allegation that Catholic princes had agreed to exterminate the Lutherans) to further negotiations for the alliance that were otherwise faltering in 1528, a relatively stable year. Philip, not Ulrich Zwingli, was the leader in attempts to forge an arrangement with the Swiss cities. The Marburg colloquy (1529) was Philip's attempt to settle religious and political differences between the parties. Philip's boldest achievement was the restoration of the Protestant Duke Ulrich of Württemberg. He gave the dethroned Ulrich sanctuary in 1526 and around 1530 made the necessary treaty arrangements for a successful campaign against the Habsburg holders of Ulrich's duchy. In the spring of 1534, Philip led an army into Württemberg and in a lightning campaign successfully compelled the Habsburgs to recognize Ulrich's sovereignty.

The main internal problem that Philip faced was the rise of radical Protestantism or Anabaptism in his territories. Hessian radicals actively criticized the established church for what they claimed was a lack of discipline and strict morality. This was a matter that the state had emphasized in Hesse, but of which the landgrave was not exemplary. Philip employed the Strasbourg reformer Martin Bucer to alleviate the pressure from the left wing. Acts demanding stricter enforcement of discipline and a more formal, methodical confirmation process were the major tools introduced under Bucer to appease the radicals.

Philip's greatest weakness was his wayward marital life and ultimate bigamy. His moral problem came to a head in 1539 when he suddenly developed the symptoms of syphilis, recalling his father's terminating experience. Philip's personal crisis combined with a scarcity of food, the Anabaptist threat, and coincidental cosmic occurrences to create an aura of divine punishment. Philip committed bigamy in 1540 with the consent of Luther, Melanchthon, and Bucer in an attempt to alleviate the situation. However, Philip's bigamy embarrassed the Protestant movement and left him culpable before imperial law, thus increasing his problems. After 1540, the landgrave ceased to be a bold, dynamic leader. The disastrous Schmalkaldic War and Philip's consequent imprisonment (1547–1552) limited his influence to strictly Hessian affairs. Philip's most remarkable characteristic was an irenic, compromising personality, so rare in the sixteenth century. When it was commonly believed that only people of the same faith could live peaceably together, Philip allowed both Zwinglian and Lutheran pastors to preach. No one was executed for religious reasons, and Philip refused to institute even the major excommunication with temporal punishment.

Works By: *Briefwechsel Landgraf Philipp des Grossmütigen von Hessen mit Bucer*, ed. Max Lenz, 3 vols. (Leipzig, 1880–1891); *Politisches Archiv des Landgrafen Philipp des Grossmütigen von Hessen*, Hessisches Staatsarchiv, Marburg an der Lahn (microfilm copy at the Center for Reformation Research, St. Louis, Missouri).

Works About: Kurt Dülfer, *Die Packschen Händel: Darstellung und Quellen* (Marburg, 1958); Ekkehart Fabian, *Die Entstehung des Schmalkaldischen Bundes und Seiner Verfassung 1524/29–*

1531/35 (Tübingen, 1962); Herbert Grundmann, *Landgraf Philipp von Hessen auf dem Augsburger Reichstag 1530* (Gütersloh, 1959); Alton O. Hancock, "Philipp of Hesse's View of the Relationship of Prince and Church," *ChH* 35 (1966): 157–69; Walter Heinemeyer,"Landgraf Philipps des Grossmütigen Weg in die Politik," *Hessischen Jb. für Landesgesch.* 5 (1955): 176–92; Hans J. Hillerbrand, *Landgrave Philipp of Hesse* (St. Louis, 1967); *Urkundlichen Quel. zur hessischen Reformationsgesch.* ed. Günther Franz, 4 vols. (Marburg, 1954).   *W. J. Wright*

See CHARLES V; HOMBERG SYNOD; KRAFFT; LAMBERT; LÜDER; LUTHER; MARBURG COLLOQUY; SICKINGEN; SCHMALKALDIC LEAGUE; SCHMALKALDIC WAR; SPEYER, DIET OF 1526; ULRICH OF WÜRTTEMBERG; ZWINGLI.

PHILIP OF SWABIA-HOHENSTAUFEN, (c.1176–1208), youngest of the five sons of Frederick I and Beatrice of Burgundy, was originally destined for an ecclesiastical career, but in 1193 he gave that up in favor of a political life. Two years later his brother Henry VI made him duke of Tuscany and in 1196 duke of Swabia. In 1197 Philip married Irene, also called Maria, daughter of Isaac Angelus of Constantinople. Under obscure circumstances, probably because of an encroachment on papal territory, he suffered excommunication, which put him in the Church's bad graces at the crisis of Henry VI's death in 1197. Back in Germany Philip initially struggled to maintain the succession rights of Henry's infant son, Frederick, whom he and the princes had previously acknowledged as king of the Romans. Now the boy's absence in Sicily, his tender age, and the challenge of an anti-Hohenstaufen faction organized by Adolf of Cologne convinced Philip that he should accept the kingship himself, as urged by influential princes in an election at Mühlhausen on March 8, 1198. At Mainz on September 8 the archbishop of Tarantaise performed the coronation ceremony. The unusual circumstances of Philip's election and coronation provided pretexts for his foes to deny their validity while promoting their own candidate, Otto of Brunswick. The majority of the princes and the French king supported Philip, yet he could not win a decisive victory in the early fighting.

The Hohenstaufen faction considered the election dispute a purely German affair, but Otto IV and the foreign allies of both candidates begged for Pope Innocent III's intervention. With some show of reluctance, the pope entered the dispute. He reasoned that Philip was unsuitable because of his excommunication and his perjury in breaking his oath to Frederick and because the Hohenstaufen dynasty had previously threatened the papacy. Hence on March 1, 1201, Innocent declared his support for Otto and soon thereafter put Philip and his followers under the ban of the Church. Some of Philip's adherents fell away, but other princes—Adolf of Cologne, Henry of Brabant, and Henry of the Palatinate—switched from Otto to Philip. On January 6, 1205, the archbishop of Cologne recrowned Philip in Aachen, thus correcting the defects of place and person in the original ceremony. Slowly Philip's military position improved. On July 27, 1206, at Wassenberg near Cologne, he defeated Otto and drove him from the Rhineland.

Simultaneously Philip opened negotiations with Innocent III. Philip had already offered concessions while the pope recognized the impending collapse of Otto's cause. On November 1, 1207, he lifted the ban against Philip as a prelude to reconciliation. Details of a compromise were agreed upon, including marriage between one of Philip's four daughters and the pope's nephew. Before the reconciliation was officially announced, however, Philip was assassinated at Bamberg on June 21, 1208, by Otto of Wittelsbach, enraged at losing to Innocent's relative the princess previously promised to him. Philip left no sons to continue the struggle against Otto of Brunswick.

Works About: Friedrich Baethgen, "Die Excommunication Philipps von Schwaben," *Mediaevalia, Aufsätze, Nachrufe, Besprechungen,* 1 (Stuttgart, 1960): 85–92; and F. Kempf, ed., *Regestrum Innocentii III papae super negotio Romani imperii* (Rome, 1947) and F. Kempf, "Der *favor apostolicus* bei der Wahl Friedrich Barbarossas und im dtsch. Thronstreit (1198–1208)," in C. Bauer et al., eds., *Speculum Historiale, Gesch. im Spiegel von Geschichtsschreibung und Geschichtsdeutung* (Munich, 1965), pp. 469–78; R. Schwemer, *Innocenz III. und die dtsch. Kirche während des Thronstreites, 1198–1208* (Strasbourg, 1882); E. Winkelmann, *Philipp von Schwaben und Otto IV. von Braunschweig,* vol. 1: *König Philipp von Schwaben 1197–1208* (Leipzig, 1873).   R. H. Schmandt

See DISPUTED ELECTION; FREDERICK II; INNOCENT III; OTTO IV.

PICCOLOMINI, OTTAVIO (1599–1656), count and military leader during the Thirty Years War, was born at Florence and died at Vienna. He was an offspring of a Sienese family that had produced two popes during the Renaissance, Pius II (1458–1464) and Pius III (1503). Ottavio was barely seventeen years old when he began his military career as a soldier in the Spanish army in northern Italy. During the Bohemian revolt, he and his older brother Aeneas were each in command of a regiment of cuirassiers sent by Grand Duke Cosimo II to support Emperor Ferdinand II. The two brothers fought under General Marradas in southern Bohemia; Aeneas lost his life in combat in August 1619. Ottavio fought in the Battle of the White Mountain (November 1620) under Bucquoy. He then served under Carafa (1623), rejoined the Spanish briefly, and, through the mediations of Ramboldo Collalto, president of the *Hofkriegsrat,* became a captain of Wallenstein's bodyguard (1627). He fought in the Mantuan War (1629–1630), was briefly interned as a hostage at Ferrara (until September 1631), won honors in the Battle of Lützen, and was promoted to major general (1632). Throughout these years he maintained close contacts with the Spanish government and the papal curia. He initiated and headed the conspiracy that led to Wallenstein's assassination (1633–1634). The emperor awarded Piccolomini for his services by elevating him to the rank of field marshal and giving him as a present 100,000 imperial dollars and the large estate of Nachod in Bohemia.

Piccolomini again distinguished himself on the battlefield at Nördlingen (1634). He won the greatest military triumph of his career at Diedenhofen (Thionville) where he destroyed the army of the inept Marquis de Feuquières

(July 7, 1639). For this victory, the emperor named him to the imperial privy council (where, however, Piccolomini never carried much influence) and, in addition, the king of Spain awarded him with the duchy of Amalfi. After the imperial defeat at Breitenfeld (1642), he reentered Spanish service. He was honored with the Order of the Golden Fleece (1643) but was not very successful in defending Spanish interests in the Netherlands. He ended the Thirty Years War as commander-in-chief of the imperial forces, a post to which he had aspired for years but which had eluded him until 1648.

Piccolomini distinguished himself by his personal bravery and organizational talents. He also had considerable diplomatic ability. As a subordinate to Wallenstein, he handled many of the general's negotiations. After the war he led the imperial delegation to the congress that met at Nuremberg (1649–1650) to determine the execution of the Peace of Westphalia. He was made an imperial prince (*Reichsfürst*) in 1650; four years later he was admitted to the curia of princes of the imperial diet. Piccolomini married late (1651) and died without direct heirs.

Works By: Friedrich Parnemann, ed., *Der Briefwechsel der Generale Gallas, Aldringen und Piccolomini im Januar und Februar 1634* (Berlin, 1911). **Works About:** Otto Elster, *Piccolomini Studien* (Leipzig, 1911); Hermann Hallwich, ed., *Briefe und Akten zur Gesch. Wallensteins,* 4 vols. (Vienna, 1912); and "Piccolomini," *ADB,* 26:95–103; Henry F. Schwarz, *The Imperial Privy Council in the Seventeenth Century* (Cambridge, Mass., 1943), pp. 318–20; Heinrich Ritter von Srbik, *Wallensteins Ende* (Salzburg, 1952).   *Bodo Nischan*

See FERDINAND II; PIUS II; THIRTY YEARS WAR; WALLENSTEIN, ALBERT.

PIRCKHEIMER, CHARITAS (1467–1532), abbess of the Order of the Poor Clares in Nuremberg (1503–1532), became the arch defender of her convent's rights and of the monastic life when the imperial city of Nuremberg accepted the Lutheran Reformation in 1525. Charitas opposed the city council's efforts to force the nuns to become Lutheran and to disestablish their community, thereby impeding the council's attempt to unify the ecclesiastical structure of the city within its jurisdiction. The steadfastness of the Clares while the majority of other religious communities in the city were abandoning their houses was imbedded in the tradition to emulate the foundress of the order, St. Clare of Assisi, in the history of the order in the city itself, and in the life and character of Charitas Pirckheimer. It was her piety, learning, and intellectual depth— evidence of the influence of the *devotio moderna* and Christian humanism—that provided the catalyst for a determined resistance against the dissolution of the convent.

Mature and educated beyond her years, twelve-year-old Charitas (born Barbara) Pirckheimer, the eldest child of a pious and distinguished Nuremberg patrician family, chose to enter the contemplative Poor Clare cloister to become a choir nun and to continue her education. Here Charitas developed and expanded her intellectual capabilities and practiced the piety her devout parents had taught her. The nuns not only led active spiritual lives but eagerly cultivated the Scriptures and humanistic disciplines. Little is known of her early years in the convent except that as mistress of novices, she was instrumental in carrying on the religious instruction of the sisters and in promoting their understanding of the Mass, the breviary, Scripture, and the works of the church fathers. Schooling in theology, Scripture, and in the reading and writing of Latin became an integral part of the program in the novitiate. The constant initiative to keep the sense that learning was for the honor and glory of God came from within the convent walls.

When Charitas was elected mother superior in 1503, she continued this pedagogical tradition and broadened the education of the nuns by extensively instructing them in the humanistic methods. Her contacts with the clerical humanists and with the circle of friends surrounding her famous brother, Willibald Pirckheimer, strengthened the role of the convent in the intellectual community of the city and the Empire. Yet these affiliations did not take her or the cloister outside the discipline of the rule.

The conflict of 1525 between the convent and the council was not merely a segment of the Reformation in Nuremberg but a chapter in the "waning of the Middle Ages." It was a struggle that represented the best of the past meeting the best of the present. The city council was not removing a decrepit religious community from its environment but a cloister that lived according to the standards expounded by contemporary reformers, in particular, Erasmus of Rotterdam. Instead of using the convent as an example for other religious to follow, the council set out to destroy it, and it encountered the resourceful actions of the abbess.

Subjected to numerous indignities and ridicule, the Clares stood firm and rebuffed the council's harsh and unfair actions. As abbess, Charitas could have chosen the road of least resistance, as did the other monastic leaders in Nuremberg, by consenting to dissolution and to the transfer of the dispossessed. The strength of her resistance came from the traditions of her order, mysticism, the *devotio moderna,* and the concept of *imitatio*. Charitas had been taught to follow in the footsteps of St. Clare of Assisi and was therefore predisposed to act in a certain fashion. Because she was psychologically conditioned to imitate the foundress of the order, she entered the conflict with the council in the hope of saving her convent.

Although the Nuremberg council ultimately succeeded in dissolving the cloister of St. Clare in 1590, sixty-five years after the Reformation of the city, the Clares were also successful in that they never left their cloister. As long as they lived, they kept the traditions of their order alive in Nuremberg. Doomed to dissolution, this community nonetheless continued to represent the finest traditions of medieval monasticism in a reformed city.

Works By: Joseph Pfanner, ed., *Das Gebetbuch der Caritas Pirckheimer*, vol. 1: *Die Denkwür-digkeiten*, vol. 2: *Briefe*, vol. 3 (Landshut, 1961–1966). **Works About:** Sigmund Beale, "The World of Charitas Pirckheimer," *Review of Religion* 15 (1950): 128–43; Franz Binder, *Charitas Pirckheimer*, 2d ed. (Freiburg im Breigau, 1878); J. Kist, *Charitas Pirckheimer* (Bamberg, 1948); Gerta Krabbel, *Caritas Pirckheimer* (Munster, 1947); Wilhelm Loose, *Aus dem Leben der Charitas Pirckheimer* (Dresden, 1870); C. B. Ryan, "Charitas Pirckheimer" (Ph.D. diss., Ohio State University, 1976).   *C. B. Ryan*

See ERASMUS; HUMANISM; NUREMBERG; PIRCKHEIMER, WILLIBALD.

PIRCKHEIMER, WILLIBALD (1470–1530), German humanist and Nuremberg patrician, was born in Eichstätt, where his father was serving as a legal adviser to the bishop. His early development was almost entirely outside Nuremberg. He traveled extensively with his father on diplomatic missions and was later trained in military practices at the court of the bishop of Eichstätt. Following his father's advice, he studied law in Italy at the universities of Padua and Pavia from 1488 to 1495, although, as evidenced in his mastery of Greek, he was more interested in humanistic studies than in law. At his father's request, he returned to Nuremberg and, in 1496, following the customary procedure for the patricians, was elected to the ruling city council. With the exception of a brief resignation, he remained on the council until 1523.

Pirckheimer's background and training prepared him well for a career in the city council. In 1499, as a result of his knightly training and military experience, he was made leader of the contingent of troops Nuremberg contributed to Emperor Maximilian in his war with the Swiss Confederation. Pirckheimer was involved directly in only two serious military encounters and later wrote a literary description of this campaign (*Bellum Suitense*). He was also rewarded by the emperor by being appointed an imperial councillor. In 1502, Pirckheimer again provided military leadership in Nuremberg's conflict with the margrave of Brandenburg.

The most important function Pirckheimer performed for the city council was as a diplomat. His judicial knowledge, oratorical abilities, and splendid memory served him well. He was a respected negotiator and was often entrusted with ambassadorial journeys in the foreign affairs of the city. In 1505 he and Anton Tetzel represented Nuremberg at the diet of Cologne, where, in the presence of the emperor, he successfully affirmed Nuremberg's claims to possessions acquired in the Bavarian War of Succession of 1504. In its dispute with the margrave of Brandenburg over territorial rights and jurisdictions, the council often relied on Pirckheimer's diplomatic fervor. He was most active in defending Nuremberg's interests against the Franconian landed nobility. In 1514 he was the city's representative at the emperor's court at Innsbruck, and in 1519 he went to Switzerland to gain an alliance with the Swiss Confederation. In addition to his diplomatic activity, Pirckheimer was also intimately involved in the day-to-day business of governing Nuremberg. He was especially preoccupied with the city's educational system.

In the midst of pursuing an active political career, Pirckheimer managed to continue his humanistic concerns. He did, of course, achieve renown primarily because of his literary humanistic activities. Contemporaries placed him in the company of Erasmus and Reuchlin as a group from whom one might expect a "better and greater future for all Christendom." The extent and nature of his correspondence alone attest to his stature and fame in Germany and Europe in the first three decades of the sixteenth century. He acted as a patron of the arts, especially for his close friend Albrecht Dürer. His house was usually filled with guests, including princes, scholars, and theologians. Most of Pirckheimer's literary activity consisted of translations from Greek into Latin and from Greek and Latin into German. His translations include the dialogues of Lucian, the moral treatises of Plutarch, works of Xenophon, Aristophanes, Thucydides, Aristotle, Galen, Ptolemy, and especially the Greek Church fathers and other Greek theologians, particularly his favorite author, Gregory of Nazianzus. Like Luther, Pirckheimer maintained that translation must render the sense of the original, not the exact wording. His own writings include a satire in praise of gout, the *Apologia seu Laus Podagrae*, his single major original composition, a historical geography of Germany, a brief autobiography, and numerous treatises on theological and moral issues.

The last decade of his life was embittered by the controversies of the Reformation. Initially he defended Luther and in a letter to Pope Adrian VI in 1522, Pirckheimer blamed John von Eck and the Dominicans for the religious turmoil in Germany. Even before the Reformation, Pirckheimer, in company with many other humanists, had attacked the scholastic theologians and called for ecclesiastical and theological reform. But the aristocratic patrician came to feel that the supporters of Luther were indulging in excesses that threatened the foundations of civilization. Two controversies especially determined his rejection of the Reformation after 1525. The attempt by the city council of Nuremberg to dissolve the monasteries and convents led Pirckheimer, who had a number of female relatives in various convents, to defend monastic life. In a dispute with John Oecolampadius over the interpretation of the eucharistic sacrament, he clearly departed from Luther. "It is frivolous to fall away from the old church," he wrote. His retreat to Catholicism was not complete, however; he continued until his death in 1530 to attack the weaknesses of his old faith.

Works By: Willehad Paul Eckert and Christoph von Imhoff, *Willibald Pirckheimer, Dürers Freund* (Cologne, 1971); Melchior Goldast and Konrad Rittershausen, eds., *Opera politica, historica, philologica et epistolica* (Frankfurt, 1610, rpr., 1969); Emil Reicke, *Willibald Pirckheimers Briefwechsel*, 2 vols. (Munich, 1940–1956). **Works About:** Hans Rupprich, "Willibald Pirckheimer: A Study of His Personality as a Scholar," in Gerald Strauss, ed., *Pre-Reformation Germany* (London, 1972), pp. 380–435; Jackson Spielvogel, "Willibald Pirckheimer's Domestic Activity for Nürnberg," *Moreana* 25 (1970), 17–29, and "Patricians in Dissension: A Case Study from Sixteenth-Century Nürnberg," in L. Buck and J. Zophy, eds., *The Social Hist. of the Reformation* (Columbus, 1972), pp. 73–90; Lewis Spitz, "Pirckheimer-Speculative Patrician," in *The Religious Renaissance of the German Humanists* (Cambridge, Mass., 1963), pp. 155–96.   *J. J. Spielvogel*

See ADRIAN VI; DÜRER; ECK; HUMANISM; LUTHER; MAXIMILIAN I; PIRCKHEIMER, CHARITAS; SWISS WARS OF INDEPENDENCE.

PIUS II (1405–1464, pope from 1458) was an Italian pope who spent much of his prepapal career in Germany, and his papacy was fatally involved in German affairs. Born Enea Silvio de' Piccolomini of a noble Ghibelline Sienese family at Corsignana, he studied at Siena and Florence. He took service as a secretary to an Italian bishop and went with him to the Council of Basel in 1432. During the next several years, Enea Silvio worked as secretary to various prelates attending the council. In 1436 he became an official of the council itself and became a prominent partisan of conciliar supremacy in the confrontation with Pope Eugenius IV. After the council elected Felix V as antipope in 1439, Enea Silvio became his secretary. In July 1442, while on an embassy to an imperial diet at Frankfurt am Main, Enea Silvio was crowned poet laureate by King Frederick III and invited to join the imperial chancery.

Enea Silvio's service in the court of Frederick III in Vienna and Wiener Neustadt coincided with a spiritual midlife crisis. In late 1444, he had decided to become a priest, though he was not ordained until 1446. In 1447 he was made bishop of Trieste. Enea Silvio was a major figure in the negotiations between Frederick III and Pope Eugenius IV, which culminated in the Concordat of Vienna in 1448 and Frederick's imperial coronation in 1452. Enea Silvio also undertook important missions for Frederick to Milan and Bohemia. In 1450 he became bishop of Siena. The Turkish conquest of Constantinople in 1453 made Enea Silvio an ardent partisan of crusade.

In May 1455, Enea Silvio went to Rome to stay, and he was created a cardinal in December 1456. He worked in the curia as a specialist for central European matters. He was elected pope on August 19, 1458, as an Italian candidate promoted to counter a serious French bid to recover the papacy.

Pius II worked obsessively to mobilize the resources of Christendom for a great crusade against Islam, but the problems of central Europe continued to plague him. Efforts to settle the status of the Hussites in Bohemia led nowhere, and Pius finally excommunicated the Bohemian king, George of Podiebrady. The opposition to heavy papal taxes by the archbishop of Mainz, Dieter von Isenburg, led to public denunciations of Roman financial exactions. Pius promoted another candidate for the see of Mainz, but he was installed only after a devastating war in the Rhineland. Finally a power struggle in the Tyrol between the Habsburg duke Sigismund and the bishop of Brixen, Nicholas of Cusa, sparked princely protests against clerical meddling in secular politics. Pius attempted to quash dispute and shift public interest to his crusade project by various acts, most notably by the publication of the bull *Execrabilis* (January 18, 1460). *Execrabilis* threatened anyone who appealed from a pope to a council with excommunication. In another bull of 1463, Pius formally retracted the antipapal opinions that he himself had held as a younger man, to prevent enemies from quoting Enea Silvio against Pius.

Enea Silvio de' Piccolomini was one of the most gifted writers of the fifteenth century, and he was virtually the first Italian to interest himself in central Europe. He wrote histories of the Council of Basel, the Hussite wars, and the early reign of Frederick III. His *Commentaries* are a rare personal narrative of mid-fifteenth-century politics and culture. His defense of papal politics toward the German church, the *Germania*, made him a major target of hostility in the Empire during the Reformation.

Works By: Albert R. Baca, tr., *Selected Letters of Aeneas Silvius Piccolomini*, San Fernando Valley State College Renaissance Ed., no. 2 (Northridge, Cal., 1969); Florence Alden Gragg, tr., and Leona C. Gabel, ed., *The Commentaries of Pius II*, Smith College Studies in History, vol. 22, nos. 1–2, vol. 25, nos. 1–4, vols. 30, 35, 43 (Northampton, Mass., 1937–1957), abridged as *Memoirs of a Renaissance Pope* (New York, 1959); Denys Hay and W. K. Smith, tr. and ed., *De gestis concilii Basiliensis commentariorum libri II* (Oxford, 1967). **Works About:** A. Bachmann, *ADB*, 26:206–19; Rosamond J. Mitchell, *The Laurels and the Tiara: Pope Pius II* (London, 1962); Ludwig Pastor, *The History of the Popes*, tr. Frederick Antrobus (St. Louis, 1898), vol. 3; John B. Toews, "The View of Empire in Aeneas Silvius Piccolomini," *Traditio* 24 (1968): 471–87; Georg Voight, *Enea Silvio de' Piccolomini*, 3 vols. (Berlin, 1856–1862); Klaus Voigt, *Ital. Ber. aus dem spät-mittelalterlichen Dtschld.*, Kieler hist. Stud., vol. 17 (Stuttgart, 1973), pp. 77–153; Berthe Widmer, *Enea Silvio Piccolomini in der sittlichen und politischen Entscheidung*, Basler Beitr. zur Geschwiss., vol. 88 (Basel, 1963).   *S. W. Rowan*

See FREDERICK III; NICHOLAS OF CUSA.

POLISH SUCCESSION, WAR OF THE (1733–1735), was a minor European conflict initiated with the death of King Augustus II the Strong Wettin (1670–1733) of Poland. Stanislaus I Leszcynski (1677–1766), former king (1706–1716) forced out by Russia, was elected by a majority of Polish nobles in September 1733 and backed by France through his daughter Marie, queen of Louis XV, and later Spain and Sardinia. But Augustus' son, who had succeeded his father as Frederick Augustus II, elector of Saxony, was elected by a minority of nobles as Augustus III (1696–1763) and was backed by Holy Roman Emperor Charles VI (1685–1740) and by Czarina Anna (1693–1740) of Russia. Stanislaus was besieged in Danzig by the Russians and Saxons (February–June 1734), but warfare between the major powers continued on the Rhine and in Italy. The Rhine fighting between the French and Austrians, the latter under the elderly Prince Eugene of Savoy (1663–1736), was desultory, the French finally taking Philippsburg. In Italy the fighting was harder though indecisive. By the Treaty of Vienna (October 3, 1735, ratified in 1738), Augustus kept Poland; Stanislaus retained the title of king but was given the duchy of Lorraine, Francis of Lorraine (1708–1765), later Holy Roman emperor, being compensated with the grand duchy of Tuscany; and Austria ceded Naples and Sicily to Spain, in return for the latter's claim to Parma.

Works About: C. W. Böttiger and T. Flathe, *Gesch. des Kurstaates und Königreichs Sachsen* (Gotha, 1867–1873); R. Röpel, *Polen um die Mitte des 18. Jahrhunderts* (Gotha, 1876).

A. H. Ganz

See CHARLES VI; EUGENE OF SAVOY; FRANCIS I; FREDERICK AUGUSTUS.

PRAGMATIC SANCTION (1713), or Pactum Mutuae Cessionis et Successionis, was first formulated in 1703 and amended in 1713 by Holy Roman emperor Charles VI. In essence the pact declared that all of the Habsburg possessions were indivisible and hereditary in both the male and the female line. Both Charles and his elder brother Joseph had agreed to abide by this pact during the reign of their father, Leopold I. If Archduke Charles, Leopold's youngest son, was successful in winning the Spanish Empire (War of the Spanish Succession, 1701–1713), Leopold would recognize the separation of the Spanish line from the German-Austrian-Hungarian-Bohemian line represented by the eldest son, Joseph. If either of the two lines should become extinct, one line should succeed the other. Although in both the Spanish line and the Austrian line, the male line had precedence, the right of female succession was also recognized.

After the deaths of his father and his brother, Charles VI modified the pact and made it public. Charles wanted to ensure that his territories would pass undivided to his children in both the male and female line and to establish the precedence of his own line over that of his brother. Both of Joseph's daughters, Maria Joseph, who married Frederick Augustus II of Saxony (1719), and Maria Amalia, who married Charles Albert of Bavaria (1722), had formally renounced their claims to the throne when they married. Only if Charles' line died out would Joseph's children have the right to inherit. As the years passed, it became apparent that Charles would have no male heirs. His only son, Leopold, had died at birth in 1716. His heir, Maria Theresa, was born the following year. The problem of securing recognition for Maria Theresa's succession preoccupied Charles. Charles attempted to obtain the consent not only of his crown lands but also of foreign powers. The process of gaining acceptance by the various estates was slow and cumbersome, but in the 1720s the various estates assented: in 1720 Austria and Bohemia, in 1721 Croatia, in 1722–1723 Hungary and Transylvania, and in 1724–1725 the Austrian Netherlands and Lombardy. In order to persuade the European powers to accept the Pragmatic Sanction, Charles VI was forced to make concessions. He abandoned the Ostend Company in exchange for England's assent. He supported Frederick Augustus' candidacy to the Polish throne in order to obtain Saxony's assent. All of the major European powers recognized the Pragmatic Sanction in the 1720s and the 1730s. The problem of ensuring that the Habsburg lands as an indivisible whole would pass to his daughter obsessed Charles to the exclusion of everything else; he refused to listen to Prince Eugene of Savoy who advised him to build up his army and his treasury and not to rely on written guarantees. Unfortunately Charles did not heed Eugene's advice. Charles VI died in October 1740. In less than two months, his daughter, Maria Theresa, young and inexperienced, found herself at war with Prussia, Bavaria, Saxony, Spain, and France (War of the Austrian Succession). Although many of the foreign powers had repudiated their pledges to respect the Pragmatic Sanction, the Habsburg estates accepted Maria Theresa as the legitimate heir and recognized the indivisibility of the Habsburg lands; this in itself was no mean achievement for Charles.

Works About: Hajo Holborn, *A Hist. of Modern Germany, 1648–1840* (New York, 1969); Karl A. Roider Jr., "The Pragmatic Sanction," *Austrian Hist. Yearbook* 8:153–158; Gustav Truba, *Grundlagen der Pragmatischen Sanktion* (Leipzig, 1912) and *Gesch. des Thronfolgerechtes in aller habsburgischen Ländern bis zur Pragmatischen Sanktion Kaiser Karls VI, 1156–1732* (Heidelberg, 1923), and ed.   *L. S. Frey and M. L. Frey*

See AUSTRIAN SUCCESSION; CHARLES VI; EUGENE OF SAVOY; MARIA THERESA.

PUFENDORF, SAMUEL (1632–1694), legal theorist and historian, was born at Chemnitz in Saxony to a family that had produced a long line of Lutheran pastors. Although the family had only limited means, young Samuel was sent to school and in 1650 went to the University of Leipzig for six years. At Leipzig, he turned from theology to the study of Roman law, as well as history and philology. Pufendorf then moved on to Jena, where he lived in the home of Erhard Weigel, a well-known mathematician and physicist. Disdaining the existing state of professional scholarship, he decided not to take a doctorate.

Through the influence of his brother, Samuel secured the post of tutor in the household of Peter Julius Coyet, a Swedish nobleman who in 1658 went on diplomatic business to Copenhagen. While there, Pufendorf was taken prisoner by the Danes after a Swedish attack and spent eight months in prison meditating on the works of Thomas Hobbes and Hugo Grotius. His next two years were spent at the Hague, where he began to publish works on legal theory. His scholarship attracted favorable notice from Elector Charles Louis of the Palatinate, who awarded him a professorship at the University of Heidelberg.

While a professor at Heidelberg, Pufendorf did his main work on the constitution of the Holy Roman Empire, *De statu Imperii Germanici* (1664 or 1665). This book came to be considered the outstanding systematic work on imperial public law, although it was considered highly controversial and was eventually banned by the imperial censor. Pufendorf had not signed his own name to the work but came to be generally recognized as its author. He argued that Germany was not an aristocracy but a political entity located midway between a monarchy and a system where supreme power was exercised only by a general agreement of the estates, or a *systemata civitatum*. Although critical of the Habsburgs, he did not push for the immediate abolition of the office of emperor.

In 1668 Pufendorf journeyed to Sweden to accept the chair of natural law at the new University of Lund. He spent much of the next twenty years of his life in Sweden, serving for a time as the royal historian in Stockholm writing a history of that country from the reign of King Gustavus II to Charles X Gustavus. His other works included *De Jure Naturae et Gentium Libri Acto* (1672), which argued that all men have a right to equality and freedom. Although criticized by Leibniz, Pufendorf enjoyed a European-wide reputation. In 1688 now a baron, he returned to the Empire as a historian to the elector of Brandenburg at Berlin, and it was there that he died.

Works By: *De jure naturae et gentium libri acto* (London, 1688, 1934); *De officio hominis et civis juxta legem naturalim libri duo* (New York, 1927); *Elementorum jurisprudentiae universalis libri duo* (Oxford, 1931); *The Present State of Germany* (London, 1690). **Works About:** Harry Bresslau, "Pufendorf," *ADB,* 26:701–11; Hans Gross, *Empire and Sovereignty: A Hist. of the Public Law Literature in the Holy Roman Empire, 1599–1804* (Chicago, 1975); Leonard Krieger, *The Politics of Discretion: Pufendorf and the Acceptance of Natural Law* (Chicago, 1965); Hans Welzel, *Die Naturrechtslehre Samuel Pufendorfs* (Munich, 1958); Erik Wolf, *Grotius, Pufendorf, Thomasius: Drie Kapitel zu Gestaltgesch. der Rechtswissenschaft* (Tübingen, 1927).   *J. W. Zophy*

See FREDERICK III, ELECTOR; FREDERICK WILLIAM; LEIBNIZ.

r

RAINALD OF DASSEL (c. 1118–1167), Frederick Barbarossa's chancellor and archbishop of Cologne, was the second son of a count of modest origins. Intended for a career in the Church, young Rainald was trained in philosophy and theology at Hildesheim and Paris. He served as provost of several religious houses in Germany and cultivated a love of ancient literature. An affable personality, Rainald may have met Emperor Frederick in Würzburg in 1149, where he made a favorable impression on a number of members of the imperial court.

An able administrator, Rainald was selected as chancellor of the Empire in May 1156 and remained at the side of the emperor for the next decade. As chancellor, he encouraged Frederick in his efforts to create an imperial structure in Italy. Rainald wanted to reinvigorate the imperial Church through military control over Italy and by bringing pressure to bear on the papacy. Although at times overly belligerent and fond of military adventure, Rainald was a skilled diplomat and negotiator. Frederick rewarded him for his loyal service by making him archbishop of Cologne in 1159. He died of malaria in the midst of the collapse of Frederick's plans for Italy.

Works About: W. Föhl, *Studien zu Rainald von Dassel, JKGV,* 17 (1935); K. Hampe, *Germany under the Salian and Hohenstaufen Emperors,* tr. R. Bennett (Totowa, N.J., 1973); R. M. Herkenrath, "Rainald von Dassel als Verfasser und Schreiber von Kaiserurkunden," *MIÖG,* 72 (1964); 34–62; Peter Munz, *Frederick Barbarossa* (Ithaca, 1969); Marcel Pacaut, *Frederick Barbarossa,* tr. A. J. Pomerans (New York, 1970).   *J. W. Zophy*

See COLOGNE; FREDERICK I.

REISCH, GREGORY (c. 1467–1525), encyclopedist, religious leader, and father confessor to Emperor Maximilian I, was born at Balingen in Swabia. He was already a cleric when he entered Freiburg University in 1487, and he completed his M. A. in 1489. He taught in the arts faculties at both Freiburg and Heidelberg, and he was briefly at Ingolstadt.

By 1500, Reisch had joined the Carthusian order, and he was elected prior of the house at Freiburg im Breisgau in 1502. He soon became visitor of the Rhenish province of the Carthusians, and he used his office to locate rare manuscripts for scholars and publishers. In Freiburg he taught mathematics, cosmography, Hermetic philosophy, and Hebrew to a select few. Reisch's students included the cartographers Matthias Ringmann Philesius and Martin Waldseemüller, as well as the theologian John Eck. Reisch began the edition of St. Jerome, which was transferred to Erasmus by the publishers in 1514. Erasmus hailed Reisch's support of his new edition of the New Testament as vital for gaining general approval in Germany.

In late 1510, Emperor Maximilian named a commission that included Reisch, Pius Hieronymus Baldung of the Austrian government at Ensisheim, and Angelo de Besutio, law professor at Freiburg, to review opinions filed by German universities concerning John Reuchlin's objections to the proposal to confiscate all nonbiblical Hebrew writings. The commission found unanimously against Reuchlin. After the start of the Reformation crisis, Reisch gained a reputation as a determined foe of Lutheran tendencies within the Carthusian order.

Emperor Maximilian I summoned Reisch from Freiburg to Wels to be with him as he died. Reisch confessed Maximilian, and he carried out Maximilian's bizarre and self-abasing burial instructions after the emperor died on January 12, 1519.

Reisch's major work was the *Philosophic Pearl (Margarita philosophica),* an illustrated encyclopedia handbook of the liberal arts in Latin, stressing mathematics and the natural sciences (completed 1496, published 1503). It was one of the most popular schoolbooks of the sixteenth century. He also published a compilation of the statutes of the Carthusian order in 1510.

Works About: Percy Stafford Allen et al., eds., *Opus epistolarum Desiderii Erasmi Roterodami,* 12 vols. (Oxford, 1906–1958); Eduardus Böcking, ed., *Ulrichi Hutteni equitis operum supplementum,* 2 vols. (Leipzig, 1864–1869); John Ferguson, "The Margarita Philosophica of Gregorius Reisch: A Bibliography," *Library,* 4th series, vol. 10 (1929):194–216; Karl Hartfelder, "Der Karthäuserprior Gregor Reisch, Verfasser der Margarita philosophica," *Z. für die Gesch. des Oberrheins* 44 (1890):170–200; Alfred Hartmann, *Die Amerbachkorrespondenz* (Basel, 1942–1947), vols. 1–3; Gustav Münzel, "Der Karthäuserprior Gregor Reisch und die Margarita philosophica," *Z. des Freiburger Geschver.* 48 (1937): 1–87; Robert Ritter von Srbik (Alphonse Lhotsky, ed.), *Maximilian I. und Gregor Reisch, Arch für österr. Gesch.* vol. 122 (Vienna, 1961).

S. W. Rowan

See ECK; ERASMUS; MAXIMILIAN I; REUCHLIN.

REUCHLIN, JOHN (1455–1522), humanist Hebrew scholar, was born at Pforzheim and educated at the universities of Freiburg, Basel, and Paris. Trained as a lawyer, he taught for a while and then entered into the service of Duke Eberhard of Württemberg. During this period, Reuchlin was able to take three trips to Italy, where he came into contact with such leading humanists as Pico della Mirandola and Marsilio Ficino. From 1502 until 1513, he served as head jurist for the Swabian League. His last years were spent as a professor of Greek and Hebrew at the universities of Ingolstadt and Tübingen.

A fine scholar, Reuchlin became a leading humanist through such works as *On the Wonder-Working Word, On the Cabalistic Art,* and *Rudiments of Hebrew* (1506), which made it possible to learn Hebrew in Europe. His interest in Jewish thought eventually involved him in controversy with a converted Jew, John Pfefferkorn, who argued that all Hebrew books should be confiscated. When Pfefferkorn attacked Reuchlin personally, the humanist defended himself in an essay, *The Eye Mirror*, which was later condemned by both Pope Leo X and Emperor Maximilian. While the controversy was at its height, two of Reuchlin's humanist admirers, Crotus Rubeanus and Ulrich von Hutten, published their *Letters of Obscure Men*, a devastating satire on Reuchlin's opponents, who included a number of Dominican theologians from Cologne. Reuchlin accepted the discipline of Church and was aloof and then hostile to the Reformation.

Works By: *Johannes Reuchlins Briefwechsel*, ed. Ludwig Geiger (Stuttgart, 1875). **Works About:** Max Brod, *Johannes Reuchlin und seine Kampf* (Stuttgart, 1965); Ludwig Geiger, *Johann Reuchlin* (Leipzig, 1871); Manfred Krebs, ed., *Johannes Reuchlin* (Pforzheim, 1955); Ernst Mayerhoff, *Johann Reuchlin und seine Zeit* (Berlin, 1830); James Overfield, "A New Look at the Reuchlin Affair," *Studies in Medieval and Renaissance Hist.* 8 (1971); 165–207; L. W. Spitz, *The Religious Renaissance of the German Humanists* (Cambridge, Mass., 1963).   *J. W. Zophy*

See HUMANISM; HUTTEN; MAXIMILIAN; SWABIAN LEAGUE.

RHEGIUS, URBANUS (489–1541), reformer and polemicist, was a native of Langenargen near Constance. Urbanus, although from a family of modest means, managed to gain admittance to the University of Freiburg in 1508, where he studied under Ulrich Zasius, Wolfgang Capito, John Rhagius, and John Eck, Luther's opponent. After receiving his B. A. in 1510, Rhegius followed Eck to the University of Ingolstadt. There he devoted himself increasingly to theology, along with poetry and rhetoric.

Ordained a priest in 1519, he became spiritual vicar to the bishop of Constance, where he became increasingly supportive of Martin Luther. This did not stop him from accepting a post as cathedral preacher at Augsburg. Writing against those who burned Luther's books, he was ousted from his office in late 1521. He later surfaced as a preacher at Hall in the valley of the Inn, where his pro-Lutheran writings alienated Archduke Ferdinand and resulted in his departure in 1524.

Returning to Augsburg where the Reform movement was growing apace, Rhegius became a pastor, administered the sacrament in both kinds, and married. A participant in the diet of Augsburg of 1530, he preached to a number of the visiting princes and dignitaries. However, on June 16, Emperor Charles ordered the dismissal of Rhegius and the other evangelical preachers, and the Augsburg government complied. Fortunately, Rhegius was soon offered a church in Celle by Duke Ernest of Brunswick-Lüneburg. He did so well that he was appointed court preacher and then general superintendent in 1531, an office he filled with great vigor. His activity extended even into the city of Hanover, for which he drew up a church order.

Works About: Douglas B. Hampton, "Urbanus Rhegius and the Spread of the German Reformation" (Ph.D. diss., Ohio State University, 1973); H. Ch. Heimburger, *Urbanus Rhegius* (Gotha, 1851); O. Seitz, *Die theologische Entwicklung des Urbanus Rhegius* (Gotha, 1898); Gerhard Uhlhorn, *Urbanus Rhegius* (Elberfeld, 1862); Paul Tschackert, "Rhegius, Urbanus," *Schaff-Herzog*, 10:22–23.   *J. W. Zophy*

See AUGSBURG, DIET OF; CHARLES V; ECK; FERDINAND I; LUTHER.

RHINE LEAGUE OF CITIES was founded on July 13, 1254, in order to help keep peace in Germany. Germany in the mid-thirteenth century was plagued by interminable feudal wars and marauding robbers, who made the roads unsafe for trade and travel. Emperor Frederick II, who was heavily involved in Italo-Sicilian affairs, was of little help in keeping the peace in the north. His son and successor, Conrad IV, was preoccupied trying to win and hold his crown.

Finally a group of episcopal towns in the Rhine valley, including Basel, Cologne, Mayence, Metz, Speyer, Strasbourg, and Worms, joined together in a general pact to keep the peace for a ten-year period and to reduce toll restrictions to commerce. The league had been formed under the leadership of ecclesiastical princes like Archbishops Gerhard of Mayence and Conrad of Cologne, but a number of secular nobles and other towns such as Nuremberg also joined in. The Rhine League was of great value in keeping relative calm during the Great Interregnum (1254–1273) and in providing a measure of stability for Emperor Rudolf I of Habsburg.

Works About: E. Bielfeldt, *Der Rheinische Bund von 1254. Ein Erster Versuch einer Reichsreform* (Cologne, 1937). Louis Snyder, ed., *Documents of German Hist.* (New Brunswick, N.J. 1958). *J. W. Zophy*

See CONRAD IV; FREDERICK II; INTERREGNUM; RUDOLF I.

RIEMENSCHNEIDER, TILMAN (c. 1460–1531), sculptor, was born in Osterode near Hildesheim in the Harz Mountains of Saxony. In 1483 Tilman was admitted to the guild of painters, sculptors, and glaziers of Würzburg. He became a member of the city council in 1504 and from that time on held various civic offices. During the Peasants' Revolt of 1524–1526, Riemenschneider was openly sympathetic to the peasants and decried the use of force by their opponents. For this he was put on trial and tortured but was soon released and back at work. One of the leading artists in the Empire, Tilman Riemenschneider is especially noted for his altar pieces.

Works About: Justus Bier, *Tilmann Riemenschneider* (Vienna, 1948); K. Gerstenberg, *Tilmann Riemenschneider* (Munich, 1955); Hubert Schrade, "Tilman Riemenschneider," *DGD*, 1:332–42; Martin Weinberger, "Riemenschneider," *EWA*, 12:215–18. *J. W. Zophy*

See PEASANTS' WAR.

ROMAN LAW, reception of, in the Empire, represents a historiographical problem. The significant interpretive points of dispute revolve around the causes and consequences of the reception, the relationship between Roman civil principles and indigenous Germanic ones, and the apparent inevitability of the reception. Despite these contentions, there is little controversy that the reception occurred, that it received a substantial impetus in the legislation creating the Imperial Cameral Court in 1495 *(Reichskammergerichtsordnung),* and that it became increasingly popular during the course of the sixteenth century.

With the demise of the Roman Empire, the emperor and imperial law lost their effectiveness. In the resulting void, various European peoples developed their own, largely unwritten, legal norms. Not until the recovery of Emperor Justinian's (527–565) civil digest (Pandects) in the late eleventh century and the slightly later canonical codification by Gratian *(Decretum Gratiani)* did there emerge two bodies of law that had pretensions of being applicable to all of Europe. There existed similarities in content in these compilations, especially within the sphere of procedural law.

The almost simultaneous appearance of these codes marked a new stage in European historical development, one that prepared the bases for the high Middle Ages. Dicta in them served as models for the subsequent development of law in many parts of Europe, and their study and attendant glosses led both to a revival of jurisprudential thought and to growing numbers of trained jurists.

Secular authorities throughout Europe appropriated much Roman law, especially where it could be harmonized with existing legal custom (and thereby evoking little disturbance) or where the power of the prince remained relatively uncontested. Roman law was largely secular, it was written, and it transcended local boundaries. For these reasons it was superior to customary law. Its use appealed both to princes bent on maintaining and centralizing their power and to individuals and corporations involved in supralocal affairs. Roman law thus penetrated most European countries, although its reception by, or introduction into, the Empire came relatively late in comparison with the rest of the western Europe.

Because of the diffuse political nature of the Empire, there existed a bewildering variety of laws, customs, and jurisdictions, some of them overlapping. Princes, cities, and villages, among other political units, had their own privileges and traditions, and these most often differed. Both with the growth in power of these units and with the expanding economy that characterized the Empire in the late Middle Ages, there developed a need to systematize legal relationships among them. The emergence of legal codes whose principles extended beyond local boundaries and the formal study of law at many universities came together. As a result more and more Roman legal practices developed in the Empire during the fifteenth and, especially, the sixteenth centuries. The spearhead for this development is difficult to pinpoint. Certainly the emperor and many princes found Roman law congenial. It is also evident that litigious parties began to employ formally trained lawyers in their actions because court justices began to render decisions based on Roman and canonical procedure.

The adoption of Roman legal principles and Roman canon law procedures produced considerable dissatisfaction among certain groups in the Empire. In some areas, such as Saxony which possessed a written territorial code, the *Sachsenspiegel,* from the thirteenth century, the Roman civil code encountered entrenched opposition. Others, such as the free imperial knights and the peasantry, railed against the imposition of an alien—both Roman law and its modifications by Italian jurists—set of principles that they felt did not accord with native conditions; their reactions played a part in both the Knights' War (1522–1523) and the Peasants' War (1524–1526). It is perhaps noteworthy that Roman criminal procedure in the Empire received its formal elaboration in the *Carolina* issued by Emperor Charles V (1519–1556), a code that followed closely on these wars.

Despite the reaction to the reception and in spite of the problems attendant upon the interpretation of it, Roman law fused with Germanic traditions. This is manifest in the sphere of procedural law with its emphasis on written, notarial documentation and evidence. For the most part the Empire received Roman law not by legislation, but through application by justices.

Works About: Georg von Below, *Die Ursachen der Rezeption des römischen Rechts in Deutschland* (Munich, 1905, rpr. 1964); Helmut Coing, *Die Rezeption des römischen Rechts in Frankfurt am Main, Ein Beitrag zur Rezeptionsgesch.*, 2d ed. (Frankfurt, 1962); Paul Koschaker, *Europa und das römische Recht*, 4th ed. (Munich, 1966); Hermann Kraus, *Kaiserrecht und Rezeption* (Heidelberg, 1952); Paul Vinogradoff, *Roman Law in Medieval Europe*, 3d ed. (Hildesheim, 1961); Gerhard Wesenberg, *Neure dtsch. Privatrechtsgesch. im Rahmen der europäischen Rechtentwicklung*, 3d ed. (Lahr, 1976).   *P. N. Bebb*

See CHARLES ; IMPERIAL CAMERAL COURT; NUREMBERG *REFORMATION*; PEASANTS' WAR.

ROSSBACH, a village in Saxony, was where Frederick II of Prussia routed a Franco-imperial army twice the size of his, on November 5, 1757, during the Seven Years War. Surrounded by foes on four fronts, Frederick adopted a strategy of operating on interior lines, striking at his enemies separately, before they could unite against him. In the autumn of 1757, Frederick forced a crossing of the Saale at Weissenfels to engage a Franco-imperial army under Charles de Rohan, prince de Soubise (1715–1787), and Joseph Frederick William, duke of Saxe-Hildburghausen (1702–1787), respectively. Although they outnumbered the Prussians forty-two thousand to twenty-two thousand, the French troops were of low quality and of lower morale, the German forces comprised disparate elements, and the two commanders were agreed only in their caution. Nonetheless the allied army marched south late in the morning of November 5 from Mücheln to cut off Frederick's army, encamped between Bedra and Rossbach, from the Saale crossings. Upon seeing the movement, Frederick believed the allies were retreating, but as they turned east at Zeuchfeld he realized they were advancing instead. He in turn struck his tents and disappeared beyond the Janus Hill, leading the allies to believe the Prussians were retreating. Encouraged, the intended right-wing allied cavalry trotted ahead in pursuit, leaving the infantry columns, which had gotten entangled, behind. Suddenly thirty-eight squadrons of Prussian cavalry, led by Major General Frederick William von Seydlitz (1721–1773), swept over the Pölzen Hill and slashed into the surprised allied advance guard. As the cavalry melee drifted southward, Prussian infantry descended the Janus Hill, supported by eighteen heavy guns, in left oblique order and smashed the infantry columns with platoon volleys as they vainly tried to deploy. Then Seydlitz, though wounded, who had rallied his cavalry in a hollow near Tagewerben, charged a second time and broke the allied right flank, sending the army fleeing. In an hour and a half of battle, the allies had lost 10,900 soldiers, including 5,000 prisoners; the Prussian casualties were a mere 548. Rossbach discouraged the French from future operations against "Old Fritz," but Frederick was already hastening to Silesia to meet a new Austrian threat.

Works About: Austrian official *Die Kriege unter der Regierung der Kaiserin Marie Theresia* (Vienna, 1896–1914); Prussian official, *Die Kriege Friedrichs des Grossen,* 20 vols. (Berlin, 1890–1913).   *A. H. Ganz*

See FREDERICK II, THE GREAT; SEVEN YEARS WAR.

RUDOLF I OF HABSBURG (1218–1291), Holy Roman emperor from 1273 to 1291, was the son of Count Albert IV. Through most of his youth, Rudolf had been an adventurer who had taken part in all the wars of Germany since the time of Frederick II. Rudolf was heir to the county of Habsburg in the Aargau and through his marriage to Gertrude of Hohenberg obtained a great estate in Alsace. Although Rudolf's reign was not among the most illustrious in the history of the Holy Roman Empire, he did lay solid foundations for the future of his dynasty, which played a major role in southern Germany until the nineteenth century. This was accomplished partly through wars and partly through prudent marriages and subsequent inheritances that increased the paternal domain of the Habsburgs.

Rudolf did not come from a family of princely rank. His election reflected the decline of the old houses, duchies, nations, and kingdoms and the rise of new and more numerous noble families. These families had risen in power and wealth based upon allodial inheritance, their position as imperial functionaries, and their feudal territorial jurisdictions. By 1273 imperial elections had come to be vested in seven electors: three spiritual and four lay. The lay electors represented the various jurisdictions within the Empire. These included the imperial jurisdiction of the count Palatine, feudal in the king of Bohemia, national in the duke of Saxony, and margraviate in Brandenburg.

When elected to the German throne, Rudolf was no stranger to the various power struggles within the Empire. Following the death of Frederick II in 1250, Rudolf had sided with Conrad IV and risen to the office of marshal of the court of Ottocar, king of Bohemia. From Bohemia he returned to Alsace and was elected general of the Strasbourgers in their war against their bishops from 1261 to 1269. Subsequently he held the same office at Zurich and even later led one of the factions of the city of Basel against its bishop.

When the electors met at Michaelmas in 1273 at Frankfurt under some pressure from Pope Gregory X, the throne had been vacant more than a year.

Although Bavaria voted for Ottocar, king of Bohemia, no real candidate for the crown emerged. Finally it was decided that Louis of Wittelsbach, the count Palatine, should make the election. He announced Rudolf, count of Habsburg, as his choice. Rudolf was crowned on October 24, 1273, at Aachen as king of the Romans.

Unlike many of his predecessors, Rudolf was either not interested or realized the futility of reviving imperial dreams, especially in Italy. The two main policies of his reign were to strengthen his position in Germany and to increase the power of his own family.

Rudolf inaugurated a principle of cordial union between imperial and papal interests. He wanted papal recognition of his crown and minimal involvement in Italian affairs. The pope wanted an extension of the Church's temporal power, especially in southern Italy from which the Hohenstaufen emperors had so often threatened the papacy, and imperial support for a crusade to Palestine.

At the Council of Lyons in 1274, the pope received the ambassadors of Alphonse of Castile and Ottocar of Bohemia who were asking for the Empire. The pope, who seems to have had some influence in the election of Rudolf, withheld his recognition until Rudolf had made certain concessions. These included the surrender of the Romagna, the exarchate, the inheritance of the Countess Matilda and the suzerainty of Sicily, Sardinia, and Corsica. Gregory X then made the journey to Lausanne to bestow his benediction on Rudolf on October 18, 1275. Rudolf was then to go to Rome for the imperial crown and continue on crusade to Palestine. Rudolf never made it to Rome, which led Gregory X to complain of broken faith and thence to excommunicate Rudolf. Gregory X died in 1276, and by 1278 Rudolf had gained absolution from Nicholas III in return for Bologna and its appurtenances.

Having minimized German involvement in Italy, Rudolf turned to the securing of a firm foundation for his own family in Germany. One of his first acts as king was to bestow in marriage three of his six daughters on the three lay electors who had supported him. The later marriages of the other three also served to consolidate the family interests.

Throughout most of 1275, Rudolf was occupied putting down the robber counts of Saxony. Between 1276 and 1278 he did battle with his strongest rival, Ottocar of Bohemia, finally defeating him on August 26 in a battle near Vienna. Ottocar was killed in the battle, leaving a twelve-year-old child as heir. Rudolf took his lands and gave them to various members of his family, thus laying a solid basis for the future growth of the Habsburg family.

After 1282 Rudolf did little except pacify ancient feuds, which continued after his death. Although Rudolf was a prudent and generally competent king, he was not able to strengthen his position enough to get his son elected as successor in 1290. The princes maintained that the kingdom was too poor to support two kings. Rudolf died on July 15, 1291, at Germersheim and was buried at Speyer with the Franconian kings.

Works About: G. Barraclough, *The Origins of Modern Germany* (New York, 1946); A. Gerlich, *Studien zur Landfriedenspolitik König Rudolfs von Habsburg* (Mainz, 1963); F. Heer, *The Holy Roman Empire* (New York, 1968); *MGH Legum Sectio IV, Constitutiones et Acta Publica,* ed. J. Schwalm (Hanover, 1904–1906), vols. 2–4; Oswald Redlich, *Rudolf von Habsburg: Das Dtsch. Reich nach dem untergange des alten Kaisertums* (Aalen, 1965).   *D. B. Mapes*

See ALBERT I; CONRAD IV; FREDERICK II; INTERREGNUM; VIENNA.

RUDOLF II (1552–1612), Holy Roman emperor from 1576 to 1612, was born in Vienna the eldest son of Emperor Maximilian II and Mary, the daughter of Emperor Charles V. Rudolf was a great patron of the arts and sciences but not a particularly impressive political leader.

Much of his childhood was spent at Munich, a thriving cultural center. From 1563 to 1571, he and his brother Ernest lived in Spain at the insistence of their uncle, Philip II of Spain, who wanted to free them from the Protestant influences that had marked their father's upbringing. Rudolf grew up to be a competent linguist like his father and could use German, Spanish, Italian, Latin, French, and some Czech.

Rudolf was made king of Hungary in 1572 at Pressburg and king of Bohemia in Prague in 1575. At that time he was also acknowledged as king of the Romans. On October 12, 1576, he became Holy Roman emperor. As emperor, Rudolf II supported the Counter Reformation and waged an underfinanced and indecisive war against the Turks (1591–1606). He wanted to achieve an international balance of power but lacked the will to carry out a sustained policy, especially in his later years when he was troubled by ill health and psychological problems. Despite lengthy marriage negotiations concerning Philip II's daughter, Isabella, Rudolf II remained a bachelor, who increasingly disappeared from the larger imperial stage for his castle in Prague.

An aloof but intelligent man, Rudolf II expressed himself best in his support for the arts and sciences. He made Prague a great cultural center during his reign. There he pursued his great passions for art, music, literature, science, and the occult. His favorite artists were Albrecht Dürer and Peter Brueghel, and he sent agents all over Europe to purchase their work and that of others for his growing collection at Castle Hradschin. Rudolf seemed to want to salvage as much of Europe's art as he could before another outbreak of iconoclasm took place. He also loved beautiful things and collected clocks, jewels, and many other objects. The emperor enjoyed the company of artists, and they were among his confidants. Rudolf II encouraged a host of writers including the English poetess Elizabeth Jane Weston (1582–1612).

Rudolf II is also renowned for his interest in science and the occult. It was the emperor who brought the astronomer Tycho Brahe to Prague; Brahe recommended John Kepler for the post of court astronomer. Kepler worked for Rudolf and honored the emperor with his *Tabulae Rudolphin*. John Dee, the famous mathematician and court astrologer, was in Bohemia from 1583 to 1589 at the behest of the emperor. The highly superstitious Habsburg maintained a stable of astrologers and alchemists.

Despite his great work as a collector and patron, Rudolf's political and mental position deteriorated toward the end of his reign. He became increasingly stubborn, apathetic to political concerns, and at times mentally unbalanced. In 1609 Rudolf was forced to issue a "Letter of Majesty," which gave the Bohemians protection against any religious imposition, thereby reversing an earlier edict banning the Bohemian Brethren. A quarrel with his brother resulted in the emperor's forced recognition of Matthias as king of Bohemia in 1611. Matthias then succeeded Rudolf II as emperor following his death on January 20, 1612, in Prague.

Works By: *Divi Rudolphi Imperatoris . . . epistolae ineditae,* ed. B. de Pace (Vienna, 1771). **Works About:** P. Erlanger and E. Neweklowsky, *L'Empereur insolite, Rudolphe II de Habsburg* (Paris, 1971); R. J. W. Evans, *Rudolf II and His World: A Study in Intellectual History* (Oxford, 1973); Anton Gindely, *Rudolf II und seine Zeit,* 2 vols. (Prague, 1862–1865); H. Moritz, *Die Wahl Rudolfs II, der Reichstag zu Regensburg und die Freistellungsbewegung* (Marburg, 1895); Gertrude von Schwarzenfeld, *Rudolf II, der saturnische Kaiser* (Munich, 1961).   *J. W. Zophy*

See DÜRER; KEPLER; MATTHIAS; MAXIMILIAN II.

RUPERT I (1352–1410), also Ruprecht; German king and (uncrowned) Holy Roman emperor (1400–1410), Elector Rupert III of the Palatinate (1398–1410), was born at Amberg (Upper Palatinate).

Rupert sought to use the Wittelsbach power base in the Palatinate to revive the powers of emperor, greatly weakened by the ineffectiveness of Wenceslaus (1378–1400), and to forestall advancing anarchy in Germany. In 1400, the Rhineland electors took the lead in acting on their concerns, assumed the authority to set Wenceslaus aside, and elected Rupert king of the Germans and next emperor (August 21). Pope Boniface IX in Rome withheld recognition—a precondition for coronation as emperor—and sought in the curia to set aside Rupert's election. Rupert decided to undertake a royal procession into Italy.

Ostensibly and publicly, his objective was to rid Italy of the vigorously expansive dictator of Milan, Giangaleazzo Visconti. Beyond that he expected to establish effective imperial presence in northern Italy, acquire sufficient credibility with the papacy to gain the imperial crown, and legitimize among his fellow rulers in Germany his election by his effectiveness.

The progress went slowly and not well. It was to be financed largely by Florence, a promised 200,000 gulden and credits for more. In fact, Rupert realized 50,000 gulden, payable in Italy. By the time he reached Trent (October 14, 1401), Visconti had fortified Brescia and Verona. Bad leadership was a major factor in a defeat on October 21. That was accompanied by a drying up of Florentine finance and a pullout from his army by two key allies, Archbishop Frederick of Cologne and Duke Leopold of Austria.

Rupert broke off the invasion and moved into winter quarters at Padua. Unable to move Venice from neutrality, to get more money from Florence, or to negotiate recognition by the pope, he abandoned the venture, recrossed the Alps, and arrived in Munich on May 2, 1402. Rupert's scheme to resurrect the imperial role in Italy was paralleled in failure by the much more threatening work of Giangaleazzo Visconti to forge a Milan-based kingdom in north and central Italy. The despot died of plague on September 3, 1402.

The challenge of Rupert's progress inspired Wenceslaus to a show of activity by looking toward a Rome journey for himself. He renewed his designation of Sigismund as imperial vicar and endowed him with regency in Bohemia during his absence. The brothers were not reconciled, however, as Sigismund seized the deposed emperor and turned him over to the Habsburgs for pawn.

Rupert's opportunity for coronation now seemed ripe, if approbation from Boniface IX could be secured. But again the pope declined, which helped to deflect Rupert's momentum once again. His enthusiastic activity in ruling Germany aroused animosities among the estates fearing further losses of freedom. On September 14, 1405, the Marburg League was formed. The leader of this group of cities and territories was Elector Archbishop John of Mainz, who had been a key figure in the politics that created Rupert German king in 1400.

Mainz claimed that Rupert was violating the special relationship between electors and king. But Rupert's principal problem simply was that the Palatinate alone did not afford a sufficient power base for independent European action. This made him vulnerable at home and the Empire vulnerable abroad. France and others clearly recognized his problem; Brabant already was lost to the new Burgundian state. Realizing that Rupert had too little rather than too much power, the duke of Gelderland opened the gates of Aachen and let Rupert occupy the throne of Charlemagne on November 14, 1407.

Rupert's last major engagement was the Council of Pisa in 1409. Wenceslaus aligned himself with the cardinals at Pisa, but Rupert felt necessarily bound to support the Roman pope. He stayed out of the council while stimulating arguments from scholars at the University of Heidelberg that only a general council could resolve the Church's needs and that he as German king had authority to call such a general council.

The Council of Pisa resulted in three competing popes. Schism for the first time invaded Germany as Rupert was unable to maintain religious unity among the estates. Leader of the opposition in the controversy was Elector Archbishop John of Mainz, increasingly persuaded that Rupert must go. As the two prepared for armed conflict, Rupert died. His power had been insufficient for the task of ruling Germany, but it was sufficient to make effective Gregory XII's summons of the long-awaited general Church council in the German imperial city of Constance. His rule in the Palatinate was beneficial and expansive.

Works About: *BW*, 2409–12; *DRTA*, Ältere Reihe (Berlin, 1877–1888), vols. 3–6; Ludwig Häusser, *Gesch. der rheinische Pfalz nach ihren politische, kirchenlich und literar. Verhältnissen*, 2d ed., 2 vols. (Heidelberg, 1856); August Thorbecke, "Ruprecht III," *ADB*, 29:716–26.   *K. C. Sessions*

See SIGISMUND; WENCESLAUS.

RUPERT, PRINCE (1619–1682), count Palatine of the Rhine and duke of Bavaria was also duke of Cumberland, earl of Holderness, commander in the Thirty Years War, Royalist general in the English Civil War, first lord of the admiralty, and twice on the privy council. Rupert's entire life, reputation, and accomplishments were fruits of military activity.

Third son of Frederick, elector Palatine, and Elizabeth, daughter of James I (England), Rupert was born in Prague shortly after Frederick's coronation as king of Bohemia. Following the Battle of the White Mountain (1620), Rupert's family took residence in Holland. Little is known of his education. His career began in England around 1635 to 1637, where he created a good impression at the court of Charles I.

Rupert fought for his brother, elector Palatine, in 1638, was captured, and was imprisoned at Linz, Austria. Released unconditionally through the efforts of England, Rupert returned there July 1642. His courage and enthusiasm were well known; his usefulness to Charles early in the civil war was ensured by victories on September 23, 1642, at Worcester and at Edgehill in October. His subsequent actions were not decisively victorious but displayed his unshakable valor and magnified his reputation. Charles created him earl of Holderness and duke of Cumberland on January 24, 1644.

Rupert's military and political fortunes eroded thereafter. Ordered by Charles to defend him at York, he suffered crushing defeat at Marston Moor on July 12, 1644. Though made commander in chief, his defeat at Naseby (June 14, 1645) led him to counsel peacemaking. Rupture with Charles, later reconciled, was the consequence of that stance.

Parliament exiled him in June 1645 because his royal service showed ingratitude toward England. He gained favor at the English court in exile and sailed from Holland on January 11, 1649, as commander of the royal fleet. Three years of plundering English and Spanish merchant shipping brought small advantage, however. Rupert withdrew to his German estates in 1654.

He returned to England and high favor following the Restoration. Admitted to the privy council (April 28, 1662), made admiral of the fleet in the third Dutch maritime war (1672–1674), and first lord of the admiralty (1673–1679), he was appointed again to the privy council.

Rupert died November 29, 1682. He never married but left two natural children.

Works About: C. M. H., "Rupert, Prince," *DNB*, 17:405–17; Patrick Morrah, *Prince Rupert of the Rhine* (London, 1976); Eliot Warburton, *Life of Prince Rupert*, 3 vols. (London, 1849).   *K. C. Sessions*

See FREDERICK V; THIRTY YEARS WAR.

SACHS, HANS (1494–1576), beloved poet and dramatist, was an influential supporter of Luther. The son of a tailor and a native of Nuremberg, Sachs attended Latin school and then began an apprenticeship as a shoemaker in 1508. After a period of wandering and study both of shoemaking and song, he returned to Nuremberg as a master shoemaker and author, remaining there for the rest of his life. Prolific and popular, Sachs composed more than four thousand *Meisterlieder* ("master songs"), seventeen hundred tales and fables in verse, and two hundred dramas. Many of his writings are distinguished by their colorful use of language, charm, and wit. A strong and influential supporter of the Reformation, Sachs wrote four prose dialogues defending the movement and the popular poem, "The Wittenberg Nightingale," as a tribute to Luther. The support of such a well-regarded literary figure was most important to the success of Lutheranism in Nuremberg and elsewhere.

Works By: F. M. Ellis, ed., *The Early Meisterlieder of Hans Sachs* (Bloomington, Ind., 1974); A. von Keller and E. Goetze, eds., *Hans Sachs*, 26 vols. (Tübingen, 1870–1908). **Works About:** F. M. Ellis, *Hans Sachs Studies* (Bloomington, Ind., 1941); Walter French, *Medieval Civilization as Illustrated by the Fastnachtspiele of Hans Sachs* (Baltimore, 1925); *Hans Sachs und Nürnberg*, ed. H. Brunner, G. Hirschmann, and F. Schnelbogl (Nuremberg, 1976); Niklas Holzberg, *Hans Sachs Bibliographie* (Nuremberg, 1976); Barbara Könneker, *Hans Sachs* (Stuttgart, 1971); Eli Sobel, *The Tristan Romance in the Meisterlieder of Hans Sachs* (Berkeley, 1963).   *J. W. Zophy*

See LUTHER; NUREMBERG.

SCHEURL, CHRISTOPH (1481–1542), humanist, professor of law, diplomat, and legal adviser to his native Nuremberg, studied at Heidelberg and Bologna, where he acquired a doctorate in Roman and canon law. While in Italy he had acted as translator for Emperor Maximilian I (1493–1519) and came into contact with close associates of Elector Frederick the Wise of Saxony (1486–1525). After taking his doctorate, he became professor on the law faculty of the new University of Wittenberg, a position he occupied from 1507 to 1512. While at Wittenberg he served as adviser to the Saxon princes and as assessor at their courts. In 1512, he returned to Nuremberg where he received an appointment as legal adviser to the government, an influential post he retained until his death.

Because of his studies and teaching and due to the prominence of Nuremberg as a mercantile and intellectual center, Scheurl had contact with a number of the most influential figures in the early sixteenth century. Among these were Luther, John Eck, Melanchthon, Campeggio, Staupitz, Cajetan, Spalatin, Matthew Lang, Dürer, and Pirckheimer. His experience at Wittenberg naturally brought him into association with people who subsequently espoused Protestantism. Similarly his participation in Nuremberg's humanist circle, of which he eventually became spokesman, exposed him more to the major themes of humanist activities; it was this group that acted as the spearhead for Nuremberg's acceptance of Protestantism, and Scheurl presided at the religious colloquy in 1525 that resulted in the city's introduction of the Reformation. Although Scheurl never became Protestant himself and, in fact, his closest friends were Catholic proponents, he maintained correspondence and acquaintance with evangelicals to his death.

As legal adviser to Nuremberg's government, Scheurl was influential not only in local affairs that concerned both religious and secular developments but also events that affected the city, its neighbors, and the Empire at large. Perhaps most significant were his commission from Nuremberg in 1519 to Spain in order to welcome the newly elected emperor, Charles V (1519–1556), and to argue the city's causes before him; his appointment by the Imperial Council of Regency in 1522 as the only representative of a city to negotiate in Vienna about Turkish affairs; and his 1523 appointment to an embassy that presented the cities' complaints at the imperial court in Spain about recent decisions of the Nuremberg diet. These and other commissions made Scheurl one of the most important officials inside and outside Nuremberg, and because of them he eventually became an adviser to Ferdinand and the emperor.

Scheurl wrote extensively. Most well known to students of the Empire is his extensive correspondence, but equally significant is his description of Nuremberg's government, his chronicle, and his edition of Staupitz's Advent sermons. In addition, he wrote and edited a large number of humanist works. Above all he was responsible for transmitting to John Eck Luther's Ninety-five Theses, which he thought Eck might enjoy.

Works By: Christoph Scheurl, "Geschichtebuch der Christenheit von 1511 bis 1521," *Jb. des dtsch. Reichs und der dtsch. Kirche im Zeitalter der Reformation,* ed. J. K. F. Knaake (Leipzig, 1872), 1:3–179; Franz von Soden and J. K. F. Knaake, eds., *Christoph Scheurls Briefbuch. Ein Beitrag zur Gesch. der Reformation und ihrer Zeit*, 2 vols. (Potsdam, 1867–1872, rpr. 1962). **Works About**: Phillip N. Bebb, "The Lawyers, Dr. Christoph Scheurl, and the Reformation in Nürnberg," in *The Social Hist. of the Reformation*, ed. Lawrence P. Buck and Jonathan W. Zophy (Columbus, 1972), pp. 52–72; Wilhelm Graf, *Doktor Christoph Scheurl von Nürnberg* (Leipzig and Berlin, 1930); Ernst Mummenhoff, "Scheurl," *ADB*, 31:145–154; Franz von Soden, *Christoph Scheurl der Zeite und sein Wohnhaus in Nürnberg* (Nuremberg, 1837).   *P. N. Bebb*

See CHARLES V; ECK; FERDINAND I; FREDERICK III, THE WISE; HUMANISM; LUTHER; MAXIMILIAN I; NUREMBERG; STAUPITZ.

SCHILLER, JOHN CHRISTOPH FREDERICK (1759–1805), dramatist, poet, historian, and philosopher, was born at Marbach in Württemberg. His father worked as a barber and surgeon before becoming an army captain and, finally, overseer of the estate of Duke Charles Eugene of Württemberg. Coming

from a very religious family, young Frederick intended to become a clergyman and accordingly attended the Latin school of Ludwigsburg in preparation for that career. However, in 1773 Duke Charles Eugene insisted that the boy enter his military academy at Castle Solitude. Since theology was not in the course of study, Schiller first studied law and then medicine when the school was moved to Stuttgart in 1775.

In 1780 while serving as a regimental surgeon, Schiller completed his first drama, *The Robbers*. When first performed by Baron Herbert von Dalberg in 1782, the play was greeted by a wildly enthusiastic audience. Unfortunately the author was sentenced to fourteen days' detention and was prohibited from publishing anything except medical treatises by Duke Charles for having attended two performances of his own play. Chafing under such military discipline and unable to renounce his love for literature, Schiller fled to Mannheim hoping to find help from Dalberg. But Dalberg feared the wrath of the duke and refused to employ the poet. Schiller, in great distress, received help from Henrietta von Wolzogen, the mother of a classmate. At her home in Bauerbach, he published a collection of poems and completed several political dramas.

Since Duke Charles Eugene had not pursued Schiller, Dalberg gave him employment for one year, which was followed by a financially unsuccessful stint as a journalist. Unexpected support came from an admirer, Christian Gottfried Körner, father of the poet Theodore, who invited Schiller to Leipzig and then to Dresden. During this period Schiller's great tragedy, *Don Carlos* (1787), was finished. In 1789, he secured an appointment as professor of history at Jena upon the nomination of Goethe. The financial security of this position allowed him to marry Charlotte von Lengefeld with whom he found enduring contentment. Prior to his appointment, he had immersed himself in historical studies and writing. Fascinated by the history of the Holy Roman Empire, Schiller began writing a *History of the Thirty Years War*, during which he fell ill from a serious lung infection. Throughout the remainder of his life, Schiller struggled against chronic illness.

Illness had forced him to give up his professorate at Jena, but relief came in the form of a generous pension from Prince Frederick Christian von Schleswig-Holstein and Count Ernest von Schimmelmann. The three-year pension allowed him to study the thought of the philosopher Immanuel Kant and to write a number of influential works on the history of aesthetic theory.

In 1794 Schiller established the literary journal *Die Horen*, to which Goethe contributed. Although the journal failed, Schiller's friendship with the sage of Weimar endured. He moved to Weimar in 1799, where he assisted Goethe at the court theater. There he finished his trilogy, *Wallenstein*, which not only returned him to the subject of imperial history and the Thirty Years War but also proved to be one of the finest historical dramas in German literature. Although continually plagued by ill health, Schiller managed to produce a drama almost every year, including the ever-popular *William Tell* (1804), which presents the struggle of the Swiss against tyranny, a favorite theme of the author. Schiller remains one of Germany's greatest and most beloved literary figures.

Works By: *Friedrich Schiller: An Anthology for Our Time*, ed. Frederick Ungar (New York, 1959); *Schillers Samtliche Werke*, ed. E. von der Hellen, 16 vols. (Stuttgart, 1904–1905); *Schillers Werke*, ed. Julius Petersen and Hermann Schneider, 11 vols. (Stuttgart, 1943–). **Works About**: Ilse Graham, *Schiller's Drama* (New York, 1974); Charles E. Passage, *Friedrich Schiller* (New York, 1975); Benno von Wiese, *Friedrich Schiller* (Stuttgart, 1963).   *J. W. Zophy*

See GOETHE; KANT; THIRTY YEARS WAR; WALLENSTEIN, ALBERT.

SCHMALKALDIC LEAGUE, a union of Protestant estates that lasted until the Schmalkaldic War, emerged in February 1531 partially as a result of previous Protestant attempts at alliance but more specifically as a result of the recess of the diet at Augsburg in 1530. Among other statements, the recess declared the enforcement of the Edict of Worms, suppression of heretical (Lutheran, Zwinglian, Anabaptist) innovations, and adherence of Protestants to these demands by April 15, 1531. Failure to follow these dictates would result in the use of force and prosecution at the Imperial Cameral Court (*Reichskammergericht*). Due to Emperor Charles V's recent alliance with Pope Clement VII, Charles' first appearance in Germany since 1521, his somewhat favorable relations with France, and the decidedly Catholic emphasis found in the recess, Protestants felt themselves to be on the brink of imminent attack. As a consequence, Landgrave Philip of Hesse and Elector John of Saxony, leaders of the Protestant estates, convoked a planning session in December 1530. This was held at the town of Schmalkald in the Thuringian forest, and it was from this town that the league took its name. The original members of the league included seven north German princes, to which Hesse and electoral Saxony belonged, and the cities of Magdeburg and Bremen. Later the league added many new members, and it remained the major Protestant confessional alliance until the outbreak of the Schmalkaldic War in 1546.

In its charter the league established its existence for six years. This was extended for another ten years in December 1535. Although it had adopted the Augsburg Confession as its doctrinal statement, some subsequent league members and associates held diverse views; this applied especially to efforts, largely made by Philip of Hesse, to enlist the support of Bavaria, France, England, and a number of south German cities partial to Zwinglianism. The charter claimed that an attack on any member was an attack on everyone and must be resisted by the full force of the league. To this end graduated assessments of its members supplied a military force of ten thousand infantry and two thousand cavalry. The resultant militia was led by Philip and the elector as captains. In 1535 an added provision stated that this force was to be doubled in the event of emergency. The league also adopted measures to hinder processes lodged with the Imperial Cameral Court.

Many Protestant estates were hesitant at first to join the league because its existence implied opposition to the imperial sovereign. As Luther and other theologians and jurists gradually accepted the constitutional validity of resistance, however, objections began to vanish. In addition, two specific occurrences augmented league membership: The first was the emperor's desire to placate Protestant estates because he needed their support to carry out his foreign policies; Protestants interpreted Charles' desire as an indication that he would not proceed against them on the basis of religion as long as they agreed to his policies. Second, the estates reacted negatively to what they regarded as Habsburg familial versus imperial concerns, seen especially in Ferdinand's election as king in January 1531 and Turkish military encroachments in Austria. Even Catholic estates, notably Bavaria, were opposed to making the imperial throne hereditary in the Habsburg house, and they were averse to expending the Empire's resources in order to strengthen Austria and Spain. Thus these considerations and the growth of resistance theory played a role in increasing league numbers. All of the prominent Protestant estates, with the exception of Nuremberg and Brandenburg-Ansbach, eventually joined the league.

Much of the success that the Schmalkaldic League enjoyed was in fact due to Charles V's policies. The emperor's pressing need for money and arms to fight the Turks and Valois gave the Protestants leverage. They threatened to withhold their subsidies if Charles turned against them. The emperor did not press the issue. He did not follow through on the April 15, 1531, deadline specified in the recess, and in the next year he agreed to the so-called Nuremberg peace, according to which he quashed processes in the Imperial Cameral Court and promised no action against the Protestants until a meeting of a general Church council. The resulting standstill gave the Protestants time to win over more estates and organize the league more fully.

By the mid-1540s when Charles had reached a kind of moratorium with the Turks and had concluded another chapter in the Habsburg-Valois rivalry by the Treaty of Crépy, much of the Empire was Protestant and belonged to the league. The Habsburgs had lost Württemburg in 1534 when the duchy was restored to the Protestant Duke Ulrich; under Ulrich the duchy joined the league in 1536. A further blow occurred with the death of the Catholic Duke George of Saxony in 1539. Henry, his brother and successor, made the duchy Lutheran and joined the league in the same year. By the time that Charles turned his attention to the Empire's religious problems, most of the electors had already adopted Protestantism or were leaning toward it, and most of northern Germany and large portions of southern Germany belonged to the Schmalkaldic League.

Works About: Ekkehart Fabian, ed., *Die Schmalkaldischen Bundesabschiede 1530–1532* and *Die Schmalkaldischen Bundesabschiede 1533–1536*, Schriften zur Kirchen und Rechtsgesch., vols. 7–8 (Tübingen, 1958), and *Die Beschlüsse oberdtsch. Schmalkaldischen Städtetage, Quellenbuch zur Reformations- und Verfassungsgeschichte Ulms und der anderen Reichsstädte des oberländischen Schmalkaldischen Bundeskreises*, Schriften zur Kirchen- und Rechtsgeschichte, vols. 9–10, 14–15,

21–24 (Tübingen, 1959–1960); *Quel zur Gesch. der Reformationsbündnisse und der Konstanzer Reformationsprozesse 1529–1548,* Schriften zur Kirchen- und Rechtsgeschichte, vol. 34 (Tübingen, 1967); Ekkehart Fabian, *Die Entstehung des Schmalkaldischen Bundes und seiner Verfassung 1524/ 29-1531/35*, Schriften zur Kirchen- und Rechtsgeschichte, vol. 1, 2d ed. (Tübingen, 1962), H. J. Grimm, *The Reformation Era, 1500–1650*, 2d ed. (New York, 1973); Hajo Holborn, *A Hist. of Modern Germany*, vol. 1: *The Reformation* (New York, 1959); *The Cambridge Modern Hist.*, vol. 2: *The Reformation* (Cambridge, 1903), chaps. 7–8.   *P. N. Bebb*

See AUGSBURG, DIET OF; CHARLES V; FERDINAND I; IMPERIAL CAMERAL COURT; JOHN OF SAXONY; PHILIP OF HESSE; SCHMALKALDIC WAR; ULRICH.

SCHMALKALDIC WAR (1546–1547) was a series of skirmishes between the imperial forces of Charles V and the Schmalkaldic League. The war, which Charles ostensibly won, appeared to mark the decisive defeat of Protestantism in the Empire. Charles' victory, however, was more hollow than sound since the Protestant religion and church organization had become too entrenched to be eradicated by military means and the resultant imperial decrees. Nevertheless the war probably marked the high point of Charles' personal reign in the Empire.

Despite the development of the Catholic League at Nuremberg in 1538, Charles' need to conciliate the Protestant estates in order to advance his interests offered the Protestants some fifteen years to consolidate their position after the diet of Augsburg in 1530. His apparent mediating attitude in the religious sphere was further manifest by his authorization of religious conferences at Hagenau, Worms, and Regensburg in 1540 and 1541. But by 1545–1546 Charles was finally in a position to put down the evangelical heresies. He had recently concluded the Treaty of Crépy with Francis I of France (1515–1547), reached an armistice with the Turks, and come to an accord with Pope Paul III (1534–1549), who had just opened the Council of Trent (1545–1563).

In face of the superior military forces of the Schmalkaldic League, Charles had to bargain shrewdly. He had alienated many imperial estates, Catholic as well as Protestant, by pushing Habsburg dynastic interests vis-à-vis the imperial constitution. By various means he won over and/or neutralized some of these estates. He now concluded an agreement, for example, with the duke of Bavaria who was Catholic but who had regularly seen in Charles' policies the aggrandizement of Austria and the Habsburgs at the expense of Bavaria and the Wittelsbachs. Charles also promised leadership roles and rewards to princes and estates in return for their backing. The fact that he maintained the ensuing war was not for religious reasons but to enforce the imperial constitution also convinced some estates.

Both positive and negative factors help explain Charles' victory. Perhaps the largest positive factor was that he acquired the support of the Protestant Duke Maurice of Saxony (1541–1553), successor to his father, Henry, in ducal Saxony and son-in-law of Landgrave Philip of Hesse (d. 1567). Charles promised Maurice the electoral title in addition to other concessions, and Maurice, antagonistic toward his cousin Elector John Frederick (d. 1554), accepted. Although Lutheran himself, Maurice was more concerned with advancing the Albertine branch of the Wettin family.

Several negative factors also contributed to Charles' success. Among these were the difficulties of coordinating a united league defense against the imperial troops and habitual delays of troop payment and military supplies to the Protestants. Although outnumbering Charles' forces in the south while the emperor resided at Regensburg, league armies allowed Charles to increase his militia because there was no common plan against him.

The war itself lasted only for a short period of time. When Maurice invaded electoral Saxony in November 1546, Elector John Frederick rushed north with his troops, thereby truncating the Schmalkaldic armies. Charles thus was able to assume control of southern Germany and the Rhineland. Then in response to the elector's successes in defending Saxony, Charles moved to relieve Maurice, surprising and capturing the elector at the famous Battle of Mühlberg in April 1547. A few weeks later in May, the emperor extracted the Wittenberg capitulation from John Frederick by which the electoral title and much of the elector's territory passed to Maurice. In the next month, the new elector persuaded Philip of Hesse to surrender. Consequently the two major leaders of the Schmalkaldic League were in Charles' custody, and even though a few northern cities, such as Magdeburg, continued to resist, the emperor's victory appeared complete.

By this time, however, the international situation had changed once again, endangering the prospects for a religious settlement in the Empire. Charles began to encounter increasing hostility from the papacy and France who were fearful of Charles' plans for the Empire. With a few exceptions his reform legislation introduced at the diet of Augsburg in 1547 were rejected by the estates as infringements on the Empire's constitution. Similarly the imposition of the Augsburg Interim in 1548, which was officially accepted by most of the estates, could not be enforced. The entrenched interests of the German estates wrecked Charles' goal of reform and gave his victory its hollow sound. The emperor certainly came to this realization by the time of the outbreak of the so-called second Schmalkaldic War in 1552 in which the princes, led by Maurice and backed by Henry II of France (1547–1559), were arrayed against him.

Works About: Karlheinz Blashke, *Sachsen in Zeitalter der Reformation*, Schriften des Vereins für Reformationsgesch, vols. 185 (Gütersloh, 1970); Erich Brandenburg, ed., *Politische Korrespondenz des Herzogs und Kürfursten Moritz von Sachsen*, 2 vols. (Leipzig, 1900–1904); Karl Brandi, *The Emperor Charles V*, tr. C. V. Wedgwood (New York, 1939); Fritz Hartung, *Karl V. und die dtsch. Reichsstände 1546–1555* (Halle, 1910, rpr. 1971); Adolf Hasenclever, *Die kurpfälzische Politik in den Zeiten des Schmalkaldischen Krieges (Januar 1546 bis Januar 1547)*, Heidelberger Abhandlungen zur mittleren und neueren Gesch., vol. 10 (Heidelberg, 1905); Hajo Holborn, *A Hist. of Modern Germany)*, vol. 1: *The Reformation*, (New York, 1959); Max Lenz, ed., *Briefwechsel Landgraf Philipps des Grössmutigen von Hessen mit Bucer*, 3 vols. (Leipzig, 1880–1891, rpr., 1965); Alfred Schüz, *Der Donaufeldzug Karls V. im Jahre 1546* (Tübingen, 1930).   *P. N. Bebb*

See CHARLES V; JOHN FREDERICK; MAURICE; PHILIP OF HESSE; SCHMALKALDIC LEAGUE.

SCHWENCKFELD, CASPAR (1489–1561), controversial reformer, was born at Ossig in Silesia to a distinguished German family. At age sixteen Caspar began his studies of the liberal arts at Cologne and canon law at Frankfurt. Later he served his native principality as a diplomat until 1523 when increasing deafness forced him to abandon that career.

While still a diplomat, Schwenckfeld was converted by the writings of Martin Luther and others to the evangelical cause. Although remaining a layman, he felt he had the right to preach and did so, converting many prominent Silesians, including Duke Frederick II, who became his patron and protector. Support was needed for Schwenckfeld was unable to convince Luther of his interpretation of the Eucharist and was branded a sacramentarian.

His position in Silesia was further undermined in 1528 when Ulrich Zwingli published one of his books with a favorable preface, proving to his enemies that Schwenckfeld was a Zwinglian and thus a dangerous radical. Although the charges were untrue, he went into voluntary exile, ending up in Strasbourg, where for a time he was well received. Finally theological differences forced him to leave in 1534 for Ulm. There too the mild-mannered Schwenckfeld proved a lightning rod for theological disputes. Nevertheless despite fierce condemnations by Luther and others, he continued to preach and write, winning a small but loyal band of devoted followers.

Works About: *Corpus Schwenckfeldianorum*, ed. Hartranft, Johnson, and Schultz, vols. 1–15[1] (Leipzig, 1907–1939), vols. 15[2]–19 (Pennsburg, Pa., 1959–61). **Works By**: Karl Ecke, *Kaspar von Schwenckfeld* (Blaubeuren-Ulm, 1965); Paul L. Maier, *Caspar Schwenckfeld on the Person and Work of Christ* (Assen, 1959); Joachim Seyppel, *Schwenckfeld, Knight of Christ* (Pennsburg, Pa., 1961).   *J. W. Zophy*

See FRANKFURT; LUTHER; STRASBOURG; ULM; ZWINGLI.

SEVEN YEARS WAR (1756–1763), a worldwide European conflict, was fought over two separate issues: the Anglo-French colonial and maritime rivalry in North America and India and the Austro-Prussian struggle for hegemony in Germany. War over the first was precipitated by a colonial clash in America in 1754, the second by King Frederick II (1712–1786) of Prussia's invasion of Saxony in 1756; conflict was ended by the treaties of Paris and Hubertusburg, 1763, respectively. The war saw England, Hanover, and Prussia aligned against France, Austria, Russia, Saxony, Sweden, and, after 1762, Spain. Unlike the indecisive War of the Austrian Succession (1740–1748), the later war confirmed Prussia's status as a major European power and England's status as the leading maritime power.

The prelude witnessed the diplomatic revolution by which Bourbon France and Habsburg Austria, traditional rivals, emerged as allies. Austria was already allied to Russia (June 2, 1746) against the emergent Prussia because Empress Maria Theresa (1717–1780) was obsessed with regaining Silesia, and Czarina Elizabeth (1709–1762) was determined to take East Prussia (and give it to Poland in exchange for Courland) and reduce Frederick to his electorate of

Brandenburg. In 1750 Austrian minister Prince Wenceslaus von Kaunitz (1711–1794) sought French adherence, but Louis XV (1710–1774) at that time would not be reconciled with Russia (over Poland) and was not prepared to strengthen Austria by helping destroy Prussia.

The English continental policy of the duke of Newcastle (1693–1768) was determined by King George II's (1683–1760) desire to protect his native Hanover. Because Austria was reluctant to make a commitment, the English got an agreement from Russia at St. Petersburg, September 30, 1755, in exchange for an annual subsidy of £100,000, but simultaneously negotiated with Prussia, resulting in the Convention of Westminster (January 16, 1756), by which each would respect the other's territory.

The Anglo-Prussian agreement shocked their respective allies, Russia and France, and Kaunitz skillfully aligned those states with Austria. In April Russian Chancellor Alexis Bestuzhev offered Austria eighty thousand troops for an attack on Prussia, and in the First Treaty of Versailles (May 1, 1756), France and Austria concluded a military alliance. Frederick's intelligence system made him aware of Kaunitz's maneuverings, but he apparently did not believe that France and Austria could be reconciled (Kaunitz, in fact, was ready to give away the Austrian Netherlands for French support against Prussia), nor was he aware how his witticisms infuriated his female opponents, Elizabeth, Maria Theresa, and Madame de Pompadour (1721–1764), the ambitious and influential mistress of Louis XV.

Finally convinced that his three opponents were uniting to destroy him, Frederick decided to strike first; he invaded Saxony on August 29, 1756. Although he coveted Saxony and even considered offering Elector Frederick Augustus II Wettin (1696–1763; also king of Poland as Augustus III after 1736) Bohemia in exchange (after he conquered it), the invasion resulted from military considerations: defensively Saxony was a threat to Berlin, only thirty miles distant, and operations in Silesia were hampered by Saxony on the flank; offensively it provided resources and a base of operations for campaigns in Bohemia and Germany. Frederick entered Dresden on September 10, while the Saxons fell back to the entrenched plateau at Pirna; they capitulated October 16 after Frederick defeated Austrian Field Marshal Maximilian von Browne (1705–1757) on October 1 at Lobositz in Bohemia.

The armies of the period were generally small, comprising personnel impressed, harshly disciplined, and trained to precision, with a high proportion of cavalry. Infantry musketeer and fusilier regiments were divided tactically into their two battalions, while their grenadier companies were combined into separate grenadier battalions, the infantry being armed with a heavy, inaccurate flintlock musket and socket bayonet. Infantry battalions advanced and fired in three lines or formed squares against cavalry attack. The cavalry operated in squadrons from their parent regiments, heavy (breastplated cuirassier), medium (dragoon), and light (hussar). The troopers had flintlock carbines and pistols but generally relied on the sword. The Austrians and Russians also employed Croat and Cossack irregulars, respectively. The artillery comprised small battalion pieces; massed battery pieces; and heavy siege pieces, firing solid roundshot, grapeshot, and caseshot or canister; and howitzers also firing powder-filled explosive shell and carcass fire bombs. The armies were divided into two or three wings, with a cavalry wing on either flank. Frederick II of Prussia had developed tactics of marching by columns onto the battlefield parallel to his opponent, deploying by wheeling (facing) into line, and then advancing in an oblique (or staggered, *en echelon, in Staffeln*) formation of battalions against the enemy's flank, the refused wing available to cover retreat or reinforce success.

If Frederick thought his aggression would intimidate his enemies, the effect was the opposite. A preemptive attack is as likely to be precipitive as preventive. But if his opponents were planning to attack him anyway (he failed to find confirmation in the Saxon archives at least), aggression formalized by the Austro-Russian offensive Second Treaty of Versailles of May 1, then perhaps his action was at least strategically justified. Russian troop movements were hampered by French concern about Poland's status, and France was preoccupied by its overseas conflict with England. Frederick advanced on Prague defeating Browne and Prince Charles of Lorraine (1712–1780), the empress' brother-in-law, nearby on May 6 (Browne being killed), and besieging the city; but then Field Marshal Leopold von Daun (1705–1766) advanced to relieve the city, and Frederick met him at Kolin on June 18, 1757. Frederick intended his army to advance in oblique order against the Austrian right flank; but the advance became disjointed, the whitecoats held the high ground, and then Austrian cavalry overwhelmed the Prussian cavalry and advance guard. The defeat cost Frederick 13,768 (including 5,000 captured) of 32,000, to Daun's 9,000 casualties of 44,000, and the raising of the siege of Prague.

Elsewhere a French army defeated a Hanoverian army under William Augustus, duke of Cumberland, at Hastenbeck on the Weser (July 26, 1757), the latter capitulating on September 8 at the convention of Klosterzeven; a Russian army under General Apraksin invaded East Prussia and crushed Hans von Lehwaldt at Gross-Jägerndorf on August 30; the Swedes invaded Prussian Pomerania in September; the Austrians defeated a Prussian force in Silesia on September 7 at Moys, and on October 16 General Haddick's light troops even raided Berlin, leaving the next day with a ransom payment of 215,000 thalers.

Because the most serious threat was a Franco-German army invading Saxony, Frederick, operating on interior lines, marched to meet them. At Rossbach on November 5, 1757, the Prussian cavalry, led by General Frederick William von Seydlitz (1721–1773), slashed into the advancing enemy columns and routed them. But in Silesia the duke of Brunswick-Bevern (1765–1781) was defeated at Breslau by Prince Charles on November 22, Bevern himself being captured two days later, and the fortress city fell on November 25. Frederick force marched his troops 170 miles in twelve days over poor roads to meet Prince

Charles at Leuthen on December 5, 1757. In the greatest victory of his career, Frederick marched to attack the south (left) flank of his foe, the infantry advancing in perfect oblique order, the artillery giving constant support, and the cavalry meeting all counterattacks and then propelling the defeated whitecoats into flight. Charles, defeated for the fifth time in two wars by Frederick, was relieved of his command and succeeded by Daun, the victor of Kolin.

Frederick's victories encouraged the English who, under William Pitt, the first earl of Chatham (1708–1778) and prime minister since November 1756, repudiated Cumberland's capitulation and reinforced the Hanoverians, occupying the French. Lehwaldt drove the Swedes back into their fortress at Stralsund, and the Russians had already retired, apparently because Czarina Elizabeth was rumored to be ill, and her successor, Peter, was an ardent Prussophile. Thus Frederick entered 1758 optimistically, especially as the British promised an annual subsidy of £670,000 (four million thalers) in a new treaty signed April 11, and an Anglo-Hanoverian army under Ferdinand, duke of Brunswick (1721–1792), crossed the lower Rhine and defeated the French at Krefeld on June 23. Frederick himself cleared Silesia and then invaded Moravia and invested Olmütz.

Nonetheless the Austrians ambushed Frederick's supply column, and in any case a new Russian army under the Scottish émigré William Fermor, was plundering its way toward the Oder. Frederick rapidly marched to that river and crossed it below Küstrin to flank Fermor but was fought to a stalemate at Zorndorf (August 25, 1758). Logistical difficulties caused the greencoats to withdraw, and Frederick was able to rush to Saxony to assist his brother, Prince Henry, against a new Austrian advance. Daun surprised Frederick, encamped at Hochkirch, on October 14 but was too cautious to exploit his victory, and Frederick still held Saxony and Silesia at year's end.

The war of attrition was having its effect on Prussia, however, and the spring of 1759 found another Russian army under General Saltykov advancing into Brandenburg. As one Prussian force was defeated at Züllichau (or Kay) on July 23, Frederick rushed up to attack at Kunersdorf on August 12. But the Russians had been reinforced by the Austrians, Frederick's columns lost their way in the forests and attacked independently, and Frederick suffered the worst defeat of his career. Yet again the Russians withdrew, and an exhausted Frederick raced to Saxony where Daun had taken Dresden on September 14. A depressing campaign season ended when Prussian General Frederick von Finck (1718–1766) was trapped at Maxen and forced to surrender to Daun on November 21.

For England, conversely, 1759 had been a year of success. French armies crossed the Weser into Hanover, but they were lured into an attack on Ferdinand of Brunswick's Anglo-Hanoverian army at Minden (August 1) and shattered by the stoutness of six British infantry regiments. A French plan to invade England itself was foiled by the Royal Navy when the Toulon fleet was scattered off Lagos, Portugal (August 19), and the Brest fleet was wrecked at Quiberon Bay,

Brittany (November 21). Seapower enabled the British to prevail in Canada, where Quebec had been won September 13, and also in India.

Three columns were converging on Prussia in 1760: Austrians under Daun in Saxony and under Gideon Ernest Loudon (1717–1770) in Silesia, and Russians under General Chernyshev from Poland. Frederick countermarched to hold Daun by threatening Dresden, and then doubled back to Silesia, evaded an attack by Loudon at Liegnitz (August 15), mauling him in the process and discouraging Chernyshev. Frederick reentered Breslau on August 17, but in the autumn had to march for Berlin, sacked by the cossacks of General Totleben's raid (October 8–13). The last threat was posed in Saxony by Daun, who had advanced to Torgau. Frederick attacked his entrenched position on November 3, suffering heavy losses; but then Hans Joachim von Zieten's (1699–1786) wing belatedly arrived, and by nightfall Daun, thrice victor over Frederick, finally retreated. In western Germany, Ferdinand's Anglo-Hanoverian army defeated the French at Warburg on July 31, 1760, but his advance across the Rhine was stopped at Klosterkamp on October 16.

Mutual exhaustion brought tentative peace negotiations in 1761, but they came to naught. Neither were campaigns fought to a decision. In Westphalia Ferdinand's advance was stopped at Grünberg on March 21, while a French advance in turn was checked at Vellinghausen (July 15). In Silesia Frederick maneuvered against the Russians and Austrians who, however, refused to attack him when he took up an entrenched position at Bunzelwitz. But by year's end the Austrians were inexorably advancing in Saxony and Silesia, and on December 16 the Russians captured the fortress port of Kolberg on the Pomeranian coast. English support for Prussia was also wavering. Pitt resigned on October 5 because of the vacillation of the government and the animosity of the new king, George III (1738–1820). Indeed England faced a new potential foe in Spain, encouraged by France to join the fray in foreign minister (1758–1770) Etienne François, duke de Choiseul's (1719–1785), family compact (between Bourbons Louis XV and Carlos III of Spain, 1716–1788) of August 1761.

Frederick's prospects were at their bleakest when Elizabeth of Russia died suddenly on January 5, 1762, and Frederick's admirer ascended the throne as Peter III (1728–1762). On May 5 Peter made peace with Frederick, mediated a Prusso-Swedish treaty (of Hamburg) on May 22, and in June allied his armies with the Prussians. He was deposed and murdered in July, but his widow, Catherine II (1729–1796), did not rejoin the anti-Prussian coalition. Austria alone continued the struggle, but in Silesia Daun was defeated at Burkersdorf and Reichenbach on July 21 and August 16, respectively, trying to relieve Schweidnitz, which fell to Frederick on October 9. In Saxony the Austrians were defeated at Freiberg on October 29 by Prince Henry and signed an armistice on November 24, 1762.

Spain's involvement resulted in its invasion of Portugal but its loss of Havana and Manila to British seapower. As Ferdinand of Brunswick advanced against the French, entering Cassel on November 1, France agreed to peace preliminaries with Great Britain at Fontainebleau on November 3. The Seven Years War formally ended with the Treaty of Paris (February 10, 1763), by which colonial possessions were traded but France lost Canada, and the Treaty of Hubertusburg in Saxony (February 15, 1763), by which the status quo of 1748 was restored, Frederick keeping Silesia (in this third Silesian war), and Saxony being returned to its elector. More significant was the evident decline of France and Austria, the rise of England and Prussia, and the increasing role of Russia in European affairs.

Works About: *Die Kriege unter der Regierung der Kaiserin Marie Theresia,* 9 vols. (Vienna, 1896–1914); Frederick II, *Politische Correspondenz Friedrichs des Grossen,* 46 vols. (Berlin, 1879–1939); E. I. Masslowski, *Der Siebenjährige Krieg nach russischer Darstellung,* 3 vols. (Berlin, 1889–1893); Prussian General Staff, *Die Kriege Friedrichs des Grossen,* 20 vols. (Berlin, 1890–1914), esp. *Der Siebenjährige Krieg,* vol. 13 (completed through 1759).   *A. H. Ganz*

See AUSTRIAN SUCCESSION; FREDERICK II, THE GREAT; KAUNITZ; MARIA THERESA; ROSSBACH.

SFORZA, BIANCA MARIA (1472–1510), second wife of Emperor Maximilian I, was born in Pavia, the daughter of Galeazzo Maria Sforza, duke of Milan, and Bona of Savoy. Attempts to marry her to Philbert, duke of Savoy, Albert of Bavaria, and the eldest son of King Matthias Corvinus of Hungary all failed for various reasons. After the assassination of her father, Bianca's uncle, Ludovico il Moro Sforza, became regent and ruler of Milan and sought a matrimonial alliance for her that would gain him support against the French. Emperor Maximilian was the logical choice, and Ludovico offered him the hand of his niece, "one of the richest brides in the world," with a dowry of 400,000 ducats. Maximilian agreed to marry Bianca for purely political reasons. This connection with Milan, he believed, would close the gates to the French in Italy, protect imperial rights in Italy, and through the dowry provide support for his wars against the Turks.

After marriage by proxy at Milan, Bianca traveled to Innsbruck where she had to wait several months before she was joined by Maximilian for another marriage ceremony in March 1494. Maximilian made very little effort to achieve a lasting relationship with her. He found her to be nervous, capricious, indulgent, sickly, and gloomy. Soon the emperor ignored her. Bianca became ever more lonely and was, in fact, only occasionally invited to the great court ceremonies. The couple had no children. Unloved and neglected, the empress led a joyless existence without attaining any political influence. After an illness she died in 1510 and was buried in Innsbruck.

Works About: E. Bock, "Bianca Maria," **NDB**, 2:214; Felice Calvi, *Bianca Maria Sforza-Visconti* (Milan, 1888).   *J. J. Spielvogel*

See MAXIMILIAN I.

SICKINGEN, FRANZ VON (1481–1523), leader of the Knights' Revolt of 1522–1523, was born at castle Ebernburg, the only son of a knight. Franz received some training from the humanist John Reuchlin. His wife, Hedwig of Florsheim, died after twelve years of wedded life, leaving him three sons and three daughters. He refused to marry again and instead began a career as a knight errant.

Sickingen was concerned about the declining fortunes of the imperial nobility and felt that his class must assert itself against the growing power of the princes and the towns. He began by attacking the city of Worms, creating havoc with its trade and capturing vast stores of booty. In April 1515 Emperor Maximilian put him under imperial ban but was unable to enforce it. Later the ban was withdrawn on condition that Sickingen make peace with Worms. He later attacked the cities of Metz and Frankfurt, as well as Landgrave Philip of Hesse. His assaults ceased only after the payment of large indemnities.

Following the death of Maximilian, Sickingen found his services sought after by King Francis I of France, whom he had already fought for, and the newly elected emperor, Charles V. Germanic feeling triumphed this time, and he threw in his lot with Charles, even loaning him 20,000 gulden for his coronation. During this same period he also came to the defense of his old teacher Reuchlin. His humanist friend Ulrich von Hutten converted him to the cause of Martin Luther. Sickingen offered his support to Luther, who refused it, but did dedicate a small book to him. Others such as Hutten, Martin Bucer, and Oecolampadius did accept his protection.

Sickingen's own plans for reform included the idea of secularizing the wealthy archbishopric of Trier. Those plans were shelved for a time as Sickingen accepted a commission as general from Charles V for a war against the French. The campaign failed, and, to make matters worse, the imperial government defaulted on a second loan from Sickingen of 76,000 gulden. He was forced to send home many of his soldiers with empty promises.

In order to recoup his losses in prestige and fortune, Sickingen revived his scheme for the attack upon Richard von Greiffenklau, archbishop of Trier, an old enemy. He hoped to rally many of the knights and, even more naively, some of the cities to his banner. Despite limited support from the former and none from the latter, the campaign against Trier commenced on August 29, 1522. The archbishop, who had allied with Philip of Hesse and Count Palatine Louis, proved an able foe. The knights soon found themselves driven back to their own castles, which fell one by one to the artillery of the allied princes. Sickingen died during the siege of his castle at Landstuhl.

Works About: William R. Hitchcock, *The Background of the Knights' Revolt, 1522–23* (Berkeley, 1958); Heinrich Ulmann, *Franz von Sickingen* (Leipzig, 1872).   *J. W. Zophy*

See CHARLES V; HUTTEN; LUTHER; MAXIMILIAN I.

SIGISMUND (1368–1437), also known as Siegmund, Sigismundus, (Latin), and officially as Sigmund, was Holy Roman emperor from 1410 to 1437, as well as king of Hungary and Bohemia. Throughout his career, Sigismund sought crusade against the Ottoman Turks, security and rule in Hungary and Bohemia, and Christian unity in Germany under imperial leadership.

The son of Emperor Charles IV, he was betrothed to Maria, the daughter of King Louis of Hungary and Poland (died 1386). Sigismund then overcame rival claimants and a great deal of internal opposition to be crowned king of Hungary on March 31, 1387. To mount a crusade against the Turks who threatened his lands, he mortgaged one of his possessions, electoral Brandenburg, to Margrave Jobst of Moravia for five years. Sigismund suffered a crushing defeat at Nicopolis by Sultan Bayazid I on September 28, 1396. Now endangered by Jobst, he resumed Brandenburg, mortgaged Neumark to the Teutonic Knights (1402), and received rule in Bohemia from his brother Wenceslaus (1402). Efforts failed to placate Jobst, who invaded Hungary, and Sigismund turned to peacemaking in the east.

Elected Holy Roman emperor on July 21, 1411, to replace Rupert of Bavaria (he dated his election from September 20, 1410), Sigismund's early years were occupied with the diplomacy of the Council of Constance (1414–1418), which he hoped would bring peace to a Church traumatized by the Great Schism. He endorsed the bull, *Sacrosancta* (April 6, 1415), which asserted conciliar authority; secured the elimination of the three rival popes; and accepted the election of a new pope, Martin V, to end the schism (November 11, 1417) without a precondition of Church reform.

The Council of Constance presided over by Sigismund is also famous for the trial and burning of John Hus, which touched off the relentless opposition of his Bohemian followers. The reformer had accepted Sigismund's invitation and safe conduct to Constance. The emperor arrived at the council to find Hus imprisoned for heresy and revoked the safe conduct he had granted to preserve the Council. Although Sigismund was the only heir of Wenceslaus, who died on April 16, 1419, the Bohemian estates refused him recognition as king. A campaign in Bohemia in 1420 and 1421 failed and stimulated the majority of Hussites to adopt the unifying Articles of Prague. Severe defeat in 1427 convinced Sigismund that only compromise could resolve the Hussite crisis. This would require agreement of the pope, and Sigismund set his sights on the forthcoming Council of Basel (1431–1439). He secured adoption of the Compacts of Prague (1433), which the council had negotiated with representatives of the Bohemians. After implementing the compacts and making Bohemia secure, Sigismund entered Prague on August 24, 1436. He left amid great hostility in 1437.

Emperor Sigismund died on December 9, 1437. He was a leader and a planner, but he did not occupy himself with implementation. The constant pressure of eastern problems prevented him from giving long-range attention to German issues. However, several of his actions did have a lasting impact, most significantly the investiture of Brandenburg in the Hohenzollern house and Saxony in the Wettin house. Sigismund tried several ways of forming a power base in Germany, relying at the outset on the electors, shifting to the imperial cities later, but in the end he found himself frustrated by German parochialism. His most important accomplishment was the Council of Constance, which he arranged, guided, and held together. Yet it generated the Bohemian crisis, which dramatically underscored the need for constitutional reform in the Empire. Nevertheless he kept Bohemia unified and in the Empire. By contrast Sigismund was an ineffective king of Hungary, who never attained his high goal of defeating the Ottoman Turks.

Works About: W. Altmann, *Die Urkunden Kaiser Sigmunds*, 2 vols. (Vienna, 1896–1900); J. von Aschbach, *Gesch. Kaiser Sigmunds*, 4 vols. (Vienna, 1838–1845, rpr., 1964) *DRTA* (Stuttgart, 1908–1916), vols. 7–9; A. Main, *The Emperor Sigismund* (London, 1903); Theodor Lindner, "Sigmund," *ADB*, 34:267–82; *MGH: SRG, Geschichtschreibern der dtsch, Vorzeit*, ed. H. Mencken and tr. J. von Hagen (Hanover, 1886), vol. 1.   *K. C. Sessions*

See CHARLES IV; CONCILIARISM; HUS; RUPERT I.

SILESIUS, ANGELUS or JOHN SCHEFFLER (1624–77), mystic, poet, and propagandist, was born in Breslau, the capital of Silesia. He studied medicine and philosophy at Strasbourg and Leiden. His mysticism was influenced by the writings of Meister Eckhart, Jacob Boehme, and Abraham von Franckenburg. After a surprising conversion to Roman Catholicism in 1652, Silesius gave up his position as the personal physician to the Protestant duke of Württemberg. He adopted the name Angelus Silesius and eventually became physician to Emperor Ferdinand III. Ordained a priest in 1661, Silesius became a fanatical propagandist for the Counter Reformation. He was also regarded as one of the leading poets of his era.

Works By: *Sämtliche poetische Werke und eine Auswahl aus seinen Streitschriften*, ed. Georg Ellinger, 2 vols. (Berlin, 1923); *Selections from the Cherubinic Wanderer*, tr. J. E. Crawford Flitch (London, 1932). **Works About**: Georg Ellinger, *Angelus Silesius* (Breslau, 1927); M. H. Godecker, *Angelus Silesius' Personality through His Ecclesiolagia* (Washington, D.C., 1938); Jeffrey L. Sammons, *Angelus Silesius* (New York, 1967).   *J. W. Zophy*

See BOEHME; ECKHART; FERDINAND III.

SOPHIE CHARLOTTE (1668–1705), the daughter of Ernest Augustus and Sophie of Hanover, married Frederick III, elector of Brandenburg and later king in Prussia, in 1684. Her black hair, which she never powdered, blue eyes, regular features, and fair complexion earned her the sobriquet the "beautiful queen." Her personal charm and her interest in literature and philosophy helped to make Berlin a cultural center, which attracted intellectuals such as Leibniz. One of the most beautiful and intelligent women of her day, the spirited queen attempted to control the more sedate, sober, and pious Frederick. She resented the influence of Eberhard von Danckelmann, the competent prime minister, and helped to engineer his downfall in 1697. Her death in 1705, though widely regretted, occasioned no alteration in court affairs because of her failure during the latter years of her life to influence court politics and because of the increasingly pronounced estrangement between the king and the queen.

Works By: Ernst Berner, *Aus dem Briefwechsel König Friedrichs I, von Preussen und seiner Familie* (Berlin, 1901). **Works About**: Bernard von Brentano, *Sophie Charlotte und Danckelmann* (Weisbaden, 1949); Karl August Ludwig Philip Varnhagen von Ense, *Biographische Denkmale* (Leipzig, 1872); J. P. Erman, *Mémoires pour servir à l'histoire de Sophie Charlotte, reine de Prusse* (Berlin, 1801); Linda Frey and Marsha Frey, "Frederick I and His Court, 1703–1710," *Révue de l'Université d'Ottawa* 45 (1975): 478–90; R. Koser, "Sophie Charlotte, die erste preussische Königin," *Dtsch. Rundschau* 52 (1926): 353–69; Otto Krauske, "Königin Sophie Charlotte," *Hohenzoll. Jb.* 4 (1900): 110–26; J. Toland, *An Account of the Courts of Prussia and Hanover* (London, 1705), pp. 22–24.   L. S. Frey and M. L. Frey

See FREDERICK III, ELECTOR; LEIBNIZ.

SPALATIN (real name Burckhardt), GEORGE (1484–1545), jurist and Lutheran reformer, was born in the town of Spalt near Nuremberg (hence the assumed name Spalatin), the son of a wealthy tanner. He studied law at the universities of Erfurt and Wittenberg and became a member of the humanist group associated with Conrad Mutian. In 1505 he was appointed a teacher at the cloister Georgenthal near Gotha; in 1508 he was ordained a priest. Shortly thereafter he was called into the service of Frederick the Wise, elector of Saxony, as a tutor to the young prince John Frederick. In 1512 he was made director of the castle library at Wittenberg. In time he became Frederick's closest and most trusted adviser, serving the elector in a wide range of capacities: as private secretary, historiographer, court chaplain, and father confessor. It was from this unique position of personal influence within the Saxon court that he was able to promote effectively the cause of religious reform. He served as an indispensable go-between for the elector (who seems never to have spoken personally with Luther) and the reformer, and continually labored to secure for the latter Frederick's goodwill and protection.

Spalatin's activities on behalf of his friend Luther date from the early days of the reform movement. In 1518 when Luther was called to defend his teaching at Heidelberg, Spalatin secured for him from Frederick the Wise a secure escort through the elector's own territories and effective letters of recommendation to neighboring rulers. Early in 1519 he mediated the important negotiations between Luther and the papal nuncio, Karl von Miltitz. Spalatin's role was especially important in the events leading up to and during the diet of Worms (1521), and it was partly due to his influence that the highly cautious elector of Saxony persevered in gaining the emperor Charles V's consent to a public hearing for Luther before the estates of the Empire.

Although Spalatin left the electoral court in 1525 to accept a pastorate in Altenburg, he continued to play a part in Saxon religious diplomacy. He was present at the diet of Augsburg (1530), where he helped write the Augsburg Confession, and he attended meetings of the Schmalkaldic League leaders. In the meantime, he had emerged as a major influence in the organizational development of the Lutheran state church. Although he was unsuccessful in persuading Frederick the Wise to undertake a magisterial reform, his proposal of governmental intervention in ecclesiastical affairs received a more positive response from Frederick's successors, who decided to promote and direct the Reformation throughout their lands. Spalatin himself was particularly involved in the implementation of the church visitation program.

Although not an especially creative author, Spalatin made many useful translations of the writings of others, including Luther, Melanchthon, and Erasmus. Among his own compositions, the works on Saxon history are most important.

Works By: Georg Berbig, *Spalatiniana* (Leipzig, 1908); Peter Drews, "Spalatiniana," *ZKG* 19 (1899): 69–98, 486–514, and 20 (1900): 467–99; Georg Mentz, "Die Briefe G. Spalatins an V. Warbeck, nebst ergänzenden Aktenstücken," *ARG* 1 (1903–1904): 197–246; Christian Gotth. Neudecker and Ludwig Preller, eds., *Georg Spalatins hist. Nachlass und Briefe*, 1: *Friedrichs des Weisen Leben und Zeitgesch.* (Jena, 1851); Georg Spalatin, *Annales Reformationis oder Jb. von der Reformation Lutheri* (Leipzig, 1718). **Works About**: Georg Berbig, *Georg Spalatin und sein Verhältnis zu Martin Luther auf Grund ihres Briefwechsels bis zum Jahre 1525* (Halle, 1906); Willy Flach, "Georg Spalatin als Geschichtsschreiber," in *Zur Gesch. und Kultur des Elb-Saale-Raumes: Festschrift für Walter Möllenberg*, ed. Otto Kerne (Burg, 1939), pp. 211–30; Irmgard Höss, *Georg Spalatin 1484–1545* (Weimar, 1956), and "Georg Spalatins Verhältnis zu Luther und der Reformation," *Luther: Mitt. der Luthergesch.* (1960), 67–80; Georg Müller, "Georg Spalatin," *ADB*, 35:1–29; Hans Volz, "Bibliographie der im 16. Jahrhundert erschienenen Schriften Georg Spalatins," *Z. für Bibliothekswesen* 5 (1958): 83–119.   *C. C. Christensen*

See CHARLES V; FREDERICK III, THE WISE; LUTHER; SCHMALKALDIC LEAGUE.

SPANISH SUCCESSION, WAR OF THE (1701–1714), one of the major wars of the eighteenth century, sought to resolve the greatest diplomatic issue of the day: the deposition of the Spanish empire. The death of Carlos II, the "last pallid relic of a faded dynasty" on November 1, 1700, brought the whole problem of the succession dramatically to the fore. The question was tangled and difficult. In the Spanish empire, Castilian law clearly stipulated that in default of male heirs to the throne, females should inherit in order of primogeniture. Furthermore ever since 1559 when Charles V had divided his kingdom between the two branches of the house of Habsburg, there had been a series of mutual family agreements that if one branch should die out, the other would succeed it.

To ensure a Habsburg succession, the Austrian heir married the eldest Spanish infanta. If, however, the eldest infanta married into another house, she renounced her claim to the Spanish throne, and the Austrian heir married her next elder sister, thereby ensuring the succession. In the seventeenth century, two infantas married into the house of Bourbon: Anne of Austria, daughter of Philip III (married Louis XIII in 1615), and Maria Theresa, daughter of Philip IV (married Louis XIV in 1659). Both infantas renounced their claims to the throne, and their younger sisters married Austrian Habsburgs: Maria, the daughter of Philip III, married Emperor Ferdinand (1631), and Margaret, the daughter of Philip IV, married Emperor Leopold I (1666). The problem of the succession was complicated because Maria Theresa's renunciation of the throne was conditional on the full payment of her dowry and because Margaret, Emperor Leopold's wife, had left only a daughter, Maria Antonia, who married the elector of Bavaria (1685) and had a son, the electoral prince Joseph Ferdinand. Leopold had extracted a private, personal renunciation of the Spanish throne from Maria Antonia.

There were then three claimants for the Spanish throne. The electoral prince Joseph Ferdinand rightly claimed that Maria Antonia's renunciation was invalid, while the dauphin, son of Maria Theresa, maintained that his mother's was contingent on the payment of her dowry. Emperor Leopold alleged that he was the legitimate heir because both Maria Theresa and Maria Antonia had renounced their claims and because his mother, Maria, wife of Emperor Ferdinand III, passed her rights on to him. Leopold would in turn transfer his to Archduke Charles, his second son.

In order to prevent a general European war from developing, England, France, and the United Provinces signed the Partition Treaties of 1698 and 1700. Both Spain and Austria, however, repudiated these treaties. Emperor Leopold had resolved to "sink or swim with the Spaniards," who vigorously opposed any division of their lands. The first Partition Treaty allocated Spain, the Netherlands, and the colonies to Joseph Ferdinand, the Milanese to Archduke Charles, and the two Sicilies to the dauphin. In an attempt to avoid partition of his empire, Carlos II made a will leaving his entire empire to Joseph Ferdinand. The death of the electoral prince in 1699 rendered both settlements abortive. In a vain effort to reach a peaceful settlement, William III negotiated a second Partition Treaty. By this treaty, Spain, the Netherlands, and the colonies would go to Archduke Charles, while the Milanese and the two Sicilies would go to the dauphin.

In one last desperate counter move, Carlos II, in order to detach the Bourbons from the policy of partition, made a will leaving his entire empire to Philip of Anjou, provided that the crowns of Spain and France should never be united. If Philip did not accept the will, the entire inheritance would pass to Archduke Charles. Louis XIV repudiated the partitions and recognized his grandson Philip of Anjou as king of Spain on November 15, 1700. Later England and the United Provinces also recognized Philip as king of Spain. Austria, both exasperated and disappointed with Carlos II's will, immediately sent troops to Italy.

The emperor, convinced of his inalienable right to the Spanish throne, firmly believed that God would aid him in his cause. In the hope of winning the

Spanish inheritance for the Habsburgs, Leopold tried to secure aid from the various German princes. Louis XIV tried to persuade many of them to remain neutral by emphasizing that the Spanish succession was only a dynastic question, a private quarrel that concerned only the Bourbons and the Habsburgs, not the Empire. Leopold, on the other hand, stressed that the growing power of France threatened every German prince and that the whole Empire should come to his aid, particularly after France's illegal seizure of the imperial fiefs in Italy.

By the end of 1701, self-interest, fear of French hegemony, hope of allied subsidies, and loyalty of such men as Lothar Franz Schonborn, elector of Mainz and archchancellor of the Empire, and Christian Ernest of Bayreuth, imperial field marshal, had secured for Leopold the support of Frederick, elector of Brandenburg, king in Prussia; George, elector of Hanover; and the elector Palatine. Duke Anton Ulrich of Brunswick-Wolfenbüttel, head of the elder Guelph dynasty, Joseph Clemens, elector and archbishop of Cologne, and his elder brother, Max Emmanuel, elector of Bavaria, of the Wittelsbach dynasty allied with Louis XIV. Celle and Hanover quickly overpowered Anton Ulrich, who fled while his brother Rudolph Augustus concluded an accord that allowed Brunswick-Wolfenbüttel troops to be taken into the emperor's service.

Meanwhile John Churchill, later duke of Marlborough, was negotiating the Grand Alliance at the Hague. Although the emperor continued to insist on his right to inherit the whole Spanish empire, he nevertheless signed the treaty. By this pact of September 7, 1701, Austria, England, and the United Provinces accepted the rule of Philip V over Spain and the Spanish Indies on condition that the crowns of Spain and France should never be united. They also agreed to obtain "a just and reasonable satisfaction" for the house of Habsburg in the form of Milan, Naples, Sicily, the Spanish Mediterranean islands, and the Netherlands. The United Provinces would acquire "a Dyke, Rampart and Barrier to separate France and the United Provinces" in the Spanish Netherlands. Article 8 stipulated that England and the United Provinces must enjoy the same trading privileges in Philip's dominions as they enjoyed under Carlos II and that France must not possess or trade with the Spanish Indies. Later the allies agreed that the emperor should bring eighty-two thousand men into the field against France, the United Provinces one hundred thousand, and England forty thousand.

In 1701, Austria was not prepared financially, administratively, or militarily to enter the war. Rampant corruption in the central government and administration, fluctuating tax yields, especially from the land tax, incorrect tax estimates, declining trade, and imminent bankruptcy severely limited the Habsburg war efforts. The allies were increasingly exasperated with the emperor's slowness, irresolution, and seeming indifference concerning his military preparedness. As of June 1701, the emperor had only ten thousand troops in the field. By November 1701 he had only fourteen thousand.

The year 1701 also revealed the allies' basically irreconcilable views on strategy. England and the United Provinces wanted the emperor to center the main war effort on the Rhine rather than on Italy. Leopold, along with his advisers, thought that once Italy was conquered, the rest of the Spanish dominions would follow quickly and easily. Italy's proximity to the hereditary countries made it strategically important for the Habsburgs. In May 1701, the emperor took the initiative and sent Prince Eugene of Savoy into Italy to overrun the Franco-Spanish positions. Eugene assembled his army in Tyrol on March 27, 1701. By marching through Vincenze, neutral Venetian territory, he surprised Marshal Catinat and forced him to retreat to the Oglio. The new commander, Villeroi, was defeated at Chiari. The supply routes to central Italy and Germany were now under imperial control. In a daring maneuver, Eugene made his way into Cremona, the winter headquarters of the French, and captured the marshal (February 1702). There was little decisive action on land or sea in the first two years of the war; Marlborough overran parts of the lower Rhine, Lewis of Baden seized Landau, and Eugene outmaneuvered Vendôme in Italy. A revolt (1703–1711) led by Rákóczi in Hungary threatened to divert badly needed men and supplies. Marshal Villars led a strong force through the Black Forest, but the elector of Bavaria chose to invade the Tyrol, where fierce resistance forced him to withdraw. The allies detached Portugal from its French alliance in 1703 but thereby committed themselves to placing Charles on the Spanish throne. In that same year, they won the alliance of Duke Victor Amadeus of Savoy. In 1704, the double offensive launched by the Hungarian rebels and the Franco-Bavarian troops toward Vienna was repulsed only by the victory of Blenheim, the first of a series of defeats that marked the end of French military superiority. Vienna was saved, Bavaria was in allied hands, and the French were on the defensive. In 1705, there were no decisive battles. In 1706, Marlborough's victory at Ramillies and Eugene's at Turin ensured allied control of the Netherlands and Italy. In 1707, Louis XIV ordered Vendôme to operate in the lowlands and Villars to raid Bavaria. In Spain, Berwick defeated the Anglo-Portuguese forces. In 1708, Vendôme moved into the Spanish Netherlands, but found himself outmaneuvered at the Battle of Oudenarde. Lille then fell to the allies. Negotiations opened at the Hague, but allied demands made peace impossible. In 1709, the battle of Malplaquet was won at enormous cost to both the allied victors and the defeated French. Negotiations were reopened at Gertruydenberg in 1710 but soon collapsed. Louis refused to send troops against his grandson if Philip refused to abdicate. Louis preferred, he said, "to make war on my enemies rather than on my children." Continental victories had not brought peace. The destruction of the Marlborough-Godolphin ministry, the fall of the Whigs, and the death of Emperor Joseph paved the way for negotiations, which began at Utrecht in 1712. Peace was made by a series of treaties signed in 1713, 1714, and 1715. In effect, the plenipotentiaries partitioned the Spanish empire. The Holy Roman Empire still remained at war with France. The Emperor Charles VI, finally realizing the futility of continuing the struggle, concluded peace at Rastatt and Baden (March and September 1714).

Works About: Max Braubach, *Prinz Eugen von Savoyen*, 5 vols. (Vienna, 1963–65); Winston S. Churchill, *Marlborough, His Life and Times* (London, 1947); M. R. R. de Courcy, *La coalition de 1701 contra la France* (Paris, 1886); Eugene Francois, Prince of Savoy, *Feldzuge des Prinzen Eugen von Savoyen*, 20 vols. (Vienna, 1876–1892); A. Gaedeke, *Die Politik Österreichs in der spanischen Erbfolgefrage*, 2 vols. (Leipzig, 1906); Max Immich, *Gesch. des europäischen Staatensystems von 1660 bis 1789* (Berlin, 1905); A. Legrelle, *La diplomatie française et la succession d'Espagne*, 4 vols. (Ghent, 1888–1892); F. A. M. A. Mignet, *Négociations relatives à la succession d'Espagne, sous Louis XIV*, 4 vols. (Paris, 1835–1842); Sir George Murray, ed., *Letters and Dispatches of John Churchill, First Duke of Marlborough, from 1702–1712*, 5 vols. (London, 1845); C. G. Picavet, *La diplomatie française au temps de Louis XIV, 1661–1715* (Paris, 1930); G. F. Preuss, "Österreich, Frankreich, und Bayern in der spanischen Erbfolgefrage," *Hist. Vierteljahrschrift* 4 (1901): 309–33, 491–503; H. L. Snyder, eds., *The Marlborough-Godolphin Correspondence*, 3 vols. (Oxford, 1976); F. E. Vault and J. J. G. Pelet, *Mémoires militaires relatifs à la succession d'Espagne sous Louis XIV*, 11 vols. (Paris, 1835–1842).

L. S. Frey and M. L. Frey

See BLENHEIM; CHARLES VI; EUGENE OF SAVOY; JOSEPH I; LEOPOLD I; UTRECHT.

SPENGLER, LAZARUS (1479–1534), council secretary of the imperial city of Nuremberg, was born the ninth of twenty-one children on March 13, 1479. George Spengler, his father, was a native of Donauwörth who came to Nuremberg in 1475, where he was council secretary from that year until his death in 1496.

At sixteen years of age, Lazarus went to the University of Leipzig to study law. Because of the death of his father two years later, he returned to Nuremberg to help support his family, working as a secretary in the municipal court. In 1501, he married Ursula, the only child of Hans and Margaretha Sulmeister. The couple had nine children, only four of whom were living when he made his last will and testament in 1529. Lazarus sent his most promising son, his namesake, to the University of Wittenberg, but since the young man had no inclination to study, he sent him to the Netherlands to to begin a career as a merchant. This took him to Portugal and eventually to South America.

In 1501, the city council made Spengler secretary in the chancellery, where he was in charge of the municipal records. In 1507 it made him first *Ratsschreiber*, or council secretary, a position that he held until his death. In 1516 it made him a member of the large city council. At the opening of the third diet of Nuremberg in 1524, Ferdinand, in the name of his brother Emperor Charles V, improved the coat of arms of Lazarus and his brother George in recognition of their services to the Holy Roman Empire.

It was in the role of first secretary of the city council that Spengler assumed his position of leadership, not only at home but also in the Holy Roman Empire at large. Although he had been unable to complete his university studies, he was so widely read and well informed that the city council depended much on him for advice. Having charge of the council's official records, he became thoroughly acquainted with its activities. Often serving in a diplomatic capacity at imperial diets, diets of the Swabian League, and various meetings of princes and cities, he became familiar with the important issues and leaders of his day.

Spengler's interest in cultural and religious matters was evinced by his participation in the discussions of the city's intellectual circle. Early in his career as secretary, he came into contact with a group interested in humanism. It included such prominent men as Willibald Pirckheimer, one of Germany's best-known humanists; Christoph Scheurl, the city's chief jurisconsult who had taught law at the University of Wittenberg; Anton Tucher and Hieronymus Ebner, two of the most influential councilmen; and Albrecht Dürer, Germany's best-known artist. This circle, referred to as the *Sodalitas celtica* because of the frequent visits to Nuremberg of the outstanding humanist Conrad Celtis during the second decade of the century, soon came under the spell of the preaching of John Staupitz, vicar-general of the Augustinian Eremites and Luther's mentor. It then came to be known as the *Sodalitas staupitziana*. Later its members were called *Martinianer* because of their support of Martin Luther. As early as 1514, Spengler published his translation from Latin into German of the pseudo-Eusebius biography, *The Life and Death of St. Jerome*, for which Dürer provided his woodcut "Jerome in the Grotto." His friendship with Dürer led to the publication in 1520 of his *Admonition and Instruction for a Virtuous Life*, written in rhyme and dedicated to the artist.

Spengler's interest in the Reformation was stimulated by Luther's visits to Nuremberg on his way to and from his hearings before Cajetan in Augsburg in 1518. He resented the attacks upon Luther so keenly that he wrote one of the first well-known pamphlets in his defense, *Defense and Christian Reply of an Honorable Lover of the Divine Truth of Holy Scripture*. It was published anonymously in 1519. Because of this *Defense* and the fact that John Eck believed that Spengler had translated into German Pirckheimer's attack on him, this foremost opponent of Luther included Spengler with Pirckheimer in the papal bull *Exsurge domine* against the Reformer, threatening them with excommunication, and in the bull *Decet pontificem romanum*, excommunicating them. Although both eventually were absolved, this experience helped influence Spengler to play a leading role as a lay reformer. He was one of the city's delegates to the diet of Worms in 1521. He wrote memorandums for the city council, the councils of other German cities, and various rulers, giving advice with respect to making changes designed to conform with evangelical doctrines. He made important contacts with rulers attending the meetings of Imperial Cameral Court and the three meetings of the imperial diet in Nuremberg from 1522 to 1524. He supported the Lutheran provosts and preachers of Nuremberg in their changes in church services and doctrines. He was spokesman for the council at the religious colloquy of 1525, the outcome of which led the council to support the Reformation openly and to break with Rome. Following Luther's advice, he took an active part in establishing in Nuremberg a gymnasium, or higher school of learning, with the active assistance of Melanchthon. To consolidate Reformation changes in Nuremberg and help attain doctrinal and ecclesiastical unity among Protestants, he was the driving force behind the cooperation with Margrave George of Brandenburg-Ansbach, which resulted in the publication of the Brandenburg-Nuremberg Church Order of 1533.

In addition to his many activities in his official capacity as city council secretary, Spengler continued to write pamphlets and also hymns in support of the Reformation. In 1522, he wrote *The Main Articles Through Which Christendom Has Been Misled*, concerned with practical Christian ethics. In 1529, he produced his well-known *Excerpts from Papal Laws* for which Luther wrote a foreword and which the reformer had published in Wittenberg in 1530. Equally influential was his *Confession of Faith*, attached to his last will and testament. Luther considered it such an excellent summary of faith that he provided it with a laudatory introduction and had it published in Wittenberg in 1535. His best-known hymn is "Through Adam's Fall," included in Lutheran hymnals from 1524 to the present.

While supporting the Reformation, Spengler remained loyal to the Holy Roman Empire. He thereby followed not only the traditional policy of Nuremberg, which depended upon the emperor for security in the face of the ambitions of surrounding territorial princes, but also his religious commitments. Convinced that a German Christian did not have the right to resist the emperor by force, even in defense of his religion, he played an important part in keeping Nuremberg out of the Schmalkaldic League of Lutheran princes and cities and loyal to the Holy Roman Empire until its absorption by Bavaria in 1806.

Works By: Paul Kalkoff, *Die Reformation in der Reichsstadt Nürnbergs nach den Flugschriften ihres Ratsschreibers Lazarus Spenglers* (Halle, 1926); Gerhard Pfeiffer, ed., *Quel. zur Nürnberger Reformationsgesch. . . . (Juni 1524–Juni 1525)*, Einzelarbeiten aus der Kirchengeschichte Bayerns, 45 (Nuremberg, 1968); Theodor Pressel, *Lazarus Spengler: Nach gleichzeitigen Quel.* (Elberfeld, 1862). **Works About**: Harold J. Grimm, *Lazarus Spengler, A Lay Leader of the Reformation* (Columbus, Ohio, 1978); Urbanus Gottlieb Haussdorff, *Lebens-Beschreibung eines christlichen Politici, nehmlich Lazari Spenglers* (Nuremberg, 1741); Hans von Schubert, *Lazarus Spengler und die Reformation in Nürnberg*, ed. Hajo Holborn (Leipzig, 1934).   *H. J. Grimm*

See DÜRER; ECK; FERDINAND I; LUTHER; MELANCHTHON; NUREMBERG; PIRCKHEIMER, WILLIBALD; SCHEURL; STAUPITZ.

SPEYER, DIET OF 1526, opened on June 25 and concluded its business late in August. This was the first diet to meet since the conclusion of the third diet of Nuremberg in 1524, and, following upon the religious statements contained in the Nuremberg recess, Protestantism had made significant gains in the Empire. This advance indicated that the evangelical movement had not lost popular support.

During the interval between the Nuremberg diet and that of Speyer, a number of occurrences had taken place. Most significant among these were the Battle of Pavia in February 1525 in which Emperor Charles V captured, imprisoned, and eventually ransomed King Francis I (1515–1547) of France. The emperor thereby appeared to have his hands free to turn to the affairs of the Empire. A second development was the princes' creation of defensive leagues for purposes of maintaining religious practices and peace. The first alliance was the Catholic Regensburg Union, and this was followed in the north by the Catholic League of Dessau and the Protestant League of Gotha-Torgau. Other leagues, such as the existing Swabian League, had become transconfessional in that its membership included both Catholic and Protestant estates. A final series of events that prepared the backdrop for the diet of Speyer were the disturbances caused by the Knights' and Peasants' wars. These conflicts had been put down by religiously neutral associations, an indication that relative peace could prevail despite religious differences.

As a result of these occurrences, the princes began to realize their own power vis-à-vis the emperor's. The princes, through their alliances, had been able to secure relative peace in the Empire without the emperor's aid. By the time the diet opened, the international situation had changed once again, and the emperor now confronted renewed hostilities from France, the papacy, and the Turks, which turned his attention away from the Empire. Thus there appeared little hope of effecting the imperial proposition that dealt chiefly with the religious question and asked for the eradication of heresy and rebellion, enforcement of the Edict of Worms, and postponement of any final religious decision pending the meeting of a council.

Because of Charles' foreign involvements and the princes' fear that by strengthening the power of the emperor they might endanger their own privileges, the estates at Speyer stood in concert. In the recess of August 27, they declared unanimously that until the meeting of a general council or national assembly, each estate was to treat the Edict of Worms in such a manner as to account for its actions "before God and his imperial majesty." This decision allowed individual estates to deal with religious problems on a territorial basis. It therefore increased the estates' power, and Protestantism continued to make further inroads in the Empire. Although the second diet of Speyer in 1529 overturned this declaration, and the subsequent recess of the diet of Augsburg in 1530 promised action against the Protestants, the emperor was powerless to settle the religious question without the concomitant help of the estates. For this reason the diet of Speyer in 1526 was a harbinger of the religious peace of Augsburg in 1555.

Works About: Theodor Brieger, *Der Speierer Reichstag von 1526* (Leipzig, 1909); B. J. Kidd, ed., *Documents Illustrative of the Continental Reformation* (Oxford, 1911); Walter Friedensburg, *Der Reichstag zu Speier 1526*, Hist. Untersuchungen, vol. 5 (Berlin, 1887, rpr. 1970); Julius Ney, "Analakten zur Gesch. des Reichstags zu Speier im Jahre 1526," *Z. für Kirchengesch.* 8 (1886):300–17 and *Der Reichstag zu Speier 1526* (Homburg, 1889) and "Speyer, Diets of," *Schaff-Herzog*, ed. S. Jackson (New York, 1911), 11:43–46.   *P. N. Bebb*

See AUGSBURG, RELIGIOUS PEACE OF; CHARLES V; FERDINAND I; NUREMBERG, DIETS OF 1522-1524; PEASANTS' WAR; SPEYER, DIET OF 1529.

SPEYER, DIET OF 1529, was the first formal meeting of the imperial estates since that at Speyer in 1526. Catholic estates were predominant at this diet, which lasted from the middle of March to the middle of April. The prevalence of Catholics at Speyer was due in large measure to the Emperor Charles V's military successes, his new relationship with the pope—which resulted in an announced plan to convoke a general council in the near future—and his pending return to the Empire. Injuries to the dignity of spiritual princes by Landgrave Philip of Hesse also produced a conservative reaction among some estates.

Although the main object of the diet was to decide on levies to oppose the Turks, most of its work centered on the religious situation in the Empire. In the imperial proposition, modified and read by Ferdinand to the estates on March 15, the emperor demanded the revocation of the Speyer recess of 1526 because it had led to tumult and the enforcement of the Edict of Worms where it was feasible. A majority of estates supported the proposition, voted the revocation, and outlawed any further religious innovation. The recess, dated April 22, banned the introduction of Zwinglianism in the Empire and condemned to death anyone convicted of practicing adult baptism. In territories already partial to Luther's teaching, nothing further was to be done in opposition to the Catholic church, and the celebration of the Mass was not to be prohibited. The recess also stated that until the meeting of a general council, no one was to be coerced or restrained from pursuing the exercise of true religion.

This majority decision was unacceptable to a minority of evangelical estates, and they produced a minority decision, thus raising the ancient constitutional problem of majority versus minority rights. Such a decision was a protest, and the minority estates became known as protesting estates, or Protestants. The protest, signed by a small number of princes and fourteen cities, held that a decision of a majority (recess of the present diet) could not nullify a unanimous decision (recess of Speyer in 1526) and that, in any event, one's conscience in religious affairs was bound to God, not to human decisions.

Many have taken the view that the estates that affixed their signatures to the protest performed a courageous act because they ran the risk of losing their privileges and status by opposing the emperor's desires. Certainly there existed only a few arguments justifying constitutional resistance to the emperor at this point in time.

The result of the diet of Speyer forced evangelical estates to attempt closer alliances. Theological differences, however, hindered the attempt. Neither Luther nor Zwingli, the two major leaders of the evangelical movement, had come to an agreement of the correct interpretation of the Bible and sacraments. The ensuing Marburg colloquy in October made explicit their disunity. Consequently some evangelical estates, especially south German imperial cities partial to Zwingli, had no firm foundation on which to ally with Lutheran ones.

Works About: Hist. Kommission bei der Bayerischen Akademie der Wissenschaften, ed., *DRTA, Jüngere Reihe*, vol. 7: *DRTA unter Kaiser Karl V.*, ed. Johannes Kühn (Stuttgart, 1935, rpr.

Göttingen, 1963); B. J. Kidd, ed., *Documents Illustrative of the Continental Reformation* (Oxford, 1911), pp. 239–45); Johannes Kühn, *Die Gesch. des Speyer Reichstags 1529*, Schriften des Vereins für Reformations–gesch., vol. 146 (Speyer, 1929); Julius Ney, *Gesch. des Reichstages zu Speier im Jahre 1529* (Halle, 1880), and Julius Ney, ed., *Die Appellation und Protestation der evangelischen Stände auf dem Reichstage zu Speier 1529*, Quellenschriften zur Gesch. des Protestantismus, 2 vol. 5 (Leipzig, 1906, rpr. 1967). *P. N. Bebb*

See AUGSBURG, RELIGIOUS PEACE OF; CHARLES V; FERDINAND I; LUTHER; MARBURG COLLOQUY; PHILIP OF HESSE; SPEYER, DIET OF 1526; WORMS; ZWINGLI.

SPIEGEL, JACOB (1483–c. 1547), Alsatian humanist, jurist, and imperial bureaucrat, was born in Sélestat (Schlettstadt). His father was a baker, his mother a sister of the humanist priest Jacob Wimpfeling. He studied briefly at the famous municipal school at Sélestat, but after his father's death his uncle took him to live in Speyer. Spiegel studied at Heidelberg (1497–1500), and from 1500 to 1504 he studied law at Freiburg under Ulrich Zasius.

Spiegel entered the newly reorganized Imperial Chancery in 1504 under the patronage of the financial officer Jacob Villinger, who was also from Sélestat. He returned to the study of law in 1512, and he was briefly a professor of law at Vienna. He then served as personal secretary to Maximilian I until the emperor's death on January 12, 1519. In March 1520, Spiegel became a secretary to Emperor Charles V, and in 1522 a recommendation from Erasmus helped gain him a post with the court of Archduke Ferdinand. He left Ferdinand's court in 1526, passing his position as secretary to his half-brother John Meier. Spiegel returned to Sélestat to live on an ecclesiastical pension, but he continued to attend imperial diets and perform other occasional services for Archduke (later King) Ferdinand into the 1540s.

Spiegel was a friend at court for humanist literary activities. He edited and commented on a large number of works by other humanists, including many that advocated the reform of the Church and the defense of German national pride. In 1520 he published Jacob Wimpfeling's pamphlet on behalf of limiting the powers of the Roman curia in Germany.

Spiegel's major literary accomplishment was his popular *Lexicon of Civil Law*, first published in Strasbourg in 1538. It distilled the humanist approach to Roman law into the form of a dictionary, citing many contemporary jurists. It was an important tool in a period when Roman law was being accepted as the common law of the Empire.

Works By: Percy Stafford Allen et al., eds., *Opus epistolarum Desiderii Erasmi Roterodami*, 12 vols. (Oxford, 1906–1958); Emile Arbentz and Hermann Wartmann, eds., *Vadianische Briefsammlung*, 6 vols. (St. Gallen, 1890–1908); Adalbert Horawitz and Karl Hartfelder, eds., *Briefwechsel des Beatus Rhenanus* (Leipzig, 1886); Joseph von Riegger, *Udalrici Zasii . . . epistolae* (Ulm, 1774). **Works About**: Thomas Burger, "Jakob Spiegel," J. D. diss., University of Freiburg im Breisgau (Augsburg, 1973); Joseph Gény, *Die Reichstadt Schlettstadt* (Freiburg, 1900); Gustav Knod, *Jacob Spiegel aus Schlettstadt*, 2 pts. (Strasbourg, 1884–1886), and *ADB*, 35:156–58. *S. W. Rowan*

See CHARLES V; ERASMUS; FERDINAND I; MAXIMILIAN I; ROMAN LAW; VILLINGER; WIMPFELING; ZASIUS.

STAHREMBERG, ERNEST RÜDIGER VON (1638–1701), count, was a notable Austrian field marshal and knight of the Golden Fleece. He fought under Montecucculi in the Turkish wars in the 1660s, distinguishing himself at the Battle of St. Gotthard, and in the wars against Louis XIV in the 1670s. In 1680 Leopold I appointed him commandant in Vienna and colonel of the city guard. He served the Habsburgs illustriously as governor of Vienna during the Turkish siege of 1683. It was Stahremberg who recruited men for the garrison and who persuaded the emperor to spend more money on the old, inadequate fortifications of the city just before the Turkish onslaught. With a mere twelve thousand men, the strong-willed Stahremberg was able to prevent Vienna's capitulation to the Turks under the command of the grand vizier, Kara Mustapha. Had Mustapha vigorously pressed the attack, he could have taken the city. He preferred to wait for the city to surrender; exhaustion, plague, and famine, he thought, would compel Vienna to capitulate. This strategy almost worked. In spite of his valiant efforts, Stahremberg was forced to give up the ravelin on September 3 and on September 9 the moat. The situation was desperate. Fortunately the relief army under the command of Joh III Sobieski, king of Poland, and Duke Charles V of Lorraine arrived on September 12 and raised the siege. For his heroic defense of the city, Leopold promoted Stahremberg to field marshal and in 1691 to president of the Council of War. Known for his courage, probity, forcefulness, and loyalty, Stahremberg died at the onset of the War of the Spanish Succession (1701–1714).

Stahremberg was part of an illustrious family; his father, Conrad Balthazar, acted as *statthalter* from 1663 to 1687, his cousin Guidobald fought courageously during the Turkish wars in the 1680s and the 1690s and during the War of the Spanish Succession, and his brother Gundaker served as president of the *Hofkammer* and finance minister for Joseph I, Charles VI, and Maria Theresa. Both of his sons by his first marriage died in the Turkish wars.

Works By: Onno Klopp, ed., *Corrispondenza epistolare tra Leopold I Imperatore* (Graz, 1888), V. Renner, ed., *Vertrauliche Briefe der Grafen Ernst Rüdiger von Stahremberg* (Vienna, 1890–1891). **Works About**: *ADB*, 35:468–70; Thomas Barker, *Double Eagle and Crescent: Vienna's Turkish Siege and Its Historical Setting*, (Albany, 1967); Onno Klopp, *Das Jahr 1683 und der folgende Turkenkrieg bis zum Frieden von Carlowitz, 1699* (Graz, 1882); Reinhold Lorenz, *Türkenjahr* (Vienna, 1933); Oswald Redlich, *Weltmacht des Barock; Öesterreich in der Zeit Leopolds I* (Vienna, 1961); John Stoye, *The Siege of Vienna* (New York, 1964). *L. S. Frey and M. L. Frey*

See LEOPOLD I; SPANISH SUCCESSION; VIENNA, SIEGE OF.

STAUPITZ, JOHN VON (1460/69–1524), influential Church leader and theologian, was born at Motterwitz in Saxony to a noble family. Educated at Leipzig and Cologne, John joined the Order of the Hermits of Saint Augustine.

His order sent him to Tübingen to complete his theological education and to serve as prior of the Augustinian house. Within three years he completed his doctorate.

In 1500 Staupitz left Tübingen for Munich, where he became prior of the Augustinian cloister. Two years later he was called by Duke Frederick the Wise of Saxony to become professor of Bible and dean of the theological faculty at his newly founded University of Wittenberg. Charged with organizing the university, Staupitz did a great deal to create an atmosphere where individual ideas and beliefs, even if controversial, could be expressed. In addition to his duties at Wittenberg, he was named vicar-general of the Reformed congregation of the Hermits of Saint Augustine.

Since his administrative duties began to take so much of his time, Staupitz encouraged Martin Luther to earn a doctorate and fill his professorship. For a number of years Staupitz had served as Luther's confessor and spiritual adviser. His views on grace and predestination influenced Luther. Although far milder in spirit than Luther, Staupitz stood by him when the indulgence controversy first broke out in 1517. As the situation became more polarized, he released Luther from his vows and resigned his own office as vicar-general in 1520.

Staupitz accepted Cardinal Matthew Lang's offer to become a preacher and adviser at his court in Salzburg. His last years were spent there as an abbot of a Benedictine monastery. Even though he had put a good deal of distance between himself and the Protestants, his works were placed on the index of prohibited books by Pope Paul IV in 1559.

Works By: *Staupitz, Tubinger Predigten*, ed. Georg Buchwald and Ernst Wolf (Leipzig, 1927); *Johannis Staupitii: Opera . . . Dtsch. Schriften*, ed. J. F. K. Knaake (Potsdam, 1867). **Works About**: Alfred Jeremias, *Johannes von Staupitz, Luthers von Staupitz und die Anfange der Reformation* (Leipzig, 1888); T. Kolde, *Die Dtsch. Augustiner-Congregation und Johann von Staupitz* (Gotha, 1879); David C. Steinmetz, *Misercordia Dei: The Theology of Johannes von Staupitz in Its Late Medieval Setting* (Leiden, 1968); Ernst Wolf, *Staupitz und Luther* (Leipzig, 1927).   *J. W. Zophy*

See FREDERICK III, THE WISE; LANG; LUTHER.

STEPHEN IX (c. 1000–1058, pope from 1057), a pope from Lorraine whose rule marked a stage in the growing independence of the papacy from German control, was born as Frederick, son of Duke Gozelo of Lorraine. He was educated in Liège and became a canon there. In early 1051 Frederick went to Italy and served as librarian and chancellor to Pope Leo IX. Frederick went to Constantinople in early 1054 as a papal legate in the negotiations that ended on July 15, 1054, in what was to become the definitive schism between the Eastern and Western churches.

Frederick retired to Monte Cassino shortly after his return to Rome, largely because the Emperor Henry III was engaged in a struggle with Frederick's brother Godfrey the Bearded, who had married Countess Beatrice of Tuscany.

Henry III died in October 1056, and Frederick was elected abbot of Monte Cassino in May 1057 under the auspices of the papal reform party. Pope Victor II soon made him a cardinal. In August 1057 after Victor died, Frederick was elected pope by acclamation as part of a political reaction against imperial influence in Italy. He took the name of Stephen. The election was virtually an act of rebellion, and the reformers had great difficulty persuading the Empress Agnes to accept it.

The brief reign of Stephen IX was marked by strong initiatives to impose celibacy on the clergy of Rome itself. Stephen also explored the idea of allying with popular protests against the allegedly corrupt established clergy in Milan. Stephen appears to have been trying to forge a political league with his brother Godfrey against the Normans and possibly against the Empire when he died at Florence on March 29, 1058. The brief pontificate of Stephen IX foreshadowed many of the policies that were to mature under Nicholas II and Gregory VII, specifically the move to virtually complete independence from the German monarch.

Works By: Jacques Paul Migne, *Patrologia latina* (Paris, 1853), vol. 143, cols. 865–884. **Works About**: Giovanni B. Borino, "L'arcidiaconato di Ildebrando," *Studi gregoriani* 3 (1948): 463–516; A. Clerval, *Dictionnaire de théologie catholique*, 5: 980–91: 15 vols. (Paris, 1903–1950); Georges Despy, "La carrière lotharingienne du pape Etienne IX," *Revue belge de philologie et d'histoire* 31 (1953): 955–72; Augustin Fliche, *La réforme grégorienne et la reconquête chrétienne*, Hist. de l'église, vol. 8 (Paris, 1950); Hubert Jedin and John Patrick Dolan, *Handbook of Church Hist.*, vol. 3 (London, 1969); Theodor Lindner, *ADB*, 36:62–64; Ulysse Robert, "Le pape Etienne X," *Revue des questions historiques* 20 (1876):49–76.   S. W. Rowan

See BEATRICE; GREGORY VII; HENRY III; LEO IX.

STOSS, VEIT (1447–1553), artist, of whose early life little is known, may have been born in Nuremberg. Stoss spent some time in Cracow, receiving a number of important commissions as a painter, sculptor, and engraver. In 1496 he returned to Nuremberg, where he lived until his death. His career there was successful artistically but marred by a legal case in 1503 that resulted in his being branded for forging a signature of a merchant who owed him money. Further punishment was stopped after the intercession of Emperor Maximilian, much to the annoyance of some in Nuremberg. The Reformation damaged Stoss' career further, as a result of his Catholicism and a reduction in commissions for artists.

Works About: Theodor Müller, "Veit Stoss," *DGD*, 5:73–80; Martin Weinberger, "Stoss," *EWA*, 13:434–38.   *J. W. Zophy*

See MAXIMILIAN I; NUREMBERG.

STRALSUND, PEACE OF, was agreed upon in 1370. In 1367 a number of member cities of the Hanseatic League joined together with King Albert of Sweden, the duke of Mecklenberg, and the counts of Holstein in the Cologne confederation to combat the aggression of King Valdemar of Denmark and his ally, King Haaken of Norway. Eventually the allies were successful, and Valdemar sued for peace. Final settlement was not achieved until May 24, 1370. By the terms of the Peace of Stralsund, thirty-seven Hansa towns and all other towns associated with the league were given unmolested freedom to trade in Denmark and the Skåne on the payment of certain fixed duties. In addition the Hanseatic League received certain salvage rights and trading privileges in connection with the Skåne. Those terms helped keep the northern lands open to trade under league domination.

Works About: David K. Bjork, "The Peace of Stralsund, 1370," *Spec.* 7 (1932): 447–76; Karl N. Schwebel, *Der Stralsunder Friede (1370) im Spiegel der hist. Literatur: Eine Übersicht* (Bremen, 1970).   *J. W. Zophy*

See HANSEATIC LEAGUE.

STRASBOURG, located at the branching Ill River on the left bank of the Rhine, was originally the site of an ancient Celtic settlement. Captured by the Romans, Argentoratum, as it was called in Latin, was a garrison outpost and administrative center. It was pillaged by the Alemanni in 355 A.D.. Recovered in the following year by Julian, it remained a well-populated entrepôt until the Alains, Vandals, and Franks ravaged the left bank of the Rhine on their march to Rome in 406.

Strasbourg remained a fortified crossroad under the Frankish kings. It may have owed its existence to the bishopric, which was founded in the fourth century as suffragan to the archbishop of Mainz and which may have been reestablished by Dagobert II. Its history is obscured by pious legends. A text by Gregory of Tours contains the earliest reference, in 489, to the city. There is little evidence to support the assertions of patriotic German historians of the Renaissance that Strasbourg was prominent under the Merovingians or that it was especially favored by Charlemagne. These claims originate in part from documents forged in the Middle Ages to sustain claims to ancient trading privileges on the Rhine.

In 842, Louis II and Charles the Bald, with their troops encamped and waiting to go to battle, ended hostilities at Strasbourg and swore an oath of alliance against Lothar I, which led eventually to the dissolution of the Carolingian empire. Strasbourg emerged from this conflict as part of the *regnum Lotharingiae* in the Treaty of Verdun in 843 and was brought to the German Empire by Lothar II, although not securely until the eleventh century.

An imperial grant in 874 by Otto II gave full seigneurial rights over the city to Bishop Rathold as a reward for exceptional military services in Italy. The bishop claimed the right to invest the magistracy with their offices, controlled key fiscal and administrative positions in the municipal government, tried all cases except those under imperial jurisdiction, regulated the guilds, and named their officers. Each citizen owed five days of labor as well as specific special services. And according to the patent granted in 874, the bishop held the Strasbourg mint and appointed its chief officer. Tension between the city and the bishop rose as the bourgeoisie prospered, while the emperors, who were often at odds with the Church, proved their devotion to such a powerful and strategically placed city by chipping away at the bishops' seigneurial rights. In 1201, Count Rudolf of Habsburg, the bishop of Strasbourg and a leading bourgeois, came to an agreement that allowed the citizens limited rights of consultation and consent in the drafting of municipal statute law. Several years later, in 1214, Frederick II attempted to deprive the city of its lay courts and reestablished the full authority of the bishop's regime but had to retract his decree the following year. During his conflict with Innocent IV, Frederick went full circle, extending the city's privileges and freeing its citizens from all but imperial taxes in 1236.

Bishop Gauthier von Geroldseck, attempting to reassert seigneurial rights, was expelled from the city in 1261 and defeated at the Battle of Hausbergen in March 1263. He was forced to recognize a municipal council of twelve members and promise not to build any fortification in the city. His successor, selected from among the clerics who had supported the city during the revolt, signed a capitulation that gave over rights to select the magistracy, required that fiscal officers be selected from among the bourgeois, turned over the communal lands and the hospital to the council, and recognized the city's right to defend the common good. The bishop lost the mint in 1437 when Sigismund turned that too over to the city.

Strasbourg became one of the seven former seats of bishoprics that enjoyed a uniquely independent position in the Empire. The city, whose claim to be called free and imperial was recognized by Charles IV's chancery in 1359, paid no imposts to the Empire and did not appear on imperial lists of tributary cities after 1381. It refused to make any financial contribution to the Empire until 1458, when Frederick III managed to extort a grant for his Turkish campaigns. It enjoyed full internal autonomy and had its own foreign policy, which included diplomatic missions to the king of France and dukes of Burgundy. Its sole uncontested obligation was to provide a contingent of troops to accompany the emperor to Rome.

Under the rule of a patrician oligarchy, Strasbourg was by no means the stepchild of the Empire. It was invited to the diet of Mainz as a prince or lord to agree to the Public Peace of 1278 and acted as one of its guarantors. Its rulers continued to struggle against the Church, attempting to close the city to the religious orders in 1276 and seizing inheritable property left by main-morte to the Church in 1287. The guilds seized the right to name their own masters in 1263. And the commons, so recently seized from the Church, became the source of disputes between the patrician oligarchy and the citizenry of Strasbourg, who accused them, in turn, of expropriating it in 1275.

In 1332, the more powerful guilds and artisans took advantage of a long-standing feud between patrician factions to displace the patricians from their monopoly of power. Accusing the patricians of disturbing the public peace and governmental malfeasance, the insurgents established a council of wealthy bour-geois and representatives of each guild, disarmed the patricians, and placed them under house arrest. They reorganized the municipal government, adding a general council and a Senate. While the patricians were not excluded from government, their influence was diluted by the presence of nonpatrician elites and by the new office of *ammeister*, a rotating, nonpatrician official who pre-sided over nearly all units of government. Specialized privy councils emerged from the Senate in the fifteenth century. Both the Council of the Thirteen, which was originally devised to direct military affairs, and that of the Fifteen, originally to revise the laws, became standing executive bodies directing the highest policy decisions and the internal administration of the city. Each year the citizens were to read a descriptive resume of the government; the first was read on October 17, 1334. Revised over the years along with the magistracy itself, the final version of the *Schworbrief* was promulgated in 1482 and was publicly read for the last time in 1789.

A second abortive popular uprising in 1349 proved the resilience of the new regime, but the revolt turned into a pogrom against Strasbourg's considerable Jewish population. The Jewish quarter was burned, debts owed to Jews were cancelled, and their property was seized. When Charles IV reminded the mag-istracy that the victims were imperial wards and of their responsibility to protect them and their property, Strasbourg joined a defensive league with the bishop, the counts of Württemberg and Freiburg, and local seigneurs against him.

The city was associated with the Rhenish Urban League, formed in 1380, which included Speyer, Mainz, Worms, Schlettstadt, and Frankfurt. Directed against the imperial knights and the territorial princes, the Rhenish league and the Swabian Urban League merged in 1383. They were defeated in several decisive battles by the dukes of Bavaria and the count Palatine in 1383 and they declined thereafter.

Far more useful were the regional tactical alliances, such as the league with Duke René II of Lorraine, which was provoked by the invasion of the Armagnacs in 1439. This trickle of troops, freed by peace in France to forage wherever prosperity could be found, turned into organized invasion under the dauphin Louis when Frederick III foolishly asked France for assistance against the Swiss in 1444. Strasbourg led the mobilization of local seigneurs against cities to defend Alsace against them. In 1474, Strasbourg helped found the League of Constance to defend the rights of the imperial cities against Charles the Bold, who had purchased rights to Habsburg holdings on the Rhine from Archduke Sigismund in 1469.

Strasbourg responded to the Lutheran Reformation in 1523 and 1524 under the leadership of Martin Bucer and Wolfgang Capito, although the Mass was not abolished until 1529. The magistracy itself took some initiative, under con-siderable pressure from parishioners, by seizing control of cloisters and Church foundations, taking over the collection of alms, and appointing fiscal officers to supervise church finances. They established a church commission in 1531 under Bucer's direction and adopted the Augsburg Confession in 1533. In 1538, they established a gymnasium to replace the parish schools; in 1566 this became an academy and in 1621 the University of Strasbourg. Jacob Sturm directed Strasbourg successfully through the perils confronting adherents to the Schmalkaldic League and relaxed into the Interim of Augsburg without serious confrontation with the emperor.

The only major disturbance of the tense peace between the two religions occurred in 1583 when the Protestants attempted to seize control of the Grand-Chapter electing the bishop of Strasbourg and invited intervention by Rudolf II. While the emperor tried to threaten the magistracy into prosecuting this violation of the ecclesiastical reservation, it was the Catholic imperial princes who actually menaced the city. Elections in 1585 and 1586 proved inconclusive and the Bishops' War in Strasbourg from 1592 to 1604 mobilized sentiments and party alignments, which led in turn to the outbreak of the Thirty Years War.

The Peace of Westphalia and Nimwegen left the disposition of Alsace a negotiable item and, despite Strasbourg's claims for imperial protection, the Chambers of Reunion forced its capitulation on October 4, 1681, to Louis XIV. Strasbourg retained special privileges in matters of religion, self-government, and trade under the French. The magistracy continued to run the internal affairs of the city, including taxation, and the Rule of Government of 1752 shows how thoroughly the crown honored Strasbourg's special status in the realm. But in 1687, Louis XIV issued a *lettre de cachet* requiring equal Catholic representation in all municipal positions, and this requirement effectively broke the monopoly of the established Protestant elite. Despite Strasbourg's claim to be a free royal city, in practice, it was subject to the royal court established at Ensisheim in 1658, at Breisach in 1674, and finally resting at Colmar in 1698. Its privileges were lost in the Revolution, and Strasbourg became a provincial capital.

Works About: Thomas A. Brady, Jr., *Ruling Class, Regime, and Reformation in Strasbourg, 1520–1555*, Studies in Medieval and Reformation Thought, 22 (Leiden, 1978); Miriam Chrisman, *Strasbourg and the Reform: A Study in the Process of Change* (New Haven, Conn., 1967): Karl Theodore Eheberg, *Verfassungs-, Verwaltungs-, und Wirtschaftsgesch. der Stadt Strassburg bis 1861*, vol. 1; *Urkunden* (Strasbourg, 1899); Franklin Ford, *Strasbourg in Transition: 1648–1789* (Cambridge, Mass., 1958); Francis Rapp, *Réforme et Reformation à Strasbourg: Eglise et Société dans le Diocese de Strasbourg (1450–1525)* (Paris, 1974); Rodolph Ruess, *Histoire de Strasbourg depuis ses origines jusqu'à nos jours* (Paris, 1922): Hans Virck, *Politische Correspondenz der Stadt Strassburg im Zeitalter der Reformation (1517–1555)* (Strasbourg, 1882–1928), vols. 1–5; Wilhelm Wiegand, *Urkundenbuch der Stadt Strassburg (600–1400)* (Strasbourg, 1879–1890), vols. 1–7; Gerhard Wunder, *Das Strassburger Landgebiet, Territorialgesch. . . . 13 bis 18 Jh.* (Berlin, 1967). *S. A. Garretson*

See BUCER; CAPITO; CHARLES IV; FREDERICK II; FREDERICK III; LOUIS II; OTTO II; RUDOLF II; SCHMALKALDIC LEAGUE; SIGISMUND; STURM; VERDUN; WESTPHALIA.

STRIGEL, BERNHARD (c. 1460–1528), court painter for Emperor Maximilian I, was born in Memmingen to a family of painters. He worked for a while in Ulm with Bartholomew Zeitblom, who was known for elevated and spiritual tendencies in his art. The first reference to Strigel's presence back in Memmingen is in 1506. By 1507, he was in contact with Emperor Maximilian, for whom he made repeated trips to Augsburg, Innsbruck, and Vienna. A pronounced sensibility for elegance and adornment made him a desirable court painter, and he soon became the favorite portrait painter of Maximilian. He held several important positions in Memmingen, and the city council sent him on business to other cities on many occasions.

The numerous paintings of Strigel are noticeable for a lack of sharpness of observation. All of his figures have the same basic type of face with distinctive pointed chins and rather distorted hands. His use of clear and warm colors is especially appealing. His most famous works are paintings of political figures. To mark the occasion of the succession treaty concluded between the Habsburgs and Jagiellos at Vienna in 1515, he did a portrait of Emperor Maximilian I and his family. He also did paintings of King Louis II of Hungary, the Habsburg Ferdinand I, the humanist and diplomat John Cuspinian, and the Augsburg patrician Conrad Rehlinger. In his backgrounds Strigel emphasized the fashionable elegance of Swabian towns.

Works About: W. Schmidt, "Strigel," *ADB*, 36: 589–90.   *J. J. Spielvogel*

See CUSPINIAN; FERDINAND I; MAXIMILIAN I.

STURM, JACOB (1489–1553), statesman, was born in Strasbourg to a prosperous patrician family. Jacob received an excellent education at Heidelberg and Freiburg. His interests and education were in part shaped by the humanist Jacob Wimpfeling, a family friend. Active in humanist circles in Strasbourg, Sturm also served as a librarian and secretary to the cathedral provost.

When he converted to the evangelical religion in 1523, Sturm abandoned his clerical career and entered into the council of Strasbourg. This led to a break with Wimpfeling, to whom Sturm declared, "If I am a heretic, that is what you made me." His movement through the ranks of Strasbourg's government was sure and certain. In 1526 he became a life member of the influential Council of the Thirteen for War, where he helped shape Strasbourg's foreign policy until his death. Active as a diplomat on ninety-one missions, Sturm became one of the leading urban politicians. He consistently supported the evangelical faith and was one of the founding fathers of the Schmalkaldic League. After the defeat of the league, Sturm urged Strasbourg to make peace with the emperor and accept the Augsburg Interim. To Sturm the survival of Strasbourg was more important than maintaining every facet of the new religion. Once again the practical realism of Sturm and his supporters prevailed, and Strasbourg survived the crisis of 1547–1548. Sturm also aided the humanist pedagogue, John Sturm (1507–1589), in the founding of his famous school in Strasbourg.

Works About: Hermann Baumgarten, *Jakob Sturm* (Strasbourg, 1867); Thomas A. Brady, Jr., "Jacob Sturm of Strasbourg (1489–1553) and the Political Security of German Protestantism, 1526–1532" (Ph.D. diss., University of Chicago, 1968), "Jacob Sturm of Strasbourg and the Lutherans at the Diet of Augsburg, 1530," *Ch* 42 (1973): 183–202, and *Ruling Class, Regime and Reformation at Strasbourg, 1520–1555* (Leiden, 1978); Otto Winckelmann, "Jakob Sturm," *ADB*, 37:5–20.   *J. W. Zophy*

See SCHMALKALDIC LEAGUE; STRASBOURG; WIMPFELING.

STÜRTZEL, CONRAD (1435–1509), a leading member of the early government of Maximilian I, was born to a burgher family in Kitzingen. He earned his B.A. and M.A. at Heidelberg between 1455 and 1458. He went to Freiburg im Breisgau as one of the founding members of the university there in 1458. He taught at first in the arts faculty, but after receiving a doctorate in canon law, he entered the law faculty.

From 1474 on, Stürtzel served Archduke Sigismund of Austria-Tyrol as a counselor as well as ambassador, and in 1481 he resigned his law professorship at Freiburg to become a full-time member of Sigismund's government at Innsbruck. In this capacity he represented Sigismund at imperial diets and on embassies abroad. In 1487, when the Tyrolean estates meeting at Meran forced Sigismund to purge his administration of unpopular noble members, Stürtzel became aulic chancellor. In 1488 he was instrumental in thwarting Sigismund's plan to sell the Tyrol and other western Habsburg lands to the dukes of Bavaria, and in 1490 he helped arrange Sigismund's resignation in favor of King Maximilian I. Stürtzel continued to head the government at Innsbruck, which became the center of Maximilian's administration when he succeeded his father, Emperor Frederick III, as sole head of the Empire in 1493. Stürtzel seems to have lost enthusiasm for some of Maximilian's policies in the late 1490s as a result of his increased sympathies with the imperial reform proposals of Berthold von Henneberg, elector archbishop of Mainz. Stürtzel retired from active political life in 1500, though he continued to hold the title of aulic and Tyrolean chancellor and to draw a large pension until his death.

Stürtzel retired to Freiburg, where he had built a palatial home. He was frequently called out of retirement to consult with the Austrian government on negotiations with the Swiss Confederation and on questions of Alsatian administration. In 1504 he was a major participant in a trumped-up blood accusation against the Jews of Waldkirch arising out of a child murder that had taken place in his area of feudal jurisdiction. The thesis that Stürtzel was the author of the radical reform tract, *The Book of a Hundred Chapters and Forty Statutes,* has not gained general support.

Works About: Georg Buchwald, *Konrad Stürtzel von Buchheim aus Kitzingen* (Leipzig, 1900); Jürgen Bücking, "Das Geschlecht Stürtzel von Buchheim (1491–1790)," *Z. für die Gesch. des Oberrheins* 118 (1970): 239–78 and "Der 'oberrheinische Revolutionär' heisst Conrad Sturtzel," *Arch. für Kulturgesch.* 56 (1974): 177–97; Friedrich Pfaff, "Die Kindermorde zu Benzhausen und Waldkirch im Breisgau," *Alemannia* 27 (1900): 247–97; Hermann Wiesflecker, *Kaiser Maximilian I.* (Munich, 1971–1977), vols. 1–3.   *S. W. Rowan*

See BERTHOLD; FREDERICK III; FREIBURG; MAXIMILIAN I.

SWABIAN LEAGUE (1488–c. 1534), an organization of great princes, lesser territories, and cities in south Germany, had a unique character as the outgrowth of direct imperial action. Frederick III issued a mandate for a league in Swabia on June 26, 1487. It acquired members quickly and came to include most of the area's secular and ecclesiastical entities. During its height after 1500, the powerful electors of Mainz, Trier, and the Palatinate, as well as Württemberg, Hesse, and Bavaria, adhered. At its peak, its constitution provided for a legislative assembly, a judicial system, a military arm, and rudimentary taxation procedures, though most finances were proportional assessments.

The league was controversial throughout its career and identified with imperial reform movements: that seeking to reconstitute the powers of the German king as well as that seeking to reforge a new, federated Empire based on the great states. Neither of these contradictory thrusts directly precipitated the collapse of the league. Reformation forces ultimately led members to pursue individual objectives over league goals. The end was written in 1534 when Philip of Hesse, allied with Francis I of France under the Treaty of Bar-le-duc, invaded Württemberg.

From 1488, the constitution of the league provided for an assembly of all members and a smaller league council (*Bundesrat*), for a system of courts and a chief legal officer, and for a mutual sharing of league costs. Because it assumed authority to itself and acted decisively, the league acquired considerable sovereignty and prestige. But the long-range problem of territorial politics emerged early. League concerns expanded to include dealing with each other as well. Strong efforts for imperial reform led by Elector Archbishop Berthold of Mainz to bring about a federated unity encountered the reform politics of resettling the Empire upon the great princes. And persistently the smaller members, particularly the cities, maneuvered to prevent domination of the league by the great states. Constitutional reform in 1496 improved legal and judicial matters but not political cohesion or the problem of equitable financing.

Formation of the Swabian League by Frederick III has been represented as reform, an effort to stabilize the political map of south Germany and enhance domestic peace under the German king. In reality, the league initially was a move by the Habsburg emperor to counter Bavaria and always remained a component of Habsburg politics. By 1500, political contradictions in the league and the needs of the Habsburgs led Emperor Maximilian to seek to make it a direct instrument. Reaffirmation of the constitution attended significant revisions in the league council and the court system tending toward greater balance among the several groups making up the league. In following years, decisions and initiative tended to devolve upon the league council, where concern became less unity than defense of self-interest. Especially in times of military action, the council met almost permanently.

In contrast to its political and constitutional uncertainties, the league enjoyed considerable strength militarily. By 1525–1526, the army of the league was the largest and strongest military force in the Empire. But by then its main concerns had altered from domestic peace and defensive security to deep involvement in imperial politics. In 1519, the league army undertook a Habsburg mission against Duke Ulrich of Württemberg; in 1522–1523, it responded to the Sickingen feud and the Knights' War. And in 1525–1526, the army was the principal agent in restoring south German authorities to control over the peasants.

The Peasants' Revolt illuminates clearly the dilemma that plagued the league. The army's victory strengthened the territorial rulers and the cities but did little for the emperor. Thus was the league an instrument of Habsburg house politics, managed—especially after 1500—by Maximilian as duke of Austria and contrary to effective imperial reform. Other member states sought to use the league similarly. In 1534 Bavaria persuaded the league not to resist Philip of Hesse over Württemberg. Habsburg troops were decisively defeated, and Lutheran Duke Ulrich was restored. The persistent dynamic of territorial politics over Habsburg machinations and imperial nostalgia, when fired by the convictions of the Reformation, ultimately ended any capacity for league effectiveness.

The historical significance of the Swabian League is greater than its duration of apparent success. Its very existence signifies the end of the Holy Roman Empire as a unity. Its career measures the real strength of the imperial office even in the very locale of greatest imperial presence. Thus it was not at all an element of reform but an active agent of territorialism. In assuming legislative, judicial, military, and fiscal powers to itself, the league was playing the part of any major territorial power by diminishing the emperor. In the end, however, the league must be credited with a significant historical role in maintaining domestic peace and suppressing social revolution.

Works About: Ernst Bock, *Der Schwäbische Bund und seine Verfassung 1488–1534* (Breslau, 1927); Christian Greiner, "Die Politik des Schwäbischen Bundes während des Bauernkrieges 1524/1525," *Z. des hist. Ver. Schwaben* 68 (1974): 7–94; Helmo Hesslinger, *Die Anfänge des Schwabischen Bundes* (Stuttgart, 1970); K. A. Klüpfel, eds., *Urkunden zur Gesch. des Schwäbischen Bundes*, 2 vols. (Stuttgart, 1846, 1853); Thomas F. Sea, "The Economic Impact of the German Peasants' War: The Question of Reparations," *SCJ* 8 (1977): 75–97, and "The Swabian League and the German Peasants' War" (Ph.D. diss., University of California, 1974).   *K. C. Sessions*

See BERTHOLD; FREDERICK III; MAXIMILIAN I; PEASANTS' WAR; PHILIP OF HESSE; SICKINGEN; TRUCHSESS; ULRICH.

SWISS WARS OF INDEPENDENCE, also known as the Swabian War, was a series of military encounters in 1499 between members of the Swiss Confederation on the one side and the forces of Emperor Maximilian I and the Swabian League on the other. By the treaty concluded at Basel in September 1499, the confederation gained virtual independence from the Empire although the legal recognition of this independence did not come until the Peace of Westphalia in 1648.

As part of the medieval Holy Roman Empire, the districts that formed Switzerland suffered the same vicissitudes experienced by other members of the Empire. Similar to Germanic attempts to solve native peace problems by creating leagues, three Swiss forest cantons (Uri, Schwyz, Unterwalden) formed the Everlasting Pact in 1291. This union became the basis of the Swiss Confederation, and subsequently other cantons attached themselves to the original core: Lucerne (1332), Glarus (1351), Zurich (1351), Zug (1352), Bern (1353), Solothurn (1481), and Fribourg (1481). Non-Habsburg emperors granted various privileges and freedoms to the cantons in order to isolate the neighboring Habsburgs, and these grants served to strengthen cantonal governments and the notion of Swiss particularism.

Because of the proximity of the confederation to Austria, an enmity developed between the two, especially when the Habsburgs acquired the imperial title. As emperors, the Habsburgs attempted to crush the emerging separateness of the Swiss and to subordinate parts of Switzerland to Austria's control. This became particularly manifest in jurisdictional contentions along the Tyrolese border where the Habsburgs, as rulers of Tyrol, had valid claims to places within Rhaetia. To counter these claims, inhabitants in Rhaetia formed three separate leagues, two of which joined the confederation in 1497 and 1498. The best organized of these, the Grey League, became the name by which the canton was known afterward, Graubünden or Grisons.

Since the Habsburgs wished the demise of the confederation, they employed all of the Empire's means at their disposal. These techniques involved refusals to renew and recognize traditional Swiss privileges, effecting anti-Swiss military alliances, and attempting to impose the results of imperial legislation on the Swiss. Two specific occurrences at the end of the fifteenth century accelerated the movement to war. The first was the creation in 1488 of the Swabian League, a union of south German princes and cities authorized by Maximilian to preserve the peace and to act as a counterweight to the dukes of Bavaria. Maximilian thus had a military force at his disposal, one that might also be used against the confederation. The second was the constitutional reform measures passed by the diet of Worms in 1495, which were to apply to the Swiss territories. Although the Swiss were not represented in the diet, they were required to acknowledge the competency of the newly created Imperial Cameral Court, observe the eternal peace, and pay the Common Penny, which defrayed the cost of both.

The confederation's refusal, tantamount to a declaration of war, was at the same time an expression of confidence in its strength. Because many of the abuses that the Worms' decrees attempted to correct in the Empire at large did not apply to the Swiss, the confederation viewed the decrees as foreign importations. Furthermore the Swiss had created the most noted militia in Europe, the famed pikemen, feared by foes and acknowledged by such political analysts as Machiavelli and Guicciardini. These were the famous Swiss mercenaries who continued to characterize so much of subsequent Swiss history.

The result of Maximilian's desire and the confederation's confidence was the Swabian War. In a stunning series of victories over numerically much stronger opponents, the confederation acquired its freedom from Habsburg constraints.

This spirit of independence was evoked in Schiller's *William Tell*, the most famous legend in the country's history.

Works About: C. Jecklin and F. Jecklin, *Der Anteil Graubündens am Schwabenkrieg* (Davos, 1899); W. Oechsli, *Die Beziehungen der schweizerische Eidgenossenschaft zum Reiche bis zum Schwabenkrieg* (Bern, 1890); Konrad Pellikan, *Chronikon*, ed. B. Riggenbach (Basel, 1877); Willibald Pirckheimer, *Schweizerkrieg*, ed. K. Ruck (Munich, 1895); H. Ulmann, *Kaiser Maximilian I*, 2 vols. (Stuttgart, 1884–1891).   *P. N. Bebb*

See MAXIMILIAN I; SCHILLER; SWABIAN LEAGUE.

SYLVESTER II or GERBERT (945–1003), pope, was born of humble parentage near Aurillac, France. Gerbert was taught grammar, rhetoric, arithmetic, and music by Raymond Lavaur, later abbot of Aurillac, where the pupil became a monk. He continued his education in Spain at the abbey of Ripoll, where he had gone in 967 in the company of Count Borrell of Barcelona. Three years later he traveled with Borrell to Rome, where he impressed Pope John XIII. Pope John recommended him to Emperor Otto I. After two years' service at Otto's court, Gerbert went to Reims, where he was ordained and served as a secretary to Archbishop Adalbero. In Italy with Adalbero in 980, his public debate about philosophical divisions of knowledge delighted Emperor Otto II, who made him abbot of Bobbio. After Otto's death in 973, Gerbert found himself without sufficient support to withstand the enmity of local nobles and clergy and fled to Reims to resume his first love, teaching.

After failing to secure the archbishopric of Reims for himself, Gerbert went to the court of Otto III in 997. His earlier support of Otto's claim to the throne was greatly appreciated, as were his administrative and teaching abilities. Otto used him in both capacities before making Gerbert archbishop of Ravenna. When the German pope, Gregory V, died unexpectedly in 999, Otto named his good friend Gerbert pope. Styled Sylvester II, he proved to be a vigorous and active pontiff denouncing simony and nepotism and insisting upon celibacy. Sylvester II also made contributions in mathematics and philosophy, especially in interpreting Muslim thought.

Works By: *Oeuvres de Gerbert, pape sous le nom de Sylvestre II*, ed. A. Olleris (Clermont-Ferrand, 1867); *The Letters of Gerbert with His Papal Privileges as Sylvester II*, tr. H. P. Lattin (New York, 1961). **Works About**: O. G. Darlington, "Gerbert the Teacher," *AHR* 52 (1946–1947): 456–76; H. P. Lattin, "Sylvester II," *New Catholic Encyclopedia*, (New York, 1967) 13:858–60; Horace K. Mann, *The Lives of the Popes in the Early Middle Ages*, 17 vols. (London, 1925), 5:1–120   *J. W. Zophy*

See GREGORY V; OTTO I; OTTO II; OTTO III.

t

TEUTBERGA (THEUTBERGA) (b. about 835–840, d. after 869), daughter of Count Boso, married Lothar, king of Lorraine (825–869), the second son of Emperor Lothar I. At the time of their engagement (c. 855) Lothar had already taken a concubine named Waldrada. In 857 Lothar initiated proceedings to have his marriage to Teutberga dissolved. His efforts to divorce her continued until his death and became a divisive issue in imperial and ecclesiastical politics. Although Teutberga was defended by her brother, Abbot Hucbert of St. Maurice, and Archbishop Hincmar of Reims, upheld by popes Nicholas I and Adrian II, and aided by Lothar's uncle, Charles the Bald, her personal life was a succession of humiliating circumstances. Lothar first accused Teutberga of having an incestuous relationship with her brother before her marriage. Later he charged her with barrenness. Finally his appeals argued that she of her own free will wanted the divorce. When Lothar was compelled to take Teutberga back after the first confrontation, she underwent trial by ordeal (hot water) before her testimony of innocence was accepted. A confession of her guilt was forcibly extracted from her when Lothar reiterated his charges before a synod of Lotharingian bishops at Aachen in 862. The synod granted the divorce, and Lothar quickly married Waldrada, who had already born him a son, Hugo. Pope Nicholas I summoned a synod of Frankish bishops at Metz (863) to review the Aachen judgment. The bishops upheld the divorce. Nicholas I reversed the decisions of both synods, demanding that Lothar give up Waldrada and take Teutberga again as his wife.

Throughout the 860s Lothar and Waldrada appealed for a reversal of the pope's decision. Nicholas I refused to change his ruling and threatened Lothar, Waldrada, and the bishops who supported them with ecclesiastical sanctions. In 869 Teutberga appealed to Pope Adrian II to grant the divorce. She said that she would rather live with the heathens than go back to Lothar. Nevertheless Adrian II still urged reconciliation. Lothar died in Italy on August 8, 869, on his way home from an audience with Adrian II about the divorce. Waldrada took the veil after Lothar's death, and Teutberga spent her final years at the convent of St. Glodesindis in Metz.

Works About: E. Dümmler, *Gesch. des Ostfränkischen Reiches* (Leipzig, 1887–1888), vol. 1; E. Mühlbacher, *Die Regesten des Kaiserreichs unter den Karolingern* (Innsbruck, 1881), and "Lothar II," *ADB* 19: 241–51; M. Sdralek, *Hincmar's von Rheims canonistisches Gutachten über die Ehescheidung des Königs Lothar II.* (Freiburg, 1881).   J. W. Gates

See LOUIS II.

TEUTONIC KNIGHTS is the popular English name of the religious-military crusading society officially entitled the Brothers of St. Mary's Hospital of the Germans in Jerusalem, or simply the German Order. The order was one of twelve such congregations founded in Europe between 1100 and 1300 for the dual purpose of waging holy war against infidels or pagans and supplying medical or social services to others engaged in that enterprise.

The German Order originated in 1190 during the Third Crusade. To care for sick pilgrims, some citizens of Bremen and Lübeck present at the siege of Acre organized a hospital and placed it under the administration of a chaplain and his clerical and nonclerical aides. Pope Clement III on February 6, 1191, gave official recognition of the German hospital, which soon acquired houses in Acre, Gaza, Jaffa, Ascalon, Rama, and Zamsi. Early in 1198 the Germans who came to the Holy Land on Henry VI's crusade added a military branch to the order in imitation of the Templars and Hospitallers, whose constitutions served as the basis for the rule of the German Order. Pope Innocent III on February 19, 1199, sanctioned this development. From this time there was a division within the order between the nobles or knights, whose chief occupation was military, and the nonaristocratic members, some of whom were ordained clergy, who conducted its spiritual and medical services. Women were also admitted in the latter capacity.

The order grew rapidly but always retained its German character. Through the generosity of Europe's Christians, it acquired and maintained about three hundred houses or foundations (*Kommenden*) by 1300. Under commanders (*Komture*), these foundations were grouped into commanderies or provinces (*Balleien*), of which there were thirteen in Germany, three in Italy, and one each in France, Greece, and Syria, plus the two states of Prussia and Livonia, which were added by conquest from non-Christians. District commanders (*Landkomture*) administered the provinces except in Germany, Livonia, and Prussia where district or territorial masters (*Landmeister*) performed that function. At the order's head was an elected grand master (*Hochmeister*), a layman like most of the governing group and, like them, observing the traditional monastic vows. A staff of advisers (*Grossgebietiger*) and administrators assisted him. The castle of Montfort near Acre served as headquarters until 1271. Over the centuries the order's central office was transferred to Acre, Venice, Marienberg, Königsberg, Mergentheim, and finally Vienna. Most of the order's work consisted of routine medical or pastoral service, but its spectacular achievement as a political power in the eastern Baltic area, particularly in Prussia, has captured the attention of later generations and created the romanticized image of the Teutonic Knights as the most ruthless exponents of the *Drang nach Osten* (Drive to the East).

The initial step in the order's move toward territorial sovereignty was the experience gained in Hungary between 1211 and 1224. Andreas II invited the Knights into his kingdom to help defend it against the Cumans. After the Cumans' defeat, the king revoked the order's privileges and confiscated its castles, and so it departed. In 1226 Duke Conrad of Masovia in northwestern Poland similarly requested the Knights' aid against the savage Prussians who had defeated the military and spiritual efforts of Bishop Christian and who were devastating Masovia. Grand Master Hermann von Salza (1209–1239) declined to accept this new field of activity until he had secured, as he did in 1230, Conrad's grant of full sovereignty to the order for all lands it might conquer from the Prussians. Additional liberties and guarantees from Frederick II and Pope Gregory IX strengthened its legal independence. Prussia was not to be a fief of the Holy Roman Empire nor was the grand master to be the emperor's vassal.

In 1233 the territorial master, Hermann Balk, began the actual conquest of Prussia. In 1237 the order absorbed the Brethren of the Sword, a similar crusading association that had already begun the conquest of Livonia and Estonia but was faltering. Thus almost the entire eastern coast of the Baltic came under the order's jurisdiction. A frontier was established with Russia when the Knights were defeated at the Battle of Lake Peipus, April 5, 1242. The suppression of a violent native uprising (1260–1290), left it secure in its own domains.

As conquest yielded to colonization and internal development, the usual religious institutions and the influence of the German settlers affected the religious and ethnic character of the region. Literature and the arts were cultivated. Hanseatic commercial influences made themselves felt. The order erected imposing specimens of Low German brick Gothic architecture, much of which survived until World War II. Militarily the order attained its peak with the occupation of Gotland (1398–1408); thereafter it declined rapidly as stronger monarchies emerged on its borders because of the Union of Kalmar (1397) and the personal union of Poland and Lithuania (1386). With the latter states, warfare was endemic. Defeated by them at Tannenberg on July 15, 1410, the order's power was further strained by internal dissension and protracted hostilities that ended in 1466; the Peace of Thorn reduced Prussia to the condition of a fief of the Polish crown.

During the Reformation Grand Master Albert of Brandenburg-Ansbach (1511–1525) became a Lutheran and secularized Prussia as a duchy. The Livonian district master, Gotthard Kettler, followed his example and in 1561 accepted Courland as a hereditary duchy, also under Polish overlordship. The territorial role of the German Order thus ended, but its medical and social work elsewhere continued, although much curtailed by the religious controversies. From 1525 to 1809 its headquarters were at Mergentheim, where it also maintained a seminary for the training of its priests. Napoleon Bonaparte suppressed its work in Germany altogether, and the order then moved to Vienna. Remaining vestiges of its chivalric and medieval origin the order survived even the Nazi era. In 1974 it numbered 876 members, including nuns, in three provinces: Germany, Austria, and south Tyrol, with a prefecture in Rome.

Works About: Th. Hirsch. M. Töppen, and E. Strehlke, eds., *Scriptores rerum Prussicarum, Die Geschichtsquellen der preussischen Vorzeit bis zum Untergange der Ordensherrschaft,* 5 vols.

(Leipzig, 1861–1874, rpr. 1965); Hanns H. Hoffmann, *Der Staat des Deutschmeisters* (Munich, 1966); Erich Joachim and Walter Hubatsch, eds., *Regesta historico-diplomatica Ordinis S. Mariae Theutonicorum, 1198–1525*. 3 vols. (Göttingen. 1948–1950); Karl H. Lampe and Klemens Wieser, *Bibliographie des Dtsch. Ordens bis 1529* (Bonn-Godesberg, 1975); Max Perlbach, ed., *Die Statuten des Dtsch. Ordens nach den ältesten Handschriften* (Halle, 1890); Peter G. Thielen, *Die Verwaltung des Ordensstaates Preussen vornehmlich im 15. Jahrhundert* (Köln-Graz, 1965); Marian Tumler, *Der Dtsch. Orden im Werden, Wachsen und Wirken bis 1400 mit einem Abriss der Gesch. des Ordens von 1400 bis zur neuestern Zeit* (Vienna, 1955); Erich Weise, ed., *Die Staatsvertrage des Dtsch. Ordens in Preussen im 15. Jahrhundert*, 2 vols. (Königsberg and Marburg, 1939–1953); Klemens Wieser, ed., *Acht Jahrhunderte Deutscher Orden in Einzeldarstellungen* (Bad Godesberg, 1967).   *R. H. Schmandt*

See HENRY VI; INNOCENT III; VIENNA.

THIRTY YEARS WAR (1618–1648), a series of wars between 1618 and 1648, resulted from the religious divisions within Germany and the constitutional conflict between the imperial estates and the Habsburg emperor. What began as a civil war soon became an international conflict between Europe's leading powers that left Germany devastated and the Empire powerless and disunited. *Background:* The Holy Roman Empire was politically and religiously split into over three hundred principalities and cities. The Peace of Augsburg (1555) gave Catholic and Lutheran princes the right to determine the religion of their subjects. Protestants were allowed to keep all Church properties seized before 1552; an ecclesiastical reservation, however, forbade the further alienation of Church lands. In spite of this provision, Lutheran princes continued to secularize Catholic church properties, particularly in northern Germany. At the same time the Catholics, led by Jesuits and the dukes of Bavaria, became increasingly aggressive in their quest to regain what had earlier been lost to the Protestants. The spread of Calvinism, a faith excluded from the Peace of Augsburg, added a further source of friction.

These growing political and ideological divisions resulted in the complete breakdown of all imperial institutions. To protect their interests, a group of evangelical princes and cities in 1608 founded the Protestant Union under the leadership of Frederick V, the militant Calvinist ruler of the Palatinate. In response the Catholics organized the Catholic League under Duke Maximilian of Bavaria. By 1609 two military alliances thus faced each other in the Empire, each determined to keep the rival religion from making any more gains and, to complicate matters further, each looking to outside powers for military and political support.

Foreign interests aggravated the Empire's internal problems. The Spanish were preparing to reconquer the Dutch after their twelve-year truce was due to expire in 1621. By cooperating closely with the Austrians, they hoped to consolidate the Habsburg position in central Europe. This move in turn would antagonize the French, who feared a strong Empire and Habsburg encirclement. In the north the kings of Denmark and Sweden sought to establish their dominion over the Baltic. The Danish king also claimed control of several secularized north German bishoprics.

A harbinger of things to come was the Jülich-Cleves succession dispute (1609–1614), which revealed how closely intertwined the Empire's problems had become with international issues. A major war at this time was avoided only because Germany's princes were too weak and Europe's powers not yet ready for a showdown.

The Bohemian-Palatinate Phase, 1618–1623: The war began in an unexpected corner of the Empire, the kingdom of Bohemia. In 1617, Archduke Ferdinand of Styria, nephew of Emperor Matthias, had been accepted as king designate by the Bohemian estates. As a zealous Catholic who had rooted out heresy in his domain, Ferdinand clashed almost immediately with Bohemia's Protestant nobility when he began to curtail their religious rights, which had been guaranteed by Emperor Rudolf II's Letter of Majesty. The estates' unhappiness grew when it became clear that the new king was determined to centralize the country at the expense of their constitutional liberties and privileges. Provoked by these actions, a group of Bohemian nobles on May 23, 1618, tossed two of Ferdinand's imperial commissioners from a window of the royal castle in Prague. This Defenestration of Prague marked the beginning of the Thirty Years War.

The Bohemian rebels were soon joined by Protestants from neighboring Austria, Moravia, Silesia, and Lusatia. When Ferdinand sent troops to restore his authority, the Bohemians deposed him and, on August 26, 1619, offered the crown to Frederick V of the Palatinate, the head of the Protestant Union.

Frederick's acceptance of the crown was foolhardy and turned the local rebellion into an outright civil war. The new king soon made the bitter discovery that neither his father-in-law, King James I of England, nor the Dutch, nor even the German estates were prepared to back his Bohemian venture. The only foreign aid he received came from Duke Charles Emmanuel of Savoy who sent a small mercenary army under the command of Count Ernest von Mansfeld.

Frederick's cause suffered a further blow when the German electors picked Ferdinand, the man whom the Bohemians had just jilted, to succeed Emperor Matthias (who had died earlier in the year). Ferdinand's elevation strengthened his hand in dealing with the rebels. Maximilian of Bavaria, head of the Catholic League and strongest among the German princes, immediately pledged his support to the new emperor. So did John George of Saxony, the "foremost Lutheran prince in the Empire," whose blind hatred of Calvinism and hope for territorial gain drove him into the imperial camp. Important also was the aid that Emperor Ferdinand II received from the Spaniards, who saw in Frederick's foolish venture a welcome excuse to entrench themselves in the Rhineland and thereby build up their position against the French and the Dutch.

The Bohemian revolt came to an ignominious end on November 8, 1620, in the Battle of the White Mountain near Prague. Here the Catholic forces under the command of Count John Tsercleas von Tilly won an overwhelming victory.

Frederick, henceforth ridiculed as the Winter King, fled and eventually found refuge in the Hague. An absolute Catholic Habsburg monarchy was established in Bohemia; Protestantism and the estates' constitutional rights were ruthlessly suppressed.

Frederick's homeland, the Palatinate, fared not much better. It was overrun by Bavarian forces and Spanish troops under the command of General Ambrogia Spinola. The Protestant Union officially dissolved in May 1621. In September 1622 Tilly's troops stormed Heidelberg, and the Palatinate war was over. Emperor Ferdinand II, his power greatly strengthened, could now act in Germany. As rewards for their support, he granted the disgraced Frederick's electoral title to Maximilian of Bavaria and the province of Lusatia to John George of Saxony.

The Lower Saxon-Danish Phase, 1623–1630: The lead in Protestant affairs soon was taken by King Christian IV of Denmark, who as Duke of Holstein was a member of the Lower Saxon Circle of the Empire. The Danish king intervened partly to aid his coreligionists but primarily to pick up some bishoprics in northern Germany. France, England, and the United Provinces encouraged his intervention yet provided no significant military or financial assistance. Christian thus entered the war as ill prepared as Frederick had been when he joined the Bohemian rebels, and the effects were equally disastrous.

To counter the Danish–Lower Saxon alliance, Emperor Ferdinand II accepted the offer of Albert von Wallenstein, a Bohemian parvenu, to raise an army of twenty thousand men. Wallenstein, who had no particular religious convictions, wanted to build a Habsburg military machine strong enough to operate independently of all other forces in the Empire, including the Catholic League. Wallenstein's and Tilly's armies won decisive victories at Dessau and Lutter in 1626, and Christian's position soon became hopeless. In the Peace of Lübeck (May 22, 1629) he was forced to renounce his ambitions in Germany but was allowed to retain his hereditary lands.

The Protestant estates in northern Germany were in serious trouble. Interpreting his recent victories as a divine mandate to impose both his will and religion on the German Protestants, Ferdinand decided to move forcefully and turn the Empire into a centralized Catholic Habsburg monarchy. He declared the rights of the dukes of Mecklenburg forfeited because they had actively supported King Christian IV. The emperor then gave their duchy to Wallenstein who was not even a prince of the Empire. Even more ominous was the Edict of Restitution, which Ferdinand issued on March 6, 1629. It threatened the very survival of Protestantism by ordering the restoration to the Catholic church of all church properties that had been secularized since 1552. The Protestant electors of Brandenburg and Saxony, who had valiantly tried to stay out of the war, became increasingly alarmed about the emperor's intentions. The Catholic princes too, especially Maximilian of Bavaria, began to fear Ferdinand's power and demanded the dismissal of Wallenstein, whose army had grown to one hundred thousand. Ferdinand initially hesitated but, wishing to retain the goodwill of his allies, reluctantly agreed at the Regensburg electors' meeting (1630) to let his powerful general go. Wallenstein's dismissal, it soon became evident, could not have occurred at a more inopportune moment for the emperor and his allies.

The Swedish Phase, 1630–1635: Among those most concerned about the growth of Habsburg power in the Empire were the French and the Swedes. Richelieu was still busy consolidating his position in France. It was left therefore to Sweden to block Ferdinand's rising power. Its Lutheran king, Gustavus Adolphus, was one of the ablest rulers of his generation. Though Sweden was sparse in population and resources, Gustavus Adolphus had built one of the best armies of the day and had developed Sweden into a Baltic empire. Politics and religion were closely connected for him. He regarded Ferdinand's growing might in northern Germany as a threat to Lutheranism generally and to his own empire more specifically.

On July 6, 1630, Gustavus Adolphus landed a small but well-disciplined army on the Pomeranian coast. Although the German Protestants showed great enthusiasm for the Swedish king, their princes, particularly the electors of Brandenburg and Saxony, were not eager to fight on his side. The two Protestant electors instead sought to pursue a policy of armed neutrality between the Swedish and imperial camps. Their failure to support the king led to one of the greatest catastrophes of the war, the fall of Magdeburg on May 20, 1631. Tilly, whose troops had conquered the city, refused to recognize the electors' neutrality and thereby forced them to join the Swedes. A few weeks later, on September 17, 1631, Gustavus Adolphus won an overwhelming victory over Tilly at Breitenfeld near Leipzig. His army then marched triumphantly to the Rhine and from there pushed into southern Germany where it deliberately devastated the Bavarian countryside in the spring of 1632.

Since the Catholic position was deteriorating rapidly, Ferdinand II decided in December 1631 to recall Wallenstein as supreme commander. Under his able leadership, the imperial army soon grew in strength. Early in September 1632 the imperial forces showed they could hold their own in a clash with the Swedes that occurred near Nuremberg. Wallenstein then moved on to Saxony where he planned to spend the winter. Gustavus Adolphus followed him and on November 16, 1632, the two armies met in a furious battle at Lützen (near Leipzig). In the encounter, Gustavus Adolphus lost his life. Maddened with grief the Swedes fought on under the command of Duke Bernhard von Saxe-Weimar and eventually won the battle. Gustavus Adolphus' ultimate aims will always remain uncertain. He had kept Ferdinand from imposing a Catholic monarchical regime on the Empire and apparently had hoped to become the ruler of a great reorganized Protestant empire that would include Scandinavia and north Germany.

The conduct of the Swedish war effort now devolved upon Chancellor Axel Oxenstierna, the late king's chief adviser. The first efforts of Oxenstierna were aimed at organizing Sweden's allies and consolidating the king's conquests in Germany. In April 1633 he founded the Heilbronn League, an alliance of south German Protestant states. He also renewed the alliance with France that Gustavus Adolphus had concluded in 1631.

The imperial war effort in the meantime was weakened by Wallenstein's treacherous conduct. The general had virtually ceased to fight the Swedes and Saxons. Instead he had opened private negotiations with them hoping to create an independent position for himself. The emperor, finally convinced of his treachery, ordered the general seized dead or alive. In the night of February 25, 1634, Wallenstein was murdered at Eger in Bohemia.

The general's removal restored unity within the imperial army, which now was placed under the command of Ferdinand III, the young heir to the throne. The Habsburgs' position was further strengthened by the Protestants' unwillingness to cooperate fully with Oxenstierna. On September 6, 1634, at Nördlingen, an imperial army, reinforced by Spanish troops, defeated the Swedish army. The Battle of Nördlingen was a blow to the Swedes and destroyed their hopes for control of Germany. The Heilbronn League was scattered. Practically all of southern Germany again fell back into the hands of the imperialists, and German Protestantism once more was seriously threatened.

John George of Saxony, always a reluctant Swedish ally, signed the Peace of Prague with Ferdinand II on May 30, 1635. The Edict of Restitution was virtually suspended, but Calvinists were not included in the agreement. There were to be no more special military alliances among the princes; instead they would help finance the imperial army. The treaty aimed at restoring peace in the Empire and removing foreigners from German soil. Other princes were invited to join, and all, with the exception of Bernhard of Saxe-Weimar and William of Hesse-Cassel, eventually signed the treaty.

The Swedish-French Phase, 1635–1648: The Peace of Prague was an important victory for the emperor. With the Habsburg position greatly strengthened and the Swedes beaten at Nördlingen, Richelieu decided that France had to intervene directly in the fighting. The war therefore continued not because the German princes wanted it but because their powerful foreign neighbors refused to give peace a chance. Germany was about to enter the last, most painful, and most destructive phase of the war, one in which its soil became the battlefield and prize of outside powers as French, Swedish, and Dutch armies fought against the Spanish and Austrian Habsburgs.

French intervention in 1635 did not immediately change the tide of war. After 1638, however, Richelieu's fortunes improved. In that year Bernhard of Saxe-Weimar, whom the French had taken into their service, won significant victories at Rheinfelden and Breisach, thereby interrupting Spanish communications between Milan and the Netherlands. Spain was further weakened by the Catalonian uprising and the rebellion of Portugal in 1640. On May 19, 1643, the French won a crushing victory over the Spanish at Rocroi on the border of the Spanish Netherlands. Simultaneously the Swedes once again pushed deep into the Empire.

The new emperor, Ferdinand III (1637–1657), meanwhile found himself increasingly isolated in Germany. In 1640 Frederick William, the young elector of Brandenburg, broke away from the alliance with the emperor, which he together with other German princes had joined in 1635, and commenced armistice negotiations with Sweden. John George of Saxony soon followed his example. Only Bavaria remained an active ally of the emperor and as such had to endure the brunt of the suffering and destruction in the war's final years.

The resentment against foreigners and the desire for peace had been mounting steadily in Germany for years. At Christmas 1641, Ferdinand III agreed to commence peace negotiations with the French at Münster and the Swedes at Osnabrück. But the vicissitudes of war, which encouraged all parties to hope for more favorable conditions, delayed the actual opening of the conference for three more years. The carnage finally ended in the fall of 1648 when the treaties of Westphalia were signed and peace again returned to Germany.

Consequences: The war left the Empire weak and divided and Germany physically wrecked. Its population losses have been estimated at 30 to 40 percent; the material and cultural losses were practically incalculable. At this heavy price the advance of the Catholic Counter Reformation and Habsburg monarchical ambitions had been stopped. The emperor's power was further weakened by the Peace of Westphalia, which permitted individual German princes to conclude alliances with foreign states. The emergence of a modern nation-state in Germany thus was delayed for several centuries.

Internationally the war marked the end of the age of Spanish preponderance. The victory of the French Bourbons over the Habsburgs was confirmed in 1659 when the Peace of the Pyrenees concluded the fighting between France and Spain. The Thirty Years War that had begun as a religious conflict wound up as Europe's first modern political struggle. A new era in European history had been launched.

Works About: Johann Philipp Abelin, *Theatrum Europaeum*, 3d ed. (Frankfurt am Main 1662–1707), vols. 1–5; E. A. Beller, "The Thirty Years War," in *The New Cambridge Modern Hist.* (Cambridge, 1970), 4:306–58; G. Benecke, ed. *Germany in the Thirty Years War (New York, 1979); Briefe und Akten zur Gesch. des Dreissigjährigen Krieges, N.F. Die Politik Maximilians I von Baiern und seiner Verbündeten, 1618–1651* (Munich, 1907–); Hans Jacob Christoffel von Grimmelshausen, *The Adventure of a Simpleton (Simplicius Simplicissimus)* (New York, 1963); *Documenta Bohemica Bellum Tricennale Illustrantia*, 7 vols. (Prague, 1971–); Jean Dumont, ed., *Corps Universel Diplomatique du Droit des Gens* (Amsterdam, 1728), 5: pt. 2, 6: pt. 1; Günther Franz, *Der Dreissigjährige Kriege und das deutschen Volk*, 3d ed. (Stuttgart, 1961); Henri Hauser, *La prépondérance espagnole, 1559–1660* (Paris, 1933); Michael Caspar Londorp, ed., *Der Römischen Kayserlichen Majestät und dess Heiligen Römischen Reichs . . . Acta Oublica* (Frankfurt am Main, 1668), vols. 1–5; Georges Pagès, *The Thirty Years War* (New York, 1971): J. V. Polišenský, *The Thirty Years War* (Berkeley, 1971), and *War and Society in Europe, 1618–1648* (Cambridge, 1978); M. Ritter, *Dtsch. Gesch. im Zeitalter der Reformation und des Dreissigjährigen*

Krieges (Stuttgart, 1908); S. H. Steinberg, *The Thirty Years War and the Conflict for European Hegemony 1600–1660* (New York, 1966); C. V. Wedgwood, *The Thirty Years War* (London, 1938).   *Bodo Nischan*

See CATHOLIC LEAGUE; BERNHARD; EDICT OF RESTITUTION; FERDINAND II; FERDINAND III; FREDERICK V, ELECTOR; GEORGE WILLIAM; GRIMMELSHAUSEN; JOHN GEORGE; LEIPZIG CONVENTION; MANSFELD, ERNEST; MATTHIAS; MAXIMILIAN I, DUKE; MUNSTER TREATY; NORDLINGEN; NUREMBERG; OSNABRÜCK; PAPPENHEIM; PICCOLOMINI; TILLY; WALLENSTEIN, ALBERT; WESTPHALIA.

TILLY, JOHN TSERCLAES VON (1559–1632), count, Bavarian military commander during the Thirty Years War, was born at Castle Tilly in Brabant and died at Ingolstadt, Bavaria. Jesuit educated, he had originally wished to enter the order himself but decided to serve the Catholic church on the military battlefield instead. As a general, Tilly became known for his unswerving devotion to the Virgin Mary and the strict morality and discipline that he sought to maintain among his troops.

Tilly began his military career in the Spanish army of Alexander Farnese during the Dutch revolution. He fought in the Cologne War against Gebhard Truchsess von Waldburg (1583–1584) and participated in the French religious wars. After 1600 he served the Austrian Habsburgs in Hungary against the Turks; for his services he was promoted to colonel (1602) and field marshal (1605). During the Austrian succession dispute (1608), he supported Emperor Rudolf II against Archduke Matthias.

In 1610, Duke Maximilian of Bavaria appointed Tilly to lead and organize the forces of the recently created Catholic League. As general lieutenant of the league army, he helped suppress the Bohemian revolt that started the Thirty Years War. Tilly's army routed the rebel forces in the Battle of the White Mountain near Prague (November 8, 1620). He then pursued Count Ernest von Mansfeld, whose mercenaries had aided the rebels, into the Palatinate, home of Frederick V, Bohemia's disgraced Winter King. Mansfeld kept eluding him, but Tilly won major victories over his allies at Wimpfen and Höchst (1622); in September his forces stormed Heidelberg, the principality's capital. As an award for his services the emperor made Tilly a count (1622).

After the conquest of the Palatinate, Tilly marched his army north into Hesse to counter the moves of ''Bishop'' Christian, the impetuous administrator of Halberstadt and younger brother of the ruling duke of Brunswick, who was exhorting the imperial estates of the Lower Saxon Circle to rise in defense of their German liberties. The Halbersstädter received little response from the north German princes who, for the moment at least, preferred to stay neutral. On August 6, 1623, the Catholic forces caught up with Christian at Stadtlohn, not far from the Dutch border, and practically annihilated the so-called mad bishop's army.

The Lower Saxon princes meanwhile had become increasingly alarmed about the progress of Catholic arms. Tilly's troops, known as papist bloodhounds, were viewed by many Protestants as a threat to their religious interests and political neutrality. In order to be ready for a possible confrontation, they decided to arm and elect the duke of Holstein, King Christian IV of Denmark, captain of their imperial circle (May 1625).

The war for which both sides had been preparing came in 1626. Tilly received some assistance from an imperial army led by Duke Albert von Wallenstein, but the decisive battles were fought and won by his forces. The league troops conquered Göttingen and Hanover; on August 27, 1626, they crushed the army of King Christian in a battle that was fought at Lutter (south of Brunswick). The Lower Saxon princes soon sued for peace; only the dukes of Mecklenburg stayed with the Danish king. In the next two years, Tilly's and Wallenstein's forces cooperated (not always very harmoniously) in pushing King Christian out of Germany. Tilly felt that the terms of the Treaty of Lübeck (1629), which ended the Danish war, were too lenient. He interpreted his recent victories as a divine mandate for the re-Catholization of Germany and supported the emperor's Edict of Restitution (1629).

Wallenstein's growing army had made it increasingly difficult for Tilly to supply and quarter his troops. Not surprisingly therefore, the league princes, particularly Maximilian of Bavaria, fearful of the emperor's power, now demanded that Ferdinand reduce the size of his army and let his powerful general go. Ferdinand initially hesitated, but, wishing to retain the goodwill of his allies, finally agreed to dismiss Wallenstein and to appoint Tilly in his stead (1630).

The imperial and league armies were at last unified in command, but Tilly inherited none of Wallenstein's vast powers and privileges, only his problems and obligations, and the biggest of these was King Gustavus Adolphus of Sweden. In the summer of 1630 Gustavus had landed a small, well-disciplined army in Pomerania to counter the Habsburgs' growing might, which he perceived as a threat to his own Baltic empire. In order to keep the German Protestants from joining the king, Tilly decided on a show of force in northern Germany. After a long siege, he conquered and destroyed Magdeburg (May 20, 1631), the well-fortified Lutheran citadel that Gustavus Adolphus had pledged to defend. He tried to intimidate neutral Saxony but instead drove its Lutheran ruler into the arms of the waiting Gustavus Adolphus. When the two concluded an alliance, Tilly invaded Saxony. His army captured Leipzig, but then, very suddenly and unexpectedly, the tide turned. In a battle fought at the village of Breitenfeld, north of Leipzig, on September 17, 1631, Tilly, thus far seemingly invincible, suffered a humiliating defeat at the hands of Gustavus Adolphus.

The league general withdrew via Hesse to Franconia and Bavaria where he hoped to regroup. Morale among his soldiers ran low; in the winter of 1631–1632, they deserted in increasingly large numbers. On April 15, 1632, while trying to block the Swedish advance into Bavaria, Tilly suffered a serious injury during a cannonade at Rain on the Lech. Mortally wounded, the seventy-three-year-old general was taken to Ingolstadt where he died two weeks later (April

30). Tilly lacked the charisma and political visions of his great contemporaries Wallenstein and Gustavus Adolphus. But to the end he remained a faithful Catholic, a "monk in armor," who gave all he had in the defense of the old faith.

Works About: *Briefe und Akten zur Gesch. des Dreissigjährigen Krieges* (Munich, 1870–1909; new series, 1907–); *Documenta Bohemica Bellum Tricennale Illustrantia* (Prague, 1974–1977). vols. 3–5; Georg Gilardone, *Tilly, der Heilige im Harnisch* (Munich, 1932); Hermann Hallwich, ed., *Briefe und Akten zur Gesch. Wallensteins,* 4 vols. (Vienna, 1912); Onno Klopp, *Tilly im dreissigjährigen Kriege,* 2 vols. (Stuttgart, 1861); Julius O. Opel, *Der niedersächsischdänische Krieg* (Halle, 1872); "Tilly," *BW* 3:2910–12; Antoine C. H. Villermont, *Tilly; ou, La guerre de trente ans de 1618 à 1632* (Paris, 1860); Karl Wittich, *Magdeburg, Gustav Adolf und Tilly* (Berlin, 1874), and "Tilly," *ADB*, 38:314–50.   *Bodo Nischan*

See FREDERICK V, ELECTOR; MANSFELD, ERNEST; MATTHIAS; MAXIMILIAN I, DUKE; RUDOLF II; THIRTY YEARS WAR; WALLENSTEIN, ALBERT.

TITLES commonly used in the Holy Roman Empire include emperor, king, archduke, duke, margrave, landgrave, and count. Each one of them has a long and complex history and has meant different things at different times to different people. They will be described here only in a broad, general sense.

The title emperor was derived from the ancient Roman military title *Imperator,* which was conferred on Augustus Caesar in 27 B. C. by the Roman senate to recognize his unlimited power of command (*imperium*) in the provinces. In earlier times the title *Imperator* and the power of command were considered only temporary. The term "emperor" began to be used to designate Augustus Caesar and his successors. The German word *Kaiser,* which means emperor, is in part a corruption of the Latin *Caesar,* which came to be used interchangeably with the term emperor. The later Roman emperors continued to use the titles Imperator, Caesar, and Augustus. All of these Roman titles and many others were borrowed by many of the men who ruled the Holy Roman Empire.

Charlemagne styled himself "Carolus serenissimus Augustus, a Deo coronatus, magnus et pacificus imperator, Romanum gubernans imperium, qui et per misericordiam Dei rex Francorum et Langobardorum." Subsequent Carolingian emperors were usually entitled simply "Imperator Augustus." Some like Conrad I and Henry I were only German Kings (Latin *Rex* , German *König*.). Many of the later emperors were addressed as king before their coronation and "Imperator Augustus" after their coronation at Rome.

From the eleventh century until the sixteenth, the usual practice was for the monarch to be called "Romanorum rex semper Augustus" until his coronation at Rome by the pope. Following the coronation in Rome, the monarch invariably came to be addressed as "Romanorum Imperator semper Augustus." In 1508 Maximilian I, after having been refused passage to Rome by the Venetians, obtained a bull from Pope Julius II permitting him to call himself "Imperator electus" (*erwählter Kaiser* in German; elected emperor in English). Ferdinand

I and all succeeding emperors took this title immediately after their German coronation and it was until 1806 their strict legal designation. However, the term "elect" was usually omitted in formal documents when the sovereign was addressed or spoken of in the third person. In ordinary practice he was simply "Roman Emperor."

Maximilian I also added the title "Germaniae rex" (German king). A great many other titles of less consequence were added from time to time. Charles V had seventy-five titles, which reflected not only his imperial honors, but his worldwide hereditary possessions as well.

The title "King of the Romans" (*Romischer König* in German) came to be used to designate the heir-apparent to be crowned during his father's lifetime, so that at the death of the latter he might step at once into his place.

The title "Archduke" (*Erzherzog* in German) refers to a duke, who is more important than a regular duke or who rules a larger than normal or more prestigious dukedom. An example of this would be the archdukes of Austria; many of whom like Ferdinand I became emperors. A duke, of course, is simply someone who rules over a large territory or dukedom. Some of the early Medieval tribal kingdoms, such as that of the Saxons, came to be called stem duchies and the ruler of the Saxons came to be known as the duke of Saxony.

A margrave or marquess (*Markgraf*) is the term used to designate a count (*Graf*), who administers a march province (*Markgrafschaft*). A march province is one located near the frontier of the Empire and often in need of strong military leadership. A landgrave is a count who administers a rural territory; for example Landgrave Philip of Hesse. The term "count" (*Graf*) itself was also widely used in the Empire, sometimes merely as an honorific title, which did not automatically confer rule over a grant of land.

Works About: James Bryce, *The Holy Roman Empire* (New York, 1961); H. Grundmann, *Betrachtungen zur Kaiserkrönung Ottos I* (Munich, 1962); F. Heer, *The Holy Roman Empire*, tr. J. Sondheimer (New York, 1968); W. G. Sinnigen and A. E. R. Boak, *A History of Rome*, 6th ed. (New York, 1977).   *J. W. Zophy*

See AACHEN; CHARLEMAGNE; CHARLES V; CONRAD I; FERDINAND I; GOLDEN BULL OF 1356; HENRY I; IMPERIAL REGALIA; MAXIMILIAN I; PHILIP OF HESSE.

TORGAU, a fortified town in Saxony on the left (west) bank of the Elbe, was where Frederick the Great of Prussia defeated an Austrian army on November 3, 1760, during the Seven Years War. Beset by enemies on all sides, Frederick had rapidly shifted his army to reinforce threatened areas in Saxony, Silesia, Brandenburg, and Pomerania. In October he had marched from Silesia to drive off the Austro-Russian raid on Berlin and then to Saxony, where Field Marshal Leopold von Daun (1705–1766) had united with General Franz Moritz von Lacy's (Lascy, 1725–1801) corps from Berlin on October 24 at Torgau, fortifying a position on a plateau west of the town. Frederick divided his army, sending a column under hussar general Hans Joachim von Zieten (1699–1786) to feint from the southwest, while Frederick marched around to attack from the northeast. The movement began early on November 3 in pouring rain. But Zieten delayed to engage Croats and other light troops, and Frederick, hearing the gunfire on the strong south wind, threw his troops into the attack piecemeal as they arrived. Daun, thrice victor over the Prussians, had shifted his troops and guns to meet Frederick's attack. Of 6,000 grenadiers in the advance guard, only 600 survived the caseshot and musket volleys that swept the approaches. Both Frederick and Daun were wounded and evacuated, each believing the Prussians had been repulsed. But at dusk Zieten located an unguarded causeway across the Röhr, and his infantry finally broke the Austrian line. The whitecoats retreated to the fortress and then across the Elbe. Frederick had lost heavily, 16,670 of 50,000, the Austrians 15,697 of 53,400. Torgau had decided little since Daun still held southern Saxony, but, given the exhaustion of the belligerents, Torgau was to be the last major battle of Frederick's career.

Works About: Austrian official, *Die Kriege unter der Regierung der Kaiserin Marie Theresia* (Vienna, 1896–1914).   *A. H. Ganz*

See FREDERICK II, THE GREAT; SEVEN YEARS WAR.

TRAUTTMANSDORFF, MAXIMILIAN VON (1584–1650), count, member of the Imperial Privy Council, one of the most outstanding Austrian diplomats in the seventeenth century, was born in Graz and died in Vienna. He was the son of John Frederick von Trauttmansdorff, a privy councillor and minister of war at the court of Archduke Charles of Inner Austria. Originally Lutheran, his family converted to Roman Catholicism when Maximilian was still a boy. He served briefly with the imperial army in Hungary and, as captain of the cavalry, with the Spanish in the Netherlands. In 1612, Emperor Rudolf II named him to the Imperial Aulic Council. Shortly afterward, Emperor Matthias appointed him first minister at the court of Empress Anna; he later held the same post under Ferdinand II and Ferdinand III. From 1637 until his death he served as director of the privy council.

Trauttmansdorff was endowed with a lively mind and breadth of vision. As a statesman he made his most notable contribution in the field of diplomacy. In 1617–1618 he helped Archduke Ferdinand to secure the elective crowns of Bohemia and Hungary; he also played a leading role in getting Ferdinand elected as Holy Roman emperor (1619). He influenced decisively imperial policy during the Thirty Years War. Trauttmansdorff recognized early the importance of Bavaria and played a considerable part in winning for Ferdinand II the support of Duke Maximilian I and the Catholic League. In 1622 he concluded the Peace of Nikolsburg with Bethlen Gabor, the half-independent ruler of Transylvania, who had joined the Bohemian rebels against Ferdinand. After the fall of the Palatinate, he arranged the transfer of the Upper Palatinate and the electoral title from the disgraced Elector Frederick V, Bohemia's Winter King, to Maximilian of Bavaria. In 1628 he persuaded Maximilian to return Upper Austria, which Ferdinand had pawned earlier to the Bavarian as compensation for his military efforts. After 1627 he served intermittently as imperial ambassador to the Saxon court in Dresden. He was one of Ferdinand's main advisers at the Regensburg electors' meeting (1630). His influence at the imperial court grew after the murder of the imperial general Albert von Wallenstein in 1634 (whom Trauttmansdorff had opposed but in whose assassination he was not implicated). The resulting demise of the court party of Prince Hans Ulrich von Eggenberg enabled Trauttmansdorff to emerge as the leading minister in Vienna. In that capacity he negotiated the Peace of Prague (1635) with Elector John George of Saxony; the treaty aimed at restoring peace in the Empire and removing foreigners from German soil.

Trauttmansdorff performed his most important diplomatic mission as the chief imperial envoy to the Westphalian Peace Congress, which concluded the Thirty Years War. He arrived at the conference in 1645 and actively paticipated in the negotiations for the next one and a half years. A tolerant and patient man, Trauttmansdorff was ideally suited to reconcile the many conflicting claims and interests at the congress. He had to contend with the constantly mounting demands of the French and the Swedes and the suspicion of the Spanish, who feared, not unjustly, that he would sacrifice their country's interests to achieve peace for the Empire. Trauttmansdorff understood realistically that France and Sweden had to be satisfied if the conference were to succeed. His sincerity and genuine commitment to peace earned him the respect of friend and foe alike. When Trauttmansdorff left the congress in 1647 to return to Vienna, he had negotiated draft treaties with France and Sweden essentially identical with those that the Empire would sign with the two powers one year later.

Works About: Max Braubach and Konrad Repgen, eds., *Acta Pacis Westphalicae* (Münster, 1962–), vol. 1; Fritz Dickmann, *Der Westfälische Frieden*, (Münster, 1972), passim; Egloffstein, "Trauttmansdorff," *ADB*, 38:531–36; Hermann Hallwich, ed., *Briefe und Akten zur Gesch. Wallensteins*, 4 vols. (Vienna, 1912); Henry F. Schwarz, *The Imperial Privy Council in the Seventeenth Century* (Cambridge, Mass., 1943), pp. 372–74; "Trauttmansdorff, Maximilian," *Wurzbach*, 47:76– 79   *Bodo Nischan*

See FERDINAND II; FERDINAND III; MATTHIAS; MAXIMILIAN I, DUKE; RUDOLF II; THIRTY YEARS WAR; WALLENSTEIN, ALBERT; WESTPHALIA.

TRUCHSESS, GEORGE III VON WALDBURG (1488–1531), statesman and military leader, was born to a noble family at Waldsee in Swabia. His formal education for the most part was limited to three years' instruction by a canon at the court of his mother's brother, Frederick von Zollern, bishop of Augsburg. George also learned a good deal about politics and diplomacy by accompanying the bishop on trips to neighboring principalities and towns. His first military experience came during the Bavarian War of Succession in 1504, when he served first as a page and then as a cavalryman.

In 1508 Truchsess joined the service of Duke Ulrich of Württemberg. He served with Ulrich in the suppression of an agrarian rebellion in southern Germany, known as the "poor Conrad" revolt of 1514. Truchsess broke with Ulrich shortly after the murder of Hans von Hutten by Ulrich and joined the service of the dukes of Bavaria. In 1516 he commanded the Bavarian contingent serving with Emperor Maximilian in Italy.

Truchsess found himself fighting against his former patron as a lieutenant to Duke William of Bavaria, who commanded the forces of the Swabian League in the 1519 campaign, which deprived Ulrich of his duchy. Following this campaign, George allied himself with the house of Habsburg. In the spring of 1523, Archduke Ferdinand gave him command of the Swabian League army assembled to attack the Franconian robber knights. He also served the Habsburgs as a diplomat at the 1524 diet of Nuremberg and as a member of the Imperial Council of Regency.

During the Peasants' Revolt of 1524–1526, Truchsess achieved great fame as the commander of the forces of the Swabian League. Firm and highly effective in dealing with the rebels, he was made chief regent (*Statthalter*) of Württemberg, a post he held until his death. In Württemberg he attempted to suppress the public appearances of the evangelicals but without using excessive cruelty. Truchsess also rendered valuable service to the Habsburgs as a spokesman and negotiator on religion at the diets of Speyer (1526 and 1529) and at Augsburg (1530).

Works About: Virginia DeMarce, "The Official Career of Georg III Truchsess von Waldburg" (Ph.D. diss., Stanford University, 1967); Joseph Vochezer, *Gesch. des fürstlichen Hauses Waldburg in Schwaben* (Kempten, 1888–1907); August Willburger, *Georg III. Truchsess von Waldburg* (Stuttgart, 1934).   *J. W. Zophy*

See FERDINAND I; MAXIMILIAN I; PEASANTS' WAR; SWABIAN LEAGUE; ULRICH OF WÜRTTEMBERG.

TUSCAN MARCH, an administrative district in Italy, encompassed the major cities, and the territories of Lucca, Pisa, Pistoia, Siena, Florence, and probably also Arezzo and Volterra, governed by a margrave. This official evolved by the time of the later Carolingians, superseding the earlier count, and exercised control over all Tuscany. From the end of the tenth century (Otto I) to the late twelfth century, the margrave was the most powerful representative of the imperial sovereign in the Italian kingdom. By a slow process the city of Florence, which had begun to merge with Fiesole in the ninth century, replaced Lucca as the center of margravial administration. Subsequent to the death of Matilda in 1115, Margrave Rabodo transferred his capital to the center of Tuscany, San Miniato del Tedesco, where the Arno and Elsa rivers met. By this time, however, the heyday of the Tuscan March in imperial affairs was past. The territory became a source of contention among the expanding Tuscan communes. During the Renaissance, Florence once again became the center of Tuscany, but the district was independent from the Empire.

The Tuscan March played a considerable role in the history of the early Empire, although none so important as that which occurred during the investiture controversy and the ensuing Welf-Waiblingen struggles. The origins of Tuscan estrangement from the Empire were found in the mid-eleventh century when Duke Godfrey of Upper Lorraine, disappointed with Emperor Henry III's refusal to give him Lower Lorraine, married Beatrice, widow of Margrave Boniface. Boniface, the head of the Canossa family, had been one of the pope's most powerful supporters in Italy. Godfrey continued his predecessor's alliance, especially after his brother became Pope Stephen IX.

When Matilda, the daughter of Boniface, succeeded both Godfrey as leader of the margraviate in 1069 and her father as heiress of the Canossa family holdings in Lombardy, she began a reign that dominated much of Italy and, indirectly, Germany for more than forty years. Even though she held her office by consent of the emperor, she sided with Gregory VII against Henry IV in the contention over investiture. Matilda's castle at Canossa was the scene of Henry IV's memorable submission in January 1077. When she died childless in 1115, her testament made the pope heir of her allodial properties but reserved her imperial territories to her successor. This led to ongoing difficulties between emperors and popes. It also led to problems between emperors and their opponents in the Empire, especially during the Welf-Waiblingen controversies.

Florence, almost alone in the march, remained faithful to the papacy, a faith that had considerable benefits for the city in the future. Because of Florence's allegiance, other Tuscan cities received imperial grants and privileges in an attempt to neutralize Florence's power. Thus most of Tuscany allied with the Empire. Eventually these opposing alliances developed into the communal contests observed during the Guelf-Ghibelline struggles, the Italian theater in Tuscany of the Welf-Waiblingen contention in Germany. By the end of the twelfth century, after the Welf margrave deserted to the papacy and Frederick Barbarossa appointed new administrators, the influence of the march in German affairs waned.

Works About: Antonio Falce, *Il marchese Ugo di Tuscia* (Florence, 1921), and *Bonifacio di Canossa, padre di Matilda,* 2 vols. (Reggio Emilia, 1926–1927); A. Overmann, *Gräfin Mathilde von Tuscien, Gesch. ihres Gutes von 1115–1230* (Innsbruck, 1895); Ferdinand Schevill, *History of Florence* (New York, 1936, rpr. 1961); F. Schneider, *Die Reichsverwaltung in Toscana, von der Gründung des Langobardenreiches bis zum Ausgang der Staufer (568–1268)* (Rome, 1914, rpr. 1966).   *P. N. Bebb*

See GREGORY VII; FREDERICK I; HENRY III; HENRY IV; MATILDA OF TUSCANY.

ULM, a major town of southern Germany, was a free imperial city from the thirteenth century until 1802. Situated at a vital crossing of the Danube, Ulm first appears in a Carolingian charter of the year 854, where it is described as a *Pfalz,* or royal palace. A market settlement soon grew up around the palace. The Salian emperors frequently held court in Ulm, but during the investiture conflict in the late eleventh century the community came under the domination of the Welfs and other foes of Emperor Henry IV. After 1100 Ulm was controlled by the Hohenstaufen in their capacity as dukes of Swabia. Although Ulm was attacked and destroyed by a Welf army in 1134, the Hohenstaufen rapidly rebuilt the settlement, and by 1181 it had been granted the status of a city.

The new city flourished under Hohenstaufen patronage. During the interregnum of 1254–1273 following the collapse of the Hohenstaufen, Ulm was able to assert its status as a free imperial city. In 1274 Rudolf of Hapsburg granted Ulm the same privileges enjoyed by the free city of Esslingen; "Ulmer Recht" was subsequently awarded to a number of other Swabian cities.

Beginning in 1316, the old wall surrounding Ulm was replaced by a new one that quadrupled the size of the city. The optimism implied by this undertaking was justified by Ulm's rapid development as a major commercial center and seat of textile production. The city's growing wealth was demonstrated from 1377 onward by the construction of the minster of Ulm, one of the great achievements of German Gothic architecture. (The 162-meter-high spire, however, was added only in the nineteenth century.) Decades of political conflict between patricians and guild members finally came to an end with the adoption of the *Schwörbrief* of 1397, under which all citizens pledged loyalty to a constitution giving guild masters a majority of seats in both the small and the large city council.

Ulm was deeply involved in the political alliances and conflicts of southern Germany during the late Middle Ages. As a founding member of the league of Swabian cities in 1376, Ulm played a dominant role in the league's affairs until its defeat by the count of Württemberg in 1388. In 1449–1450 Ulm was again allied with other cities in an unsuccessful war against Württemberg. From 1488 to 1534 the city was active in the Swabian League.

Beginning in the late fourteenth century, the city of Ulm undertook an ambitious program of territorial expansion in the surrounding region, primarily by purchasing land from indebted noble families. By the end of the Middle Ages, Ulm ruled over an extensive territory stretching northwest from the city, whose population substantially exceeded that of the city itself.

The Reformation found enthusiastic support among many of Ulm's citizens in the 1520s. The city government at first took a cautious stance, but in 1530, forced to decide for or against the recess of the diet of Augsburg, the magistrates submitted the question to the citizenry as a whole. The ensuing poll, carried out through the guilds, showed 87 percent of the citizens in favor of the Reformation. The next year Protestant worship was systematically introduced.

The city joined the Schmalkaldic League in 1531 and participated in the war of 1546–1547 against Charles V. In 1548, to punish the city, Charles V abrogated the constitution of 1397 with its strong representation by the guilds and instituted a single city council with predominantly patrician membership. The city also submitted briefly to the emperor's Interim of 1548, but after a few years the magistrates pressed forward again with the Reformation.

In 1609 Ulm joined the Protestant Union. Throughout the Thirty Years War, the city and its hinterland experienced frequent campaigns. Early in the war armies of the union and the Catholic League gathered near the city, but a direct conflict between them was averted by the Treaty of Ulm of 1620. In 1632 the city entered into an alliance with Gustavus Adolphus and accepted a Swedish garrison, but in 1635, following a lengthy siege by imperial troops, the city subscribed to the Peace of Prague. The region continued to be a focus of military activity until the end of the war in 1648.

After the Thirty Years War, Ulm served as the customary seat for meetings of the Swabian circle. Despite its political importance, however, Ulm suffered a gradual economic decline. The city's debts from the Thirty Years War were aggravated by new financial burdens imposed during the War of the Spanish Succession, when Bavarian and French troops occupied the city from 1702 to 1704.

In the late eighteenth century the patrician government of Ulm came under bitter attack from citizens who felt excluded from decision making. An appeal by the citizens to the *Reichshofrat* from 1778 to 1787 resulted in some political reforms. But a second appeal, launched in 1794, was broken off by the events of the Napoleonic era. In 1802 Ulm was annexed by Bavaria, and the *Reichsdeputationshauptschluss* of 1803 confirmed the city's loss of imperial status. In 1810 the city was transferred to the kingdom of Württemberg.

Works About: Gottfried Geiger, *Die Reichsstadt Ulm vor der Reformation: Städtisches und kirchliches Leben am Ausgang des Mittelalters* (Ulm, 1971); Carl Mollwo, ed., *Das Rote Buch der Stadt Ulm* (Stuttgart, 1905); Gerold Neusser, *Das Territorium der Reichsstadt Ulm im 18. Jahrhundert: Verwaltungsgeschichtliche Forschungen* (Ulm, 1964); Eugen Nübling, *Die Reichsstadt Ulm am Ausgange des Mittelalters* (1378–1556), 2 vols. (Ulm, 1904–1907); Friedrich Pressel, Gustav Veesenmeyer, and Hugo Bazing, eds., *Ulmisches Urkundenbuch* (854–1378), 3 vols. (Stuttgart and Ulm, 1873–1900); Hans Specker, *Ulm: Stadtgesch.* (Ulm, 1977); Gustav Veesenmeyer, ed., *Fratris Felici Fabri Tractatus de civitate Ulmensi* (Tübingen, 1889).   *C. R. Friedrichs*

See CHARLES V; HENRY IV; IMPERIAL CITIES; RUDOLF I; SCHMALKALDIC LEAGUE; SCHMALKALDIC WAR; SPANISH SUCCESSION; SWABIAN LEAGUE; THIRTY YEARS WAR.

ULRICH OF WÜRTTEMBERG (1487–1550), duke who introduced the Protestant Reformation to his lands, was born in Reichenweiler (Riquewihr) in Alsace, the son of Count Henry of Württemberg and Countess Elizabeth of Zweibrücken. Because his father was mentally unstable, young Ulrich was brought to Stuttgart and raised by relatives until 1498, when the Swabian estates compelled the ineffective Duke Eberhard II to resign in favor of his younger nephew. Holy Roman Emperor Maximilian I selected a bride for Ulrich, the six-year-old Sabina of Bavaria, whom he passionately detested but eventually married in 1511.

During the following years, Ulrich assisted Maximilian militarily in several wars as a member of the Swabian League. In 1514 his extensive debts and growing unrest in Württemberg forced Ulrich to conclude the Treaty of Tübingen with the provincial estates (*Landtag*). His subsequent murder of Hans von Hutten, a courtier, because of his fascination with the latter's beautiful wife, and the flight of Duchess Sabina to her Bavarian relatives that same year (1515) led the emperor to place Ulrich under the ban in 1516 and again in 1518. The duke's precipitous conquest of Reutlingen, an imperial free city, in 1519 caused the Swabian League to drive Ulrich into exile; his lands were awarded to Austrian occupation forces. In 1522 the new Holy Roman emperor, Charles V, placed Württemberg in the care of his brother Ferdinand. From now until 1534, Ulrich's lands remained under Austrian domination, while the duke continued to make armed forays from safe border refuges, notably in 1525 at the head of some armed peasant bands.

Finally in 1534 Ulrich, who had embraced the Lutheran Reformation during his exile, led a force of twenty thousand men, assisted by Landgrave Philip of Hesse and French financial subsidies, to reclaim his lands and to introduce the Reformation to Württemberg. The Treaty of Kaaden on June 29, 1534, restored the duke to his former position as ruler and allowed him a free hand in regulating the religious settlement. Only a few feudal ties with Austria remained in need of further clarification. The Lutheran Erhard Schnepf and the Zwinglian Ambrosius Blarer introduced the religious reformation of the territory, which was crowned in 1536 with the completion of a comprehensive ecclesiastical ordinance (*Kirchenordnung*). A pedagogium in Tübingen and Latin schools throughout the land were established to educate young men for service to the church and to the state, funded from confiscated monastic properties and incomes. Even though he became a member of the rival Schmalkaldic League, Ulrich took care to remain on good terms with Emperor Charles V during the Schmalkaldic War, but to no avail, since he still had to pay a sum of 300,000 gulden to the emperor and was compelled to accept the Augsburg Interim, which attempted to restore Catholicism as the sole religious faith. This conflict remained unresolved at the time of Ulrich's sudden death on November 6, 1550, when he was succeeded by his recently reconciled only son, Christopher. Ever moody and mistrustful, Ulrich, by his stubborn refusal to admit defeat, eventually won the grudging admiration of his countrymen.

Works About: L. F. Heyd, *Ulrich, Herzog zu Württemberg: Ein Beitr. zur Gesch. Württemberg und des dtsch. Reichs im Zeitalter der Reformation,* 3 vols. (Tübingen, 1841–1844); Bernhard Kugler, *Ulrich, Herzog zu Württemberg* (Stuttgart, 1865); Karl Pfaff, *Gesch. Wirtenbergs* (Stuttgart, 1819); vol. 7; C. F. Sattler, *Gesch. des Herzogthums Würtenberg unter der Regierung der Herzogen* (Ulm, 1770–1771), vols. 2–3; Eugen Schneider, "Ulrich, Herzog von Württemberg," *ADB,* 39:237–43; C. F. von Stälin, *Wirtembergische Gesch.* (Stuttgart, 1873); Karl Weller and Arnold Weller, *Württembergische Gesch. im südwestdeutschen Raum,* 6th ed. (Stuttgart and Aalen, 1971).   *L. J. Reith*

See CHARLES V; CHRISTOPHER; FERDINAND I; MAXIMILIAN I; PHILIP OF HESSE; SCHMALKALDIC WAR; SWABIAN LEAGUE.

UNIVERSITIES, institutions of higher education that gradually assumed the Roman law denotation of corporations or juristic persons, owed their foundations to specific acts by emperors or popes. Each generally comprised four faculties authorized to confer degrees: an undergraduate liberal arts faculty and three graduate ones in law, theology, and medicine. Universities within the Empire occurred relatively late in comparison with the rest of Europe, an event perhaps explained by the Empire's political decentralization.

The following is a list of universities within the Empire—excluding those developed in Switzerland after the Swiss Wars of Independence—and their foundation dates: Prague, 1348; Vienna, 1365; Heidelberg, 1386; Cologne, 1388 (to 1798; reformed, 1919); Erfurt, 1392 (to 1816); Leipzig, 1409; Rostock, 1419; Löwen, 1426; Greifswald, 1456; Basel, 1456; Freiburg, 1457; Ingolstadt, 1472 (transferred to Landshut, 1802); Trier, 1473 (to 1795); Mainz, 1476 (to 1798; reformed, 1946); Tübingen, 1477; Wittenberg, 1502 (transferred to Halle, 1815); Frankfurt am Oder, 1506 (transferred to Breslau, 1811); Marburg, 1527; Königsberg, 1544 (to 1945); Dillingen, 1554 (to 1802); Jena, 1558; Helmstedt, 1575 (to 1809); Olmütz, 1576 (to 1782); Würzburg, 1582; Graz, 1586; Giessen, 1607 (to 1945); Paderborn, 1614 (to 1809); Molsheim, 1618 (to 1701); Rinteln, 1619 (to 1809); Strasbourg, 1621 (to 1792; reformed 1872–1918, 1941–1944); Altdorf, 1623 (to 1807); Salzburg, 1623 (to 1810); Osnabrück, 1630 (to 1633); Dorpat, 1632 (to 1710; reformed, 1802–1893); Bamberg, 1648 (to 1803); Herborn, 1654 (to 1817); Duisburg, 1655 (to 1818); Kiel, 1655; Innsbruck, 1672 (to 1810; reformed 1826); Halle, 1694; Breslau, 1702 (reformed 1811–1945); Fulda, 1734 (to 1805); Göttingen, 1737; Erlangen, 1743; Münster, 1773 (to 1818; reformed 1902); Stuttgart, 1781 (to 1794); Lamberg, 1784 (to 1871); Bonn, 1786 (to 1797; reformed 1818); Landshut, 1802 (from Ingolstadt; transferred to Munich, 1826).

Works About: Heinrich Denifle, *Die Entstehung der Universitäten des Mittelalters bis 1400* (Berlin, 1885, rpr. 1956); Wilhelm Erman and Ewald Horn, eds., *Bibliographie der dtsch. Universitäten,* 3 vols. (Leipzig and Berlin, 1904–05); Georg Kaufmann, *Gesch. der dtsch. Universitäten,* 2 vols. (Stuttgart, 1888–1896, rpr. 1958); Hastings Rashdall, *The Universities of Europe in the Middle Ages,* ed. F. M. Powicke and A. B. Emden, 3 vols. (Oxford, 1936, rpr. 1969); Hellmuth Rössler and Günther Franz, eds., *Universität und Gelehrtenstand 1400–1800* (Limburg/Lahn, 1970).   *P. N. Bebb*

See COLOGNE; FREIBURG; STRASBOURG; VIENNA.

UTRECHT, PEACE OF, consisted of a series of treaties signed in 1713, 1714, and 1715 ending the War of the Spanish Succession (1701–1714). In this conflict, the allies—Austria, Great Britain, the United Provinces, the Holy Roman Empire, Prussia, Savoy, and Portugal—contested Philip V's (Louis XIV's grandson) claim to the entire Spanish monarchy. Peace overtures began in 1709 and 1710 but failed. By 1711, however, the situation changed: the hawkish Whigs fell from power in Great Britain; war weariness increased throughout Europe; the allies realized that it would be virtually impossible to oust Philip from Spain; and the death of the Holy Roman emperor, Joseph I, in 1711 raised the specter of a personal union between Spain and the Danubian lands under Charles VI, the Habsburg claimant to the Spanish monarchy. The allies were as averse to a union between Spain and the Habsburg lands as they were to one between Spain and France. In 1711 and 1712, Louis XIV's heirs, the dauphin, Louis, duke of Burgundy, and Burgundy's son, the duke of Brittany, died. Only a sickly child stood between Philip V of Spain and the crown of France. The very real possibility that Philip V would hold both crowns alarmed the allies.

Both sides were eager for peace in January 1712 when the congress opened at Utrecht. The principal negotiators were Thomas Wentworth, earl of Strafford, and John Robinson, bishop of Bristol for Great Britain; Marshal d'Huxelles, Abbé Polignac, and Nicholas Mesnager for France; Willem Buys and Bruno van der Dussen for the United Provinces; and Count Sinzendorf and Baron Casper Florentine von Consbruch for the Holy Roman Empire. The guiding precept of the diplomats was preservation of the balance of power. The allies acknowledged Philip V as king of Spain with the proviso that the Spanish and French thrones never be united under one monarch. Louis, in turn, recognized Frederick as king in Prussia, accepted the Protestant succession in Great Britain, and promised to give no further succor of shelter in France to the Stuart pretender. The Spanish promised, but did not honor, an amnesty to the Catalans who had so courageously aided the allies.

The treaties of Utrecht were in effect but another partition treaty; the representatives agreed to dismember the Spanish empire. Philip V kept Spain while the Habsburgs got Milan, Naples, and the Netherlands. The duke of Savoy regained Savoy and Nice, which the French had taken, and received Sicily, which he later exchanged for Sardinia. Great Britain acquired not only Gibraltar and Minorca from Spain, but from France Nova Scotia, St. Kitt's, the Hudson Bay territory, and Newfoundland, where the French retained their fishing rights. France received the principality of Orange. Neuchâtel, Valengin, and Upper Guelderland went to Prussia. The French also agreed to demolish Dunkirk, a privateering base, and fill in the harbor. The Wittelsbachs in Bavaria and Cologne, who had allied with Louis XIV, recovered their lands and titles in the Empire. The United Provinces received their "barrier," a string of fortresses in the Netherlands of Namur, Tournai, Menin, Furnes, Warneton, Ypres, and Knoque and the right to garrison Dendermonde in part. The Dutch were allowed a garrison force of thirty-five thousand in the Netherlands, three-fifths of the costs being carried by the emperor and the remainder by the Dutch. They would use the barrier as a bulwark against French aggression and as a device to exploit the trade of the area.

Commercially the Dutch also received favored-nation status in France and Spain, as did Great Britain. Spain also granted Great Britain the Asiento, the lucrative trade in Spanish America for thirty years. France gave up all commercial advantages in Spain.

The Utrecht peace benefited Great Britain most of all; the British got the majority of the colonial, commercial, and strategic spoils of the war. Although the treaty was later bitterly denounced by the Whigs, it marked the expansion of the British colonial and commercial empire.

Neither Austria nor the Holy Roman Empire ratified any of the treaties. Charles refused because the pacts disregarded Habsburg claims to Spain. But the situation called for peace: the French had crossed the Rhine; the Catalans had been defeated in Spain; and plague had broken out in Vienna. France too was weary of war and financially exhausted. Prince Eugene of Savoy recognized the impossibility of carrying on the conflict without allied assistance and urged Charles to open negotiations. Charles deputized Prince Eugene to act for him, and Louis XIV sent Marshal Villars to begin discussions at Rastatt, the castle belonging to the deceased margrave of Baden. On March 7, 1714, these two soldiers signed the treaty for their respective monarchs. The agreement essentially followed the lines of the settlement at Utrecht except that the emperor did not acknowledge Philip as king of Spain and Philip in turn refused to recognize Charles' acquisition of the Netherlands, Milan, and Naples. France received Alsace but abandoned all claims to territory east of the Rhine. The representatives of the Holy Roman Empire essentially confirmed the settlement at Baden in September 1714.

Works About: *Actes, mémoires et autre pièces authentiques concernant la paix d'Utrecht* (Utrecht, 1714–1715); Jean Baptiste Colbert, marquis de Torcy, *Mémoires* (The Hague, 1757); Roderick Geikie and Isabel Montgomery, *The Dutch Barrier, 1705–1719* (Cambridge, 1930); C. Giraud, *La Paix d'Utrecht* (Paris, 1847); O. Weber, *Der Friede von Utrecht* (Gotha, 1891); Geoffrey Holmes, *British Politics in the Age of Anne* (London, 1967); C. W. von Koch and F. Scholl, *Histoire abregée des traités* (1817–1818); A. Legrelle, *La Diplomatie française et la Succession d'Espagne* (Paris, 1892).   *L. S. Frey and M. L. Frey*

See CHARLES VI; EUGENE; SPANISH SUCCESSION

VERDUN, TREATY OF, was concluded in 843. Throughout the reign (814–840) of Charlemagne's successor, Louis the Pious, the Empire of the Franks retained a precarious nominal unity. When he died on an island near Ingelheim on June 30, 840, a power struggle among his sons followed immediately. Lothar, the oldest, was king of Italy and the area east of the Meuse; Louis the German was expanding from Bavaria to control much of the Frankish empire east of the Rhine; Charles the Bald was king of Aquitaine and the area west of the Meuse. One of the three older sons of Louis the Pious, Pepin, had died in 838, and his son, Pepin II, was contesting the donation at Worms in 839 of his father's domains to Charles the Bald by Louis the Pious.

Lothar, originally named coemperor with his father in the *divisio imperii* of 817, rushed north to claim the imperial title. One chronicler says the dying emperor named him his successor; if so, this had no impact on his brothers. Lothar immediately crossed the Rhine to deal with Louis. However, rather than risk a major battle, Lothar and Louis made a truce in July and agreed to meet again on November 3 to decide the matter, by arms if necessary, at the same place. While Louis strengthened his position across the Rhine, Lothar moved against Charles. Since Charles was only seventeen, Lothar undoubtedly preferred to face the apparently less formidable opponent first. A number of lords between the Seine and the Loire quickly switched loyalties to Lothar, and an embassy from Charles opened negotiations at Orleans. The envoys included Nithard—whose mother was a daughter of Charlemagne—the main source for this conflict. Charles was temporarily allowed Aquitaine, Septimanie, Provence, and ten counties between the Loire and the Seine. A meeting was scheduled for May 8, 841 (it was now November 840) at Attigny, to which Louis would also be summoned, to work out a comprehensive settlement.

In May only Charles and Louis appeared, and they joined in an alliance against their common enemy. Lothar himself was waiting to link forces with Pepin II, then contesting Charles for Aquitaine. They joined forces on June 24, 841. The next day the expected battle took place at Fontenoy. Lothar needed a decisive victory, but the result was indecisive and very bloody. One chronicler gives the losses for Lothar and Pepin at over forty thousand, a figure both exaggerated and revealing.

Shortly afterward the armies of Louis and Charles separated, the former going to the Rhine, the latter to the Loire. Lothar, based mostly in Worms, made slight gains (recaptured Aachen) against both during the winter. This caused

Louis and Charles to meet again at Strasbourg to strengthen their alliance. On February 14, 842, Louis and Charles swore oaths of fidelity and brotherhood to each other in the presence of their generally illiterate troops. Each brother addressed the followers of the other in their own language. Thus Louis spoke in the *lingua romana* and Charles the *lingua teudisca,* the ancestors of French and German. In March the combined armies again marched against Lothar and took Aachen, which Lothar had abandoned to head south. When they reached Chalon (probably -sur-Saône), envoys from Lothar met them. Since all sides were tired of the war (the Viking raids were increasing) and Lothar still had considerable support, he proposed peace terms that would give him a third of the Empire plus some more both because of the imperial title given him by his father and the imperial grandeur (*dignitas*) that his grandfather had joined to the Frankish throne. The three brothers met on June 15 near Mâcon, and in November at Koblenz forty representatives from each faction began a peace conference. The peace and resulting partition were enacted at Verdun the following August.

In reference to an earlier division, Nithard states that it was done not so much on the basis of fertility of the land or strictly equal shares as on relationship (*affinitas*) and convenience (*congruentia*). So in this case care was taken to ensure that no vassal of one king was included in the domains of another. Louis was given most of the lands (*Francia orientalis*) beyond the Rhine, as well as the dioceses of Speyer, Worms, and Mainz. Lothar's territory (*Francia media* or just *Francia* as befitted the emperor) was generally bounded on the east by the Alps, the Aar, and Rhine rivers; he also obtained Frisia and some counties across the Rhine near Cologne. The boundaries to the west were the Rhone, Saône, and Scheldt rivers; to the north the North Sea; and to the south the duchy of Benevento. Charles received the rest of the Empire (*Francia occidentalis*) up to the Spanish border. Although Lothar had the title of emperor, the brothers treated each other as equals.

This treaty has probably been considered more significant than its participants could have imagined. Dividing property among sons was an old Frankish custom, and the Empire had been divided a number of times earlier in the century. Ecclesiastical officials, who saw a unified Empire as a worthy parallel to a unified Church, lamented it (the opportune death of Pope Gregory IV in January 844 may have eased its implementation); modern scholars, examining the linguistic divisions displayed in the Strasbourg oaths, have seen the prefiguring of modern Europe. More likely it reflects the growing strength of vassals and more regional interests as well as the logical outcome of the policies of Louis the Pious. The state of affairs created by Verdun did not endure. The lines were drawn again at Meersen in 870; Charles the Bald absorbed most of Lothar's domains; and Charles the Fat gained back virtually all of Charlemagne's Empire. Perhaps the separate kings chosen by the East and West Franks (887–888) to succeed Charles the Fat more appropriately mark the splintering of the Empire.

Works About: G. Barraclough, *The Crucible of Europe* (Berkeley, 1976); *Carolingian Chronicles: Royal Frankish Annals and Nithard's Hist.*, ed. B. W. Scholz, with B. Rogers (Ann Arbor, 1970); E. Dümmler, *Gesch. des Ostfränkischen Reiches* (Darmstadt, 1960); Nithard, *Histoire des fils de Louis le Pieux*, ed. and tr. P. Lauer (Paris, 1926); U. Penndorf, *Das Problem der "Reichseinheitsidee" nach der Teilung von Verdun, 843*, Münchener Beitr. zur Mediävistik und Renaissance-Forschung, 20 (Munich, 1974); W. Wattenbach, W. Levison, and H. Löwe, *Deutschlands Gesichtsquellen im Mittelalter, Vorzeit und Karolinger*, 3 and 4 (Weimar, 1957, 1963).   *C. J. Dull*

See CHARLEMAGNE; CHARLES III; LOUIS I; LOUIS II.

VIENNA, a city of great importance for the history of the later Holy Roman Empire, lies in the northeastern corner of the modern nation of Austria on the Danube River where the Alps give way to the broad Pannonian Basin of eastern Europe. In 881 the name *Wenia* appeared for the first time in the Salzburg *Annals*. After a period of slow growth, Wien, or Vienna, was chartered as a town in 1137. Ten years later work on St. Stephen's Cathedral was begun. The town already had a major church in St. Ruprecht's, dating from the eighth century.

In 1156 the dukes of Babenberg made Vienna their capital. It was there that Leopold VI Babenberg proclaimed himself, by the grace of God, duke of Austria and Styria in 1208. The port on the Danube became an important distribution center for both Bohemia and Hungary. As an imperial city, Vienna retained a measure of independence from the Babenbergs. Emperor Frederick II also granted the town a trade monopoly as a staging point for the crusades. Later the Teutonic Knights made Vienna their headquarters. Swept by a damaging fire in 1258, Vienna made a rapid recovery.

After the extinction of the Babenberg line in 1246, Vienna began its long association with the Habsburg dynasty. Emperor Rudolf I of Habsburg renewed the city's privileges as an imperial city. From 1279 on the Habsburgs began work on their Hofburg palace there. The ransom paid Duke Leopold VI for the return of King Richard the Lion Heart of England helped to pay for the construction of the city's walls. Vienna was helped greatly by Rudolf IV of Habsburg, duke of Austria (1339–1365). Rudolf ordered the reconstruction of St. Stephen's in Gothic style and persuaded Pope Urban V to issue a bull for the endowment of a university. The University of Vienna went on to become a leading intellectual center. Rudolf also helped the commercial life of Vienna by granting trade privileges to foreign merchants.

Vienna's rise to prominence was by no means always certain. Other cities, such as Prague and Graz, were often its rivals. Not all of the Habsburgs or all of the emperors favored the city on the Danube. However, Emperor Maximilian I did make Vienna the administrative capital of Lower Austria. In the fall of 1529 the city withstood a two-week siege by a large Turkish army led by Suleiman the Magnificent. Only timely rains, which foreshadowed an early winter and made Suleiman decide to retreat, saved Vienna from more serious damage.

Emperor Maximilian II lived in the city from 1564 to 1576 and helped to revitalize Vienna. Emperor Ferdinand II (ruled 1619–1637) moved the chancellery there from Prague. Vienna managed to avoid any serious damage during the Thirty Years War. However, it was Emperor Leopold I (1658–1705) who had perhaps the most significant lasting impact upon the city on the Danube of any of the other emperors. During Leopold's reign, Vienna withstood a second siege by the Turks in 1683 after having been ravished by plague in 1679. Both the city and the emperor achieved great prestige for having withstood the Turks. Vienna became the virtual capital of the Habsburgs' Danubian empire and was recognized as one of the great cities of the Holy Roman Empire as well. Because Leopold I had a passion for music, Vienna became a leading musical center. A host of great musicians, including Beethoven, Haydn, and Mozart, came to live and work in the city. Leopold also gave an impetus to the further architectural development of the city. He sought architectural grandeur and beauty as a means of reaffirming his imperial dignity and the glory of his reign.

What Leopold had encouraged was continued by later emperors and the nobles who wanted to live near the imperial family. Vienna soon experienced a great construction boom, which filled the city with a host of glorious buildings, many of which were designed by its brilliant native sons: John Lucas von Hildebrandt, John Fischer von Erlach, and his son, Josef Emmanuel. Great garden palaces such as the Belvedere by Hildebrandt for Prince Eugene of Savoy and Fischer's Schonbrünn rivaled Louis XIV's Versailles.

By the death of Emperor Charles VI in 1740, the bustling commercial, cultural, and governmental center had grown to one hundred thousand inhabitants. Vienna had become famous for its coffee, a commodity that traces its origins in the city to the Turkish siege of 1683 when captured green beans were roasted on the advice of a spy and brewed. The Danube continued as an important commercial waterway, and Vienna was a busy port. It remained an important governmental center as Emperor Francis I and Empress Maria Theresa ruled their respective territories from that base and raised sixteen children in the Schönbrunn. Their descendants continued to live and reign in Vienna even after the dissolution of the Empire in 1806 by Napoleon. The Corsican conqueror impudently attempted to reorder the city and even affixed the French imperial eagles to the Schönbrunn while leveling the great walls of Vienna. Fortunately the city of music managed to survive both the dissolution of the Holy Roman Empire and the fall of Napoleon.

Works About: Ilsa Barea, *Vienna, Legend and Reality* (London, 1966); Franz Baltzarek et al., *Wien an der Schwelle der Neuzeit* (Vienna, 1974); Christa Esterhazy, *Vienna* (London, 1966); Egon Gartenberg, *Vienna: Its Musical Heritage* (University Park, Pa., 1968); Richard Grover, *Wien wie es war* (Vienna, 1965); Ann T. Leitich, *Vienna gloriosa, Weltstadt des Barock* (Vienna, 1963); Fred Hennings, *Das Barocke Wien*, 2 vols. (Vienna, 1965); A. Levetus, *Imperial Vienna* (New York, 1965); Richard Waldegg, *Sittengesch. von Wien* (Stuttgart, 1957).   *J. W. Zophy*

See FERDINAND II; FISCHER; FRANCIS I; FRANCIS II; HAYDN; LEOPOLD I; MARIA THERESA; MOZART; TEUTONIC KNIGHTS; VIENNA, SIEGE OF.

VIENNA, SIEGE OF (1683), was the second time that the Turks had assaulted the city; Sultan Suleiman had attempted and failed to take the city in 1529. In the 1680s, however, the Habsburgs were ill prepared for the Turkish offensive; their lands had been decimated by bubonic plague and war in the west. Leopold and his court were far more concerned about the threat from the west; they were convinced that war with France was inevitable. Accordingly, they underestimated the impending danger from the east. They did, however, instruct their minister in Constantinople, Albert Caprara, to adopt a conciliatory policy toward the Turks.

The Turks were convinced that it was an ideal time to take Vienna, which they viewed as a staggeringly rich and attractive prize. They hoped to capitalize on Louis XIV's aggression in the west and Hungarian disaffection in the east. Imre Tököly organized the Hungarian insurrection and declared war on Leopold I, who had alienated the Hungarians by his attempts to increase control from Vienna and restrict the liberties of Protestants. The situation delighted Kara Mustapha, who succeeded his father-in-law, Fazil Ahmed, as grand vizier in 1676. Mustapha, who was intensely, arrogantly ambitious had decided on war and assembled a large army, estimated at between one hundred thousand and two hundred thousand men at Adrianople in 1683. Sultan Mehmet IV stayed at Belgrade while Kara Mustapha moved toward the capital.

As the Turks marched through the Danubian valley, the population, helpless, scattered before them. Even the ancient system of defense by which beacons flashed across the countryside to warn of enemy attack had not been used. By mid-July government had collapsed throughout the region, and Leopold I and his court had abandoned the capital and moved to Passau. By July 14 the Turks were at the gates of the city. The Habsburgs were poorly prepared for the onslaught from the east. The old, inadequate fortifications around the capital were only gradually being refurbished, troops only slowly levied. If Kara Mustapha had hurried, he could have taken the unprepared city by storm. He preferred, however, to wait for the city to capitulate; exhaustion, plague, and famine, he thought, would compel Vienna to surrender. This strategy almost worked; by mid-September the situation in Vienna was desperate. But the delay proved fatal for the Turks and the grand vizier.

By this time Duke Charles V of Lorraine, who had been appointed field commander, realizing that his force of thirty thousand could not hope to withstand the Turks, retreated to the northern bank of the Danube and left the defense of the city to Count Ernest Rüdiger von Stahremberg, a soldier who had distinguished himself in earlier campaigns against the French. He was the son of the rich and influential nobleman, Conrad Balthazar Stahremberg, *statthalter* from 1663 to 1687. In February 1680 Leopold had appointed Stahremberg commandant in Vienna and colonel of the city guard. It was Stahremberg who recruited men for the garrison and persuaded Leopold to spend more money on the fortifications. By mid-July Stahremberg had only thirteen thousand men in the garrison. Fortunately the troops were supported by the citizenry, particularly the students at the University of Vienna and prominent citizens such as Major Andreas Liebenberg, who died during the siege, and Bishop Leopold Kollonitsch.

On reaching Vienna, the bold but thoroughly unimaginative Kara Mustapha ordered the capital to surrender. Upon Stahremberg's refusal he began the total encirclement of the city, which was to cut off communication between Lorraine and Stahremberg almost entirely. The grand vizier, who had difficulty controlling his own men, never tried to mask his plans or even stage a feint attack. By the end of August, the walls around the city were seriously damaged by Turkish mining and bombardment. On September 3 Stahremberg was forced to give up the ravelin. On September 9 the Turks entered the moat in force. The situation was desperate.

By this time, the population was psychologically exhausted, worn out by the constant bombardment and decimated by dysentery. The strong-willed Stahremberg had done all he could to prevent the city's capitulation. He ordered the paving stones dug up to bolster the fortifications and to lessen the damage done by Turkish shot, he recruited civilians to help with the guard duty and do repair work on the defenses; and he even forbade the ringing of bells and chimes in the city except for the striking of the hour. If the Turks penetrated the citadel, the civilians would be warned by the ringing of the bells of St. Stephen's Cathedral. Problems of garbage disposal, burial of the dead, and acute shortage of food plagued the commander. Sorties out from the city were less and less successful because of the ever-vigilant Turkish infantry. According to the tradition, Stahremberg daily climbed to the top of St. Stephen's to watch for the relief force, which almost arrived too late.

Charles of Lorraine was vividly aware of the crisis in the capital. Throughout the siege Lorraine concentrated on urging the gathering Christian army to hurry toward the city, heroically defending Pressburg from Tököly and interrupting Turkish communications. All that he could do with his small force was retreat and carry out delaying operations. He kept pressing Leopold to relieve the city, but the emperor repeatedly ordered him not to move against the much larger Turkish force.

While the relief army was slowly gathering, Leopold was negotiating with the other powers in Europe to come to his assistance. Innocent XI, who had earlier urged the Christian states in Europe to take the initiative against the Turks, provided the emperor with both moral and financial aid. Leopold also concluded pacts with Bavaria, Saxony, and Poland. King Joh III Sobieski had already agreed that if the Turks laid siege to Vienna, he would immediately come to Leopold's aid. Fortunately Sobieski was already preparing for a campaign when news reached him of the Turkish bombardment of Vienna. The relief army, composed of Austrians, Bavarians, Saxons, Poles, and volunteers from all parts of Europe, totaling about sixty-five thousand, was assembled in mid-September. Sobieski, ever anxious to consolidate his position at home and abroad, held the supreme command. Brave and experienced, he was recognized as the uncontested head of this army. Charles of Lorraine, Prince Eugene of Savoy, and Max Emmanuel of Bavaria served with distinction.

On September 12 the armies clashed. The ensuing battle was a series of confused encounters, but it was obvious that the Turks had been outgunned and outmaneuvered. The siege collapsed, and the Turks, in a headlong route, retreated toward Hungary. The grand vizier, bitter, desperate, defeated, was later executed by the sultan. In describing the ensuing melee, Sobieski wrote the pope, "We came, we saw, God conquered." The extremely ambitious and assertive Sobieski insulted Leopold I by entering the city before him, underlining the Habsburgs' desertion of their capital. The Turkish defeat aroused a new militancy in the Habsburg attitude toward the east. In the 1680s and 1690s, the Habsburgs lead a counteroffensive down the Danube, taking Budapest in 1686, and defeating the Turks at Mohács (1687) and Zenta (1697). The debacle of 1683 marked the beginning of the Ottoman retreat from Europe.

Works About: Thomas Barker, *Double Eagle and Crescent: Vienna's Turkish Siege and Its Historical Setting* (Albany, 1967); Otto Forst de Battaglia, *Jan Sobieski: König von Polen* (Zurich, 1946); Onno Klopp, *Das Jahr 1683 und der folgende grosse Turkenkrieg bis zum Frieden von Carlowitz 1699* (Graz, 1882), and ed., *Corispondenza epistolare tra Leopold I Imperatore I* (Graz, 1888); O. Laslowski, *Jan III Sobieski* (Lwow, 1933); Reinhold Lorenz, *Türkenjahr 1683* (Vienna, 1933); J. B. Morton, *Sobieski, King of Poland* (London, 1932); V. Renner, ed., *Vetrauliche Briefe der Grafen Ernst Rudiger von Stahremberg* (Vienna, 1890–1891); John Stoye, *The Siege of Vienna* (New York, 1964).   L. S. Frey and M. L. Frey

See EUGENE OF SAVOY; LEOPOLD I; MOHÁCS; PASSAU; STAHREMBERG; VIENNA; ZENTA.

VIGNA, PIER DELLA (PETRUS DE VINEA) (?–1249) was born in Capua toward the end of the twelfth century to an impoverished but well-respected family; his father, Angelo, at least in later life, had been a judge. Although his family's straitened circumstances allowed Piero no help in his education, a stipend granted by the university, or by the commune, of Bologna, allowed him subsistence while he pursued the study of canon and civil law in that city. His later demonstrations of skill in Italian rhyme and Latin prose prove that he must also have studied the art of writing there. Upon della Vigna's elegantly written request, Archbishop Bernardo of Palermo, an intimate associate and adviser of Frederick II, introduced the future minister to the emperor, most probably in 1221. Della Vigna's extraordinary gifts in linguistic style and his knowledge of the law were the immediate grounds for an appointment to the imperial chancery. He developed a close friendship with the emperor because of their shared cultural, philosophical, artistic, and social interests; his climb through the ranks of the imperial civil service was swift. From 1225 until 1247, officially della Vigna filled only the position of judge of the high court; but from 1238 to 1247 his real post was that of *familiaris,* or privy councillor to the emperor, since he had in actual practice ceased to function in his office of judge of the court of appeal in 1234. Important imperial documents bear della Vigna's stylistic imprint. Of his fashioning is the charter founding the University of Naples in 1224. The most significant effect of his tenure in Frederick's entourage, however, was the royal constitution promulgated at Melfi in 1231; this *Liber Augustalis,* which was a practical synthesis of Roman, Romano-Byzantine, Justinian, and common legal tradition, and an assertion of Frederick's absolute power over Sicilian society, was formulated, at least in the greater part, by della Vigna. His close association with the emperor and his primacy among the notaries of the chancery allowed him to hold sway over imperial decisions and privileges granted from about 1239 to 1246. Through him passed all of the emperor's private correspondence, and he drew up the edicts and manifestos of the emperor's virulent quarrel with the papacy. In May 1247, after the death of his peer and colleague Taddeo da Suessa in the tragic siege of Parma, della Vigna was given at last the official title of his full administrative authority, protonotary of the imperial court and logothete of the kingdom of Sicily. Though never styled chancellor, he became in effect the head of the imperial chancery, the emperor's spokesman in all matters legal, diplomatic, social and political, and director of the Empire's finances. He formed the sole link between the emperor and the people for petitions and pleas. In the royal palace in Naples, a wall fresco was painted to depict him in this role.

Della Vigna's professional success was coupled with extraordinary personal gain. Some estimates placed his fortune at 900,000 Neapolitan ducats and others at 10,000 pounds in gold *Augustales.* Such sums do not include, among other landed properties, his large palace in Naples, his vast gardens outside the city, and his huge conglomerate of estates near Capua. As historians have seen, his position presented great temptations for self-aggrandizement at the expense of the public coffers, temptations made even greater by the fact that the monarch allowed him to act upon his own initiative in many matters. The contemporary astrologer, Guido Bonatti, avers that della Vigna regularly subverted the emperor's orders. It is probable that Frederick began to see his minister as a threat to his own aims of absolutism in the kingdom of Sicily and even of the Empire. Suddenly in February 1249, under circumstances that seem to have been intentionally shrouded in mystery by the crown, della Vigna fell from grace. Arrested in Cremona and blinded, he was led from town to town on an ass to be mocked by the populace until the death sentence was to be executed. In May 1249, however (accounts differ about the precise location and method), Piero cheated the emperor's legal retribution and, in despair, dashed his own skull against a stone wall or column in San Miniato.

Various chronicles present conflicting versions concerning the cause of his fall and death. That the logothete was not involved in a plot to poison the emperor and that he was not in league with the pope appears clear, but that he was avaricious and engaged in other crimes just as sinister and thus, ultimately, as treasonable, is borne out by existing evidence. The imperial register shows not only that Piero was especially involved with the administration of property and the exaction of duties and taxes but that he dealt most often with the prosecution of accused traitors and with the confiscation of their belongings. Della Vigna's power and greed appear particularly in the methods he used in 1244 to enlarge his estate in Capua at the expense of a hostel, the Ospedale di San Jacopo di Altopascio, the seat of the Order of the Knights of St. James, engaged in the care of pilgrims and the sick. The logothete used the enormous pressure of the strongest office in the imperial government to force the hostel-hospital to cede its Capuan property against its will.

That the logothete had indeed seized and embezzled the property of subjects is also made clear by a letter of the emperor: Piero's continual, years-long embezzlements had led the state to the brink of destruction. Frederick's letter recommends that the greatest care and secrecy be used henceforth in ascertaining the guilt of any subject accused of treason, for not only had this care not been used in the past but great wrongs had been inflicted upon the innocent. He pointed to della Vigna as an example of previous abuses of power.

Fifty years after Pier's death, the Florentine poet Dante Alighieri placed Frederick's adviser among the avaricious, violent suicides of *Inferno* XIII. Nineteenth- and twentieth-century historians agree that della Vigna's crimes were avarice, bribery, and embezzlement.

Works By: G. Hanauer, "Material zur Beurteilung des Petrus de Vinea, Briefe," *MIÖG* 21 (1900):527–36; Jean L. A. Huillard-Bréholles, *Vie et correspondance de Pierre de la Vigna ministre de l'empereur Frederic II* (Paris, 1864). **Works About:** Friedrich Baethgen,"Dante und Petrus de Vinea: Eine kritische Studie," *Sitzungsberichte der Bayrischen Akademie der Wissenschaften*, Philosophisch-hist. Klasse (1955): 3–49; Antonio Casertano, *Un oscuro dramma politico del secolo XIII: Pier della Vigna* (Rome, 1928); Thomas Curtis Van Cleve, *The Emperor Frederick II of Hohenstaufen: Immuatator Mundi* (Oxford, 1972); Ernest Kantorowicz, *Kaiser Friedrich der Zweite*, 2 vols. (Berlin, 1927, 1931, rpr. 1963); Friedrich Schneider, "Kaiser Friedrich II. und Petrus von Vinea im Urteil Dantes," *Dtsch. Dante-Jb*. 27 (1948): 230–50.   *A. K. Cassell*

See DANTE; FREDERICK II.

VILLINGER, JACOB (?–c. 1528), a major figure in the late government of Emperor Maximilian I, was born to a modest burgher family in Sélestat (Schlettstadt) in Alsace. His early life is quite obscure, but he is known to have attended the notable municipal school at Sélestat under Crato Hofmann. He was working as a bookkeeper for Queen Bianca Maria Sforza by 1500, but he soon moved over into the financial administration of King (later Emperor) Maximilian. In September 1504, Maximilian knighted Villinger for conspicuous bravery on the field of battle at the Wenzenberg near Regensburg. He was head of the Aulic Chamber by 1509, and in 1512 he was formally named grand treasurer. He was in charge of finances in the last hectic decade of Maximilian's government when expenditures chronically outran resources. Villinger had married into the family of Philip Adler, a business rival of Jacob Fugger the Rich in Augsburg, and Villinger appears to have tried to wean the government away from total dependence on the Fugger banking firm. Efforts to develop alternate sources of credit had failed by 1515, and the imperial government ended up even more closely tied to Fugger than before.

In Maximilian's last years, Villinger served as a special envoy for crucial negotiations with King Charles of Spain and Louis XII of France. After Maximilian's death in early 1519, Villinger raised vast sums of money to elect Charles V as emperor. Villinger's importance faded after the diet of Worms in 1521, and he had fallen into disfavor with Archduke Ferdinand by late 1523. Villinger was an avid entrepreneur and speculator in his own right, investing in logging and mining, as well as in real estate. He became one of the major creditors of the imperial government, holding a fortune in Burgundian jewels and assorted lands as security. Villinger was widely accused of having enriched himself at the emperor's expense.

Villinger retired to his luxurious townhouse in Freiburg to manage his many enterprises, and in 1525 he helped launch a new national mercury cartel. Erasmus lived in Villinger's house when he moved to Freiburg in 1529, shortly after the grand treasurer's death.

Works About: Sigmund Adler, *Die Organisation der Centralverwaltung unter Kaiser Maximilian I*. (Leipzig, 1886); Clemens Bauer, "Jakob Villinger Grossschatzmeister Kaiser Maximilians. Ein Umriss," *Syntagma Friburgense. Hist. Studien Hermann Aubin dargebracht*, Schriften des Kopernikuskreises, vol. 1 (Lindau and Constance, 1956); Paul Kalkoff, *Der Wormser Reichstag von 1521* (Munich and Berlin, 1922); Götz von Pölnitz, *Jakob Fugger*, 2 vols. (Tübingen, 1949–1951); Hermann Wiesflecker, *Kaiser Maximilian I*. (Munich, 1977); vol. 3.   *S. W. Rowan*

See CHARLES V; ERASMUS; FERDINAND I; FUGGER; MAXIMILIAN I; SFORZA.

VOLPRECHT, WOLFGANG (?–1528), prior of the Augustinian monastery in Nuremberg, introduced liturgical changes advocated by Lutheran reformers before the Nuremberg city council endorsed the Reformation in 1525. Little is known of Volprecht's early life. When he enrolled at the university in Ingolstadt (1507), he was already a monk at the Nuremberg cloister. By 1521 he was prior of the chapter and most certainly a member of the humanist-evangelical circle of clergymen and patricians meeting at the cloister since 1517. While the imperial diet was meeting in Nuremberg in 1523, Volprecht served Communion in both kinds to a small circle within the monastery. At Easter 1524 it was reported that the four thousand Nurembergers received Communion in both kinds at the Augustinian chapel, and in May 1524 Volprecht began to read the Mass in German. On September 19, 1524, the bishop of Bamberg tried to excommunicate Volprecht, Dominicus Schleupner, preacher at St. Sebald's church, and Andreas Osiander, preacher at St. Lawrence's church, for introducing changes in the liturgy. The city council took steps to protect the three men and in March 1525 held a colloquy between the Lutheran and Catholic parties. The council approved Lutheran reforms and ordered the dissolution of the Nuremberg cloisters. Volprecht had already offered to put the chapter's endowment into the city poor chest on December 24, 1524, and the transfer took place at the conclusion of the colloquy. Volprecht believed that monks should take pastoral appointments, become citizens of their communities, and be permitted to marry. Volprecht was appointed preacher at the Sutte chapel in the New Spital (Hospital). He married Katherina Meder in 1526 and is probably the author of the early reformation pamphlet, *Wie alle closter* (1524) published under the pseudonym, Noricus Philadelphus.

Works About: Irmgard Höss, "Das religiöse Leben vor der Reformation," in G. Pfeiffer, ed., *Nürnberg: Gesch. einer europäischen Stadt* (Munich, 1972); Bernhard Klaus, "Die Nürnberger Dtsch. Messe 1524," *Jb. für Liturgik und Hymnologie* 1 (1955); Gerhard Pfeiffer, "Entscheidung zur Reformation," in Pfeiffer, ed., *Nürnberg*.   *J. W. Gates*

See NUREMBERG; OSIANDER.

W

WALLENSTEIN (OR WALDSTEIN), ALBERT WENZEL EUSEBIUS VON (1583–1634), a soldier who raised himself from the minor aristocracy to the rank of duke of Friedland and Mecklenburg, and during the Thirty Years War served Emperor Ferdinand II twice as his commander-in-chief, was born on September 24, 1583, at Hermaniz in Bohemia into the Lutheran family of Waldstein (Czech name: Valdšteyn). An orphan at age thirteen, he was brought up by an uncle who sent him to the celebrated Protestant University of Altdorf. His grand tour (1600–1602) led him through France and Italy where he attended lectures at the universities of Bologna and Padua. He converted to Catholicism in 1606 but had no strong religious convictions. His faith was in astrology (John Kepler cast horoscopes for him.) In 1609, Wallenstein married an elderly wealthy widow, Lucretia von Wičkow, who after her death five years later left him immense estates in Moravia that made him rich. By administering his properties unusually well, he was able to increase his wealth even further.

Wallenstein brought himself to the attention of Ferdinand of Styria, the future Emperor Ferdinand II, when he aided the archduke in his war against Venice (1617) with a mercenary army that Wallenstein had raised at his own expense. During the Bohemian rebellion, which started the Thirty Years War, he remained loyal to Austria. However, his military exploits during the revolt were less notable than his shrewd business sense and administrative ability. He provided Ferdinand with much needed financial aid, and the emperor repaid him in land and dignities. Wallenstein profited immensely from the Habsburgs' victory. He obtained more than fifty estates that had been confiscated from rebellious Bohemian nobles and became the wealthiest man in the country. The emperor appointed him governor of the kingdom of Bohemia and quartermaster general of the army. Wallenstein added further to his influence and power in 1623 when he married Isabella Katharina, the daughter of Charles von Harrach, one of the emperor's most influential advisers. In 1625 Ferdinand bestowed upon him the title duke of Friedland with the right of coinage.

When King Christian IV of Denmark threatened to intervene in the war, Ferdinand II readily accepted Wallenstein's offer to raise an independent imperial army of twenty thousand troops at his own expense. He appointed Wallenstein *capo* (captain) of all his forces and authorized him to levy contributions in conquered places for the support of his army. The new commander-in-chief soon proved his military ability when he beat Count Ernest von Mansfeld in the Battle at the Dessau Bridge (April 25, 1626). In conjunction with Tilly, the league general, he then conquered Mecklenburg, Holstein, Schleswig, and Denmark. The emperor reimbursed Wallenstein for his expenses by giving him the Silesian principality of Sagan. He also awarded him the duchy of Mecklenburg as a hereditary fief (1629) after the dukes of that principality had been outlawed for their support of Christian IV. Wallenstein had reached the zenith of his career.

His elevation to the rank of an imperial prince and overwhelming military power in northern Germany encouraged Wallenstein to press further and pursue a more independent policy. As general of the Oceanic and Baltic seas (an appointment that he had obtained from Ferdinand in 1628), he now tried to extend his control over the Baltic Sea, where he planned to form a great trading empire in which the emperor, Spain, and the Hanseatic cities would cooperate against the Dutch and the English. But this scheme failed when the cities, particularly Stralsund, refused to cooperate. Wallenstein's increasing independence also showed itself in his unwillingness to back the Edict of Restitution (1629), whereby Ferdinand sought to expand and strengthen both his religion and power in Germany.

The general's arrogance, wealth, new titles and power, and particularly the oppressive size of his army, which by the end of the decade had swollen to one hundred thousand men, antagonized not only the emperor's enemies but increasingly also his friends. Catholic and Protestant princes alike began to demand his dismissal, Ferdinand initially hesitated, but, wishing to retain the goodwill of his allies (the German princes had threatened to combine against Ferdinand under French leadership) and anxious to gain acceptance of his son as Roman king, or prospective heir to the throne, he reluctantly agreed at the Regensburg electors' meeting on August 13, 1630, to let his powerful general go. The imperial army, reduced in size, was placed under the command of General Tilly. Wallenstein never forgave Ferdinand for this act and from then on was determined to wreak vengeance on the emperor and on Maximilian, whom he held primarily responsible for his dismissal.

The duke spent the next two years on his princely estates in Bohemia. Meanwhile King Gustavus Adolphus of Sweden had entered the war and had inflicted a number of disastrous defeats on the imperial army. By December 1631, the situation had deteriorated so badly that Ferdinand decided to reinstate Wallenstein as commander-in-chief. In return, the duke promised to raise an army of fifty thousand men. The selection of officers was to be his prerogative; large financial guarantees were given by the emperor; and, most significant of all, Wallenstein was authorized to enter into direct peace negotiations with Saxony.

Within a short time Wallenstein had raised and equipped one hundred thousand men. He liberated Bohemia and forced the Swedes out of Bavaria and Franconia in summer 1632. Then he occupied Saxony in order to detach its ruler, Elector John George I, from the Swedish alliance. On November 16, 1632, the Swedish and the imperial forces met in a furious battle at Lützen (near

Leipzig). Gustavus Adolphus lost his life in the encounter, but his army still won the battle.

After Lützen, Wallenstein clearly degenerated in mind and body. He negotiated and intrigued with the Saxons, Brandenburgers, Bohemians, Swedes, and French, going far beyond the instructions that the emperor had given him earlier. He made different and often contradictory offers to various parties and soon lost credit with all. Meanwhile his military leadership deteriorated rapidly. He ignored Ferdinand's entreaties to detail forces to southern Germany where the Swedes had gained superiority. The emperor, urged on by the Bavarian and Spanish governments, finally decided to dismiss his recalcitrant and unsuccessful commander-in-chief. Wallenstein, aware that Vienna was planning his deposition, sought to assure himself of the loyalty of his army. In the Pilsen Declaration (January 12, 1634), forty-nine of his generals pledged to stand with him; however, his leading officers (Ottavio Piccolomini, Matthias Gallas, and John von Aldringen) remained loyal to the emperor. Ferdinand correctly interpreted this declaration as treachery and ordered Wallenstein seized dead or alive. Desperate, the latter now tried to speed up his negotiations with the emperor's enemies. He increasingly lost control of his army. With his troops he had moved to Eger (in western Bohemia) to await the Swedes and Saxons. There he and his remaining confidants were murdered in the night of February 25, 1634. An English captain, Walter Devereux, ran his halberd through Wallenstein, thus ending the life of the man who had dazzled Europe and terrified Vienna.

Precisely what motives and goals inspired Wallenstein, particularly during his second generalship, has been the subject of much scholarly debate. Revenge against Ferdinand and Maximilian, and an appetite for personal power and gain, possibly even for the royal crown of Bohemia, undoubtedly influenced him. Equally important, though, was his desire for peace and the resentment he felt against foreigners who had turned the Empire into the battleground and prize of international power politics. Not surprisingly, therefore, Wallenstein has been portrayed both as a loyal servant and traitor of the emperor, as a soldier of fortune as well as a Bohemian nationalist and German patriot.

Works By: Friedrich C. Förster, ed., *Albrechts von Wallenstein, des Herzogs von Friedland und Mecklenburg, ungedruckte, eigenhändige, vertrauliche Briefe und amtliche Schreiben aus den Jahren 1627–1634*, 3 pts. (Berlin, 1828–1829); Hermann Hallwich, ed., *Briefe und Akten zur Gesch. Wallensteins*, 4 vols. (Vienna, 1912); Georg Irmer, ed., *Die Verhandlungen Schwedens und seiner Verbündeten mit Wallenstein und dem Kaiser von 1631 bis 1634*, 3 vols. (Leipzig, 1888–1891). **Works About:** *Documenta Bohemica Bellum Tricennale Illustrantia* (Prague, 1972–1974), vols. 2–4; Hellmut Diwald, *Wallenstein: Eine Biographie* (Munich, 1969); Golo Mann, *Wallenstein: His Life Narrated* (New York, 1976); Josef Pekář, *Wallenstein 1630–1634; Tragödie einer Verschwörung* (Berlin, 1937); Leopold von Ranke, *Gesch. Wallensteins* (Leipzig, 1880); Heinrich Ritter von Srbik, *Wallensteins Ende* (Salzburg, 1952); "Wallenstein," *BW*, 3:3025–31; K. Wittich, "Wallenstein," *ADB*, 45:582–641.

Bodo Nischan

See ALDRINGER; EDICT OF RESTITUTION; FERDINAND II; KEPLER; THIRTY YEARS WAR; TILLY; WALLENSTEIN, ISABELLA.

WALLENSTEIN, DUCHESS ISABELLA KATHARINA VON (1602–?), second wife of the imperial commander-in-chief Albert von Wallenstein, was the daughter of Count Charles von Harrach, one of the most important advisers of Emperor Ferdinand II. Isabella became the wife of Wallenstein in 1623 (his first wife had died nine years earlier). The marriage was important because it enhanced Wallenstein's prestige and influence at the Vienna court. Isabella was an attractive and intelligent woman whose lifelong devotion to her husband is reflected in the letters she wrote during the general's many lengthy military campaigns away from home. Wallenstein returned these feelings of love and tenderness, but unfortunately none of his letters to Isabella has survived. The duchess was innocent of her husband's "conspiracy" against the emperor. (Wallenstein was assassinated in February 1634.)

Works About: Hellmut Diwald, *Wallenstein: Eine Biographie* (Munich, 1969), pp. 207–11; Friedrich C. Förster, *Wallenstein, Herzog zu Mecklenburg, Friedland, und Sagan als Feldherr und Landesfürst in seinem öffentlichen und Privatleben* (Potsdam, 1834), pp. 320 ff; Hermann Hallwich, ed., *Briefe und Akten zur Gesch. Wallensteins* (Vienna, 1912), vol. 4; Golo Mann, *Wallenstein: His Life Narrated* (New York, 1976), passim.   *Bodo Nischan*

See FERDINAND II; WALLENSTEIN, ALBERT.

WALTHER VON DER VOGELWEIDE (c. 1170–1230) was a lyric poet of obscure origins. He came to Vienna in 1190, where he was introduced to Duke Leopold VI by his friend and fellow poet Reinmar von Hagenau. There he found patronage until 1198 when his last princely patron died, and he quarreled with Reinmar. During the struggle for the imperial throne between Philip of Swabia and Otto of Brunswick, Walther sided with Philip and participated in his coronation. Following Philip's assassination in 1208, the poet-singer attempted to win the favor of Otto IV.

He vigorously attacked Pope Innocent III in verse for intervening in imperial affairs, fearing that the Empire would be weakened and subjugated to the papacy. Walther had Innocent tell his cronies, "We've done all right for ourselves, for we have two Swabians fighting over the same crown and destroying the Empire in the process. Meanwhile we fill our coffers. Their German money flows into our pockets. Let the German swine fast as we, O priests, partake of fat hens and good wine!"

Although Walther was disappointed in the rewards he received from Otto, he fared much better under Frederick II, who granted him a fief. A political poet, Walther also supported the emperor's cause at the diet of Nuremberg of 1224–1225 and repeatedly urged Frederick to join the crusade of 1228. His poems were not only popular but highly influential.

Works By: Walther von der Vogelweide, *Die Lieder*, ed. F. Maurer (Tübingen, 1962); *Gedichte*, ed. Helmut Protze (Halle, 1963); *The Poems*, tr. E. H. Zeydel and B. Q. Morgan (Ithaca, N. Y., 1952). **Works About:** Helmut de Boor, "Walther von der Vogelweide," *DGD*, 1:114–29; Kurt H. Halbach, *Walther von der Vogelweide* (Stuttgart, 1965); G. F. Jones, *Walther von der Vogelweide*

(New York, 1968); D. A. Wells, "Imperial Sanctity and Political Reality: Bible, Liturgy, and the Ambivalence of Symbol in Walther von der Vogelweide's Songs under Otto IV," *Spec.* 53 (1978): 479–510.   *J. W. Zophy*

See DISPUTED ELECTION; FREDERICK II; INNOCENT III; OTTO IV; PHILIP OF SWABIA-HOHENSTAUFEN.

WAR OF THE LEAGUE OF AUGSBURG (also called the War of the Grand Alliance, King William's War, and War of the Succession in the Palatinate) was the third of Louis XIV's wars. In this conflict (1688–1697) Louis hoped to consolidate his gains in the Holy Roman Empire before Leopold made peace with the Turks. After recent imperial successes against the Turks (raising the siege of Vienna, taking Belgrade, and defeating the Turks at Mohács), Louis declared war on the Empire (September 2, 1688). Louis denounced the alliances formed against him and Leopold's hostility toward the claims of his sister-in-law in the Palatinate and demanded the destruction of the fortifications of Philippsburg, financial settlement for the Palatinate claims, and confirmation of the French candidate von Fürstenberg as archbishop of Cologne. Louis did offer to return Philippsburg after the fortifications were razed and Freiburg, as long as it remained disarmed. These offers were conditional upon the Empire's acceptance of the armistice of Regensburg (1684) as a definitive peace.

On the very day that Louis declared war, Louvois ordered French troops to enter the Rhineland and besiege Philippsburg. France was unprepared for a long conflict; Louis and Louvois were misled if they expected an easy victory. On October 18, 1688, Leopold declared war; on October 22 Frederick III of Brandenburg, who had earlier concluded a secret alliance with Leopold, John George III of Saxony, Ernest Augustus of Hanover, and Charles of Hesse-Cassel, formed the Magdeburg concert and sent an army of over twenty-two thousand to the Rhine; months later, the Holy Roman Empire too went to war, as did England, the Netherlands, Savoy, Spain, and Sweden. The allies hoped to force Louis to give up the territories that he had seized since 1659.

Louis stood alone against most of Europe. His revocation of the Edict of Nantes (1685) had alienated the Protestants. The Glorious Revolution of 1688, which had deposed the pro-French James, placed Louis' bitter foe, William of Orange, on the English throne. French colonial and commercial policy aroused the antagonism and jealousy of the maritime powers, England and the United Provinces. Louis' interference in the Palatine succession and the election of the archbishop of Cologne increased German hostility. Louis' support of the exiled James II's claim to the English throne ensured English involvement. In 1688 no German prince allied with Louis. Fortunately for France, the bickering and dissension among the allies outweighed their preponderant military advantage. Leopold, for example, refused to submit to pressure and conclude peace with the Turks.

The ensuing war extended from the Rhine to the Netherlands, to Italy, to Ireland, to North America, to the Caribbean, and even to India. Duke Charles

V of Lorraine, Margrave Ludwig of Baden, and the dukes of Luxembourg, Villars, and Vauban took part in the conflict.

War had begun on the Rhine where the French, encountering little resistance, seized the Palatinate, Trier, and Mainz, until the Magdeburg concert forced the French to retreat behind the Rhine. As they retreated, the French wasted the countryside and dispersed the population. In the beginning of 1689 Duke Charles V of Lorraine took Mainz and the elector of Brandenburg took Bonn, thus freeing the lower and middle Rhine. The situation on the upper Rhine remained precarious for the allies. After the death of the superb tactician Charles V of Lorraine (1690), the war degenerated into one of position rather than movement.

In the Netherlands the French were more successful. Marshal Luxembourg defeated the allies under the command of Prince George Frederick Waldeck at Fleurus (1690) and later William III at Neerwinden in 1693. But by 1694 the war in the Netherlands had also reached a stalemate. In Ireland the English were able to close one front by their victory at Boyne over James II and his Irish supporters (1690). In Spain the French took Barcelona, and in the Alps they forced Savoy to negotiate an early peace.

On the sea, the French were not as fortunate. Although they had defeated the Anglo-Dutch fleet at Beachy Head in 1690, by 1692 the French had lost their supremacy at sea. The vastly superior Anglo-Dutch fleet destroyed the French fleet under Tourville at La Hogue (1692). This victory revealed the weakness of the French navy and marked the beginning of English naval superiority. Overseas fighting took place at Pondicherry, Jamaica, Martinique, Santa Domingo, and North America, where the French with their Indian allies retained the initiative.

In 1693 France, tired and impoverished, initiated peace overtures. These failed, but Louis, playing on the dissensions in the alliance, was able to ensure Italian neutrality by concluding peace (Treaty of Turin, 1696) with Victor Amadeus II of Savoy. Louis agreed to cede two important fortresses, Cassale to Mantua and Pinerola to Savoy, and to marry his heir to the duke's daughter, Adelaide. Louis astutely continued to play the allies against one another. He agreed to grant favorable trade conditions to the Dutch and to allow them to garrison fortresses in the Netherlands. To England he offered to return all colonial gains, to recognize William II as king of England, and to stop supporting James II and the Jacobites. He enticed Spain with easy terms: the full withdrawal of all French troops from Spain and the return of Luxembourg and Barcelona. Louis also would relinquish Lorraine and all territory that he had seized on the right bank of the Rhine—Philippsburg, Kehl, Freiburg, and Breisach—but he refused to give up Strasbourg or Alsace. Leopold, who had fared badly at the congress, had no recourse but to sign the treaty. The allies signed the peace in late September and October 1697. Some of the Protestant states had refused to sign the agreement because of the famous Ryswick clause, which provided that the religious status of the lands that France returned to the Empire remain Catholic. The French had flagrantly violated the earlier armistice of 1684 and propagated Catholicism in those regions. With certain exceptions the peace at Ryswick signaled a return to the status quo ante bellum. In France the war had highlighted the danger of diplomatic isolation.

Works About: Max Braubach, *Prinz Eugen von Savoyen* 5 vols. (Vienna, 1963–1965), and *Versailles und Wien von Ludwig XIV bis Kaunitz* (Bonn, 1952); J. S. Corbett, *England in the Mediterranean 1603–1713* (London, 1904), vol. 2; J. Dumont, *Corps universel diplomatique du droit des gens* (The Hague, 1726–1731); B. Erdmanndsörffer, *Dtsch. Gesch. vom Westfälischen Frieden bis zum Regierungsantritt Friedrichs der Grossen, 1648–1740* (Berlin, 1892); R. Fester, *Die ausgsburger Allianz von 1686* (Munich, 1893); Hugo Hantsch, *Die Gesch. Österreich* (Vienna, 1947), and *Die Entwicklung Österreichs-Ungarns zur Grossmacht* (Freiburg im Breisgau, 1933); A. Legrelle, *Notes et Documents sur la paix Ryswick* (Lille, 1894); F. A. M. Mignet, *Negociations relatives à la succession d'Espagne sous Louis XIV* (Paris, 1835–1842); A. Saint-Leger and P. Sagnac, *La Prepondérance française, Louis XIV, 1661–1715* (Paris, 1935); John P. Spielman, *Leopold I of Austria* (New Brunswick, N.J., 1977); H. Srbik, *Wien und Versailles, 1692–1697* (Munich, 1944).   *L. S. Frey and M. L. Frey*

See LEOPOLD I; LUDWIG WILLIAM; PETERWARDEIN.

WARTENBERG, JOHN CASIMIR KOLBE VON (1643–1712), count, governed by means of his personal access to Frederick III, elector of Brandenburg, later Frederick I, king in Prussia. Born in Metz, the son of an exiled Palatinate noble, he entered the service of Brandenburg in 1688. After the overthrow of Eberhard von Danckelmann in 1697, Wartenberg directed policy for fourteen years. Although never a member of the privy council, Wartenberg controlled the state council. The eclipse of the privy council, which was now divorced from the ascendant *Staatsconferenz,* ensured his dominance. After Frederick's coronation as king in Prussia (1701), he appointed Wartenberg prime minister.

Frederick the Great, expressing the general consensus on Wartenberg, condemned him as a greedy, corrupt, self-seeking opportunist, who enriched himself at the expense of the state and who governed by exploiting the talents of others. Wartenberg's wife, the mistress of Frederick, alienated the court and helped estrange many potential allies of her husband by her haughty manner, pride, and avarice. An investigation of Wartenberg's scandalous and corrupt administration, instigated by the crown prince Frederick William led to his downfall and exile in 1711.

Works About: Christophe, Count von Dohna, *Mémoires originaux sur la règne et la cour de Frédéric I, Roi de Prusse* (Berlin, 1883), p. 306; Charles-Lewis, Baron de Poellnitz, *Memoirs* (London, 1745), 3:237; Reinhold August Dorwart, *The Administrative Reforms of Frederick William* (Cambridge, 1953), p. 28; Frederick II, *Oeuvres* (Berlin, 1789), vol. 2; Linda Frey and Marsha Frey,"Frederick I and His Court, 1703–1710," *Revue de l'Université d'Ottawa* 45 (1975): 478–90; Albert Waddington, *Histoire de Prusse* (Paris, 1911), 2:162; "Wartenberg," *ADB* 16:463–66.   *L. S. Frey and M. F. Frey*

See FREDERICK II, THE GREAT; FREDERICK III, ELECTOR.

WELF-WAIBLINGEN CONTROVERSY, also known in its Italianized form as the Guelf-Ghibelline struggle, refers to conflicts between two German families that lasted from the eleventh to the thirteenth centuries and led to contentions for the royal office. The origins of the controversy predated the investiture problem, were accelerated during the investiture wars, and remained until the demise of the Hohenstaufen under Emperor Frederick II (1211–1250). During Emperor Henry IV's reign (1056–1106), the dukes of Saxony from the house of Billung proved troublesome. Henry deposed and imprisoned the hereditary duke and raised to his place a noble, Lothar of Supplinburg, who eventually became Emperor Lothar II (1125–1137).

While this was taking place in northern Germany, there emerged in the south two families whose names gave rise to the Welf-Waiblingen controversey. In Bavaria the house of Welf acquired the duchy. A Welf son, Henry the Proud (d. 1139), succeeded in marrying the daughter of Lothar, and thus the Welfs had claims both to Bavaria and Saxony. In Swabia, near Bavaria, the Hohenstaufen family, which came from the village of Waiblingen, had risen to power as dukes. Frederick (d. 1105), duke of Swabia, married the daughter of Emperor Henry IV. Two important children resulted from this marriage: one married the sister of Henry the Proud, the issue of whom was the future Emperor Frederick I (Barbarossa, 1152–1190); the other was Conrad who became the first of the Hohenstaufen emperors as Conrad II (1138–1152), successor to Lothar II.

Because of the proximity of Bavaria and Swabia, animosity developed between the two houses. This resulted in civil war in the Empire, one exacerbated by the rival claims of the Welfs and Hohenstaufen to both the imperial dignity and to territories within the Empire. In 1125, for example, Duke Frederick of Swabia, the obvious successor to Emperor Henry V (1106–1125), was rejected by the electors as a result of a Welf alliance that put forth Lothar. Similarly in 1138, Henry the Proud, heir designate of Lothar, lost the election to the Hohenstaufen Conrad. Civil war ensued between their factions and lasted sporadically for more than one hundred years.

When Frederick Barbarossa became emperor, his election seemed to augur well for the end of the Welf-Waiblingen controversy. His father was a Hohenstaufen, his mother a Welf. Frederick, overturning Conrad's acts with regard to Henry the Proud, recognized Henry's successor, Henry the Lion (d. 1191), in Saxony and Bavaria and Welf administration in the Tuscan March. Henry the Lion, however, refused aid to the emperor during the latter's Italian campaigns. Another round of civil war broke out. Frederick finally subdued Henry, confiscated his territories, and dismembered Saxony. Never again did the Welfs have such power even though Henry's son, Otto IV (1201–1218), successfully vied with Frederick's son, Philip of Swabia (1197–1208), as rival claimants for the royal title. With the election of Frederick II as king and the deposition of Otto IV, the Welf-Waiblingen struggles in Germany came to a gradual conclusion.

The convoluted nature of the controversy admits of no easy generalization, and for this reason it has been variously interpreted. Some view the Hohenstaufen destruction of Welf claims to Bavaria, Saxony, and Tuscany as signifying the end of the one German family with sufficient power to offset German particularism. But the continued rebellion on the part of the Welfs against the Hohenstaufen emperors offered virtually no other solution, especially as intermarriage brought into the scenario other European powers. In a sense the Waiblingen faction encountered papal hostility because it was successful in acquiring the royal dignity. Hence Welf (Guelf) signified papal supporters, and Waiblingen (Ghibelline) signified imperial ones. Even without the royal title, however, the Welfs persisted in the duchy of Brunswick, whereas the Hohenstaufen died out shortly after Frederick II's reign.

Works About: Geoffrey Barraclough, *The Origins of Modern Germany* (Oxford, 1946, rpr. 1963); Johannes Bühler, *Die Hohenstaufen, Nach zeitgenössischen Quel.* (Leipzig, 1925); Karl Hampe, *Germany under the Salian and Hohenstaufen Emperors,* tr. Ralph Bennett (Oxford, 1973); Peter Munz, *Frederick Barbarossa, A Study in Medieval Politics* (New York, 1969); Otto of Freising, *The Deeds of Frederick Barbarossa by Otto of Friesing and His Continuator, Rahewin,* tr. C. C. Mierow and Richard Emery, Records of Civilization, Sources and Studies, vol. 49 (New York, 1953, rpr. 1966); James Westfall Thompson, *Feudal Germany* (Chicago, 1928, rpr. 1962).

P. N. Bebb

See CONRAD II; FREDERICK I; FREDERICK II; HENRY IV; HENRY V; HENRY THE LION; INVESTITURE CONTROVERSY; LOTHAR II; OTTO IV; PHILIP OF SWABIA-HOHENSTAUFEN.

WENCESLAUS I (1361–1419), emperor from 1378 to 1400, was the eldest son of the Luxembourg emperor Charles IV and Anna of Silesia-Schweidniz. He succeeded to the crown of Germany and Bohemia, both of which his father had secured for him prior to his death. He was elected king of the Germans on June 10, 1376, at Frankfurt and crowned at Aachen on July 6. He was crowned king of Bohemia on June 15, 1363, at Prague. Charles' death on November 29, 1378, made him heir to the duchy of Luxembourg as well, although his succession there was postponed until his uncle Wenceslaus died in 1383. He later added Artois and the Franche-Comté to his holdings. Wenceslaus' devotion to dynastic interests brought him some success early in his reign; it became a major fault later and contributed to the disasters that befell him.

Wenceslaus' chief dynastic interests lay in Bohemia and Hungary in the eastern part of the Empire, but intense rivalry between him, his cousin Jobst of Moravia, and his half-brother Sigismund, margrave of Brandenburg, made it nearly impossible to control the area. His crown in Bohemia was secure for a time, although, as always, the Bohemian nobility resented the intrusive presence of a francophile German ruling house on their throne. However, the Hungarian succession absorbed Wenceslaus' attention almost immediately after his coronation as king of Germany and prevented his coronation as emperor in Rome. The death of Louis of Hungary and Poland in September 1382 brought both crowns into a tripartite succession dispute between a Habsburg, an Angevin, and Sigismund. Although the Polish estates preferred to choose their own king and eventually repudiated all of the candidates, Wenceslaus seized the crown for Sigismund, who married Maria, Louis of Hungary's elder daughter, in 1385 and acceded to the crown in 1387. Sigismund had to mortgage the margraviate of Brandenburg to Jobst of Moravia in order to gain control of Hungary and remained in dire fiscal and political straits thereafter.

Wenceslaus' support in Bohemia drifted away in the meantime and, when a quarrel with Archbishop John II of Prague led the king to instigate the murder of his vicar-general, an uprising occurred, led by Jobst of Moravia. Wenceslaus was imprisoned for several months in 1394 while Jobst ruled with a royal council of Bohemian nobles and high clerics. The protests and threats of the German estates and the more active intervention of Wenceslaus' brother John of Görlitz secured his release.

By 1396, Wenceslaus' growing disrepute, coupled with Sigismund's growing popularity, led the king to name his half-brother vicar general of the Empire. But Sigismund's defeat by the Turks at Nicopolis in 1396 lost him the crown of Hungary for a time and cost him the margraviate of Brandenburg, which now went to Jobst of Moravia, until he died in 1411. All of this turmoil enbroiled Wenceslaus in intrigue and made it impossible for him to assert his authority in the western Empire. After 1389 he paid little attention to imperial affairs, despite pressing issues and frequent demands by the princes and electors that he attend to them.

Chief among these issues was the relationship of the Empire to the two churches at Avignon and Rome. Wenceslaus continued his father's support of the Roman pope, Urban VI, although the league formed in his name by the electors and princes on February 27, 1370, would have proceeded with or without him. The league helped ease relations between the Luxembourg and Wittelsbach dynasties, however, and thus submerged some of the rivalry that might have disrupted Wenceslaus' early reign.

Committed to reducing Avignon's influence in Germany, the league settled the persistent conflict over the archbishopric of Mainz in favor of Adolf of Nassau. Its hegemony was further extended by the death of Leopold of Austria, an adherent of Clement VII, at the Battle of Sempach in 1386. And Wenceslaus allied with Richard II against France in 1381, a move that struck indirectly at Avignon but accomplished little more than delivering English subsidies for Wenceslaus' planned coronation at Rome.

The king's real disagreement with the electors was revealed after Urban's death in 1389. The election of Boniface IX in Rome and Benedict XIII at Avignon revived conciliar sentiments prominent in Louis the Bavarian's reign. Theoretically argued by the Parisian magisters Conrad of Gelnhausen and Henry of Langenstein, the conciliar argument failed to convince many influential German princes, who preferred to support Rome. Wenceslaus, however, joined with Charles VI of France in supporting the deposition of both popes, despite the appeals and threats of Boniface.

Even more embarrassing than Boniface's refusal to abdicate was Wenceslaus' own abdication, or so it was seen, in northern Italy. When Giangaleazzo Visconti of Milan purchased the office of imperial regent in May 1395, he stood toe to toe against the Florentine League. France rushed to support the league, which chose to interpret this sale of office as imperial intervention in Italy. In Germany, just the opposite opinion prevailed, and Wenceslaus was denounced for alienating imperial rights, an illegal, if not immoral, act.

Worse, the Empire was troubled by internecine conflict between the cities and the territorial princes. In the absence of imperial authority, demands for the establishment of a king's peace alternated with the creation of associations for self-protection and self-help. In Swabia, fourteen cities led by Ulm joined together in an alliance for mutual aid in 1376. Regensburg, hard pressed by the dukes of Bavaria, joined in 1381, and Nuremberg followed in 1384. By 1388, the Swabian Urban League had over forty members. Its example was followed by the Rhenish League, composed of Frankfurt, Mainz, Worms, Strasbourg, and Speyer, which finally associated itself with the Swabians in 1381 in order to defend itself against the imperious dukes Eberhard of Württemberg and Leopold of Austria. Alsatian and Saxon leagues were founded in 1379 and 1382 to protect the free imperial status of their members. Even the imperial knights formed federations to protect their freedom, although they identified the cities as their major opponents.

Nor was Wenceslaus an ally of the cities. He wanted to settle disputes but lacked the resources to enforce his judgments. His proposals to divide the Empire into four districts, advanced in March 1383 at Nuremberg, struck directly at the urban leagues, which would be broken into regional units governed by the great princes. They therefore refused to participate, and their abstention made the reforms little more than princely counteralliances. Both the cities and the princes sought, however, to forestall conflict in a truce established at Heidelberg in 1384.

Preferring to play the fair broker and parlay royal favor into municipal loans for his dynastic intrigues in Hungary and Bohemia, Wenceslaus convinced himself that he was on the right side of the conflict when the Swiss defeated Leopold of Austria at Sempach (1386) and Näfels (1388). Wenceslaus put himself at the head of the Swabian Urban League at Würzburg in 1387. Shortly thereafter, Eberhard of Württemberg defeated the Swabians at Döffingen in August and Rudolf II of the Palatinate defeated the Rhenish league twice near Worms in 1388. Regretting his blunder, Wenceslaus demanded dissolution of the leagues at Eger on May 5, 1389, in exchange for a general truce for six years. The king had isolated himself still more.

Wenceslaus' absence from the Empire after 1389, combined with his brief support of the urban leagues and his unpopular policies toward Rome and in

Italy, made his removal an immediate possibility. The electors of Cologne and the Palatinate entered negotiations with Richard II of England to claim the German crown in 1394. More significant, however, was a meeting between Duke John of Nassau and the count Palatine, Rupert III, at Oppenheim on March 24, 1396. Rupert agreed to convince Boniface IX to support Nassau's claim to the archbishopric of Mainz in exchange for the electoral vote. The installation achieved, they met with the archbishop of Cologne and representatives of Trier and Saxony at Boppard on April 11, 1399, established a union for the protection of their electoral prerogatives, and summoned Wenceslaus to appear before them at Oberlahnstein in August 1400. When he ignored the summons, the Rhenish electors, along with Stephen III of Bavaria-Ingolstadt and Burggrave Frederick VI of Nuremberg, declared him deposed. They elected Rupert III king the following month.

Wenceslaus made no effort to resist and remained king in Bohemia. He quarreled with Sigismund in 1403 and was imprisoned in Vienna for nineteen months and forced to abdicate. Freed in 1404, he regained the crown of Bohemia and supported Sigismund's election as king of Germany in 1411. He died in Prague on August 16, 1419.

Documents: *DRTA*, Ältere Reihe, ed., Julius Weizacker (Munich, 1867–1877); vols. 1–3. Works About: K. A. Fink, *Die Konziliare Idee im späten Mittelalter,* Vörtrage und Forschungen, 9 (Darmstadt, 1965); August Gerlich, *Hapsburg-Luxembourg-Wittelsbach im Kampf um die dtsch. Königs Krone* (Wiesbaden, 1960); Hermann Heimpel, *Studien zur Kirchen; und Reichsreform des 15. Jahrhunderts* (Heidelberg, 1929); D. Hindeschiedt,"Wenzel, Ruprecht und der Städtekampf in Sudwestdeutschland," *Z. GORh,* NF, 13 (1898); 197–254; Theodor Lindner, *Gesch. der Dtsch. Reiches unter König Wenzel* (Braunschweig, 1875–1880), vols. 1–2; Heinz Rider, *Wenzel: Ein unwurdiger König* (Vienna, 1970); H. Weigel, "König Wenzels persönliche Politik," *Dtsch. Archiv für Gesch. des Mittelalters* 7 (1944): 133–99.   *S. A. Garretson*

See ADOLF OF NASSAU; CHARLES IV; CONCILIARISM; RUPERT I; SIGISMUND.

WESTERBURG, GERHARD (?–1558), was an anabaptist leader, whose religious career spans the radicalism of the early Anabaptist movement and ends with the conversion to the Reformed church. Although the date of his birth is unknown, Westerburg's parents were members of the Cologne merchant aristocracy. Receiving a thorough education first at the University of Cologne and finally at Bologna, Gerhard was awarded a doctor's degree in both civil and ecclesiastical law. Despite his patrician background, Westerburg showed a deep interest in the plight of the underprivileged and the burning religious questions of his time. Perhaps this dual concern led him to become involved in Anabaptism, a movement that displayed religious and social overtones.

In the 1520s he developed contacts with the noted Zwickau Prophets, especially the revolutionary Nicholas Storch. Yet it was Andreas Karlstadt in Wittenberg who attracted him, and Westerburg became an ardent follower. Typical of his devotion to Karlstadt was his defense of this radical in a short pamphlet,

Vom Fegfeuer (1522), from which he earned his nickname Dr. Purgatory. Expelled from Saxony in 1524, Westerburg traveled to Zurich where he became associated with the early Anabaptist leaders Conrad Grebel and Felix Manz. In 1525 Westerburg became the leader of a Reformation movement in Frankfurt am Main. It was here that the events of the Peasants' War touched him.

Westerburg was instrumental in the writing of the famous forty-two Frankfurt Articles in April 1525. These articles were basically demands by which the artisans and lower classes of the city hoped to improve their status. Besides religious demands, certain political and social reforms, such as the election of one of the two burgomasters from among the poor and changes in the court system, were contained. Although the articles were accepted and printed, the defeat of the peasant uprising ended their chances and forced Westerburg to return to Cologne.

In his native city, Westerburg was attacked for his open religious views but was permitted to continue his pastoral career when a local imperial court ruled in his favor. Soon he, along with his brother, Arnold, became the head of the growing Anabaptist community in Cologne. His involvement in the Münster affair, which was superficial because he did not participate in the revolt but rather visited the city and was rebaptized there, led to increasing suspicion by the Cologne authorities, and eventually he would leave the city. Between 1535 and 1542 his life is obscure, but in that time he converted to the Reformed church. He appears after 1542 in Königsberg as a Reformed preacher and on later travels to Emden and East Friesland. Except for his efforts to work with Herman of Wied, his life until his death in 1558 was quiet and uneventful.

Works By: Gerhard Westerburg, *Von dem grossen Gottdienst der löblichen Statt Cöllen* (Strasbourg, 1545). **Works About:** Harold S. Bender, *The Mennonite Encyclopedia*, 4 vols. (Scottdale, Pa., 1955–1959); Hans H. Th. Stiasny. *Die strafrechliche Verfolgung der Täufer in der freien Reichstadt Köln 1529 bis 1618* (Münster, 1962); George H. Williams, *The Radical Reformation* (Philadelphia, 1962).   *C. T. Eby*

See ANABAPTISM; KARLSTADT; MÜNSTER AFFAIR; PEASANTS' WAR.

WESTPHALIA, PEACE OF, concluded the Thirty Years War (1618–1648). Its main provisions are contained in two treaties that were negotiated in the Westphalian towns of Münster and Osnabrück between representatives of King Louis XIV of France, Queen Christina of Sweden, and Emperor Ferdinand III and the German estates. The treaties were signed on October 24, 1648, and significantly affected both the Empire and its neighbors. They provided a framework for the European state system until the time of the French Revolution. The peace marked the end of the era of religious wars and inaugurated the modern phase in European history in which relations among sovereign states are governed by international law.

General Nature of the Peace Talks: The international congress to end the war to central Europe began in 1644. The German princes and their subjects were desirous of peace, yet the actual negotiations proceeded very slowly because of several complicating factors. A major handicap was that the talks were conducted while the fighting continued, permitting the fluctuations of war to influence the discussions. Battlefield victories, for instance, served to encourage parties to raise their demands or harden their positions. Particularly difficult to satisfy were the French and the Swedes, who demanded major territorial concessions from the Empire as compensation for their war efforts. The situation was further complicated by the fact that German problems were discussed jointly with international issues. All the major powers save England, Poland, Russia, and Turkey sent representatives to the congress to lobby for their interests. Münster and Osnabrück lay thirty miles apart, and communications between the various parties were sometimes difficult and always time-consuming.

The representatives of the German Protestant estates gathered at Osnabrück, where Sweden served as their leader; the Catholics went to Münster, where they followed the lead of either France or the emperor. The chief negotiators were the imperial representative Count Maximilian von Trauttmansdorff, the French diplomats Abel Servien and the Marquis d' Avaux, and Sweden's Adler Salvius and Axel Oxenstierna, the son of the Swedish chancellor. At Münster, the papal nuncio Fabio Chigi, who later became Pope Alexander VII, and the Venetian ambassador Aluise Contarini served as mediators; there were no mediators at Osnabrück. Negotiations between the Catholic and Protestant estates followed the very cumbersome style of the diet of the Empire. The estates, acting as two sections of the diet, had to concur on all questions before an agreement could be promulgated as a law of the Empire.

The instruments of peace that finally were adopted at Münster and Osnabrück were largely the result of foreign mediation and dictation. The Empire's internal problems therefore were settled in the light of the power interests of Europe's leading states.

Territorial Provisions: In the west, France obtained the Habsburgs' rights and possessions in Upper and Lower Alsace. These rights were so ill defined and confused that they later led to trouble. Strasbourg, the chief city of Alsace, over which the emperor did not exercise any authority, was not ceded but was seized by Louis XIV in 1681. France's sovereignty over the three Lorraine bishoprics of Metz, Toul, and Verdun which the French had occupied for a century, was recognized. In addition it gained control over the Rhenish fortress cities of Breisach and Philippsburg. None of these territorial concessions gave France a seat in the imperial diet.

Sweden's demands were more difficult to satisfy since it claimed all of Pomerania, a duchy to which Frederick William of Brandenburg had incontestable legal claim after the death of the last Pomeranian ruler in 1637. The elector's fierce resistance and the emperor's willingness to appease Sweden in the end produced a compromise. The disputed territory was divided. Sweden took control of western Pomerania, including the mouth of the rivers Oder and Stettin and the islands of Rügen, Usedom, and Wollin. In return for letting Brandenburg have eastern Pomerania, the Swedes obtained the Mecklenburg port city of Wismar and the secularized bishoprics of Bremen and Verden, which together comprised the lands between the Elbe and Weser rivers. Sweden thus gained control over the estuaries of the three major north German rivers and strengthened its position along the southeastern shores of the Baltic. It received these territories as fiefs of the Empire, thereby gaining the right to send representatives to the diet. In addition Sweden obtained an indemnity of 5 million imperial dollars for the demobilization of its army in Germany; it had demanded 20 million imperial dollars.

Brandenburg received eastern Pomerania. As compensation for the loss of western Pomerania, Federick William gained the secularized bishoprics of Kammin, Halberstadt, and Minden and the archbishopric of Magdeburg, which was to revert to Brandenburg on the death of its Saxon administrator. These territorial gains were important for they helped bridge the gap between the electorate and the Rhenish-Westphalian territories that the Hohenzollerns had acquired earlier in the century. Next to the Habsburgs, Frederick William now was the ruler of the largest territory in the Empire.

Saxony, which was dismayed at the loss of Magdeburg, kept only Lusatia, ceded to it earlier. Mecklenburg was compensated for the loss of Wismar by the bishoprics of Ratzeburg and Schwerin. Hesse-Cassel received the abbey of Hersfeld and the county of Schaumburg. Maximilian of Bavaria retained both the electoral dignity and the Upper Palatinate. Charles Louis, the eldest son of the disgraced Frederick V, Bohemia's Winter King, received the Rhenish Palatinate and a new eighth electorate especially created for him. The independence of the United Provinces of the Netherlands and the Swiss Confederation from the Empire was officially recognized.

Confessional Provisions: The Peace of Westphalia effectively checkmated the Catholic Counter Reformation in Germany. Generally the provisions of the Peace of Augsburg of 1555 were confirmed, but they were broadened and clarified. Calvinism was now officially recognized together with Lutheranism and Catholicism. The princes' right of reformation was reaffirmed. A distinction was made, however, between the public practice of religion, which the princes could regulate, and peoples' private practice of religion at home, where the rulers would not seek to impose their authority.

The restitution provisions regarding secularized church territories of the Edict of Restitution (1629) and the Peace of Prague (1635) were abandoned in favor of a new formula that made 1624 the determining date for the ownership of church properties and offices. Provision was made for parity between Catholics and Protestants in religiously divided cities such as Augsburg and Regensburg. The ecclesiastical reservation that Protestants had strongly opposed since the peace of 1555 was extended to Protestant bishoprics: a Protestant administrator from now on would have to resign just like a Catholic bishop if he changed his faith. Protestant administrators were given the right to send representatives to the imperial diet.

Religious disputes that came before the imperial diet henceforth could not be resolved by majority vote. Instead the diet's Catholic and Protestant members, the *corpus catholicorum* and the *corpus evangelicorum*, were to hold separate deliberations and resolve their differences through peaceful negotiations. Similarly an equal number of Catholics and Protestants were to be appointed to the Imperial Cameral Court to prevent any one religious group from imposing its will there. Protestant judges also were to be brought into the Imperial Aulic Council.

Constitutional Provisions: The emperor's monarchical and centralistic ambitions were as effectively blocked as the Catholic Counter Reformation. The territorial princes were the chief winners of the Peace of Westphalia. The German estates, over three hundred in number, were granted full sovereignty, including the right to conclude alliances among themselves and with foreign powers. This right was limited only by the futile clause that such alliances were not to be directed against the emperor or the Empire. The treaty stipulated further that the emperor was not to issue any new laws, levy taxes, recruit soldiers, or make war without the consent of the Empire's estates.

Since agreement among the three hundred estates was virtually impossible, the principle of self-determination, or medieval constitutional liberties, served to undermine the Holy Roman Empire as an effective political unit. While other European states were moving toward unification, the emergence of a modern nation-state in Germany was delayed for several centuries. New centers of power emerged instead in Austria and Brandenburg-Prussia, and these were to influence the course of German and European affairs decisively in years to come.

Works: Max Braubach and Konrad Repgen, eds., *Acta Pacis Westphalicae* (Münster, 1962–); Konrad Müller, ed., *Instrumenta Pacis Westphalicae. Die Westfälischen Friedensverträge 1648*, Quell. zur neueren Gesch. (Bern, 1949), vols. 12–13; Karl Zeumer, ed., *Quellensammlung zur Gesch. der deutschen Reichsverfassung in Mittelalter und Neuzeit*, 2d ed. (Tübingen, 1913), 2:395–443. **Works About:** Max Braubach, *Der Westfälische Friede* (Münster, 1948); Fritz Dickmann, *Der Westfälische Friede*, 3d ed. (Münster, 1972); Hajo Holborn, *A Hist. of Germany: The Reformation* (New York, 1959), pp. 361–74; A. W. Ward, "The Peace of Westphalia," pp. 395–433, in *The Cambridge Modern Hist.*, vol. 4 (New York, 1934); Fritz Wolff, *Corpus Evangelicorum und Corpus Catholicorum auf dem Westfälischen Friedenskongress*, Schriftenreihe zur Erforschung der neueren Gesch., 2 (Münster, 1966).   *Bodo Nischan*

See FERDINAND III; MÜNSTER TREATY; OSNABRÜCK; THIRTY YEARS WAR.

WILLIAM V (1548–1626), duke of Bavaria from October 1579 to 1597, was one of the leading Catholic princes in the Holy Roman Empire during the late sixteenth century. His avid support of the Catholic cause in Germany led to a rather distorted image of William V created largely by the nationalistic German historians of the nineteenth century. Traditionally his reign has been labeled "the paradise of ultramontanism." Particularly emphasized was his reliance upon the Jesuits who were influential in shaping his thought and policies. It is true that the Jesuits affected William's life. Dominicus Mengin, a Jesuit, was William's confessor for twenty-nine years. In addition, he was educated at the Jesuit-staffed University of Ingolstadt. Nonetheless William V was not a puppet; he was a man of ability and some foresight whose political decisions furthered the Catholic cause and the fortunes of the house of Wittelsbach.

Information about his childhood is scanty. His father, Albert V, carefully designed a program for the young prince's instruction in his duties as a prince to uphold the interests of his family and Catholicism. It was also from Albert that William inherited his love for the Renaissance. The elegant balls, hunts, and the extensive collection of paintings, especially those of Dürer and Michelangelo, placed Bavaria, already strained by his father's spending, on the verge of bankruptcy and contributed to his eventual abdication. The role that his mother, Renata of Lorraine, played in William's life is not clear.

William V continued his father's policy of allying the interests of the Bavarian state with that of Catholicism. Despite his devotion to the old faith, William did not ignore the territorial opportunities. The acquisition of bishoprics for family members was a good example. In 1573 William acquired the bishopric of Hildesheim for his brother, Ernest, already bishop of Freising. In 1581 Ernest added Luttich, Stablo, and Malmedy. Alexander Farnese, the Spanish governor, encouraged these moves, hoping to win Bavarian support in the Netherlands. The papacy was also clearly behind Bavaria. In 1583 when Gebhard Truchsess attempted to Protestanize the archbishopric of Cologne, the papacy ignored the Tridentine decree against pluralism and permitted Ernest to take over Cologne. Spanish and Bavarian troops under the command of Ferdinand of Bavaria made sure that the Protestant cause failed in Cologne. Finally in 1585 Ernest became bishop of Münster.

After the Cologne war, William's policy centered around an attempt to form a Catholic union. He also continued to annex territories for family members. Although his attempt to control the city of Strasbourg failed, between 1581 and 1584 he re-Catholicized the district of Hohenwaldeck. In 1595 he influenced the election of Philip of Bavaria as bishop of Regensburg.

The cost of these ventures was high. Seven hundred thousand gulden were needed to finance the Cologne war alone. William's luxurious life-style, combined with his father's previous debt of over two and one-half million gulden, prompted a financial crisis in Bavaria. Unable to cope with the problem, William in 1593 slowly began to transfer power to his son Maximilian. Other factors affecting his decision were ill health and a desire to devote more time to his religious life. On October 5, 1597, William V formally abdicated his power.

Works About: Berndt Baader, *Der Bayerische Renaissancehof Herzog Wilhelms V. 1568–1579* (Leipzig, 1943); Julius Cohen, *Der Kampf der Bayerherzog gegen die reformatorische Bewegung in sechzehnten Jahrhundert* (Nuremberg, 1930); Heinz Dollinger, *Studien zur Finanzreform Maximillian I von Bayern in den Jahren 1598–1618* (Göttingen, 1968); Helmut Dotterwuch, *Der Junge*

Maximilian (Munich, 1963); Max Lossen, *Der Kölnische Krieg 1565–1586,* 2 vols. (Munich and Gotha, 1882–1897); Wolfgang Quint, *Souveranitätsbegriff und Souveranitätspolitik in Bayern* (Berlin, 1971); Max Spindler, ed., *Handbuch der Bayerischen Gesch.* (Munich, 1969), vols. 2, 3.   *C. T. Eby*

See ALBERT V; COLOGNE.

WILLIAM V (1602–1637), landgrave of Hesse-Cassel, was born at Cassel and died in East Frisia. After a grand tour and studies at the universities of Strasbourg, Basel, and Geneva, young William was named administrator of the abbey of Hersfeld (1617). He married Amalia Elizabeth, daughter of the duke of Hanau and a niece of William of Orange (1619).

Hesse-Cassel, a member of the Palatinate-led Protestant Union, suffered bitterly during the early years of the Thirty Years War. The principality's staunchly Lutheran estates refused to provide Maurice (William's father), their Calvinist ruler, with the necessary financial means to defend the country adequately against the Catholic League. Maurice's difficulties were compounded by his rivalry with neighboring Hesse-Darmstadt whose Lutheran landgrave generally sided with the emperor. In 1623 the Imperial Aulic Council adjudicated an inheritance dispute between the two principalities by granting all of Upper Hesse to the Darmstadt line. Count Tilly, whose Catholic forces occupied much of Hesse-Cassel, added further to Maurice's woes by persuading the country's nobility to remain neutral while their landgrave attempted, in vain, to defend his realm against imperial and league forces.

Faced with an almost hopeless political situation, Maurice finally abdicated in favor of his son William (1627). From the beginning the new ruler's efforts were aimed at stabilizing and strengthening his country. William immediately signed an accord normalizing relations with Hesse-Darmstadt. He reorganized his country's administration and military and became a leading advocate of a more forceful Protestant defensive policy. When Gustavus Adolphus of Sweden entered the war, he was one of the first to join the foreign king (1631). The Hessian army started to push back the Catholic forces even before Gustavus had won his overwhelming victory over the league at Breitenfeld. After liberating Hesse, the landgrave's troops invaded Westphalia and aided Gustavus in the siege and conquest of Mainz. William supported the Swedish-dominated Heilbronn League but did not join it formally. Sweden's defeat at Nördlingen (1634), however, caused him to look more to France for financial and military aid. William was one of the few German princes who did not accept the Peace of Prague (1635); he objected to the agreement because it excluded Calvinists. Instead he signed a formal alliance with France (1636) and continued his war against the emperor. Ferdinand responded by placing William under the imperial ban and invading his country. The landgrave and his family were forced to flee Cassel (1637). Shortly afterward, William fell ill. He died on September 21 at his military headquarters at Leer in East Frisia. William's policy of active resistance against the emperor was continued, and in the end vindicated, by his very able wife, Amalia Elizabeth, who succeeded him as landgravin of Hesse-Cassel.

Works About: Hermann Hallwich, ed., *Briefe und Akten zur Gesch. Wallensteins,* 4 vols. (Vienna, 1912); Walter Keim, "Landgraf Wilhelm V von Hessen-Kassel vom Regierungsantritt 1627 bis zum Abschluss des Bündnisses mit Gustav Adolf 1631 unter besonderer Berücksichtigung der Beziehungen zu Schweden," *Hessisches Jb. für Landesgesch.* 12 (1962): 130–210, 13 (1963): 141–210; Kretzschmar, "Wilhelm V," *ADB,* 43:39–54; *Rikskansleren Axel Oxenstiernas Skrifter och brefvexling* (Stockholm, 1895), vol. 7; Walter Struck, *Das Bündniss Wilhelm von Weimar mit Gustav Adolf* (Stralsund, 1895); Louise van Tongerloo, "Beziehungen zwischen Hessen-Kassel und den Vereinigten Niederlanden während des Dreissigjährigen Krieges," *Hessisches Jb. für Landesgesch.* 14 (1964): 199–270.   *Bodo Nischan*

See THIRTY YEARS WAR; TILLY.

WIMPFELING, JACOB (1450–1528), the leader of the Rhenish humanist sodalities at Strasbourg and Schlettstadt, pedagogical reformer, historian, and clerical reformer, was born in Schlettstadt to a relatively wealthy agrarian family. He was educated at Louis Dringenburg's grammar school there. Upon his father's death in 1463, he was sent to Freiburg to stay with his uncle, a cleric, and entered the university. There he met Geiler von Kaysersberg, the reforming preacher who was to bring him to Strasbourg. He continued his studies at Erfurt and Heidelberg in canon law and then theology.

An associate of the count Palatine's chancellor, John von Dalberg, at Heidelberg, Wimpfeling was both court poet and secretary to Frederick I and became rector and vice-chancellor of the university in 1481 and 1482. Troubled by severe attacks of conscience, he occasionally planned retreats to the Black Forest with his close friend, the reforming bishop of Basel, Christoph von Utenheim. In 1498, he composed and organized the presentation of six dialogues on the duties of princes entitled *Philippica* and, since the elector's son Louis missed the performance, wrote a second *Fürstenspiegel* (Looking Glass for Princes), the *Agatharchia.*

His most famous work, *Germania,* contained a proposal for the creation of a gymnasium in Strasbourg and the first national history of Germany. Published in 1500, it provoked a controversy with Thomas Murner, who found parts of Wimpfeling's historical argument for German hegemony over Alsace farfetched. The quarrel involved all of Wimpfeling's friends and students and became a small cause célébre. The argument for establishing a humanist school in Strasbourg was rejected by the magistracy.

Wimpfeling had turned down an offer by Christoph von Utenheim to help reform the diocese of Basel in order to help Geiler on his new edition of Gerson's works. Among the many texts written while in Strasbourg, the *Apologia pro republica Christiana,* composed in early 1504 to dissuade two sons of his patrician patrons, Jacob Sturm and Franz Paulus, from the study of canon law, contained a controversial attack on the legal profession. He also involved himself in the quarrel between Jacob Locher (Philomusus) and George Zingel in defense of theology between 1503 and 1505. Wimpfeling's cautious attitute toward the teaching of pagan literature, expressed in his *Contra turpem libellum Philomusi defensio theologiae* in 1510, was and remained a central part of his pedagogical program.

Wimpfeling's major pedagogical texts, aside from *Germania,* were *Isidoneus Germanicus* (1497), *Adolescentia* (1500), and *Diatriba de proba institutione puerorum* (1514). He emphasized the constructive role of education in conveying genuine piety and strong moral character. The first was to be accomplished by thorough reading in patristics, carefully edited classics, specific contemporary texts, which supposedly remedied the defects of pagan authors, and Scripture. The second was to be accomplished by the regulation of daily life, which was governed by maxims and regulae drawn from disparate sources: pagan literature, Scripture, and the corpus juris. This thorough reformation of education was to serve patriotic ends.

In 1510, Wimpfeling received an imperial commission through Jacob Spiegel, his nephew and imperial secretary, to adapt the Pragmatic Sanction to German conditions. The political situation that generated this commission shifted, however, and Wimpfeling's *Medulla pragmaticae sanctionis* was never applied. Spiegel published it, along with his uncle's revised edition of Martin Mair's *Gravamina,* in 1520.

Wimpfeling played no part in the Reuchlin controversy and retired to Schlettstadt in 1515. Briefly favorable to Martin Luther, he contributed a dedication to Erasmus' public letter to Archbishop Albert of Mainz on Luther's behalf in 1520. He soon broke with the evangelicals over their rejection of ceremonials and defended the cult of the Virgin. He conducted a minor polemical battle with Martin Bucer and Wolfgang Capito. He died in Schlettstadt on November 17, 1528.

Works By: Otto Herding, ed., *Adolescentia,* Opera Selecta, vol. 1. (Munich, 1965); Emil von Borries, ed., *Wimpfeling und Murner im Kampf um die ältere Gesch. des Elsasses* (Heidelberg, 1926). **Works About:** T. A. Brady, "The Themes of Social Structure, Social Conflict, and Civic Harmony in Jakob Wimpheling's *Germania,*" *SCJ* 3 (1972): 65–76; Joseph Knepper, *Nationaler Gedanke und Kaiseridee bei den elsassischen Humanisten* (Freiburg, 1898), and *Jakob Wimpfeling. Sein Leben und seine Werke* (Freiburg, 1902); Charles Alois Schmidt, *Histoire Littéraire de l'Alsace à la fin du XVe et au commencement du XVIe siècle* (Paris, 1879); L. W. Spitz, *The Religious Renaissance of the German Humanists* (Cambridge, Mass., 1963).   S. A. Garretson

See BUCER; CAPITO; ERASMUS; HUMANISM; KAYSERSBERG; LUTHER; REUCHLIN; SPIEGEL; STRASBOURG; STURM.

WITCHCRAFT, or rather the suppression of this alleged blend of sorcery and heresy from c. 1450 to 1750, provided a focus for the rising tide of misogny in the Holy Roman Empire and elsewhere in Europe and North America. Witchcraft came to be perceived as an infectious and seditious threat to civil and religious authority. It simultaneously offered convenient scapegoats (mostly single women) for the natural disasters and personal failures of the period. Witchcraft supposedly combined sorcery's use of rituals and formulas to produce negative supernatural effects with heresy's repudiation and perversion of Christian rites and practices. Thus the practice of witchcraft embodied in the witches' *malefica,* or evil spells, constituted a dual criminal offense, which initiated excessive, even unbridled, punishment at times.

Although witchcraft theories have support in classical and medieval sources, with the distillation of witchcraft theory in the mid-fifteenth century came the impetus for wide-scale witch-hunting and the attendant horrors for its often hapless victims. In 1484 Pope Innocent VIII issued his *Summis desiderantis affectibus,* a papal bull that validated the existence of witchcraft in the Empire and effectively suppressed local opposition to the investigation of these evils by papal inquisitors. Thus duly authorized, the Dominican friars Henry Institoris and Jacob Sprenger executed forty-eight witches within the diocese of Constance by 1486 and completed their manual and summary of existing witchcraft theory, the *Malleus Maleficarum* (Hammer of witches), which also prescribed the methods for prosecuting witches through the secular courts. The Protestant Reformation brought no respite for the victims of witch-hunting, for Martin Luther, among other reformers, helped to perpetuate the fear and hatred of witches.

Despite these pronouncements, no clear orthodoxy on witchcraft had been established by the middle of the sixteenth century. The secular courts limited trial and punishment to attested cases of harmful magic, although the medieval Inquisition deemed all magic capital heresy. Emperor Charles V's *Constitutio Criminalis Carolina* (1532), which formed the basic criminal law of the Empire, codified this ambiguity by disallowing the capital punishment required for harmful magic in cases of magic that produced no physical harm. However, in the second half of the sixteenth century, many legislators, jurists, and theologians ceased to make such distinctions. When applying the electoral Saxon criminal constitutions of 1572, which were an attempt to clarify the *Carolina,* German courts systematically convicted witches of both a pact with the devil and specific damage and thus avoided such technicalities.

Eventually a minority position in opposition to the witch-hunts emerged. One group challenged the basic presuppositions of witchcraft theory: the witch's pact with the devil, demonic power over the laws of nature, and divine permission for the use of that demonic power. Other writers attacked the legal abuses inherent in the witch trials.

The publication of *De Praestigiis Daemonum* in 1563 established Dr. John Weyer as the leader of the former group. Weyer asserted that the devil's extensive powers required no human aid; confessed witches were little more than deluded persons, who mistakenly thought they had magical powers. He argued that what these women instead needed was Christian education and held that only those guilty of murder by poison deserved death regardless of other magical practices. Although Weyer himself was accused of being in league with the devil, his writings did inspire others to challenge the witch-hunts. By the eighteenth century the phenomenon had spent itself, but not before thousands of innocent victims had been tortured, tried, and often executed during the several centuries that the witch hysteria prevailed in the Empire.

Works About: Julio Caro Baroja, *The World of Witches,* tr. O. Glendinning (Chicago, 1965); Norman Cohn, *Europe's Inner Demons* (New York, 1975); J. Hansen, *Zauberwahn, Inquisition und Hexenprozess im Mittelalter* (Munich, 1900); H. C. E. Midelfort, *Witch Hunting in Southwestern Germany, 1562–1684* (Stanford, 1972); E. W. Monter, ed., *European Witchcraft* (New York, 1969); *Quel. und Untersuchungen zur Gesch. des Hexenwahns und des Hexenverfolgung im Mittelalter,* ed. Joseph Hansen (Bonn, 1901); J. B. Russell, *Witchcraft in the Middle Ages* (Ithaca, 1972); Keith Thomas, *Religion and the Decline of Magic* (New York, 1971); *Witchcraft in Europe, 1100–1700: A Documentary Hist.* ed. A. Kors and E. Peters (Philadelphia, 1972).   *A. H. Zophy*

See CHARLES V; KEPLER; LUTHER.

WOLFRAM VON ESCHENBACH (c. 1165–1220), epic poet, began life in the village of Eschenbach near Ansbach in Franconia. An impoverished knight, Wolfram depended, like other poets of the period, upon princely patronage such as that of Landgrave Herman of Thuringia, a friend to many poets. Although a devoted husband and father, much of his life was spent in travel.

Wolfram became known as one of the greatest German poets. He began his career as a singer of *Minnelieder* (love songs, 1200–1210) but moved on to write the long epic poem, the *Parzival.* The *Parzival* tells the story of one of King Arthur's knights, who becomes the ruler of the Grail community, an ideal state where worldly pleasures are combined with Christian virtues. This and his other writings, as well as his personality, were immensely popular throughout the Middle Ages.

Works By: *The Parzival of Wolfram von Eschenbach,* tr. E. H. Zeydel and B. Q. Morgan (Chapel Hill, 1960); *Wolfram von Eschenbach,* ed. Karl Lachmann (Berlin, 1926). **Works About:** Joachim Bumke, *Wolfram von Eschenbach* (Stuttgart, 1966); Margaret Richey, *Studies of Wolfram von Eschenbach* (Oxford, 1957); H. Sacker, *An Introduction to Wolfram's Parzival* (Cambridge, 1963).   *J. W. Zophy*

See GOTTFRIED VON STRASBOURG; HARTMANN VON AUE.

WORMS, DIET OF, 1521, first meeting of the imperial estates with the recently elected Emperor Charles V (1519–1556), opened on January 27; and its recess (*Abschied*), or decisions, was signed on May 26. Due to Luther's appearance and the resultant Edict of Worms issued against the reformer, the significance of the diet has often been seen in conjunction with the Reformation. Although the diet was certainly important for the Reformation, the religious problem was only one of a number of pressing issues facing the estates. Moreover since Charles left the Empire for nine years immediately after the conclusion of the diet, the estates' actions at Worms prepared the bases for imperial governance during the interim.

Although it contained many points, the imperial proposition read to the estates concerned the organization of imperial government, maintenance of public peace, and tax assessments. Almost incidently the diet was to concern itself with Luther's rebellion. In treating the proposition's major points, the diet provided for reestablishment of the Imperial Council of Regency (*Reichsregiment*) and reconstructed the Imperial Cameral Court (*Reichskammergericht*), both of which fulfilled part of Charles' capitulations of elections made to the electors in 1519. The recess tied these institutions closely together, provided for their installation at Nuremberg, and established greater royal control over their operations. In the realm of public peace, the diet largely recapitulated the laws of the Empire promulgated during the reign of Charles' predecessor, Maximilian I (1493–1519). Thus the Eternal Peace (an agreement between Maximilian I and the estates to maintain law and order) was reaffirmed, feuds outlawed, and violations of the peace submitted to the court for judgment. To support Charles financially and militarily, especially with regard to his impending war with France, the estates drew up a tax register; this assessment remained the tax basis for most of the estates throughout Charles' reign. While the diet debated numerous other proposals touching on the economy, administration, and judiciary, these concerns appeared less important than those dealing with Luther.

Despite Luther's condemnation in the papal bull *Exsurge domine* of 1520, the final form of the formal bull of excommunication, *Decet pontificem romanum,* did not appear until late in 1521 after the diet had accepted the Edict of Worms. This famous edict resulted from Luther's refusal to recant his views when he was summoned to appear before the emperor and estates. Luther based his refusal on the point that he had not been proven incorrect either by the Scriptures or reason, and therefore he must not act against his conscience. Various entreaties to Luther to change his mind proved unsuccessful. The edict that banned Luther from the Empire bore the date of May 6, although the emperor and the few estates that remained in Worms did not sign and issue it until the end of that month. Since the edict declared that Luther "is to be regarded as a convicted heretic," the estates acted as a de facto church council because the formal excommunication had yet to be issued.

Due to the fact that only a few estates remained to conclude the diet and that Charles left the Empire to pursue his policies, there appeared little hope of carrying out the edict's provisions. Luther's partisans and many noncommitted estates felt the reformer had been judged without a hearing and that his views had not been refuted. These opinions augmented the cry for a free church council to meet and decide on the religious issue, a cry frequently reiterated during the diets of the 1520s and 1530s.

Works: Hist. Kommission bei der Bayerischen Akademie der Wissenschaften, ed., *DRTA, Jüngere Reihe,* vol. 2: *DRTA unter Kaiser Karl V.,* ed. Adolf Wrede (Gotha, 1896, rpr. 1962); B. J. Kidd, ed., *Documents Illustrative of the Continental Reformation* (Oxford, 1911), pp. 79–89. **Works**

About: Roland H. Bainton, *Here I Stand: A Life of Martin Luther* (New York, 1950); De Lamar Jensen, *Confrontation at Worms* (Provo, Utah, 1973); Fritz Reuter, ed., *Der Reichstag zu Worms von 1521, Reichspolitik und Luthersache* (Worms, 1971)   *P. N. Bebb*

See CHARLES V; IMPERIAL CAMERAL COURT; IMPERIAL COUNCIL OF REGENCY; LUTHER.

Z

ZASIUS, ULRICH (1461–1535), humanist jurist and civil servant, was born in the burgher Zäsi family in Constance and studied at Tübingen, starting in 1481 and leaving after a few years with a B.A. He became town clerk at Buchhorn (Friedrichshafen) in the late 1480s. He then became town clerk at Baden im Aargau (1489–1494) where he also kept the Latin correspondence of the Swiss Confederation. He then moved to Freiburg im Breisgau to serve as town clerk (1494–1496), and at this point he determined to seek a more prestigious career than municipal administration. After serving as the master of the Freiburg Latin School, Zasius registered as a law student at the university in 1499. He rapidly received a doctorate in civil law, and he used his popularity with students and with the town government to obtain a professorship from the faculty in 1506. Zasius was generally regarded as one of the three leading humanist jurists of Europe, along with Guillaume Budé and Andrea Alciati. Zasius trained many of the most important administrators and practicing lawyers of the next generation in the German southwest.

Zasius became involved in a bitter dispute with his former student John Eck between 1517 and 1519, which tended to identify Zasius as a partisan of Martin Luther. Zasius rejected Luther's doctrines after the Leipzig disputations in 1519, but he never lived down his reputation as a crypto-Lutheran in ultra-Catholic Freiburg. Zasius' friendship with Desiderius Erasmus of Rotterdam culminated in Erasmus' residence in Freiburg (1529–1535).

Zasius spent much of his later life working for governments and private clients preparing legal opinions (*consilia*). He was retained as a legal consultant by the town of Freiburg in 1502, named imperial counsel by Maximilian I and Charles V, and acted as a consultant to King Ferdinand. He was the chief author of the new law code of Freiburg published in 1520. His consilia dealt with such diverse subjects as the disputes between Maximilian I and the Venetians, the limitations on executive power in the constitutional settlement at Worms in 1495, the use of the death penalty for Anabaptists, and whether Alsace was subject to German law.

Zasius' surviving writings consist mostly of voluminous lectures, treatises on Roman law, controversial and occasional writings, and letters. Zasius wrote a defense of the power of the state to baptize Jewish children against the will of the parents in 1505, and it was published in 1508. His letters are an important source of political and intellectual history of the German southwest between 1495 and 1535.

Works By: Percy Stafford Allen et al., eds. *Opus epistolarum Desiderii Erasmi Roterodami,* 12 vols. (Oxford, 1906–1958); Alfred Hartmann, ed., *Die Amerbachkorrespondenz,* 6 vols. (Basel, 1943–1967); Joseph von Riegger, ed., *Udalrici Zasii . . . epistolae* (Ulm, 1774); Johann Ulrich Zasius and Joachim Münsinger von Frundeck, eds., *Udalricus Zasius, Opera omnia,* 7 vols. (Lyons, 1550–1551). **Works About:** Steven Rowan, "Ulrich Zasius and the Baptism of Jewish Children," *SCJ* 6 (October 1975): 3–25, "Ulrich Zasius and John Eck," *SCJ* 8 (suppl., 1977): 79–95; and "The German Works of Ulrich Zasius," *Manuscripta* 21 (1977): 131–43. Roderich (von) Stintzing, *Ulrich Zasius* (Basel, 1857; rpr. Darmstadt, 1961); Hans Winterberg, *Die Schüler von Ulrich Zasius* (Stuttgart, 1961).   *S. W. Rowan*

See CHARLES V; ECK; ERASMUS; FERDINAND I; FREIBURG; LUTHER; MAXIMILIAN I.

ZENTA, BATTLE OF (1697), proved to be the decisive victory for Leopold I in his long war against the Turks. Zenta was part of a larger campaign that began in 1683 when the Turks under grand vizier Kara Mustapha invaded Habsburg Hungary and besieged Vienna, the capital of the Holy Roman Empire. With approximately two hundred thousand troops, the Turks tried to seize the city. Failing, they hastily and disastrously retreated. In 1686, Budapest fell to the imperialists as did Pécs, Szeged, and Arad. In 1687, Duke Charles V of Lorraine defeated the Turks at Mohács and in 1688, Max Emmanuel, elector of Bavaria, seized the capital of Serbia, Belgrade. The Turks recouped their losses under the personal leadership of the sultan, Mustafa II, who reconquered Belgrade in 1690 and defeated the imperialists at Lugos in eastern Hungary. The Turks then proved unwilling to sue for peace. In order to break this stalemate, Leopold appointed Prince Eugene of Savoy as commander-in-chief of the imperial forces in Hungary in 1697; this was Eugene's first independent command. With an army of fifty thousand, Eugene pursued the Turks who intended to seize the imperial garrison at Szeged. Learning of the imperialist pursuit, the sultan feared that he would be outflanked by Eugene on his rear and the imperialists at Szeged, so he ordered his army to cross the rapidly flowing Tisza at Zenta. On September 11, Eugene caught up with the Turks, who were still crossing the river. Even though it was late afternoon, Eugene ordered the attack. The sultan sent some of the cavalry back to aid the struggling infantry, but this only increased the confusion among the Turks and further blocked their retreat. Approximately twenty thousand Turks, including the grand vizier, were killed and ten thousand drowned in the ensuing melee. The Turkish infantry was totally destroyed; the remaining Turks fled to Temesvár, abandoning their camp and their guns. Eugene, who had outmaneuvered the Turks, captured an immense amount of loot, including the sultan's personal treasure chest. Although skirmishing continued throughout 1698, Zenta effectually ended the Turkish war. Peace was finally concluded at the Treaty of Karlowitz (1699), which confirmed Leopold's victories of the last sixteen years.

Works About: Max Braubach, *Prince Eugen von Savoygen,* 5 vols. (Vienna, 1963–1965); Eugene-François, prince of Savoy, *Feldzüge des Prinzen von Savoyen,* 20 vols. (Vienna, 1876–1892), 2:144–54; Nicholas Henderson, *Prince Eugene of Savoy* (London, 1964); Franz Krones, ed., *Hand-*

buch der Gesch. Österreich von der altesten bis der neuesten Zeit (Berlin, 1879), vol. 3; Derek McKay, Prince Eugene of Savoy (London, 1977); Helmut Oehler, Prinz Eugen im Urteil Europas (Munich, 1944); Oswald Redlich, Weltmacht des Barock, Österreich in der Zeit Kaiser Leopolds I (Vienna, 1961); John P. Spielman, Leopold I of Austria (New Brunswick, N.J., 1977).   L. S. Frey and M. L. Frey

See EUGENE; LEOPOLD I; KARLOWITZ; VIENNA, SEIGE OF.

ZORNDORF (POLISH SARBINOWO), village of Prussia in the Oder valley, northeast of Küstrin (Kostrzyn), was the site of a bloody battle between Frederick the Great's Prussians and the Russians on August 25, 1758, during the Seven Years War. Giving up the invasion of Moravia and the siege of Olmütz, Frederick left Prussian Field Marshall James Keith (1696–1758) to occupy the position of Austrian Field Marshal Leopold von Daun (1705–66) and hastened to Frankfurt-on-the-Oder. A large Russian army under Scottish émigré General William Fermor (1704–1771) had overrun Prussia and was besieging General Christoph von Dohna's (1703–1762) garrison in the fortress of Küstrin. Frederick crossed the Oder below Küstrin but, finding Fermor ensconced on the hills behind the swamps of the Mützel River valley, marched around his right flank, Fermor changing front to match him, until the Russians were facing south on three cramped plateaus with the Mützel at their back. On August 25 Frederick launched a frontal attack in oblique order after a two-hour cannonade. But General von Manteuffel's grenadiers became separated from the rest of General von Kanitz's left wing, and the refused right wing under Dohna inclined too far off to the east. The greencoats were stubbornly holding their own when Frederick William von Seydlitz (1721–1773) finally crossed the difficult Zabern Grund on the left with thirty-six squadrons, and his cuirassiers began to hack the Russians down. Frederick reoriented Dohna, who also closed with the Russians, but at darkness the two armies drew apart. Frederick had lost over a third of his army, 12,797 of 36,000, Fermor 18,500 of 43,300. The Russians drew back to a new position the next day, the Prussians too exhausted to reengage; and only on August 27 did Fermor, with supply difficulties, slowly retreat from West Prussia. Frederick, disconcerted at the Russian doggedness, was already marching to Saxony to ward off another Austrian threat.

Works About: E. J. Masslowski, Der Siebenjährige Krieg nach russischer Darstellung, 3 vols. (Berlin, 1889–1893); Prussian official, Die Kriege Friedrichs des Grossen, 20 vols. (Berlin, 1890–1913), esp. Der Siebenjährige Krieg, vol. 13.   A. H. Ganz

See FREDERICK II, THE GREAT; SEVEN YEARS WAR.

ZWINGLI, ULRICH (1484–1531), church reformer, was born at Wildhaus, a village in the eastern part of the Swiss Confederation under the jurisdiction of St. Gall, in the county of Toggenburg. After his early education at Wesen, Basel, and Bern, he studied at the University of Vienna and then at the University of Basel where he became baccalaureate in 1504 and master of arts in

1506. In 1506 he was ordained and appointed parish priest at Glarus. By this time clearly under the influence of Erasmus, Zwingli spent much time during his ten years at Glarus immersing himself in the Latin classics, the Church fathers, and the Bible. He also improved his knowledge of Greek and began to learn Hebrew. In 1515 he was chaplain for the Swiss army at the Battle of Marignano against the French, where ten thousand Swiss were killed. This experience resulted in his lifelong abhorrence of the mercenary traffic in the confederation. In 1516 he moved to Einsiedeln, where he utilized his mastery of Greek in his sermons and continued his Hebrew studies. Then, in late 1518, he was appointed stipendiary priest (*Leutpriester*) at the Grossmünster in Zurich.

The first two years of Zwingli's Zurich ministry were marked by frequent preaching, based on the Bible, from a radical Erasmian perspective. Like other young Erasmians, he perceived Luther not as a leader but as a colleague in reform. By 1522, apparently independent of Luther, Zwingli had moved from his Erasmianism to an evangelical position. Slowly, and in concert with the Zurich council, Zwingli led the Zurich Church to an evangelical reform. The disputation of January 1523 brought the formal support of the council for reform. The Reformation in Zurich was completed with the abolition of the Mass on April 13, 1525. By this time, Zwingli's reform was under fire from the radical fringe, the Anabaptists. Three disputations, the third from November 6–8, 1525, resulted in the victory of the Zwinglian party.

Zwingli's quarrel with Luther stemmed from Zwingli's view of the Eucharist as a sign and a commemoration, with emphasis on the mystical and spiritual presence of Christ in the elements. After some years of controversy, Zwingli and Luther met personally at Marburg in 1529 to debate the issue of Eucharist. The Marburg colloquy was arranged by Philip of Hesse in the face of the emperor's determination to enforce the Edict of Worms, according to the decision of the second diet of Speyer (March 1529). There was no compromise at Marburg. The Protestant movement was split into two camps, which had important consequences for the later Reformation in the Empire.

This eucharistic quarrel between Zwingli and Luther was reflected in the competition for the allegiance of the imperial cities. The eucharistic teachings were important (Zwingli's doctrine was quite popular with the people in the republican cities), but the competition involved much more than theology. It also made clear the basic differences in approach to ecclesiastical, political, and social issues. Zwingli's emphasis on the Christian community and his high regard for republicanism held a great attraction for the guild cities of upper Germany and the Swiss Confederation, whereas Luther's appeal was largely limited to the more aristocratic cities of the north and those in Franconia in the south.

Within the confederation, Zwinglianism found support in most of the cities and in some country areas. Bern, the leading military power in the confederation, was reformed early in 1528. After a disputation in which Zwingli was the leading figure. Zwingli's dream was to evangelize the entire confederation, and thus he hoped for an effective military alliance with Bern. Although the Bernese rejected Zwingli's political plan, Bern did join together with Zurich and Constance for mutual defense in the Christian Civic Union (*das Christliche Burgrecht*). The Catholic states (Uri, Schwyz, Unterwalden, Lucerne, and Zug) soon formed their own defensive league, the Christian Alliance (*die Christliche Vereinigung*), which stipulated that Ferdinand of Austria would provide military aid should the Catholic states be attacked.

In 1529, Zwingli urged a preventive military strike against the Catholic states. Although Bern resisted such a move, the Zurich council, fearful of a Catholic attack, fielded an army in 1529, which faced the inferior Catholic forces at Kappel in mid-June. However, instead of war, and against Zwingli's wishes, the first peace of Kappel was negotiated. The treaty called for religious freedom, stipulated that the Catholics break their alliance with Ferdinand, and froze the religious lines in the confederation. Bern's policy of restraint had won out; Zwingli's dream of a united, Reformed confederation was destroyed. Without Bern, Zurich arranged a defensive alliance with Strasbourg and Hesse in November 1530.

None of the stipulations of the treaty of Kappel was followed: the Zwinglians continued to evangelize, and the Catholic states kept their alliance with Austria. Zwingli wanted to attack the Catholic states in the spring of 1531, but Bern insisted on an economic blockade. Pressed by the blockade and incensed by the advance of Zwinglianism in the territories east of Zurich, the Catholic states attacked on October 11, 1531. Zurich received no aid from its allies; the battle at Kappel was a quick and decisive victory for the Catholics. Zwingli, an armed combatant, died on the field of battle.

Works By: Emil Egli et al. eds., *Huldreich Zwinglis sämtliche Werke,* 14 vols. (Berlin-Leipzig-Zurich, 1905–). **Works About:** J. W. Cottrell, "Covenant and Baptism in the Theology of Huldreich Zwingli" (Ph.D. diss., Princeton Theological Seminary, 1971); Georg Finsler, ed., *Zwingli-Bibliographie* (Zurich, 1897); Ulrich Gäbler, *Huldrych Zwingli im 20. Jahrhundert. Forschungsbericht und annotierte Bibliographie 1897–1972* (Zurich, 1975); Martin Haas, *Huldrych Zwingli und seine Zeit* (Zurich, 1976); René Hauswirth, *Landgraf Philipp von Hessen und Zwingli* (Tübingen, 1968); Walther Köhler, *Zwingli und Luther,* 2 vols. (Leipzig and Gütersloh, 1924–1953); B. Moeller, *Imperial Cities and the Reformation,* tr. H. C. E. Midelfort and M. Edwards (Philadelphia, 1972); G. R. Potter, *Zwingli* (Cambridge, 1976); Arthur Rich, *Die Anfänge der Theologie Huldrych Zwinglis* (Zurich, 1949); R. Walton, *Zwingli's Theocracy* (Toronto, 1968).   *J. W. Baker*

See BULLINGER; ERASMUS; LUTHER; MARBURG COLLOQUY; PHILIP OF HESSE.

APPENDIX A The Holy Roman Emperors and Their Predecessor Kings

Charlemagne (800–814) (dates given for total reign as king and/or emperor)
Louis I, the Pious (814–840)
Louis II, the German (840–876), king of East Frankland
Carloman (876–880), king of Bavaria
Louis (876–882), king of Saxony
Louis (880–882), king of Bavaria
Charles III, the Fat (880–887), reunited the Empire and was crowned emperor
Arnulf (887–899), was crowned emperor
Louis the Child (899–911), last Carolingian king of East Frankland
Conrad of Franconia (911–918), king of East Frankland

SAXON KINGS OF EAST FRANKLAND, 919–973

Henry I, the Fowler (919–936)
Otto I, the Great (936–973)

SAXON EMPERORS, 968–1024

Otto I, the Great (962–973)
Otto II (973–983)
Otto III (983–1002)
Henry II, the Saint (1002–1024)

FRANCONIAN EMPERORS, 1024–1125

Conrad II, the Salian (1024–1039)
Henry III, the Black (1039–1056)
Henry IV (1056–1106)

SAXON EMPEROR, 1125–1137

Lothar II (III) (1125–1137)

HOHENSTAUFEN EMPERORS, 1138–1254

Conrad III (1138–1152)
Frederick I., Barbarossa (1152–1190)
Henry VI (1190–1197)
Philip of Swabia-Hohenstaufen (1198–1208), not crowned, rival of Otto IV, of Brunswick-Welf
    (1198–1215), rival of Philip
Frederick II (1211/1215–1250), rival of Otto IV, 1211–1215; also king of Sicily, 1197–1250
Conrad IV (1250–1254), not crowned

THE GREAT INTERREGNUM IN GERMANY, 1254–1273

HABSBURG, LUXEMBOURG, AND OTHER EMPERORS, 1273–1556

Rudolf I, of Habsburg (1273–1291), not crowned
Adolf I, of Nassau (1292–1298), not crowned
Albert I, of Austria (Habsburg) (1298–1308), not crowned
Henry VII, of Luxembourg (1308–1313)
Louis IV, of Bavaria (1314–1347)
Charles IV, of Luxembourg-Bohemia (1347–1378)
Wenceslaus of Luxembourg (1378–1400), not crowned
Rupert of Bavaria (1400–1410), not crowned
Sigismund of Luxembourg (1410–1437)
Albert II, of Austria (Habsburg) (1438–1439), not crowned
Frederick III, of Styria (Habsburg) (1440–1493), last emperor crowned at Rome
Maximilian I, of Habsburg (1493–1519)
Charles V (Habsburg) (1519–1556)

HABSBURG EMPERORS, 1556–1740

Ferdinand I (1556–1564)
Maximilian II (1564–1576)
Rudolf II (1576–1612)
Matthias (1612–1619)
Ferdinand II (1619–1637)
Ferdinand III (1637–1657)
Leopold I (1658–1705)
Joseph I (1705–1711)
Charles VI (1711–1740)

BAVARIAN EMPEROR, 1742–1745

Charles VII (1742–1745)

LORRAINE EMPEROR, 1745–1765

Francis I (1745–1765), husband of Maria Theresa

HABSBURG-LORRAINE EMPERORS, 1765–1806

Joseph II (1765–1790), son of Francis I and Maria Theresa
Leopold II (1790–1792)
Francis II (1792–1806)

APPENDIX B Chronology

Items in capitalized letters can be found in separate entries in the essays section.

800	Coronation of CHARLEMAGNE
843	TREATY OF VERDUN divides the Carolingian empire
c. 787–925	Scandinavian invasions
955	OTTO I ends the Magyar invasions at the battle of Lechfeld
1054	Schism of West and East in the church
1066	Norman Conquest of England
1073–85	Pope GREGORY VII
1075–1122	INVESTITURE CONTROVERSY
1095	First Crusade
12th century	Rise of towns; coming of Arabic and Greek science
1190	Death of FREDERICK I, BARBAROSSA on the Third Crusade
1198–1216	Pope INNOCENT III
1215	Fourth Lateran Council; Magna Carta
1231	FREDERICK II issues the constitutions of Melfi
1225–1274	Thomas Aquinas
1265–1321	DANTE
13th century	Rise of parliaments
1305–1378	The Babylonian Captivity (popes at Avignon)
1337–1453	The Hundred Years War between England and France
1348	Black Death (plagues)
1378–1417	The Great Schism of the Western Church
1414–1417	Council of Constance (SIGISMUND and HUS)
1420–1431	Hussite Wars
c. 1450	GUTENBERG and movable type
1453	Fall of Constantinople to the Ottoman Turks
15th century	The Renaissance at its height
1452–1519	Leonardo da Vinci
1466–1536	ERASMUS
1469	Marriage of Ferdinand of Aragon and Isabella of Castile
1469–1527	Machiavelli
1475–1564	Michelangelo
1471–1528	DÜRER
1492	First voyage of Columbus
1497–1499	Voyage of Vasco da Gama
1517	LUTHER's Ninety-five Theses begin the Reformation
1519–1556	Emperor CHARLES V
1519–1522	Magellan circumnavigates the globe
1524–1526	PEASANTS' WAR in Germany
1529	Turks besiege VIENNA
1531	First stock exchange at Antwerp
1540	Founding of the Jesuits
1543	Copernicus and Vesalius publish
1541–1564	Calvin at Geneva
1545–1563	Council of Trent
1555	Religious Peace of AUGSBURG

1568–1648	Revolt of the Netherlands
1571	Defeat of Turks at Lepanto
1572	St. Bartholomew's Massacre
1564–1616	Shakespeare
1588	Spanish Armada
1598	Edict of Nantes
1618–1648	The THIRTY YEARS WAR
1648	Peace of WESTPHALIA
1649–1658	Rule of Cromwell
1661–1715	Age of Louis XIV
1682–1725	Czar Peter the Great
1683	Turks threaten VIENNA
1687	Newton's *Principia*
1688–1697	WAR OF THE LEAGUE OF AUGSBURG
1701–1714	WAR OF THE SPANISH SUCCESSION
18th century	Age of Englightenment
1740–1780	MARIA THERESA
1740–1787	FREDERICK II of Prussia
1740–1748	WAR OF THE AUSTRIAN SUCCESSION
1740–1760	Voltaire at his peak
1749–1832	GOETHE
1756–1763	SEVEN YEARS WAR
1761	Rousseau's *Social Contract*
1762–96	Catherine II of Russia
1772	First partition of Poland
1776	Adam Smith's *Wealth of Nations*
1778–1783	War of American Independence
1789	Beginning of the French Revolution
1792–1802	FRENCH REVOLUTIONARY WARS
1806	End of the Holy Roman Empire

APPENDIX C The House of Hohenzollern

Items in capitalized letters can be found in separate entries in the essays section.

Frederick I, elector of Brandenburg and ruler of Bayreuth and Ansbach (1417–1440)
Frederick II, "Iron Tooth" (1440–1470)
Albert Achilles (1470–1486)
John Cicero (1486–1499)
Joachim I (1499–1535)
Joachim II (1535–1571)
John George (1571–1598)
Joachim Frederick (1598–1608)
John Sigismund, elector and duke of Prussia (1608–1619)
GEORGE WILLIAM (1619–1640)
FREDERICK WILLIAM, the Great Elector (1640–1688)
FREDERICK III, margrave of Brandenburg (1688–1713), and as Frederick I, king of Prussia (1701–1713)
FREDERICK WILLIAM I, king of Prussia (1713–1740)
FREDERICK II, the Great (1740–1786)
Frederick William II (1786–1797)
Frederick William III (1797–1840)

Bibliography

Allgemeine deutsche Biographie. 56 vols. Berlin, 1875–1912.

Angermeier, Heinz. *Königtum und Landfriede in deutschen Spätmittelalter.* Munich, 1966.

Aretin, Karl O. von. *Heiliges Römisches Reich, 1776–1806, Reichsverfassung und Staatssouveränität.* 2 vols. Wiesbaden, 1967.

Atkinson, C. T. *A History of Germany, 1715–1815.* New York, 1908, rpr. 1969.

Barraclough, Geoffrey. *Medieval Germany, 911–1250: Essays by German Historians.* 2 vols. Oxford, 967.

———. *The Origins of Modern Germany.* Oxford, 1962.

Bäuml, Franz H. *Medieval Civilization in Germany, 800–1273.* New York, 1969.

Bax, E. Belfort, *German Society at the Close of the Middle Ages.* London, 1894, rpr. 1967.

Bayley, Charles C. *The Election of the Sovereign in Germany during the Thirteenth Century.* Chicago, 1938.

———. *The Formation of the German College of Electors in the Mid-Thirteenth Century.* Toronto, 1949.

Bechtel, H. *Wirtschafts- und Sozialgeschichte Deutschlands* Munich, 1967.

Becker, Otto H. *Kaisertum, deutsche Königswahl und Legitimitatsprinzip in der Auffassung der späteren Staufer und ihres Umkreises.* Frankfurt, 1975.

Becker, Winfrid. *Der Kurfürstenrat, Grundzuge seiner Entwicklung in der Reichsverfassung und seine Stellung auf dem Westfalischen Friedenskongresse.* Münster, 1973.

Benecke, G. *Society and Politics in Germany, 1500–1750.* Toronto, 1974.

Berbig, Hans Joachim. *Das Kaiserliche Hochstift Bamberg und das Heilige Römische Reich vom Westfälischen Frieden bis zur Säkularisation.* 2 vols. Wiesbaden, 1976.

Biographisches Wörterbuch zur deutschen Geschichte. Edited by K. Bosl, H. Rössler, Günther Franz, and Hanns Hubert Hofmann. 3 vols. Munich, 1973–1975.

Blanning, T. C. W. *Reform and Revolution in Mainz, 1743-1803.* London, 1974.

Blickle, Peter. *Landschaften in Alten Reich: Die staatliche Funktion des gemeinen Mannes in Oberdeutschland.* Munich, 1973.

Bock, F. *Reichsidee und Nationalstaaten Vom Untergang des Alten Reiches bis zur Kundigung des deutsch-englischen Bündnisses im Jahre 1341.* Munich, 1943.

Bog, I. *Der Reichsmerkantilismus, Studien zur Wirtschaftspolitik des Heiligen Römischen Reiches im 17. und 18. Jahrhundert.* Stuttgart, 1959.

Borchardt, F. L. *German Antiquity in Renaissance Myth.* Baltimore, 1971.

Bosl, Karl. *Die Grundlagen der modernen Gesellschaft im Mittelalter.* 2 Vols.

———. *Die Reichsministerialität der Salier und Staufer.* 2 vols. Stuttgart, 1950–1951.

Bruford, W. H. *Germany in the Eighteenth Century: The Social Background of the Literary Revival.* Cambridge, 1965.

Brunner, O. *Land und Herrschaft.* 4th ed. Vienna, 1959.

Bryce, James, *The Holy Roman Empire.* New York, 1904, rpr. 1961.

D. Bullough, "After Charlemagne: The Empire under the Ottonians," in *The Dark Ages.* Edited by D. Talbot Rice. London, 1965.

Butler, W. F. T. *The Lombard Communes: A History of the Republic of North Italy.* New York, 1969.

Büttner, Heinrich. *Zur frühmittelalterlichen Reichsgeschichte an Rhein, Main und Neckar.* Edited by Alois Gerlich. Darmstadt, 1975.

Calmette, Joseph. *Le Reich allemand au Moyen Age.* Paris, 1951.

507

The Cambridge Medieval History. 8 vols. Cambridge, 1964.

Carsten, F. L. *The Origins of Prussia*. Oxford, 1954.

———. *Princes and Parliaments in Germany*. Oxford, 1959.

Cartellieri, Alexander. *Die Weltstellung des Deutschen Reiches, 911–1047*. Munich, 1932.

Clasen, Claus-Peter. *The Palatinate in European History, 1559–1660*. Oxford, 1966.

Cohn, Henry J. *The Government of the Rhine Palatinate in the Fifteenth Century*. Oxford, 1965.

Crankshaw, Edward. *The Habsburgs: Portrait of a Dynasty*. New York, 1971.

Dahlmann, F. C., and Waitz, G. *Quellenkunde der deutschen Geschichte*. 9th ed. Leipzig, 1931.

Dannenbauer, Heinrich. *Grundlagen der mittelalterlichen Welt, Skizzen und Studien*. Stuttgart, 1958.

Deer, J. *Die Enstehung des ungarischen Königtums*. Budapest, 1942.

Deutsche Königspfalzen. Beiträge zu ihrer historischen und archäologischen Erforschung. Veroffentlichungen des Max-Planck-Institute für Geschichte. Göttingen, 1963.

Dickinson, R. E. *Germany, A General and Regional Geography*. New York, 1953.

Dictionary of Scientific Biography. 14 vols. New York, 1970–1976.

Die Grossen Deutschen: Deutsche Biographie. Edited by Hermann Heimpel, Theodor Heuss, and Benno Reifenberg. 5 vols. Berlin, 1957.

Die Grossen Deutschen Neue Deutsche Biographie. Edited by Willy Andreas and Wilhelm von Scholz. 5 vols. Berlin, 1935.

Duggan, Lawrence G. *Bishop and Chapter: The Governance of the Bishopric of Speyer to 1552*. New Brunswick, N.J., 1978.

Dunham, Samuel A. *History of the Germanic Empire*. London, 1834–1835.

Dvornik, F. *The Making of Central and Eastern Europe*. London, 1949.

Ebengreuth, A. L. von. *Die Verfassung und Verwaltung der Germanen und des deutschen Reiches bis zum Jahre 1806*. Leipzig, 1911.

Engel, H. U. *Die Strasse nach Europa. Reichskleinodien und Kaiserkrönungen*. Hamburg, 1962.

Epstein, Klaus. *The Genesis of German Conservatism*. Princeton, 1966.

Erdmannsdörffer, Berhard. *Deutsche Geschichte von Westfälischen Frieden bis zum Regierungsantritt Friedrichs des Grossen, 1648–1740*. 2 vols. Darmstadt, 1974.

Eulenberg, Herbert. *The Hohenzollerns*. Translated by M. M. Bozman. New York, 1929.

European Authors 1000–1900: A Biographical Dictionary of European Literature. Edited by S. Kunitz and V. Colby. New York, 1967.

Evans, R. J. W. *The Making of the Habsburg Monarchy, 1550-1770*. New York, 1979.

Falco, Giorgio. *The Holy Roman Republic: A Historic Profile of the Middle Ages*. Translated by K. U. Kent. London, 1964.

Fichtenau, H. *Grundzüge der Geschichte des Mittelalters*. Vienna, 1947.

Fillitz, H. *Die Insignien und Kleinodien des Heiligen Römisches Reiches*. Vienna, 1954.

Fisher, Herbert A. L. *Studies in Napoleonic Statesmanship: Germany*. 1903, rpr. New York, 1968.

———. *The Medieval Empire*. 2 vols. New York, 1898, rpr. 1969.

Fleckenstein, Josef. *Early Medieval Germany*. Translated by Bernard Smith. New York, 1978.

———, and Schmid, Karl, eds. *Adel und Kirche*. Freiburg, 1968.

Flenly, Ralph. *Modern German History*. 4th ed. New York, 1968.

Folz, R. *The Concept of Empire*. London, 1969.

Freed, J. B. *The Friars and Germanic Society in the Thirteenth Century*. Cambridge, Mass., 1977.

Frischauer, Paul. *Die Habsburger. Geschichte einer Familie*. Vienna, 1961.

———. *The Imperial Crown*. London, 1939.

Gaupp, F. *Deutsche Falschung der abendländischen Reichsidee*. Bern, 1946.

Giesebrecht, Wilhelm von. *Geschichte der Deutschen Kaiserzeit*. Edited by Wilhelm Schild. 6 vols. Leipzig, 1873–1895, rpr. 1929–1930.

Gillingham, J. B. *The Kingdom of Germany in the High Middle Ages*. London, 1971.

Goez, Werner. *Translatio Imperii: Ein Beitrag zur Geschichte des Geschichtsdenkens und der politischen Theorien im Mittelalter und in der frühen Neuzeit*. Tübingen, 1958.

Gooch, G. P. *Germany and the French Revolution*. London, 1920.

Gross, Hans. *Empire and Sovereignty: A History of the Public Law Literature in the Holy Roman Empire, 1599–1804*. Chicago, 1975.

Gross, L. *Die Geschichte der deutschen reichshofkanzlei von 1559*. Vienna, 1933.

Groves' Dictionary of Music and Musicians. Edited by Eric Blom. 10 vols. New York, 1960.

Grundmann, Herbert. *Ausgewählte Aufsatze. Monumenta Germaniae Historica*. 3 vols. Stuttgart, 1976–1978.

———. *Geschichtsschreibung im Mittelalter: Gattungen, Epochen, Eigenart*. 2d ed. Stuttgart, 1969.

Hales, E. E. *The Emperor and the Pope*. New York. 1978.

Haller, Johannes. *Das Altdeutsche Kaisertum*. Stuttgart, 1944.

———. *Epochen der deutschen Geschichte*. Stuttgart, 1922.

Hampe, Theodor. *Die Fahrenden Leute in der deutschen Vergangenheit*. Jena, 1924.

———. *Germany under the Salien and Hohenstaufen Emperors*. Translated by Ralph Bennett. Totowa, N.J., 1973.

Handbuch der deutschen Geschichte. Bruno Gebhardt. Herbert Grundmann ed. 4 vols. Stuttgart, 1954, rpr. 1967.

Handbuch der deutschen Geschichte. Leo Just. 5 vols. Constance, 1957.

Hartung, Fritz. *Deutsche Geschichte im Zeitalter der, der Gegenreformation und des 30 jahrigen Krieges*. Berlin, 1971.

Hauck, A. *Kirchengeschichte Deutschland*. 5 vols. Leipzig, 1922–1929.

Heer, Friedrich. *Die Tragödie des Heiligen Reiches*. Stuttgart, 1952.

———. *The Holy Roman Empire*. Translated by Janet Sondheimer. New York, 1968.

Hellmann, E. *Die Reichsidee in deutschen Dichtungen der der Salier und frühen Stauferzeit*. Berlin, 1963.

Henderson, Ernest F. *A History of Germany in the Middle Ages*. New York, 1894, rpr. 1968.

Herzstein, Robert E., ed. *The Holy Roman Empire in the Middle Ages: Universal State or German Catastrophe?* Boston, 1966.

Hill, Boyd H., ed., *Medieval Monarchy in Action: The German Empire from Henry I to Henry IV*. New York, 1972.

———. *The Rise of the First Reich: Germany in the Tenth Century*. New York, 1969.

Hofmann, Hanns Hubert. *Adelige Herrschaft und souveräner Staat*. Munich, 1962.

———. *Quellen zum Verfassungsorganismus des Heiligen Römischen Reiches Deutscher Nation, 1495–1815*. Darmstadt, 1976.

Holborn, Hajo. *A History of Modern Germany*. 3 vols. New York, 1959–1970.

Holtzmann, Walther. *Das mittelalterliche Imperium und die werden den Nationen*. Cologne, 1953.

Huch, Ricarda. *Römisches reich deutscher nation*. Berlin, 1934, rpr. 1954.

Hugelmann, K. G. *Stamme, Nation und Nationalstaat in deutschen Mittelalter*. Würzburg, 1955.

Huysten, Albert. *Die Aachener Krone der Goldenen Bulle das Symbol des alten Deutschen Reiches*. Weimar, 1938.

Instinsky, H. U. *Bischofsstuhl und Kaiserthron*. Munich, 1955.

Janssen, Johannes. *History of the German People at the Close of the Middle Ages*. 16 vols. St. Louis, 1925, rpr. New York, 1966.

Just, Leo. *Deutsche Geschichte bis zu Ausgang des Mittelalters*. Frankfurt, 1957.

Kaegi, W. *Chronica Mundi*. Einsiedeln, 1954.

Kämpf, H. *Das Reich im Mittelalter*. Stuttgart, 1950.

———. *Die Entstehung des deutschen Reiches*. Darmstadt, 1956.

Kann, Robert A. *A History of the Habsburg Empire, 1526–1918*. Berkeley, 1974.

Kern, Fritz. *Kingship and Law in the Middle Ages*. Translated by S. B. Chrimes. New York, 1956.

Keutgen, Friedrich. *Der deutsche Staat des Mittelalters*. rpr. Aalen, 1963.

Kieckhefer, Richard. *Repression of Heresy in Medieval Germany*. Philadelphia, 1979.

Kienast, Walther. *Deutschland und Frankreich in der Kaiserzeit, 900–1270*. 3 vols. Stuttgart, 1974.

Knüll, B. *Historische Geographie: Deutschland im Mittelalter*. Breslau, 1903.

Koenigsberger, H. G. *The Habsburgs and Europe*. Ithaca, New York, 1971.

Leeper, A. W. A. *A History of Medieval Austria*. Oxford, 1941.

LeGates, Marlene Jahss. "The Knights and the Problems of Political Organizing in Sixteenth-Century." *Central European History,* 7 (1974): 99–136.

Leuschner, Joachim. *Germany in the Later Middle Ages*. Translated by Sabine MacCormack. New York, 1978.

Lindner, Theodor. *Deutsche Geschichte unter den Habsburgern und Luxemburgern, 1273–1437*. 2 vols. Darmstadt, 1970.

Loewenstein, Prince Hubertus zu. *The Germans in History*. New York, 1970.

Lortz, Joseph. *The Reformation in Germany*. Translated by R. Walls. 2 vols. New York, 1968.

Lutz, Heinrich. *Frankreich und das Reich im 16. und 17. Jahrhundert*. Göttingen, 1968.

Maehl, William H. *Germany in Western Civilization*. University, Ala., 1979.

Maschke, R. *Der Kampf zwischen Kaisertum und Papsttum*. Constance, 1955.

Mayer, Theodor ed. *Adel und Bauern im deutschen Staat des Mittelalters*. Leipzig, 1943.

————. *Fürsten und Staat*. Weimar, 1950.

Meinecke, Friedrich. *The Age of German Liberation, 1795–1815*. Edited and translated by Peter Paret. Berkeley, 1977.

Mitteis, H. *The State in the Middle Ages: A Comparative Constitutional History of Feudal Europe*. Translated by H. F. Orton. New York, 1975.

Moeller, Bernd. *Deutschland im Zeitalter der Reformation*. Göttingen, 1977.

Mommsen, K. *Eidgenossen, Kaiser und Reich*. Stuttgart, 1958.

Mommsen, W. "Zur Bedeutung des Reichsgedankens." *Historische Zeitschrift,* 174 (1952).

Neue deutsche Biographie. 10 vols. Berlin, 1974–.

New Catholic Encyclopedia. 16 vols. New York, 1967–1970.

Obermann, Karl; Scheel, Heinrich; Stoecker, H.; Töpfer, B; and Zschäbitz, G. *Biographisches Lexikon zur Deutschen Geschichte*. Berlin, 1967.

Offler, Hilary S. *Empire and Papacy: The Last Struggle*. London, 1958.

Propyläen Weltgeschichte Eine Universalgeschichte. Edited by Golo Mann and August Nitschke. 10 vols. Berlin, 1964.

Rassow, P. *Die geschichtliche Einheit des Abendlandes*. Cologne, 1960.

————. *Forschungen zur Reichsidee im 16. und 17. Jahrhundert*. Cologne, 1955.

————. *Honor imperii*. 2d ed. Cologne, 1961.

Rauch, Günter. *Die Bündnisse deutscher Herrscher mit Reichsangehörigen von Regierungsantritt Friedrich Barbarossas bis zum Tod Rudolfs von Habsburg*. Aalen, 1966.

Reinhardt, Kurt F. *Germany 2000 Years*. 2 vols. New York, 1962.

Reuter, Timothy, ed. and tr. *The Medieval Nobility: Selected Essays*. New York, 1978.

Ritter, Moritz. *Deutsche Geschichte im Zeitalter der Gegenreformation und des dreissigjährigen Krieges*. 3 vols. Stuttgart, 1889–1905.

Rohden, R. R. *Die Idee des Reiches in der europäischen Geschichte*. Oldenburg, 1943.

Sagara, Eda. *A Social History of Germany, 1648–1914*. New York, 1978.

Santifaller, Leo. *Zur Geschichte des Ottonisch-Salischen Reichskirchensystems*. Cologne, 1964.

The New Schaff-Herzog Encyclopedia of Religious Knowledge. 12 vols. New York, 1968.

Schieder, Theodor, ed. "Beiträge zur Geschichte des mittelalterlichen deutschen Königtums." *Historische Zeitschrift* Beiheft 2 (Neue Folge). Munich, 1973.

Schneider, Fedor. *Die neueren Anschauungen der deutschen Historiker über die Kaiserpolitik des Mittelalters*. 6th ed. Weimar, 1943.

Schramm, Percy E., with Mütherich, Florentine. *Denkmale der deutschen Könige und Kaiser*. Munich, 1962.

————. *Herrschaftszeichen und Staatssymbolik*. 3 vols. Stuttgart, 1954–1956.

————. *Kaiser, Rom und Renovatio*. Darmstadt, 1957.

————. *Sphaira, Globus und Reichsapfel*. Stuttgart, 1958.

Schubert, Friedrich H. *Die deutschen Reichstage in der Staatslehre der frühen Neuzeit*. Göttingen, 1966.

Schwarz, Henry F. *The Imperial Privy Council in the Seventeenth Century*. London, 1943.

Skalweit, Stephan. *Reich und Reformation*. Berlin, 1967.

Srbik, Heinrich von. *Deutsche Einheit*. 4 vols. Munich, 1935–1942.

Staats, Reinhart, *Theologie der Reichskrone: Ottonische "Renovatio imperii" im Spiegel einer Insignie*. Stuttgart, 1976.

Steinhausen, G. *Geschichte der deutschen Kultur*. 3d ed. Leipzig, 1929.

Steinmetz, Max. *Deutschland von 1476 bis 1648*. Berlin, 1965.

Stengel, E. H. *Abhandlungen und Untersuchung en zur Geschichte des Kaisergedankens im Mittelalter*. Cologne, 1965.

Stern, Leo, and Bartmuss, Hans-Joachim. *Deutschland in der Feudalepoche von der Wende des 5./ 6. Jh. bis zur Mitte des 11. Jh*. Berlin, 1965.

———— and Voight, Erhard. *Deutschland in der Feudalepoche von der Mitte des 13. Jh. bis zum ausgehenden 15. Jh*. Berlin, 1965.

Stieber, Joachim. *Pope Eugenius IV: The Council of Basel and the Secular and Ecclesiastical Authorities in the Empire*. Leiden, 1978.

Strauss, Gerald. "The Holy Roman Empire Revisited," *Central European History*, 11 (1978): 290–301.

————. *Luther's House of Intellect: Indoctrination of the Young in the German Reformation*. Baltimore, 1978.

————, ed. *Pre-Reformation Germany*. New York, 1972.

————. *Sixteenth-Century Germany: Its Topography and Topographers*. Madison, 1959.

Stubbs, William. *Germany in the Later Middle Ages, 1200–1500*. Edited by Arthur Hassall. New York, 1969.

Sybel, Heinrich von. *Universalstaat oder Nationalstaat*. Edited by Friedrich Schneider. Innsbruck, 1941.

Tapie, Victor-L. *The Rise and Fall of the Habsburg Monarchy*. Translated by Stephan Hardman. New York, 1971.

Tellenbach, Gerd. *Church, State and Christian Society*. New York, 1970.

————. *Die Entstehung des deutschen Reiches*. Munich, 1947.

Thompson, James Westfall. *Feudal Germany*. Chicago, 1928, rpr. 1962.

Tout, Thomas F. *The Empire and the Papacy, 918–1273*. London, 1965.

Uhlirz, M. *Handbuch der Geschichte Österreichs*. 4 vols. Vienna, 1927–1944.

Ullmann, Walter. "Reflections on the Medieval Empire." *Transactions of the Royal Historical Society* 14 (1964): 89–108.

Valentin, V. *The German People: Their History and Civilization*. New York, 1946.

Van Caenegem, R. C., with Ganshof, F. L. *Guide to the Sources of Medieval History*. New York, 1978.

Vann, J. A. *The Swabian Kreis: Politics and Privilege in the Holy Roman Empire, 1648–1715*. Brussels, 1976.

————, and Rowan, Steven W., eds. *The Old Reich: Essays on German Political Institutions, 1495–1806*. Brussels, 1974.

Waas, A. *Der Mensch im deutschen Mittelalter*. Cologne, 1964.

————. *Herrschaft und Staat im Frühmittelalter*. Berlin, 1938.

Waitz, G. *Deutsche Verfassungsgeschichte*. 8 vols. Kiel, 1874–85.

Walder, E. *Das Ende des alten Reiches*. Bern, 1948.

Wandruszka, A. *The House of Habsburg*. Translated by C. Epstein and H. Epstein. New York, 1964.

Wenkebach, Heinz. *Bestrebung zur Erhaltung der Einheit des Heiligen Römischen Reiches in der Reichsschlüssen von 1663 bis 1806*. Aalen, 1970.

Wieruszowski, Helene. *Reichsbesitz und reichsrechte im Rheinland, 500–1300*. Bonn, 1926.

———. *Von imperium zum nationalen Königstum.* Bonn, 1933.

Wines, Roger. "The Imperial Circles, Princely Diplomacy and Imperial Reform, 1681–1714." *Journal of Modern History,* 39 (1967): 1–29.

Zeydel, Edwin H. *The Holy Roman Empire in German Literature.* New York, 1918.

Index

Alexander II, pope, 9, 187–188, 202
Alexander III, pope, 143–144, 215
Alexander VI, pope, 57, 314
Alexander VII, pope, 328, 485
Alexander of Roes, 17; writings of, 17
Alexius III, Byzantine emperor, 146, 212
Alfani, Gianni, 101
Algau; rebels of, 366
Alighieri, Beatrice, 46, 101
Alighieri, Dante, 46, 101–105, 213, 371, 469;
    Commedia of, 46, 101, 104, 469; other writ-
    ings of, 101–104
Alighieri, Giovanni, 101
Alighieri, Jacopo, 101
Alighieri, Pietro, 101
Allstedt, 329–330
Almaric of Cyprus, 211
Alphonse of Castile, 241–242, 393
Alps, 24, 61, 72, 98, 138, 147, 171–172, 209–
    211, 214, 239, 270, 285, 299, 396, 462–463,
    477; army of the, 170
Alsace, 5, 42, 70, 83, 261, 279–280, 289, 321,
    328, 431, 460, 485, 490, 496
Altdorf, university of, 267, 361, 458, 472
Altdorfer, Albrecht, 17
Altenburg, 415; university of, 348
Altranstädt, Treaty of 1706, 162, 339
Alt-Seidenberg, 47
Alva, duke of, 309
Alvintzy, Joseph von Barbarek, 170
Amalfi, 377
Amalia Elizabeth, 489–490
Amberg, 395
Amberger, Christoph, 56
Ambras, fortress of 131, 310
Amiens, Treaty of 1802, 169, 172, 332
Amsdorf, Nicholas von, 18, 53, 259
Amsterdam, 267
Anabaptism, 18–20, 28, 54, 105–107, 224–
    225, 229–230, 259, 302–303, 327, 330,
    374, 483, 496
Anabaptists, 302, 326, 348, 499
Anacletus, 277
Ancona, 37, 239
Andalo, Brancaleone degli, 98
Andreae, Jacob, 20–21, 84, 288
Andreae, John Valentin, 21–22, 114; writings
    of, 22
Andreas I, king of Hungary, 9, 270
Andreas II, king of Hungary, 118, 439
Angilbert, 3
Anna, empress, 127, 315, 317
Anna, czarina of Russia, 31, 382
Anna, duchess of Bavaria, 13
Anna, queen of Poland, 132
Anna Maria, duchess of Württemberg, 83, 288
Anna of Mecklenburg, 373

Anna of Schweidniz-Jauer, empress, 71, 73,
    372, 480
Anna of Tyrol, empress, 310, 451
Anne, electress of Brandenburg, 178
Anne, queen of England, 193
Anne of Austria, 416
Anno, archbishop of Cologne, 9, 201–202
Ansbach, 37, 114, 347, 493
Anselm, archbishop of Canterbury, 308
Anton Ulrich, duke of Brunswick-Wolfenbüttel,
    417
Apollo, 105
Apraksin, 407
Apulia, 99
Aquasparta, Matteo d', 102
Aquinas, Thomas, 16, 57, 101, 116
Aquitaine, 280–281, 461
Arabia, 362; culture of, 147; science of, 16
Arad, 258, 324, 497
Aragon, 7, 75
Aragona, Giacoma d', 46
Architecture, 4, 135–136, 464; Baroque, 157,
    271; Byzantine, 4, 68; Dutch, 163; Gothic,
    440, 455, 463, Oriental, 4, 68; Roman, 4;
    Romanesque, 68
Ardvin of Ivrea, 198
Arezzo, 214, 371
Argonne, 169
Aribo, archbishop of Mainz, 181
Aristophanes, 380
Aristotle, 16, 101, 303, 380
Arles, 72
Armagnacs, 430
Arnim, Hans George von, 23
Arnold of Brescia, 126, 142
Arno River, 103
Arnstadt, 35; New Church in, 35
Arnulf, emperor, 23–25, 61, 70, 283
Arnulf, count, 24
Arnulf, duke of Bavaria, 94, 283
Arqua, 372
Artois, 305, 313–314, 480
Ascalon, 439
Aschaffenburg, 191
Asiento, 460
Askanian dynasty, 284
Aspelt, Peter von, 213
Aspern-Essling, Battle of 1809, 138
Astrologers and astrology, 262, 365, 394–395,
    472
Atlantic Sea, 345
Attigny, 281, 461
Atto, 5
Auersberg, Leopold William, 296
Augsburg, 25–29, 56, 59, 106, 113, 117, 173–
    174, 180, 224, 229–230, 237, 266, 280,
    302–303, 372–373, 388, 432, 452, 486; diet

Notes on the Contributors

E. John B. Allen is an associate professor of history at Plymouth State College in New Hampshire. In addition to writing several articles, Professor Allen is the author of *Post and Courier Service in the Diplomacy of Early Modern Europe* (The Hague, 1972).

J. Wayne Baker is an associate professor of history at the University of Akron and the author of essays in such journals as the *Sixteenth Century Journal* and *Zwingliana*.

Phillip Norton Bebb is an associate professor at Ohio University. Professor Bebb has published in *The Social History of the Reformation* (Columbus, Ohio, 1972) and *Occasional Papers of the American Society for Reformation Research*.

Lawrence P. Buck is an associate professor at Widener University in Chester, Pennsylvania. He is the coeditor of *The Social History of the Reformation* and the author of a number of articles on the German Peasants' Revolt.

Anthony K. Cassell is an associate professor of Italian at the University of Illinois-Urbana. The translator and editor of Boccaccio's *The Corbaccio* (Urbana, 1975), Professor Cassell has also published in such journals as *Comparative Literature* and *Modern Language Notes*.

Mark E. Chapman is completing his theological training at the Lutheran Theological Seminary in Gettysburg, Pennsylvania.

Carl C. Christensen is a professor of history at the University of Colorado in Boulder. He is the author of *Art and the Reformation in Germany* (Athens, Ohio, 1979) and numerous articles.

Richard G. Cole is a professor of history at Luther College in Decorah, Iowa. His essays have appeared in *The Social History of the Reformation, Archive for Reformation History,* and the *Lutheran Quarterly*.

Dennis S. Devlin edits the *Journal of the Great Lakes Historical Conference* and teaches history at Grand Valley State College in Allendale, Michigan. Dr. Devlin has also taught at the University of Louisville.

Clifford J. Dull is a consultant for Standard Publishing Company of Hamilton, Ohio. Dr. Dull has taught at Carthage College, the University of Wisconsin-Madison, and the University of Colorado and has published in such journals as *Classical Philology* and the *Christian Standard*.

Charles T. Eby is an instructor at St. Joseph's University in Philadelphia, Pennsylvania.

Linda S. Frey is an associate professor of history at the University of Montana.

Marsha L. Frey is an associate professor at Kansas State University. She and her twin sister have collaborated on scholarly articles for such journals as *Austrian History Yearbook, Canadian Journal of History, East European Quarterly,* and the *Historian.*

Christopher R. Friedrichs is an associate professor of history at the University of British Columbia. In addition to publishing a number of articles on German urban history in such journals as *Past and Present,* Professor Friedrichs is the author of *Urban Society in an Age of War: Nördlingen* (Princeton, 1979).

A. Harding Ganz is an associate professor of history at Ohio State University at Newark. Professor Ganz is the author of essays that have appeared in *Armor, Germany in the Pacific, Military Affairs,* and *Militargeschichtliche Mitteilungen.*

Scott A. Garretson is completing his doctorate at the University of Chicago.

Jane Whitehead Gates teaches at the Rudolf Steiner School in New York. Dr. Gates has published in *The Social History of the Reformation.*

Harold J. Grimm is professor emeritus at Ohio State University. Considered the Nestor of Reformation studies in America, Professor Grimm's most recent books are *The Reformation Era,* 2d ed. (New York, 1973), and *Lazarus Spengler, A Lay Leader of the Reformation* (Columbus, Ohio, 1978).

Kurt K. Hendel teaches at Christ Seminary in St. Louis. Dr. Hendel has published in *Currents in Theology and Mission, Profiles in Belief,* and *The Social History of the Reformation.*

David M. Hockenbery is director of alumni relations at Capital University, where he also teaches European history. He formerly taught at Baylor University and Ohio State University.

Dorothy B. Mapes teaches at Grand Rapids College in Michigan and works for the Grand Rapids Ethnic Heritage Consortium. She is also a doctoral student at Michigan State University

Andrew M. McLean is an associate professor of English at the University of Wisconsin-Parkside in Kenosha, Wisconsin. Professor McLean is the book review editor of *Clio* and has published numerous essays in such journals as *Renaissance Quarterly, Moreana,* and *Shakespeare Quarterly.*

Bodo Nischan is an associate professor of history at East Carolina University. His essays have appeared in such journals as *Central European History, Historical Journal,* and the *Journal of Religious History.*

Louis J. Reith is a librarian at Saint Bonaventure's University. Dr. Reith is the translator of *Two Kingdoms and One World* and one of the editors of *Umdeutungen der Zweireichelehre Luthers in 19. Jahrhundert* (Gütersloh, 1975).

Steven W. Rowan is an associate professor at the University of Missouri-St. Louis. Professor Rowan is the coeditor of *The Old Reich: Essays on German Political Institutions* (Brussels, 1974) and has published in such journals as *Central European History, Manuscripta,* the *Sixteenth Century Journal,* and *Speculum.*

Catherine B. Ryan is an instructor of history at The State University of New York College at Potsdam. **John P. Ryan** is an associate professor of history at the State University of New York College at Potsdam.

Raymond H. Schmandt is professor of history at St. Joseph's University. Professor Schmandt is the coauthor of *History of the Catholic Church* (Milwaukee, 1957) and author of *Leo III and the Modern World* (New York, 1961), in addition to essays that have appeared in such journals as *Speculum* and *The Catholic Historical Review*.

Kyle C. Sessions is an associate professor of history at Illinois State University. He is the editor of *Reformation and Authority: The Meaning of the Peasants' Revolt* (Boston, 1968) and the author of *Faces in the Peasants' Revolt* (St. Louis, 1976).

Jackson J. Spielvogel is an associate professor of history at Pennsylvania State University and the author of essays that have been published in *Moreana* and *The Social History of the Reformation*.

William J. Wright is an associate professor of history at the University of Tennessee at Chattanooga. Professor Wright's essays have appeared in *Archive for Reformation History, Church History, Journal of Modern History*, and the *Sixteenth Century Journal*.

Angela Howard Zophy teaches history at the University of Wisconsin-Parkside and at Carthage College in Kenosha, Wisconsin. She has published essays in *Dialogue: Woman to Woman*.

Jonathan W. Zophy is an associate professor of history at Carthage College. He is the coeditor of *The Social History of the Reformation* (Columbus, Ohio, 1972) and has published in such journals as the *Sixteenth Century Journal*, the *History Teacher, Forum for Honors, Phylon*, and *Journal of Urban History*.